HOW WOMEN BECAME POETS

How Women Became Poets

A GENDER HISTORY OF GREEK LITERATURE

EMILY HAUSER

PRINCETON UNIVERSITY PRESS
PRINCETON & OXFORD

Published by Princeton University Press
41 William Street, Princeton, New Jersey 08540
99 Banbury Road, Oxford OX2 6JX

press.princeton.edu

All Rights Reserved

Library of Congress Cataloging-in-Publication Data

Names: Hauser, Emily, author.
Title: How women became poets : a gender history of Greek literature /
    Emily Hauser.
Description: Princeton : Princeton University Press, 2023. |
    Includes bibliographical references and index.
Identifiers: LCCN 2022042333 (print) | LCCN 2022042334 (ebook) |
    ISBN 9780691201078 (hardback) | ISBN 9780691239286 (ebook)
Subjects: LCSH: Greek literature—Women authors—History and criticism.
Classification: LCC PA3067 .H38 2023 (print) | LCC PA3067 (ebook) |
    DDC 881/.01099287—dc23/eng/20221108
LC record available at https://lccn.loc.gov/2022042333
LC ebook record available at https://lccn.loc.gov/2022042334

British Library Cataloging-in-Publication Data is available

Editorial: Matt Rohal and Alena Chekanov
Production Editorial: Theresa Liu
Jacket/Cover Design: Chris Ferrante
Production: Erin Suydam
Publicity: William Pagdatoon and Charlotte Coyne
Copyeditor: Aviva Arad

Jacket image: Eroshka/Shutterstock

This book has been composed in Classic Arno

Printed on acid-free paper. ∞

Printed in the United States of America

10 9 8 7 6 5 4 3 2 1

For Eliza and Theo, our best creations
And for Oliver, always

A radical critique of literature, feminist in its impulse, would take the work first of all as a clue to how we live, how we have been living, how we have been led to imagine ourselves, how our language has trapped as well as liberated us, how the very act of naming has been till now a male prerogative, and how we can begin to see and name—and therefore live—afresh.

—ADRIENNE RICH, "WHEN WE DEAD AWAKEN: WRITING AS RE-VISION"

ἔτι δή γε περὶ τῶν ὀνομάτων μαθεῖν σε δεῖ,
ἅττ᾽ ἄρρεν᾽ ἐστίν, ἅττα δ᾽ αὐτῶν θήλεα.

You still need to learn about names—
which are male, and which ones are female.

—ARISTOPHANES, CLOUDS

CONTENTS

PART IV. BIRD

A New Kind of Language: Women Poets in Their Own Words

NOTE ON TRANSLITERATIONS AND TEXTS

I HAVE chosen to transliterate Greek throughout in order to make this book as accessible as possible to specialists and nonspecialists alike. I have preferred the Latinate versions of transliterated Greek names for familiarity (e.g., Callistratus, not Kallistratos; Hecuba, not Hecabe), and in order to achieve consistency with more frequently Latinized forms like Hercules and Achilles. In transliterating Greek terms, I have followed the Library of Congress transliteration system except in the case of upsilon: I have rendered upsilon as "y" in *hymnos, hymnein* (not *humnos*) and *mythos, mythologein* (not *muthos*) in order to underline the connection to their English cognates, but have rendered elsewhere as "u" (e.g., *kluta*). Titles of ancient texts follow the abbreviations listed in the *Oxford Classical Dictionary*, fourth edition. Greek citations refer to the Oxford Classical Texts unless otherwise specified: see the list of abbreviations for full bibliographic details. Translations are my own throughout, unless otherwise acknowledged. Finally, parts of chapters 8 and 9 appeared earlier as an article in *Ramus* (Hauser 2016a); I am grateful to the publisher for permission to reprint.

ACKNOWLEDGMENTS

I AM so grateful for so many people—institutions, colleagues, friends, and family—who have made this book possible. I undertook the foundational research for the book as a Junior Fellow at the Harvard Society of Fellows in 2017–18: I benefited hugely not only from the dedicated research time provided by the fellowship and Harvard's outstanding facilities and library, but also the stimulating conversation of both Junior and Senior Fellows, in particular Gregory Nagy, who has been a generous mentor and brilliant critic from the very beginning. The Harvard Classics Department was enormously welcoming and I owe them much gratitude: for conversations with Kathleen Coleman, Richard Thomas, and Naomi Weiss, as well as Julia Judge, Marco Romani Mistretta, Gil Renberg, James Zainaldin, and many others, and the generous feedback of the Technical Traditions workshop. At the same time, I have been fortunate enough to benefit from the support of many mentors and friends at other institutions, who have provided guidance and encouragement at various stages of the project: at Yale, Emily Greenwood (both a stellar advisor and hugely thoughtful reader), as well as Egbert Bakker, Joshua Billings, Diana Kleiner, Irene Peirano Garrison, and Joseph Solodow; also Ruby Blondell, Anna Busetto, Nancy Felson, Markus Hafner, Judith Hallett, Andromache Karanika, Lisa Maurizio, Helen Morales, Sheila Murnaghan, José Luís García Ramón, Laura Slatkin, and Tim Whitmarsh. I am so thankful to them all for their unwavering support and willingness to share ideas.

This has been a project that has spanned many different homes, from New Haven to Boston to Exeter. I have truly found a home at Exeter over the past few years, and feel enormously grateful for my fantastic colleagues who not only make the department such a vibrant place to work and share research, but who are also wonderful people and friends. I am grateful to them all, but will mention in particular Barbara Borg, Fiona Cox, Katharine Earnshaw, Richard Flower, Gabriele Galluzzo, Maria Gerolemou, Chris Gill, Rebecca Langlands, Muireann Maguire, Karen ní Mheallaigh, Daniel Ogden, Helena Taylor, and

Matthew Wright, all of whom have either read parts of the book or had conversations with me about it at various points over the past few years; as well as my students, especially Oliver Maynard and the students of my seminar on women's writing, who have encouraged me to see old topics in new ways, and the audience of the Classical Association branch in Exeter. Many thanks to you all for your helpful suggestions, warm encouragement, and sparkling company: it is a pleasure and a privilege to benefit from your expertise and friendship.

Every book needs a home, and I could not have found a better one than at Princeton University Press. My editor, Matt Rohal, has been fantastic and has believed in the book from the very start: I am hugely thankful for his support, warmth, and advice. I am especially grateful to the Press, and Christie Henry in particular, for the award of a Global Equity Grant, which made the research for this book possible and enabled me to buy the books I needed to keep working throughout the global pandemic; the Editorial Board, and Barbara Graziosi in particular, have been instrumental in making this book better with their thoughtful feedback and encouragement. I am indebted to those experts (already mentioned above) on the various authors covered in the book, who have kindly consented to read parts or the whole of the manuscript. Above all, I owe a huge debt of gratitude to Laura McClure and Ruby Blondell, the readers for Princeton University Press, for their boundless generosity in reading and commenting on the book, their insightful feedback and their generous encouragement and support. I am enormously grateful to have been able to benefit from their expertise and critical feedback, which has been hugely helpful in improving the book: any errors that remain are entirely my own.

Finally, I wish to thank my friends and family, who have been there with me every step of the way along the journey: Gemma and Niccolò, Helena and Dave, Kim and Miguel, Muireann, Ali, Katharine, Amy, Naomi, Helena and Loukas, Zoe, Athina, Natalia and Arabella, for all their love, support, and belief in my footnotes; as well as my parents and parents-in-law, who have listened patiently to more than they probably want to about the role of the *poiētēs* in Plato. Above all, I am grateful to my amazing husband, Oliver, for always supporting and believing in me: he made this book possible (as well as everything else) by his love, patience, kindness, and insight as well as sharing in caring for our children and juggling a million other things so that I could complete it. I am so grateful every day for his unconditional love and support. Finally, I am grateful for our wonderful children, Eliza and Theo, with whom I was pregnant for most of the writing of this book, and to whom it is dedicated; I am so thankful for the sunshine that they bring to our lives.

LIST OF ABBREVIATIONS

Chantraine   P. Chantraine, *Dictionnaire étymologique de la langue grecque*, 2 vols. (Paris: Klincksieck, 1968–77).

Dilts   M. R. Dilts, ed., *Heraclidis Lembi excerpta Politiarum* (Durham NC: Duke University Press, 1971).

Dindorf   W. Dindorf, ed., *Aristides*, 3 vols. (Leipzig: Reimer, 1829).

DK   H. Diels and W. Kranz, eds., *Die Fragmente der Vorsokratiker*, 6th ed., 3 vols. (Berlin: Weidmann, 1952).

F   J. Fontenrose, ed., *The Delphic Oracle: Its Responses and Operations, with a Catalogue of Responses* (Berkeley: University of California Press, 1978).

FGrH   F. Jacoby, ed., *Fragmente der Griechischen Historiker* (Leiden: Brill, 1923–).

F-S   W. W. Fortenbaugh and E. Schütrumpf, eds., *Demetrius of Phalerum: Text, Translation and Discussion* (Oxford, New York: Routledge, 2000).

GG   *Grammatici Graeci*. 6 vols. (Leipzig: Teubner, 1878–1910).

G-P   Either: A. S. F. Gow and D. L. Page, eds., *The Greek Anthology 1: Hellenistic Epigrams*, 2 vols. (Cambridge: Cambridge University Press, 1965), or, A. S. F. Gow and D. L. Page, eds., *The Greek Anthology 2: The Garland of Philip and Some Contemporary Epigrams*, 2 vols. (Cambridge: Cambridge University Press, 1968).

H   A. S. Hollis, ed., *Callimachus: Hecale* (Oxford: Clarendon, 1990).

Hense   O. Hense, ed., *Teletis reliquiae* (Tübingen: Siebeck, 1909).

PMG   D. Page, ed., *Poetae melici Graeci* (Oxford: Clarendon, 1962).

PMGF   M. Davies, ed., *Poetarum melicorum Graecorum fragmenta*, vol. 1 (Oxford: Clarendon, 1991).

PSI   *Papiri della Società Italiana* (1908–)

Rose   V. Rose, ed., *Aristotelis qui ferebantur librorum fragmenta*, 3rd ed. (Leipzig: Teubner, 1886).

SEG   *Supplementum Epigraphicum Graecum* (1923–)

SIG   W. Dittenberger and F. Hiller von Gaertringen, eds., *Sylloge Inscriptionum Graecarum*, 4th ed., 2 vols. (Hildesheim: Georg Olms, 1960).

S-M   Either: B. Snell and H. Maehler, eds., *Pindari carmina cum fragmentis*, 2 vols. (Leipzig: Teubner, 1987–89), or, B. Snell and H. Maehler, eds., *Bacchylides* (Leipzig: Teubner, 1970).

TrGF   B. Snell, R. Kannicht, and S. Radt, eds., *Tragicorum Graecorum fragmenta*, 5 vols. (Göttingen: Vandenhoeck and Ruprecht, 1971–2004).

V   E.-M. Voigt, ed., *Sappho et Alcaeus, Fragmenta* (Amsterdam: Polak and van Gennep, 1971).

W   M. L. West, ed., *Carmina Anacreontea* (Leipzig: Teubner, 1984).

Wehrli F. Wehrli, ed., *Phainias von Eresos, Chamaileon, Praxiphanes* (Basel: Schwabe, 1957).

HOW WOMEN BECAME POETS

A Name of One's Own

JUST AS Virginia Woolf recognized in *A Room of One's Own* that women need a place in which to write, so too women writers across the ages have been in need of a name to describe—and acknowledge—what it is they do.[1] We might think debates over what to call a woman who writes ("author" or "authoress," "poet" or "poetess") are a modern-day conundrum—but the gendering of poets has an antiquity to it, that reaches right back to Sappho. Yet strangely—in spite of producing one of the most famous female writers of all time—ancient Greece began with no word with which to describe its most illustrious female poet. When Sappho sang her songs, the only word which existed to describe a poet was a male one—*aoidos*, or "singer-man." This was a word that was gendered masculine in the grammar of ancient Greek, and—as this book will suggest—ring-fenced as the property of men alone in practice. For Sappho, this term carried with it the hallmark of male social convention, the weighty masculinizing of the genre and production of epic, and the formidable example of male poets like Homer and Hesiod, who had used it to describe themselves and poets like them.

So we begin with a troubling, yet fascinating, paradox: the most famous woman poet of ancient Greece, whose craft was, itself, a craft of words, had no words with which to talk about who she was, and what she did. She had no name of her own.

This book traces the story of the invention of that name. It explores and exposes the archaeology of the gendering of the poet, following ancient Greek poets, philosophers, and historians as they developed the vocabulary for poetic authorship in the crucible of gender. It begins with the first articulations of what it meant to be a "singer-man" in Homer in the eighth century BCE,

---

1. Woolf [1929] 1989.

before moving through the centuries-long story of associations of masculinity with poetic production—and the ways that men policed, and sometimes challenged, that masculinity. It describes how male writers attempted to articulate the rise of women poets—and particularly, the prominence of Sappho—by coming up with new ways of speaking about women who wrote. And it explores how women authors from Sappho to Nossis responded by developing their own vocabulary to describe their gendered identity in counterpoint to the language spoken by men. What emerges, I argue, is a history, not just of a word, but of the construction of the gendered self in, and through, literature—the development of a name of one's own.

The problematic of all this—why it matters—is not only the inherent interest of uncovering the story of Sappho's naming as "poet" (though that is certainly interesting in its own right). This book, rather, aims to provide a new perspective on the history of Greek literature as a battleground of gender. It challenges traditional assumptions about the "canon" of Greek literature, highlighting the articulated construction of masculinity in Greek poetic texts, at the same time as it places ancient women poets back onto center stage as principal actors in the drama of the debate around what it means to create poetry. This rests, fundamentally, on a problematization of the ways that the culture and language of ancient Greece have influenced the terms we use to speak about literature and authorship, through a cultural heritage that, for thousands of years, was used to justify the linguistic and cultural hegemony of men.[2] The book thus—at the same time as it prizes open the gendering of ancient authorship—invites a reexamination of the language, the modes of thought, and the critical structures we use now as a way into rethinking the expectations and values that may be embedded in the words we speak today.

One very salient example of this is the fact that, so far, readings of ancient authorship have focused on the normative discourse—that is, the terms used by men for men in a very male world.[3] Jesper Svenbro's analysis of the genealogy of the word for "poet," and Andrew Ford's chapter on the same in *The Origins of Criticism* (2002), for example, are exclusively male focused (though

2. Beard 2017: x–xi; cf. Morales 2020: xvi. On feminism and classics, see Rabinowitz and Richlin 1993, McManus 1997, Sharrock 1997, Zajko and Leonard 2006, Zajko 2008.

3. See especially Ford 2002: 131–57, and also Weil 1884, Diehl 1940, Vicaire 1964: 1–9, Durante 1976, Svenbro 1984, Ford 1985, Morgan 1993, D. Bouvier 2003, Maslov 2009 (on which see further, chapter 9, n. 10). For more general studies, see Calame and Chartier 2004, Schmitzer 2007, Beecroft 2010, Marmodoro and Hill 2013, Fletcher and Hanink 2016, Bakker 2017, Hafner (forthcoming). On male-gendering going unnoticed in criticism, see Fögen 2004: 216, J. Gould 1980: 38, Kampen 1998: x.

neither makes mention of gender); Ford implicitly makes the same assumptions of male-gendering in ventriloquizing ancient Greek terms like "craftsman."[4] Yet there is, in fact, a whole range of vocabulary around authorship being invented, discussed, and debated in ancient texts by both male and female authors which actively engages with the gendering of the terms employed. Setting authorship terms in this context gives us a new view into ideas around gender and literary production in ancient Greece, and provides an important way into looking at the corpus of ancient literature through the lens of gender. Notions such as "canon" and ideas of authorial identity—previously studied largely through *sphragis*, or authors' "signatures"—can be reformulated in the words of ancient Greek authors, as they struggled to find a gendered vocabulary for what they did.[5] In short, this book challenges the assumption that the male canon was an inevitable aspect of Greek literature. It puts forward, instead, the argument that the maleness of Greek literature and authorship was something that had to be consistently negotiated: demonstrating how Greek authors constructed and debated their gendered sense of self through the words they used to describe themselves, each other, and their craft.[6]

A central part of this work, at the same time, lies in recovering the women writers of ancient Greece, both well known and marginal. Sappho is the best known and most influential of a line of ancient Greek female poets—and yet it has often been observed that women's voices were largely silenced in the ancient world, both literally and figuratively in their survival in the textual record.[7] From epics composed by male bards and recited by male rhapsodes, to tragedies and comedies written by men and performed by and for male audiences,

4. Svenbro 1984: 160–73, Ford 2002: 131–57. See, for example, Ford 2002: 142, where epinician poets are seen as "qualif[ying] the craftsmanly image of their art" (and note, in spite of an interesting opening example redolent with gender tensions, Ford's segregation of women's poetry as a "culture of their own" and therefore "mostly hidden from the historian" at p. 7). Note, too, that Svenbro mentions Sappho only in the context of her appearance in Herodotus (Svenbro 1984: 171); her own poetic terminology is confined to a footnote (208 n. 93).

5. On *sphragis*, see Calame 2004a, Peirano 2014, and Prins 1999: 8–13 (on Sappho), Pratt 1995 and Woodbury 1952 (on Theognis), Race 1997: 297 n. 5 (on Pindar), etc. On proper names and reference in the context of gender, see McConnell-Ginet 2003: 74–76. This book is focused on looking specifically for the presence of substantive nouns describing authorship, which therefore means the exclusion of instances of *sphragis*, though see pp. 46–47 for discussion of Hesiod.

6. On the construction of masculinity in ancient Greece, see, e.g., Foxhall and Salmon 1998a and 1998b, Arnold and Brady 2011, esp. Yarrow 2011, Rubarth 2014; see also chapter 4, n. 16.

7. For general studies on ancient women writers, see Barnard 1978, Snyder 1989, De Martino 1991, Skinner 1993, Stehle 1997: 71–118, Bowman 2004, Greene 2005, Klinck 2008; for an anthology of women writers (in translation), see Plant 2004.

the poetry that survives from ancient Greece is almost always male.[8] In a corpus
that contains at least 3,200 male writers of Greek alone, we only have the names of
under a hundred women writing in ancient Greek, many of whose work is lost
to us. Of these, just over half were poets, and—although they cover a vast span
of time between the archaic and Hellenistic periods—the poetry of a mere
thirteen women writers survives.[9] The lack of female poets compared to male is
a vivid testament to the prevailing culture of female silencing—both in the
societal expectations of women's silence, as well as the erasure of their voices
from the record through the vagaries of the male tradition.[10] This is in spite of
the evidence for at least a certain degree of literacy among (some) women—for
education was still, by and large, the preserve of men.[11] The ways in which Sap-
pho, and other ancient female poets following her, discuss their authorship and
identity is not only of value in recovering ancient women's voices and accessing
attitudes to their poetics, then. It does not only serve as a reminder that poetic
authorship in the ancient world was always set against a background of an as-
sumption of gender—so that both male and female poets were always writing
in terms of, or against, gender. It also plays a part in arguing for the centrality of
women's role in defining and shaping ideas around authorship and literary pro-
duction in Greek literature.

It was not just the social context and mechanisms of literary production that
were prone to gendering: ancient Greek, like many other languages both ancient
and modern, was grammatically gendered, meaning that gender was explicit in
its authorship terms—*ho poiētēs* (the [male] poet-man), for example, and *hē
poiētria* (the [female] poet-woman). This is a gendering that English—which

8. See, e.g., Ford 2002: 7, Greene 2005: xi–xiii, West 2014a: 315–16.

9. Plant 2004: 1 with n. 1. The count of female writers in Greek is mine, based on the list of
attested women writers at Plant 2004: 243–49. The exact figures are: fifty-seven female poets
writing in Greek, forty-two of those before the end of the Hellenistic period, and thirteen of
those before the end of the Hellenistic period who have work extant. Cf. Stephanis 1988:
593–94.

10. The paradigmatic examples from classical Athens are Thuc. 2.45.2 and Soph. *Aj.* 293;
cf. Eur. *Tro.* 643–58, and, for a later example, Plut. *Mor.* 142c–d. See McClure 1999a: 19–24 on
female silencing in classical Athens, also M. Lefkowitz 1981a: 1, R. Fowler 1983: 338, Fögen 2004:
223–24, Lefkowitz and Fant 2005: 65, 393, Beard 2017: 3–21.

11. On female literacy, see Cole 1981, Glazebrook 2005, Dillon 2014; for the papyrological evi-
dence, see Bagnall and Cribiore 2006. On women's education, see Pomeroy 1977, Wolicki 2015;
see also Bundrick 2005: 92–102. On men's education, see F. Beck 1964, Marrou 1975, Griffith 2015:
45–47, and see also pp. 116–17 with chapter 4, n. 131, and p. 126 with chapter 5, nn. 20 and 27.

has lost grammatical gender in most other respects—has retained. "Author" and "authoress," "poet" and "poetess" are well-known examples in English of explicitly gendered noun pairs, like the *poiētēs* and *poiētria* of ancient Greek—and they demonstrate just why these kinds of questions still matter.

There continues to be a notable lack of consensus in contemporary English as to which form—generic masculine "poet," or marked feminine "poetess"— should be used, both to acknowledge women, and, at the same time, to foster equality with men. For the most part, gender neutrality (or "degendering") is favored through the use of the generic masculine, as in "poet."[12] Here Sappho, however, continues to cause division: known in the Victorian period as "the Poetess," she now appears most often in criticism as a "woman/female poet," but can still be found as "poetess," particularly in opposition to Homer (the "poet").[13] In French, on the other hand, a recent ruling in 2019 by the Académie française stipulated a global approach across all French-speaking countries known as "engendering": the use of feminine counterparts for all masculine nouns—*la poétesse* as the feminine of *le poète*, and so on (so that, in one example of a contemporary French translation from an English text, Sappho is *la poétesse*, in contrast to the English "poet").[14]

Yet even in grammatically gendered languages like French or Greek, where engendering might be perceived (as the French Académie clearly sees it) as the route to equality, it is not an unproblematic solution. We can see this particularly in the case of nouns like "author" in modern French (*l'auteur*), where different feminine forms have multiplied over the centuries—and it brings up a series of important questions.[15] What do we say is the "correct" form of feminization in a gendered language, and who decides what that is? Do we

12. On nominal gender in English, see Cheshire 1985, Cheshire 2008, and Romaine 2001: 154–68; see also Wittig 1985: 3, Fögen 2004: 214.

13. For an ancient example of this tendency, see Gal. *Quod animi mores* 4.771; for discussion, see pp. 214–15 with chapter 7, n. 85. On Victorian Sappho, see Prins 1999; for Sappho as "woman/ female poet" in modern criticism, see, as only two examples, Finglass and Kelly 2021: 1, Lardinois 2021a. By contrast, a survey of "literary works" published in 2020 (which mentions Sappho only once), calls her a "love-poetess" (Reed 2020: 29); Melvyn Bragg introduced Sappho on Radio 4's *In Our Time* thus (echoing Galen's formulation): "Where Homer was the poet, Sappho was the poetess" (Bragg 2015).

14. See, for example, Russell 2020: 168, where *poétesse* is used of Sappho as a translation of "poet" from the English (Russell 2019: 168). See Académie française 2019; on grammatical gender in French, see Burr 2003.

15. Académie française 2019: 10.

plump for continued usage of the masculine noun with the masculine definite article (*l'auteur*), following historical precedents that derive from periods where men created the social hierarchy? Do we go halfway, adding a feminine definite article to a masculine noun—*la auteur*, for instance? Or do we introduce a fully feminized form (*la auteure*)—and if so, how do we go about forming it, and which of the many versions that have proliferated in linguistic usage (*l'autoresse, l'autrice*, for example) do we choose?[16] Do some feminized terms have a history of being perceived as second-rate or degrading, in a way that would make an entirely new modern coinage preferable?[17] This brings up yet another issue: How do we trace and explain the ways in which women have adopted masculine terms in grammatically gendered languages in the past, "as a way to mark their equal competence to men"?[18] And how do we understand the changes that are occurring in women's self-naming today in both genderless, natural-gender, and grammatically gendered languages—where, at least according to the Académie's claims, "a new generation of women wants their professional titles to make gender difference explicit"?[19]

All these questions matter, because what we call ourselves not only reveals ideas and assumptions about identity, gender, community; it also shapes how we think.[20] Language, and the labels we give ourselves and each other, help us to see where we fit in in society; to articulate our subjectivity as speaking individuals, what we understand our purpose, our role to be; to describe the kinds of activities we undertake.[21] In a history where women have been largely barred from higher-paying, traditionally male occupations, the ways in which women in particular use terminology to lay claim to skills and expertise in

16. Académie française 2019: 2.

17. The Académie report gives the example of *doctoresse*, the older (pejoratively) feminine-marked term, which has been replaced in common usage with *docteure*, formed from the masculine (Académie française 2019: 9).

18. "L'égalité de compétence et de mérite avec les hommes," Académie française 2019: 3.

19. "Les nouvelles générations donnant souvent la préférence aux appellations qui font droit à la différence," Académie française 2019: 3.

20. On linguistic relativity, see the collected works of Benjamin Lee Whorf in Caroll, Levinson, and Lee 2012, esp. 173–204; see also Gentner and Goldin-Meadow 2003.

21. On the connection between naming and identity, see Alford 1987, Dion 1983, Kaplan and Bernays 1999, Bucholtz and Hall 2005, Hall 2012. On language as a tool for performing gender identity, see West and Zimmerman 1987, Butler 1988, Butler 1990: 25–34, Baker 2008: 1–16, 63–89, Holmes and Wilson 2017: 167–93; see also introduction, nn. 49 and 50. On subjectivity in discourse, see Benveniste 1971, Baumgarten, Du Bois, and House 2012.

counterpoint to a generally male-dominant culture speak volumes about how women see themselves and their relationship to their work.[22] As Erica Jong puts it in her feminist essay, "The Artist as Housewife," "naming is a form of self-creation."[23]

In light of these important and highly current debates around gendered naming, ancient Greek provides a fascinating comparison and contrast to modern languages, both naturally and grammatically gendered—as the example of Sappho shows. It is part of a much wider network of discussions and patterns around gender and authorship—continued into Latin, developed in subsequent periods, and hotly debated in modern-day English, as well as other languages—which intersect in fruitful ways.[24] It equips us with a way into thinking about how we respond to the challenge of gendered language—through exploring how ancient writers, both male and female, posed such questions themselves. In large part, this is helpful because the terms we use to describe poetic authorship themselves derive from ancient words. Our "author" derives from Latin *auctor* (author); our "poet," "poetry," "poetic" from Greek *poiētēs* (poet). These terms for poetry arose in the midst of a discussion around the craft of poetic making in the fifth century BCE and were passed on over centuries of debate around poetic authorship into our own languages, from Greek to Latin *poeta* to Old French *poete* (modern *poète*), and so into English, in a tradition which has—not unproblematically—formed the basis of much of Western literature. Systems of classification for poetry and aesthetic and interpretative values, too, have been drawn from ancient criticism, from the development of genres such as epic, lyric, tragedy, and comedy in Greek poetry, to influential treatises on poetry such as Aristotle's *Poetics*.[25] If we are to understand the complexities and situatedness of being a "poet," we need to do the work of examining, and examining our own assumptions about,

---

22. Black and Juhn 2000: 450. On occupations and professions in antiquity, see Stewart, Harris, and Lewis 2020.

23. Jong 1980: 117.

24. Corbett 1991 gives a survey of grammatical gender across languages: see further, introduction, n. 50. For an example of the current debate, see the guidelines issued in 2018 by the European Parliament; for controversies in German, see Johnson 2019, Shelton 2019, Loxton 2019; in Hebrew, Tobin 2001, Ghert-Zand 2018; in Swedish, Bas-Wohlert 2012. In English, there has been increasing recognition in recent years of new gender-neutral terms like "folx" or "womxn," and the gender-neutral pronouns "they/their," to refer in a gender-neutral way to the diverse and nonbinary members of the LGBTQ+ community (Zimman 2017).

25. Ford 2002: x.

the gendered naming strategies coded into ancient Greek poetic texts. We need to undertake an archaeology of the words for "poet," then and now, to investigate exactly what it is we say when we speak, to understand how language has been used and continues to be used to express gender and identity—and how everything we say has a layered, often fraught history in the performance of gendered poetic identities. Sappho's search for a name, in other words, is just one instance of the contest over gendered naming, and what it means to be a woman, or a man, who writes.

Sappho: Poet

One of the basic premises of this book is that any statement of the word "poet" is loaded with two intertwined arguments: first, an argument for gender identity (made explicit in Greek through the gendering of the definite article and the noun ending: *ho poiētēs* [the male poet] in the masculine, *hē poiētria* [the female poet] in the feminine), and second, a reference to notions of poetic authorship. Yet defining terms like "gender" and "authorship" in relation to Greek antiquity is notoriously difficult. Every language and cultural system, ancient and modern, has its own structures, references, and values—and these need to be put in context before we can start to unravel the ways in which speakers of that language manipulate, play with, and develop their own vocabularies and identity statements. If we begin with authorship—"Sappho as poet"—there is, to begin with, the issue of the definition of the author itself: whether we can (or should) label authorship on a continuum across literature in Greek, and across different literary genres and contexts. This is particularly the case in archaic Greek poetry, where the blurring of boundaries between composition, performance, and written text begs the question at which point we pin down the "author" (if at all). We also need to examine the possibility of any continuity of perceptions of authorship between—for example—the oral circulation of texts and performances in archaic Greece, the dramatic performances of classical Greek tragedy and comedy, and the highly literary productions of Hellenistic Greece.[26] Then there is the matter of the precise location of authorial identity: in the use of

---

26. On performance in ancient Greece, see Gentili 1988, Lardinois 1996, Calame 1997, Stehle 1997, Edmunds and Wallace 1997, Kurke 2000, Bakker 2009, Carey 2009, Athanassaki and Bowie 2011, Minchin 2011, Bakker 2017. For a useful discussion of how we might see authorship engaging with oral performance, see Nagy 1996: 207–25. Bing 1988 is the classic analysis of the transi-

the first person, biographical information, self-naming (*sphragis*), self-referential terminology more broadly, or even the notoriously difficult "style."[27] And finally, there is the question of the way in which we interpret the author from a literary-critical perspective: whether we take authorial statements as biographical fact, or as constructions of a poetic persona.

Even—perhaps especially—in instances of the declaration of authorship, we have to exert caution in interpreting authorial identity. This is particularly the case in performed poetry, where the "I"-figure is just as likely to be a reflection of the poems' performance environment, or a persona projected by the poet.[28] Instead of pointing to the biographical elements of a poet's life, the ambiguity and openness of the lyric "I" seems to invite us to ask exactly what the function of statements of authorship might be within a text, and how we figure authorship in a communal and performance-based context. When Sappho says "I will sing these songs beautifully to delight my female companions" (fr. 160 L-P), is she speaking of herself performing to her companions, or ventriloquizing the voice of a female chorus collectively singing to one another?[29] How do we interpret the fragment given that it is almost certainly not what Sappho originally sang? (There is a problem of transmission in the second line.)[30] And to what extent can we take this "I"—even if it refers to Sappho—to reflect her "true" identity (inasmuch as that is ever recoverable), as opposed to a performed persona?

The questions raised by the authorial persona in ancient lyric anticipate Foucault's twentieth-century theory of the "author-function"—the construction of

---

tion from oral performance to the written texts of Hellenistic Alexandria. On the relationship of women to oral performance, see Snyder 1989: xi–xii, Stehle 1997: 71–118, Klinck 2008.

27. On the poetic *Lives*, see M. Lefkowitz 1981b, Farrell 2002, and Fletcher and Hanink 2016. Beecroft 2010: 17 summarizes the categories of authorship attribution in ancient Greek literature; on the first-person construction of gender in ancient literature, see Fuhrer and Cordes 2022. See further, introduction, nn. 3 and 5.

28. See Gentili 1990, Calame 1995: 3–26, Mayer 2003, Kurke 2007: 143, and, on the interpretation of "Sappho" in fr. 1, Purves 2014; see, for further discussion, pp. 235–44, and on Pindar, see Hauser 2022. See also introduction, n. 32.

29. τάδε νῦν ἑταίραις ταὶς ἔμαις τέρπνα κάλως ἀείσω, Sappho fr. 160 L-P = Ath. 13.571d. See Lardinois 1996: 154–55 and chapter 8, pp. 235–44 with n. 14 for discussion. For the first-person plural, see fr. 140a L-P, where the speaker asks "What should we do?" followed by an instruction to a group of "girls" (τί κε θεῖμεν; / καττύπτεσθε, κόραι), fr. 140a.1–2 L-P. Lardinois 1996: 165 argues that we may have παρθένοι mentioned at fr. 17.14 L-P (Lobel and Page give π]αρθ[εν-), but see contra Stehle 1997: 268.

30. τέρπνα in line 2 does not fit the meter: see Lobel-Page 1963 ad loc.

the authorial persona and its value for interpreting a text.[31] Shifting the biographical emphasis of previous work on ancient authors, scholarship on authorship in the ancient world has now taken a turn to look at the function or persona played by the author as a literary construction and an important element in the interpretation of the text.[32] This is the approach which will be followed in this book. Rather than searching for the "actual" authors and poets of ancient Greece, or a "real" Sappho, I look instead at the "masks" and "figures" of authorship, how they are deployed within the context of a text, and how they relate to the social construction of gender.[33] Throughout the book, I use nouns like "author," proper names like "Sappho," and gendered pronouns "s/he" as placeholders for the *function* which these names, or gendered labels, perform.

This also brings up the question of the location of authorial identity. Almost all critical studies of ancient authors and authorship focus on moments of self-naming or *sphragis*—as in the case of Sappho's use of her proper name, *Psapph'*, at fr. 1.20 L-P.[34] But in ancient Greek, a "name" (*onoma*)—used in English for proper names like Sappho and Homer—in fact referred to common nouns and proper names, and even "words" in general, too.[35] Thus, in Greek, a word like *aoidos* (bard) or *poiētēs* (poet) was an *onoma*, the same as a proper name. The importance of these "names" for poets is shored up by the fact that ancient Greek critics had much to say about the labeling of poets. Two examples will suffice (though there are many to choose from).[36] Plato's Socrates is found in one of the dialogues investigating the most appropriate "name" (*onoma*) for Protagoras—the philosopher who was credited in antiquity with dividing nouns (*onomata*) into grammatical genders—by making a

31. Foucault 1977; for summary and discussion of Barthes and Foucault, see Burke 1992; During 1992: 118–22, A. Wilson 2004, and cf. Searle 1969: 169.

32. See, by way of examples of this shift in perspective, Calame 1995: 14–15, Clay 1998, Steiner 2015, Beecroft 2010: 2.

33. I take authorship to mean the ascription of the production of discourse (including self-ascription): cf. Behme 2007: 10, and, for another definition of authorship, see Beecroft 2010: 16. For the language of "masks" and "figures" see Steiner 2015: 31.

34. τίς σ᾽, ὦ / Ψάπφ᾽, ἀδικήει; (who wrongs you, Sappho?), Sappho fr. 1.19–20 L-P. On *sphragis*, see introduction, n. 5.

35. Brunschwig 1984: 4; the absence of a distinction between "names" and "nouns" is common to most languages: see Anderson 2007: 16. For an overview of ancient grammatical theory and philosophy of language, see Taylor 1995, Blank 2000, Swiggers and Wouters 2002. For a history of the ancient study of names/nouns, see Anderson 2007: 132, Householder 1995a and 1995b.

36. For more examples, see pp. 122–26.

comparison to other well-known figures.[37] "What name [*onoma*] do we hear Protagoras being called?" he asks. "Like we hear the name 'sculptor' for Pheidias, or 'poet' [*poiētēs*] for Homer—what do people say about Protagoras?" (Pl. *Prt.* 311e).[38] In the context of exploring naming practices for professions, and in a meta-examination of the nature of names by applying a "name" to the very philosopher who first classified them, it is the example of the word "poet" which, tellingly, first comes to mind. Aristotle picks up this interest in using "poet" as an example of naming—with Homer, the paramount poet, as his exemplar—in *On Interpretation*, asking what it means to say that someone "is" something.[39] "Let's say, Homer is something—say, a poet. Does that mean he 'is,' or not? The verb 'is' applies to Homer here only incidentally. It means that he 'is' a poet, not that he 'is' in and of itself" (Arist. *Int.* 21a).[40] Aristotle's question here is not only what it means to say that someone "is" something. It also asks what it means to be a poet. When we say the word "poet," what is implicit in the term?[41] How does it relate to the identity of the person being named as a poet? In the close link through predication of the proper name and the word "poet," Aristotle demonstrates the proximity between poetic naming and identity *as* a poet. This is particularly the case with the prototypical poet Homer, where to say one was, to all intents and purposes, to say the other: Homer's name became so synonymous with poetry in antiquity that he was often termed simply "the poet" (*ho poiētēs*).[42]

---

37. τί ὄνομα ἄλλο γε λεγόμενον περὶ Πρωταγόρου ἀκούομεν, Pl. *Prt.* 311e1–2. On Protagoras's three grammatical genders, see pp. 13–16.

38. τί ὄνομα ἄλλο γε λεγόμενον περὶ Πρωταγόρου ἀκούομεν; ὥσπερ περὶ Φειδίου ἀγαλματοποιὸν καὶ περὶ Ὁμήρου ποιητήν, τί τοιοῦτον περὶ Πρωταγόρου ἀκούομεν, *Prt.* 311e1–4. On this passage, see Nagy 2009a: 519–23.

39. On Aristotle's *On Interpretation*, see Whitaker 2002: 35–70.

40. ὥσπερ Ὅμηρός ἐστί τι, οἷον ποιητής· ἆρ᾽ οὖν καὶ ἔστιν, ἢ οὔ; κατὰ συμβεβηκὸς γὰρ κατηγορεῖται τὸ ἔστιν τοῦ Ὁμήρου· ὅτι γὰρ ποιητής ἐστιν, ἀλλ᾽ οὐ καθ᾽ αὑτό, κατηγορεῖται κατὰ τοῦ Ὁμήρου τὸ ἔστιν, Arist. *Int.* 21a25–28.

41. Cf. the *Poetics*, where the first occurrence of the word ποιητής is, interestingly, with reference to the problem of naming poets (*Poet.* 1447b13–16); see Janko 2011: 271 n. 14. Aristotle uses the generalizing masculine ὁ ποιητής throughout the *Poetics*; see, e.g., *Poet.* 1451b1, 1451b27, 1460a7, 1460b1, and 1449b3 in the plural. Note also Aristotle's lost treatise on poets, *Peri poiētōn*: see Janko 2011: 317–539, M. Heath 2013.

42. On Homer as a universal authority see Graziosi 2002: 57–58, Nagy 2009a. Cf. Xenophanes DK 21 B 10, ἐξ ἀρχῆς καθ᾽ Ὅμηρον ἐπεὶ μεμαθήκασι πάντες (since from the beginning everyone learned from Homer); see also Pl. *Prt.* 311e3, Plut. *Quaest. conv.* 667f. The examples of Homer as ὁ ποιητής are too numerous to detail: see, e.g., Pl. *Grg.* 485d, Arist. *Rh.*

The final consideration in terms of ancient authorship is the performance context of much of archaic and classical Greek poetry—and it brings us closer to the question of gender, or "Sappho as woman." From the oral tradition of epic poetry to the rhapsodic recitals of Homer, the dramatic contests of fifth-century Athens, sympotic poems, choral lyric, hymns, and victory odes, Greek poetry was rooted in a culture of performance.[43] Even later poetry, written for literate readers and no longer performed, often contained reflections and refractions of poetry's performative beginnings.[44] And then there are the lost, but no less important, oral traditions of everyday sung poetry—many of which included women's genres, like lament (of which we see glimmers in surviving poetry), maiden songs, wedding songs, weaving songs, and lullabies.[45] These—because ancient (male) critics deemed them unworthy of preservation or comment—are often hidden behind the self-referential, literary, male poetry of the Greek canon in discussions of authorship and authorial persona. It is a function both of the extant evidence and the focus on the construction of poets within the literary tradition that these hidden voices can only be heard in the echoes behind some of our surviving texts. And yet, at the same time, these traditions linger suggestively in many of the women's voices analyzed in this book: the laments of the women in *Iliad* 24, for example; the weaving songs of Calypso and Circe in *Odyssey* 5 and 10 (chapter 1); the public lament at the women's festival in Theocritus's fifteenth *Idyll* (chapter 7); and Sappho's shared lamentation with her daughter at fr. 150 L-P (chapter 8). Indeed, the power—and danger—of women's lament, in particular, as the most culturally validated form of women's song, is a theme which recurs throughout this book, and appears again and again, both in male poets' attempts to appropriate women's voices in lament—thereby, of course, as we will see, acknowledging its significance—as well as in women's own voicing of their poetry.[46]

The performance context of Greek poetry implicates gender inextricably in constructions of poetic authorship, because claims of authorship made in real-time performance would have been intricately linked with the process of enacting gender. As Eva Stehle points out, "Since gender is an inevitable part

---

1365a11, 1380b28, *Poet.* 1460b2, Polyb. 9.16, schol. ad Aesch. PV 436, Phld. *Po.* 1, 87 and 93 Janko, Strabo 1.1.4, 1.1.10, 1.1.20, etc., Plut. *Quaest. conv.* 667f, Gal. *Quod animi mores* 4.771. For examples of Homer's association with the verb ποιεῖν, see Nagy 2004a: 44–45 n. 9. See further pp. 116–19.

43. See introduction, n. 26, chapter 8, n. 36.

44. See, e.g., Bing 1993 on Callim. *Hymn* 2 and its impersonation of performance.

45. For a fascinating attempt to trace a lost genre of women's work songs, see Karanika 2014; on lullabies, see chapter 5, n. 64.

46. See pp. 36–40, 57–61, 130–35, 204–7.

of self-presentation in the flesh and cultural assumptions about gender attach themselves to speakers prior to any speech and inform its reception, oral texts must be read as gendered speech."[47] The same holds true for the written "voice" in later Greek texts, where the authorial voice staged and created figures for identity, thus enabling the poet, as a gendered body, to enact and perform themselves.[48] Authorship and gender in ancient Greek poetry are thus not only performative acts (to draw on Judith Butler's theorization of the performativity of gender) in and of themselves.[49] Their performativity informs each other, where the voice of the poet and the construction of gender interplay in subtle and complex ways. Rather than attempting to recover an "authentic" or "original" Homer or Sappho, or suggesting a fixed continuity in notions of authorship, this book, then, takes the more nuanced position of assessing the construction of the gendered voice in and through the shifting, performed articulation of notions of authorship—as they meet in the performativity of the self through words.

Sappho: Woman

The performance of the self in words naturally leads to a discussion of gender and language in ancient Greece. To a speaker of ancient Greek, the world was structured through gender.[50] A poet was male (*ho aoidos* or *ho poiētēs*); so was a lamp (*ho luchnos*) or a stone (*ho lithos*). A water-jar was female (*hē hudria*). A cloak was neuter (*to himation*). Indeed, our term for "gender" itself goes back to the Greek word *genos* ("kind," via Latin *genus*).[51] The centrality of gender in structuring both the social world and the language of ancient Greek thought is

47. Stehle 1997: 11; cf. Murray and Rowland 2007: 211.

48. J. L. Austin introduced the theory of the "performative utterance" in 1962; on the performativity of authorship, see Railton 1991: 3–22.

49. Judith Butler's understanding of gender as a continuous series of "constituting acts" (1988: 519–20) maps onto the performativity of authorship and gender in archaic oral poetry. See further Case 1990: 251–330, Parker and Sedgwick 1995: 5–6; for further discussion, see pp. 260–61.

50. For grammatical gender in language, see Corbett 1991; on the application of grammatical gender in ancient Greek, see Janse 2020, and in Latin, Corbeill 2015; see Fögen 2004: 237–74 for further bibliography. For introductions to the field of language and gender studies, see Hellinger and Bußmann 2001–2003, Eckert and McConnell-Ginet 2013, Ehrlich, Meyerhoff, and Holmes 2017.

51. See Varro's definition of *genus* as derived from *generare* because "genders alone give birth" (*genera tantum illa esse quae generant*, Varro fr. 245 Funaioli). On Latin grammar and gender see Corbeill 2015, also Vaahtera 2008.

revealed by the early distinction between the categories of names (*onomata*) by the philosopher Protagoras—the same one Socrates tried to find a name for—as "male, female and objects" (*arrena kai thēlea kai skeuē*, DK 80 A 27).[52] It is uncertain whether Protagoras was referring to general classification by sex, or the more specific classes of grammatical gender—but, either way, this is probably the first attempt in Greek literature to distinguish between the three major gender classes which became the foundations of the grammar of the language.[53] Not only that, but the order set up by Protagoras—masculine first, then feminine, then neuter—established the traditional hierarchical order of the genders. Of course, the placing of male before female in Protagoras was a reflection of a world view which set men above women in every respect, from citizenship to authorship. But it also, as I will argue throughout the chapters that follow, came to be used as a resource which could be manipulated both to reinforce and to challenge the norms of gender identity structured into language.[54]

Aristotle—who maintained Protagoras's hierarchical order of the genders—also recorded another concern of Protagoras's: the proper assignment of gender to words.[55] He gives the example of *mēnis* (wrath) and *pēlēx* (helmet) in Homer (as always, the prototypical poet). Protagoras argued that, in classifying *mēnis* and *pēlēx* as feminine, Homer committed a grammatical mistake: they should, in fact, be masculine.[56] But while *pēlēx* could be argued to fit a third-declension masculine paradigm (like *phulax*), *mēnis* looks morphologically feminine—and, as an abstract concept like justice (*themis*), seems much more likely to fit the feminine gender.[57] What is interesting is that Protagoras's idea of "proper" gender assignment here does not seem to accord with noun declensions—but rather, with the semantic properties of the word. Stereotypically male qualities, like Achilles's anger, or a battle helmet, are seen as requiring masculine gender, to fit with the "maleness" of their meaning. In other words, to the earliest theorist of grammatical gender in Greek, the grammatical gender of words was not simply arbitrary, assigned according to form:

---

52. Πρωταγόρας τὰ γένη τῶν ὀνομάτων διῄρει, ἄρρενα καὶ θήλεα καὶ σκεύη, DK 80 A 27 = Arist. *Rh.* 1407b7–8.

53. Taylor 1995: 84, Janse 2020: 25–26. Corbeill 2015: 17 seems to take the passage as referring to grammatical gender; see, by contrast, Rademaker 2013: 89.

54. Corbeill 2015: 1 makes a similar argument for Latin grammar; cf. Janse 2020.

55. See Sluiter 1990: 7–8, also Ibrahim 1973: 15, Corbeill 2015: 17–18.

56. ὁ μῆνις καὶ ὁ πήληξ ἄρρεν ἐστίν, Arist. *Soph. el.* 173b = DK 80 A 28.

57. Corbeill 2015: 18, following Wackernagel 1926–1928: 2.4–5.

it needed to have a semantic grounding, too.[58] It helps to give words their meaning, and it also aligns with that meaning, associating them with qualities that are stereotypically connected to "male" and "female" attributes. The fifth-century BCE comic playwright Aristophanes famously lampoons contemporary debates over grammatical gender in his satire of Socrates's "Thinkery" in the *Clouds*, where Strepsiades goes to learn about the proper gender of nouns: "You still need to learn about names [*onomatōn*]," Aristophanes's Socrates tells him, "which are male, and which ones are female" (*Clouds* 681–82).[59] Protagoras's early association of gender qualities with grammatical gender is exploited in "Socrates's" gender lesson to create juxtapositions, subversions, and fluidities between "masculine" and "feminine" categories: females, with common-gender nouns, that look the same as males (*Clouds* 661–64); newly coined feminine terms that generate a new vocabulary for females (666); males like Cleonymus with effeminate qualities that turn them into women (Cleonyme, 680); and men like Amynias whose masculine gender is undermined by the very grammar of their names (Amynia—a feminine-looking word—in the vocative, 689–92). Later, in the fourth century, Plato goes beyond Protagoras's determination that the gendered semantic qualities of a word match its grammatical gender, to suggest that the etymologies of the words used for "male" and "female" themselves in fact describe and delineate gender roles. In the *Cratylus*, during a discussion of the origins of words—which makes it the first surviving attempt in Greek literature to construct a history of language—Socrates draws a direct parallel between the words for "man," "woman," "male," and "female" and the semantic qualities of masculinity and femininity.[60] "Masculinity" (*to arren*) and "man" (*ho anēr*) are connected to *andreia*, "courage" (but also, through its etymology, "manliness").[61]

---

58. On semantic gender assignment, see Corbett 1991: 7–32.

59. ἔτι δή γε περὶ τῶν ὀνομάτων μαθεῖν σε δεῖ, / ἅττ᾽ ἄρρεν᾽ ἐστίν, ἅττα δ᾽ αὐτῶν θήλεα, Ar. *Nub.* 681–82. On this scene, see Wackernagel 1926–1928: 2.1, Fögen 2004: 226–28, and Willi 2003: 98–100 with further bibliography.

60. Ademollo 2011: 1–22 gives an excellent introduction to the dialogue; see also Denyer 1991: 68–82, Sedley 2003. There has long been a debate on whether we should take the etymological practice represented in the *Cratylus* seriously; for an argument toward a serious reading of the dialogue, see Sedley 2003, esp. pp. 147–73. On the *Cratylus* as the first study of etymology in Greek, see Dion. Hal. *Comp.* 16.20–24; see also Partee 1972. For further discussion, see pp. 124–25.

61. On the definition and concept of ἀνδρεία, see Rosen and Sluiter 2003, esp. Bassi 2003: 25–26, 32–56, and, on the concept of courage generally, Smoes 1995. See further, on Aristophanes and ἀνδρεία, chapter 4, n. 15; on Plato, p. 128 and chapter 5, n. 26.

"Woman" (*gunē*), on the other hand, and "femininity" (*to thēlu*) are assimilated to "birth" (*gonē*) and "nipple" (*thēlē*) respectively.[62] The term for "man," then, connects men to the "masculine" quality of bravery, while women are deemed by the very fabric of the word that describes them to be associated only with birth and breastfeeding.

For us today, the binary between male and female, reflected in the masculine/feminine opposition in grammar and the enshrinement of stereotypical "masculine" and "feminine" qualities in words, is an uncomfortable one. So too is the uncompromising conflation of sex and gender: the idea that a biological male must also exhibit (and will only exhibit) socially and culturally defined "masculine" traits, and a biological female "feminine" ones, even in— among other things—the language they use.[63] This opposition between male and female, and the conflation of sex and gender, were assumptions which structured the ancient Greek world, thought, literature, and—as we have seen—even grammar.[64] And yet it is also not true to say that we do not see important moments where the boundaries of this structure are being challenged. We find depictions of women, like Helen and Andromache in the *Iliad*, Clytemnestra in Aeschylus's *Agamemnon*, Sophocles's Antigone or Diotima in Plato's *Symposium*, who attempt to take on masculine roles and speech, challenge male hierarchies, or even subvert the biology of the male body (chapters 1 and 5). We find male poets sketching male characters (indeed, other male poets) that cross gender binaries in both their language and their dress, like Aristophanes's Agathon in *Women at the Thesmophoria* (chapter 4). We see Euripides using the masculine word *aoidos*, "singer-man," for women, to explore what a world would look like in which women could appropriate culturally masculine spheres of activity (chapter 6). And we come across

62. καὶ τὸ ἄρρεν καὶ ὁ ἀνὴρ ἐπὶ παραπλησίῳ τινὶ τούτῳ ἐστί, τῇ ἄνω ῥοῇ. γυνὴ δὲ γονή μοι φαίνεται βούλεσθαι εἶναι. τὸ δὲ θῆλυ ἀπὸ τῆς θηλῆς τι φαίνεται ἐπωνομάσθαι, Pl. *Cra.* 414a1–5; cf. Arist. *Poet.* 1454a22–4.

63. Note, on men and women speaking differently, Ar. fr. 706 K-A; cf. chapter 4, n. 34. Compare Pl. *Cra.* 392c–d (on men's and women's naming of Astyanax/Scamandrius) and 418b7–419b4, where women are envisioned as preserving an older form of language (see McDonald 2016: 166, Clackson 2015: 129, Fögen 2004: 221–22); cf. *Ion* 540b10–11. See also Arist. *De poet.* fr. 63 Janko, Arist. *Poet.* 1454a31. For an overview of gender-specific language in antiquity, see Fögen 2004; on women's language in the ancient world, see Gilleland 1980, McClure 1999a, Willi 2003: 157–97, Kruschwitz 2012.

64. For an introduction to gender in the ancient world, see Holmes 2012: 1–13; see also Winkler 1990, Zeitlin 1996, Wyke 1998, McClure 2002.

women poets like Sappho, Eurydice, Corinna, and Nossis who, simply through the act of speaking, defy the cultural conventions of the "public" sphere as male, and, in their poetry, rewrite the tradition of male-authored literature (as we will see in chapters 8 and 9). These moments of gendered rupture are not outliers, I suggest: they are precisely the crucibles in which gender is both constructed and contested. In this sense, I am interested, not in gender as some kind of "fixed" or "essential" category, but in the resistances, breakages, and slippages in gendered language, where the so-called "fixed" categories that appear to structure Greek language, literature, and society are called into question.[65] This book, then, traces the constant tension between the construction of gender in language by men in ways that enforced (and reinforced) the gender opposition and binary—and the ways in which those gender norms were challenged, tested, broken down, and rewritten by women and (sometimes) men. Bonnie McElhinny asks of gender and language theorists, "When is gender relevant?"[66] The answer is that, when it comes to poetic authorship in the ancient world, gender is always relevant: because it is always implicated in the contexts of poetic production, in the performance of the gendered voice, and in the very word for "poet" itself.

What's in a Name?

Over the course of this book, I construct a history of the gendering of poets in Greek literature, from the beginnings of archaic poetry to the end of the Hellenistic period. Part I explores the earliest Greek term for poet, *aoidos*, as a "singer-man" who safeguarded poetic production as a male undertaking in counterpoint to the power of women's voices. Opening with Homer, I explore in chapter 1 how the Homeric epics forged a new vocabulary for the male poet, which would have an immense and lasting impact on the gendering of authorship across ancient Greek literature. The role of the poet, and the words he uses, are defined in Homer as "a concern for men" alone, particularly in the *Odyssey*—yet, at the same time, women's powerful voices (like that of Helen, who defines herself as *aoidimos*, "sung of") pose a distinct, and challenging, provocation to the masculinity of the bard which remains in tension, particularly

65. See Kern 1961, Livia 2003: 142–48 against inherent male/female "styles," in contrast to the influential discussion of *écriture féminine* in Cixous 1976; for a summary of the debate over the existence of "feminine" types of language, see Moi 1985, Lanser 1992: 3–24.

66. McElhinny 2003: 33.

in the triple female lament which closes the *Iliad*. Chapter 2 shows how Hesiod draws on this exploration of women's voices to develop the gendered relationship between the poet and the Muses, as a pathway to the appropriation of the female voice. The poet of the *Theogony*, as *Mousaōn therapōn* (servant of the Muses), is able both to take possession of the female creative power of the Muse and to exclude her from poetic production. Meanwhile, in the *Works and Days*, we encounter a metaphorical female voice in the fable of the hawk and the nightingale, *aēdōn* (cognate with *aeidein*, "to sing"), whose identity as a singing female and potential *aoidos* culminates in her silencing by the male hawk. Moving to the *Homeric Hymn to Hermes* in chapter 3, Hermes's evisceration of the tortoise to create the first instrument of song, the lyre, is read as a prolonged rape analogy that powerfully demonstrates the male cooption of the feminine apparatus of song.

Part II continues the thread of male poetic self-definition, but moves to the new term for poet, *poiētēs*, which emerged in the fifth century BCE. This word, I suggest, demonstrates novel ways of demarcating the masculinity of the poet, that connects the poet's role as "maker" with the "making" of men in the state—creating a new, civic vision of a male *poiētēs*, from Aristophanes's exploration of the role of the "poet-man" (*anēr poiētēs*) in shaping the men of the Athenian state (chapter 4), to Plato's insistence on the erasure of female speech and prescription of the right kind of poet in the ideal republic (chapter 5). Yet there are hints of resistance to this vision—for example, with Diotima in Plato's *Symposium*, the (ventriloquized) woman who appears to challenge the imagery of gendered poets to argue for a radical understanding of *poiētēs* as a uniquely female form of generativity and creativity.

The figure of Diotima, and her argument for a gendered interpretation of the *poiētēs*, provides the turning point to explore the possibility of a language to describe female poets. Part III charts the struggle for words as male poets attempted to come up with new terms to describe women who wrote, in a language that (as yet) had no words to do so. In chapter 6, I show how Euripides, who gives voice to a multiplicity of female experiences in his plays, explores different "othered" contexts in which the term *aoidos* might be gendered feminine. And yet, as the chorus of the *Medea* tells us, this attempt to rewrite the tradition from a female perspective in the end simply reinforces male stereotypes regarding women's speech and characterization. A pivotal moment is Herodotus's treatment of Sappho (chapter 7), whom he calls a *mousopoios* (music-maker), despite using the term *poiētēs* several times of male poets. By creating a variation on a term from Sappho's poetry—*mousopolos*, or "one who serves the Muses" (fr. 150 L-P)—Herodotus refuses to use Sappho's own vo-cabulary for herself, undercuts the gendered and poetic power of the Sapphic term, and, instead, signals a form of gender segregation that subordinates her to the male poetic community. This approach paves the way for later depictions of Sappho (and other female poets) as first a woman, second a poet: while Antipater of Sidon calls Sappho an *aoidos* (three hundred years after Herodo-tus), these two instances form the only moments where Sappho is termed "poet" in all extant male-authored Greek literature to the end of the Hellenistic period. But there is another side to the story: the chapter ends with inscrip-tional evidence for a historical *poiētria* (female poet), Aristodama of Smyrna, which indicates that women could, in certain contexts and genres, earn praise and public memorialization for their songs in their own right, to be acknowl-edged as a *poiētria*.

Part IV takes up the example of Aristodama to give voice to how women poets came up with a name of their own, through their knowing, intertextual engagement with canonical moments of male poets' gendered self-definition. It reveals how women poets demonstrated their ability to generate new, supple terms to express their gendered identities in their own words, and suggests that they lay claim to a special association with the Muses through their gen-der, involving aspects of maternity, community, and authorial identity. In chapter 8, I explore the metaphor of mother and daughter as a figure for women's poetic creation and intertextual relationships between women poets—from Sappho's *mousopolos*, which suggests an involved relationship with the Muses as well as a participation in a close-knit community character-ized by the mother-daughter bond, to an oracle on Homer's mother and an epigram by Eurydice that rewrites motherhood into notions of authorship. Finally, chapter 9 looks back to the term *aoidos* with which the book began, showing how women contest the masculinity of poet-terms which had become canonically male. I explore how women poets from Sappho to Corinna to the Delphic oracles reject male poet-terms, and instead critique and stage the sys-tems through which women are compared to men—as well as, in an epigram of Nossis, coming up with a new, allusive vocabulary of the female nightingale (*aēdonis*) to lay claim to a powerful, yet subversively masked, connection be-tween female gender and song.

It is a reflection both of the norms of male authorship in antiquity, and the amount of evidence we have, that there should be more chapters analyzing texts by male poets than female. This is an unfortunate, but unavoidable, limi-tation, due to the fact that women were far less likely than men to be writers in the ancient world, and that what they wrote was far less likely to survive—and it reflects the systematic male-gendering of poetic authorship in ancient Greece, which makes up much of the story of this book. And yet, by looking at gendering across the board, and incorporating female-authored sources (some of them unusual and little known) alongside male, I hope not only to draw attention to the concerted strategies that led to norms of male authorship in Greece and beyond—but also to point us toward the resourceful, inventive women authors of the ancient world who wrote back against these strategies, to come up with new words for themselves. In balancing two parts of the book on men with two parts on women, then—even if only one of those is women writing in their own voices—I aim to do justice to the women poets of the ancient world, whose extradition from norms of male authorship and resultant rewriting of their gendered identity in words this book attempts to trace.

The power of the words we use for ourselves and each other—the power of names, in other words—is a central theme. As such, each part of the book has been given a single word which brings into play the powerful signifiers and metaphors which are often used by poets in their self-identity, signposting the power of the words we use not only for ourselves, but to describe the world around us. Part I, "Lyre," draws on the image of the poet's instrument—gendered feminine in Greek—to symbolize the gender struggles of the archaic bard, and the appropriation of the lyre to the male poet's cause. In part II, "Tool" becomes a link between the advent of the new "maker," *poiētēs*, and the vision of poetry as a means for educating men in the state. The "Wreath" of part III gestures to the symbolic appropriation of women poets by men; while part IV, "Bird," calls on the figure of the nightingale as a reconceptualization of women's voices and relationship to poetry.

This book, then, is not simply about reading individual poets, but addresses multiple themes in the performance of gender—the manifold ways in which each poet engages with gendering. The ultimate aim is an exploration of the gender strategies of Greek literature, not simply a new way of reading Homer, Plato, or Sappho—though it is my hope that looking at gender strategies will feed back into our understanding of these texts in new and interesting ways, and shed new light on familiar texts. In so doing, many themes recur throughout the book, crossing between the different linguistic and gender strategies of the poets analyzed. A particularly frequent topic is that of the Muses, and the way in which the gendered relationship between the (mostly male) poet and the female Muses frames the gender of the poet. Another is the conceptualization of mother/fatherhood as a gendered model of literary lineage—

either in the relationship between poet as mother/father and poem as child, or in the sequence of the literary tradition with previous poetic forebears modeled as "parents." Other themes include the voice, agency (particularly in relation to women characters and poets), community, gender-bending, imitation, performance, and the body; cross-references are included throughout the text as much as possible, to facilitate interactions between the different genres, texts, and periods covered. This book can therefore be read in two ways—front-to-back, as a diachronic history of the gendering of Greek poets; or crossing between different themes to make connections and relationships between different texts and intertexts. My hope is that this enables the survey of Greek poets to be accessible to a reader who might not be familiar with the source material, while those who are can feel free to jump between the texts to take stock of the overarching thematic connections. It is, then—to borrow a metaphor from the economist Colin Camerer—a book for both snorkeling and diving: snorkeling for those who want to get an overview of the way gender and poetics interact in Greek literature without the need for an intimate knowledge of ancient philology, or those who might be interested in applying the same general methodologies to other areas, time periods, or texts; and diving for those who want to go deep into the text, and perhaps draw their own conclusions or take further the initial thoughts advanced here.[67]

In a project such as this, it is impossible to cover everything. Precedence has therefore been given to tracing the wider story of the gendering of the poet in Greek literature, rather than to a comprehensive account of every occurrence of each term in every genre and time period. In other words, this is a narrative, not a concordance. The focus here is on a new and interactive understanding, bridging across different texts and time periods, rather than encyclopedism. At the same time, by narrowing my scope to the terms for poetic authorship (rather than the many adjectives, verbal periphrases, metaphors, and mechanisms surrounding literary production) and instituting the chronological end point of 31 BCE, I have done my best to be able to include here the most important instances of gendered poet-terms in Greek literature up to the end of the Hellenistic period.[68] Meanwhile, the focus on gendered naming means that other aspects of poetry which are clearly relevant to the construction

---

67. Camerer 2003: xiv.

68. Although it should be noted that—though beyond the scope of this study—Greek literature of the imperial period has many interesting things to say on both gender and the figure of the poet; see Dihle 1994: 312, Whitmarsh 2004: 161–76.

of gender—such as the social function of poetry, its composition and performance contexts, trends in musical developments, and so on—have necessarily had to take a sideline, though I have done my best to incorporate them as and when I could, and to point the reader to the important work that is being done on gender in these different areas. In some sense, the need to impose boundaries shows just how rich this area is as a line of inquiry—the sheer volume of evidence for poet-terms, and the continuation of the topic as a central line of thought well beyond the periods and language covered here. This inevitably means I cannot say everything—and I see that as a good thing. I am not, nor do I claim to be, an expert on all the authors I treat; rather, I am taking a particular lens to these texts and using my interest in gender and poetic authorship as a way into interpreting them in what are hopefully new and thought-provoking ways.

This book has an ambitious goal. It proposes that we can read the story of Greek literature as a continuously negotiated contest of gender. At the same time, it asks us to think about the ways that we use language today, and the power of words to shore up, and bring down, gender hierarchies. If it succeeds in challenging its readers to see old texts in new ways, if it encourages them to come to the study of the past as a site of gender negotiation, and makes them reflect on the importance of thinking through how we use words to describe ourselves and others—then it will have achieved its aims.

PART I

Lyre

THE SINGER-MAN:
MAKING POETS MALE FROM
THE BEGINNING

1

The Invention of the Singer-Man in Homer

THE STORY begins with Homer, as often in both ancient and modern criticism, where the term for "poet" first appears in Greek literature. From the very beginning, poets like Homer talked about what it meant to be a poet, depicting bard figures who sang in their own tradition of epic song—and the word they used was *aoidos*. This meant "bard" or "singer," and comes from the Greek verb *aeidein* (to sing).[1] This early term, as many have pointed out, clearly demonstrates the importance of performance and song culture in archaic Greece.[2] Bards like Homer and his predecessors sang epic poems in performance, composing and recomposing their subject matter from a wide pool of traditional mythic material.[3] Lyricists like Alcman and Sappho sang their poetry accompanied by a lyre and, at times, a singing and dancing chorus. Symposia centered around the performance of elegiac poetry like that of Alcaeus or Theognis. Victory odes by Pindar and Bacchylides were sung in celebration of athletes at the games. Even informal genres such as funerary

---

1. See Chantraine s.v. ἀείδω, *LfgrE* s.v. ἀοιδός. On the epic bard, see Svenbro 1984: 18–38, Gentili 1988: 3–23, Goldhill 1991: 56–68, Ford 1992: 90–130, C. Segal 1994a: 113–41; on the semantics of the term ἀοιδός, see Koller 1965 and Maslov 2009. The noun occurs once in the *Iliad* (24.720) and thirty-seven times in the *Odyssey* (1.325, 1.336, 1.338, 1.346, 1.347, 1.370, 3.267, 3.270, 4.17, 8.43, 8.47, 8.62, 8.73, 8.83, 8.87, 8.367, 8.471, 8.479, 8.481, 8.521, 8.539, 9.3, 9.7, 11.368, 13.9, 13.27, 16.252, 17.358, 17.359, 17.385, 17.518, 22.330, 22.345, 22.376, 23.133, 23.143, 24.439).

2. R. L. Fowler 1987: 89–100, Gentili 1988: 3, Nagy 1989: 23–4, Ford 2002: 131.

3. The major work on Homeric performance and composition is still Lord 2000; an overview of the history of the Homeric question is provided at Nagy 2001: 533. See also J. Foley 1990, Janko 1998, Nagy 2004b, R. L. Fowler 2005, Jensen 2011, Minchin 2011, West 2011, West 2014b. On the "pool of tradition," see Honko 1998: 63, 92.

lament (*thrēnos*)—typically (and unusually) the province of women—were sung. Early Greece was, truly, a song culture.[4] And this is reflected nowhere better than in the fact that poets were called "singers."

But the first word for poet in ancient Greece is also important in other respects—because, aside from its etymology and its connection to singing-in-performance, it is also gendered male. That this has gone without remark in scholarship for so long is a testament to just how successful archaic male poets in making the maleness of poetic authorship appear inevitable. But the archaic period, which gives us the earliest evidence of a sung poetic tradition that stretches back before the introduction of writing, is the place where those stereotypes were being born. This is where the gendering of poetic authorship was first being policed, contested, challenged, and the foundations for the normative language of male authorship were being laid down. This part of the book will take an overview, over the next three chapters, of the introduction of the term *aoidos* to Greek literature—to tell the beginning of the story of gendering poets.

As the originary poet, Homer set the standards for the discourse of male poetic authorship that would follow. The word *aoidos* occurs in Homeric epic at the site of powerful, challenging women's voices and stories—and even at one point, I will suggest, potentially applies to women themselves. It is used to explore the masculinity of poetic authorship, as well as to probe the power and generativity of the female voice to challenge a male-gendered system of poetics. This is particularly true, not only because of the rich examples of female voices in Homer, but, as we will see in the chapters that follow, because of the generativity of the feminine apparatus around song: from the female Muses (chapter 2) to the feminine lyre (*chelus*, chapter 3).[5] Homer's *aoidos*, then, begins a history of strategies to respond to women's voices and creativity, to explore—but also to set up a long discourse of challenging and problematizing—the invention of the "singer-man."

The Song of the Bard in *Odyssey* 1: All about Men

The *Odyssey* is often noted for the prevalence of its portrayals of poets, with its memorable depictions of the bards Phemius and Demodocus, and Eumaeus's mention of *aoidoi* as one of the class of men "workers" (*dēmioergoi, Od.*

4. See introduction, n. 26.

5. On the depiction of women in Homer, see, inter alia, Arthur 1981, B. Cohen 1995, Felson and Slatkin 2005, Hauser (forthcoming).

17.383–85).[6] Just over three hundred lines into book 1 of the *Odyssey*, we find the first bard of the poem: Phemius. There is already a clear interest in poetic names with Phemius's name, which comes from the Greek *phēmē*, meaning "word": essentially, he is a poet whose name is "Word-man."[7] But Phemius is first introduced, not by his proper name (which occurs over ten lines later), but by his occupation—*aoidos*: "among the men sang [*aeide*] the much-heard singer [*aoidos*]" (*Od.* 1.325).[8] As this introduction shows, it is not only the bard's personal name which has an etymology underlining his connection to poetic song. The verb for "sang" here, *aeide*, is the word from which "bard" or "singer" is derived in Greek, and the two words are juxtaposed to emphasize the link: *aoidos aeide*, or "the singer sang." With this first occurrence of the term in the *Odyssey*, its derivation is explained to highlight the importance of the word, and Phemius's status as a singer and poet. He is also given an adjective, *periklutos*, or "much-heard," "much-famed," which has another marked poetic etymology, from the verb *kluein* (to hear). This verb gives the noun form *kleos* (thing heard, renown)—which not only becomes a central defining feature of Homeric heroes, who aim to win "deathless glory," but also of Homeric poetry itself, which tells the "glorious deeds of men" (*klea andrōn*).[9] *Kleos*, in other words, is both the glory won by Homeric heroes and the poetry which endows those heroes with renown. Phemius, in being "much-heard," is thus intricately connected into the value system of Homeric poetry: he himself has renown, but, as an *aoidos*, he is also the one who gives it, through singing of the deeds of men in poetry.

So the first instance of a poet being named in the *Odyssey* is carefully defined, both in his personal name as "Word-man," the etymologizing of his professional occupation as a "singer who sings," and his connection to the *kleos* which epic poems uniquely endow. But this first definition of a poet is also emphatically gendered male. His connection to *kleos*, through the adjective *periklutos*, recalls the subject matter of Homeric poetry, the *klea andrōn*

6. τίς γὰρ δὴ ξεῖνον καλεῖ ἄλλοθεν αὐτὸς ἐπελθὼν / ἄλλον γ', εἰ μὴ τῶν οἳ δημιοεργοὶ ἔασι, / μάντιν ἢ ἰητῆρα κακῶν ἢ τέκτονα δούρων, / ἢ καὶ θέσπιν ἀοιδόν, ὅ κεν τέρπῃσιν ἀείδων, *Od.* 17.382–85. Steiner 2015: 36 suggests that this identifies the bard as a "professional summoned from without"; Ford 2002: 50 connects to Solon fr. 13.43–62 *IEG*; see also Nagy 1990a: 56–67, and cf. Hes. *Op.* 25–6, Soph. *Trach.* 1000.

7. Rüter 1969: 233, Pucci 1987: 196, West ad *Od.* 1.154 (Heubeck, West, and Hainsworth 1988).

8. Τοῖσι δ' ἀοιδὸς ἄειδε περικλυτός, *Od.* 1.325.

9. On the etymology of κλέος and its relation to epic poetry, see Nagy 1974: 231–55, 1979: 16–18; see also Katz 1991: 6, Pucci 1998: 224–30. See *Il.* 9.189, 9.524, *Od.* 8.73 for the κλέα ἀνδρῶν, and cf. Hes. *Theog.* 100; see C. Segal 1994a: 86.

(renown of men)—sung by Achilles to the lyre in book 9 of the *Iliad*, and the subject matter of the Odyssean bard Demodocus, before he tells the story of the quarrel between Odysseus and Achilles.[10] In these cases, it is just as much the fact that epic's subject matter is *of men* (*andrōn*) that is emphasized, as the *klea*—the connection between glory and epic poetry. And Phemius is no exception to telling stories of men: his theme is "the homecoming of the [male] Greeks" (*Achaiōn noston, Od.* 1.326).

If this were not explicit enough, we are given a gendered commentary on both Phemius's subject matter and his intended audience by the entrance of Penelope. Phemius is introduced as singing "among the men" (*toisi*, 1.325) about the "[male] Greeks" (1.326).[11] Penelope, on the other hand, intrudes from the female-marked space of the upper quarters, accompanied by two female slaves, and described as superlative among and representative of her gender class: "noble among women" (*dia gunaikōn*, 1.332). She shows herself highly aware of the gender marking of epic poetry. In her opening line she defines Phemius's subject and the subject of all bards: "the deeds of men [*andrōn*] and gods, which singers [*aoidoi*] make renowned [*kleiousin*]" (1.338).[12] Although she uses the term "deeds" (*erga*), rather than *klea*, Penelope adds a further qualification that describes the role of bards (*aoidoi*): to "make the deeds of men renowned," using the verb *kleiein*—cognate with *kluein* and *kleos*. So Penelope's formulation links the *aoidos* directly with the *klea andrōn* for the first time in Homeric epic—defining what bards do as celebrating the deeds of men through poetry. Not only this, but the masculine *andrōn*—"men"—seems to be a marked choice for the bard's subject matter, in contrast to the non-gender-specific ability of poetry to "charm mortals [*brotōn*]" (1.337)—including Penelope herself, who has been listening to Phemius's song along with the suitors. It seems clear, then, that this is a marked moment of gendered poetic commentary—as a woman listens to a male bard, and is the first to comment on the songs of *aoidoi* as the tales of men.

If the subject matter of epic poetry is masculine, however, then so is its intended audience. Penelope may think that the aim of poetry is to "charm mortals"—that is, men and women alike. But Telemachus's response to Penelope's intervention is a highly gender-specific rebuke (*Od.* 1.356–59):[13]

---

10. *Il.* 9.189, *Od.* 8.73; on Demodocus's first song, see Nagy 1979: 15–25. See further pp. 33–35.

11. Cf. the all-male audience of Demodocus among the Phaeacians: see pp. 33–34.

12. ἔργ᾽ ἀνδρῶν τε θεῶν τε, τά τε κλείουσιν ἀοιδοί, *Od.* 1.338.

13. ἀλλ᾽ εἰς οἶκον ἰοῦσα τὰ σ᾽ αὐτῆς ἔργα κόμιζε, / ἱστόν τ᾽ ἠλακάτην τε, καὶ ἀμφιπόλοισι κέλευε / ἔργον ἐποίχεσθαι· μῦθος δ᾽ ἄνδρεσσι μελήσει / πᾶσι, μάλιστα δ᾽

but go into the house and attend to your own tasks,
the loom and the distaff, and order your female slaves
to busy themselves at the task; words are the concern of
all men, and me most of all, since the rule in this house is mine.

Here we have the first depiction of a bard in the epic framed by a discussion
around gendered access to and interpretation of poetry, with Telemachus set-
ting Penelope and the feminine world of weaving against the "men" (358) who
control speech. Speech, and poetry, in particular, are thus demarcated from
the first as gendered acts. If Penelope was attempting to intercept the bard
Phemius's song (she asks him to sing a different song, 339), her misconcep-
tions as to the gendering of poetry are quickly corrected.[14] Telemachus's reply,
"words are men's concern," becomes almost a programmatic statement of the
male-gendering of literature in the ancient world.

This is emphasized through Telemachus's use of the word *mythos*, which
can refer in Greek to both "words," "speech," and "poetic narrative."[15] On one
level there is the overt meaning, where *mythos* refers back to Penelope's own
transgressive attempt to comment on Phemius's song: "words [about poetry]
are for men." However, the fact that *mythos* can be used for both "words, dis-
cussion" and "poetry" itself blurs Telemachus's critical voice and the creative
voice of Phemius the (male) bard, suggesting male control over both poetry
and its transmission and criticism. Women are neither meant to pronounce
on poetry, nor to attempt (as Penelope is doing here) to direct its content: in
this sense, the phrase would read, "words [that is, poetry] are for men." And
finally, there is the potential of *mythos* to refer to "speech, language" as a whole:
"words [that is, language in general] are for men." The enlargement from poetic
commentary to poetic speech to all language enables Telemachus to transition
from Penelope's non-gender-appropriate intervention to his own power over
words as both poetic commentator, bard-equivalent, and social head of the
household ("since the rule in this house is mine," 360)—each of which is di-
rectly founded on his masculinity as one among a social group of male bard
and male audience ("words are the concern of all men, and me most of all,"

ἐμοί· τοῦ γὰρ κράτος ἔστ᾿ ἐνὶ οἴκῳ, Hom. *Od.* 1.356–59. For an interpretation of this scene as
a critical commentary on poetry, see Ford 2002: 5–8 and West ad *Od.* 1.346 ff. (Heubeck, West,
and Hainsworth 1988); as evidence of the poem's approaches to teleology, Hauser 2020: 39–42;
as female silencing, Beard 2017: 3–9.

14. τῶν ἕν γέ σφιν ἄειδε, "sing one of these [songs] to them instead," *Od.* 1.339. On Penelope
as a bard figure, associated with the poet, see Winkler 1990: 156, Mueller 2007: esp. 359.

15. Martin 1989: 12 and passim.

359–60). The final twist that brings the performance home is the fact that the word *mythos* is, itself, grammatically gendered masculine. Not only access to poetry, then, or the social conventions of authorship and the usage of language, but even the word for language itself is male. The male-gendered "word" is, indeed, a concern for men alone.[16]

If a woman is the first to identify a bard's song in the *Odyssey* as the "deeds of men," then, she is also swiftly silenced. "Words are men's concern" becomes programmatic, not only for men's ability to pronounce on poetry, but their ability (like the male *aoidos* Phemius) to generate the words that form poetry itself—which, in turn, amplify men's glory. It is a closely controlled mechanism and interrelationship between the male bards who control words, the male audiences who listen to and interpret those words, and the tales of male deeds, which promulgate masculine glory. And, when threatened by the intrusion of female speech, it leads to a forceful redelineation of gender roles. Men do words; women do not. The *aoidos*, as this programmatic passage argues, is a man who sings about men, to men, as a means to reinforce those men's status and power—and any attempt on the part of a woman to intercept that mechanism is swiftly silenced.

The Singer-Man: Safeguarding the Man's Tale in *Odyssey* 3

If Phemius, the masculine glory his song promotes, and the reception of his male audience all serve to emphasize the *aoidos* as emphatically a man, the next occurrence of a bard-figure in the *Odyssey* drives the message home. Telemachus, now journeying in search of his father, has arrived at the court of Nestor in Pylos and inquires after the death of Agamemnon. Nestor tells how Agamemnon, when he departed for Troy, left his wife Clytemnestra with a "singer-man" (*aoidos anēr*) whose job it was "to guard his wife" (*Od.* 3.267–68).[17] Aegisthus, however, left the bard to die on an island, so that he and Clytemnestra could start plotting their rule over Mycenae and Agamemnon's death.

---

16. See Ford 2002: 7: "To become a man among men, Telemachus asserts himself as a man over women"; cf. Goldhill 1991: 60–61.

17. πὰρ δ᾽ ἄρ᾽ ἔην καὶ ἀοιδὸς ἀνήρ, ᾧ πόλλ᾽ ἐπέτελλεν / Ἀτρεΐδης Τροίηνδε κιὼν εἴρυσθαι ἄκοιτιν (And with her was a singer-man, under strict orders from the son of Atreus to guard his wife when he went to Troy), *Od.* 3.267–68. For the translation of ἀοιδός as "singer-man," see Steiner 2015: 33.

There are several important elements to this story. Who was the bard to whom Clytemnestra was entrusted? Why leave Clytemnestra in the charge of a bard at all—surely not the best equipped of Agamemnon's palace officials to guard against a coup? Why specify this detail so particularly, in the wider context of the story of the death of Agamemnon? And why add the word *aner* (man) to the description of the bard, when the grammatical gender of the word already marks it as masculine?[18]

These questions were, in fact, already debated in antiquity. Demetrius of Phalerum, a late fourth-century BCE orator and literary critic, suggested that this *aoidos* was none other than Demodocus, the Phaeacian bard, whom Clytemnestra so respected that she ordered him to be banished rather than killed.[19] Strabo, addressing the question of why a bard should be chosen at all to guard the king's wife, thought that it demonstrated Homer's opinion that bards were seen as the superintendents or guardians of virtue.[20] More recently, Stephen Scully has argued that the singer was selected specifically in his role as "transmitter, teacher, and constructor of . . . values," while Deborah Steiner sees an opposition between the "moral" bard, on the one hand, and the "immoral" Aegisthus on the other as a rival performer who also seduces his audience (in this case, Clytemnestra).[21] When viewed through the lens of gender and poetics, however, we can read the male bard here as put in place to enforce the "correct" story on the female character, whose fidelity is to be celebrated in his tale of the hero's return. We can see the importance of the female story for the male return through the figure of Penelope: Penelope's faithfulness to Odysseus is a prerequisite for his homecoming (*nostos*), which is, in turn, the subject of the *Odyssey* (1.77).[22] As Nancy Felson elaborates, "While [Odysseus] journeyed, he envisioned Penelope as a fixed point, a stable goal, a *telos* or 'fulfillment.'"[23] Returning to Penelope is, then, for Odysseus, the end of his *nostos*, as well as the poem

18. Cf. the common exhortation in the *Iliad* to warriors to "be men" (ἀνέρες ἔστε, *Il.* 5.529; 6.112; 8.174; 11.287; 15.487; 15.561; 15.661; 15.734; 16.270; 17.185): see Bassi 2003: 33–34, also Graziosi and Haubold 2003.

19. Demetrius of Phalerum fr. 144 F-S = Scholia ad *Od.* 3.267. See Perry 1962: 303, Steiner 2015: 32.

20. Ὅμηρος δὲ τοὺς ἀοιδοὺς σωφρονιστὰς εἴρηκε, Strabo 1.2.3.

21. Scully 1981: 78, Steiner 2015: 32.

22. ἀλλ᾽ ἄγεθ᾽, ἡμεῖς οἵδε περιφραζώμεθα πάντες / νόστον, ὅπως ἔλθῃσι, *Od.* 1.76–77.

23. Felson 1994: 44.

which tells the story of the *nostos*.[24] Meanwhile, Agamemnon's tale is set up throughout the *Odyssey* as an alternative model to that of Odysseus, the failed other-version, the "what-could-be" that threatens Odysseus if Penelope were to be unfaithful and become a Clytemnestra to Odysseus's Agamemnon.[25] The male bard, doubly male marked as *aoidos anēr* or "singer-man," is thus put in place to ensure the fidelity of the woman to the man's *nostos*-tale—ensuring that Agamemnon can have his return to his faithful wife, and that his "glorious deeds" can be celebrated in the bard's song. Of course, in Agamemnon's case his *nostos* fails. The presence of the bard here in *Odyssey* 3, and his implicit failure, explains why this is an *Odyssey*—the tale of Odysseus's return—and not the story of Agamemnon: because Agamemnon's male bard failed to safeguard the masculine tale of the hero's return by ensuring his wife's fidelity, and relaying the tale of the "glorious deeds" of that return to future generations.

The reason, then, why the bard is specified as doubly male—as both an *aoidos* and a man (*anēr*)—becomes apparent: it is because his gendered role in safeguarding the story of the "glorious deeds of men" (*klea andrōn*) is being foregrounded and shored up here. While the addition of *anēr* to *aoidos* might, at first sight, seem simply idiomatic, or a metrical redundancy, the connection between the *anēr*, the *aoidos*, the guardianship of the wife (*akoitin*, 268), and the deeds "of men" (*andrōn*) which were outlined as the bard's subject by Penelope in book 1, means this can be read as a loaded juxtaposition.[26] The bard is spoken of as an *anēr* precisely because it is the stories of *andrōn* (men)—or one particular man—which Agamemnon hopes he will vouchsafe; and this is achieved by ensuring the woman's fidelity to the man's tale of the *nostos*. In a way, the labeling of the poet with two nouns in apposition to one another— *aoidos* and *anēr*—suggests that the two are interchangeable: to be a bard is to be a man; and to be a bard is to tell about men, and so to participate in and safeguard the discourse of manhood. Just as the bard Phemius's songs were

24. Hauser 2020: 49, 53.

25. On Clytemnestra as a foil for Penelope, see Katz 1991, Felson 1994: 89, Tsitsibakou-Vasalos 2009; on Agamemnon's tale as a counterpoint to Odysseus's, Olson 1995: 24–42, and as "an alternative narrative model," Slatkin 2011: 144.

26. Other examples of appositional ἀνήρ in Homer: ἀνέρες ἀγροιῶται, *Il.* 11.549; τέκτονες ἄνδρες, *Il.* 6.315, 16.483, *Od.* 9.126. The later idiom becomes a relatively common collocation to indicate a male professional: see LSJ s.v. ἀνήρ VI.1. See Pind. *Pyth.* 1.91, 9.118, *Ol.* 8.2, *Isthm.* 6.51; ἀνδρὸς λογοποιοῦ, Hdt. 5.125.1; Callim. *Hymn* 2.43; Posidippus 9.1 G-P; Theon *Progymnasmata* 122.24; Plut. [*De mus.*] 1142b316; Paus. 3.8.2; Lucian *Philops.* 2.16; ἀοιδὸς ἀνήρ, Maximus *Dissertationes* 10.5.15, 28.1.7–8; Sext. Emp. *Pyr.* 29.189. Cf. Pl. *Ion* 539e9 on Ion as a ῥαψῳδὸν ἄνδρα.

explicitly emphasized as *by, for,* and *about* men in book 1, then, here it is another gendered relationship that structures the singer-man. And while this bard is marooned and left to die, without guaranteeing Agamemnon's *nostos* or its fame in poetry, he is tacitly supplanted by another *aoidos anēr* who is telling the story of a successful *nostos*: the bard of the *Odyssey* himself.

But there is another important takeaway: the addition of *anēr* to the supposedly already-masculine "bard" also, crucially, implies that the masculinity of the *aoidos* is not, yet, so self-evident, so proof against the danger of women's tales, that it does not need to be bolstered by the addition of the masculine marker. The shadowy background to the depiction of the *aoidos anēr* as vouchsafing Agamemnon's male *nostos*-tale is, of course, the dark side of the story: the fact that it is Clytemnestra who will be victorious and exact revenge on her husband, in an attempt to make this her own tale.[27] The danger here, as the audience familiar with the mythic material knows, is real: Clytemnestra represents the threat of the woman's story to overtake that of the male hero. The placing of the male bard as her guard, and his crucial explication as a "man," demonstrates, more than anything else, that this is an issue about gendered poetry, about the safeguarding of song as a male concern. The specific marking of the *aoidos* as male, and the equivalence of the terms "bard" and "man," thus connects the male singer to his song about men—but it also, at a crucial moment of gender subversion in which the woman's tale threatens to overtake the man's, shores up his gendered role in making sure that that song happens, by policing women and enforcing the masculinity of song.

Other Singer-Men in the *Odyssey*

The rest of the *Odyssey* is engaged in enforcing the masculinity of the *aoidos* as established in the early books. As Demodocus, the bard in the Phaeacian court, begins to sing in book 8, we have an exhibition of a traditional gender dynamic: the female Muse, who inspires the male bard, with the bard's subject matter as the *klea andrōn*: "The Muse inspired the bard to sing the glorious deeds of men [*klea andrōn*]" (8.73).[28] The Muse, of course, was called on at the very beginning of the *Odyssey* in the poet's own invocation ("sing to me, Muse, of a complicated man," 1.1), and appeared a few lines before as Demodocus's

27. As Agamemnon warns Odysseus at *Od.* 11.405–56.
28. Μοῦσ᾽ ἄρ᾽ ἀοιδὸν ἀνῆκεν ἀειδέμεναι κλέα ἀνδρῶν, 8.73; see Nagy 1979: 15–25.

patron (8.62–64).[29] Here, as Demodocus starts to sing, the gendered relationship is made particularly clear: the female Muse (*Mousa*) does not sing herself, but inspires the male bard (*aoidos*) to sing about men (the *klea andrōn*, 8.73). We will explore the gendered role of the Muse and her relationship with the male bard more in the next chapter. For now, it is simply worth noting that, once again, the figure of the male *aoidos* appears in a relationship that is marked by gender, and—against the femininity of the Muse—the subject of poetry is emphatically defined in opposition as *about men* (*andrōn*, 8.73). Meanwhile, the context of this recital of male tales is also distinctively masculine: just before Demodocus is led in, we are told that "the porticoes and courtyards and rooms were full of men (*andrōn*) assembling, and there were many of them, young and old alike" (8.57–58).[30] In book 13, Alcinous specifically defines the audience of the *aoidos* as men: "each man [*andri*] of you who drinks the gleaming wine of the elders in my halls and listens to the *aoidos*" (13.7–9).[31] And while Alcinous's queen, Arete, receives Odysseus in the court in book 7 among "the Phaeacian leaders and counsellors" (7.136), she is not identified among the audience of Demodocus's songs; indeed, she is first mentioned in book 8.419–45 just before Demodocus's third song, where she is commanded to receive and store Odysseus's gifts and organize his bath, after which Odysseus is said to "come out to join the wine-drinking men [*andras*]" (456–57).[32] (This is in contrast to the recital of Odysseus—a guest of the queen [7.53–77, 11.338], and not a professional *aoidos*—to whom Arete listens, and even comments on his performance [11.336–41].)[33] Meanwhile, Nausicaa is pictured in the next line standing "at the door-post" (8.458), giving a vivid spatial image

29. The translation "complicated" at *Od.* 1.1 is Emily Wilson's (2018 ad loc). For the relationship between bard and Muse, cf. also *Od.* 8.479–81 where Odysseus talks about the privileged relationship between bard and Muse.

30. πλῆντο δ᾽ ἄρ᾽ αἴθουσαί τε καὶ ἔρκεα καὶ δόμοι ἀνδρῶν / ἀγρομένων· πολλοὶ δ᾽ ἄρ᾽ ἔσαν νέοι ἠδὲ παλαιοί, *Od.* 8.57–58. On the exclusively male audience here, see Doherty 1992: 162 with n. 4, 163–70.

31. ὑμέων δ᾽ ἀνδρὶ ἑκάστῳ ἐφιέμενος τάδε εἴρω, / ὅσσοι ἐνὶ μεγάροισι γερούσιον αἴθοπα οἶνον / αἰεὶ πίνετ᾽ ἐμοῖσιν, ἀκουάζεσθε δ᾽ ἀοιδοῦ, *Od.* 13.7–9.

32. ἔκ ῥ᾽ ἀσαμίνθου βὰς ἄνδρας μέτα οἰνοποτῆρας / ἤιε, *Od.* 8.456–57. Doherty 1992 gives a detailed discussion of the evidence for Arete's exclusion from the audience of Demodocus's song.

33. Doherty 1991; on Odysseus as deliberately including women in his audience, see Doherty 1992, and on Arete's centrality to the Phaeacian episode, see Skempis and Ziogas 2009.

of women's place outside the hall—like Penelope in book 1—where the song is being sung.[34]

This is the context for the final song of Demodocus, which is capped by a three-word phrase: *aoidos aeide periklutos*, "the famed *aoidos* sang" (521).[35] The male *aoidos* who is *periklutos* is thus connected, like Phemius, with the *klea andrōn*, the male subject of epic. This is a loaded web of gender associations, and is marked by contrast with one of the most vivid gender reversals in the epic, where Odysseus's emotive response to Demodocus's song is compared to the weeping of a captive woman.[36] Charles Segal imagines this as a tribute to the power of song to enable its audience to cross boundaries, "to experience vicariously an inversion of role, status, and gender."[37] Yet the boundary crossing only goes one way: this kind of involvement in song is only made available to the men, like Odysseus among the other "wine-drinking men" (456), who hear the song of the male bard. In a way, then, the comparison of Odysseus to a weeping woman simply underlines the fact that the women of the court have been led away beyond the doorpost, unable to experience the emotions invoked by the male bard's song: the only war trauma a woman can experience is the actual trauma of war (as we will see in the triple lament of the women in *Iliad* 24, including Andromache's own lament for her dead husband), not Odysseus's gender appropriation of their experience. While Odysseus may respond like a woman, then, appropriating a woman's experience, women are themselves excluded from the theatre of poetry—both as audience, and as poet. Demodocus's song becomes the paradigm of the male *aoidos* who sings about, and for, men alone.

The example of Demodocus is one of the richest expositions of the gendered mechanisms of male bard, male audience, and male subject matter—but we see the masculinity of the poet being reinforced throughout the rest of the epic. The much-commented-upon association between Odysseus and the figure of the bard—in his comparison to a bard by Eumaeus in book 17, for example, in the simile comparing his stringing of the bow to that of a lyre in book 21, and, of course, in the fusion of the poet's and protagonist's voices when Odysseus follows in Demodocus's footsteps, telling his own tales and

---

34. στῆ ῥα παρὰ σταθμὸν τέγεος πύκα ποιητοῖο, *Od.* 8.458. On the symbolism of the σταθμός, see Wohl 1993.

35. Ταῦτ᾽ ἄρ᾽ ἀοιδὸς ἄειδε περικλυτός, *Od.* 8.521.

36. *Od.* 8.523–31: see H. Foley 1978, C. Segal 1994a: 121–24, Rinon 2006: 219–21, Rankine 2011.

37. C. Segal 1994a: 123.

becoming his own bard in books 9–12—creates a sympathetic masculinity throughout the poem between the bard of the epic-at-large and his main character.[38] At the same time, we see the masculinity of Odysseus's poetic world in Eumaeus's simile comparing Odysseus to an *aoidos*: he compares the experience of hearing Odysseus's storytelling to "when a man [*anēr*] looks at a bard [*aoidon*], who sings [*aeidei*] beautiful words to mortals he has learned from the gods" (17.518–19).[39] The words *anēr* and *aoidos* are juxtaposed in Eumaeus's comparison—*aoidon anēr*, 518—reminding us of the *aoidos anēr* collocation of 3.267, and further tying together the masculinity of singer and audience. (Eumaeus's delineation of Odysseus's ideal audience as a "man" neatly elides the presence of a woman, Arete, at Odysseus's recitation in Phaeacia, an experience, perhaps, that belonged to the otherworld, not the gendered structures of Ithaca.) And Eumaeus's specific identification of the audience of the *aoidos* as a "man" here is particularly targeted: he is describing the effects of Odysseus's tale-telling, with a simile comparing the all-male audience's reaction to the male bard, to Penelope, the woman who had been reminded so forcibly in book 1 that she was not privy to the world of words or the performance of the *aoidos*.

Women Singers? A New Kind of Poet in *Iliad* 24

The *Odyssey* is not alone in its depiction of *aoidoi*, however. Although the *Iliad* contains far fewer bard-figures than the *Odyssey*, it nevertheless presents us with one of the most interesting gendered occurrences of *aoidos* in Homeric epic, and a striking departure from the normative assumptions laid down in the *Odyssey*—in the only instance of the term *aoidos* in the entire poem.[40] At the very end of the *Iliad*, as Hector's body is led back into Troy by Priam, the laying-out of the body is described (*Il.* 24.720–22):

38. *Od.* 17.518–21, 21.406–9; see Rüter 1969: 237–38, Goldhill 1991: 66, C. Segal 1994a: 85–109, Louden 1997: 95, Pucci 1998: 131–78 esp. 131, de Jong 2001: 221. For an important counterargument, see D. Beck 2005.

39. ὡς δ᾽ ὅτ᾽ ἀοιδὸν ἀνὴρ ποτιδέρκεται, ὅς τε θεῶν ἒξ / ἀείδῃ δεδαὼς ἔπε᾽ ἱμερόεντα βροτοῖσι, *Od.* 17.518–19.

40. Though there is another occurrence in some editions at *Il.* 18.604: Allen's OCT and West's Teubner both athetize *Il.* 18.604–5, on the grounds that the lines do not appear in any manuscripts of the *Iliad*; the decision to include them stems from Wolf's *Prolegomena* (ch. 49 n. 49), following Athenaeus (Ath. 5.181d). See Edwards 1991 ad loc; like Tsagalis 2004: 3 n. 12, I agree with Allen and West in following the manuscript tradition.

> beside him they put singers [*aoidous*]
> leading the lament: they wailed their moaning song [*aoidēn*],
> and the women [*gunaikes*] groaned in response.[41]

The male singers—*aoidoi* (720)—are explicitly set in opposition to a group of women (*gunaikes*, 722) in what appears at first glance to be a scenario of call-and-response lamentation between the two genders: the men leading the lament, and the women acting as a chorus, responding to the men.[42] While the men are given a professional term for what they do (*aoidos*)—their masculinity is encoded within the male ending of the noun and the masculine article (*hoi . . . hoi*, 721–22)—the women are labeled only by their gender (*gunaikes*, 722). It seems, on the face of it, that lament is being tied into women's gender as a standard expectation of a woman's role—as opposed to one that allows her to lay claim to the identity of a craft, in the same way as a male *aoidos*.[43] Not only that, but the men are defined as singing a song (*aoidēn*, 721; most likely a typical funerary lament or *thrēnos*), as opposed to the women's unidentified groans (*epi de stenachonto*, 722)—apparently setting up a contrast, not only between their genders and their status as singers, but even their voices, and the ways in which they lament.[44]

So far, then, the Iliadic *aoidos* appears to construct a male community of singers, opposed against women. It seems to give a history for the term—the *aoidoi* sing an *aoidē*, providing an etymology for the word "singer"—and to endow male singers with a genre of song (the *thrēnos*), in opposition to women's unidentified groans. So far, so binary. But this picture of equally divided gendered lament—professional male singers versus groaning women—is complicated by what comes next. Immediately following these lines we have the entrance of Andromache: "Among the women white-armed Andromache

41. παρὰ δ᾽ εἷσαν ἀοιδοὺς / θρήνων ἐξάρχους, οἵ τε στονόεσσαν ἀοιδὴν / οἳ μὲν ἄρ᾽ ἐθρήνεον, ἐπὶ δὲ στενάχοντο γυναῖκες, Hom. *Il.* 24.720–2.

42. Nagy 1989: 19 reads this as an opposition "between professional *aoidoi* and what we would call 'amateur' singers"; see also Macleod 1982 ad loc., Tsagalis 2004: 2, Maslov 2009: 5–6. For the gender aspect, see Easterling 1991: 149, Alexiou 2002: 12.

43. On lament as "an art of women" see Holst-Warhaft 1992: 1; see, in general, Easterling 1991, Holst-Warhaft 1992, Murnaghan 1999, Alexiou 2002, Tsagalis 2004, Dué 2006, Suter 2008. On the capacity of women's lament to challenge or subvert male speech, see Murnaghan 1999: 207, Perkell 2008: 93 and 108 n. 1. On the laments of *Iliad* 24 in particular, see Easterling 1991: 149, Holst-Warhaft 1992: 110–13, Alexiou 2002: 12, 102–3, 182–83, Perkell 2008, Blondell 2018: 122.

44. On the θρῆνος see Alexiou 2002: 12, Richardson 1993 ad 24.719–22, Tsagalis 2004: 2–8; see also chapter 1, n. 54.

led the lament [*goos*]" (723).[45] Not only is Andromache given an explicit term for lament here (*goos*), in opposition to the men's *thrēnos*,[46] she is also described as "leading" the lament (*ērche*, 723), the verbal form of the noun applied to the men as "leaders of the lament" (*thrēnōn exarchous*, 721) only two lines earlier.[47] If the male *aoidoi* were visualized as leading a call-and-response lamentation, with the women as responders only, we now have a new model: a woman leader within a group of women. Even more interestingly, she elicits exactly the same response from her chorus of women as that elicited by the male bards: when she finishes her long lament, "the women groaned in response" (*epi de stenachonto gunaikes*, 746).[48]

If now might seem an appropriate time for the song of the professional male *aoidoi* to come in, it does not happen. Instead, after Andromache's lament, we have two more: one from Hecuba, and another from Helen. Both, like the *aoidoi* of lines 720–21, are described as "leaders" among the women's song.[49] Both cause groaning in their audience, just as the *aoidoi* make the women "groan in response" at line 722.[50] And it seems that their audience is widening from women alone: from Andromache's provocation of groaning from the women around her, we move to Hecuba simply "stirring up wailing" in general (no gender specified, 760)—and Helen's lament, the last of all, makes the whole "people" (*dēmos*) groan (776).

So the question is: Why mention the male *aoidoi* and set them up in opposition to the groaning audience of women, if it is three women—and only women—who follow with long, highly poetic lamentations for Hector that serve elaborately to mirror the themes of the (male-authored) poem as a whole?[51] And—even more troublingly—if these women are both leading songs and eliciting groans, then what differentiates them from the male singers, who were identified precisely by those characteristics? Or was the term *aoidoi* never meant to be male at all?

---

45. τῇσιν δ᾽ Ἀνδρομάχη λευκώλενος ἦρχε γόοιο, *Il.* 24.723.

46. On γόος vs. θρῆνος, see Tsagalis 2004: 2–8; on γόος as emblematic of female vocality (pace Tsagalis 2004: 5 n. 25), see Easterling 1991.

47. ἔξαρχος is an Iliadic hapax here: Richardson 1993 ad *Il.* 24.719–22.

48. Ὡς ἔφατο κλαίουσ᾽, ἐπὶ δὲ στενάχοντο γυναῖκες, *Il.* 24.746.

49. τῇσιν δ᾽ αὖθ᾽ Ἑκάβη ἁδινοῦ ἐξῆρχε γόοιο (Hecuba, *Il.* 24.747); τῇσι δ᾽ ἔπειθ᾽ Ἑλένη τριτάτη ἐξῆρχε γόοιο (Helen, 24.761).

50. Ὡς ἔφατο κλαίουσα, γόον δ᾽ ἀλίαστον ὄρινε (Hecuba, *Il.* 24.760); ὣς ἔφατο κλαίουσ᾽, ἐπὶ δ᾽ ἔστενε δῆμος ἀπείρων (Helen, 24.776).

51. Macleod 1982 ad 723–76.

In gendered languages which make use of the generic masculine (of which ancient Greek is one), "grammatically masculine nouns have a wider lexical and referential potential . . . [they] may be used to refer to males, groups of people whose gender is unknown or unimportant in the context, or even female referents."[52] Of course, this is another linguistic reflection of the assumption of male dominance: in a group of a hundred women and one man, the masculine would still predominate. But it also means that the gendered opposition set up at *Il.* 24.720–22, which seemed so forceful, between the male *aoidoi* and the responsive women, may not be a gendered binary at all. The airtime given to the three female laments that follow, and the fact that no male *aoidoi* are quoted at all, means that we are led to wonder whether it wasn't the *female* leaders of song—Andromache, Hecuba, and Helen—who were being forecasted by the plural term *aoidoi*, as a generic plural that encompasses the community of (female) lamenters, rather than a signal of male professionals. What at first appeared to be a programmatic statement of the male dominance of poetic song, and women's lack of a claim to professional terms, is turned on its head by the virtuosic performances of the three Trojan women that follow—each of which demonstrates the poetic abilities that were ascribed to the (supposedly male) *aoidoi*.

Which means that we may have been reading this passage wrong all along. The lament (*thrēnos*, 721) of the *aoidoi* here has always been read as a mourning song sung by professional male singers, responded to by an inarticulate group of women.[53] The combined facts of the grammatical masculinity of *aoidous* (720) (underlined by *hoi . . . hoi*, 721–22), the example of male bards in the *Odyssey* like Phemius and Demodocus, and the later male dominance of the identity of "poet," means that interpreters of the passage have been lured into the assumption that *aoidoi* here must mean "male singers"—and that the genre of the *thrēnos* must, consequently, be masculine (as Christos Tsagalis has most recently argued).[54] But the examples of the eloquent female laments that follow, and the ways in which they pick up on the precise characteristics of the *aoidoi* of the *thrēnos* here—their ability to lead a group of mourners, and to elicit groans in response—argues suggestively for a proleptic rereading of the

52. Hellinger and Bußmann 2001: 9, see also McConnell-Ginet 2014.

53. Macleod 1982 ad 721–22, Richardson 1993 ad 24.719–22, Easterling 1991: 149, Tsagalis 2004: 6.

54. Tsagalis 2004: 6, though he notes the counter-example of the Muses' θρῆνος at *Od.* 24.58–62; see also Easterling 1991: 149, Holst-Warhaft 1992: 102, C. Segal 1993a: 57–58.

identity of the *aoidoi* here as *female* singers—not male.[55] The virtuosic triple lament acknowledges and foregrounds the importance of women's lamentation as a genre, and garners the word *aoidos*—the very term used for the male Homeric bard in the *Odyssey*—in recognition of the power, as well as the danger, of women's voices in lament. At the same time, this performance by three women gains particular emphasis and importance as the closing act of the *Iliad*—paradoxically ending an epic (a masculine genre) that was performed by a male *aoidos*, on a male topic (the anger of Achilles and the battles of Trojans and Greeks), with the feminine genre of lament articulating women's voices and experiences of war, and performed by three female *aoidoi*.

In other words—in direct contrast to the *Odyssey*—the only time that the word for "poet" occurs in the *Iliad*, it may, in fact, be referring to women.

Helen: Singer and Song in *Iliad* 6

The layering and complication of the gender of *aoidos* in *Iliad* 24 is not, I think, a coincidence. It belies, as we have seen, an awareness on the part of the male bard, himself an *aoidos*, who was composing and recomposing these epic poems in performance, about the power of women's voices, and the urgent need to define the gender identity of the poet. The troubling power of women's voices is explored throughout the Homeric epics, from the entrancing weaving songs of Calypso in *Odyssey* 5 and Circe in *Odyssey* 10 to the "barking" of the monstrous Scylla, and—of course—the dangerous, and poetic, lure of the voices of the Sirens in *Odyssey* 12.[56] Women figure as powerfully connected to poetry throughout the epics in their role as Muses—as in the invocations with which the poems begin, or in *Iliad* 2, when the poet underlines his dependence on the Muses' omniscience.[57] And they are portrayed as dangerous creators whose ability to "weave" (a frequent metaphor

55. This argument is strengthened by comparison to the θρῆνος of the Muses and Nereids for Achilles at *Od.* 24.58–62, where it is women who are associated with the θρῆνος, not men; see Russo, Fernandez-Galiano, and Heubeck 1993 ad *Od.* 24.60.

56. Calypso, *Od.* 5.61–62; Circe, 10.221; Scylla, 12.85–87; the Sirens, 12.184–91. See Doherty 1995a: esp. 85–86, Schein 1995, and see Hauser (forthcoming) on women's association with poetry in Homer; see further chapter 1, n. 5. On the Sirens, see Pucci 1998: 1–10, who argues for the Iliadic poetic tone of the Sirens' song; cf. Schein 1995: 21. On the enchantment of the Sirens' song (*Od.* 12.40, 44) connecting to the enchantment of poets (1.337, 17.514), see Doherty 1995a: 83.

57. See pp. 46–56 with chapter 2, n. 9.

for poetic production) threatens to supplant the poet, and which (as in the example of Penelope in the *Odyssey*) serves to figure for women's subversive attempts to take the plot into their own hands.[58] And yet, in spite of men's wariness of women's voices and attempts to silence them—like Telemachus silencing Penelope in book 1 of the *Odyssey*, or Hector silencing Andromache in *Iliad* 6—women were, as we have seen, allowed one particular access to song, through lament: it was one of the few public speech genres to which they could lay claim. It is not a coincidence, then, that it is at the site of lament—and a collection of some of the longest and most important laments of the *Iliad*—that this overlap between being a woman, and being an *aoidos*, first occurs. The claim of women to be an *aoidos* presents, in other words, a very real challenge.

One of the female figures who comes closest to encroaching on the male poet's voice, across the two epics, is Helen—the third and last of the trio of lamenting women in *Iliad* 24. The most well-known example of Helen's appropriation of the authorial stance is, quite paradoxically, one in which she is entirely silent: the weaving of her web in *Il.* 3.125–28, where she describes the events of the *Iliad* in visual form.[59] The connection between the act of weaving and the act of storytelling in Homer is a common one: and Helen's web in particular, with its depiction of the battle between Trojans and Greeks, becomes a microcosm of the poem which tells the same story.[60] But Helen also adopts both the voice and the vocabulary of poetic speech.[61] She tells stories (the tale of Odysseus's disguise in *Odyssey* 4, to Telemachus), where her direct address of her audience, rather than through a male bard or intermediary (as a Muse would have to speak), "opens up the possibility

58. On the subversive nature of Penelope's weaving, see Bergren 1983: 1–9, Winkler 1990: 156, Katz 1991: 3–6, Murnaghan 2009, and, for Penelope as a poet, see chapter 1, n. 14. On women's weaving in ancient Greece, see Pantelia 1993, Barber 1994: 101–63, Fantham, Foley, Kampen, Pomeroy, and Shapiro 1994: 33–34.

59. On Helen's weaving, see Bergren 1979, Kennedy 1986, Mueller 2010: esp. 12–13; on her silence in this scene, Roisman 2006: 9–10.

60. On the long-noted connection between weaving and poetry in Homer, see Clader 1976: 6–12, Homeyer 1977: 10–11, Snyder 1981, Bergren 1983: 79, Pantelia 1993: 494, Worman 2002: 89–90, Elmer 2005: 2, Roisman 2006: 10 and 18 n., Blondell 2010a: 19, Karanika 2014: 4–5; see also Worman 2001: 30 with 37 n. for additional bibliography.

61. On Helen's voice, see Worman 2001, Roisman 2006, Blondell 2010a; on Helen as Muse, see Crane 1988: 42, Suzuki 1989: 69, Wohl 1993: 33–34, Doherty 1995b: 135–38, Worman 2001: 23. On the Homeric bard "performing" Helen, see Blondell 2018: 122.

that the subject position of bard might be available to females."[62] She is a
master of different speech genres, from self-blame to lament (as we have
seen, in *Iliad* 24) to epic—and she receives the same accolade for her epic
recitation of Odysseus's disguise (to have spoken "in good measure," *Od.*
4.266) as another epic bard, Demodocus.[63] She is able to alleviate grief
through the administration of her "drug of forgetfulness" (4.220–21), whose
effects, like the capacity of epic storytelling to alleviate grief, "are those of
epic poetry or *kleos*, which makes all trials sufferable in the heroic ethos."[64]
And she has the capacity to modulate her voice to imitate others—a key
poetic technique. Just after he approves Helen's speech as "in good measure,"
Menelaus tells the tale of Helen's guileful attempt to deceive the Greek sol-
diers inside the wooden horse by impersonating the voices of their wives
(4.279).[65] This imitative ability to impersonate voices, while certainly a sig-
nal of Helen's vocal mutability, is also a central requirement of a poet of
mimetic fiction. The most famous discussion of *mimēsis* occurs in the clas-
sical period in book 10 of Plato's *Republic*, but there is evidence for the con-
nection between imitation and poetry in the archaic period, as we will see
in chapter 3, in the *Homeric Hymn to Apollo*.[66] A chorus of Delian women is
described as "know[ing] how to represent the voices and the rhythms of all
people."[67] What is striking about both this passage and the passage in the
Odyssey is that it is vocal imitative ability that is stressed in each—and that
both depict women. In other words, this mimetic ability, while clearly a nec-

---

62. Doherty 1995b: 137; see also Doherty 1995a: 86–87. On the similarities between Helen's
tale and epic, see Bergren 1983: 79.

63. On Helen's rhetoric of self-blame at *Il.* 3.172–80 and 6.344–58 see Blondell 2010a, also
Clader 1976: 17–23, Nagy 1979: 222–42, Graver 1995, Worman 2001: 21. On Helen as elegiac
mourner, see Pantelia 2002; as epigrammatist, Elmer 2005. On Menelaus's labeling of Helen's
speech as κατὰ μοῖραν (according to measure), suggesting Helen's "conformity to epic diction
in particular," see Worman 2001: 33 with n. 45, citing Nagy 1979: 40 with n. 2, 134; on this term
as used of Demodocus (*Od.* 8.496), see Nagy 1979: 40.

64. Wohl 1993: 33; cf. Odysseus on the joy of listening to a bard, *Od.* 9.5–7.

65. On the competing narratives between Helen and Menelaus here, see Olson 1989, Katz
1991: 75–76. For other interpretations of this passage, see Clader 1976: 34, 38, Worman 2001: 34.

66. On the Delian women, see Peponi 2009; see further pp. 62–63 and chapter 3, n. 1. For
the comparison between the two passages, see Martin 2001: 56–57 and Worman 2001: 34.

67. πάντων δ᾽ ἀνθρώπων φωνὰς καὶ κρεμβαλιαστὺν / μιμεῖσθ᾽ ἴσασιν, *Hymn. Hom.
Ap.* 162–63. On the text, see chapter 3, n. 3.

essary quality for a bard, is particularly associated in Homer and the *Homeric Hymns* with *women*. It suggests, perhaps, that while Helen (and the Delian women) are performers in their own right, there is something unique about their vocality as (potential) female bards.

But Helen does not only appropriate the voice of a bard: she also adopts the vocabulary of poetic naming. In the sixth book of the *Iliad*, she comments to Hector that "in future we will be subjects of song [*aoidimoi*] for generations to come" (*Il.* 6.357–58).[68] The adjective she uses, *aoidimos*, occurs first here in Greek literature, and—like *aoidos*—derives from the verb *aeidein*, "to sing." She is, as she herself puts it, quintessentially "an object of poetry"—or, in Ruby Blondell's words, "a subject who is the object of [the poet's] song."[69] It is particularly interesting to note in this context that Helen is not only fundamentally aware of her status as a character of poetry: she also places emphasis on the fact that she is vocalized (*aoidimos*, from *aeidein*) into the existence that, in turn, gives her a voice. It is the fundamental paradox of a literary character who speaks her awareness of her dependency on speech.[70] (We might compare the inherent oxymoron to Helen's weaving, in which she "creates the text in which she herself is a character.")[71] At the same time, ironically, she states the dependency of the bard *on her*: it is her very existence as a character in poetry, who is *aoidimos*, that guarantees and ensures the poetic success of the male *aoidos*. The *aoidimos* female object of song makes the *aoidos*, by providing him with something to sing about. (It is worth noting that, while Helen's plural *aoidimoi* appears to include Hector, neither he nor any other male character in the *Iliad* conceptualizes himself in this way as a passive object of song.)

In this sense, Helen embodies both the poet and the poet's song—and she even appropriates the vocabulary of the *aoidos*, in adjectival form, to describe herself (even though she turns herself into an object of poetry by so doing), long before she merges with the lamenting *aoidoi* of *Iliad* 24. In the dangerous and powerful association of the woman's voice with imitation, storytelling, and the vocabulary of song here, then, we have the challenge to the maleness of the *aoidos* with which the ambiguous passage in *Iliad* 24 wrestles—as well

---

68. ὡς καὶ ὀπίσσω / ἀνθρώποισι πελώμεθ᾽ ἀοίδιμοι ἐσσομένοισι, *Il.* 6.357–58.

69. Blondell 2010a: 20.

70. See Clader 1976: 8, Suzuki 1989: 55 on Helen's self-consciousness.

71. Wohl 1993: 33. Compare Clader 1976: 8, Bergren 1979: 80.

as the dependence of the male *aoidos* on his *aoidimos* female "objects of song" to provide the fodder for his poetry.

The scenes in Homeric epic where the *aoidos* is identified and developed for the first time, then, take place on the battleground of gender. The *Odyssey* is deeply engaged with exploring the masculinity of the *aoidos* and shoring up the relationship between the male bard, his male audience, and his tale of the deeds of men—all in counterpoint to the powerful stories of women. The *Iliad*, meanwhile, troubles and complicates these gender norms. The three virtuosic female lamenters of *Iliad* 24 take on all the characteristics attributed to *aoidoi*: leadership of the lament, and call-and-response songs with a female chorus. Meanwhile, Helen comes dangerously close elsewhere to appropriating the speech of the bard herself, as in her vocal imitation of the wives of the Greeks in Menelaus's story of the Trojan horse—so much so that, in Demodocus's song of the fall of Troy in *Odyssey* 8, we find Helen's dangerous, imitative, near-poetic vocality excised entirely from the bard's idealized all-male version of the epic, reestablishing the masculine *aoidos* as the only one capable of imitative speech.

But the editing of Helen from Demodocus's song elicits one last, crucial observation: even if the bards of Odyssean epic are depicted as closing down the gendering of epic to a male-produced genre, the *Homeric* bard does not do so—at least, not exclusively. We find the rich, polyphonous voices of women resounding across both epics: the laments of Andromache, Hecuba, and Helen in *Iliad* 24; the interjection of Penelope in *Odyssey* 1; the tale-telling of Helen in *Odyssey* 4, to mention but a few. Female poet-figures, as we have seen, abound in both the *Iliad* and the *Odyssey*, from singing Calypso and Circe to weaving Helen to the Sirens' songs. In other words, Homer does not athetize Helen, or her counterparts, out of the story of the fall of Troy, as his character Demodocus does. Instead, the attribution of *aoidos* to the female lamenters in *Iliad* 24, and the labeling of Helen as *aoidimos* in her own speech, works to foreground and explore, not conceal, the gender battle that is going on. And it also serves to obfuscate and challenge traditional gender categorizations: the *Odyssey*, often seen as an epic more concerned with the experiences of women, enforces the masculinity of the bard; the *Iliad*, traditionally read as a "masculine" epic concerned with war and the glory of men, works to challenge the gender norms of the male poet.[72]

72. See, e.g., Schein 1984: 67–88.

What all this suggests is that, at the very beginnings of Greek epic, the masculinity of the poet—implicit in the very word *aoidos* and the social contexts of the male bard singing songs of male glory to an audience of men—was being consistently explored, challenged, and complicated by the intrusion of women's voices and agency. Some women succeeded in overcoming the bard, like Clytemnestra, with disastrous effects for the male tale; others, like Penelope, accepted defeat to return to their ascribed gender roles, and made way for the song of the men; still others, like Helen, Hecuba, and Andromache, challenged the masculinizing of the bard with their resonant, powerful voices verbalizing their own experiences of war.

Being a poet, in other words, was a battleground of gender from the very beginning.

2

Mastering the Muses in Hesiod

HOMER'S "SINGER-MAN" does not go unnoticed. The first occurrence of *aoidos* in Hesiod's *Theogony*, the epic poem describing the origins of the gods, gives the same phrase: "singer-men [*andres aoidoi*] on earth and lyre-players come from the Muses and far-shooting Apollo" (*Theog.* 94–95).[1] Where Homer's *aoidos anēr* was supplanted by the bard of the *Odyssey* himself, here we have a community of multiple "singer-men" being evoked. We are still on very familiar ground in the gender dynamics at play. The female Muses and male Apollo inspire the *andres aoidoi,* who are marked male with the appositional *andres* that serves both to underline the masculinity of the *aoidos* and to generate the image of a community of men.[2] If Homer showed the gender dynamics of a failed bard and supplanted him with his own success, then Hesiod identifies himself as one of a number of successful poets in the ranks of Homer.[3] Hesiod (or rather, his persona) is famously more present than Homer in his poetry, identified explicitly by name at the opening of the *Theogony* (*Theog.* 22).[4] Just like the fictional bard Phemius in book 1 of the *Odyssey*, his name seems to have a metapoetic meaning—here, "sender-forth of

---

1. ἐκ γάρ τοι Μουσέων καὶ ἑκηβόλου Ἀπόλλωνος / ἄνδρες ἀοιδοὶ ἔασιν ἐπὶ χθόνα καὶ κιθαρισταί, *Theog.* 94–95 = *Hymn. Hom. in Musas et Apollinem* (25) 2–3; cf. Hes. *Op.* 26, Hes. fr. 305 M-W. On the ἀοιδός in Hesiod, see Calame 1995: 58–74, Clay 2003: 67–72, Stoddard 2003, Nagy 1990b: 47–61, Nagy 1992, Nagy 2009b: 285.

2. See also the male-marked bard "whom [masc.] the Muses love" which follows: ὁ δ' ὄλβιος, ὅντινα Μοῦσαι / φίλωνται, *Theog.* 96–97.

3. On the relative dating of Hesiod and Homer, see Janko 1982, Graziosi and Haubold 2005: 35–48. Cf. Hes. fr. 357 M-W for an early example of the contest between Homer and Hesiod in the biographical tradition, on which see Graziosi 2002: 168–80.

4. On Hesiod's self-consciousness, see Griffith 1983: 37, Nagy 1992: 119, Stoddard 2003: 1 n. 1, Tsagalis 2009: 131–32, and, for the biography versus persona debate, Griffith 1983, Millett 1984,

voice."[5] The second part in particular, -odos, is connected with both audē (voice), aoidē (song), and aoidos (bard)—linking Hesiod's personal name into the professional term for "poet" and showing, as we saw in the introduction, how the boundaries between different types of names were often blurred.[6]

But there is another important element to Hesiod's description of the andres aoidoi at the opening of his epic, in addition to the intertextuality with Homer: the link between the community of male bards and the Muses, the female gods of music and poetry and inspirers of song. And this brings us to a new chapter in the self-definition of the poet in relation to gender: the much-commented-upon relationship between the male bard and the female Muse, which structures much of archaic poetry and becomes a defining feature of the male poet's inspiration.[7]

Hesiod, Servant of the Muses

It is worth noting that, in Homeric epic, the bard does not define the terms of his craft (aoidos, dēmioergos, epos) through the Muses. There are close associations, of course—most famously in the proems to the epics, where the bard calls on the Muse to "sing" (aeide, Hom. Il. 1.1) or "tell" (ennepe, Od. 1.1) his song.[8] In an important passage in book 2 of the Iliad, the Homeric bard delineates both his closeness to the Muses and the difference between the immortal Muse and the mortal limitations of the bard: "Speak, now, you Muses who have your homes on Olympus: for you are female gods [theai], and you are omnipresent and know everything, but we hear only the sounds

---

Nagy 1990b: 36–82. On the enunciative role of Hesiod's first-person statements in the Theogony, see Calame 1995: 58–74.

    5. West 1966 ad Theog. 22, Nagy 1979: 296–97, Nagy 1990b: 47.

    6. For the connection between αὐδή and ἀείδω, see Chantraine s.v. αὐδή, also Nagy 1979: 296 n. 1. By way of comparison, on Ὅμηρος as "he who fits the song together," see Nagy 1979: 296–300.

    7. On the Muses in archaic Greek epic, see Calhoun 1938, Murray 1981, Svenbro 1984: 46–73, Ford 1992: 57–89, Minchin 1995, Doherty 1995a: 82–83, Collins 1999: 242, Maslov 2016, Tulli 2019. Additional connections between women and the sung/spoken word exist in the personification of the iambic genre as a woman, Iambe (Hymn. Hom. Dem. 202), and Phanothea, the mythical inventor of the hexameter (Clem. Al. Strom. i. p. 366). On the Muses more generally, see, among others, Boyancé 1937, Otto 1954, C. Segal 1994b: 101, Spentzou and Fowler 2002.

    8. μῆνιν ἄειδε θεὰ, Hom. Il 1.1; ἄνδρα μοι ἔννεπε, μοῦσα, πολύτροπον, Od 1.1. On the invocation of the Muse in Homer, see Calhoun 1938, Minton 1960, Murray 1981, Finkelberg 1990, Ford 1992: 32–34, 57–89, Minchin 1995, Pucci 1998: esp. 44–45.

of your voice [*kleos*] and know nothing" (*Il.* 2.484–86).[9] The Muses, as immortal beings, have access to the omniscience and omnipresence which the poet needs in order to visualize his poem; the bard, meanwhile, provides the mechanics of speech, the poetry (*kleos*) that "we hear," the spoken epic.[10] The symbiosis between the Muse and the bard in Homer is thus divided between knowledge and speech, immortality and mortality, female and male: "The poet's only task seems to be that of repeating, with his own voice, word for word what the Muses tell him."[11] The Muse remembers and the poet speaks aloud, in a constant relationship between thought and sound, inspiration and production, female and male. We have already seen this mechanism played out in the *Odyssey* in the figure of Demodocus, who is "inspired to sing of the glorious deeds of men [*klea andrōn*]" by the female Muse (*Od.* 8.73). Elsewhere, in other descriptions in the *Odyssey* of Demodocus, of Odysseus himself, and the *aoidos* Phemius in book 22, the bard's art is said to be gifted or taught by "god" or "the Muse," who "cares" for the *aoidos* and inspires his song.[12] But in spite of the bard's privileged (and gendered) relationship to the Muse in the *Odyssey* and *Iliad*, and the multiple moments where the bard acknowledges or is identified by his proximity to the inspiration of the Muses, the *aoidos* is never connected to the Muse in the words he uses to define himself. The female god of song never becomes a part of his title, an integral part of the definition of the male poet.

It is Hesiod who takes that step. The *Theogony* seems to begin in a similar vein to the Homeric delineation of the relationship between Muse and bard: the Muses feature in the poem's first line ("let us start singing from the Muses of Helicon," *Theog.* 1), as in the *Iliad* and *Odyssey*.[13] In the *Theogony*, however, it is the Muses who are the opening *subject* of the epic, rather than simply tutelary deities who inspire the poet's song. The proem to the *Theogony* functions as a hymn to the Muses (and shares many features with hymns,

---

9. ἔσπετε νῦν μοι Μοῦσαι Ὀλύμπια δώματ᾽ ἔχουσαι· ὑμεῖς γὰρ θεαί ἐστε πάρεστέ τε ἴστέ τε πάντα, / ἡμεῖς δὲ κλέος οἶον ἀκούομεν οὐδέ τι ἴδμεν, Hom. *Il.* 2.484–86; see Nagy 1979: 16, and, for a different reading of πάρεστέ, Heiden 2008a.

10. Cavarero 2005: 96.

11. Pucci 1998: 44.

12. *Od.* 8.44–45, 8.62–64, 8.480–81 17.518–19, 22. 347–48.

13. Μουσάων Ἑλικωνιάδων ἀρχώμεθ᾽ ἀείδειν, *Theog.* 1. On the Muses in Hesiod, see Pucci 1977: 8–14, Marquardt 1982, Calame 1982, Pucci 1998: 31–48, Scodel 2001: 112–23, Stoddard 2003.

including some of its lines) as well as a simple invocation.[14] This hymn turns into an intensely personal consecration of the poet Hesiod (lines 22–34), who, as we have seen, is identified by name: the Muses "taught Hesiod a beautiful song . . . and breathed into me a divine voice, so that I might celebrate both the things that are to come and the things that are" (*Theog.* 22, 31–32).[15] The Muses speak to the bard personally (26–28), laying claim to their ability to "tell many lies similar to the truth, but to speak the truth when we want."[16] They are praised for their omniscient singing (36–39), their immortal voice (43), and, in particular, their song which tells of "the race of the gods from the beginning" (44–45) (and later, of mortals and giants, too).[17] At first glance Hesiod's portrayal of the Muses only corroborates Homer's picture: the emphasis on the bard's voice in collaboration with the Muses' inspiration, the juxtaposition of mortality and immortality, and the Muses' omniscience.[18] But later in the proem, in the famous "kings and singers" passage at lines 80–103, Hesiod goes into more detail about both the role and the title of the singer.[19] In this passage, kings (*basilées*) and singers (*aoidoi*) are compared in the power of their eloquence, their ability to settle quarrels (in the case of kings) and ease sorrow through song (in the case of bards).[20] And it is here, at line 94, that we have the first occurrence of *aoidos* in the epic, as Hesiod draws the contrast between *andres aoidoi* (singer-men)

14. See Friedländer 1914, Minton 1970, Nagy 1990b: 53–61, who notes (p. 55) that *Theog.* 94–97 = *Hymn. Hom. in Musas et Apollinem* (25) 2–5.

15. αἵ νύ ποθ᾿ Ἡσίοδον καλὴν ἐδίδαξαν ἀοιδήν . . . ἐνέπνευσαν δέ μοι αὐδὴν / θέσπιν, ἵνα κλείοιμι τά τ᾿ ἐσσόμενα πρό τ᾿ ἐόντα, *Theog.* 22, 31–32.

16. ἴδμεν ψεύδεα πολλὰ λέγειν ἐτύμοισιν ὁμοῖα, / ἴδμεν δ᾿, εὖτ᾿ ἐθέλωμεν, ἀληθέα γηρύσασθαι, *Theog.* 27–28; cf. the Sirens, Doherty 1995a: 83. On these much-interpreted lines, see Finkelberg 1998: 157–60, who articulates the general view that the Muses' statement represents an opposition between Homeric and Hesiodic poetry; see also Pucci 1977: 8–44, Svenbro 1984: 55–75, Clay 1988, G. R. F. Ferrari 1988, Nagy 1992: 119–30, Katz and Volk 2000, Scodel 2001, Heiden 2007.

17. αἱ δ᾿ ἄμβροτον ὄσσαν ἱεῖσαι / θεῶν γένος αἰδοῖον πρῶτον κλείουσιν ἀοιδῇ / ἐξ ἀρχῆς, *Theog.* 43–45. On the Muses' voice, see Collins 1999.

18. Compare τά τ᾿ ἐσσόμενα πρό τ᾿ ἐόντα, *Theog.* 32, with ἴστέ τε πάντα, *Il.* 2.485. On the paradox of the θέσπις αὐδή as a "divine mortal voice," see Ford 1992: 173.

19. On this passage balancing the consecration of the poet see Minton 1970: 357. On the "kings and singers" passage, see West 1966: 44, Roth 1976, Duban 1980, Stoddard 2003.

20. Stoddard 2003: 9; see also Thalmann 1984: 139–40. On the oddity of the Muses bestowing their gifts on a nonpoet, see Murray 2004: 369.

as "from the Muses and Apollo" and kings as "from Zeus." A few lines later, the bard is further defined (*Theog.* 99–101):[21]

> a bard [*aoidos*],
> servant of the Muses [*Mousaōn therapōn*], sings of the glories of the
>   people of old
> and the blessed gods who hold Olympus

An additional title is granted to the *aoidos* here. He is not just Homer's *aoidos anēr*, one in a community of male bards as we see with the *andres aoidoi* of *Theogony* 94; he is now a "servant of the Muses" (line 100), a *Mousaōn therapōn*.[22] The placement of the appositional title for the bard, literally separated over a line break, demonstrates that this is a figurative break from traditional formulations of the *aoidos*. In other words, Hesiod is doing something different here. But what does it mean to be a *Mousaōn therapōn*? How does it change how we read the bard in relation to gender dynamics?

There are several ways we can read the *Mousaōn therapōn* here. We can take a macrolevel view of the relationship between the bard and the Muses in ancient Greek poetry, and use that to read back into the *Theogony*; we can look at the *Theogony* itself and what it tells us about the poet-Muse relationship; and we can focus in on the microlevel to read from the semantics of the term *Mousaōn therapōn* itself, and what that tells us about the gendered self-definition of the bard. (This third approach is something of the modus operandi of this book.) Unsurprisingly, given the prominence of the Muses in both Homer and Hesiod and their centrality to defining the depiction of the Muses in later literature, the gendering of the relationship between Muse and bard in ancient literature has undergone a significant amount of scrutiny in (particularly feminist) scholarship. "The relationship between poet and 'Muse,'" Alison Sharrock observes, "is a gendered one. Poets are practically all men, and the 'poet's voice' is a male voice: Muses are all women."[23] Some, like Penelope Murray, see the divine attributes granted to the Muses as a positive nod to their female (as well as their religious) power, and the poet's request

---

21. ἀοιδὸς / Μουσάων θεράπων κλεῖα προτέρων ἀνθρώπων / ὑμνήσει μάκαράς τε θεούς οἳ Ὄλυμπον ἔχουσιν, Hes. *Theog.* 99–101.

22. We find the same phrase in the plural at the *Homeric Hymn to Selene* (32) 20. For other examples, see chapter 2, n. 48.

23. Sharrock 2002: 208.

for inspiration as a call for something which the male poet lacks.[24] Many, however, read the Muse as a figure for female disempowerment, a refusal of agency to women by the transferal of inspiration to the male bard and a silencing of the female voice, where, in spite of the Muses' connection to song, the male poet is the only one allowed to speak.[25] As Murray puts it, summarizing this line of argument, "man creates, woman inspires; man is the maker, woman the vehicle of male fantasy, an object created by the male imagination, incapable of any kind of agency herself."[26] Or, more succinctly, in the words of Ann Bergren: the Muse is "an appropriation by the male of what he attributes to the female."[27] There is also often an erotic charge to the Muse as passive partner.[28] This eroticism is set within the context, not only of a highly gendered relationship opposing male/female, active/passive, Muse/poet, but also, frequently, of the male appropriation of the female body and its biological generativity: as Sandra Gilbert and Susan Gubar point out, the metaphor of Muse as tool in the male poet's act of creation suggests that he is literally "'beget[ting]' art upon the (female) body of the muse."[29]

These readings of the male poet as appropriating the creative power of the female Muse, at the same time as he silences her, seem particularly salient to Hesiod.[30] If we focus in on the depiction of the relationship between Muse and bard in the *Theogony*, we see that it maps closely to the erotic objectification, as well as the disempowerment and silencing, of the Muses—even as they are praised as figures of inspiration.[31] The poem opens with a description of the Muses dancing and bathing in the mountain springs: their "soft feet" (line 3) and "tender skin" (line 5) both suggest sensual undertones, and link in to the

---

24. See, e.g., Murray 1981: 90.

25. Gilbert and Gubar 1979: 47, 49, Gubar 1981, Lada-Richards 2002: 77.

26. Murray 2006: 327.

27. Bergren 1983: 71.

28. Sharrock 2002: 208.

29. Gilbert and Gubar 1979: 49. For the example of men appropriating female biological creativity through male pregnancy, see most famously Diotima's metaphor in Plato's *Symposium*, discussed at pp. 148–61; on the consistency of male strategies of appropriation of the female, and particularly of female procreation, across different cultures, see Halperin 1990: 143–44.

30. See Arthur 1983: 111.

31. For a nuanced reading of the personification of the Muses in the *Theogony*, see Murray 2005. It has often been noted that most personifications in the ancient world were female-gendered: see Warner 1985: 63–87, Paxson 1998: 149, Stafford 1998, Hall 2000 (on Old Comedy), Stafford and Herrin 2005.

description of Aphrodite's "slender feet" later in the poem (line 195), while at line 64 the Muses are specifically associated on Mount Olympus with the personification of "Desire," implying a sexualized aspect to their portrayal.[32] Meanwhile, although the Muses are singled out for praise for their song on Olympus about "the race of the gods from the beginning" (*Theog.* 44–45), the *Theogony*—which is precisely that, a poem of the birth of the gods—is claimed by Hesiod, and not the Muses. It may be the Muses who inspired Hesiod, who "told me to sing of the race of the blessed gods who always exist" (33), but this is unequivocally Hesiod's song (as the "signature" of his name, or *sphragis*, in line 22 emphasizes).[33] Hesiod is careful to note that the effect of the Muses' song occurs explicitly (and only) within the halls of Olympus, with the "halls" or "homes" of Olympus repeated twice within three lines.[34] This locational gap between the Muses' song about the gods sung on Olympus, and Hesiod's epic poem the *Theogony* composed for us, his human audience, maps out the relationship between the Muses and the male poet: the Muses might be able to sing among the gods, but when it comes to mortals, they have to command a mortal male poet to sing for them—their voice is lost.

That this relationship is emphatically gendered, beyond the usual trope of female silencing and male appropriation which we have already seen in Homer, is underlined by Hesiod's insistence that the poet who ventriloquizes the Muses has to be male. The first time the term *aoidos* occurs in the epic, as we have already seen, his masculinity is stressed with the addition of *anēr*: "singer-men [*andres aoidoi*] on earth and lyre-players come from the Muses and far-shooting Apollo" (94–95).[35] But this line can be read another way. Rather than seeing *andres aoidoi*

---

32. Marquardt 1982: 2, see also Arthur 1983: 98–99; cf. *Op.* 519–21.

33. καί με κέλονθ' ὑμνεῖν μακάρων γένος αἰὲν ἐόντων, *Theog.* 33; αἵ νύ ποθ' Ἡσίοδον καλὴν ἐδίδαξαν ἀοιδήν, 22. For the same point, see Clay 2003: 68, 69, 72, Arthur 1983: 111, Nagy 1990b: 57; on the Muses' voice as both an emblem of power and as a mechanism of their subordination, see Collins 1999. On Hesiod's self-naming in the *Theogony*, see chapter 2, n. 4; on *sphragis*, see introduction, n. 5.

34. γελᾷ δέ τε δώματα πατρὸς / Ζηνὸς ἐριγδούποιο θεᾶν ὀπὶ λειριοέσσῃ / σκιδναμένη· ἠχεῖ δὲ κάρη νιφόεντος Ὀλύμπου / δώματά τ' ἀθανάτων, Hes. *Theog.* 40–43 (emphasis mine). Doherty 1995a: 84 suggests that this underlines the Muses' depiction as a virgin chorus closely linked to their father's house. On the local vs. Panhellenic implications of the Muses' identification as Heliconian/Olympian, see Nagy 1990b: 57–61. See also chapter 2, n. 37.

35. Note that the Muses are conjoined with Apollo here: Nagy 1979: 291 n. 1 rightly suggests, I think, that the collocation between Muses and Apollo echoes that between *aoidoi* and lyre-players, representing "the ensemble of song."

as periphrastic for *aoidos*, like Homer's *aoidos anēr*, we might instead see *aoidoi* as the predicate of *andres*: not just "singer-men are from the Muses and Apollo," but also, "men are singers from the Muses and Apollo." With this reading, the emphasis is on the fact that it is *men*—and only men—who are able to be *aoidoi*. The Muses might be female and grant the gift of song, but it is to men alone that that gift is given. So while the Muses' song is granted "to humans" (*anthrōpoisin*, line 93)—the existence of song as a condition among mortals, in other words—it is mortal *men*, in particular, who are the singers, the *aoidoi*.

The Muses, then, are doubly excluded from the kind of song that Hesiod sings, as being both immortal and female. In terms of the audience of their song, they can only sing on Olympus, and not among mortals (*anthrōpoisin*, 93). In terms of their gendered identity as singers, they are excluded from being *aoidoi* as not-men. This exclusion, or distance, of the Muses is a key element of their depiction in the *Theogony* proem. Even though Hesiod stresses that he is held high in the Muses' favor (he is a "poetic 'bridge' between the divine and mortal realms," as Kathryn Stoddard puts it), the distance between gods and mortals is consistently emphasized throughout the proem.[36] The physical distancing and separation of the poet from the Muses is often underlined: the Muses are described as having "Olympian homes" in the proem, are called "Olympian" twice and "Heliconian" once, and their song is explicitly located on Olympus.[37] By contrast, the poet's first meeting with the Muses occurs in a position of subordination, both geographically ("under holy Helicon," line 23), and in terms of his status as a shepherd (underlined by the Muses in their address to him at line 26 as a "field-dwelling shepherd").[38] This figurative distance between the planes of existence of mortal and immortal is stressed by the Muses in their speech to Hesiod, where they contrast his lowly identity as a shepherd versus their omniscient knowledge (lines 26–28). And it is demonstrated even in the architecture of the poem's lines: the *Mousaōn therapon*, when he appears later in the "kings and singers" passage, is placed in sharp opposition to the Muses at the line's beginning, versus the "gods, who hold Olympus" at the end of the line that follows (101).[39]

36. Stoddard 2003: 5.

37. Ὀλύμπια δώματ᾽ ἔχουσαι, *Theog.* 75, see also 63; Μοῦσαι Ὀλυμπιάδες, 25, 52; Ἑλικωνιάδες, 1.

38. Ἑλικῶνος ὕπο ζαθέοιο, *Theog.* 23; ποιμένες ἄγραυλοι, 26.

39. θεούς οἳ Ὄλυμπον ἔχουσιν, *Theog.* 101.

This leads us to the final approach to understanding the significance of the phrase *Mousaōn therapōn* for the bard's gendered identity: reading from the semantics of the term itself. We are used to reading *therapōn* as "servant" in later literature—Herodotus, Aristophanes, Andocides, Lysias all use it in this sense—and that is how the word is usually translated in Hesiod.[40] But we have to understand the term in its wider archaic context, where its use in Homer suggests a cultural context to the term that gives it a different undertone. Gregory Nagy, building on the work of Nadia Van Brock, argues that the etymology of *therapōn* suggests an original meaning of "ritual substitute."[41] He suggests that *Mousaōn therapōn* at *Theogony* 100 can be understood both by comparison to Patroclus's status as a "ritual substitute" for Achilles in the *Iliad*, and, more broadly, to the status of all the Achaean warriors as "attendants of Ares" (*therapontes Arēos*), as they are often called in the *Iliad*.[42] (It is worth noting that the only other time that *therapōn* occurs in the Hesiodic corpus, in a fragment of the *Catalogue of Women*, it is in the same formulation—"the Danaans, *therapontes Arēos*"—showing an assimilation between Homeric and Hesiodic uses of the word.)[43] There seem to be two strands to Nagy's argument: on the one hand, the *therapōn* is unique in his ability to act as a ritual substitute for a single person/entity; on the other, precisely because he is *only* a substitute, he also becomes a generic force who can be replaced. The *therapōn,* thus, by definition holds a secondary position (Nagy notes that its prevailing meaning in the *Iliad* is "warrior's companion" and "attendant"): as he shows with reference to Patroclus and Achilles's relationship, "Patroklos and [Achilles] are equivalent warriors, so long as Patroklos stays by his side; once he is on his own, however, the identity of Patroklos as warrior is in question."[44] So how does this relate to the poet as *Mousaōn therapōn*? "Whereas the generic warrior is the '*therápōn* of Ares,'" Nagy concludes, "the generic poet is the '*therápōn* of the Muses.'"[45] He goes on to argue that, as

40. Most's 2006 Loeb translation and West 1999 give "servant" at *Theog.* 100; Lombardo 1993 translates "a singer / Who serves the Muses." Instances of θεράπων in Greek literature in the sense "servant": Hdt. 1.30, 5.105; Ar. *Plut.* 3, 5; Andoc. 1.12; Lys. 7.34.

41. Nagy 1979: 292, paraphrasing Van Brock 1959; see also Nagy 1990b: 48, and cf. Chantraine s.v. θεράπων.

42. Nagy 1979: 292–95. The Greeks as θεράποντες Ἄρηος: *Il.* 2.110, 6.67, 15.733, 19.78.

43. Δαναοὶ θεράποντες Ἄρηος, Hes. fr. 193.6 M-W. See Cingano 2017: 39–42.

44. Nagy 1979: 292.

45. Nagy 1979: 293.

warriors experience death and cult heroization, the status of poet as *therapōn* suggests that the poet is also claiming an identity as a cult hero.[46] The combination between the privileged access and inferior status of the *therapōn* thus maps neatly onto the opposition between mortal and immortal, the distance between poet and Muse, which is established in the proem of the *Theogony*. Hesiod is not a companion of the Muses, but rather an attendant who prays to the Muses from afar for inspiration (104).

But we can go further when we look at the relationship between Muse and *therapōn* from a gendered perspective. *Therapōn* is a masculine-gendered term, set here against the feminine Muses. Nagy's "generic poet" thus differs in one crucial way from the generic warrior, as *therapōn* of Ares: the *therapōn* of Ares shares his gender with the god he fights with or for, whereas the *therapōn* of the Muses is set in direct opposition to the gender of the Muses. Even as the term *therapōn* indicates a differential in status between two parties who are engaged in the same pursuit (war, poetry), the phrase *Mousaōn therapōn* thus encodes within itself a clash of gender which is not present in the Iliadic "*therapōn* of Ares." And this gender clash represents another, greater difference between the Iliadic representation of Patroclus as *therapōn* of Achilles and the Greeks as *therapontes* of Ares. When Patroclus initiates the decision to join battle that leads to his death, as Nagy points out, he is identified with Ares; elsewhere in the epic, "Ares is designated as the god who actually takes the hero's life"; at points, he actually joins the battle himself, most notably in book 5 of the *Iliad* where he rallies the Trojans against Diomedes, fights Diomedes himself, and is wounded.[47]

The example of the Muses in Hesiod is different. Their song is limited to Olympus; they are specified as singing only for Zeus and the gods, and the mortal poet is needed to broadcast their song of the origins of the gods "to mortals" (*Theog.* 93). Whereas Ares fights among men in the sphere of war, is wounded by them, kills them—and thus, like Achilles, can have men acting as *therapontes* to him—the Muses' power in the sphere of song is limited and differentiated. There is an irony, then, a subtle twist, to Hesiod calling himself the Muses' *therapōn*. It calls attention to the fact that, unlike the *therapontes* of Ares who can act like the war-god, kill and be killed in the parry and thrust of war, the *aoidos* is more than just a substitute for the Muses: he is unique. He,

46. Nagy 1979: 295.
47. Nagy 1979: 294.

and only he—by virtue of his status as a mortal, *and* as a man—can sing to
men, about men, as one of the *andres aoidoi*. The gender difference here, then,
the status reversal of a male serving a female, thus serves to draw attention to
the paradox of the phrase—that although Hesiod claims to be lower than the
Muses in the hierarchy as their *therapōn*, the Muses' powerlessness as immor-
tals (distanced from human song) and women (unable to be male *aoidoi*)
means that the power is, in fact, in the hands of the *aoidos*. This is the precise
force of the juxtaposition between *aoidos* and *Mousaōn therapōn* over the line
break: while the male poet may posture toward serving the Muses as a
therapōn, as a male *aoidos*, he is, in fact, the only one who can sing as one of
the *andres aoidoi*. It is particularly important that we understand the gendered
polemics to this term, the ironic pose of servitude which in fact emphasizes
the male poet's agency, as it is a phrase which is picked up and used again by
other poets—including Archilochus, Theognis, and, in a different way, as we
will see later, Sappho.[48]

These, then, are the full implications of the gap between mortal and im-
mortal, Muse and poet, female and male enshrined in the *Mousaōn therapōn*
of the *Theogony*. Although the proem may seem a hymn to the Muses' divine
abilities, it is in fact a clever display of the extent to which, as a mortal and a
man, Hesiod both uses the female Muses for his own purposes and outstrips
their powers. It is a rhetorical display of the male bard's prowess in poetry,
the very vehicle he uses to create his own fame and which the Muses cannot
generate without him. The term *Mousaōn therapōn* is thus both sophisticated
and cunning: it sets the Muses up as an ideal, a higher alter ego of the poet;
but at the same time demonstrates that an ideal is all they can ever be,
because the poet can do what they cannot—poetry. The bard makes a good
show of appearing to be subservient—but, prizing apart the gender gap be-
tween Muse and *andres aoidoi*, he demonstrates, in the very lines in which
he pronounces upon the Muses, that he is, in the end, the true master of this
medium.

48. Archilochus fr. 1 *IEG* (see pp. 264–65 with chapter 9, nn. 17 and 19); for the comparison
between Hesiod and Archilochus, see Nagy 1990b: 49–50. For Theognis, see Thgn. 769 (see
Ford 2002: 133 n. 2, and see further pp. 83–85 with chapter 4, n. 3). For Sappho, see pp. 235–44.
Note that the phrase is also used parodically for an anonymous ποιητής at Ar. *Av.* 909, who calls
himself a Μουσάων θεράπων and compares himself to Homer (910): the subsequent misin-
terpretation of θεράπων as δοῦλος, turning "servant/attendant" into "slave," makes explicit the
power relationships inherent in the phrase.

Bird/Bard: A Lesson in Gendering Poets

This tension between female Muses and male bard, female inspiration and male song, is one which will recur in the delineation of the male *aoidos* as the archaic period wears on. But there are other indications that Hesiod is aware of the loaded gender of the male *aoidos* and the threat posed to the term by the female voice. In the *Works and Days*, Hesiod's didactic epic addressed to his brother Perses, the poet pauses to tell a fable at lines 202–12, ostensibly to instruct "kings." A hawk is described carrying a nightingale in its claws. The nightingale attempts to cry out, and the hawk berates her, saying that— although she is a "singer" (*aoidos*) (208)—she should acknowledge her defeat to one who is "stronger" (207).[49] A lesson to Perses follows: do not commit *hubris*, but follow the path of justice.

It is a difficult story which has occasioned many interpretations, particularly in its relationship to the exhortation to Perses which follows. Are the kings meant to be depicted by the "stronger" hawk dominating the weaker nightingale—so that the fable becomes an example of negative behavior to be avoided, or even a cynical depiction of the world simply as it is? And is the nightingale, who is described as a "singer," meant to be interpreted as an equivalent for the *aoidos* Hesiod—who perhaps felt victimized by the more powerful kings?[50]

It is the metapoetics and the gender dynamics of the scene that interest me here, however. In the opening line—"this is how the hawk spoke to the colorful-necked nightingale"—both hawk and nightingale are introduced without the definite articles which would tell us their grammatical gender (*irēx . . . aēdona, Op.* 203).[51] The nightingale, *aēdōn*, is instead given an unusual two-termination adjective, "colorful-necked" (*poikilodeiron*, 203).[52] The adjective has the same masculine and feminine endings (or rather, it uses the

---

49. δαιμονίη, τί λέληκας; ἔχει νύ σε πολλὸν ἀρείων· / τῇ δ᾽ εἶς ᾗ σ᾽ ἂν ἐγώ περ ἄγω καὶ ἀοιδὸν ἐοῦσαν (Why are you screeching, you silly woman? A much stronger man has you now; you'll have to go wherever I take you, even if you are a female singer), Hes. *Op.* 207–8. I have translated to bring out the gender dynamics in the Greek.

50. This fable and its interpretation have been much discussed: Hubbard 1995 interprets the hawk as representing the kings, and the nightingale as Perses, whereas Puelma 1972 interprets the nightingale as Hesiod (as does Pucci 1977: 62–65). See also, for a different reading, Mordine 2006.

51. ὣδ᾽ ἴρηξ προσέειπεν ἀηδόνα ποικιλόδειρον, *Op.* 203.

52. On this adjective and its translation, see Nagy 1996: 59 with n. 1.

masculine endings for both)—so it cannot be used to clarify whether the *aēdōn* is male or female. Of course, most Greeks would not have needed the help of a definite article or adjective to tell them what the gender of a word was: they would have known, through usage and experience. But the noun "hawk" (*irēx*) was one of those difficult terms ending in -*ēx* whose gender was debated, and which cropped up in *both* masculine and feminine genders. We already saw, in the introduction, Protagoras debating the gender of the noun *pēlēx* (helmet), a third-declension noun ending in -*ēx* used in the feminine in Homer, which Protagoras argued (presumably because of its male-gendered associations) should have been masculine.[53] *Irēx* is normally masculine in Homer, and it is clear that the hawk is masculine in the *Works and Days* too: in the line that follows his introduction, he is described with a masculine present participle (*pherōn*, "carrying," 204). But a simile in book 18 of Homer's *Iliad*, where Thetis is described as a hawk as she dives down from Olympus, complicates the matter. There, the article is dropped—just as in Hesiod—and we have instead a feminine article, used to refer to Thetis: *hē d' irēx hōs alto* ("she, like a hawk, jumped," Hom. *Il.* 18.616). Dropping the article for *irēx* and giving the feminine article for Thetis instead, in a simile where a female character is being compared to a hawk, seems to play on precisely that gender instability in third-declension nouns ending in -*ēx* which is later picked up by Protagoras.

The *irēx* here in Hesiod, then, although male, brings with him an undercurrent of controversies around and experiments with the gender of nouns. So what about the *aēdon*, the nightingale? The noun *aēdon* is already interesting from a gender perspective in that the nightingale was seen as generically female in the ancient Greek world—and so the word for nightingale, *aēdon*, was grammatically feminine.[54] But from a *poetic* perspective, this is especially intriguing: because the female nightingale was systematically associated with song, and thus with poetic song.[55] The earliest instance of the nightingale as

53. Protagoras DK 80 A 28, see pp. 13–16.

54. Lutwack 1994: 10, Nagy 1996: 35; note that, although most ancient writers identify the female alone as the singer, Arist. *Hist. an.* 536a28–30 has both males and females singing. Ironically, as Arnott 2007: 1 notes, it is the male bird which is in fact the singer, as a means to attract mates and protect territory.

55. On the nightingale motif in Greek and Latin literature, see Chandler 1934, Lutwack 1994: 1–16, Nagy 1996: 7–16, 32–51, 57–60, Loraux 1998: 57–66, Monella 2005, Hünemörder 2006. See, e.g., Bacchyl. 3.97–98, Democritus DK 68 B 154, Callim. *Epigr.* 2.6, *Anth. Pal.* 7.44.3, 9.184.9; see further pp. 181–82 and pp. 271–81 with chapter 9, n. 49.

singer occurs in book 19 of the *Odyssey*, where Penelope compares her inces-
sant weeping to the nightingale's mournful song: this would, later, lead the
nightingale to be associated both with female lament and male (and, as we will
see, female) poets' self-identification as singers.[56] The poetic undertones of
the nightingale were not simply buried in the connection between the night-
ingale and its well-known song, however: they were made explicit in the very
term for the nightingale itself in Greek, derived from *aeidein* (to sing)—the
same root as *aoidos*—and thus literally "female singer."[57] This etymology and
poetic connection is clearly played out in the fable of the hawk and the night-
ingale in Hesiod.[58] The hawk declares that he will not drop the nightingale
(*aēdōn*), "even though she is a singer [*kai aoidon eousan*]" (Hes. *Op.* 208). The
hawk cleverly gives the derivation of the word *aēdōn* as a "singer" (*aoidos*),
connecting her shrill cries (*lelēkas*, 207) to poetic song.

The ancient scholiast on these lines sees the identification of the nightingale
as *aoidos* as explicitly connecting her to Hesiod: "[Hesiod] compared himself
to the nightingale with good reason—for the bird is musical."[59] The song of
the nightingale and its etymological similarity to *aoidos*, in other words, invite
a double connection between bard and bird. On the other hand, from a gender
perspective, the female *aēdōn* here is called an *aoidos* by the male hawk—a
word which, as Pietro Pucci points out, "cannot evoke anything else but the
'professional poet,'" who has been identified, both in the bard figures of Ho-
meric epic, and in Hesiod's own self-definition, as male.[60] The usage of *aoidos*
here is made all the more uncomfortable—in spite of the etymological con-
nection between *aoidos* (bard) and *aēdōn* (nightingale), both derived from
aeidein—by the juxtaposition between the male *aoidon* and the female parti-
ciple *eousan*. To approximate in English, the hawk's speech literally says: "even
though you [fem.] are a [male] bard."

56. ὡς δ᾿ ὅτε Πανδαρέου κούρη, χλωρηῒς ἀηδών, / καλὸν ἀείδησιν (as when the
daughter of Pandareus, the nightingale in the green, sings beautifully), Hom. *Od.* 19.518–19; see
Nagy 1996: 7–8, and see 32–38 for the argument that the nightingale figures as a symbol for
poetic variation in composition; for the translation of χλωρηῒς, see Nagy 1996: 7 n. 1. For the
potential connection to Penelope's identity as a mother here, see Loraux 1998: 60. See further
pp. 271–81 with chapter 9, nn. 49 and 55.

57. Chantraine s.v. ἀηδών.

58. Nagy 1996: 60 with n. 2.

59. καλῶς οὖν ἑαυτὸν ἐηδόνι ἀπήκασε—μουσικὸν γὰρ τὸ ὄρνεον, schol. ad. Hes. *Op.*
202a; see Pertusi 1955: 75, J. Lefkowitz 2014: 7–8.

60. Pucci 1977: 62.

There is one potential solution. *Aoidos* could be used here as a two-termination adjective—one which uses the masculine endings for both male and female—as we saw with *poikilodeiron* five lines earlier at 203. Although this would be less common in later periods for noncompound adjectives (contrast *poikilodeiros*, which is a compound), two-termination adjectives for noncompounds like *aoidos* complies with archaic usage.[61] So the hawk, instead of saying "you are a male bard," could instead be using *aoidos* adjectivally: "you are bardic" or "musical."[62] The argument against interpreting *aoidos* as an adjective here is the one which has been made from the scholiast on: the inescapable identification which is being invited between the nightingale and Hesiod as *aoidos*. The other issue is that reading *aoidos* adjectivally does not elide the masculine-looking form of the ending in -*on*, and the emphatic juxtaposition between the masculine-appearing *aoidon* and the feminine *eousan*. It does not escape the fact, in other words, that *aoidos* here *can* be read as a noun, "male bard."

We are left, then, I think, with the conclusion that there is a deliberate exploration being made of the etymological link between *aoidos* and *aēdōn*, at the same time as there is also an awareness and exploitation of the gender clash between a *female* nightingale compared to a *male* poet. Where the gender dynamics of the opening of the *Theogony* presented an unabashedly male poet, here we have a problematically feminine figure for the poet—and the grammar demonstrates the discomfort with the connection. While the nightingale was seen as prototypically female and a feminine singer, the lack of a word for a "female singer"—aside from the word for nightingale (*aēdōn*) itself—means that the masculine vocabulary of the *aoidos* has to be uneasily appropriated across grammatical gender, just as we saw with the female lament of *Iliad* 24. The gendering of poetic roles from the opening of the *Theogony* is displaced into the world of animals to problematize and explore the issue of the threat of feminine song to male poetics—suggesting that the equation of the singer with the man may be less straightforward than it initially seemed.

And yet the gender framing of the passage deals swiftly with this discomfort. The male hawk talking to the female nightingale about the supremacy of

61. My thanks to Gregory Nagy for a series of conversations about this passage, and in particular for pointing this out.

62. This would then be the first occurrence of ἀοιδός, -όν as an adjective in Greek literature. Pucci 1977: 62 reads ἀοιδός nominally here, as I do, and instead argues for an adjectival reading of the word at *Hymn. Hom. Merc.* 25; see chapter 3, n. 7. For later examples, see chapter 6, n. 56.

might and the necessity of submission serves, on a metapoetic level, to do double duty as a statement of gendered poetics, putting the female *aoidos* back in her place. This is particularly true in that it is the hawk, and not the nightingale, who is given a voice here, conforming with accepted norms of male speech and female silencing that stretch back to Telemachus's silencing of Penelope. And the voice of the hawk is, in fact, of course, the voice of the poet, the male *aoidos*, who ventriloquizes the hawk here.[63] At the same time as the nightingale's abilities to sing are appropriated from the female into the male sphere through the use of the term *aoidos*, then, the male *aoidos* himself also reminds the female nightingale of the inevitable dominance of the male voice—both by figuratively carrying her away in the talons of the male hawk, and by literally silencing her, not giving her the chance to speak.

The term *aoidos* occurs less frequently in Hesiod than in Homer—yet, just as in Homer, it occurs at moments of marked gender tension.[64] As the fable of the nightingale in the *Works and Days* unequivocally demonstrates, attempting to meddle in male poetic song is a dangerous game for a woman to play—even an abstracted, idealized woman with the power to inspire song like the Muses, or a fabulized female bird. And it does not end well for the female "bard," silenced and carried off in the talons of the hawk. This appropriation of not only women's voices, but also their bodies, in the service of male song, will be the subject of the next chapter.

---

63. Pucci 1977: 62 does not pick up on the silencing of the nightingale, along with the fact that it is the hawk, not the nightingale, who speaks in the voice of the male poet.

64. ἀοιδός occurs seven times in the Hesiodic corpus, as compared to thirty-eight times in Homer (see chapter 1, n. 1): *Theog.* 95, 99, *Op.* 26 (twice), 208, fr. 305 M-W, fr. 357 M-W.

3

The Instruments of Song in the *Homeric Hymns*

THE ORIGIN story of the first instrument of song—the invention of the lyre—begins with another female creature, who is also called an *aoidos*. This is not, however, the only time an *aoidos* is mentioned in the *Homeric Hymns*. One of the most famous instances occurs in the *Homeric Hymn to Apollo*, where the narrator addresses a chorus of Delian women and asks them to tell everyone that a "blind man" is "the best man among poets [*aoidoi*]" (line 169).[1] The passage appears to reference Homer's status as male poet and reception as an *aoidos*.[2] At the same time, it explores the Delian women's (feminine) capacity for imitation ("they know how to imitate [*mimeisth'*] the voices and rhythmic patterns / of all peoples," 162–63), which—like Helen's vocal mutability in book 4 of the *Odyssey*, and Hesiod's Muses' ability to imitate the truth (*Theog.* 27–28)—seems to mimic that of the poet.[3] There seems to be a highly particularized

1. ἀνὴρ ἥδιστος ἀοιδῶν, *Hymn. Hom. Ap.* 169. The performance of the Delian women has been extensively discussed: for a recent interpretation, see Peponi 2009; see also A. Miller 1986: 57–65, Clay 1989: 47–56, Calame 1997: 104–10, and, on the performance aspect, Aloni 1989: 91–106, Nagy 2013, Passmore 2018. For this passage in relation to the debate over the unity of the hymn (itself a major focus of scholarship, see, e.g., Chappell 2011 for an overview), see A. Miller 1979. The text here is Richardson's (2010) unless otherwise noted.

2. Graziosi 2002: 62–66. On the identity of the ἀοιδός, commonly interpreted in antiquity as Homer, see Clay 1989: 49 n. 101, and on the deliberate lack of identification of Homer, Burkert 1987: 55; for the ascription to Cynaethus, see West 1975.

3. πάντων δ᾽ ἀνθρώπων φωνὰς καὶ κρεμβαλιαστὺν / μιμεῖσθ᾽ ἴσασιν, *Hymn. Hom. Ap.* 162–63. On the contested manuscript traditions and interpretations of these lines, see A. Miller 1986: 59, Burkert 1987: 54, Peponi 2009, Richardson 2010 ad 162–64; my translation of κρεμβαλιαστὺν (162) follows Peponi 2009. See Peponi 2009: 62–66 for a discussion as to what

discourse, available already in the archaic period, around women's imitative, creative, poetic voices. Read in this way, the Delian women—some of the earliest historically situated female poetic performers of antiquity—belong to a group of poetically charged women who are couched in terms that appeal directly to the gendered mimetic qualities of poetry—powers that, significantly, are not even attributed here to the (male) bard himself. These women even receive a poetically significant term: they are called *therapnai*, "female servants," of Apollo the "Far-shooter" (*Hymn. Hom. Ap.* 157), recalling Hesiod's self-designation as a "male servant (*therapōn*) of the Muses" (*Theog.* 100) and follower of "the Muses and far-shooting Apollo" (94).[4] This, like *mimeisthai* (to imitate), is the first occurrence of the word *therapnē* (feminine of *therapōn*) in extant Greek literature—marking out the invention of a new vocabulary to attempt to depict the Delian women's association with poetry, and its relationship to their gender.[5] The male *aoidos* in the *Homeric Hymn to Apollo*, then, is set in a complex, contested, gendered context, like the *aoidoi* of Homer and Hesiod, against the imitative female song of the Delian women.

But there is another, and more sinister, occurrence of *aoidos* in the *Homeric Hymns*, which will be the focus of this chapter. The *Homeric Hymn to Hermes* opens with Hermes's birth and the description of his prodigious talents and "renowned deeds" (*kluta erga*, *Hymn. Hom. Merc.* 16). On the day of his birth, so the hymn tells us, on his way out of the cave where he was born, the god encounters a tortoise (lines 24–38):[6]

---

this imitation entails; see also Burkert 1987: 54, who suggests that μιμεῖσθαι refers to the type of performance (also Nagy 2013) and Bergren 1982: 93. I have chosen to avoid the usual translation for the Δηλιάδες, "Delian maidens," since Thucydides refers to them as γυναῖκες (3.104.5) and therefore their identification as young unmarried women is not certain: see Stehle 1997: 110 n. 124 (who translates "women"), Nagy 2013: 237 n. 49.

4. Μουσάων θεράπων (Hes. *Theog.* 100), ἐκ γάρ τοι Μουσέων καὶ ἐκηβόλου Ἀπόλλωνος (94); Ἑκατηβελέταο θεράπναι (*Hymn. Hom. Ap.* 157) (emphasis mine). Clay 1989: 49 notes the similarity but draws the connection to the Muses, not the bard; cf. Bergren 1982: 92.

5. Richardson 2010 ad 157. On the first occurrence of μιμεῖσθαι, see *LfgrE* s.v. μιμέομαι; see Dornseiff 1933: 8.

6. ἔνθα χέλυν εὑρὼν ἐκτήσατο μυρίον ὄλβον· / Ἑρμῆς τοι πρώτιστα χέλυν τεκτήνατ᾽ ἀοιδόν, / ἥ ῥά οἱ ἀντεβόλησεν ἐπ᾽ αὐλείῃσι θύρῃσι / βοσκομένη προπάροιθε δόμων ἐριθηλέα ποίην, / σαῦλα ποσὶν βαίνουσα· Διὸς δ᾽ ἐριούνιος υἱὸς / ἀθρήσας ἐγέλασσε καὶ αὐτίκα μῦθον ἔειπε· / Σύμβολον ἤδη μοι μέγ᾽ ὀνήσιμον, οὐκ ὀνοτάζω. / χαῖρε φυὴν ἐρόεσσα χοροιτύπε δαιτὸς ἑταίρη, / ἀσπασίη προφανεῖσα· πόθεν τόδε καλὸν ἄθυρμα, / αἰόλον ὄστρακόν ἔσσο, χέλυς ὄρεσι ζώουσα. / ἀλλ᾽ οἴσω σ᾽ εἰς δῶμα λαβών· ὄφελός τι

He found there a tortoise [*chelun*], and so got an endless source of
   pleasure:
because it was Hermes who first made [*tektēnat'*] the tortoise a bard
   [*aoidon*];   25
she [*hē*] came across him at the gates of the courtyard,
grazing on the lush grass in front of the house,
waddling as she walked; the luck-bringing son of Zeus
saw her and laughed and said [*mython eeipe*]:
"Here's a good omen for me already, and not one I'll disregard!   30
Hello, lovely-looker [*phuēn eroessa*], dance-beating feast companion
   [*hetairē*],
a welcome sight! Where did you get this beautiful plaything [*athurma*],
this speckled shell you wear—a tortoise who lives in the mountains?
But I'll pick you up and take you into the house; you'll be a help to me,
and I won't slight you; you'll benefit me first of all.   35
'It's better to be at home, for there's danger outside.'
You'll be a safeguard against harmful spells
while you live; and if you die, then you'll sing [*aeidois*] beautifully."

At the opening of this passage, the female tortoise—who subsequently, in
Hermes's hands, becomes the lyre—is labeled an *aoidos*: "It was Hermes who
first made the tortoise [*chelun*] a bard [*aoidon*]" (25).[7] Just like Hesiod's
nightingale, here we have a female animal who is connected to song. Like the
nightingale, this is a female creature who is specifically gender marked: as
we saw in the previous chapter, the Greeks thought only female nightingales
sang; similarly, they believed that all tortoises were female.[8] And, like the

---

μοι ἔσσηι, / οὐδ᾽ ἀποτιμήσω· σὺ δέ με πρώτιστον ὀνήσεις. / οἴκοι βέλτερον εἶναι, ἐπεὶ
βλαβερὸν τὸ θύρηφιν· / ἢ γὰρ ἐπηλυσίης πολυπήμονος ἔσσεαι ἔχμα / ζώουσ᾽· ἢν δὲ
θάνηις τότε κεν μάλα καλὸν ἀείδοις, *Hymn. Hom. Merc.* 24–38. The text is Richardson's
(2010) unless otherwise noted: at lines 32–33 I follow West's (2003) punctuation and emenda-
tion of ἔσσο for ἔσσι (for discussion, see Vergados 2013 ad loc.). For the characterization of
Hermes in the hymn see, e.g., N. Brown 1947: 66–101, Jaillard 2007, Fletcher 2008; for the ele-
ments of humor in the poem, Vergados 2011a, Vergados 2013: 26–39. For a useful analysis of the
invention of the lyre, see Romani Mistretta 2017, who looks at the technical craft of the lyre's
creation; see also Shelmerdine 1984, Brillante 1999, and Peponi 2012: 98–127 for a reading of the
hymn as a model of citharoedic performance and aesthetic response.

   7. Pucci reads ἀοιδός adjectivally (1977: 62); Vergados 2013 ad loc. is clear that it should be
taken as a noun. See further chapter 2, n. 62.

   8. Llewellyn-Jones 2003: 190, 208 n. 5.

nightingale, the tortoise here is labeled with the term *aoidos*—the word for male bardic authorship.[9] Strangely, strikingly, the word for "bard," *aoidos*, is applied—not to the male god who is the subject of the hymn and inventor of the lyre in a passage that appears to describe the very invention of poetic song, and who, we will see later, even sings a song himself (*hupo kalon aeiden*, 54)— but to the animal (and later inanimate) female lyre which accompanies him.[10] There is one important difference to the nightingale, however: this tortoise, this *aoidos*, has no voice. The common belief among the ancient Greeks was that the tortoise was mute.[11] This is reflected in the *Homeric Hymn*: the tortoise does not produce a sound until, as we will see, she is turned into a lyre. The headline of the passage—"it was Hermes who first made the tortoise a bard" (25)—contains not one paradox, then, but two: a female creature becomes a male bard; a mute animal becomes a singing man.

These paradoxes point to a deep and fundamental discomfort, at the very moment of the invention of the poet's crucial prop, with the gendering of the paraphernalia of song. The tortoise (*chelus*) which forms the lyre is inescapably feminine. All the words for "lyre" in Greek are feminine (*phorminx*, *kithara*, *lura*, *barbitos*, and of course, *chelus*).[12] The word for "song" itself (*aoidē*) is feminine—and so is the word for voice (*audē*), as we saw with Hesiod. The Muses, inspirers of song, are also female. This generates a gendered conflict between the male singer and his masculine subject matter, and the female apparatus of singing and poetry. At this crucial locus of the invention of the lyre, where a history of poetry is retrojected into the past, we have one of the most important attempts to resolve this tension, and in a particularly sexualized and

9. For another connection between the tortoise and the vocabulary of ἀοιδός (though not in the substantive), cf. Sappho fr. 58.12 L-P: φιλάοιδον λιγύραν χελύνναν (the clear-voiced song-loving tortoise).

10. For Hermes and the invention of song here, see Vergados 2013: 4.

11. Llewellyn-Jones 2003: 190, 208 n. 5: see Arist. *Hist. an.* 536a8, 509b8.

12. Maas and Snyder 1989: xv; on the χέλυς, see West 1992: 56–57, and on its grammatical gender, see Janse 2020: 27. Note that the gender of βάρβιτος, however, is indeterminate between masculine and feminine in the early poets (and later we see it in the neuter, βάρβιτον): see Chantraine s.v.; e.g., Anac. fr. 472 *PMG*, Pindar fr. 125.1 S-M, Bacchyl. fr. 20B.1 S-M give the masculine; *Anacreontea* 23.3 W gives the feminine, but 14.34 the masculine. Note that this is the earliest instance of χέλυς; for another early example, see Sappho fr. 118 L-P (marked feminine with the adjectives δῖα, line 1, and φωνάεσσα, line 2), and see also Sappho fr. 58.12 L-P (see chapter 3, n. 9); for Erinna and the tortoise (χελύννα) of the opening lines of her fragmentary *Distaff* (*PSI* 1090), see Arthur 1980. On the femininity of the tortoise, see Llewellyn-Jones 2003: 189–91.

violent context. The masculinity of the male singer—the *aoidos*—is reclaimed from the *chelus* who tried to appropriate the vocabulary of the bard, through a prolonged rape analogy which sees the man physically eviscerating the female and claiming her power for his own.

The first signal of the replacement of the female connection with song with a man is the most basic, even before the tortoise makes her entrance: the displacement of the Muses. Although the Muse is invoked at the beginning of the hymn, she is ordered to "sing of Hermes" (*Hermēn hymnei Mousa*, line 1).[13] The assonance and alliteration between Hermes's name and the command to "sing a hymn" (*hymnei*) suggests—as with Hesiod's name in the *Theogony* and Phemius's name in the *Odyssey*—an attempt to connect Hermes's name to song.[14] From the very beginning, then, it is Hermes who is placed upfront as implicated in song, through his very name—over and above the Muses. This displacement of the Muses' connection to song by Hermes is made explicit as the hymn continues—for not only is he named as the inventor of the lyre, but he also starts to sing himself (54), thus replacing the Muses' own hymn with his own.

So how does Hermes get from a phonetic link between his name and song to actually becoming a (male) singer himself? The answer lies in his discovery of the tortoise and its transformation into the lyre. After a brief description of Hermes's birth and a summary of his "glorious deeds" (*kluta erga*, 16), he stumbles across the tortoise on his way out of the cave where he was born. The introduction to the tortoise immediately foregrounds the discomfort with the tortoise's femininity and her connection to song, which will be addressed in the following lines in the depiction of Hermes's invention of the lyre: "It was Hermes who first made the tortoise [*chelun*] a bard [*aoidon*]" (25).[15] The movement from female tortoise (*chelus*) to male bard (*aoidos*)—along with the placement of male Hermes and male *aoidon* at the start and end of the line, enclosing and surrounding the female tortoise—signals the way in which Hermes will tame the female instrument to his male purposes, to allow himself ultimately to step into the identity of the bard.

---

13. Ἑρμῆν ὕμνει Μοῦσα, *Hymn. Hom. Merc.* 1.

14. The resonance is particularly strong due to the use of the contracted form of Hermes's name (see Richardson 2010 and Vergados 2013 ad loc.), and the choice to use the less usual ὑμνεῖν over ἀείδειν; note also the implicit etymologizing of ἕρμαιον (a "lucky find") in connection to Hermes's name; see Vergados 2013 ad 24.

15. Ἑρμῆς τοι πρώτιστα χέλυν τεκτήνατ᾽ ἀοιδόν, *Hymn. Hom. Merc.* 25.

For now, however, the uneasy conjunction of female tortoise and male bard is allowed to sit. Indeed, the femininity of the tortoise is explicitly emphasized: the next line (and the next word after *aoidon*) has "her" (*hē*, 26) coming across Hermes, grazing the grass (with the feminine participle *boskomenē*, 27) and walking (feminine participle *bainousa*, 28), creating a triad of feminine agreements. This is in clear contrast to Hermes, who is described in the same line as the male son (*huios*, 28) of the male god Zeus (*Dios*, 28) with a masculine adjective (*eriounios*, 28).[16] And, as a man, it is Hermes— like Telemachus in book 1 of the *Odyssey* and the hawk in Hesiod's *Works and Days*—who is allowed to speak, as opposed to the silent tortoise: "he spoke a word" (*mython eeipe*, 29), recalling Telemachus's statement of men's control over words (*mythos*) at *Odyssey* 1.358.[17] The muteness of the female tortoise is underlined—a silence that was, as we have seen, gender enforced as particularly appropriate to a woman, as well as (in the Greek view) natural to the tortoise.[18] Faced with the tortoise who will become the lyre, it is Hermes who has already taken control of the words of poetry—and thus, his claim to be an *aoidos*.

Hermes goes on to address the tortoise, not as an *aoidos*, but as a "lovely-looker" (*phuēn eroessa*, 31).[19] This phrase is interesting for several reasons. First of all, the feminine adjective *eroessa* (lovely) again serves to emphasize the tortoise's gender. It also places her in the context of the vocabulary of sexual desire, since the adjective derives from the noun *erōs* (desire, passion).[20] This is further underlined by its juxtaposition with *phuēn* (appearance), another feminine noun and one which is cognate with the verb *phuein*—meaning both "to create, produce" and "to give birth." Hermes's appellation of the tortoise as a "lovely-looker" thus both underlines her

---

16. ἥ ῥά οἱ ἀντεβόλησεν ἐπ᾽ αὐλείῃσι θύρῃσι / βοσκομένη προπάροιθε δόμων ἐριθηλέα ποίην, / σαῦλα ποσὶν βαίνουσα· Διὸς δ᾽ ἐριούνιος υἱός, *Hymn. Hom. Merc.* 26–28.

17. Διὸς δ᾽ ἐριούνιος υἱός / ἀθρήσας ἐγέλασσε καὶ αὐτίκα μῦθον ἔειπε, *Hymn. Hom. Merc.* 28–29; on Hermes's riddling speech here, see Clay 1989: 106, also 110–11.

18. On the tortoise as a symbol of female silence, see Llewellyn-Jones 2003: 190; on women's silencing, see introduction, n. 10.

19. χαῖρε φυὴν ἐρόεσσα χοροιτύπε δαιτὸς ἑταίρη, *Hymn. Hom. Merc.* 31. On this address as ironically picking up on hymnic conventions, see Richardson 2010 ad loc.

20. The erotic charge to Hermes's address to the tortoise has often been noted (e.g., Hübner 1986: 160–61, Vergados 2013 ad loc.), although the violent undertones and symbolism of rape have thus far (to my knowledge) been ignored. Note also the sexual connotations of the tortoise's suggestive walk (σαῦλα ποσὶν βαίνουσα, 28), noted at Vergados 2013 ad 28.

gender, her sexuality, and also—as a female—her generative creative power through her ability to give birth, to produce (*phuein*) through sex (*eros*). Her feminine creativity, her sexuality, and her femaleness are what Hermes sees first: and it is these feminine creative attributes, crucially, which are what he sees as qualifying her for her creative role in song (as a "dance-beating feast companion," 31).

At the same time, the location of the encounter on a grassy meadow (27)—commonly associated with sex, and especially rape, as in the rape of Persephone in the opening lines of another Homeric hymn, the *Hymn to Demeter*—warns us that there may be more afoot here than a simple pastoral scene.[21] As Hermes's speech continues, we realize that we are, in fact, in the midst of a highly disturbing rape analogy which appropriates the tortoise's female creativity through her literal physical overpowering by the man. The label of "dance-beating feast companion [*hetairē*]" (31) which Hermes bestows on the tortoise in his opening address is not only a reference to her relationship to song.[22] The term *hetairē*—in the feminine—could refer, not only to a "companion," but to the female courtesans (*hetairai*) who were paid for their sexual favors. The qualification "feast companion" (*daitos hetairē*, 31) only serves to underline this reading, as it was at banquets and symposia that *hetairai* often accompanied aristocratic men.[23] The tortoise's femininity, her sexuality, and her generative creativity are degraded until she becomes a sexual companion (*hetairē*) at a feast where men, not women, would have recited poetic songs, from the bards we see performing at feasts in Homer, to the songs of the symposium.[24]

21. See *Hymn. Hom. Dem.* 2–21, Eur. *Hipp.* 210–11 with Knox 1952: 6 n. 8.

22. On the accentation and translation of χοροιτύπε, see Vergados 2013 ad loc. Brillante 1999: 99 argues that these terms "non possono essere attribuiti all'essere vivente, ma solo allo strumento ancora da costruire"; he thus misses the point of the slippage between tortoise as embodied female ἑταίρη and inanimate instrument which is being articulated here; cf. Hübner 1986: 161.

23. On the role of the ἑταίρη, see Kurke 1999: 178–87, E. Cohen 2006, Dover 2016: 20–21. For this interpretation of the tortoise, see Richardson 2010 ad loc, Vergados 2013: 252; cf. *Hymn. Hom. Merc.* 478, where Hermes once again labels the tortoise as a ἑταίρη. The sexualized reading of the tortoise as feminine ἑταίρη contrasts with Hermes's labeling by Apollo as (masculine) δαιτός ἑταῖρε at 436.

24. On the all-male symposium, see Ford 2002: 7, 25–45, Nagy 2010: 33, West 2014: 320, Steiner 2015: 36; see, e.g., Pind. *Isthm.* 6.1 on the ἀνδρῶν . . . συμποσίου. On the role of women (*hetairai*, flute-girls, acrobats, dancers, etc.) at the symposium in both generating sexual tension and providing sexual services and entertainment, see Fehr 1990, Kurke 1999: 178–87; note also

The movement here is not just about disempowering the female tortoise, however: it is about actively overpowering her and appropriating her skills and qualities. This is stated by Hermes: "you'll benefit me first of all" (35), showcasing how the female is to be tamed to be useful to the male.[25] More than this, he is explicit about the fact that she cannot be allowed to live and to be connected to song: the only way she will be able to sing is if she is dead ("if you die, then you'll sing [*aeidois*] beautifully," 38).[26] Ironically, she must be stripped of her life, her voice, and her agency before "she" can sing. Of course, what makes this even more pointed is that this usage of "sing" (*aeidois*, 38) here is clearly metaphorical: as we will see, it will be he, Hermes, who will sing to the accompaniment of the lyre, and all she will be able to do, as an inanimate lyre, is resound in accompaniment. The mute female will continue to be muted in a different way, singing in tune to the male song. Pointedly, her death and conversion to the cause of male song also results in the elimination of her female gender. While she is alive, she is described as "living," with the feminine participle *zōousa* (38); in death, in the nongendered second-person singulars *thanēis* (you die) and *aeidois* (you sing, 38), her gender is elided as she is incorporated into the discourse of male song.

The violence that conquers and silences the female toward the cause of male song is not only fatal—it is also sexual. The passage continues (39–51):[27]

This is what he said, and lifting [*aeiras*] her in both hands
he went back into the house, carrying [*pherōn*] his lovely plaything
  [*erateinon athurma*].   40

the flute-girl (αὐλητρίς) in Plato's *Symposium*, who is sent away as inappropriate to the men's philosophical discussion (Pl. *Symp.* 176e7–8): see chapter 5, n. 120.

25. σὺ δέ με πρώτιστον ὀνήσεις, *Hymn. Hom. Merc.* 35.

26. ἢν δὲ θάνηις τότε κεν μάλα καλὸν ἀείδοις, *Hymn. Hom. Merc.* 38.

27. Ὣς ἄρ᾽ ἔφη· καὶ χερσὶν ἅμ᾽ ἀμφοτέρηισιν ἀείρας / ἂψ εἴσω κίε δῶμα φέρων ἐρατεινὸν ἄθυρμα. / ἔνθ᾽ ἀναμηλώσας γλυφάνωι πολιοῖο σιδήρου / αἰῶν᾽ ἐξετόρησεν ὀρεσκῴοιο χελώνης. / ὡς δ᾽ ὁπότ᾽ ὠκὺ νόημα διὰ στέρνοιο περήσει / ἀνέρος ὅν τε θαμιναὶ ἐπιστρωφῶσι μέριμναι, / ἢ ὅτε δινηθῶσιν ἀπ᾽ ὀφθαλμῶν ἀμαρυγαί, / ὣς ἅμ᾽ ἔπος τε καὶ ἔργον ἐμήδετο κύδιμος Ἑρμῆς. / πῆξε δ᾽ ἄρ᾽ ἐν μέτροισι ταμὼν δόνακας καλάμοιο / πειρήνας διὰ νῶτα διὰ ῥινοῖο χελώνης. / ἀμφὶ δὲ δέρμα τάνυσσε βοὸς πραπίδεσσιν ἑῆισι, / καὶ πήχεις ἐνέθηκ᾽, ἐπὶ δὲ ζυγὸν ἤραρεν ἀμφοῖν, / ἑπτὰ δὲ θηλυτέρων οἴων ἐτανύσσατο χορδάς, *Hymn. Hom. Merc.* 39–51. There are two instances in which I have diverged from Richardson's text: I give ἀναμηλώσας at 41 (following Ruhnken and West), rather than Richardson's ἀναπηλύσας; at 51 I read θηλυτέρων (Antig. *Mir.* 7, following Vergados) over Richardson's συμφώνους: see Vergados 2013: 261–62, 269–70 and Vergados 2007 for discussion.

Then he probed into her and with a chisel [*gluphanōi*] of grey iron
gouged out the life-stuff of the mountain-dwelling tortoise.
As when a quick thought pierces the heart
of a man [*aneros*] who is visited by constant worries,
or when bright glances flash from the eyes,   45
so glorious [*kudimos*] Hermes made [*emēdeto*] his work as quick as his
    word [*epos*].
He cut reed stalks to measure [*en metroisi*] and fixed them in,
fastening their ends across the back through the shell of the tortoise.
Over it all he cleverly stretched ox-hide
and attached two arms and fitted a bridge across both   50
and stretched the gut-strings of seven female [*thēluterōn*] sheep.

Hermes physically takes control of the tortoise, picking her up (*labōn*, 34;
aeiras, 39) and carrying her (*pherōn*, 40) into the house in a grotesque parody
of a wedding ceremony. Where the bride would normally be escorted in pro-
cession to enter the husband's household, here the tortoise is taken (*pherōn*,
40) into the house by force. The perverted marriage metaphor is made even
more potent by the fact that Hermes first encounters the tortoise "as he crosses
the threshold" (23) of the cave, symbolic of the woman's liminal position and
her transfer from her previous home to that of her husband in the wedding
ceremony.[28]

   That this is a symbolic rape is emphasized by the tortoise's objectification
at the crucial point of transition into Hermes's household. Where previously
she was feminine, as we have seen, for the first time here she is turned into a
neuter object: "he went back into the house, carrying his lovely plaything [*era-
teinon athurma*]" (40).[29] The application of this neuter phrase to the living,
female tortoise is made even more jarring by the fact that the same word
was previously used to describe her inanimate shell: "Where did you get this

28. οὐδὸν ὑπερβαίνων ὑψηρεφέος ἄντροιο, *Hymn. Hom. Merc.* 23. On the ἔκδοσις, the
formal transferal of bride to groom including the procession to the bride's new home and rituals
marking the crossing of the threshold, see Redfield 1982: 186–98, G. Ferrari 2003: 28. On the
depiction of the cave as a house/palace here, see Vergados 2011b, Vergados 2013: 244, and on
the threshold, in particular, Vergados 2011b: 6–7. Llewellyn-Jones 2003: 190 notes that χελώνη
could also mean "threshold," building on the image of the tortoise carrying her house with her
in her shell: the transferal of the tortoise into Hermes's house thus becomes a potent symbol of
Hermes's transgression of her female privacy and interiority.
   29. ἂψ εἴσω κίε δῶμα φέρων ἐρατεινὸν ἄθυρμα, *Hymn. Hom. Merc.* 40.

beautiful plaything [*athurma*], this speckled shell you wear?" (32–33).[30] In essence, she has already been reduced to nothing but her shell through Hermes's physical overpowering of her, even before the actual evisceration begins. The only change between the description of her shell and the description of the objectified tortoise is the adjective, *erateinon*—again, like *eroessa*, a word which is cognate with *erōs* and which underlines the disturbing sexual undertones of the passage.

The killing of the tortoise and appropriation of her song through a metaphorical rape act comes to a head in the gory description of Hermes's gouging-out of the tortoise's innards.[31] He examines her with a probe (*anamēlōsas*, 41), gouging her out with a chisel (*gluphanōi*, 41) and "piercing" or "boring" her (*exetorēsen*, 42; *pēxe*, 47; *peirēnas*, 48)—with obvious sexual connotations.[32] More than this, the specification of the *gluphanos*, the chisel, suggests not only the rape metaphor with the symbolic penis, but also the domination of the female with the utensils of male craft and engraving: the chisel was used to engrave seals and sculpt stone.[33] The connection between Hermes's depiction as a craftsman and the tortoise as an *aoidos* is made explicit at the beginning of the passage: "It was Hermes who first made [*tektēnat'*] the tortoise a bard [*aoidon*]" (25). This looks back to the fluid categorization of *aoidoi* as "craftsmen" (*dēmioergoi*) in the archaic period, as in *Odyssey* 17.383–85, where Eumaeus groups the *aoidos* among other craftsmen like seers, physicians, and carpenters.[34] Hermes thus exploits the utensils of male craft in the context of rape specifically to debilitate the female tortoise's generative connection to song— and thus to construct his *own* identity as a craftsmanly *aoidos*.

---

30. πόθεν τόδε καλὸν ἄθυρμα, / αἰόλον ὄστρακόν ἔσσο, *Hymn. Hom. Merc.* 32–33. For the text and punctuation (following West 2003), see chapter 3, n. 6.

31. Note that Furley 2011: 225 reads this instead as a parody of an epic duel, which may very well also be the case; Shelmerdine 1984: 204–5 reads it as a form of sacrifice (see contra Clay 1989: 107 n. 39). See also Hamilton 2015: 146 on the connection between violence and the invention of instruments in Greek literature.

32. Note the textual uncertainty around ἀναμηλώσας at line 41: see chapter 3, n. 27. I follow Ruhnken and West in reading ἀναμηλώσας here, which picks up on the vocabulary of probing/piercing in the following lines.

33. This is the first extant occurrence of γλύφανος (Richardson 2010 ad 41–42). Cf. the verbal form γλύφω (see Chantraine s.v., *LfgrE* s.v. γλύφανος): Hdt. 2.46, 7.69.1, Theoc. *Id.* 1.28.

34. Romani Mistretta 2017: 9–10. For *Od.* 17.383–85, see chapter 1, n. 6; on craft metaphors for song, see Ford 2002: 93–130, cf. Fearn 2017: 19–23, 34. For later examples, see chapter 6, nn. 53 and 68.

The generativity of Hermes's metaphorical rape of the female tortoise in engendering words for song is demonstrated by the simile which follows, which almost seems to take its poetic power from the sexual and physical domination of the female tortoise: "as when a quick thought pierces the heart of a man [*aneros*] who is visited by constant worries" (43–44).[35] It is as if the poetic lines of the simile itself, and not just the overt comparison, are stimulated by Hermes's activity. Aside from the obvious connection between the "piercing" of the man by a thought in the simile and the piercing of the tortoise, the simile also makes the gendered dimension of Hermes's actions explicit. The tortoise pierced by Hermes is compared, through the force of the simile, to a man pierced by a thought. The female tortoise is thus now displaced, not only as a singer in her own right, but also as a subject of poetry, by means of the comparison: the new subject of poetry is the *man* (*aneros*, 44).

This displacement of the female as both singer and subject is made clear in the line that caps the simile: "so glorious [*kudimos*] Hermes made [*emēdeto*] his work as quick as his word [*epos*]" (46).[36] Hermes's earlier power over words (*mythos*, 29) is reemphasized with *epos* here; his ability to "devise a word" (*epos . . . emēdeto*) links to the cunning plans of gods which form the plots of Homeric epic, and thus suggests not only his divine power, but also his connection to the contrivance of song.[37] This connection of his invention of the lyre to the creation of poetry is underlined by the description of the reeds which follows, which are cut "to measure" (*en metroisi*, 47)—using a term, *metron*, which would come to be applied to the poetic meter which measured out the beats of a line.[38] And he is further linked to poetry through the epithet *kudimos* ("glorious," 46), connecting to the "glorious deeds of men"

35. ὡς δ᾽ ὁπότ᾽ ὠκὺ νόημα διὰ στέρνοιο περήσει / ἀνέρος ὅν τε θαμιναὶ ἐπιστρωφῶσι μέριμναι, *Hymn. Hom. Merc.* 43–44.

36. ὡς ἅμ᾽ ἔπος τε καὶ ἔργον ἐμήδετο κύδιμος Ἑρμῆς, *Hymn. Hom. Merc.* 46.

37. E.g., of the plans of Zeus, Hom. *Il.* 7.478, *Od.* 24.96, see Heiden 2008b: 162–85; cf. Vergados 2013: 266. On the cunning of μῆτις (cognate with μήδομαι) and its connection to the contrivance of song, see Slatkin 2011: 154–55; for an interesting interpretation of the gender differentiation of μῆτις in archaic poetry, see Holmberg 1997. On Hermes's μῆτις, see Clay 1989: 99–102. Note that ἔπος does not properly achieve the sense "epic" until the sixth century BCE: Ford 1981: 137–52, and Martin 1989: 13; also Bynum 1976: 47–54, who argues that it was Aristotle who introduced the sense of "epic" to ἔπος.

38. The history of Greek metrics appears to date to the classical period with Hippias of Elis and Damon of Oa, see Ercoles 2014; on the term *metron* in the sense "meter," see Ar. *Nub.* 638, 641, Pl. *Grg.* 502c6, *Leg.* 669d7, Arist. *Pol.* 1459a17, etc., and see Riad 2014.

(*klea andrōn*) which are the subject of epic poetry, as well as his earlier definition as a doer of "renowned deeds" (*kluta erga*, 16).[39] The capping phrase of the simile thus displaces the female tortoise to set Hermes up as both the deviser of words—the cunning contriver of plots, like the epic bard—and the doer of glorious deeds—the subject of epic poetry. More than this, it is the very act of stripping the life and sexuality of the female tortoise which has endowed Hermes with the epithet "glorious." The "renowned deeds" (*kluta erga*, 16) which the opening of the hymn forecasted he would perform are realized at the very moment that the tortoise is deprived of her body and her sex. That this is a highly gender-marked moment of power transfer is underlined by the gut strings that Hermes applies to the hollowed-out shell, which come from "female sheep" (51).[40] Not only has he eviscerated a female tortoise in aid of his transformation into a "glorious" male singer, then: he has also gutted seven other female animals, turning this into a symbolic mass disemboweling of the woman's body in the aid of male song.

The transformation of the embodied female tortoise into an inanimate object, and the power of that gender transformation to endow Hermes with his masculinity as a singer, is made abundantly clear in the following lines (52–59):[41]

> But when he had made it, he took it up, his lovely plaything [*athurma*],
> and tested the strings in a scale with the plectrum, and she [*hē*]
>   sounded out loudly
> beneath his hand; and the god sang in accompaniment a beautiful
>   song [*hupo kalon aeiden*],
> testing, improvising, like young men [*kouroi hēbētai*]   55
> sneering insults at a feast,
> about Zeus son of Cronos and beautiful-sandalled Maia,
> how before they used to talk in the easy company of sex,
> naming [*exonomazōn*] his own name-renowned [*onomakluton*] lineage.

39. See chapter 1, n. 9.

40. On the text here, see chapter 3, n. 27. Note that Antigonus of Carystus, who is our source for θηλυτέρων here, cites the passage as an example of the fact that only female sheep guts produced sound, as opposed to rams—an interesting analogue to the assumption of the muteness of female tortoises in antiquity (see chapter 3, n. 11).

41. αὐτὰρ ἐπεὶ δὴ τεῦξε φέρων ἐρατεινὸν ἄθυρμα, / πλήκτρῳ ἐπειρήτιζε κατὰ μέλος, ἣ δ᾽ ὑπὸ χειρὸς / σμερδαλέον κονάβησε· θεὸς δ᾽ ὑπὸ καλὸν ἄειδεν / ἐξ αὐτοσχεδίης πειρώμενος, ἠύτε κοῦροι / ἡβηταὶ θαλίῃσι παραιβόλα κερτομέουσιν, / ἀμφὶ Δία Κρονίδην καί Μαιάδα καλλιπέδιλον / ὡς πάρος ὠρίζεσκον ἑταιρείηι φιλότητι, / ἥν τ᾽ αὐτοῦ γενεὴν ὀνομακλυτόν ἐξονομάζων, *Hymn. Hom. Merc.* 52–59.

Again, the tortoise is called an *erateinon athurma*, a "lovely plaything" (52). Previously used at line 40 in anticipation of her objectification, the transformation into neuter object has now been realized. Yet the sexual undertones of the transaction are still uncomfortably there. As Hermes tries out the lyre, "she sounded out loudly beneath his hand" (53–54).[42] The tortoise/lyre is still referred to with the feminine pronoun (*hē*, 53), showing the continuing discomfort with the femininity of the lyre—in spite of Hermes's attempts to desexualize her and turn her into a neuter *athurma*.[43] Even more disturbingly, the collocation of "she, beneath his hand" at line 53 (*hē d' hupo cheiros*) and the "sounding out" (*konabēse*, 54) of the female suggests the sexually charged image of the man grasping her and her cry in response, connecting back to the rape metaphor earlier. And again, as with her evisceration and piercing above, it is precisely this act of sexual overpowering which enables the god to become a singer. For the first time, we see him "singing in accompaniment a beautiful song" (*hupo kalon aeidein*, 54), with the verb *aeidein*—cognate with *aoidos*. The transformation from living female tortoise as *aoidos* to Hermes, the glorious *aoidos* singing of his own glorious deeds to the accompaniment of the inanimate lyre, is complete.[44] Where previously he said that she would "sing beautifully" (*kalon aeidois*, 38), now it is he who appropriates the "beautiful singing" (*kalon aeidein*, 54)—and her voice is turned to the "crashing" or "ringing" of an inanimate object (*konabēse*, 54).[45]

So how and what does the newly minted male bard sing? First, the how: his improvisations, tellingly, are compared in a second simile to the interjections made by young men (*kouroi hēbētai*) at feasts (55–56).[46] Just as the subject of poetry was defined through the simile above as the man (*aneros*, 44), this simile also emphasizes the gendered dimension of song: here it is the

---

42. ἣ δ᾽ ὑπὸ χειρὸς / σμερδαλέον κονάβησε, *Hymn. Hom. Merc.* 53–54.

43. At lines 64 and 506, however, she is a lyre in the feminine, with the word φόρμιγξ, at 423 a λύρη, and at 509 and 515 a κίθαρις, both also feminine; interestingly, *LfgrE* s.v. λύρη notes that this is the first occurrence of the term in archaic literature (see later, e.g., Archil. fr. 93a.5 *IEG*).

44. Vergados 2013: 247 notes that Hermes is appropriating the identity of the ἀοιδός here, but, strangely, identifies the appropriation from Apollo, not the tortoise: "By making the tortoise into an ἀοιδός, Hermes already appropriates Apollo's role as the god of song."

45. See *LfgrE* s.v. κοναβῆσαι, -ίζω: the verb is used specifically of inanimate objects, e.g., ships (*Il.* 2.334 = 16.277), buildings (*Od.* 10.399, 17.542), armor (*Il.* 13.498, 21.255), helmets (*Il.* 15.648), etc.

46. ἠΰτε κοῦροι / ἡβηταὶ θαλίῃσι παραιβόλα κερτομέουσιν, *Hymn. Hom. Merc.* 55–56.

improvisations of the singers, the *kouroi hēbētai* or "young men," that are com-
pared to Hermes's song. In contrast to the tortoise, who at the opening of the
passage was put into the role of the female *hetairē* (31), sexualized companion
to the men at the feast, here Hermes becomes the sympotic male singer among
a community of men.[47] And his first song is also a gendered one: the story of
another sexual union, echoing Hermes's rape of the tortoise, this one between
Zeus and Maia. Once again, as with the overpowering of the tortoise, this is a
sexual relationship which is adduced in order to create and define the subject
of his own male glory—here, in the description of his lineage as son of Zeus
and Maia.

The importance of Hermes's tale-telling in naming and constructing his
sense of self is made explicit at this closing stage of the story of the invention
of the lyre: "naming [*exonomazōn*] his own name-renowned [*onomakluton*]
lineage" (59).[48] Two terms which derive from the word for "word" or "name"
(*onoma*) are juxtaposed: the adjective *onomaklutos*, "name-renowned," and the
verb *exonomazein*, "to announce, call by name."[49] It is a fascinating end to a
story which has been as much about the problems of the gendered naming of
poets, and the instruments of poetry, as it has been about the invention of the
lyre. Where we started with the problematic naming of the female *chelus* as an
aoidos, we have moved to Hermes identified as the sole singer (*hupo kalon
aeiden*, 54) and—more than that—the *namer* (*exonomazōn*, 59). His control
over words, hinted at the beginning with his *mythos* (29) and underlined in
his contriving of "word and deed" (*epos te kai ergon*, 46), is finally revealed as
linking male dominance over song with a dominance over all language, all
acts of naming. He is both the namer (*exonomazōn*, 59) and the named (*ono-
makluton*, 59), both the arbiter of language and the only proper subject of
speech. This line sets the ultimate seal on the man as both singer and subject
of poetry, with *onomakluton* linking back to Hermes's *kluta* erga at line 16 (the
subject of the hymn)—making explicit the fact that Hermes's self-aggrandizing
hymn praising his own origins is intended as an echo of the poet's own hymn.[50]
Hermes and the poet are thus bound together as singer-men, vouchsafed

47. On the allusion to the practice of capping songs in the symposium here, see Richardson
2010 ad 55–61.

48. ἥν τ' αὐτοῦ γενεήν ὀνομακλυτόν ἐξονομάζων, *Hymn. Hom. Merc.* 59.

49. Here ὀνομάκλυτος occurs as a two-termination adjective, although it is found with a
feminine ending at Pind. *Pae.* 6.123; see Chantraine s.v. ὄνομα.

50. On Hermes's κλυτὰ ἔργα see Clay 1989: 105, Jaillard 2007: 76–80.

through their joint male control over the feminine lyre.[51] And it emphasizes
the connection between control over poetry and control over language, over
words, over the discourse of the self, which lies at the heart of the man's desire
to dominate speech—achieved, as the overpowering and evisceration of the
female tortoise shows, through the appropriation and elimination of the body,
the voice, and the sexual creative power of the female.

Coda: Pindar's Lyre

The *Homeric Hymn to Hermes* is not the only archaic text to deliberate over the
gendered power of the lyre. The lyric poet Pindar, who bridged what we now
(arbitrarily) term the archaic and classical periods of Greek poetry, opens one
of his victory odes, *Pythian* 1, with an address to a lyre (1–4):[52]

> Golden lyre [*chrusea phorminx*], joint [*sundikon*] possession [*kteanon*]
>   of Apollo
> and the violet-haired Muses; to which the footstep listens,
>   the beginning of the celebration,
> and bards [*aoidoi*] obey your signals
> whenever quivering your strings you make ready
>   the prelude of the chorus-leading opening.

The ode provides a fitting coda to the discussion of the self-definition of the
male poet in the archaic period, and the transition to new ways of thinking and
talking about what it meant to be a male poet in classical literature in the next
part of the book. The opening to *Pythian* 1 with the invocation to the lyre was
a famous one, even in antiquity—and, with its overt femaleness, with the femi-
nine *phorminx* and feminine adjective *chrusea* (*Pyth.* 1.1), it seems to follow
on neatly from the description of the *chelus* in the *Homeric Hymn to Hermes*.
The correspondence between the two descriptions of the lyre is mirrored in
the movement from feminine to neuter, neutralizing the dangerous femininity

---

51. See, e.g., Shelmerdine 1984: 207; cf. Vergados 2013: 271 on Hermes's hymn here as a *mise
en abyme*.

52. Χρυσέα φόρμιγξ, Ἀπόλλωνος καὶ ἰοπλοκάμων / σύνδικον Μοισᾶν κτέανον· τᾶς
ἀκούει μὲν βάσις ἀγλαΐας ἀρχά, / πείθονται δ᾿ ἀοιδοὶ σάμασιν / ἀγησιχόρων ὁπόταν
προοιμίων ἀμβολὰς τεύχῃς ἐλελιζομένα, Pind. *Pyth.* 1.1–4. The text is quoted according to
the edition of Snell and Maehler 1987. On this passage, see Gantz 1974: 143–45, Skulsky 1975:
8–12, Athanassaki 2009: 246–47, Fearn 2017: 169–228.

of the lyre: though the ode opens with the feminine *phorminx*, by the next line Pindar has reduced it to a neuter *kteanon*, a "possession" (2), a condensed version of the strategy of the poet of the *Homeric Hymn to Hermes*. Similarly, the lyre is claimed for the male god Apollo in line 1, ahead of the female Muses— just as Hermes displaced the Muses in the *Homeric Hymn*—with the emphatic adjective *sundikon*, "joint" or "rightful," underlining the male god's claim to the female lyre as well as his right to come first in the list of possessors.[53] This male claim is formally asserted in the third line through the masculine bards (*aoidoi*, 3) who sing in response to the lyre's signals—in contrast to the lyre itself which, like the sounding tortoiseshell of the *Homeric Hymn to Hermes*, is only able to "vibrate" (*elelizomena*, 4), not sing. At the same time, there is a potent gender inversion: it is the bards who are said to "obey" (3) the lyre's signals—placing them in the subservient position to the feminine lyre—as well as, in the following verses, the masculine eagle of Zeus (*aietos*, 6) and the hypermale "powerful" Ares (10), both of whom are subdued by the power of the lyre's song.

The attempt to neutralize the feminine lyre in *Pythian* 1, then, is not entirely successful: her song continues to subdue men (the male bards, the male eagle, the male Ares). The dangerous power of female song and the feminine apparatus surrounding song persists, always needing to be responded to, cut back, challenged. The ending of the ode presents a solution: the omission of the lyre altogether. Where, at the start, bards (*aoidoi*, 3) were said to "obey" the lyre, here they appear again without the lyre at all: "the acclaim of glory that lives after mortals alone tells of the lives of men [*andrōn*] who are gone to chroniclers and bards [*aoidois*]" (92–94).[54] A different mechanism of song is introduced, one which omits the lyre as intermediary and presents a reciprocal relationship between male bards (*aoidoi*) and the men (*andres*) whose stories they tell. As with the male *aoidos anēr* of Homer who tells of the *klea andrōn*, and the male singer of the *Homeric Hymn to Hermes* who manipulates the lyre as a vehicle to name his own fame, here the feminine lyre is displaced to allow

---

53. σύνδικον here has occasioned controversy over its translation: LSJ s.v. gives "joint"; Fränkel 1951: 521 n. 26 argues for a reading akin to σὺν δίκᾳ; Hooker 1977 suggests "speaking on [Apollo and the Muses'] behalf"; Race 1997 ad loc. notes that the term usually means "advocate" and thus translates as "rightful" or (following Hooker) "possession who speaks on the behalf of its owner"; Maslov 2015: 221 with n. 110 gives "possession that is their partisan supporter."

54. ὀπιθόμβροτον αὔχημα δόξας / οἶον ἀποιχομένων ἀνδρῶν δίαιταν μανύει / καὶ λογίοις καὶ ἀοιδοῖς, Pind. *Pyth.* 1.92–94.

for a poetry which links male singers to the men they celebrate. This move is picked up on by later commentators: the scholiast on *Pythian* 1.1 remarks that "some say that Hieron [the dedicatee of the ode] promised a golden lyre [*kith-aran*] to Pindar, which is why the poet [*poiētēs*] began the invocation with the lyre, commemorating him [*auton*] [i.e., Hieron]."[55] A male chain of reciprocity is posited between the masculine poet and the male patron. Instead of hymning the feminine lyre, the scholiast says, we should instead read the invocation as a veiled reference to the commemoration of the male patron—replacing the praise of the female object, the lyre, with the man and his relationship to the male poet.[56]

The act of naming the bard, then, at the beginning of Greek poetry, and the construction of the poet's role, was a continually contested process. As the word for "poet" (*aoidos*) itself entered the written record, we can trace poets exploring ideas around what it meant to be a bard within the gendered contexts of poetry. The idea of the masculinity of the poet was born at transgressional sites of gender, and the naming of the *aoidos* was deployed to explore and enforce these gender boundaries.

The term *aoidos* did not die with the archaic period, though other terms—above all *poiētēs* (poet)—did displace it, as we will see in the next part of the book. Where *aoidos* continues to be used, it comes to have an archaizing flavor, referring back to the original discourse of male poetry initiated in Homer and Hesiod.[57] This is best demonstrated, once again, in Pindar, at the opening of *Nemean* 2, where it describes the Homeridae, a group of poets who claimed to be both literal (genealogical) and poetic descendants of Homer: "The Homeridae, singers [*aoidoi*] of stitched verses, most often begin from the prelude to Zeus" (*Nem.* 2.1–3).[58] The term "singers" or "bards" (*aoidoi*) here refers to a very specific genre and tradition: the poetic lineage of Homer, suggesting that *aoidos* has already acquired a specialized sense of "male epic bard." The masculinity of this tradition is underlined by the use of *Homeridae*, a male

55. Τινὲς χρυσῆν ὑποσχέσθαι φασὶ κιθάραν τὸν Ἱέρωνα τῷ Πινδάρῳ. Διὸ καὶ ὁ ποιητὴς ὑπομιμνήσκων αὐτὸν τῆς ἐπαγγελίας ἀπὸ τῆς κιθάρας ἤρξατο, schol. ad Pind. *Pyth.* 1.1. For the relationship with Hieron in this ode, see Morgan 2015: 300–358, Fearn 2017: 168–228.

56. For more discussion of Pindar's gendering of the poet, see Hauser 2022.

57. See Maslov 2009: 11 with n. 25.

58. Ὅθεν περ καὶ Ὁμηρίδαι / ῥαπτῶν ἐπέων τὰ πόλλ' ἀοιδοί / ἄρχονται, Διὸς ἐκ προοιμίου, Pind. *Nem.* 2.1–3.

patronymic—"sons of Homer"—figuring the lineage of *aoidoi* descending from Homer as a male father-to-son relationship. Pindar's usage of *aoidos* here confirms the success of the bounding moves operated by Homer, Hesiod, and the *Homeric Hymns*. Not only has the term come to be associated generically with epic (*rhaptōn epeōn*, 2), creating an etymology for the rhapsodes who recited hexameter poetry;[59] it has also become emphatically male gendered, as both the originary male term for "poet," and the source and validation of male poetic descendants within the constructed canon of Greek literature. It is to these poetic descendants and inheritors of the masculinity of the male poet, as Greek literature crosses from the archaic into the classical period and the sixth century into the fifth, that we turn next.

59. ῥαπτῶν ἐπέων . . . ἀοιδοί at *Nem.* 2.2 gives an etymology of the ῥαψῳδός (song-stitcher): see Nagy 1989: 7, Pfeijffer 1999 ad loc.

PART II

Tool

THE MAN-MAKER:
MALE POETS MAKING
MALE CITIZENS

4

How to Make Men
in Aristophanes

DURING THE fifth century BCE, the vocabulary for male poetic authorship underwent a seismic shift. The old vocabulary of the masculine *aoidos*, which had been established by male bards in the archaic period, began to disappear in favor of a new family of terms, derived from the verb *poiein* ("to make," and so "to make poetry"). Words like *poiētēs* (male poet), *poiēsis* (poetry), and *poiēma* (poem) start to make their appearance, marking a major shift in the attitude to poetry—and to the role of the male poet.

An early example of this vocabulary of *poiein* occurs in the poetry of Solon, the Athenian statesman and poet, where he orders a change of theme with the verb *metapoiein*, closely followed by *aeidein*: "Change your theme [*metapoiēson*], clear-voiced singer, and sing [*aeide*] like this" (fr. 20 *IEG*).[1] Here *poiein* and *aeidein*—making and singing—occur side by side, suggesting a transition in vocabulary for poetry and a point, in the preclassical period, where *poiein* and *aeidein* vocabulary hung in the balance. A similar fluctuation between old and new terms for poet and poetry occurs in Theognis, who describes the poet as the *Mousōn therapōn*, the "servant of the Muses" (769),

---

1. μεταποίησον Λιγιαστάδη, ὧδε δ᾽ ἄειδε, fr. 20.3 *IEG*. West argues that the change of theme is from a quotation of Mimnermus fr. 6.2 in the lines preceding this fragment, West 1974: 72–76; see also Gerber 1997: 108–9, Ford 2002: 132–33, Steiner 2015: 34–35. The attribution of Λιγιαστάδη (Diels gives Λιγυαιστάδη) is unclear: it could be both an adjective and a substantive, substituting for Mimnermus's name and thus acting as a reference to his identity as an author. Meanwhile, its derivation is also unclear: Maria Noussia-Fantuzzi suggests "clear-voiced singer" (from λιγύς and ἀείδειν) or, perhaps, "pleasing [ἀνδάνειν] with clear song" (2010: 403).

borrowing Hesiod's phrase.[2] But Theognis continues to define the poet's activity (771): "to seek, to show, to compose [*poiein*]." The text is disputed, but, if the reading of *poiein* is right, it would seem to imply an early usage of *poiein* for poetic activity.[3] Meanwhile, as I have argued elsewhere, Pindar appears to deploy a noun ending in *-poios*, "maker," to define his own craft (by contrast with sculpture) as a poetic "maker of images of men" (*andriantopoios*, *Nem.* 5.1).[4]

As the fifth century progresses, *poiētēs* seems to become more and more favored as the term for "poet," over the older *aoidos* (the exception is tragedy).[5] Herodotus's *Histories*—our first extended piece of Greek prose—showcases for the first time the sustained establishment of *poiētēs* as the word for "poet," as well as nouns composed of the *-poios* suffix (such as *epopoios*, "epic poet"; *logopoios*, "prose-writer" [literally, "word-maker"]; and *mousopoios*, "poet" [literally, "music-maker"]).[6] The verb *poiein* is also commonly used for composing poetry.[7] The term *aoidos*, by contrast, appears only once in Herodotus, to refer to an explicitly archaic bard, Arion, the inventor of the dithyramb, who was saved from drowning by the dolphins who heard his song.[8] This seems to suggest that *aoidos* had, by this point, a retrospective flavor to it, just as in Pindar's *Nemean* 2, looking back to the archaic bards who had termed themselves *aoidoi*. *Poiētēs*, on the other hand, appears six times in Herodotus (to describe Homer, Alcaeus, and Aeschylus, among others) and twice in Thucydides; it also occurs in a fragment of the tragedian Euripides,

---

2. χρὴ Μουσῶν θεράποντα καὶ ἄγγελον (the servant and messenger of the Muses), Thgn. 769.

3. ἀλλὰ τὰ μὲν μῶσθαι, τὰ δὲ δεικνύναι, ἄλλα δὲ ποιεῖν, Thgn. 771. The text given here is that of Gerber 1999a; West supplies a different text and punctuation (δεικνύναι· ἄλλα δὲ ποιῶν), which turns the translation of ποιεῖν to "doing" (see Ford 2002: 133 n. 2). See also van Groningen 1966: 297–99.

4. Οὐκ ἀνδριαντοποιός εἰμ᾿, Pind. *Nem.* 5.1; see Hauser 2022: 141–45.

5. Ford notes a lexical split whereby ποιητής and its cognates become the preserve of authors of technical treatises, historians, or parodists, and ἀοιδός remains the favored word among tragedians: Ford 2002: 137 with n. 23; cf. Torrance 2013: 163. For ἀοιδός in the tragic poets, see chapter 6, nn. 21 and 22.

6. See pp. 192–204 with chapter 7, nn. 11–13. For Herodotus's date, see chapter 7, n. 1.

7. See chapter 7, n. 9.

8. τοῦ ἀρίστου ἀνθρώπων ἀοιδοῦ (the best singer among men), Hdt. 1.24.5; note that he is also called a κιθαρῳδός at 1.23. Herodotus emphasizes the archaization of ἀοιδός by contextualizing Arion among "those alive at that time" (τῶν τότε ἐόντων, 1.23).

alongside—like Herodotus—the adjective *mousopoios*, "music-making."[9] In the extant plays and fragments of the comic poet Aristophanes, meanwhile, *poiētēs* appears more than forty times, setting the stage for the word's dominance of poet-vocabulary.[10] *Poiētēs* and nouns with the *-poios* suffix thus seem to have grown steadily in popularity from Solon, Theognis, and Pindar in the late archaic period through the fifth century; and, by the time that we reach Aristophanes (in poetry) and Herodotus (in prose), *poiētēs* and its cognates were being thoroughly established as the "new" terms for the fifth-century poet-about-town.

So why does the shift from *aoidos* to *poiētēs* matter, and what does it tell us about what it meant to be a poet? Andrew Ford argues that the derivation of the new term *poiētēs* from the verb *poiein* (to make) suggests a move toward a more artisanal, craft-focused vision of poetry.[11] With the shift in the fifth and fourth centuries away from orality toward "a sense of songs as texts to be studied rather than performed," the overwhelming preponderance of *poiētēs* and its cognates demonstrates "an increasing awareness of the lasting powers of texts [which] supported the conception of song as a stable work rather than a performance."[12] This technical, formal visualization of poetry-making came from a reconceptualization of writing (and the function and dissemination of texts) as a technical skill and lasting artifact, like craftsmanship—mostly among writers who wanted to emphasize their technical expertise, deriving from critics who were writing in the tradition of Ionian *historia*. This, in turn, enabled the increasing professionalization of literature and the continuation of a semantics for authorship rooted in *-poios* (*-maker*) suffixes into the Hellenistic period.[13]

These are all important observations for the development of critical attitudes to Greek poetry, which is the focus of Ford's analysis—but they glide

---

9. ποιητής: Thuc. 1.5.2, 1.21.1 (both of poets in general); Eur. fr. 663 *TrGF*. Wright 2010: 166 and Torrance 2013: 163 note that Euripides is the only fifth-century tragedian to use the term ποιητής. ποίησις as poetry: Thuc. 1.10.3 (of Homer). μουσοποιός: Eur. *Hipp.* 1428, *Tro.* 1119; see chapter 7, n. 24.

10. Forty-three times in total: five in *Acharnians*, four in *Knights*, three in *Clouds*, four in *Wasps*, three in *Peace*, four in *Birds*, two in *Lysistrata*, three in *Women at the Thesmophoria*, fourteen in *Frogs*, once in fragments.

11. Ford 2002: 131–57; see also Braun 1938, Vicaire 1964: 6–7, Svenbro 1984: 155–79. Graziosi 2002: 41–47.

12. Ford 2002: 154, 157.

13. Ford 2002: 134, 294.

over the gender and identity politics involved in the shift from *aoidos* to *poiētēs*, as male poets continued to explore the male-gendering of the production of poetry. This chapter, then, takes up the watershed moment in Greek poetry where male poets moved from calling themselves "singer-men" to "making-men," and—rather than focusing on the conceptual move from performance to craft—looks instead at the acts of identity creation and gender policing which structured the introduction of the new term, *poiētēs*, or "man-maker."

It is with Aristophanes, in particular, that the vocabulary of *poiētēs* becomes deeply established as the terminology for male poets speaking about poets— not only to discuss other poets (most conspicuously in the judgment of Aeschylus and Euripides in the *Frogs*), but also, as we will see, as a label for Aristophanes himself.[14] The masculinity of the male *poiētēs* is a central concern for Aristophanes, both thematically and linguistically: though *poiētēs* is itself gendered male, Aristophanes uses it multiple times in conjunction with the noun *anēr* in the phrase *anēr poiētēs*, or "man-poet."[15] Not only does this remind us of Homer's *aoidos anēr*, creating a gendered poetic lineage looking back to epic, it also showcases the three central pillars which we will see in Aristophanes's depiction of the relationship between gender and the *poiētēs*. The first is that the poet has to learn how to "become" a man—dealing with issues of imitation and identity that come with depicting both male and female characters, in order to explore his own gendered identity.[16] The second is that the poet's activity as a "maker" is directly and inherently connected to his identity as a man, underlining the male gender of the poet and connecting it to his activity as an agent of craft, with a new emphasis on the "doing" inherent in the etymology of *poiētēs*. And the third is that the poet also makes men—not simply generating men's fame in song (as the epic *aoidos*), but actually forming and shaping the men themselves: as we will see, Aristophanes claims to educate

14. Aristophanes is the major surviving source of Old Comedy, but we do have some other examples of ποιητής in Old Comedy: for a possible instance in Cratinus at P. Oxy. 663.8, see Bakola 2010: 297–300; for Eupolis, see Eup. fr. 205 K-A (on which see Lech 2012), fr. 392 K-A.

15. *Nub.* 545, *Lys.* 368, *Thesm.* 147, *Ran.* 858, 1008, 1030, 1369; cf. *Pax* 773–74. On the figure of the comic poet as "an embodiment of *andreia*" in Aristophanes, see Sluiter and Rosen 2003: 13–19, and on ἀνδρεία in Aristophanes, see Bassi 2003: 44–46, Rademaker 2003: 115 n. 1.

16. On the construction of masculinity in classical Athens, see Winkler 1990: 45–70, Bassi 1998, Fox 1998, Foxhall and Salmon 1998a and 1998b, Rosen and Sluiter 2003: 1–211; see also the introduction, nn. 6 and 61. On masculinity in Aristophanes, see Rademaker 2003, McDonald 2016 (focusing on language), and cf. Sluiter and Rosen 2003: 13–19.

men through his poetry to form the backbone of the citizenry in the democratic *polis*. These three aspects of Aristophanes's gendered *poiētēs*—the poet as a maker who has to learn how to become a man; the poet as man and maker; and the poet as maker of men—will be the focus of the discussion that follows.

From Poetess to Poet: Becoming a Man-Poet

Aristophanes's discussions of poets (and poetry) form some of the key passages for early aesthetic criticism, as in the debate over the tragic styles of Aeschylus and Euripides in the *Frogs*, for instance.[17] We have already seen in the introduction how Aristophanes engages with contemporary debates over naming and grammatical gender in the *Clouds*, and this interest in naming extends in no small part to the word for "poet," with the new fashion for *poiētēs* and -*poios* compounds.[18] The term *poiētēs* occurs over forty times in Aristophanes's extant plays and fragments (fourteen times in the *Frogs* alone), and the *anēr poiētēs* (man-poet) collocation makes an appearance seven times, in four different plays. Meanwhile, -*poios* compounds range from the apparently serious *melopoios* ("song-maker," i.e., lyric poet, *Ran.* 1250) and *tragōidopoios* (tragedy-maker, *Thesm.* 30), to the parodic *agriopoios* (maker of savages, *Ran.* 837), *krēmnopoios* (crag-making, *Nub.* 1367), and *ptōchopoios* (beggar-maker, *Ran.* 842), both mocking the tragedians' high-flown language and poking fun at the contemporary trend toward ever more complex and specific -*poios* compounds.[19]

But there is a question which must first be addressed, which lingers behind the terms used in the figuration of the *poiētēs*: How does a poet become a man, and how does the man become a poet?

To answer this question, we have to turn to the *Women at the Thesmophoria*.[20] This play, performed in 411 BCE, sees the playwright Euripides brought

17. For Aristophanes on poetry, see esp. Wright 2012; also Ugolini 1923, Snell 1982: 113–35, O'Sullivan 1992: 1–22, 106–52, Ford 2002: 188, 199–200, Silk 2002: 42–97, Zanetto 2006, Bakola, Prauscello, and Telò 2013. For Aristophanes and his comic rivals, see Harvey and Wilkins 2000 (esp. Silk 2000), Bakola 2008, Sidwell 2009, Biles 2011. For Aristophanes and tragedy, see, inter alia, Rau 1967, Taplin 1986, Heiden 1991, Calame 2004b, Nelson 2016, Farmer 2017. On literary criticism in the *Frogs*, see chapter 4, n. 119.

18. See p. 15.

19. Ford 2002: 134.

20. See the commentaries by Sommerstein 1994, Austin and Olson 2004; see also Dover 1972: 162–72, Hansen 1976, Moulton 1981: 108–43, Taaffe 1993: 74–102, MacDowell 1995: 251–73,

to judgment before the women of Athens, who feel maligned by their representation in Euripides's dramas—building on the popular assumption, often parodied in Aristophanes, that Euripides was a "woman-hater" for his portrayal of women.[21] Aristophanes uses this ingenious set-up to explore a whole host of issues around the interaction between the poet's gender and the depiction of his characters, and the kind of gender-bending required to be able to imitate other genders, both on the page and the stage. What happens to the male poet's gender when he tries to tell stories of women, and how does this affect his masculinity as a "man-poet" and "maker"? What mechanisms can he use to be able to imitate (and understand) women, without putting his own masculinity at risk? How can the poet do all these things, and still be a man—an *anēr poiētēs*?

Women at the Thesmophoria sees the women of Athens planning to decide the exact nature of their revenge against the poet at the festival of the Thesmophoria, a women's-only festival dedicated to Demeter and Persephone. Euripides, aided by his (unnamed) male In-law, therefore determines to infiltrate the festival, but in order to do so, he needs the help of a woman—so he approaches the (male) poet Agathon, a famed and (as Aristophanes portrays him) effete tragedian, to do the job for him.[22] This begins a whole series of gender reversals, which structure the play. As Alan Sommerstein notes, every significant male character (bar one) "to some extent 'becomes a woman,'" either by putting on female clothes (Agathon, In-law, Euripides) or being accepted as a near-woman due to their effeminacy (as in the case of Cleisthenes and Agathon).[23] In contrast, the women are portrayed as living out negative

Zeitlin 1996: 375–416, Bobrick 1997, McClure 1999a: 205–59, Gamel 2002, Stehle 2002, Clements 2014, McDonald 2016: 167–75.

21. On the date of the play, see Austin and Olson 2004: xxxiii–xxxvi; see also Sommerstein 1977, MacDowell 1995: 251–52. On Euripides's depiction as a woman-hater in Aristophanes, see Sommerstein 1994: 4–5, Assaël 1985, Marelli 2006, Tammaro 2006. As an example, see Ar. *Lys.* 283 on women as "hated by Euripides and all the gods" (τασδὶ δὲ τὰς Εὐριπίδη θεοῖς τε πᾶσιν ἐχθράς); cf. schol. in Ar. *Lys.* 283, μισογύνης γὰρ ὁ Εὐριπίδης καὶ πολλὰ κατ' αὐτῶν λέγων. See also *Lys.* 368–69, discussed at pp. 109–11.

22. On Agathon, see Roberts 1900, Austin and Olson 2004 ad 29–30, Wright 2016: 59–90, and, on his depiction in Aristophanes, see Muecke 1982, Saetta Cottone 2003, Duncan 2006: 25–57, Given 2007.

23. On transvestism in antiquity, see esp. Campanile, Carlà-Uhink, and Facella 2017, also Bassi 1998: 105–6, Corbeill 2015: 147–49, and on androgyny see Brisson 2002; in *Thesmophoriazusae*, see Hansen 1976: 165, Zeitlin 1996: 375–416, Bassi 1998: 138. On "unmanliness" in Aristophanes, see Rademaker 2003: 115–16.

feminine stereotypes—which means that "the gender-inversion is all one way: in this play (almost) everyone is a woman."[24]

As interesting as these gender reversals are in their own right, they are also centered around a discussion of gender and its relationship to the identity of the poet: not only in Euripides's alleged misogyny through his portrayal of the characters in his plays, but in the gender-switching of the figure of the poet. The focus throughout on the gendering of the poet-figures of the play demonstrates that it is not only the gendering of the characters written by poets, but the *gender of the poets themselves* which is at stake here. It is not a coincidence that the play begins at the house of the poet Agathon, a playwright lampooned for his unmanliness: he is depicted in *Women at the Thesmophoria* looking more like a woman than a man and singing a maiden's chorus, while his passivity in sex—the fact that he takes the "female" role—is a constant source of jokes.[25] Yet it is also Agathon who receives the first (male) poet-term of the play: Euripides introduces him as "the famous tragedy-maker" (*tragōidopoios*, 30).[26] It is a particularly layered moment in terms of metapoetic self-reference: a term for a poet written by a poet (Aristophanes), spoken by a poet (Euripides), about a poet (Agathon). This is one of those fashionable *-poios* suffix terms, and it is clearly intended here as a dig against the tragedians' propensity for creating long compounds.[27] It is followed by a pun by In-law which highlights the fashion for *-poios* terms: "Which [*poios*] Agathon is that?" asks In-law (30).[28] In-law segues directly from the poetic signifier *tragōidopoios* into the interrogative *poios* (an entirely different word, not derived from *poiein*), pointing specifically at the poet-term's *-poios*

24. Sommerstein 1994: 7.

25. Ar. *Thesm.* 35, 50, 59–62, 153, 200–201; see McClure 1999a: 215–26, Rademaker 2003. On active and passive sex roles in male same-sex relationships, see Halperin 1990: 15–40, Dover 2016: 16, 100–109, though note, cautioning against Dover's dichotomization, McClure 1999a: 206, Davidson 2007: 103–4, Masterson 2013: 23. On Agathon as potentially impersonating the lyric poet Anacreon here with his effeminate dress, see Snyder 1974.

26. ὁ κλεινὸς . . . / ὁ τραγῳδοποιός, *Thesm.* 29–30. On the exploration of ποιεῖν through the figure of Agathon, see Muecke 1982: 43; on "the self-reflexiveness of art" in the *Thesmophoriazusae*, see Zeitlin 1996: 375–416.

27. Later, τραγῳδοποιός would become one of the standard terms for tragedians, although this is its first extant occurrence in Greek literature, suggesting that it may have been Aristophanes himself who coined the term: see Chantraine s.v. Cf. τραγῳδοδιδάσκαλον, 88 (of Agathon by Euripides, clearly making fun of Euripides's love of compounds, as noted at Ford: 2002: 134).

28. ποῖος οὗτος Ἀγάθων, *Thesm.* 30.

suffix.[29] But In-law's question does not only serve to emphasize the fashion for -*poios* terms: it also means that a poetic term that is meant to specify identity ("Agathon the tragedy-maker [-*poios*]") is transformed into its opposite—a question about masculine identity ("What kind of man [*poios*] is he?"), with the explicitly male interrogative. At least part of the joke, in the repetition of the masculine *tragōidopoios poios*, is that In-law does not recognize Euripides's description of Agathon as a *tragōidopoios*, precisely because Euripides has used the masculine, a category into which Agathon does not fit. This grammatical confusion caused by Agathon's gender-blurring is made explicit when Agathon appears on stage sixty or so lines later, dressed as a woman and surrounded by female paraphernalia, and about to launch into song in the voice of a female chorus. As Agathon comes in and Euripides says, "he's right here" ("this man" [*houtos*], 96), In-law claims that he still cannot see the man referred to by Euripides: "Which man [*poios*] is he? I can't see any *man* [*andra*] there at all" (96–98).[30] In-law's move is both to draw on the earlier gendered-poetic pun between *tragōidopoios* and *poios* at lines 30–31 with *poios* at line 96, and to pick up on Euripides's masculine *houtos* (96), making Euripides's assumption of Agathon's male gender explicit with the noun *anēr* (98). Once again, the source of the confusion is In-law's inability to make Agathon fit grammatical gendered categories because of his fluid gender: all he can see, In-law claims, is "Cyrene" (98)—a feminine name, and the name of a famous female courtesan to boot.[31] The joke—just like the changing of Cleonymus's name to the feminine Cleonyme in *Clouds* which we saw in the introduction—is that grammatical gender, performed social gender, and biological sex have, in Agathon's case, failed to line up.[32]

In the fragmentation of the masculine *tragōidopoios* into the interrogative male *poios* that introduces this gender-bending sequence, then, terms for poets are literally being parsed and taken apart to ask how they contribute to gendered identity. A word which seems to signify a poet as a male "doer" and to

29. For a similar usage, compare *Thesm.* 621: τὸν δεῖνα; ποῖον; (What's-his-name? Which what's-his-name?).

30. [Κη.] καὶ ποῖός ἐστιν; [Εὐ.] οὗτος οὑκκυκλούμενος. / [Κη.] ἀλλ᾽ ἦ τυφλὸς μέν εἰμ᾽· ἐγὼ γὰρ οὐχ ὁρῶ / ἄνδρ᾽ οὐδέν᾽ ἐνθάδ᾽ ὄντα, Κυρήνην δ᾽ ὁρῶ, 96–98. I follow the text of Hall and Geldart's OCT here; Austin and Olson 2004 give καὶ ποῦ 'σθ' at line 96, following Meineke, see comm. ad loc.; N. Wilson, in the revised 2007 OCT, gives ποῦ ⟨'cτιν.

31. See McClure 1999a: 222.

32. See p. 15.

endow him with a specific gendered identity is turned, by the association of the *-poios* suffix with the interrogative *poios*, into one big question mark around gender and naming—just as Agathon's claim to be a man through his male name is twisted into the female name, Cyrene. The figure of Agathon thus serves a central role in introducing some of the key themes around gender, naming, and poetics which will structure the rest of the play.[33] Names, poets, and their relation to gender are, Agathon shows us, not all they seem.

The mismatch between grammatical gender, social gender, and biological sex is a continued source of humor throughout the play. As the characters gender-switch, changing into women's clothes and taking on the parts of women as they parody Euripides's plays (first *Helen*, then *Andromeda*), the correctness of grammatical gender comes under scrutiny and the difficulties in maintaining "correct" linguistic gender for effeminate cross-dressing men playing the parts of women starts to show.[34] At first, grammatical gender conforms with the explicit gender that is being performed, either in implicit performances where men inhabit women's roles (the cross-dressing trick) or explicit stagings of female characters from well-known tragedies: thus In-law, dressed as a woman to infiltrate the Thesmophoria, is referred to in the feminine until he is revealed as a man (his phallus is revealed at line 643), after which he is spoken of in the masculine.[35] When Agathon first enters (looking more like a woman than a man), his song is a maiden's chorus in which he alternates between female leader and chorus of young women, and—keeping to his part—he uses the feminine to refer to himself.[36] When In-law acts the part of Helen in the *Helen* parody during a first rescue attempt after his capture and imprisonment, he and Euripides (who performs Menelaus) both refer to In-law (acting Helen) in the feminine—that is, they acknowledge the fiction of his feminine role. On the other hand, their spectator Critylla, herself a woman, refuses to deny the biological male sex behind the fiction, and uses the masculine for In-law as Helen, until eventually In-law is forced to give up

---

33. Hansen 1976: 167.

34. On the use of gendered (and cross-gendered) speech in Aristophanes, see Sommerstein 1995, McClure 1999a: 205–59, Willi 2003: 157–97, McDonald 2016. See also introduction, n. 63.

35. Sommerstein 1994: 7–8, McClure 1999a: 231 n. 107; for "mistakes" in In-law's speech that undermine his feminine persona, see Taaffe 1993: 87, McClure 1999a: 227–28, 231–34.

36. δεξάμεναι ("women receiving," 101), κλῄζουσα ("a woman celebrating in song," 116), ὀλβίζουσα ("a woman glorifying," 117, with Hall and Geldart's text); see McClure 1999a: 222, McDonald 2016: 167–68. For Agathon performing both leader and chorus here, see Rau 1967: 106, Muecke 1982: 47.

and applies the masculine to himself, too (925).[37] As the parodies progress, and In-law moves on to act out Andromeda from Euripides's play of the same name, gender starts to get seriously confused: he moves back and forth between the masculine and feminine in referring to himself, fusing his biological male sex and his performed female gender as Andromeda; he even mistakenly addresses the (female) god Echo in the masculine (implicitly drawing attention to the male actor behind the mask), to the extent that the Scythian Archer, who stands as In-law's guard, gets so confused by the interplay of acting and reality that he makes a mistake of gender in almost every line he has.[38]

These kinds of gender mistakes not only tease out the basic paradox of the dissonance between the actor and his persona, however—they also get to the root of the vexed gendered identity of the poet, who has to be able to adopt and adapt to different genders in order to be able to compose in both male and female voices.[39] The joke around Agathon, as a poet-figure in particular, is that his fluid gender and passive sexuality is precisely what enables him to compose poetry in the voice of a woman. Another example of Agathon's flexible, gender-inverted poetic terminology comes up only a few lines after the dissection of his gender as *tragōidopoios* at line 30. Just before the poet's entrance, his slave announces his imminent arrival, claiming that the "band of the Muses" is busy "making songs" (*melopoiōn*, 42) within Agathon's home.[40] Here he uses another compound word from *poiein*, just like *tragōidopoios*; and he describes the Muses with a typically high-flown lyric noun in the masculine, "band" (*thiasos*), used for groups of singers from Alcman on. Gender reversal is again at play, forecasting the gender reversal which Agathon will embody in his entrance a few lines later: instead of the usual male poet-bards who worship the Muses (like Hesiod's *Mousaōn therapōn*), here it is the female Muses (coming together in a masculine "band" [*thiasos*]) who are gathered in celebration of the (male) poet.

37. See Sommerstein 1994: 7 with n. 46 for examples.

38. See, for example, line 1077, where In-law addresses Echo as "my good man" (ὦγάθ'), apparently referring to the gender of the (male) actor playing Echo; see Hall 1989a: 49–50, McClure 1999a: 235 n. 120.

39. Sommerstein 1994: 8, cf. Taaffe 1993: 4–10, 23–47, 82 and Duncan 2006: 25–57 (on Agathon in particular); also Zeitlin 1996: 385–86, Bassi 1998: 138, McClure 1999a: 224, McDonald 2016: 168 n. 25, and, on tragedy, Zeitlin 1996: 341–74 esp. 346, Griffith 2001.

40. ἐπιδημεῖ γὰρ / θίασος Μουσῶν ἔνδον μελάθρων / τῶν δεσποσύνων μελοποιῶν, *Thesm.* 40–42.

But there is another, deeper issue of gender here. The problem is that *melopoiōn* in this grammatical form could be either a masculine nominative singular participle (from *melopoiein*), agreeing with *thiasos*—"the [male] song-making band of the Muses"—or a feminine genitive plural noun or adjective (from *melopoios*)—"the [male] band of the [female] song-maker/song-making Muses." Colin Austin and S. Douglas Olson, in their commentary on the *Women at the Thesmophoria*, state that it should be taken as the masculine participle rather than the feminine noun.[41] But surely the interest lies in the fact that the two can be confused—that gender is so fluid here that we are unsure, even before the effeminate Agathon enters, whether his gender-fluid Muses are being gendered with a male noun and participle, or a female one. Even more interestingly, if we *do* take *melopoiōn* as a feminine here, its root—*melopoios*—is a masculine-looking second-declension noun: in fact, Aristophanes makes use of it elsewhere for a male poet in the *Frogs*, where Euripides describes Aeschylus as a "bad song-maker" (*Ran.* 1250).[42] We would therefore have to understand *melopoios* here in *Women at the Thesmophoria* as an unusual feminine that looks like a masculine—precisely the *opposite*, in fact, of Agathon, who, as we have already seen, is a man who looks like a woman. If we tie *melopoiōn* down to one or the other—masculine or feminine, as Austin and Olson do—we are missing the fundamental joke and problem here: language which creates a dichotomy between male and female is unequipped to deal with boundary crossers like Agathon and his Muses. Agathon is a woman-like man; his Muses, as that rare breed of female singers, need to appropriate the male language of poetic creativity that either turns them into a male *thiasos* or gives them a masculine-looking noun, *melopoios*, to describe what they do. Moreover, if *melopoiōn* is taken as a feminine noun rather than a masculine participle, it would be the first occurrence of the term "song-maker," *melopoios*, in extant Greek literature, as with *tragōidopoios* at *Thesm.* 30, suggesting the clustering of an invention and exploration of new vocabulary around poetic "making" in the figuration of Agathon. It is in stretching language to its limits, then,

41. Austin and Olson 2004 ad loc.

42. κακὸν / μελοποιὸν ὄντα, *Ran.* 1249–50; cf. μελοποιῶν, *Ran.* 1328. μελοποιός, as a two-termination adjective used as a substantive, is applied to both women and men; the application to women poets, particularly Sappho, becomes more common in the imperial period, e.g., Dion. Hal. *Comp.* 23.51–52, Lucian *Imagines* 18.2 (see chapter 7, n. 47), though note [Eur.] *Rhes.* 550 where the adjectival form is applied to the song of the feminine nightingale (ὑμνεῖ... / μελοποιὸν ἀηδονὶς μέριμναν, 548–50), suggesting a connection between the nightingale and the figure of the poet (on which see chapter 2, n. 55, and chapter 9, n. 49).

as Aristophanes does, that some of the most fundamental issues of poetic gender identity are revealed.

That this gender confusion around *melopoios/melopoiein* is meant to be connected to Agathon is in no doubt, since the next occurrence of the term applies to him. Again anticipating Agathon's arrival, his slave announces that "he's preparing to compose a song [*melopoiein*]" (67).[43] If *melopoiein* was used before to describe the song of the Muses, it seems appropriate that it now forecasts Agathon's song—which, when it begins a few lines later (101–29), is not only feminine in its accoutrements (see In-law's reaction to Agathon's entrance at 97–98), but also in the voice used, which is explicitly female. The poet emerges singing in the guise of the women of Troy, celebrating the end of the Greeks' siege, taking on the voice both of the choral leader and of the chorus of young women who sings in response. He opens with an address to the female chorus, "young women" (*kourai*, 102), and at one point even uses the feminine participle *klēizousa* ("invoking," 116) in the nominative to refer to himself. In-law comments on the feminine gendering of the song with a newly coined word, *thēludriōdes* or "woman-smelling" (131), just to underline the explicit effeminacy of Agathon's "song-making" (*melopoiein*, 67).[44] And again, Agathon's gender-bending feminine song is linked to his passive sexual role: In-law caps the performance with an endorsement that it was so effective that it "titillated his arse" (133), almost luring him into Agathon's passive sexuality.[45] Like In-law later when he acts the part of Helen, Agathon has fully adopted a female (and sexually passive) persona, voice, and song. In-law labels him a *gunnis*, a "womanish man" (136), and, unable to identify him by external markers of sex/gender like a penis, clothing, or objects (sword or mirror, for example), claims that he has to fall back on identifying his gender "from his song" alone (144).[46] For a poet, in other words, voice and song become one of the key markers of gender; for, unlike In-law, who merely parodies Euripides, Agathon is both composer and performer here—highlighting the confusion triggered by the cross-gendered voice he

43. καὶ γὰρ μελοποιεῖν ἄρχεται, *Thesm.* 67.

44. Cf. *Thesm.* 136 on Agathon as a γύννις (womanish man); 192, γυναικόφωνος (woman-voiced).

45. ὑπὸ τὴν ἕδραν αὐτὴν ὑπῆλθε γάργαλος, *Thesm.* 133; see McClure 1999a: 223, Wright 2012: 121.

46. ἐκ τοῦ μέλους, *Thesm.* 144. At the same time, this is also a parody of Aeschylus's *Edonians*: see Austin and Olson 2004 ad loc.

takes on when he impersonates female song "with a male voice" (125).[47] "Doing" song (*melopoiein*, 67) is well and truly gender confused in Agathon's case, and the question mark *poios*—"what kind of man is he?"—continues to define Agathon as *poiētēs*, too.

It is this awareness of the connection between Agathon's gender-bending identity and his ability to sing a women's song which leads him, in the lines that follow, to come up with a theory of mimetic performance, and what it means to be a poet. "A man-poet" (*poiētēn andra*), he says, "must match his way of life to the drama he writes [*poiein*]" (149–50).[48] At this crucial juncture, where Agathon's gender has been so significantly questioned both in his appearance and his song, he makes an important claim to normative male gender with the resonant phrase *poiētēs anēr*, "man-poet."[49] Not only does this serve to remind In-law, who has consistently questioned whether Agathon should be seen as an *anēr* at all, that his gender is masculine, after all; it also, in the apposition of a poet-term and the noun *anēr*, evokes the discourse of masculine-gender poetic identity which goes back to Homer's *aoidos anēr*.[50]

But, typically, Agathon subverts our gender expectations. Instead of the normative man-poet laying down the law on men's roles, as we see elsewhere, he instead proclaims that what defines a man-poet is precisely his ability to cross genders: so that, "if he's composing [*poiēi*] dramas about women [*gunaikeia . . . dramata*], he must embody their way of life" (*Thesm.* 151–52).[51] Here he again uses the verb *poiein*, "to compose," a handy gloss on *poiētēs* at line 149 at the opening of his poetic minitreatise and a lesson in

47. The designation of the male voice is given (humorously) to Agathon's lyre: κίθαρίν τε ματέρ' ὕμνων / ἄρσενι βοᾷ δοκίμων (the lyre, mother of songs known for their masculine voice), *Thesm.* 124–25. The text here is Schöne's, followed by Austin and Olson 2004 (see ad 125) and N. Wilson 2007; see also Hansen 1976: 169, Muecke 1982: 48. For the gendering of the lyre, see p. 65 with chapter 3, n. 12, pp. 76–78.

48. χρὴ γὰρ ποιητὴν ἄνδρα πρὸς τὰ δράματα / ἃ δεῖ ποιεῖν, πρὸς ταῦτα τοὺς τρόπους ἔχειν, *Thesm.* 149–50. On this passage, see Muecke 1982, Zeitlin 1996: 375–416, Given 2007.

49. On the theme of gender identity in this speech, see Bobrick 1997: 180, Moulton 1981: 119, Zeitlin 1996: 383–86.

50. It also ties in with Euripides's characterization as an ἀνὴρ . . . ποιητής at *Lys.* 368 (see p. 109), as well as forecasting Dionysus's and Aeschylus's discussions of the ἀνὴρ ποιητής in the *Frogs* (*Ran.* 858, see pp. 114–16; *Ran.* 1008, 1030, 1369, see pp. 117–20).

51. αὐτίκα γυναικεῖ' ἢν ποιῇ τις δράματα, / μετουσίαν δεῖ τῶν τρόπων τὸ σῶμ' ἔχειν, *Thesm.* 151–52; cf. 167, ὅμοια γὰρ ποιεῖν ἀνάγκη τῇ φύσει.

etymology after the first occurrence of the verb *poiein* in the play at line
149.[52] And yet there is more to it than simply unpacking the etymology of
the *poiētēs*. The double repetition of *poiēi tis* at lines 151 and 154, and the as-
sociation of the phrase each time with performing and embodying gender
("if someone's composing [*poiēi tis*] about women [*gunaikeia*], he must em-
body their way of life," 151–52; "if someone's composing [*poiēi tis*] about men
[*andreia*], *this* is right at hand in his body," 154), suggests that there is more
going on.[53] What I would argue, in fact, is that Aristophanes is exploiting
the juxtaposition between *poiēi* and *tis* to join them together and coin a new,
fictional word: *poiētis*, or "female poet."[54] This would work as a noun pair
with *poiētēs* along the lines of *lachanopōlētria* (female greengrocer), the femi-
nine of the masculine *lachanopōlētēr* (greengrocer)—which one of the
women, incidentally, later humorously uses for Euripides's matronymic,
thereby inverting male naming practices.[55] Elsewhere in Aristophanes, we
find *artopōlis* (female baker) at *Frogs* 858, feminine of the masculine *artopōlēs*
(baker); similarly to *artopōlis*, *poiētis* would, technically speaking, be a per-
fectly valid feminine equivalent to the male *poiētēs*.[56] In other words, having
just declared himself a "poet-man," a *poiētēs anēr*, Agathon now makes the
humorous mistake of coining a new term for himself as a "female poet," a
poiētis. It is as if he has embodied the first lesson he is trying to teach—the
necessity of taking on the body of a woman in order to represent her in
poetry—and has therefore created a new term for himself as a poet, in order
to become a female poet. And, comically, of course, this carries on even
when he is talking about how easy it is to embody men (*andreia d'ēn poiēi tis,*

52. Occurrences of ποιεῖν in this passage: *Thesm.* 150, 151, 153, 154, 157, 158, 167, 168, 169, 170,
174. The term ποιητής first occurs in In-law's warning to Agathon's slave as he threatens him
with a double male rape against both him and "your lovely-worded poet" (τοῦ τε ποιητοῦ /
τοῦ καλλιεποῦς), *Thesm.* 59–60; the emasculation of the poet here connects to Agathon's gen-
dering of the ἀνὴρ ποιητής at 149. See also chapter 4, n. 60.

53. αὐτίκα γυναικεῖ᾽ ἢν ποιῇ τις δράματα, / μετουσίαν δεῖ τῶν τρόπων τὸ σῶμ᾽ ἔχειν,
Thesm. 151–52; ἀνδρεῖα δ᾽ ἢν ποιῇ τις, ἐν τῷ σώματι / ἔνεσθ᾽ ὑπάρχον τοῦθ᾽, 154–55.

54. Aristophanes is clearly interested in this play in coining new words for "being a woman,"
as, e.g., 131 θηλυδριῶδες ("woman-smelling," of Agathon), 192 γυναικόφωνος ("with a woman's
voice," of Agathon), 268 γυναικιεῖς (from γυναικίζω, "play the woman," see Austin and Olson
2004 ad loc.), and cf. 863 γυναίκισις (imitation of women).

55. Εὐριπίδου τοῦ τῆς λαχανοπωλητρίας (Euripides, son of the female greengrocer),
Thesm. 387; cf. *Ran.* 840. See Willi 2003: 170.

56. Though it is not attested; see pp. 114–16 on the ἀρτόπωλις.

154)—the joke being, of course, that for him as a feminizing "female-poet," it is not as easy to cross back into the male body.[57]

So Agathon's paradoxical declaration is nothing less than this: that the poet-man (*poiētēs anēr*) should also be able to become a female poet (*poiētis*) in order to embody the female experience. This is not simply about inhabiting the female body through modes of dress or sexual positions (though much of the humor directed at Agathon from In-law focuses on this aspect of Agathon's poetic identity): it is also about inhabiting the female *identity* to be able to say, in the first person, that you are a *poiētis*—in other words, inhabiting the female voice. At line 192 Euripides explicitly says that Agathon is "female-voiced" (*gunaikophōnos*), with a word probably coined by Aristophanes that occurs in Greek literature only here.[58] Later on, advising Agathon's proxy, In-law, who is about to go undercover as a woman (and who is not as adept as Agathon at looking and sounding like a woman), Euripides repeats the necessity of imitating the female voice: "When you talk, make sure you do a good job of sounding like a woman [*gunaikieis*] with your voice" (267–68).[59] For Agathon, then, proper poetic "doing" is being able to transcend gender to inhabit the body, the voice, and the poetic identity of both sexes. The *anēr poiētēs* is the one who can "do" (*poiein*) gender as both a *poiētēs* and a *poiētis*: "doing" women, "doing" men through poetic composition in the gendered voice.[60]

If Agathon gives us a neat outline of what he thinks it means to be an *anēr poiētēs*, Euripides, by contrast—whose predicament in being charged as a misogynist poet by the women he characterizes is what initiates the entire

---

57. Cf. the fact that he appears to lack male genitalia: see Austin and Olson 2004 ad 141–43.

58. Austin and Olson 2004 ad loc; see also McDonald 2016: 168. See chapter 4, n. 54.

59. ἢν λαλῇς δ᾽, ὅπως τῷ φθέγματι / γυναικιεῖς εὖ καὶ πιθανῶς, *Thesm.* 267–68. On λαλεῖν as a critical reference to Euripides's colloquial style, see Denniston 1927: 115, McDonald 2016: 177; as a marker of women's speech, see McDonald 2016: 161, 168–69.

60. In-law, on the other hand, proposes a version of ποιεῖν that revolves around sexual dominance: see the double male rape at *Thesm.* 59–62 in which In-law gives the first instance of ποιητής in the play (see chapter 4, n. 52); the conflation at line 153 of "doing" a female character in a play and taking her position in sex (ὅταν Φαίδραν ποιῇς, "doing a Phaedra," 153); and, finally, at 157–58, In-law's offer to "collaborate" with Agathon (συμποιεῖν): ὅταν σατύρους τοίνυν ποιῇς, καλεῖν ἐμέ, / ἵνα συμποιῶ σοὔπισθεν ἐστυκὼς ἐγώ (When you do [ποιῇς] satyrs, give me a call, so that I can do it with you [συμποιῶ], from behind with my hard-on), 157–58.

drama—is never once called by a poet-term (*poiētēs* or otherwise) in the
whole play. The lack of poet-terms for Euripides is made particularly salient in
that Agathon, by contrast, is labeled a "tragedy-maker" (*tragōidopoios*, 30),
"tragic poet" (*tragōidodidaskalon*, 88), and a *poiētēs* (59)—and, as we have
seen, he also gives his own lengthy discourse on the function of the "poet-
man" (*anēr poiētēs*) in his treatise on gender and poets (149, 159).

   The only time that Euripides describes himself as "composing" poetry
(*poiein*), on the other hand, it is as an event that took place in the past—"when
I began to compose poetry" (174), he says, referring to his similarity to Ag-
athon as a younger poet. His comment follows immediately on the heels of
Agathon's poetic doctrine on gender imitation and the *anēr poiētēs*, and it is
used to align Euripides with Agathon's feminine characteristics. "I was just like
him at his age, when I started composing poetry [*poiein*]," Euripides remarks
(173–74).[61] And though Euripides may simply mean, by comparing himself to
Agathon, that he was similarly good-looking, or talked like Agathon, In-law in
his response immediately jumps to the conclusion that Euripides was similarly
effeminate ("I don't envy you your 'boy's education'" [175], he replies, with
significant innuendo).[62] In-law's interpretation of Euripides's comment con-
nects his poetic training with male prostitution, poking fun at Agathon and
Euripides by suggesting a shared sexually deviant past. In-law's response thus
links Euripides's early career to Agathon's effeminate poetics, through the im-
plications of a shared gender-bending sexual background. At the same time, it
is surely significant that the only time in the play that Euripides describes him-
self as "composing poetry" (*poiein*) is in looking back to a past that is no longer
the case—the beginning of his career as a younger poet: note the past tense in
the imperfect at 174, "I *began* [*ērchomēn*] composing poetry." The comparison
with Agathon thus serves to bind Euripides's younger self to Agathon's gender-
bending poetics—but, at the same time, highlights the gap between them:
Euripides as he was then, and Euripides as he is now. And these current poetics
are, according to the charge of the women at the Thesmophoria, marked by a
predilection for "find[ing] stories on purpose where the woman turned out
bad—creating [*poiōn*] Melanippes and Phaedras; but he's never made [*epoiēs'*]
a Penelope, because she was a woman known for her virtue" (546–48).[63]

---

61. καὶ γὰρ ἐγὼ τοιοῦτος ἦν / ὢν τηλικοῦτος, ἡνίκ᾽ ἠρχόμην ποιεῖν, *Thesm.* 173–74.

62. Sommerstein 1994: 9 and 171 ad 173–74 argues that the joke is that Agathon and Euripides
were male prostitutes.

63. ἐπίτηδες εὑρίσκων λόγους, ὅπου γυνὴ πονηρὰ / ἐγένετο, Μελανίππας ποιῶν
Φαίδρας τε· Πηνελόπην δὲ / οὐπώποτ᾽ ἐποίησ᾽, ὅτι γυνὴ σώφρων ἔδοξεν εἶναι, *Thesm.*

The manipulation of poet-vocabulary in *Women at the Thesmophoria*, then, shows that Euripides's problem in the play is more basic even than the initial crime with which he is accused, that of vilifying women in his poetry. His major dilemma—the one which Agathon, the other poet-figure in the play and Euripides's counterpart, shows up—is that he has lost sight of what it means to be a poet at all, in losing the gender fluidity of his younger poetic self: and that is precisely why he is never called a "poet" within the play. Being able to compose poetry, as Agathon has shown in his treatise on gender imitation and the *anēr poiētēs*, means being able to "do" both men and women. To be a *poiētēs*, you have to be able to "'do' plays about women" (*gunaikei' ēn poiēi tis dramata*, 151), and "'do' plays about men" (*andreia d' ēn poiēi tis*, 154). "We have to compose (*poiein*) the same way we are," Agathon finishes at the end of his poetic exposition (167)—just a few lines before Euripides pronounces that he used to be the same as Agathon when he started to write poetry (*poiein*, 174).[64] Euripides's description of his past activities of *poiein* (and its connection to gender-bending by In-law), without a poet-term, right on the heels of Agathon's delineation of the gender-mimetic activities of the *poiētēs*, suggests that it is precisely the loss of his gender-mimetic poetic identity (similar to Agathon) that has led to the current problem of his misogynistic representations of women—and thus to the present charge against him by the women at the Thesmophoria. Agathon might, then, look like a double for Euripides at first glance; but he is, in fact, the opposite.[65] He serves to demonstrate just where Euripides fails, in his inability to be gender flexible—both in his poetic representation of women, and in the vocabulary which names him as a poet.

There is hope for Euripides, however. At the end of the play, the poet who was charged with misrepresenting women exits the stage, dressed as an old woman carrying a harp, promising never to slander women again. This final act of cross-dressing is in aid of Euripides's last endeavor to rescue In-law, who has been imprisoned for his attempt to infiltrate the women's festival and is being guarded by a Scythian archer.[66] Euripides, in disguise as an old harp-carrying woman, uses a young dancing girl to distract the Archer and manages to release In-law, with the help of the chorus of women who has finally come

---

546–48. ποιεῖν is used twice elsewhere in the play by other characters of Euripides (*Thesm.* 193, 450).

64. ὅμοια γὰρ ποιεῖν ἀνάγκη τῇ φύσει, *Thesm.* 167.

65. On Agathon as a double for Euripides, see Sommerstein 1994: 9.

66. On the figure of the Archer, see Hall 1989a.

to his aid after his promise to stop insulting them in his plays. The assumption of female dress by Euripides marks a progression toward closure, because Euripides has never previously dressed as a woman, in contrast to the cross-dressing of other characters in the play.[67] Agathon was introduced looking more like a woman than a man (97–98, 136) and singing a "woman-smelling" song (131). In-law dressed as a woman to infiltrate the Thesmophoria, and took on the feminine gender to refer to himself, both during his disguise and after, during the parodies of Euripides's tragedies. Now, at last, Euripides, too, appears dressed as a woman—and an old woman at that, who lacks the negative meretricious associations of her dancing-girl associate, and thus embodies a less threatening vision of womanhood.[68] Where Agathon led the way at the play's opening with his feminine dress and his treatise on gender imitation as a necessary foundation for the *anēr poiētēs*, Euripides now follows. The play achieves closure with a poet who seems finally to have learned Agathon's lesson: that inhabiting both genders is the key to being able to write both men and women. And it is this which enables him to promise the women of the Thesmophoria that he will no longer slander them in his plays.

Crucially, this gender flexibility is about adopting and inhabiting a female name, just as much as it is about cross-dressing and inhabiting a female body. We saw above how In-law's opening identification of Agathon as a woman, rather than a man, rested on renaming Agathon as the female prostitute Cyrene (98). Names and their relation to gender continue to be a theme throughout the play. In the parabasis—a moment of "stepping forward" where the chorus could address the audience directly, establishing a relationship between the audience, the players on the stage, and the poet—just after In-law has been caught in female dress and his disguise revealed, the chorus of women engages in a direct "comparison of the names [*tounom'*] of women [*tēs te gunaikos*] and men [*tandros*]" (803), in order to demonstrate (through a series of humorous etymologies of women's proper names, like Aristomache [best-fighter]) that

---

67. Note that some (e.g., Rau 1967: 79, Hansen 1976: 182–83, MacDowell 1995: 269 n. 44, Austin and Olson 2004 ad 1056–57) argue that Euripides acts the part of Echo in the parody of the *Andromeda* (1010–1126). Sommerstein 1994: 8 n. 47 and comm. ad 1056–97 suggests that this is highly unlikely: there is no time for Euripides to change from his costume as Perseus, while Echo speaks of Euripides as a different person (1060–61); Gilula 1996: 162–63 argues that Echo must have been onstage (cf. Sommerstein 1994: 227), and cannot therefore have been acted by Euripides, who appears as Perseus immediately after at 1098. For the argument that Echo was offstage in Euripides's original play, see chapter 6, n. 78.

68. See J. Henderson 1987a on older women in Attic comedy.

women "are much better than men" (810).[69] And we end the play with another significant instance of renaming in the feminine, as Euripides—the poet who never received a poet-term, and the man who has finally learned to represent and inhabit women—takes on a new name for himself in his guise as the old woman. "What's your name [*onoma*]?" In-law's guard, the Archer, asks "old-woman" Euripides (1200). "Artemisia," Euripides replies. "Hm—I'll remember that name [*tounom'*]: Artamuxia," the Archer replies (1201).[70] There is more at stake here than the simple joke of the Archer's mistake in misremembering (and barbarizing: Artamuxia has a Persian flavor to it, hinting at the Archer's Scythian background) Euripides's made-up name.[71] A few lines later, after "old-woman" Euripides has successfully left the stage along with In-law, the Archer returns to find his captive gone. "Where's the old lady? Artamuxia!" he calls (1216). "What—you mean the old woman with the harp [*pēktidas*]?" the chorus leader responds (1217).[72] The chorus leader has to clarify who the Archer is calling for, because he uses the wrong name for her in more ways than one: a misremembered name (Artamuxia) for a false name (Artemisia) for Euripides. In this sense, the reason that the Archer cannot recall Euripides is because he uses the wrong name to summon him—demonstrating just how powerful naming can be in conjuring identity, as well as how an incorrect name means that Archer fails to summon his quarry: Euripides never reenters the stage from this point on.

But there is also a point to Euripides's false name. The name Artemisia would have brought up associations with the fifth-century BCE Greek queen Artemisia I of Caria (a Persian satrapy on the western shores of Asia Minor), who had fought as an ally of the Persians in the second Persian War—and this is no doubt part of the joke. Euripides's new *onoma* suggests an Eastern, feminine identity, a Greek woman from Asia Minor. At the same time, Artemisia was a woman who crossed gender boundaries (as Herodotus had already pointed out in his *Histories*), a woman who fought alongside men and led

---

69. παραβάλλουσαι τῆς τε γυναικὸς καὶ τἀνδρὸς τοὔνομ' ἑκάστου, *Thesm.* 803; οὕτως ἡμεῖς πολὺ βελτίους τῶν ἀνδρῶν εὐχόμεθ' εἶναι, 810. On the significance of the women's names, see Moulton 1981: 129–30.

70. [Το.] ὄνομα δέ σοι τί ἐστιν; [Εὐ.] Ἀρτεμισία. / [Το.] μεμνῆσι τοίνυν τοὔνομ'· Ἀρταμουξία, *Thesm.* 1200–1201.

71. See Austin and Olson 2004 ad 1200–1201, and Hall 1989a on the barbarizing caricature of the Archer, esp. 38–40; for his mistakes of grammatical gender, as at *Thesm.* 1188 καλή τό σκῆμα, see Hall 1989a: 49, McClure 1999a: 235 with n. 120.

72. τὴν γραῦν ἐρωτᾷς ἢ 'φερεν τὰς πηκτίδας; *Thesm.* 1217.

armies—making her an ideal choice for a man cross-dressing as a woman.[73] But when the Archer's incorrect use of the name Artamuxia at line 1216 fails to summon his quarry, the chorus leader glosses the name: "an old woman with a harp [*pēktidas*]" (1217). We may remember that Agathon entered the stage at the very beginning dressed looking like a woman and carrying a harp (*barbitos/lura*).[74] Agathon, in fact, singing his own female chorus, had specifically gendered his harp female—picking up on anxieties around the femininity of the lyre which resonate from the *Homeric Hymn to Hermes*—calling it the "mother of songs known for their masculine voice" (124–25), setting up a gender contrast between female lyre and male voice which neatly encapsulates Agathon's trademark gender-bending.[75] Now, at the play's end, Euripides, too, is seen in female dress, and also carrying a harp. In this final scene, then, he is associated with the figure of the gendered poet and his accoutrements: both by his connection with Agathon, and in associating him with the poet's typical (and female-gendered) prop, the lyre. But Euripides's harp—a *pēktis*—has even more layers to its female-gendering than its relation to Agathon's "mother of songs." This was a harp that was said to have been invented in the east, in Lydia, and which receives several mentions in the archaic poets, including Sappho—who, as a resident of Lesbos to the west of Asia Minor, neighbored Lydia.[76] A later tradition, recorded by the fourth-century BCE historian Menaechmus of Sicyon, even related that Sappho was the inventor of the *pēktis*—underlining the interrelationship between this instrument and the female poet from Lesbos.[77] If Euripides's initial given name in his disguise, Artemisia, connected him with Greek women in the East more generally, then his redefinition by the chorus leader as "an old woman with a *pēktis*" might just hint at a connection to Sappho, the most famous female poet who had written about the *pēktis*, and gives him a distinctly gender-poetic flavor.[78]

73. Hdt. 7.99.1, cf. 8.88.3; see Munson 1988, Harrell 2003: 80–88.

74. *Thesm.* 137–38; see Austin 1990: 17–18. On words for the lyre, see chapter 3, n. 12.

75. κίθαρίν τε ματέρ᾽ ὕμνων / ἄρσενι βοᾷ δοκίμων, *Thesm.* 124–25; see chapter 4, n. 47.

76. See Maas and Snyder 1989: 40–41, 147–49. For Sappho on the πηκτίς, see fr. 156 L-P, along with the hypothetical, but almost certainly correct, reading πᾶ]κτιν at fr. 22.11 L-P; cf. Alc. fr. 36.5 L-P, Anac. frr. 373.3 and 386 *PMG*, Pind. fr. 125.3 S-M. On Eastern cultural stereotyping of Sappho, see Yatromanolakis 2007: 171–97.

77. Menaechm. *FGrH* 131 F 4 = Ath. 14.635b; see Kivilo 2010: 193.

78. Cf. *Ran.* 1308 for a connection between Euripides's Muse and "doing the Lesbian thing" (αὕτη ποθ᾽ ἡ Μοῦσ᾽ οὐκ ἐλεσβίαζεν, οὔ); see chapter 4, n. 111.

As Euripides takes on his final successful guise with a new female name (*onoma*), then, it is not only to become a poet—but a potential *female* poet, with subtle intimated connections to Sappho. It seems that Euripides has learned Agathon's lesson after all: that to be able to represent women, you have to become a woman poet. And that, at last, in his final disguise, may be what Euripides achieves.

This might appear a positive ending for the story of gender and the male poet. Euripides has learned his lesson, promises not to slander women, and has even been able to integrate Agathon's creed to "become" a woman poet. And yet, among all the talk around gender, what is clear throughout *Women at the Thesmophoria* is that, at the end of the day, it is masculinity that is at stake here: even though there are different ways of approaching gender and Agathon may cross genders, the only poets in the play are male. Even for Agathon, a *poiētēs* has to be an *anēr poiētēs*: the question is simply how a man tells the stories of women as well as men. And when he recommends, through subtle allusion and punning, that a male *poiētēs* learn to become a female "*poiētis*," it is, crucially, not in recognition of female poets, but rather the opposite: it is a direct appropriation of the figure of the female *poiētis* by the male *poiētēs*, so that he can become the single, authoritative voice capable of imitating both male and female gender.

Even Aristophanes's women at the Thesmophoria are subject to the same gender bias. They are not annoyed that it is not a woman telling their story: their complaint is simply that the man who does it doesn't do it right. In a strange way, the opposition between Agathon's poetics and the charge against Euripides thus only serves to underline the fact that, even though they may dress up as women, or may have to learn to tell stories about women, they are always men, just like the actors of comedy themselves: it is a performance and imitation of gender that they assume for a specific end (the imitation of gendered characters), like a mask or costume, rather than any significant change in or exploration of their own gender identity. Ultimately, and paradoxically, Agathon's gender bending is precisely a function of his poetic creed as a "man-poet." The unmasking of In-law as a man, Agathon's dressing up in female paraphernalia, and Euripides's appropriation of Sappho's *pēktis* are thus metaphorical for the poet: he may impersonate women; he may even appropriate their voices for his own ends; but he is always, in the end, assumed to be a man.

This ability to impersonate women, but still to remain an *anēr poiētēs*, is not a static quality in Aristophanes's depiction of the poet: it is, in fact, one which he presents as developing over time. Thus, Euripides, in *Women at the Thesmophoria*, looks back to a time when he used to be more gender fluid like Agathon, who (as Aristophanes makes clear throughout the play, with jokes about Agathon's boyish appearance) is also young: his gender fluidity is, in part, connected to his youth, and his effeminacy and the jokes about his passivity in sex are contextualized in the role of the younger lover in a pederastic relationship.[79] In other words, you can expect gender fluidity from a young poet—in fact, as Agathon argues, it is essential for learning how to imitate different genders; but, as he has to grow into his manhood, so the poet has to grow into the role of *anēr poiētēs*. This is made explicit in another play, in the figure of another poet: Aristophanes, no less. In the parabasis of the *Clouds*, the chorus assumes the voice of the poet and speaks, unusually, in the first person, allowing us to examine Aristophanes's depiction of the persona of the poet up close.[80] Where, elsewhere in Aristophanes's plays, we see the chorus referring to "our poet," *Clouds* is unique in giving us a poet in the first-person singular naming *himself* as a poet, laying claim to poet-vocabulary.[81] And what does he call himself? Not a *didaskalos* (poet-director), as the chorus calls him in the parabases of *Acharnians* and *Peace*, or even simply a *poiētēs*, as the chorus labels him in the *Acharnians* ("the poet says . . . ," 633).[82] Here in the *Clouds*, in the first person, Aristophanes gives himself the full title, *anēr poiētēs*: "Although I'm the same kind of man-poet [*anēr poiētēs*], I don't give myself airs," the chorus says (545).[83]

79. On Agathon's older male lover, Pausanias of Kerameis (mentioned at Plato *Prt.* 315d–e, *Symp.* 177d, 193b–c; Xen. *Symp.* 8.32), see Austin and Olson 2004 ad 29–30. For Agathon's boyish appearance, see *Thesm.* 31, 33, 134 (νεάνισκος, "young man"), and 191.

80. See Biles 2011: 12–55, Gilula 1997: 141–42; O'Regan 1992: 178 n. 8 and Wright 2012: 10–16 note, quite rightly, that it would be wrong to assume that these statements represent the historical Aristophanes: see further Bakola 2008, and see chapter 4, n. 39.

81. On "our poet," see *Ach.* 628, ὁ διδάσκαλος ἡμῶν = *Pax* 738; cf. ὁ ποιητής at *Ach.* 633, *Eq.* 509, *Vesp.* 1016. See Dover 1968 ad 518–62, Biles 2011: 177–78, who connects to *Clouds*' revision.

82. *Ach.* 628, ὁ διδάσκαλος ἡμῶν = *Pax* 738; φησὶν . . . ὁ ποιητής, *Ach.* 633. Cf. the Poet of the *Birds*: πάντες ἐσμὲν οἱ διδάσκαλοι / Μουσάων θεράποντες ὀτρηροί (We are all poet-directors, ready servants of the Muses), *Av.* 912–13, looking back to Hes. *Theog.* 100. On the διδάσκαλος, see Rogers 2014.

83. κἀγὼ μὲν τοιοῦτος ἀνὴρ ὢν ποιητὴς οὐ κομῶ, *Nub.* 545. I take it, following Halliwell 1980, that this reference is to Aristophanes, not Callistratus who produced the play; see also Gilula 1990 (esp. 101 n. 2).

But Aristophanes doesn't leave it at that: he gives us an account of the education and creation of the (persona of the) man-poet, and what it took to get there. The parabasis of the *Clouds* serves as a sketch of Aristophanes's career trajectory, in that it justifies the revision and re-presentation of the play. Although originally performed in 423 BCE, some of the references in the parabasis (for example, the designation of "this play" having been presented before and failing) show that this part, at least, must have been revised, following its initial last-place defeat.[84] The function of the parabasis, then, in some part, is to bridge the gap between the earlier and later versions of the *Clouds*, to give an account of the (male) poet's career, and to place the two versions of the play in the context of his present status as an *anēr poiētēs* worthy of winning the dramatic contest against his (male) poetic rivals. And Aristophanes gives us a fascinating account of the gender mechanisms, in particular, that got him to the point of being the *anēr poiētēs* among men that he is now (545). The lead-up to his self-depiction as an *anēr poiētēs* is a description of his development as a poet that is mapped not only onto the metaphor of aging through the stages of life, but also a gender development from female to male (530–52):[85]

> I was still an unmarried girl [*parthenos*] and couldn't (or shouldn't)
>   give birth,
> so I exposed my child, and another girl took it up,
> and you all brought it up nobly and educated it.

Most commentators on this passage have focused on the biographical events, which seem to depict a young Aristophanes either unable or unwilling to present his plays at an early stage of his career, and having them produced by another older man (in this case, Callistratus).[86] More interesting in terms of gender, however, is the way in which Aristophanes specifically uses the example of the development and birth of a child in a woman as a metaphor for

---

84. See Dover 1968: lxxx–xcviii; for the current parabasis as revised, see Dover 1968: lxxx–lxxxii, Dover and Hubbard 1986, Tarrant 1991: 158–59, Marshall 2012, though see contra C. Segal 1969: 144. See further, on the revision of the *Clouds*, Revermann 2006: 326–32 (esp. 327), Biles 2011: 167–210 (esp. 176–81).

85. κἀγώ, παρθένος γὰρ ἔτ᾽ ἦν, κοὐκ ἐξῆν πώ μοι τεκεῖν, / ἐξέθηκα, παῖς δ᾽ ἑτέρα τις λαβοῦσ᾽ ἀνείλετο, / ὑμεῖς δ᾽ ἐξεθρέψατε γενναίως κἀπαιδεύσατε, *Nub.* 530–32. See Hall 2000: 407–8; on the manipulation of grammatical gender, see Janse 2020: 30–31.

86. Dover 1968: xvii n. 2 and comm. ad 530–32, Halliwell 1980, MacDowell 1982.

his own poetic production—applied (with clear irony) to the male poet.[87] This is the first time we have come across the gendered metaphor of birth for the poet's creativity, and it is one which we will see explored repeatedly—both appropriated by male poets who are unable to experience physical birth as a form of androgynous creation, and claimed by women poets as a unique connection between their gendered and poetic identities.[88]

The force of the comparison here in *Clouds* sees an unmarried girl (the youthful Aristophanes) having a baby outside social convention (having written the script of a play which he is either too young or too inexperienced to produce), exposing it and seeing it found by another girl (produced by another man) and reared in a communal household (performed and judged in front of the Athenian audience).[89] It is only once he has been through this process in the earlier plays that now—in the second performance of the *Clouds*—he can reflect, fifteen lines later, on how he has come to be an *anēr poiētēs* (545). In other words, his elevation to the status of "man-poet" was dependent both on his aging from a young man (the equivalent of a female *parthenos*, an unmarried girl)—and his transcendence and subsuming of the category of the female (just like Agathon and Euripides in the *Women at the Thesmophoria*), to become a man among men.

This flexibility and maturation from female to male is forecasted—typically, for Aristophanes—by a joke on grammatical gender. This is perhaps unsurprising, given Aristophanes's interest in gendered language in the *Clouds*: the passage where Strepsiades learns "which nouns are male and which are female" (681–82) comes just over a hundred lines later.[90] The noun *hē parthenos*, "virgin" or "unmarried girl," is a second-declension feminine noun: it has a masculine-looking ending, but is in fact grammatically feminine.[91] This is the force of Socrates's joke on *hē kardopos* (trough) later in the play: he corrects Strepsiades's attribution of *kardopos* to the (masculine-looking) second declension, saying, "you're calling a *kardopos* masculine when it's actually

87. Cf. the lyre as "mother of songs" (ματέρ᾽ ὕμνων) at *Thesm.* 124; see chapter 4, n. 47.

88. See Hansen 1976: 184–85, Ford 2002: 247. Cf. Ar. *Ran.* 96, 98 where Dionysus states his intention to find a γόνιμον δὲ ποιητὴν (fertile poet): for γόνιμος as an early literary-critical term, see Denniston 1927: 113, Wright 2012: 122, and cf. Pl. *Tht.* 148e–151e at pp. 159–60. See further pp. 156–61 with chapter 5, n. 150 and pp. 244–47.

89. On παρθένος as "unmarried girl" here rather than "virgin," see Dover 1968 ad loc., and on the παρθένος generally, Sissa 1990.

90. See p. 15.

91. Janse 2020: 30.

feminine"—as the feminine definite article demonstrates (670–71).[92] Here, at line 530, *parthenos* with its masculine ending is used without a definite article—meaning that it looks grammatically masculine, even as it is semantically feminine (*parthenos* is used of unmarried or virgin girls). The joke, then, is that Aristophanes uses a masculine-looking word for himself which, semantically and biologically, can never apply—as the following statement, "I couldn't give birth," proves.[93] The joke of line 530, "I couldn't (or shouldn't) give birth," is thus a double one: not only was Aristophanes, as a young man, not allowed to produce his plays himself—but he also literally was *unable* to give birth, as a male. The double force of the Greek *ouk exēn*—both "it wasn't allowed" and "it was impossible"—therefore serves to underline the comparison between the young Aristophanes and the unmarried girl, both isolated by convention (in the sense "it wasn't allowed").[94] But it also, in the sense "it was impossible," exposes the biological fault lines in the comparison which will enable Aristophanes to emerge, supremely, as a male poet giving birth to metaphorical plays. The metaphor of the female giving birth is used to stand in for the maturation of the male poet, exploited through the metaphor of birth creativity, and eventually discarded as the *anēr poiētēs*, the male "maker" of plays, not children, emerges as the fully realized ideal end product.[95]

So Aristophanes's depiction of his career is organized, just like Agathon's, around a gender development, maturing from a gender-bending *parthenos* who appropriates female creativity in order to become, ultimately, an *anēr poiētēs*. This transition into the world of the *anēr poiētēs* is emphatically figured as Aristophanes's introduction into the world of men, not only as a "man-poet" himself, but as a "man-poet" among *other* men—his rivals, his audience, and his characters. First off, his competitors (those who bested him in the original dramatic contest): "I was defeated by vulgar men [*hup' andrōn*]" (524–25), the chorus says, specifying Aristophanes's rivals as *andres*.[96] The same is true of the audience: referring back to his first play *Banqueters*, performed in 427 BCE,

92. τὴν κάρδοπον / ἄρρενα καλεῖς θήλειαν οὖσαν, *Nub.* 670–71; see Janse 2020: 29–30.

93. The same joke is made at *Nub.* 531, where Callistratus is called a παῖς (a common noun defined through agreement as feminine). On the gender disjunction here, see Janse 2020: 31.

94. On the translation of ἐξῆν, see Dover 1968 ad loc., Janse 2020: 32.

95. Note also the feminine personification of Comedy (Κωμῳδία, *Nub.* 534–36), on which see Hall 2000: 407–8.

96. ὑπ' ἀνδρῶν φορτικῶν / ἡττηθείς, *Nub.* 524–25. I agree with Biles 2011: 181–87 (contra Perusino 1986: 54 n. 57) that this must refer to Aristophanes's poetic competitors, rather than the judges or audience.

Aristophanes claims through the chorus that his play was praised "here [sc. in the theater] by men [*hup' andrōn*]" (528).[97] Whether these "men" (*andres*) constituted a select group of individual judges or the audience as a whole is hardly the issue: what matters is that Aristophanes is claiming here that his poetry is intended *for men*.[98] (This also bypasses the vexed question as to whether women were present in the audience or not: as Martin Revermann points out, the reason why all addresses to the audience by comic choruses are specifically to men seems to be because "only men were thought to matter," thus making men the poet's intended or notional audience.)[99] Defeated "by men" (524) in the last contest, he reminds the audience with the same phrase (*hup' andrōn*, 528) that men are not only his competition—they are also his intended audience and the judges of his poetic worth, whether that means a private group of individuals or the public collective audience.[100] Male competitors and male audience—the next step is male characters, which is where Aristophanes goes next. What the *andres* liked about his *Banqueters*, he says, were his "Virtuous Man" and his "Bugger-Man" (529)—not, this time, qualified with the noun *anēr*, but still identified as male by their masculine definite articles.[101] This fully realized male poet, then—the *anēr poiētēs* who has grown from a gender-fluid *parthenos* into a man among men—writes against his male competitors for a male audience about male characters.

Man-Poet: The Man and the Maker

Gender is thus the key to the poet learning how to become an *anēr poiētēs*: both enabling him, through his early gender fluidity, to appropriate female identities, voices, and creativity through birth in order to learn how to imitate both women and men, and schooling him as he moves to become a fully realized *anēr* to act among the other men of the *polis*, producing poetry for and

---

97. ἐνθάδ᾽ ὑπ᾽ ἀνδρῶν, *Nub.* 528.

98. See Halliwell 1980: 38–39, MacDowell 1982: 23.

99. Revermann 2010: 73. For discussion of the question of women's attendance at the Great Dionysia, see Goldhill 1994a, arguing persuasively (contra J. Henderson 1991) that the main issue at stake is the wider context of women's lack of participation in the construct of democracy.

100. See esp. the collected essays in Winkler and Zeitlin 1990, in particular Goldhill 1990 and J. Henderson 1990; see also Griffin 1998, Ford 2002: 277–82, Carter 2011, Wright 2012: 46–60, Carey 2019. For a moderated view, see Rhodes 2003.

101. ὁ σώφρων τε χὠ καταπύγων, *Nub.* 529.

about men. This section turns to the characterization of the fully developed *anēr poiētēs* in Aristophanes. I look at how the term *poiētēs* was specifically marked male by Aristophanes, bounding poetry as the province of men. I also suggest that Aristophanes was particularly aware of and interested in the verbal root of the new term *poiētēs*—*poiein*, "to make/do"—and that he associated it specifically with a gendered agency ("making" and "doing") that was unique to men and men's poetry. A new kind of male poet thus emerges—one as emphatically masculine as the archaic poet, with an underlying emphasis on his identity as a male maker and doer.

As with *Women at the Thesmophoria*, it is particularly at the boundaries of identity, where gender is under threat, that we find the masculinity of the poet being explored. Another key place to look for gender threats and reversals is the *Lysistrata*, originally performed in 411 BCE (the same year as *Women at the Thesmophoria*)—and, like *Women at the Thesmophoria*, *Lysistrata* is concerned with the relationship between women and men.[102] The play opens with the titular character, Lysistrata, calling a women's council, where the women of different city-states come together to instigate a sex ban in order to force the men to declare peace from the ongoing Peloponnesian War. The women take over the citadel, which the chorus (made up of old men) attempts to recover. Much of the comedy derives from the reversal of gender stereotypes, where women now take on political and military roles, and the men are forced to beg for sex.[103] The women should have stayed at home, the chorus of old men claims, obeying the men's orders, rather than trying to entangle themselves in battles and affairs of state. To back up their point, they quote (or appear to quote) Euripides: "There's no man-poet [*anēr poiētēs*] with better judgment [*sophōteros*] than Euripides: for there's no beast [*thremm'*] as shameless [*anaides*] as women [*gunaikes*]" (*Lysistrata* 368–69).[104] The opposition between the chorus of old men and the women defending the acropolis—who have so far gone against the natural order of gender as to take over power in

102. Austin and Olson 2004: xxxii, cf. Taaffe 1993: 74, Zeitlin 1996: 375, McClure 1999a: 206–7, Stehle 2002: 403. For the connection between the two plays' female choruses, see Hansen 1976: 184.

103. On the depiction of women in the *Lysistrata*, see Taaffe 1993: 48–73, Stroup 2004, Faraone 2006.

104. οὐκ ἔστ' ἀνὴρ Εὐριπίδου σοφώτερος ποιητής· / οὐδὲν γὰρ ὧδε θρέμμ' ἀναιδές ἐστιν ὡς γυναῖκες, *Lys.* 368–69. It is uncertain whether this is an actual quote from Euripides or a paraphrase invented by Aristophanes: see J. Henderson 1987b ad loc., Sommerstein 1990 ad 369.

the state—is seemingly encapsulated in this one quote which generalizes the dichotomy between men and women, contrasting the "man" poet Euripides (*anēr*, 368) and the "women" (*gunaikes*, 369) he is said to denounce.[105] This, in turn, builds on Euripides's portrayal in Aristophanes, as we have seen, as a "woman-hater"—which makes the poet the perfect source for a misogynistic quote about women.[106]

There are several linguistic and thematic contrasts being drawn in this "quote" from Euripides, which serves so succinctly to pit the genders against each other. First, as we have seen, there is the basic opposition between men and women: the noun *anēr* near the start of line 368 is set against *gunaikes* at the end of line 369, mirroring the stand-off between male and female choruses. Next is the contrast between the qualities that define men and women: wisdom for men (the adjective *sophōteros*, 368) and women's lack of shame (the adjective *anaides*, 369). And finally, finishing off the chiastic structure at the center of the pair of lines, we have two nouns defining men's and women's roles and occupations: men as civilized poets (*poiētēs* at the end of 368), versus women as uncontrolled wild beasts (*thremma* near the start of 369). Three male qualities characterize the chorus's portrayal of Euripides: his male gender (*anēr*, A), his good judgment (B) and his credentials as a poet (*poiētēs*, C); women, on the other hand, are placed on a different plane of existence as wild beasts (C) characterized by lack of control (B) and their female gender (*gunaikes*, A). The chiasmus, setting up the opposition of the two genders as men versus women, civilized versus wild, human versus beast, is complete.

But there is more going on. Different types of linguistic gender also come into play here to confuse and blur the neat chiastic structure of the male/female opposition. Euripides is defined in line 368 as masculine on multiple levels: grammatically (*anēr*, *Euripidou*, *sophōteros*, and *poiētēs* are all grammatically masculine); discursively (he is described in the masculine discourse of the male chorus); and semantically (*anēr* signifies "man"). When the male chorus speaks about women, on the other hand, they are described as grammatically and semantically feminine (*gunaikes*, 369) *and* neuter (*thremm' anaides*), turning them from gendered women into genderless wild beasts, like the transfigured tortoise of the *Homeric Hymn to Hermes*. Even the feminine gender which sets them below men in the hierarchy is taken away from them—

105. Revermann 2010: 73.
106. See chapter 4, n. 21.

indeed, ironically, it is precisely their identity *as* women which is what the poet says turns them into genderless beasts.

If men use language and grammatical gender to shore up their position as civilized males against nonmale, nonhuman women, there is one final step in the contrast being made here: that between the poet and his subject. The oppositions between men and women, civilized and wild, human and beast are summed up in the contrast between the *anēr poiētēs*, the "man-poet" who is adduced to describe the women, and the characters he constructs (the women themselves). The male poet-creator (here, Euripides—but we are inevitably reminded of the *anēr poiētēs* Aristophanes, too) is drawn on as the ultimate authority to define and circumscribe his characters—women—as objects: not just as neuter animals similar to beasts, but also as the objects of his poetry, circumscribed and encapsulated as they are in a quote by the male poet. In the world of male superiority drawn by the male chorus, the *anēr poiētēs* reigns supreme, an emblem of good judgment and masculinity and the power of the male voice, while the women are relegated to the status of spoken-of objects. In the end, the rhetorical power of this line is not merely its content—comparing the women to shameless beasts—but its performative power through the gender dynamics at play: reminding the women who have dared to speak in Aristophanes's play that they, too, are the objects of a male poet's imagination. It serves as a warning to the female members of the chorus that their identity as gendered beings is constructed by men. The "man-poet," *anēr poiētēs*, is set up as the ultimate authority and agent—precisely through his power to create and characterize gender through language.

This gender opposition, setting up the proper male poet by contrast to the female, is demonstrated in another gender contrast in Aristophanes: the age-old relationship between the Muse and the poet.[107] Like the women who are "shameless beasts" in the *Lysistrata*, the Muses are also compared through metaphor to animals. In the parabasis of the *Wasps* (produced in 422 BCE), the *poiētēs* (through the voice of the chorus leader) sets forward a defense of his poetic career and contrasts himself with other *poiētai* (*Vesp.* 1018).[108] After

107. On the Muses in Aristophanes, see Uchida 1992, Hall 2000: 410–12, De Simone 2008: 481–88; see further chapter 4, n. 111.

108. Aristophanes calls himself ποιητής twice in the passage (1016, 1049), as opposed to the other ποιηταί (1018); for the identity of these ποιηταί, see Starkie 1897 ad loc., Russo 1962: 26. Aristophanes's defense relates to the failure of the *Clouds* in 423 BCE: see pp. 105–6.

some years where his plays were produced by others, Aristophanes says, he eventually came forward to produce his own plays, "holding the reins on the mouths of his own Muses, not other people's" (1022).[109] The metaphor is taken from chariot driving, with the Muses figured as horses to be tamed and controlled by the male poet.[110] The celebration of the poet's independence and demonstration of his prowess as a male *poiētēs*—as he has had the chorus leader introduce him at line 1016 ("the poet")—appears to derive from his subordination and total control of the female Muses, his ability to turn them into animals and make himself their tamer.[111]

Aristophanes may boast a few lines later that "he doesn't turn the Muses he uses [*chrētai*] into pimps" (1028), to sort out lovers' spats in his plays. And yet the poet spectacularly undermines his own point: the word "uses" (*chrētai*) has a sexual undertone to it which comically subverts the poet's protestations that he is not manipulating the Muses' sexuality for his own purposes, and suggests that he may, in fact, be doing just that.[112] Meanwhile, in the *Knights* (424 BCE), the Muses' sexuality is brought to the fore as a way of bolstering the masculinity, not only of the male *poiētēs*, but also of his audience. The chorus leads into the parabasis by appealing to the audience's poetic experience: "you," they say, turning to the spectators, "have got experience [*peirathentes*] in your own right with every kind of Muse [*mousēs*]" (*Eq.* 505–6).[113] There is an inescapable double entendre going on here. On the one hand, "experience of different types of *mousa*" can gesture, quite innocently, to the audience's literary connoisseurship, their acquaintance with

109. οὐκ ἀλλοτρίων ἀλλ᾽ οἰκείων Μουσῶν στόμαθ᾽ ἡνιοχήσας, *Vesp.* 1022.

110. MacDowell 1971 ad loc.; the metaphor continues at line 1050.

111. Biles and Olson 2015 ad 1021–22. For another poet's Muse in Aristophanes, see Μοῦσ᾽ Εὐριπίδου, "the Muse of Euripides," *Ran.* 1306, figured as something between a Sapphic poetess and a sexual deviant (αὕτη ποθ᾽ ἡ Μοῦσ᾽ οὐκ ἐλεσβίαζεν, οὔ, "this Muse never played the Lesbian—oh no she didn't!," *Ran.* 1308); see Dover 1993 ad 1308, and Hall 2000: 408–9, De Simone 2008, Gilhuly 2018: 98–99. Rather than invoking the band of Muses who inspire all poets' song, Aristophanes seems to have assigned a Muse to personify individual poets' qualities: see MacDowell 1971 ad 1022, Harvey 2000: 106–8, Murray 2005: 150, Biles and Olson 2015 ad 1027–28.

112. τὰς Μούσας αἷσιν χρῆται μὴ προαγωγοὺς ἀποφήνῃ, *Vesp.* 1028. On the sexual undertones of χρῆται here, see Biles and Olson 2015 ad 1027–28, and see LSJ s.v. χράω. Cf. Pindar's denunciation of the "mercenary Muse" (ἁ Μοῖσα γὰρ οὐ φιλοκερδής πω τότ᾽ ἦν), Pind. *Isthm.* 2.6.

113. ὦ παντοίας ἤδη Μούσης / πειραθέντες καθ᾽ ἑαυτούς, *Eq.* 505–6. For the translation of καθ᾽ ἑαυτούς, see Neil 1901 ad loc.

different genres and types of music, song, and poetry encapsulated by the term *mousa*, as an appellative informed by the qualities of the Muses. On the other hand, if we take *Mousa* as a proper noun, the male audience's "experience" with all kinds of female Muses takes on a rather different, more sexual, connotation, through the personification of the Muses as embodied women.[114] This sexualized reading of feminine abstractions is driven home a few lines below, where the same verb, *peiraō*, is used in the active, to describe the many passes that poets have made at the personified female "Comic Production" (*Kōmōidodidaskalia*) in the attempt to produce good comedies: "Many have had a go [*peirasantōn*] at her, but she's only handed out her favors [*charisasthai*] to a few" (517).[115] The use of *peiraō* here to mean "make a sexual attempt on someone" is well established, as are the erotic undertones of *charizein* as "giving sexual favors."[116] Here, in addition to the male audience "having sexual experience" with different Muses, it is Aristophanes and his fellow male poets who are "trying it on" with Comic Poetry, and the feminine abstraction of Comedy who accepts or denies their advances. The effect of this is thus to bind the male audience and the community of male poets, including Aristophanes, as men who have all had the same sexual experience of the Muses and female Poetry personified, and thus the same "taste" in music. It creates a men's club where their sexual prowess as men is equivalent to their literary expertise. That this is related, both to manhood and to the identity of being a *poiētēs*, is underlined throughout the passage. The parabasis begins with the chorus claiming that they wouldn't have made this kind of speech for any old kind of "comic-producer-man" (*anēr . . . kōmōidodidaskalos*, 507).[117] As with the characterization of Euripides in the *Lysistrata* and the *andres* of Aristophanes's rivals in the *Clouds*, *anēr* underlines the masculinity of Aristophanes's poetic peers. And while, in contrast to the other *kōmōidodidaskaloi* (producers of comedy), the chorus calls Aristophanes their *poiētēs* (509), a few lines later he is just a "man" ("the man [*anēr*]

114. On the personification of the Muses, see Hall 2000, Murray 2005.

115. πολλῶν γὰρ δὴ πειρασάντων αὐτὴν ὀλίγοις χαρίσασθαι, *Eq.* 517; see Wright 2012: 121–22, and cf. the personification of Comedy at *Nub.* 534–36: see chapter 4, n. 95.

116. For πειράω as "make an attempt on," see Neil 1901 ad 517, LSJ s.v. A.IV.2 (e.g., Pind. *Pyth.* 2.34, Ar. *Plut.* 150, 1067, Lysias 1.12, etc.). On the erotic sense of χαρίζω, see LSJ s.v. A.3 and cf. Ar. *Eccl.* 629.

117. τις ἀνὴρ τῶν ἀρχαίων κωμῳδοδιδάσκαλος (one of the old comic-producer-men), *Eq.* 507; see Biles 2011: 54–55.

says . . . ," 514), as if the two words—*poiētēs* and *anēr*—are interchangeable.[118] Masculinity connects not only the poet and his audience, fused through their sexual encounters with a personified Muse, but also the identity of the poet Aristophanes himself, in his gendered self-presentation as both a man and a poet.

The association between the *anēr* and the *poiētēs* occurs again, perhaps most prominently, in one of Aristophanes's most explicitly poetry-focused plays, the *Frogs*.[119] Staged in 405 BCE, *Frogs* has the god Dionysus traveling to the Underworld to bring back the poet Euripides. Now that Euripides has died, Dionysus says, all the clever poets are gone, and Athenian tragedy is in dire straits. Dionysus arrives in the Underworld to find that Euripides has taken over the throne of poetry—which used to belong to Aeschylus—and is asked to judge a poetic contest between the two; unable to choose, he determines to bring back "whoever gives the city some useful advice."[120] Finding Aeschylus to be superior, he determines to take him back with him to Athens instead of Euripides and so to "save the city."[121]

  The poets begin their contest by hurling insults at each other. Euripides's first barb is to create a new poetic term to describe Aeschylus as an *agriopoios* ("maker of savages," *Ran.* 837), playing on the fashion for creating new coinages from the *-poios* suffix.[122] Aeschylus returns the insult with interest, generating two *-poios* coinages of his own for Euripides: *ptōchopoios* or "beggar-maker" at 842 and *chōlopoios* (lame-maker) at 846.[123] So far, it seems to be a mere opposition of poetic registers and character types that is at stake. But gender enters the game very quickly. Dionysus rebukes the poets for their insults: "It isn't appropriate," he says, "for men-poets [*andras poiētas*] to rail at each other like baker-women [*artopōlidas*]" (857–58).[124] Looking back to Euripides's characterization as an *anēr poiētēs* in the *Lysistrata*, as well as Aristophanes himself in the *Clouds*, Dionysus reminds them with the salient juxtaposition of *anēr* (man) and *poiētēs* that they have an authoritative gender role

118. νῦν δ᾿ ἄξιός ἐσθ᾿ ὁ ποιητής, *Eq.* 509; φησὶ γὰρ ἀνὴρ, 514.

119. On literary criticism in the *Frogs*, see Heiden 1991, O'Sullivan 1992: 7–22, Dover 1993: 24–37, R. Rosen 2004, Hunter 2009: 10–52.

120. ὁπότερος οὖν ἂν τῇ πόλει παραινέσειν / μέλλῃ τι χρηστόν, *Ran.* 1420–21.

121. ἡ πόλις σωθεῖσα, *Ran.* 1419.

122. ἄνθρωπον ἀγριοποιὸν, *Ran.* 837.

123. πτωχοποιὲ, *Ran.* 842; χωλοποιὸν, 846.

124. λοιδορεῖσθαι δ᾿ οὐ πρέπει / ἄνδρας ποιητὰς ὥσπερ ἀρτοπώλιδας, *Ran.* 857–58.

to uphold. The force of the phrase, with the normative "it isn't appropriate" (*ou prepei*), is that "poets should be real *men*." And this depiction of what it means to be a real man and a real poet is, as in the *Lysistrata*, created in direct contrast to the roles of women. Where men and poets are not meant to abuse one another, that kind of behavior, Dionysus suggests, is entirely appropriate for a "bakeress"—using a feminized term, *artopōlis*, the feminine of the male *artopōlēs* (baker). As in the passage in the *Lysistrata*, the opposition works on many levels. The male *anēr poiētēs* is contrasted with the female "bakeress," setting male and female gender, as well as the gendered terms that describe them, in opposition. The expectations of normative behavior for each group are contrasted: proper conduct for men (*prepei*, "it is appropriate"), poor behavior for women. Within this proper conduct, discourse in particular is targeted: the male poets are encouraged to engage in high poetic discourse (Dionysus follows his rebuke with a simile, comparing Aeschylus's roaring to that of a mighty oak, 859), whereas women's discourse is seen as lowly and abusive (*loidoreisthai*, "to rail at each other," 857). And finally, summing it all up, there is the contrast between two different modes of professionalism, two different poles on the spectrum of the professional "maker": the male "maker" *poiētēs*, distinguished by his masculinity, his high discourse, and his proper conduct; and the female bread-maker, characterized by her femininity, her abusive low discourse, and her "unacceptable" behavior. Poetry and masculinity are set up as "high" civilized endeavors of "making," versus the "low" menial task of female bread-making.[125]

These oppositions are enshrined, not only in the genders assigned to each group, their occupations, or the behaviors they exhibit, but in the very grammar and make-up of the words used to describe them. On the one hand, we have a male-professional word, *poiētēs*, for the man (ending in the masculine *-ēs*); on the other, a female-professional word, *artopōlis*, for the woman (ending in the feminine *-is*; contrast the masculine *artopōlēs*). And, as the feminine suffix, *-is*, appears in opposition to the male *-ēs* ending of *poiētēs*, the challenge

---

125. Cf. *Nub.* 1357–58: ὁ δ᾽ εὐθέως ἀρχαῖον εἶν᾽ ἔφασκε τὸ κιθαρίζειν / ᾄδειν τε πίνονθ᾽ ὡσπερεὶ κάχρυς γυναῖκ᾽ ἀλοῦσαν (But he said straight away that it's old-fashioned to play the lyre and sing while drinking like a woman grinding barley); see also *Ran.* 1368–69: εἴπερ γε δεῖ καὶ τοῦτό με, / ἀνδρῶν ποιητῶν τυροπωλῆσαι τέχνην (if I really have to do this, and deal with the craft of men-poets as if I'm selling cheese). On women's work in ancient Greece, see Karanika 2014: 10–15; on the proverbial abusive/shrill tone of the female baker in ancient Greece, see chapter 7, n. 37.

to the masculinity of *poiētēs* is defended and girded by the addition of the noun *anēr*, "man"—so that no one can challenge the unequivocal masculinity of the poet-man, in opposition to the quarreling, lowly bakeress. As in the case of the male chorus of the *Lysistrata* who are threatened by the overweening chorus of females, the male gender of the poet is underlined through the addition of *anēr* at the very moment where male identity is seen to be under threat, as Aeschylus and Euripides here give way to unacceptable "female" insults.[126] Dionysus's reminder is nothing short of a warning to Aeschylus and Euripides of what is at stake if they allow themselves to engage in female abusive speech discourses, recalling them to their roles of *man* and *poet* with a triple warning that reminds them of their male gender, their masculine discourse, and their male-poetic profession. It is a crucial moment of normative gendering that works on multiple levels. The gendering of professional terminology—*poiētēs* versus *artopōlis*—becomes a shorthand for the superiority of men over women; "high" male professions of making poetry over the menial making tasks of women; and high-flown male poetic discourse over the artisanal abusive speech practiced by women. "Men-poets," Dionysus seems to say, need to live up to their name—as men, and as makers.

Man-Poet: Maker of Men

If these passages show how the masculinity of the man is connected to his identity as "maker," it remains to be seen exactly *what* he is "making." The final step in Aristophanes's characterization of the "man-poet" is his depiction of the poet as a maker of men in the democratic *polis*: crucially, he argues that the chief function of poets is to "make people better" (*Ran.* 1009–10).[127]

This "educational" aspect of poetry was a wider central tenet of male poets' role in constructing and defining masculinity: the works of the "good (male) poets" (*poiētai agathoi*) were presented to male students to be learned by heart, from which they were expected to learn everything from technical

---

126. Dionysus's comment might seem to run counter to the speech practices of male and female characters in Aristophanes, where we find a greater number of obscenities in male speech (see McClure 1999a: 206–15, Willi 2003: 157–97 esp. 193–97, McDonald 2016); λοιδορεῖσθαι, however, refers to speech register in general (cf. e.g., λαλεῖν, see chapter 4, n. 59), and women's speech is seen as "lower-class" in contrast to "high" male speech genres like oratory and poetry: see McClure 1999a: 32–69, 228–35.

127. Snell 1982: 115; see also Dover 1974: 29–30, Taplin 1983, J. Henderson 1990, Ford 2002: 199–201, D. Bouvier 2004, Hunter 2009: 25–29, Wright 2012: 17–24.

expertise to moral lessons.[128] Aeschines, the fourth-century BCE orator, describes how it was usual for "boys to learn the sayings of the poets [tōn poiētōn] by heart, so that when we become men [andres] we can make use of them" (In Ctes. 135).[129] In this sense, it was the act of reading the (male) poets which enabled boys to become men, and inducted them into life as a man in Greece. This was particularly true of Homer, who was commonly seen as the "educator of Greece," and his epics a guide to how to live life properly (Pl. Rep. 10.606e).[130] Homer's status as the "bible of the Greeks," and the role played by the Iliad and the Odyssey in shaping everything from education to military strategy to language gave poetry, in particular, a central place in male education: reciters of Homer and other poets were described as being brought to Athens "to educate the (male) citizens."[131] And what Homer and the poets taught, as we will see, were quintessentially male values: "battle-lines, manly deeds, the arming of men" (Ar. Ran. 1036).[132] Here, however, I suggest that Aristophanes went one step further in closing the loop of the poet's connection to man-making in the state. On the one hand, he connects the male poet and his masculine-gendered agency to the politics of the dēmos by emphasizing the poet's "making" attributes as a "maker of men." But, at the same time, he also directly assimilates the new term poiētēs to the politēs (citizen) through their joint identity as men, suggesting a deep and direct connection between the poet and his fellow citizens.[133] This, then, argues for a very fifth-century Athenian vision of the male poiētēs as educator of male citizens and cocreator of the polis with other fellow poiētai-politai—united through their masculinity.

The key passage for "man-making" in Aristophanes occurs in the Frogs, a hundred or so lines after Dionysus has exhorted Aeschylus and Euripides to behave like proper "men-poets" (andras poiētas, 858). Aeschylus now asks

128. See Pl. Prt. 325e–326a, and see introduction, n. 11.

129. διὰ τοῦτο γὰρ οἶμαι ἡμᾶς παῖδας ὄντας τὰς τῶν ποιητῶν γνώμας ἐκμανθάνειν, ἵν' ἄνδρες ὄντες αὐταῖς χρώμεθα, Aeschin. In Ctes. 135.2–4; cf. Lycurg. Leoc. 107.1.

130. τὴν Ἑλλάδα πεπαίδευκεν οὗτος ὁ ποιητής, Pl. Rep. 10.606e2–3; see pp. 122–26 and chapter 5, nn. 20 and 27.

131. παιδεύειν τοὺς πολίτας, Pl. [Hipparch.] 228c4; cf. the reports that Lycurgus brought the Homeric poems to Sparta because of their educational value (Dio Chrys. 2.44, cf. Plut. Lyc. 4.4; Ael. VH 13.14). On Homer as the "bible of the Greeks," see Graziosi 2002: 246–47.

132. τάξεις, ἀρετὰς, ὁπλίσεις ἀνδρῶν, Ar. Ran. 1036; see pp. 118–21. Cf. Pl. Ion 540d–541d on Homer teaching generalship, and Isoc. Paneg. 159.

133. On Aristophanes's politics, see e.g., M. Heath 1987, McGlew 2002 esp. 6–24, Sidwell 2009, Major 2013.

Euripides "on what grounds a man-poet [*andra poiētēn*] should be admired" (1008).[134] His phraseology echoes Dionysus's earlier reprimand about the proper speech of "men-poets," showing that Aeschylus, at least, has internalized Dionysus's warning. Euripides's reply is an important one in delineating the role of the *anēr poiētēs*: "cleverness and giving good advice," he says, "and because we make [*poioumen*] people [*tous anthrōpous*] better in the state" (1009–10).[135] Euripides, too, has clearly absorbed Dionysus's reminder: his answer is nothing less than a gloss on Aeschylus's and Dionysus's term, *anēr poiētēs*, explaining and unpacking exactly what it means to be an *anēr poiētēs*. First, he verbalizes the noun *poiētēs* into its root verb, *poiein*, "to do, make": "we make" (*poioumen*, 1009), he says. He thus provides an etymology of *poiētēs*, as well as using the inclusive first-person plural to group himself and Aeschylus together as members of the élite tribe of poets; whatever their opposing views, they have a shared identity in the vocabulary of masculinity and poetic agency. The verbal aspect of *poiētēs*—agency and making—is, Euripides seems to argue, a key element of being a poet, a "maker." But it is also about *what* you make: and, for (Aristophanes's) Euripides, what a poet makes is men. Here he uses the more general *anthrōpoi*, "people," rather than *andres*, "men"— but the qualification that follows makes it clear that it is "men" that are signified here. These people operate "in the state" (*en tais polesin*), the poet says: that is, the democratic civic sphere of the *polis* in which only male citizens could fully participate.[136] In other words, what determines a good "man-maker" (*anēr poiētēs*) is in the term itself: it is precisely that he *makes men*—and, more than that, the kinds of men who make up the state. The link between male gender, poetic identity, and the act of "making" in the definition of the poet as *anēr poiētēs* describes, not only who the poet *is*, but what he *does*. He is a man and a maker, who makes (civic) men.

This man-making activity is further defined a few lines later, where Aeschylus—having agreed with Euripides's judgment on what makes a good "man-poet" or "man-maker"—goes on to demonstrate the kinds of men he

134. τίνος οὕνεκα χρὴ θαυμάζειν ἄνδρα ποιητήν; *Ran.* 1008.

135. δεξιότητος καὶ νουθεσίας, ὅτι βελτίους γε ποιοῦμεν / τοὺς ἀνθρώπους ἐν ταῖς πόλεσιν, *Ran.* 1009–10. See Dover 1993: 15–16, Ford 2002: 200, D. Bouvier 2004; see further chapter 4, n. 127.

136. For an overview of classical Athenian citizenship, see Blok 2017, and for the limitation of participation in politics to men, see Manville 1990, Cartledge 2000; for the democratic individual in Old Comedy, see McGlew 2002.

and other poets have depicted, and the manly qualities they display to the men of the audience. He looks back on the characters of his own plays, whom he says were depicted as statuesque noble warriors (1013–17), which in turn taught men to be noble (1019). After seeing his *Seven against Thebes*, for example, Aeschylus boasts, "every man [*anēr*] in the audience was desperate to go to war" (1022).[137] "This," he says—that is, training men in war—"is what men-poets [*andras . . . poiētas*] should practice" (1030).[138] He gives examples of other "poets" (*poiētōn*, 1031) who gave different types of manly advice: the institution of rites and laws (Orpheus, 1032); healing (Musaeus, 1033); farming (Hesiod, 1033–34); and "men's" (*andrōn*) battles (Homer, 1034–63). The tight interweaving of male poets, manly qualities, and male audience is highlighted—as in the parabasis of the *Clouds*—by the repetition of *anēr* and the ring composition between poets as *andres* (1030) and their subject "of men" (*andrōn*, 1036). The identity of the *poiētēs* as an *anēr* (*andras . . . poiētas*, 1030) and his depiction of manly qualities (*andrōn*, 1036) is precisely what connects him to his audience of men (*anēr*, 1022), and justifies him to be their educator. "Just as boys [*paidarioisin*] have a teacher who advises them," Aeschylus says a few lines later, "so adults have poets" (1054–55).[139]

And it is not just manly activities which Aeschylus argues should be taught by poets, but examples of men, too. "My brain modeled and made [*epoiēsen*] many examples of brave deeds—Patrocluses, lion-hearted Teucers—so I could urge the man-citizen [*andra politēn*] to match himself to them" (1040–42).[140] Aeschylus now deftly fuses the subject of his earlier question at 1008—"what makes a great *anēr poiētēs*?"—and the object of Euripides's answer—"men in the state [*polis*]"—to come up with a new noun phrase: the *anēr politēs*, or "man-citizen" (1041).[141] Aeschylus's argument is an example of Euripides's

137. ὃ θεασάμενος πᾶς ἄν τις ἀνὴρ ἠράσθη δάϊος εἶναι, *Ran.* 1022.

138. ταῦτα γὰρ ἄνδρας χρὴ ποιητὰς ἀσκεῖν, *Ran.* 1030.

139. τοῖς μὲν γὰρ παιδαρίοισιν / ἔστι διδάσκαλος ὅστις φράζει, τοῖσιν δ᾽ ἡβῶσι ποιηταί, *Ran.* 1054–55.

140. ὅθεν ἡμὴ φρὴν ἀπομαξαμένη πολλὰς ἀρετὰς ἐποίησεν, / Πατρόκλων, Τεύκρων θυμολεόντων, ἵν᾽ ἐπαίροιμ᾽ ἄνδρα πολίτην / ἀντεκτείνειν αὐτὸν τούτοις, *Ran.* 1040–42.

141. The collocation is undoubtedly an intertextual dig at Aeschylus: the noun phrase occurs for the first time at Aesch. *Sept.* 605, ξὺν πολίταις ἀνδράσιν; cf. *Ag.* 855 where Clytemnestra addresses the ἄνδρες πολῖται. Cf. also Soph. *OT* 512, *OC* 1579, Eur. *Bacch.* 270–71, Eur. fr. 512 *TrGF*, Eup. frr. 117, 129 K-A, Ar. *Eq.* 943–45, 1304, Antiph. 1.1.4, Thuc. 6.54.3. See Blok 2017: 147–62 on the semantics and gendering of the term πολίτης; for πολίτης in Aristophanes, see Blok 2017: 153 with n. 28, 155 with n. 35.

point, that a poet's job is to teach men in the state. Here, however, the masculinity of the *anēr poiētēs* is directly connected to that of the male citizenry, visualized in the singular (completing the parallel) as a "man-citizen," an *anēr politēs* (1041). The phonetic similarity between *poiētēs* and *politēs*—both begin with *po-* and end with *-tēs*, with only the central syllable different—and the formulation of the noun phrase with *anēr* mean that the parallel being drawn between the poet as "man" and the "man" citizenry he teaches is unavoidable.[142] The poet is a man and teacher of "men-citizens," then, but as a participant in the democracy he is also a "man-citizen" as well as a "man-poet." The slippage between *anēr poiētēs* and *anēr politēs* underlines both the poet's role as maker of male citizens, and his identity as a man in a band of male political citizenry.

We see this slippage occurring elsewhere in Aristophanes's plays—for example, in the *Acharnians* (425 BCE), where we have another parabasis where the chorus steps forward to talk about "our poet" (*ho didaskalos hēmōn*, *Ach.* 628).[143] The first part (628–58) serves as a defense against the charge of having slandered the Athenians. Everything that was done by "the poet" (*ho poiētēs*, 633), the chorus argues, was intended for the Athenians' benefit, and, in particular, to educate them. He has taught them in his plays not to be "empty citizens" (*chaunopolitas*, 635), shown them not to be taken in by foreign ambassadors (636–40), fought for justice in his comedies (655), and pointed the way to happiness without flattering or praising them (656–58).[144] "In doing all this [*poiēsas*], he has done you and the citizens in the city-states [*en tais polesin*] a great service," the chorus goes on, "showing what it is to be a democracy" (641–42).[145] Line 641 paraphrases the introduction to the poet's services rendered to the state at line 633 above ("the poet [*ho poiētēs*] says that he has done you a great service"), this time replacing the noun *poiētēs* with the verb *poiēsas*—both delineating the poet's activity.[146] There is a point in the change

142. For other examples of ποιητής–πόλις/πολίτης puns, see *Ran.* 1418–19, 1528–30.

143. ὁ διδάσκαλος ἡμῶν, *Ach.* 628. Dover 1968: xix and MacDowell 1982: 23–24 argue that διδάσκαλος and ποιητής refer to Callistratus, who produced the play; see contra Halliwell 1980: 43–44, Hubbard 1991: 48. On the parabasis of the *Acharnians*, see A. Bowie 1982, Hubbard 1991: 47–56.

144. For the hapax χαυνοπολίτας, see Hubbard 1991: 51 with n. 29, Olson 2002 ad loc.

145. ταῦτα ποιήσας πολλῶν ἀγαθῶν αἴτιος ὑμῖν γεγένηται / καὶ τοῖς δήμοις ἐν ταῖς πόλεσιν, δείξας ὡς δημοκρατοῦνται, *Ach.* 641–42.

146. φησὶν δ᾿ εἶναι πολλῶν ἀγαθῶν αἴτιος ὑμῖν ὁ ποιητής, *Ach.* 633. Bentley has αἴτιος, which I follow (as Olson 2002 ad loc.), rather than ἄξιος (as Wilson 2007).

from noun to verb, however. In the first instance, the poet claimed his status as a *poiētēs*, pointing to his identity in his introduction; in the second instance, having described examples of how his poetry has effected changes in the citizenry, he has moved from a poet to a doer (*poiēsas*), drawing out the verbal undertones of the noun. This "doing" is connected to the politics which he claims to shape by the subtle connection of the verb and its sphere of influence through alliteration: *poiēsas . . . en tais polesin* (641–42); *dēmous . . . deixas . . . dēmokratountai* (642). The activities of the poet are thus tied into those of the *polis*, and *poiētēs* and *politēs* are once more aligned through the chorus's rhetoric. At the same time, the delineation of the citizens as male *dēmoi*, and their sphere of influence "in the cities" (642), emphasizes that this interconnection is based on a shared gender between *ho poiētēs* and *hoi dēmoi*, the male poet who speaks, the male chorus who ventriloquizes him, and the male citizens who are his audience.[147]

This exploration of the interaction between poet-terms and gender in Aristophanes reveals many different layers to the relationship between gender and the identity of the poet, as Aristophanes depicts it. Surveying the trajectory of the poet's career and the lessons he learns in imitative art, the depictions of Agathon and Euripides in *Women at the Thesmophoria*, and (the persona of) Aristophanes himself in the *Clouds*, demonstrate a poetics whereby the fluidity of gender in a young male poet enables him to learn to imitate both men and women by inhabiting the female gender as well as the male. This totalizing power of the male poet's voice is fully represented in the depiction of the mature "poet-man," the *anēr poiētēs*, setting the poet up as a figure of masculine discourse, professionalism, and agency in the construction of poetry—underlining the male poet as a gendered "maker." And finally, the connection between the male poet's "making" and the men of the audience leads to the male poet is seen as the ultimate "maker" of men in the state. "Making" or "doing" in Aristophanes is not just about poetics, then, nor about the gendered agency of men; it is the interaction between the totalizing "making" power of the male voice, the agency of the male "maker" in constructing characters in poetry, and the shared masculinity between poet and audience as makers and citizens—where the male poet's ability to "make" (*poiein*) poetry enables him to shape his male audience of fellow citizens as shared "doers" in the state.

147. On the politics of the play, see e.g., Edmunds 1980, Carey 1993, Fisher 1993, Sidwell 2009: 107–54.

5

The (Gendered) Problem of Plato and the Poets

WITH PLATO, we move away from poets talking about their own identity, to a philosopher who was famously skeptical of poets and their craft—and this shift marks a move from the self-definition of the persona of the poet (what the poet is, defined in poetry as the poet engages in their craft), to an interest in using language to explore and define exactly what the poet should (and should not) be.[1] Plato's views on poetry were both wide-ranging and influential, setting the tone for much of the subsequent debate on literary criticism, the importance of poetry and the role of the poet in education and the state—in particular, his discussion of the "old quarrel between philosophy and poetry" (*Rep.* 10.607b6–7).[2] His attack on Homer and the poets, and the banning of almost all poetry from the ideal state in book 10 of the *Republic*, is so well known that it needs little introduction.[3] Here, I will approach Plato's much-discussed views on the poets from a different angle, through an analysis of the words he uses to try to describe (and circumscribe) the figure of the male poet.

---

1. For a summary of terms for the poet and poetry in Plato, see Vicaire 1964.

2. παλαιὰ μέν τις διαφορὰ φιλοσοφίᾳ τε καὶ ποιητικῇ, Pl. *Rep.* 10.607b6–7; see T. Gould 1990, Most 2011. On Plato's influence, see, e.g., Whitehead on the tradition of European philosophy as "a series of footnotes to Plato" (1978: 39); on literary criticism in particular, see Murray 1996: 24–32.

3. See the collected essays in Destrée and Hermann 2011, and for a general introduction, Murray 1996: 1–32; see also Partee 1970, Murdoch 1977, Belfiore 1982, Moravcsik and Temko 1982, Elias 1984, Moravcsik 1986, G. R. F. Ferrari 1989, Asmis 1992, Janaway 1995, Naddaff 2003, Janaway 2006, Moss 2007, Halliwell 2011, and, for further bibliography, see the references given in Griswold 2003. On the approach to poetry in *Republic* 10 in particular, see Griswold 1981, Nehamas 1982, Halliwell 1988: 1–16, Moss 2007.

By focusing attention on Plato's struggle for words as he endeavors to come to terms with the role of poets and their relation to the construction of gender, I suggest that we can throw new light on the old problem of Plato and the poets, through the lens of gender. As we move down to the level of words, we can watch Plato "on the ground," as it were, focusing on the dynamics of the construction of a vocabulary to describe his views on what male poets should and should not be. We see the philosopher struggling for words as he attempts to move beyond the established word for "male poet," *poiētēs*, whose association with making (and thus imitation), as well as the politically situated making of citizen men, no longer suited his purposes. And we watch as Plato reshapes the poet's relation to gender, and what it means to make men (and women) in the state.

Words matter for Plato's Socrates. The idea that if you cannot define something properly, you cannot understand it, resounds throughout the dialogues.[4] So it's worth paying attention to the terms Plato uses: the way he manipulates and marshals words gives us a deeper insight into the way things are or should be, revealing the structure of his thought world on a lexical level—some words are truer representations than others, while some miss the mark. The first feature which anyone looking at the words for poets in Plato will notice is the sheer range and flexibility of the terms he employs (a characteristic of Plato's style elsewhere, too)—more so than in any other classical author.[5] Nouns (and their associated verbs) to describe the poet range from the familiar *poiētēs*

4. Wolfsdorf 2003, Blackburn 2006: 25, Benson 2013: 136.

5. Nominal terms for "poet" in Plato include: ἀοιδός ("singer/bard," rarely, see below: *Lysis* 215c7, quotation of Hes. *Op.* 26; *Leg.* 670c9); κωμῳδοποιός ("comedy-maker, comic poet," as a substantive: *Ap.* 18d2, *Phd.* 70c1, *Symp.* 223d5, *Rep.* 10.606c8, [*Alc.*] 121d1); λογοποιός ("story-teller, speech-writer": *Euthyd.* 289d2, 289d9, 289e2, *Rep.* 392a12); μελοποιός ("song-maker, lyric poet": *Ion* 533e8, 534a1, 534a6, *Prt.* 326a7); μουσικός ("musician," as a substantive: e.g., *Grg.* 449d5, 460b4, *Cra.* 424a3, *Rep.* 1.349e10–11, 2.398e1, 3.402d8, *Phdr.* 243a7, 268d7, *Tht.* 144e3, 178d5, *Soph.* 253b3); μυθόλογος ("story-teller": *Rep.* 392d2, 398b1, *Leg.* 664d3, 941b5); μυθοποιός ("story-maker," as a substantive: *Rep.* 377b11); ποιητής ("poet": passim, e.g., *Ap.* 22a9, *Euthphr.* 3b2, 12a8, *Grg.* 485d6, *Hp. mi.* 370e1–2, *Ion* 530b8, 10, 534b4, 534e4, 536a1, *Prt.* 311e3, 325e5, 327d4, 339a1, *Lysis* 214a1, *Cra.* 391d1, 394e10, 407b1, *Euthyd.* 275d1, 305d8, *Meno* 95d1, *Phdr.* 234e6, 236d5, *Tht.* 194e2, *Soph.* 234a2, *Symp.* 186e3, 196e1–4, 205c2, 4, 9, 209a4, *Rep.* 1.328e6, 1.330c3, 2.366b1, 2.378e7, 3.387b2, 3.392a12, 3.393c8, 3.398b1, 8.568b6, 10.596d4, 10.597d2, 10.597d11, 10.599a4, 10.601b9, 10.605b6, 10.606e3, *Ti.* 28c3, *Leg.* 656c4, 660e2, 669c2, 700d4, 801c2, 810e6, 811a1, 817a3, 817b2); τραγῳδοποιός ("tragedy-maker, tragic poet," as a substantive: *Cra.* 425d5, *Symp.* 223d5, *Rep.* 3.408b8, 10.597e6, 10.605c10, 10.607a3). Cf. also λογογράφος ("speech-writer, prose-writer": *Phdr.* 257c6, 258c2).

(and *poiein*), to *logopoios/logopoiein* (prose-writer, word-/story-maker), *mythologos/mythologein* (story-teller), and *mythopoios* (story-maker), to the adjective *mousikos* ("musical" / "of the Muses," and so in the substantive, "musician").[6] (*Aoidos*, as an outdated term, is hardly ever used.)[7]

Even the seemingly innocuous *poiētēs* has a huge range of meanings in Plato.[8] We find a particular interest in the etymology of the word, as in *Euthyphro*, where Socrates caps a poetic quotation along the lines "the poet poet-ed poet-ing" (or, "the maker made making"), parsing the verbal root of *poiētēs* twice.[9] A similar juxtaposition of *poiētēs* and its verb occurs in the *Lesser Hippias*, where Socrates asks which hero, between Achilles or Odysseus, "was better poet-ed/made by the poet/maker" Homer.[10] *Poiētēs* in its basic meaning, "maker" or "inventor" appears, again, in the *Euthyphro*, where Socrates refutes the accusation that he is a "maker" of gods.[11] This activity of "making" in its broadest sense, and the man who makes, is specifically defined at the beginning of the *Sophist*, in which Plato explores theories of being: "We term it 'making' [*poiein*] when a man [*tis/ton*] turns what wasn't before into something that is, and 'being made' [*poieisthai*] for the thing that's turned into something" (*Soph.* 219b).[12] This applies naturally to the ultimate creator (artistic and otherwise) who can produce men and animals, the "maker [*poiētēs*] of living beings."[13] Meanwhile, in the *Cratylus*—the dialogue on the

---

6. μουσικός as an adjective in Plato usually means "musical," "harmonious" (e.g., *Alc.* 108d8, 108e1, *Lach.* 188d2, *Cra.* 405a6, *Symp.* 187b2, *Rep.* 10.620a9, *Leg.* 2.658a3, 7.802b6); at *Phd.* 105d9 it means rather "cultivated, educated." In the few instances where μουσικός is used as a substantive it refers to musical ability, with some crossover into poetry, but with an emphasis on sung poetry (see, e.g., *Grg.* 449d5, *Cra.* 424a3); see Vicaire 1964: 73–74, 143–44.

7. ἀοιδός occurs in a quotation of Hes. *Op.* 26 at *Lysis* 215c7; the only other occurrence (outside the spuria) is at *Leg.* 670c9.

8. See Vicaire 1964: 147–54.

9. ὁ ποιητὴς ἐποίησεν ὁ ποιήσας, *Euthphr.* 12a8.

10. πεποίηται τῷ ποιητῇ, *Hp. mi.* 370e1–2.

11. φησὶ γάρ με ποιητὴν εἶναι θεῶν, καὶ ὡς καινοὺς ποιοῦντα θεούς, *Euthphr.* 3b2; cf. *Euthyd.* 305d8 on the orator as a ποιητὴς τῶν λόγων (maker of words). For a similar usage of ποιητής in the sense of "maker, contriver," see Xen. *Cyr.* 1.6.38.

12. πᾶν ὅπερ ἂν μὴ πρότερόν τις ὂν ὕστερον εἰς οὐσίαν ἄγῃ, τὸν μὲν ἄγοντα ποιεῖν, τὸ δὲ ἀγόμενον ποιεῖσθαί πού φαμεν, *Soph.* 219b5–6. See also 234a1 on ποίησις as "the act of creation," and, similarly, ποιητική at 219d1, 265a4, 265a12, 265b4, 265e5, 266a1, 266d5.

13. καὶ γὰρ ζῴων αὐτὸν εἶπες ποιητήν, *Soph.* 234a2; ὁ θεός, βουλόμενος εἶναι ὄντως κλίνης ποιητὴς ὄντως οὔσης, *Rep.* 10.597c11–d1; τὸν μὲν οὖν ποιητὴν καὶ πατέρα τοῦδε τοῦ παντὸς εὑρεῖν, *Ti.* 28c3. See Vicaire 1964: 78–79.

origin of names which we encountered in the introduction—the debate around "making" words coincides with the activity of the poet as "maker" of characters and names. This was part of a much wider awareness of the importance of literature in shaping the language and culture of the ancient Greeks, and its seminal role—particularly in the case of Homer—in determining proper language usage: conclusive proof of the "proper" usage of a word or its etymology could be provided by a simple reference to *ho poiētēs*, "the poet."[14] Poets were seen, not just as arbiters of language, but even its inventors: Andromenides, a third-century BCE critic, is cited as claiming that "working out language and naming [*onomasia*] is the job of poets"; while Pausimachus, another critic (this time of the second century BCE), went even further to argue that "poets compose by nature when they give a name to things"—thus identifying poets as originary name-makers.[15] In Plato's *Cratylus*, the "name-giver"—imagined to have given names to all things—is suggestively juxtaposed, at one point, with the poet as similar "makers of names": Homer, "the poet" (*ton poiētēn*), is said to have "made" (*pepoiēkenai*) some names a certain way, and "the man who made names [*ho ta onomata poiōn*] seems to have thought the same," says Socrates (407b).[16] The poet is thus connected, through the verbal root of *poiētēs* and its link to "the name-maker," to issues around naming and authority over words.

All these examples demonstrate exactly why the figure of the *poiētēs* is so important to Plato from a philosophical standpoint. The concept of "making," and its association with bringing something into being, points to the core of

14. For Homer as an etiological/etymological source in antiquity, see Schironi 2018: 340–76; see also introduction, n. 42.

15. ποηταῖς] ἐπιπρέπει[ν τ]ὰ[ς τῆς τε δι]αλέκτου καὶ τῆς ὀνομασίας ἐξεργασίας, Andromenides F 17 Janko = Phld. *Po.* 1, 131.2–3 Janko, see Janko 2000: 349 n. 4; φύσιει̣ δὲ ὅταν εἰς τὴν εὐγενῆ φωνὴν καὶ πρώτην καὶ εἰς πάντ' ἐναρμόττουσαν οἱ ποιηταὶ ἐμπεσόντες ὀνομάζ ̓ω ́σι<ν> (But poets [compose] by nature when they name [things] by coming upon the word that is nobly born, primary, and entirely appropriate), trans. Janko, Phld. *Po.* 1, 117.16–21. Cf. Antiphanes fr. 189.17–18 K-A = Ath. 6.222e–223a, Antiphanes fr. 207 K-A, Dion. Hal. *Comp.* 16.3–5, 11–13.

16. καὶ γὰρ τούτων οἱ πολλοὶ ἐξηγούμενοι τὸν ποιητήν φασι τὴν Ἀθηνᾶν αὐτὸν νοῦν τε καὶ διάνοιαν πεποιηκέναι, καὶ ὁ τὰ ὀνόματα ποιῶν ἔοικε τοιοῦτόν τι περὶ αὐτῆς διανοεῖσθαι, Pl. *Cra.* 407b1–4. The name-giver is also called a δημιουργὸς ὀνομάτων at 390e1–2, recalling its use for poets elsewhere in Plato as well as in Homer: see chapter 5, n. 37. For the connection between name-giver and poet, see Pearson 2016: 20–21; for the various names of the name-giver, see Ademollo 2011: 117–25, Demand 1975.

metaphysics (as the definition of *poiein* in the *Sophist* shows), while ideas around making, creating, imitating, and describing in words (as in the *Cratylus*) lead to questions about the nature of truth and representation.[17] There is, therefore, much at stake in understanding exactly what a *poiētēs* does, and the nature of the words made by a *poiētēs*.

Stephen Halliwell writes that "in the case of Plato, an engagement with the culturally powerful texts and voices of poetry is so evident, so persistent, and so intense as to constitute a major thread running through the entire fabric of his writing and thinking."[18] Even narrowing the scope of inquiry to the word *poiētēs* constitutes a daunting task. (The term occurs over two hundred times in Plato's dialogues, and fifty-two times in the *Republic* alone.)[19] But the reason why Plato engages with the poets so extensively is precisely because there is so much at stake. As we saw in the last chapter, poetry is important because it forms the backbone of the education of male citizens, and thus of the state: it is a highly political project. Plato makes this much clear:[20]

> The praisers of Homer say that this poet [*poiētēs*] educated Greece: you should take him up to learn about the administration and teaching of human affairs, and build your whole life on what this poet [*poiētēs*] says.

Homer's central position in education highlights the dangerous power the *poiētēs* has been allowed.[21] And, for Plato's Socrates in the *Republic*, that needs to change.

---

17. E.g., *Rep.* 10.597e6–8; see Partee 1972: 114.

18. Halliwell 2000: 94.

19. On ποιητής in the *Republic*, see Vicaire 1964: 75.

20. Ὁμήρου ἐπαινέταις . . . λέγουσιν ὡς τὴν Ἑλλάδα πεπαίδευκεν οὗτος ὁ ποιητὴς καὶ πρὸς διοίκησίν τε καὶ παιδείαν τῶν ἀνθρωπίνων πραγμάτων ἄξιος ἀναλαβόντι μανθάνειν τε καὶ κατὰ τοῦτον τὸν ποιητὴν πάντα τὸν αὑτοῦ βίον κατασκευασάμενον ζῆν, *Rep.* 10.606e1–5. Cf. *Ion* 542b4 on Ion as a "praiser of Homer" (περὶ Ὁμήρου ἐπαινέτην); for Homer's centrality to education in Plato, see also *Ion* 531c1–d2. Cf. p. 117 with chapter 4, nn. 131 and 132.

21. See Ford 2002: 201 n. 51 on Plato's use of Homer to refer to the entire poetic tradition. As many have commented, however, Plato's relationship to Homer can be read as ambivalent: see Elias 1984, Halliwell 1988: 3; cf. Partee 1970 esp. 215, G. R. F. Ferrari 1989: 141–48, Halliwell 2011. On the difference between Plato's and Socrates's approaches to Homer, see Blondell 2002: 154–64. For Plato's poetic images, see, e.g., Griswold 1981: 150, Bloom 1991: 398, and for poetic citations, Halliwell 2000.

Struggling for Words: Gender and
the Poet in Plato's *Republic*

The need to control and redefine the role of the *poiētēs* lies at the heart of the discussion of poets in the *Republic*. This is the text which defines Plato's attitude toward poetry, its place in politics, and its relation to gender, and so will be the focus of my analysis, although I will also adduce examples from other dialogues that shed light on Plato's argument. In approaching Plato's argument against the poets in the *Republic*, it would be easy to assume that his attitude is uniformly negative and therefore straightforward or unambiguous.[22] Poetry is dangerous, as it is imitative and can lead men to follow bad examples; poets should therefore be banned, in the main, from his ideal state (with two important exceptions: "hymns to the gods and eulogies of good men," *Rep.* 10.607a).[23] There are two major arguments against poetry here: first, that it teaches bad examples (books 2 and 3 of the *Republic*) and so is ethically inadequate from a philosophical standpoint and as an educational tool; second, that it is an imitation of an imitation (it imitates physical beings, which are in turn imitations of the Forms) and so is metaphysically deficient (elaborated in the argument of book 10).[24] It is the first point, the ethical dimension of the poet and his relationship to the educational and social structure of the state, which will occupy this chapter—for it is in the discussion around education and the ethical example of poetry that the connection between the poet and gender comes to the fore.

By focusing in on the word for "poet," we are able, in fact, to see that the banning of the poets as bad educational examples is only part of the story. Plato is not just banning poets: he is attempting to alter the category of the male poet altogether, by changing the word for "poet" itself. The term *poiētēs* is simply no longer fit for purpose. The archaeology of the word contains links to old forms of man-making through education, typified by Homer, established over the fifth century and concretized in Aristophanes in the *poiētēs* as

22. See, e.g., Halliwell 1988: 3, and cf. Halliwell 2000: 112, Halliwell 2011; as an example of the view of Plato's attitude toward poets as "bald and uncompromising," see Nehamas 1982: 47.

23. μόνον ὕμνους θεοῖς καὶ ἐγκώμια τοῖς ἀγαθοῖς ποιήσεως παραδεκτέον εἰς πόλιν, *Rep.* 10.607a3–5, on which see Ford 2002: 259.

24. On imitation (*mimēsis*) in Plato, see, in particular, Tate 1928, Tate 1932, Kirby 1991, Melberg 1995: 10–50, M. Miller 1999, Halliwell 2002: 37–148, Moss 2007; see also, for a discussion of μίμησις and the poets in book 10 of the *Republic*, Nehamas 1982, Belfiore 1983, Moss 2007, Marušič 2011.

"maker of men." Plato's issue is that the kinds of lessons taught by these male poets—and the kinds of men they made—are highly problematic in his eyes: the men, especially Achilles, represented in poetry show unrestrained grief, they cry, they complain (3.388a–b), they are greedy (390e–391a), they insult their superiors (390a) and the gods (391a–c).[25] All this teaches cowardice, Plato's Socrates argues, and lack of self-control—which is the very opposite of what true "courage" and "manliness" (the word *andreia* in Greek means the same thing, as we saw defined in the *Cratylus* in the introduction) should be.[26] Indeed, the analysis of the right kinds of *mythoi* to be told in the ideal state opens with the essential requirement that, if the subjects are to be "manly" (*andreioi*, 3.386a6), then the stories that "must be told" must also encourage them to "be courageous/manly" (*genesthai andreion*, 3.386a8). This concern with poets as the proper educators of men, and the need to make sure they depict the right kinds of manliness, is not confined to the *Republic* alone: it is a theme which transcends the *Republic* to infiltrate many of Plato's other dialogues.[27] We therefore need a new definition of manliness, and a new definition of a poet who can teach these lessons in a new poetry that is circumscribed by a proper understanding of what gender roles should be.[28] It is significant, then, that the only poems to be left in the state, alongside hymns to the gods, are "eulogies of good men" (10.607a)—that is, poetry that praises the right kind of manliness.[29]

Rather than trying to reappropriate the term *poiētēs* from old associations with a negative kind of manliness, Plato takes a more difficult route and seeks

25. *Rep.* 3.386a1–392a2. See Hobbs 2000: 199–219, also Murray 2011: 180.

26. See pp. 15–16. Plato's *Laches* is the dialogue most concerned with the definition of ἀνδρεία, on which see C. Gould 1987, Schmid 1992, Tessitore 1994, Hobbs 2000: 76–112, Sluiter and Rosen 2003: 5–8. On ἀνδρεία in Plato, see esp. Hobbs 2000, Bassi 2003: 50–52, and in the *Republic* in particular, see Sluiter and Rosen 2003: 9–12, Hobbs 2000: 199–249; for the education of the guardians as fostering courage, see Murray 2011: 178.

27. For examples of poets as educators of men in Plato, see *Lysis* 214a, *Grg.* 485d, *Meno* 95d, *Leg.* 656c, 660e, 719b, 810e, *Prt.* 319a, 325e–326a, 339a, 339b.

28. For a new definition of ἀνδρεία as steadiness of purpose, see *Rep.* 4.429a8–430c7: see Hobbs 2000: 22–23, and 23, 96–98 on Plato's "ambivalence" toward traditional norms of gender.

29. See chapter 5, n. 23 for the text. The *Protagoras* makes the masculinity of the subject matter even more explicit with the addition of ἀνήρ: ἐγκώμια παλαιῶν ἀνδρῶν ἀγαθῶν, *Prt.* 326a2–3.

entirely to redefine the types of gendered lessons that will be told in poetry, as well as the word that will be used to describe this new gendered poet. But it is not a straightforward task. Later in book 3, having censored the wrong types of masculinity from poetry, Socrates gives an example of the kind of tale (the "noble lie") which *should* be told in his ideal state to foster courage and virtue in the men of the state.[30] This is presented as a kind of "Phoenician tale" (3.414c), referring to the lying tales told by Odysseus in the *Odyssey*—making explicit the analogy that is being created between the lie fabricated by Socrates here and the fiction of poetry.[31] Socrates, however, is rather embarrassed at the lie, and hesitant to articulate it. As he launches into the tale, he foregrounds his struggle for words: "I'll tell you—but I don't know how I'll get the daring to do so, or what words [*poiois logos*] I'll use" (414d).[32] This struggle for the right terms is reflected in the difficulty he has in naming the tale itself: he calls it variously a lie, a Phoenician tale, and a myth/story (*mythos*), while the second half is introduced with a verb for the act of "storytelling" (*mythologountes*, 415a).[33] This is a term whose fluid meaning—between the dangers of story-telling as pleasant nonsense, and the important business of forming identity through original myths—Plato exploits elsewhere: in the *Greater Hippias*, *mythologein* describes old women's pleasant (but silly) tales, whereas in the *Timaeus* and *Laws* we see it in the sense of "telling original myths."[34] The gendering of *mythologein* in the *Greater Hippias* (where it is applied to old

30. Pl. *Rep.* 414b8–415d4: see Hahm 1969, G. R. F. Ferrari 1989: 112–14, Schofield 2007.

31. Φοινικικόν τι, *Rep.* 3.414c4. For the connection between lying and poetry (cf. Hesiod's Muses in the *Theogony*, p. 49), see Gill and Wiseman 1993, Pratt 1993, and, in Plato, see Halliwell 2002: 49–50 with 49 n. 31 for further bibliography.

32. λέγω δή· καίτοι οὐκ οἶδα ὁποίᾳ τόλμῃ ἢ ποίοις λόγοις χρώμενος ἐρῶ, *Rep.* 3.414d1–2.

33. A lie (ψεῦδος): τῶν ψευδῶν τῶν ἐν δέοντι γιγνομένων, *Rep.* 3.414b7–8; τὸ ψεῦδος, 414e6. A Phoenician tale: Φοινικικόν τι, 414c4. A myth/story (μῦθος): ἀλλ᾿ ὅμως ἄκουε καὶ τὸ λοιπὸν τοῦ μύθου, 415a1–2. Schofield 2007: 138 argues for the translation "lie." For storytelling, see *Rep.* 3.415a2–3, ὡς φήσομεν πρὸς αὐτοὺς μυθολογοῦντες (as we will tell them when we tell our story); cf. also 2.376d9–10, discussed at p. 146. On μῦθος in Plato, see chapter 5, n. 84.

34. Old women's tales: *Hp. mai.* 286a2 (cf. *Rep.* 1.350e2–3). Telling original myths: *Ti.* 22b1, *Leg.* 682e5. Other instances in Plato: *Grg.* 493a5, 493d3, *Phd.* 61e2, *Phdr.* 276e3, *Rep.* 2.359d6, 2.376d9, 2.378e3, 2.379a2, 2.380c2, 3.392b5, 3.415a3, 6.501e3, 9.588c2; cf. Isoc. *Ad Nicoclem* 49, *Archidamus* 24, *Euag.* 36, Xen. *Symp.* 8.28. For Socrates specifically described with the verb μυθολογεῖν, see Pl. *Grg.* 493d3, *Phd.* 61e2, *Rep.* 2.376d9, 3.415a3, 6.501e3 (for further discussion,

women's speech) prepares us for the fact that the "noble lie" in the *Republic*, too, is a gendered act of story-making: it fosters the right kind of gender roles in order to encourage unity in the state (415d1–2). The myth which Socrates constructs is told to make "the citizens like brothers" (414e4–5: note the grammatically and semantically masculine "brothers").[35] Conversely, the state is feminized (playing off the feminine noun *polis*) and made into a passive "mother and nurse" (414e3) of the citizen-brothers who are called to defend her, and to see each other "like brothers and children of the earth" (414e6).[36] Plato's Socrates demonstrates in practice the search for a vocabulary—"what words I'll use" (414d1–2)—to describe this new kind of censored storytelling, this new kind of originary mythmaking, this new kind of gendered poetry. And in so doing, the old poets are displaced: stripped of their title altogether, they are lumped together with other "craftsmen" (*dēmiourgoi*) and are relegated, along with farmers, to the bottom rung of society.[37]

This struggle for words structures Plato's response to the poets, their gendered identity, and their role in gender creation. It is not a confusion or a lack of precision (as Paul Vicaire has argued) which causes this linguistic aporia, but rather an awareness of the need for a new word, and a new definition, of the male poet, when poetry is charged with conveying a new vision of gender.[38] So what exactly is Plato's gender vision in relation to poetry?

There are several aspects to gender and the poets in Plato—and the first is the banning of female characters and voices from poetry. If the imitation of women was essential for Aristophanes's male poet to depict female characters and subsume the role of female poets, so that he could emerge as a true "man-

---

see chapter 5, n. 94); cf. Xen. *Symp.* 8.28. For μυθολόγος, see *Rep.* 3.392d2, 3.398a–b, *Leg.* 664d3, 941b5; see further pp. 144–45.

35. ὑπὲρ τῶν ἄλλων πολιτῶν ὡς ἀδελφῶν ὄντων καὶ γηγενῶν διανοεῖσθαι (to care about the other citizens as though they were brothers and born from the earth), *Rep.* 3.414e4–5. On the aspect of brotherhood here, see Hahm 1969.

36. For the autochthonic myth, see Loraux 1993: 37–71.

37. σίδηρον δὲ καὶ χαλκὸν τοῖς τε γεωργοῖς καὶ τοῖς ἄλλοις δημιουργοῖς ([The god put] iron and bronze in the farmers and the other craftsmen), *Rep.* 3.415a6–7. For the poet as δημιουργός in Plato, see *Ap.* 22d5–6, 23e5, *Symp.* 205c2, 209a4–5, *Rep.* 10.596d3–4; see Stern-Gillet 2004: 176. Cf., for the poet as δημιουργός in Homer, chapter 1, n. 6, and see also chapter 3, n. 34.

38. Vicaire 1964: 77.

poet," Plato takes the opposite approach. All imitation or "representation" of women by men in the state is to be forbidden, in order to encourage the "men" to become "good" (*andras agathous*) (3.395d–e):[39]

> "So we will not allow," I said, "those who we say are in our charge (and who must become good men themselves) to imitate a woman, since they're men—whether a young woman or an old one, or a woman who rails at [*loidoroumenēn*] her husband, or quarrels with the gods and boasts because she thinks she's happy, or has misfortune, grief, and laments; and we'll certainly keep far from a woman who is sick, or in love, or in labor."

Female characters are thus to be removed from literature. Men and male poets are not allowed figuratively to imitate women and their voices; the physical imitation of women by men on the stage in drama is similarly forbidden.[40] All the different aspects of a woman's experience are summarily dismissed (childbirth; love; illness; relationships with men and the gods; even emotions, from happiness to grief). Women's discourse, women's voices, are pinpointed in particular.[41] A major problem is the imitation of a woman's voice, whether she is "railing at" (*loidoroumenēn*) her husband, "boasting," "lamenting," or even in the throes of sex or childbirth. Lament, as we have seen, was a key female speech genre.[42] But there are hints of other female discourses here: the verb *loidoreisthai*, "to rail at," is reminiscent of Dionysus's gendered rebuke of the two *andres poiētai* in Aristophanes's *Frogs* not to "rail at [*loidoreisthai*] each other like baker-women," suggesting a woman's unprofessional, unmasculine, lowly discourse.[43] Meanwhile, the mention of a woman sick, in love, or in labor conjures a sound landscape of nonverbal screams of passion in sex or pain in labor, circumscribing even the sounds that women make, and setting limits on women's dangerous fertility and creativity in connection to their

---

39. οὐ δὴ ἐπιτρέψομεν, ἦν δ᾽ ἐγώ, ὧν φαμὲν κήδεσθαι καὶ δεῖν αὐτοὺς ἄνδρας ἀγαθοὺς γενέσθαι, γυναῖκα μιμεῖσθαι ἄνδρας ὄντας, ἢ νέαν ἢ πρεσβυτέραν, ἢ ἀνδρὶ λοιδορουμένην ἢ πρὸς θεοὺς ἐρίζουσάν τε καὶ μεγαλαυχουμένην, οἰομένην εὐδαίμονα εἶναι, ἢ ἐν συμφοραῖς τε καὶ πένθεσιν καὶ θρήνοις ἐχομένην· κάμνουσαν δὲ ἢ ἐρῶσαν ἢ ὠδίνουσαν, πολλοῦ καὶ δεήσομεν, *Rep.* 3.395d5–e2.

40. See Murray 2011, also G. R. F. Ferrari 1989: 115–16.

41. On differences between male and female discourse in Plato, see introduction, n. 63.

42. See pp. 36–40 with chapter 1, n. 43; on women's lament in the *Republic* in particular, see Murray 2011, and cf. *Rep.* 3.387e–388a.

43. *Ran.* 857–58, see pp. 114–16.

voice.[44] In the circumscription of the right kind of male-voiced poetry, all women's voices appear to be silenced.

Yet it is worth noting that, although Plato defines the subjects of his decree against the imitation of women specifically as men ("since they're men," *andras ontas*, 395d7), he later dictates—in an apparently radical move—that women and men alike are capable of undertaking the same roles in governing the state.[45] And it follows, Socrates argues, if that is the case, that the female guardians should receive the same education as the men (5.451d–452a, 456b–c): "If we use men and women for the same jobs, then they should be taught the same things" (5.451e5–6), in particular, the same training in *mousikē*—that is, music, song, and poetry (5.452a2). In the male-gendering of the subjects of poetry and the removal of imitations of women, then, not only are all female influences to be removed from the men; all female role models are to be taken away from the female guardians, too.[46] The apparent revolution which Plato proposes, that women should be capable of holding the same offices as men and thus of receiving the same education (5.455d–e), is arguably undercut by the fact that the training which the female guardians are to receive is the educational program of the male guardians, outlined in books 2 and 3—which had the stated aim of producing "good *men*" (*andras agathous*, 3.395d6).[47] In aid of this ambition, any traces of female voices, experiences, and literary representations are thus to be removed from their education. Rather than turning the female guardians into "gender-neutral" bodies, then, as Stephen Halliwell argues, it is more a case—as Penelope Murray puts forth—"that what is required of the female guardians is that they should simply turn themselves into

44. See further pp. 156–61.

45. Interpretations of Plato's attitude to women in the *Republic* vary, from Plato as the first feminist (Canto 1985, Vlastos 1989), to a more complex/moderated approach (Calvert 1975, Pomeroy 1975, Allen 1975, Hobbs 2000: 245–48, Brisson 2012), to Plato as antifeminist or largely exclusionary of women (Annas 1976, Buchan 1999, Murray 2011). For a comprehensive overview, see Tuana 1994 and, for bibliography on the question of Plato's feminism, Zoller 2021: 57–58; see also, for a general introduction, Halliwell 1993: 9–16, 138–69, Buchan 1999: 28–31.

46. Hobbs 2000: 245–48, Murray 2011: 188. Hobbs 2000: 248 n. 80 notes that the only positive female role model recommended for emulation is Alcestis (*Symp.* 179b–c), though Alcestis's praise is given in the mouth of Phaedrus and is thus arguably a rhetorical cliché.

47. Hobbs 2000: 247 n. 79 notes that Socrates makes it clear in book 5 (451c, 456a) that his discussion of the education of the guardians in books 2 and 3 was aimed at male guardians only. See Halliwell 1993 ad 452a2, Murray 2011: 179 on the educational program here as a reference to that already outlined for the (male) guardians in books 2 and 3 of the *Republic* (2.376e–3.412a).

men, since the paradigm of human nature that Plato is dealing with is a masculine one."[48] Both men and women who are educated in the state are supposed, by virtue of the male-voiced poetry and masculine paradigms they are given, to learn how to become the right kinds of *men*.

So female characters are removed from poetry, and the women who are educated receive only masculine paradigms to become like men. But Plato's banishment of imitations of women goes one step further—abolishing not only female characters composed in the male voice, and male actors who imitate women in drama, but also, it appears, female *poets*. The reference to "a woman who is sick, or in love" (3.395e3) evokes, on one level, the well-known female characters from tragedy who suffer the pangs of doomed love, like Euripides's Medea or Phaedra. But it also, perhaps, reminds us of Sappho fr. 31 L-P, where the physicality of the suffering of a woman in love ("my ears thrum, sweat pours off me, and trembling seizes my whole body," 11–14) connects female passion and physical illness.[49] And this link between Sappho and the passion of love is, in fact, made directly elsewhere in Plato's dialogues, in the only passage where Sappho is mentioned by name, at the beginning of the *Phaedrus*.[50] In response to Phaedrus's quotation of the orator Lysias's speech on the *mania* of love, Socrates professes that "the wise men and women [*sophoi andres te kai gunaikes*] of old" (*Phdr.* 235b7) have written better on such matters, and cites "the beautiful [*kalēs*] Sappho, or the wise [*sophou*] Anacreon, or even some of the prose-writers [*sungrapheōn*]" (235c3–4) as the best examples of love's *mania*.[51] While Lysias (and authors in general) are called *poiētai* throughout the *Phaedrus*, in the ensuing discussion of the connection between madness, inspiration, love, and poetry, Sappho never receives such a term.[52] Instead, she acquires the feminine adjective *kalē*, "beautiful," tying her

48. Murray 2011: 176, with Halliwell 1993: 15; cf. Saxonhouse 1994: 68–76, Hobbs 2000: 248, though note Hobbs 2000: 246 with n. 76, where she seems to argue for a gender-neutral view.

49. ἐπιρρόμ- / βεισι δ᾽ ἄκουαι, / κὰδ δέ μ᾽ ἴδρως κακχέεται, τρόμος δὲ / παῖσαν ἄγρει, Sappho fr. 31.11–14 L-P; I cite Campbell's (1982) text here.

50. The only other potential mention of Sappho is a spurious epigram ascribed to Plato, *Anth. Pal.* 9.506, on which see p. 208.

51. παλαιοὶ γὰρ καὶ σοφοὶ ἄνδρες τε καὶ γυναῖκες περὶ αὐτῶν εἰρηκότες καὶ γεγραφότες, *Phdr.* 235b7–8; ἤ που Σαπφοῦς τῆς καλῆς ἢ Ἀνακρέοντος τοῦ σοφοῦ ἢ καὶ συγγραφέων τινῶν, 235c3–4. On Sapphic references in the *Phaedrus*, see Pender 2007, and on this passage in particular, Pender 2007: 8–14, Coo 2021: 266–69.

52. At *Phdr.* 234e5 ποιητής is used in a general sense of the "author" of a λόγος, but occurs in the context of Phaedrus's praise of Lysias; Yunis 2011 ad loc. suggests that this is a dig at

to norms of female beauty and reducing her status as a writer to an object of the male gaze, as well as—in contrast to Anacreon, who is called "wise"—excluding her from the company of the "wise critics" whom Socrates purports to cite.[53] What it seems to suggest is that, when Sappho joins in—when men *and women* poets are quoted—Plato refuses to use a word to differentiate the woman poet or to describe the qualities of female, as opposed to male, poetry, which might endow them with a kind of power or recognition. Instead of granting Sappho a term recognizing her as a poet—"male and female poets"—Socrates instead uses a periphrasis—"the wise men and women of old who spoke and wrote" (235b7–8). The denial of a feminine term to Sappho is made apparent by contrasting a passage in the *Meno* where Socrates uses a similar phrase: "I have heard from wise men and women [*andrōn te kai gunaikōn sophōn*] on divine affairs" (*Meno* 81a5–6).[54] When Meno presses him for the identity of these "men and women," Socrates reveals them with their gendered professional titles: "The speakers were priests [*hiereōn*] and priestesses [*hiereiōn*]" (81a10), he says, using the masculine and feminine versions of the same professional term.[55] Sappho receives no such courtesy. The struggle for words to define a woman poet, in a world where women poets were not the norm, means that the term *poiētēs* is denied her. And this act of taking away the term for *poiētēs*, I suggest, becomes a removal of power from the female poet. This ties into the undercurrent of irony to Socrates's apparent praise of the lyric love poets in the passage from the *Phaedrus*: as Elizabeth Pender points out, "Socrates' actual point is that the irrational desire graphically presented by the poets provides far stronger arguments *against* love even than those of Lysias."[56] But his denial of a poet-term to Sappho and ironic undermining of her authority is also part of a much more powerful appropriation and subsuming of her voice and identity into his own. His description of the effects of love

---

Lysias's artistic pretensions, although there are contemporary parallels in the orators of ποιητής being used to praise good style in oratory (not just poetry): see Isoc. *Euag.* 8, *Antid.* 192, Alcidamas *Soph.* 34, and cf. Dion. Hal. *Lys.* 3.38, *Dem.* 51.18. ποιητής occurs elsewhere in the *Phaedrus* at 234e5, 236d5, 245a7, 247c4, 258b3, 258d10, 278e1.

53. Pace Yunis 2011 ad 235c3, Coo 2021: 269. On the appropriation of the female (including Sappho) in the *Phaedrus*, see duBois 1988: 170–78.

54. ἀκήκοα γὰρ ἀνδρῶν τε καὶ γυναικῶν σοφῶν περὶ τὰ θεῖα πράγματα, *Meno* 81a5–6.

55. οἱ μὲν λέγοντές εἰσι τῶν ἱερέων τε καὶ τῶν ἱερειῶν, *Meno* 81a10.

56. Pender 2007: 10, original emphasis; cf. Rowe 1986 ad loc.

at *Phdr.* 251a–b—shuddering, sweating, heat, the power of the gaze—is an unmistakable ventriloquization of the trembling, sweat, fire beneath the flesh, and agonizing gaze of Sappho fr. 31 L-P.[57] But, yet again, Sappho goes unacknowledged—here not just denied a poet-term, but not even mentioned by name.

So poets like Sappho are renowned for their depictions of the dangerous *mania* of love, which is precisely the kind of imitation which is to be banished from the *Republic* (the "woman in love" of *Rep.* 3.395e3). Socrates's solution in the *Phaedrus* is not simply to ignore these kinds of women's imitations, but to engage in a totalizing erasure of the woman poet: by denying her a poet-term; by reducing her to a beautiful body, an object of the male gaze; and ultimately by ventriloquizing her voice into his own. Sappho's treatment in the *Phaedrus* thus forecasts the banishment of female voices and female poets in the *Republic,* and points out the most conspicuous banishment of female poets of all: that while Sappho may be mentioned in the *Phaedrus* only to be deprived of a poet-term, reduced to a "beautiful" body over a voice, and finally ventriloquized by the male, women poets and women's voices are so diminished in the *Republic* as not even to warrant a mention. The sweeping banishment of all imitations of women covers both female characters and, inevitably, given the focus of their subject matter and their use of the female voice, female poets, too—but female poets have already been excluded so effectively that they are not even spoken of, let alone given a poet-term. This kind of resonant absence of a word for a woman poet demonstrates as much as the proliferation of poet-terms for men does in the rest of the *Republic*: women's voices, and women poets, seem not to be given any space in the world of the *Republic.*

Even if women are not to be poets, and they are not to be imitated in literature, there is some discussion of the correct kind of women's discourse in relation to poetry. This is in women's informal discourse, in their roles as nurses and mothers, and the kinds of stories they tell their children.[58] In book 2, Socrates is launching into the discussion of the necessity of determining the (male) guardians' education (leading up to the pronouncements against the poets' depictions of gods, heroes, and men that includes Achilles), and argues that it is important to censor the kinds of tales told by "story-makers" (*mythopoiois*),

57. duBois 1988: 177, Coo 2021: 268.
58. See Calvert 1975: 233, Murray 2011: 177.

in order that the young guardians are only taught "what is good" (2.377c).[59] "Nurses and mothers" are then to be forced, he pronounces, to tell these censored stories to their children (2.377c3–4).[60]

Two features stand out here. The first is the marked creation of new poet-vocabulary to describe this gendered mechanism of poetic dissemination through women. The use of *mythopoios* here at 2.377c1 is the only occurrence of the term in all of Plato—and, more than that, it is the earliest instance of the word in extant Greek literature.[61] This unusual term, with the *mythos* prefix looking ahead to the kinds of *mythoi* which Plato will admit in his state (like the noble lie, called a *mythos* at 3.415a2), and the *-poios* suffix looking back to the old kinds of *poiētai*, works as an ideal catch-all to describe both the kinds of tales that will be allowed, and the kinds that will not.[62] Its uniqueness marks this out as a loaded moment of word creation and definition, particularly in juxtaposition with the gendered censorship of women's stories—it is nurses and mothers, in particular, who are to be charged with passing on these kinds of tales. This highlights the second feature of the passage, which is the ambivalence—just like the term *mythopoios*—of the attitude toward women's voices. On the one hand, they are to be given an important role in the early poetic education of the guardians of the state; we might even go so far as to say that they are being assimilated into the roles of *mythopoioi*, "storytellers," themselves, as those who are "telling stories" (*legein . . . tois mythois*, 2.377c4–5) to the future guardians, and thus receiving a verbal analogy for poet-vocabulary.[63] On the other hand, the circumscription of even women's private songs to their children—we might imagine lullabies and bedtime stories being included in this category—and their replacement with the kinds of stories which are judged right by the male

---

59. πρῶτον δὴ ἡμῖν, ὡς ἔοικεν, ἐπιστατητέον τοῖς μυθοποιοῖς (We must first, then, it seems, censor the story-makers), *Rep.* 2.377c1.

60. τοὺς δ᾽ ἐγκριθέντας πείσομεν τὰς τροφούς τε καὶ μητέρας λέγειν τοῖς παισίν (And we will make the nurses and mothers tell their children the stories that have been approved), *Rep.* 2.377c3–4. Cf. *Prt.* 325c–d, *Leg.* 887d.

61. Bloom 1991: 449 n. 37 notes ποιεῖν at 2.377c2, but not μυθοποιός; the term does not occur again in the classical period, and does not become established until the imperial period.

62. For μῦθος, see, e.g., *Rep.* 2.376d9, 377b5, 377c5, 3.415a2, 415c7: see chapter 5, n. 84, and cf. the use of μυθολόγος/μυθολογεῖν (see chapter 5, n. 34).

63. On μυθολογεῖν, see chapter 5, n. 34.

leaders seems to be a negative infringement on any freedom of female speech, specifically in connection to poetry.[64]

If the speech of women in their roles as mothers and nurses is circumscribed, so too is that of older women. Denigrating the negative treatment of the gods in Homer—which is to be censored—Socrates proclaims that only stories encouraging pious and peaceful behavior between citizens should be allowed, and that "such stories should, preferably, be told straight away to children by old men and women, and—for when they get older—poets [*poiētas*] too should be forced to make stories [*logopoiein*] like these ones" (2.378c8–d2).[65] Again, we have a stipulation of the proper kind of woman's speech (here conjoined with men), and again, it is combined with an exploration of poetic vocabulary. On the one hand, old women and men should tell their stories when children are young; when the children are older, they will be passed into the hands of the *poiētai* who must "make stories" (*logopoiein*) in the way the state prescribes. Yet again, women's (as well as men's) colloquial and informal speech is ring-fenced into a new monogendered speech that is aimed at creating the generic masculinized citizen (*politēs*, 2.378c7).[66] And again, the prescription is accompanied by an exploration of a new kind of poetic vocabulary, with the verb *logopoiein*. This verb is made up of *logos*, "word" or "story," and *poiein*, "to make" and, as we have seen, "to make poetry." While its cognate noun *logopoios* was commonly used to mean "prose-writer," and we find the verb in Plato's *Euthydemus* in the sense of "writing speeches," *logopoiein* seems to be used before Plato's time and by his contemporaries mostly to denote negative and untruthful tale-telling (rather than prose writing specifically).[67] Isocrates uses it to denigrate the made-up stories about the

---

64. On the lullaby as women's monodic poetry, see Colesanti 2014: 102–6; on women's tale-telling in general (with reference to Plato), see Buxton 1994: 18–21.

65. τοιαῦτα μᾶλλον λεκτέα πρὸς τὰ παιδία εὐθὺς καὶ γέρουσι καὶ γραυσί, καὶ πρεσβυτέροις γιγνομένοις καὶ τοὺς ποιητὰς ἐγγὺς τούτων ἀναγκαστέον λογοποιεῖν, *Rep.* 2.378c8–d2.

66. The aim of the stories is to persuade the citizens that "no [male] citizen ever fell out with another" (οὐδεὶς πώποτε πολίτης ἕτερος ἑτέρῳ ἀπήχθετο), *Rep.* 2.378c6–7.

67. λογοποιός occurs four times in Herodotus, once of Aesop (2.134.15, probably in the sense "fable-teller" rather than "prose-writer") and three times of Hecataeus (2.143.1, 5.36.2, 5.125.1); see chapter 7, nn. 13 and 22. Isoc. *Bus.* 37 has the plural in the sense "chroniclers." At Pl. *Euthyd.* 289d2, 289d9, 289e2 we have λογοποιοί as "speech-writers," with the verb λογοποιεῖν as specifically "writing speeches" versus delivering them (289d5, 289d9); for λογοποιός at *Rep.* 3.392a12, see pp. 141–44 with chapter 5, n. 79, and see Vicaire 1964: 77.

gods—exactly the kinds of tales which Plato is trying to proscribe here. Thucydides had used it of untrue tale-telling specifically by men (*andres*), and Andocides follows suit. Even Plato himself uses *logopoiein* in the *Laws* to describe the (negative) invention of the myth of Ganymede.[68] Yet here in the *Republic* (and, like *mythopoios*, this is the only time it appears in the *Republic*), the verb is used specifically of the type of poetry that will *not* tell these kinds of outrageous stories about the gods.

There seems to be a deliberate dissonance again here, then, occasioned—I would suggest—by the intrusion of women into the picture and the struggle to come up with a vocabulary for this new vision of gendered poetry. *Mythopoios* was used above to describe both the old kind of poets whose stories will be censored, and the new appropriate kinds of storytellers (among whom the "nurses and mothers" may, or may not, belong). Now, as we return to the proscription of women's speech with the tales told by old women and men, we have a shift in vocabulary to *poiētai* who *logopoiein*. The use of *logopoios* to mean "prose-writer" suggests the paradoxical translation "poets who write prose"; the typical negative associations of *logopoiein* to refer to untrue or undesirable stories about the gods are turned around to mean the opposite, the creation of new positive stories about gods and men by the new *poiētai*. A word for prose is used for poetry; a term for negative fanciful compositions is used for the strictly factual compositions of the new state. Most importantly of all, the contrast between old women and men's tale-telling to the young and the storytelling of the *poiētai* when they grow up sets women in opposition to the activities of the male *poiētēs*—however this is envisioned, and whatever words are used to try to describe his new role. As Plato struggles for words to describe the new male poet, one thing is clear: not only is women's discourse in poetry circumscribed, women's informal discourses are also vetted to be brought into line with the right kind of masculinized poetry. Women's poetry is banned, and women's songs are turned into men's poetry.

The precise danger of what happens when women are allowed free speech—and access to poetic idioms—is demonstrated in book 8 of the *Republic*. Socrates is engaged in outlining how different types of constitutions degenerate, and—having given a description of the timocratic man at 8.548d–549c—he moves on to give an example of how such a young man (and such a state) might go into decline.[69] His mother would start to complain about her

---

68. Isoc. *Bus.* 38, Thuc. 6.38.2, Andoc. *De myst.* 54, *De pace* 35, Pl. *Leg.* 636d1.
69. See Hobbs 2000: 27–31, Murray 2011: 191.

husband (anēr), the young man's father: she would say that she is slighted among other women, and that her husband is "unmanly" (anandros, 8.549d6)—"all the kinds of things," Socrates says, "that women love to harp on about [hymnein] with regards to men like this" (8.549d7–8).[70] It is the mother's specifically gendered discourse as a woman and her concern with gender (her reputation in women's speech; her accusation of her husband's lack of masculinity) which appears to set things wrong. Moreover, her speech is described with a markedly poetic word, hymnein—"to sing a hymn"—which links her dangerous woman's speech directly to the poets who compose hymns. We might remember that "hymns" are to be admitted as one of the only two types of poetry (along with "eulogies of good men") in the ideal state (10.607a)—and perhaps this is precisely the danger here: when the woman (and mother) is allowed to talk freely, without the prescription of the censored tales of the mythopoioi which Plato had outlined in book 2, deeply intertwined problems of gender, politics, and poetics arise.[71] Her gendered speech and claims about gender lead men astray; her aspiration to speech both connects her to the dangerous imitation of the poets and shows how she aims to turn her colloquial discourse into a genre which should be reserved only for the best kind of (male) poetry in the state. Women's attempts at poetry, in other words, gender embedded as they are, can destroy men, and take down cities with them.

So female voices—whether characters or poets—are banned; women's colloquial discourse is circumscribed into the poetry of men; and even male poets' output is gender constrained. They are not to imitate women, as we saw above at 3.395d–e, but are instead to focus on examples of good men, so that male and female guardians alike may be educated in the right kind of masculine paradigms. In this world, the new gender-censored poet has a central role in displaying correct examples of "the good man" (epieikēs anēr, 3.387d5). This poet is no longer like the poets of old, like Homer, who is commonly called "the poiētēs" throughout Plato and who has been criticized in book 3 for supplying negative examples of manliness (andreia).[72] In accordance with this

---

70. καὶ ἄλλα δὴ ὅσα καὶ οἷα φιλοῦσιν αἱ γυναῖκες περὶ τῶν τοιούτων ὑμνεῖν, Rep. 8.549d7–8.

71. Ford 2002: 259 notes the terminological innovation at 10.607a, with ὕμνος used for the first time "in the specific sense of 'song for a god,'" making this a marked vocabulary.

72. See p. 218 with chapter 7, n. 94 for specific examples of Homer as ὁ ποιητής in Plato.

new role, Plato needs to find a new vocabulary to describe the gender-censored male poet who imitates good men for the proper education of the state, in opposition to the masculinity represented by the old *poiētēs* like Homer. Immediately following the passage ordering the silencing of women's voices in imitation (that is, poetry), we seem to have a definition of this new kind of male poet (3.396b–c):[73]

> "There is some kind of speech [*lexeōs*] and narrative, which the man who is really good and true [*kalos kagathos*] would use in his narrative whenever he had to say something, and another different kind, which the man who had been born and brought up in the opposite way would always use to tell a narrative."
>
> "What kinds are these?" he asked.
>
> "In my opinion, when a measured man [*metrios anēr*] comes in his narrative to some speech or deed of a good man [*andros agathou*], he will want to relate it as if he himself is that man, and he won't be ashamed at this kind of imitation [*mimēsei*]."

The term for poet, *poiētēs*—which only a few sections ago had been used of Homer—is elided here.[74] But this is not, as with female poets, a complete removal of the poet, but an act of renaming, as the first part of Socrates's speech makes clear: he is addressing *lexis* or "word choice," not only *by* the poet, but *for* the poet, too. This act of renaming turns the poet from the *poiētēs* into a new phrase: a "measured man," a *metrios anēr*.[75] Not only does this explicitly emphasize the male gender of the poet which was implicit in the masculine *poiētēs*, underscoring the gendered project of poetry for Plato, and bringing to its logical conclusion the tradition of placing *anēr* in apposition with a poet-term from Homer to Aristophanes: now the masculinity of the term has reached out and subsumed the entire identity of the poet, becoming his main defining feature. The phrase also contains a neat pun which underlines exactly the kind of renaming which is going on, and the reclaiming

---

73. ἔστιν τι εἶδος λέξεώς τε καὶ διηγήσεως ἐν ᾧ ἂν διηγοῖτο ὁ τῷ ὄντι καλὸς κἀγαθός, ὁπότε τι δέοι αὐτὸν λέγειν, καὶ ἕτερον αὖ ἀνόμοιον τούτῳ εἶδος, οὗ ἂν ἔχοιτο ἀεὶ καὶ ἐν ᾧ διηγοῖτο ὁ ἐναντίως ἐκείνῳ φύς τε καὶ τραφείς. ποῖα δή, ἔφη, ταῦτα; ὁ μέν μοι δοκεῖ, ἦν δ᾿ ἐγώ, μέτριος ἀνήρ, ἐπειδὰν ἀφίκηται ἐν τῇ διηγήσει ἐπὶ λέξιν τινὰ ἢ πρᾶξιν ἀνδρὸς ἀγαθοῦ, ἐθελήσειν ὡς αὐτὸς ὢν ἐκεῖνος ἀπαγγέλλειν καὶ οὐκ αἰσχυνεῖσθαι ἐπὶ τῇ τοιαύτῃ μιμήσει, *Rep.* 3.396b9–c9.

74. *Rep.* 3.394b5; see also 3.394c2 and 394d2 on poets in general.

75. See Blankenship 1996: 72–73, Murray 2011: 188.

of the role of the old (negatively male) poet into Plato's new masculine world. *Metrios* means "measured, reasonable" in a philosophical sense, and ties into notions of self-control which Plato's Socrates advocates throughout the dialogues—including in the *Republic* as a crucial component of the guardians' education.[76] But it derives from *metron*, "measure"—a word commonly used in Plato (and elsewhere) for the meter of poetry, and in the plural even for poetry itself.[77] So Plato's new poet is a "man who speaks in meter" (a wordy periphrasis for "poet"); but he is also a "measured man," a man who has the philosopher's self-control and thus ties in with the ideals of the good man he celebrates in poetry. This interconnection between the poet as man and his "goodness," on the one hand, and the good man he tells of in his narrative, is underscored by the repetition of the noun *anēr* for both the poet and his subject. The *metrios anēr* (measured/good man) tells of the deeds of an *anēr agathos* (good man, 396c7–8). And the aim of this poetry? We have already seen it in the preceding section: to produce good men (*andres agathoi*, 395d6). The discourse of the old male *poiētēs* and the negative examples of masculinity he represents is thus removed and replaced with a new vocabulary for moderate, virtuous men relaying positive examples of manhood to each other.

This rejection of the term *poiētēs* builds on an earlier passage, at the beginning of the discussion about the appropriate tales to be told "about humans" (3.392a9) as opposed to gods and heroes. The old kinds of "poets [*poiētai*] and word-makers [*logopoioi*]" (392a12), Socrates says, composed their poems incorrectly by imparting false moral lessons.[78] (These are the same kinds of examples of emotional weakness, injustice, and cowardice of which Plato's Socrates has recently accused Homer's Achilles.) *Logopoios* is often translated as "prose-writer" here, but—as we saw above with *logopoiein* at 2.378d2—this translation does not fully do justice to either the etymology or the usage of

---

76. On self-control (σωφροσύνη), see *Rep.* 4.430e–431b. For the connection between being μέτριος and self-controlled (σώφρων), see North 1966: 9, 15 n. 54; see also Blondell 2002: 188 n. 81, Wilberding 2012: 140.

77. As "meter": *Soph.* 237a7, *Symp.* 205c6, *Phdr.* 258d10–11, 267a5, 277e7, *Grg.* 502c6, *Leg.* 809b6, 810b5, 810e8, 858d1, 886c1, *Rep.* 2.380c2, 3.393d7, 10.607d5, 10.607d8. In plural as "poetry": *Lysis* 205a9. See Chantraine s.v.

78. καὶ ποιηταὶ καὶ λογοποιοὶ κακῶς λέγουσιν περὶ ἀνθρώπων τὰ μέγιστα (Both poets and word-makers speak wrongly about people in the most important matters), *Rep.* 3.392a12–b1.

the word, constructed from *logos*, "word," and the *-poios* suffix, "maker."[79]
While it is possible, then, to take the terms *poiētai* and *logopoioi* as separate
(even opposite) categories—"poets and prose-writers"—the range and flex-
ibility of *logopoios* also allows for a reading that links the two words: "poets,
that is to say, word-makers."[80] Indeed, the presence of *-poios* in close conjunc-
tion with *poiētai* serves to bind these two terms together and to underline the
precise danger of word-making, whether in poetry or prose: "doing words"
encourages men to "do" the right or wrong kinds of things in the state. We see
this connection made explicit later in book 10: "Just as when, in a state [*polei*],
a man makes [*poiōn*] bad men powerful and gives them the state [*polin*], he
destroys the better men; shall we say that the imitative poet [*poiētēs*], too,
makes [*empoiein*] a bad constitution [*politeian*] in the soul of each individual
man?" (10.605b).[81] Plato's Socrates returns to the initial impetus for the de-
scription of the ideal republic, the comparison between virtue in the soul and
the well-run state. The comparison between the poor ruler "making" (*poiein*)
the bad *polis* and the worst kind of *poiētēs* "making" (*empoiein*) the bad con-
stitution (*politeia*) is forged through the punning, alliterative similarity be-
tween *poiētēs* and *politeia*, and the creative power of the verb *poiein*.[82] The
poet is a "maker" of the wrong kind of men; this "making" of bad men encour-
ages them, in turn, to "make" bad states. The making of the soul is not just *like*
the making of a state; it *causes* it.

So back in book 3 at 392a–b, it is precisely the "doing" of the *poiētēs* and his
status as a "maker of words" that is at stake and needs to be refuted. Just as
with the *metrios anēr* of 3.396c, Plato follows his denigration of the *poiētai* and
logopoioi with a new vocabulary for the new kind of poetry. "We will forbid
them to say such things," Socrates says (referring to the immoral lessons es-
poused by the old kinds of *poiētai*), "but instead we will command them to

79. For the translation of λογοποιοί as "prose-writers," see Shorey 1930, Bloom 1991, Ford
2002: 215 n. 19, Emlyn-Jones and Preddy 2013 ad loc.; see, by contrast, Vicaire 1964: 61, who
translates "conteurs." Note that this is the only time that the noun occurs in the *Republic*: for
λογοποιός and λογοποιεῖν elsewhere, see chapter 5, nn. 67 and 68, and for λογοποιεῖν at *Rep.*
2.378d2, see pp. 137–38.

80. In this sense the καὶ would be epexetic.

81. ὥσπερ ἐν πόλει ὅταν τις μοχθηροὺς ἐγκρατεῖς ποιῶν παραδιδῷ τὴν πόλιν, τοὺς δὲ
χαριεστέρους φθείρῃ· ταὐτὸν καὶ τὸν μιμητικὸν ποιητὴν φήσομεν κακὴν πολιτείαν ἰδίᾳ
ἑκάστου τῇ ψυχῇ ἐμποιεῖν, *Rep.* 10.605b3–7.

82. Cf. pp. 116–21 on Aristophanes, and esp. Ar. *Ach.* 641–42.

sing [*aidein*] and story-tell [*mythologein*] exactly the opposite" (3.392b4–5).[83] Now, instead of the pun for "poet-man" presented by *metrios anēr*, we have two verbs replacing the nouns *poiētai kai logopoioi*: *aidein*, the verb from which the archaic term for the bard, *aoidos*, derives; and *mythologein*. It is as if the old *poiētēs* is being replaced by the verbal form *aidein* in Plato's new prescription, and *logopoios* by the verb *mythologein*. There is both irony and subtlety here. The move from nouns to verbs demonstrates the move to a new kind, almost a new class of vocabulary. The transition from *logopoios* (word-maker) to *mythologein* (story-tell) is particularly subtle. Both include forms derived from *legein* (to speak)—but the new kind of *mythologein* dispenses with the old *-poios* suffix, emphasizing the movement away from the old kind of *poiētēs* and his vocabulary, and replaces *logos* with another word for "word," *mythos*.[84] *Mythologein*, meanwhile, anticipates Socrates's use of the very same verb later in the book, when he describes his own act of storytelling (the relation of the "noble lie") as *mythologountes* (3.415a3)—suggesting that *mythologein* might be the right word for the new kind of virtuous philosophical tale-telling.[85] The spanner in the works to this simple story, and the source of irony, however, lies in the other displacement, from *poiētēs* to *aidein*. The derivation of *aoidos* from *aidein* means that this movement from *poiētēs* to *aoidos* seems not only to move back in time to the bards of old, but also ironically to look to exactly the word which Homer (the example par excellence of the wrong kind of poet) had used for the male bard. It is as if, in conjoining these two terms and setting them against two others, Plato is creating a commentary on the difficulty of coming up with new words to describe this new kind of poetry. As we have seen in the prelude to Socrates's attempt at the right kind of poetry, the noble lie, where he articulated the difficulty of finding "what words I'll use" (3.414d1–2), this is as much about the search for words to define and enshrine this complex new vision of the poet's gendered role as it is about landing on any one term.

83. καὶ τὰ μὲν τοιαῦτα ἀπερεῖν λέγειν, τὰ δ᾽ ἐναντία τούτων προστάξειν ᾁδειν τε καὶ μυθολογεῖν, *Rep.* 3.392b4–5.

84. The μῦθος/λόγος opposition is a central one: see esp. Lincoln 1997; also Nestle 1940, Martin 1989: 12, Buxton 2001: 1–24, Calame 2001, Most 2001, R. L. Fowler 2011. On μῦθος and λόγος in Plato, see Naddaf 1998: x–xi, Halliwell 2000, and see also Halliwell 2002: 49–50, Schofield 2007: 143 for the relationship between μῦθος and ψεῦδος, or fiction and lies (on which see further pp. 129–30 with chapter 5, n. 31). On the definition of μῦθος in Plato, see Brisson 1998, Murray 1999; on Plato's myths generally, see Frutiger 1930, Elias 1984: 119–238, Morgan 2000: 132–289, Partenie 2009, and Collobert, Destrée, and Gonzalez 2012.

85. See p. 129 with chapter 5, n. 34.

Rather than indicating a confusion or imprecision on Plato's part, then, this has more to do with illustrating the (often messy) process of working out a new vocabulary: it is a metacommentary on the slipperiness of words and the importance of coming up with a right, and true, definition.

But this is not the end of Plato's search for a new term for the male poet and his censored gendered storytelling. A little later, just two sections after the description of the *metrios anēr*, Socrates contrasts the sort of "man" (*andra*, 3.398a1) who is able to imitate everything indiscriminately and who would not be allowed in the ideal republic, with the kind of "more austere and less pleasing poet [*poiētēs*] and storyteller [*mythologos*]" whom they would admit, who "would imitate the speech [*lexin*] of a good man" (3.398a–b).[86] Now it is the *anēr*, deprived of a poet-term, who is the imitator of bad examples like the old *poiētai*; and a new kind of *poiētēs* and *mythologos* who is the upholder of the right kind of imitation to mimic and create good men. The tables seem, once again, to be turned on the vocabulary which Socrates had defined at 3.392a–b and 3.396c. The *anēr* is now the wrong kind of poet (as opposed to the *metrios anēr* of 3.396c); the *poiētēs* is now joined with the *mythologos*, rather than setting the two identities against each other (as at 3.392b). Here, however, we have the noun *mythologos* instead of the verb *mythologein*. The nominal form is significant. It occurs only four times in Plato's dialogues, only twice in the *Republic*, and, markedly, each time with a different meaning—both in terms of its definition (what it is, and what it is defined against), and its value (whether it is presented as positive or negative, a representation of Plato's new order of poets or the old stereotypes). A few sections earlier at 3.392d (just after the prescription that the new kinds of poets should *aidein te kai mythologein* at 392b5), we have *mythologoi* set alongside, but as a separate category from, poets: "the narrative of *mythologoi* or *poiētai*."[87] Both are used (ironically, given the command a few lines above to the new poets to *mythologein*) to denote the old kinds of poets, like Homer (from whom Socrates famously proceeds to quote the opening of the *Iliad*). At 3.398b1, on the other hand, we have our "more austere and less pleasing *poiētēs* and *mythologos*." Now the categories are fused—not

86. αὐτοὶ δ᾽ ἂν τῷ αὐστηροτέρῳ καὶ ἀηδεστέρῳ ποιητῇ χρώμεθα καὶ μυθολόγῳ ὠφελίας ἕνεκα, ὃς ἡμῖν τὴν τοῦ ἐπιεικοῦς λέξιν μιμοῖτο, *Rep.* 3.398a8–398b2.
87. ἆρ᾽ οὐ πάντα ὅσα ὑπὸ μυθολόγων ἢ ποιητῶν λέγεται διήγησις οὖσα τυγχάνει ἢ γεγονότων ἢ ὄντων ἢ μελλόντων; (Isn't everything that story-tellers and poets say a narrative either of the past, present or future?), *Rep* 3.392d2–3.

mythologos or *poiētēs*, but *mythologos* and *poiētēs*—and they are used in opposition to the kind of *anēr* (like former poets and Homer) who imitates everything, to denote the new kind of poet in Plato's *Republic*. In other words, the meaning of *mythologos* as Plato uses it is fluid, as he attempts to work out a new way to denote the opposition between his new man-poet and the old bards.[88] It moves from the old kind of man-maker, aligned with and yet separate from the former *poiētai* like Homer, to the new *mythologos* and *poiētēs*, set *against* the old *anēr*.

The final connection between the new kind of man-maker, the men of the state and the right kind of "manly" virtues comes in the middle of this fiery debate over words for poets and the poetic making of men. At 3.395b–c Socrates defines the only kinds of virtuous men which the guardians will be allowed to imitate: men who are "brave [*andreious*], self-controlled, pious, free—all these kinds of things" (3.395c5–6).[89] We have, once again, the stipulation of bravery and its etymological connection to manliness, suggesting the "right" kind of masculinity that needs to be imitated in poetry. But the guardians are also given a new term, which aligns them with this very streamlined version of the kinds of imitations they are allowed to practice. They are to be, Socrates stipulates, "craftsmen [*dēmiourgous*] of the freedom of the state," letting go of all other kinds of "craft" (*dēmiourgiōn*) (3.395b–c).[90] The term *dēmiourgoi*, of course, looks back to the description of the bard among the *dēmiourgoi* at *Odyssey* 17.383–5, and, as we have seen, is used in the "noble lie" in the *Republic* to refer to the class of poets as well as other craftsmen.[91] Socrates could hardly make a stronger statement of the displacement of the old poets—the *dēmiourgoi* of Homer—by these new kinds of craftsmen of masculinity, the guardians, who are themselves the imitators of the right kind of virtuous manliness (*andreious*). The poets, it seems, have not been banished; they have been superseded.

This displacement of the poets (and other craftsmen along with them) continues to the highest level. In book 6 we find the philosopher-king himself

---

88. For other instances, see chapter 5, n. 34.

89. μιμεῖσθαι . . . ἀνδρείους, σώφρονας, ὁσίους, ἐλευθέρους, καὶ τὰ τοιαῦτα πάντα, *Rep.* 3.395c4–6.

90. τοὺς φύλακας ἡμῖν τῶν ἄλλων πασῶν δημιουργιῶν ἀφειμένους δεῖν εἶναι δημιουργοὺς ἐλευθερίας τῆς πόλεως πάνυ ἀκριβεῖς (Our guardians must abandon all other kinds of craft and be, in a very strict sense, craftsmen of the freedom of the state), *Rep.* 3.395b9–c1; cf. *Prt.* 327c7.

91. See chapter 1, n. 6, p. 130 with chapter 5, n. 37.

described as a *dēmiourgos* ("a craftsman of self-control and justice and every common virtue," 6.500d7–9).[92] And this brings us to the final point in the struggle for words in defining the new role of poets in relation to gender. If the poets' goals are to be aligned with those of the philosopher—exploring only examples of the good in aid of the proper education of men (or, as we have seen, women who are to be like men)—then the new poet becomes like the philosopher, and the philosopher the new poet, in his gender principles—with Plato, of course, as the ultimate philosopher-poet.[93] We return to Plato's Socrates's observation, with which we began, that in dictating the "noble lie" towards the right kind of masculinity he himself is "storytelling" (*mythologountes*, 3.415a3). This fusion of philosopher and poet in their gender aims appears elsewhere in the *Republic*.[94] Opening the debate over the education of the guardians in book 2, Socrates speaks as if he himself is their teacher (not merely prescribing their education), and uses *mythologein* once again: "Come, then, let's educate the men [*tous andras*] in our discourse as if we were telling a story in fable [*en mythōi mythologountes*] and had ample leisure" (2.376d9–10).[95] Once again, the *mythologein* of the poet is appropriated by the philosopher and, as with the noble lie, is connected to the proper education of men in the new order. Elsewhere, in book 8, Socrates even appropriates the gendered relationship between Muse and poet to invoke the Muses, "like Homer" (8.545d7), to imagine the potential decline through stasis of the ideal city, looking back to the proem of the *Iliad* and the beginning of Achilles's and Agamemnon's quarrel.[96] And while, on one level, this is an association of

92. δημιουργὸν ... σωφροσύνης τε καὶ δικαιοσύνης καὶ συμπάσης τῆς δημοτικῆς ἀρετῆς, *Rep.* 6.500d7–9.

93. Hobbs 2000: 158–62, 240–49.

94. Tate 1928: 23, G. R. F. Ferrari 1989: 141–48, Halliwell 2000, Ford 2002: 224, Naddaff 2003. For other examples, see *Rep.* 2.369c9, 2.378e7–379a1, 5.453d8–10 (Socrates as Arion), 6.501e3; see also *Leg.* 817b2.

95. ἴθι οὖν, ὥσπερ ἐν μύθῳ μυθολογοῦντές τε ἅμα καὶ σχολὴν ἄγοντες λόγῳ παιδεύωμεν τοὺς ἄνδρας, *Rep.* 2.376d9–10; note the etymologizing of μυθολογεῖν with ἐν μύθῳ. On μυθολογεῖν, see chapter 5, n. 34; on μῦθος, see chapter 5, n. 84.

96. ἢ βούλει, ὥσπερ Ὅμηρος, εὐχώμεθα ταῖς Μούσαις εἰπεῖν ἡμῖν ὅπως δὴ πρῶτον στάσις ἔμπεσε (Shall we invoke the Muses, like Homer, to tell us "how the quarrel first began"?), *Rep.* 8.545d7–e1; see Meulder 1992, Cavarero 2002, Murray 2002. The most extensive treatment of the Muse-poet relationship in Plato occurs in the *Ion*, see Partee 1971, Murray 1996: 6–12, Gonzalez 2011; cf. *Phdr.* 245a. For other invocations of the Muse or suggestions of inspiration by a Muse by Socrates, see *Cra.* 409d, 428c, *Phdr.* 237a, *Euthyd.* 275d. For the Muses generating gendered poetry, see *Leg.* 669c3–5.

poetry with the negative kinds of strife which must be purged from the ideal state (as Penelope Murray notes), it also works to create a negative association between the female Muses as we know them and the "wrong" kind of poetry.[97] This is what leads, in book 10, to the banishment of "the sweetened Muse in lyric or epic," and the admission only of "hymns to the gods and eulogies of good men" (10.607a) to the state.[98] Female poetic voices, once again, are banned, and replaced with the discourse of masculinity. But, as with the *poiētēs*, the Muses are not fully banished by Plato: instead, they are *redefined* into the proper, streamlined, "true kind of Muse of words and philosophy" (8.548b–c).[99] The philosophical, not the poetic, Muse, then, is the only kind of Muse who should rule his ideal state.[100]

The final appropriation of poetic vocabulary by the philosopher is, perhaps, the most explicitly gendered. Just as Socrates had to address the role of women in poetry (that is: none), he also, as we have seen, had some apparently radical propositions for the education of women as well as men, allowing the female guardians the same education as men (though with all-male exemplars). As he moves from the education of the men to discussing the women, Socrates effects the transition with a particularly striking gendered poetic metaphor: "Now that we have completely gone through the male drama [*andreion drama*], we should go through the female [*to gunaikeion*]" (5.451c1–3).[101] There is a striking parallel with Agathon's discussion of gendered drama in Aristophanes's *Women at the Thesmophoria*, where he talks about embodying women in *gunaikeia* and *andreia dramata* ("dramas about women" and "men," *Thesm.* 151, 154).[102] This may be a direct jibe by Plato against the creed of gender imitation espoused by Aristophanes's Agathon—particularly given that the banning of gendered imitation in poetry, as we have seen, lies at the heart

97. Murray 2011: 192.

98. τὴν ἡδυσμένην Μοῦσαν . . . ἐν μέλεσιν ἢ ἔπεσιν, *Rep.* 10.607a5–6; cf. *Leg.* 802c5–6, τῆς γλυκείας Μούσης.

99. τῆς ἀληθινῆς Μούσης τῆς μετὰ λόγων τε καὶ φιλοσοφίας, *Rep.* 8.548b8–c1; cf. *Cra.* 406a3–5, 409d1–2, 428c7, *Phlb.* 67b5, *Phd.* 61a3–4, *Phdr.* 259d.

100. ὅταν αὕτη ἡ Μοῦσα πόλεως ἐγκρατὴς γένηται, *Rep.* 6.499d3–4; see Vicaire 1964: 50.

101. μετὰ ἀνδρεῖον δρᾶμα παντελῶς διαπερανθὲν τὸ γυναικεῖον αὖ περαίνειν, *Rep.* 5.451c1–3. Note that δρᾶμα here plays on the verbal root of the word, δρᾶν (doing), connecting the "roles" of men/women in the state and the dramatic metaphor.

102. See pp. 95–96. For the parallels between *Republic* 5 and Aristophanes, see Halliwell 1998: 224–26.

of Plato's plans for the guardians' education. As Murray notes, the use of *andreion* for the male drama thus serves double purpose in Plato: both to emphasize the masculine quality of the guardians' education, but also to outline the purely male virtues, like *andreia* (courage), which they are to imitate.[103] But it also points us to the fact that the use of *drama* here in the *Republic*—the term for the poetic productions of the stage—may be more than a metaphor: it is an act of displacing the poets entirely, so that the only gendered drama that remains is that which is under the control of the philosopher-poet Plato, who dictates the correct forms of imitation, and the correct forms of gender.

"People Love Getting a Name": A Woman Speaks Back in Plato's *Symposium*

There is a twist to the tale, however. While the struggle for words for "poet" in the *Republic* gives a particular vision of the male-gendered poet, another dialogue shows a somewhat different picture—both complicating the straightforward narrative we have seen so far, and looking ahead to what happens when women enter the scene.

In the *Symposium*, we hear a woman's voice (albeit ventriloquized through a man), as Plato's Socrates recounts the teachings of "a woman from Mantinea" called Diotima.[104] In contrast to the one-track male-gendered vision of poetry in the *Republic*, Diotima espouses a more complex view: "You know that *poiēsis* is a thing of many facets," she admonishes Socrates (*Symp.* 205b).[105] Socrates's Diotima here makes a pointed philosophical move, connecting directly to the topic at hand—the nature and properties of erotic love. Her precise argument is that, if everyone shares a love of "the good" (and she and Socrates agree that they do, because good things bring happiness), then we should surely say that

103. Murray 2011: 178; see p. 128 and chapter 5, n. 26.

104. γυναικὸς Μαντινικῆς Διοτίμας, *Symp.* 201d2. On Diotima and the question of her historicity, see Wider 1986: 44–48, Irigaray 1989, Nye 1989, Flower 2007: 212–13; the point at stake here, at least for the purposes of this chapter, is not whether Diotima was a real person or fictional character, but the gender politics of her representation as a female speaker in a male-authored text, ventriloquized by a male character (see further chapter 5, nn. 119 and 142). See also Vlastos 1981, Freeman 1986, Halperin 1990: 113–51 (to whose argument for Diotima's appropriation by men I am strongly indebted), Nye 1990, S. Rosen 1999: 197–277, Nussbaum 2001: 176–84, Hunter 2004a: 81–98, Evans 2006, Gill 2016.

105. οἶσθ᾽ ὅτι ποίησίς ἐστί τι πολύ, *Symp.* 205b8. For the meaning of ποίησίς here, see Stern-Gillet 2004: 173–76.

everyone is "in love"—but clearly, we don't (204d–205b).[106] The truth is, she says, that although "love of the good" should be the true definition of *erōs*, in common usage we only apply the word (*onoma*) *erōs* to a narrow subset of the semantic range of love—erotic desire (205b4–6). It is the same, she goes on, with the word *poiēsis*: "It is a thing of many facets," and can include anything from the general act of creation, to the specific expertise of different kinds of craftsmen (*dēmiourgoi*) and poets (*poiētai*) (205b–c).[107] In other words, in attempting to make a claim about the range and flexibility of names, Diotima turns—intriguingly—straight to the example of poets.

It is clear that the comparison to poetry here is not incidental: citations of poets litter each and every speech by the symposium's participants, and there are several poets present to hear Socrates's presentation of Diotima's views on *poiēsis*, including the host, Agathon—the same poet whose parodic treatise on poetry featured in Aristophanes's *Women at the Thesmophoria*—as well as Aristophanes himself.[108] Nor is Diotima the first in the dialogue to use *poiēsis*, and the metaphor of poetry, to describe the creative power of love. Just before Socrates's relation of Diotima's philosophy of love, Agathon gives his own view: "Love," he argues, "is a poet [*poiētēs*]"—both because he "makes" men into poets when they fall in love, and because he "creates" all forms of life through *poiēsis* (196e–197a).[109] As we see elsewhere in Plato's dialogues, Plato plays on the sense of *poiein* as "making" to connect poetry to the act of creation.[110]

Diotima's discussion of *poiēsis* thus picks up on Agathon's discourse on love and poetry—in fact she is the next in the dialogue (and the last) to use the word *poiētēs*.[111] But while Agathon twists the etymology of *poiēsis* to work for him while implicitly incorporating and endorsing the male-gendering of the

---

106. See Dover 1980: 144–45, Rowe 1998: 177–78.

107. For the text, see chapter 5, n. 117.

108. See Belfiore 2011, also Halliwell 2000: 96.

109. On Love as a poet: ποιητὴς ὁ θεὸς σοφὸς οὕτως ὥστε καὶ ἄλλον ποιῆσαι· πᾶς γοῦν ποιητὴς γίγνεται, "κἂν ἄμουσος ᾖ τὸ πρίν," οὗ ἂν Ἔρως ἅψηται (The god [of love] is a clever enough poet [*poiētēs*] to make other men poets [*poiētēs*], too: we know that every man becomes a poet, "even if the Muses were unknown to him before," when love touches him), *Symp.* 196e1–3. Note the quotation of Eur. fr. 663 *TrGF*. On Love as creator: καὶ μὲν δὴ τήν γε τῶν ζῴων ποίησιν πάντων τίς ἐναντιώσεται μὴ οὐχὶ Ἔρωτος εἶναι σοφίαν (And who will deny that the making [*poiēsis*] of all living things is Love's art), *Symp.* 196e6–197a2.

110. See pp. 124–25 with chapter 5, nn. 12 and 13.

111. ποιητής occurs thirteen times in the dialogue, with five of those (i.e., over a third) in Diotima's speech.

poiētēs—Agathon's *poiētēs* is always masculine, as underlined by all the sur-
rounding adjectives and pronouns—Diotima goes deeper to examine the pre-
cise range of the word for "poet" itself, and its relationship to gender.[112] Plato
has, in fact, already had Socrates begin his quotation of Diotima's teachings with
a pointed reference to her gender: she is, he says, a "woman [*gunaikos*] from
Mantinea" (201d).[113] The adjective which qualifies her identity as a woman,
Mantinikē, "from Mantinea," also contains the word *mantis*, "seer"—suggesting
Diotima's prophetic ability, and tying in her female gender and prescient fe-
male speech with prophecy.[114] (As we will see in chapter 8, the connection of
female speech to oracular ability has a long history, in particular at the oracle at
Delphi.)[115] So even the act of Diotima's speech on poetry is gendered female
from the start, through its connection to female prophetic speech—even if (or
perhaps because) it is ventriloquized through a man.

Socrates's account of Diotima's lesson on love focuses around her famous
"ladder of love," which forms the heart of the debate in the *Symposium* and has
an important place in Plato's metaphysics.[116] But if we hone in on her argu-
ment around creativity (*poiēsis*), we find that it is aimed at unpacking exactly
the range and dynamism of the terms *poiēsis* and *poiētēs* which both enthrall
and challenge Plato in other dialogues. While the words "poetry" and "poet"
are individual words, Diotima points out, just like love, they can signify
many different things: "You know that *poiēsis* is a thing of many facets: after
all, the cause of something going from not-being to being is *poiēsis*, which is
why the work of all the crafts is also *poiēsis*, and their craftsmen [*dēmiourgoi*]
are all *poiētai*" (205b–c).[117] She gets directly to the heart of the issue around
the *poiētēs* which we have seen throughout Plato: the capacity of the word
to stretch to "making" and "creating," and the ramifications this has for our

112. For Agathon's poet as masculine, see ἄλλον (*Symp.* 196e2), πᾶς (196e2), ἄμουσος
(196e2), οὗ (196e3).

113. γυναικὸς Μαντινικῆς Διοτίμας, *Symp.* 201d2.

114. Dover 1980: 137, Rowe 1998: 173, Evans 2006: 8. On the figure of the seer, see Bremmer
1996, Griffith 2009: 475–82

115. See pp. 250–51 with chapter 8, n. 65; cf. Nye 1989: 53–54.

116. See Gill 1990, G. R. F. Ferrari 1992, Osborne 1994: 86–116, Sheffield 2001 and 2006,
R. Foley 2010: 60–2.

117. οἶσθ' ὅτι ποίησίς ἐστί τι πολύ· ἡ γάρ τοι ἐκ τοῦ μὴ ὄντος εἰς τὸ ὂν ἰόντι ὁτῳοῦν
αἰτία πᾶσά ἐστι ποίησις, ὥστε καὶ αἱ ὑπὸ πάσαις ταῖς τέχναις ἐργασίαι ποιήσεις εἰσὶ καὶ
οἱ τούτων δημιουργοὶ πάντες ποιηταί, *Symp.* 205b8–c2. For δημιουργός in Plato, see chap-
ter 5, nn. 37 and 92.

understanding of human creation versus ultimate creation and the creation of
reality, means that the term has to be very carefully understood and applied.
It goes beyond our own "poet" to cover all kinds of makers, and all acts of
making. And yet there is a dissonance between the capaciousness of the term
and the way it is used, as Diotima points out. The reality that all makers are
poiētai, she says, is not borne up by popular usage: just as we do not call every-
one "lovers," even though everyone "loves" the good, only a subset of crafts-
men, the writers of metrical verse and song, are called poets (most makers "are
not called *poiētai*, but have different names [*onomata*]," *Symp.* 205c4–5).[118] There
is, in other words, a conflict between the potential reference of words, the way
those words are actually used, and the reality of the things to which they refer.
Diotima is facing up to the limits of words to properly name the objects they
describe.

And it is no coincidence that this challenge occurs in the voice of the
woman—because, as we have seen, one of the greatest limitations of the word
poiētēs is its gender. This point is driven home by Diotima's gendered voice,
and her ventriloquization by a man (her "absent presence") in the dialogue.[119]
Even as she critiques the limitations of words like *poiētēs* to accurately de-
scribe the range of people who inhabit it, her capacity for speech is taken
away from her as her words are given in the voice of a man. That this is not
really a woman's voice at all—and that women's voices would not be allowed
into the all-male venue of the symposium, without being channeled through
a man—is emphasized at the very start of the discussion, where the female
entertainer (*aulētris*) is sent away to "entertain herself or the women in their

118. ἀλλ᾽ ὅμως, ἦ δ᾽ ἥ, οἶσθ᾽ ὅτι οὐ καλοῦνται ποιηταὶ ἀλλὰ ἄλλα ἔχουσιν ὀνόματα,
ἀπὸ δὲ πάσης τῆς ποιήσεως ἓν μόριον ἀφορισθὲν τὸ περὶ τὴν μουσικὴν καὶ τὰ μέτρα τῷ
τοῦ ὅλου ὀνόματι προσαγορεύεται. ποίησις γὰρ τοῦτο μόνον καλεῖται, καὶ οἱ ἔχοντες
τοῦτο τὸ μόριον τῆς ποιήσεως ποιηταί ("Nevertheless," she said, "you're aware that makers
aren't called *poiētai*, but have other names: one bit has been separated off from *poiēsis* as a whole,
the part that has to do with music and verse, and has been given the name of the whole. After
all, this is the only thing called *poiēsis*, and those who have this part of *poiēsis* are called *poiētai*"),
Symp. 205c4–9.

119. On Diotima's ventriloquization by Socrates, see Dubois 1988: 182, Irigaray 1989: 32, 38,
Halperin 1990, Evans 2006: 8; note, however, Nye 1989, who attempts to restore Diotima to a
role as "host" of the symposium. Freeman 1986: 172 makes the interesting point that Socrates's
channeling of Diotima can be viewed as transvestism; cf. duBois 1988: 177, 182. For another
example of a ventriloquized woman's speech in Plato, see Socrates's "quotation" of Aspasia at
Menex. 235e–249c; see D'Angour 2019: 187–91. Compare also the ventriloquization of Sappho
in the *Phaedrus*: see pp. 133–35 with chapter 5, n. 57.

quarters" (*Symp.* 176e7–8).[120] Her gender, a woman among women (*gunaixi*, 176e8) just like Diotima (*gunaikos*, 201d2), sets her quite literally outside the kind of philosophical discussion to be had by men. Diotima's point, that *poiētēs* has a much greater capacity for reference to different kinds of people than it is used, becomes rather ironic in the voice of a man. And the identity of the audience receiving her critique only serves to underline this irony: for Plato's Socrates is speaking only *to* men, and at the house of, and in response to, one of the very male verse-making *poiētai* who represent the narrow definition of *poiētēs* which Diotima is critiquing. Agathon, of course, who makes Love into a *poiētēs*, has no reason to critique the term. He benefits from it; as we see from Aristophanes's *Women at the Thesmophoria*, he has learned how to *become* it. Diotima's voice represents a resistance to the self-congratulatory male poetic identity of Agathon (and of course the other poet in the audience, Aristophanes, too): but it is a resistance that is, nevertheless, conveyed in the voice of a man.[121]

The problem with this is that, not being there to speak for herself, she cannot engage in a direct rebuttal when the all-male symposiasts—including her ventriloquist, Socrates—flagrantly ignore her point about the potential capaciousness of words in comparison to the way they are actually used. This much becomes clear when we look at the terms applied to her and others. Agathon and Aristophanes are both called poets in the dialogue, in exactly the narrow sense which Diotima criticizes.[122] On the other hand, Diotima, who draws attention to the narrowness of (male) professional terms, is never given one herself. She is not, in spite of the fact that she is regularly referred to by modern commentators as a "priestess" or "prophetess," actually called a female priest or prophet: we are left to infer this from her name, which means "honoring/honored-by Zeus," and her epithet, *Mantinikē*, with its

120. εἰσηγοῦμαι τὴν μὲν ἄρτι εἰσελθοῦσαν αὐλητρίδα χαίρειν ἐᾶν, αὐλοῦσαν ἑαυτῇ ἢ ἂν βούληται ταῖς γυναιξὶ ταῖς ἔνδον (I think we should send away the flute-girl who just came in, and she can entertain herself or the women in their quarters), *Symp.* 176e6–8; see Freeman 1986: 172, Halperin 1990: 128–29. On the all-male symposium and the role of female entertainers, see chapter 3, n. 24. Ford 2002: 7 and West 2014a: 320 both cite this passage as potential evidence for women having a separate musical culture; see further pp. 281–85.

121. For Agathon as self-congratulatory, see *Symp.* 196d6–e1. Diotima's resistance to the male rhetoric which conveys her message ties into a wider theme of the *Symposium*, which explores the relationship between the surface appeal of a speech and its truth content: see Hunter 2004a: 36–37.

122. ὥς φασιν οἵδε οἱ ποιηταὶ (as these poets here say), *Symp.* 186e2–3.

resonance with the female *mantis*.[123] (We might contrast the passage we saw above in the *Meno*, where Socrates talks about the "wise men and women" he has heard, and gives them masculine and feminine professional terms, *hiereus* and *hiereia*, *Meno* 81a10.)[124] The nouns which are given to her instead delineate her by her gender—*gunē*, "woman" (201d2)—and her gendered otherness: Socrates calls her "female stranger" (*xenē*, 201e3, 204c7, 211d2).[125] The single time she comes close to receiving a term that acknowledges her identity as a philosopher, thinker, and creator equal to the men at the symposium is in *comparison* to men: she gives an answer "like a perfect sophist," Socrates says (*Symp*. 208c1).[126] Yet there are several problems with this. The first is that she is not given a term at all: she is only compared to a male professional, not given a word to describe an identity of her own. The second is that the comparison is to men, with a masculine noun (*ho sophistēs*); the gender disjunction is made particularly clear in the Greek with the juxtaposition of the feminine definite article and masculine noun (equivalent to something like, "and she, like a perfect male sophist"). And finally, for anyone familiar with Plato's depiction of Socrates's views on the sophists, the comparison to a sophist is a backhanded compliment at best: it is "a thoroughly slippery term, ranging in connotation from 'expert' to 'sophistical,' 'tricksy.'"[127] So Plato's Socrates, far from exploring the capaciousness of terms to explore identity as Diotima invites, seems to close down Diotima by refusing her a term of her own, forcing her gender into the same mold as men—men, at that, of whom Socrates often disapproves.[128]

However, Diotima does not let this go. She seems to respond to Socrates's comment, suggesting a deliberateness in the provocative comparison. "Don't forget," she warns him a few lines later, "that people love getting a name for themselves [*tou onomastoi genesthai*]" (*Symp*. 208c5).[129] Diotima appears

---

123. Evans 2006: 8; see also Dover 1980: 137, Halperin 1990: 120–21, Rowe 1998: 173, Nussbaum 2001: 177, 467 n. 28; and see further chapter 5, n. 114.

124. See p. 134 with chapter 5, n. 55.

125. ἡ ξένη, *Symp*. 201e3; ὦ ξένη, 204c7; ἡ Μαντινικὴ ξένη, 211d2. See Rowe 1998: 173.

126. καὶ ἥ, ὥσπερ οἱ τέλεοι σοφισταί (and she, like a perfect sophist), *Symp*. 208c1. Dover 1980 ad loc. suggests that τέλεοι almost has the sense "professional" here.

127. Rowe 1998 ad loc.; for an example of Plato's major critique of the sophists, see *Soph*. 218b–233c.

128. Or at least, Plato through Socrates, as Broadie 2003: 96 suggests.

129. εἰ μὴ ἐννοεῖς, ἐνθυμηθεὶς ὡς δεινῶς διάκεινται ἔρωτι τοῦ ὀνομαστοὶ γενέσθαι, *Symp*. 208c4–5.

directly to rebuke Socrates's approach toward naming, in the very speech which Socrates had prefaced by denying her a proper term through a less than flattering comparison. At the same time, she also looks back to her earlier discussion of the proper terminology (*onomata*, 205c5) to describe what people do. The word for "getting a name for themselves," *onomastoi* (208c5), is an adjectival form directly connected to *onoma*, "word" or "term," and *onomazein*, "to give a name."[130] These are precisely the terms Diotima had used above in her critique of the terminology of love and, by analogy, *poiēsis*. We give the name (*onomazomen/onoma*), she argued, of the whole of love to just a part of it (205b5, 205d7), while we attribute different names (*onomasin*) to the other parts (205b6); similarly, although all poets should be called *poiētai*, we give different names (*onomata*) to the subclasses of craftsmen (205c5); we apply the word (*onomati*, 205c7) *poiēsis* to poetry only, when it should really apply to all kinds of creative activity.[131] When Diotima uses the term *onomastoi* at 208c5, then, the term not only brings with it the overt meaning of "getting a name, being renowned," but also refracts back onto the conversation about what it means to give names at all earlier in Diotima's speech.

This suggests an undertone of both irony and deliberate polemic to Diotima's point here. Her argument is not simply about people's love of being famous (although this is the surface content of the topic at hand, which deals with the desire for immortality through renown, *kleos*, as with the example of Achilles's choice in the *Iliad*). The choice of the term *onomastoi* suggests that Diotima is also interested in commenting on naming practices—the fact that people like to have names and terms applied to them. She thus effects a metaliterary critique of Socrates's own questionable naming practice a few lines earlier, where the only term given to her in the dialogue was in a backhanded comparison to men.

But Diotima is also interested—looking back to the application of *onoma* to the *poiētēs* in particular—in *poetic* naming practices. The link between "getting a name" here at 208c5 and the earlier discussion of the naming of the *poiētēs* is made explicit by the fact that she immediately breaks into poetry to

---

130. See Chantraine s.v. ὄνομα, and cf. pp. 10–11 with introduction, n. 35.

131. For other examples of ὄνομα in the *Symposium*, see 179c3 (Phaedrus on Alcestis, see chapter 5, n. 46), 186c3, 189e2, 3, 5, 193a1, 198b5, 199b4, 221e2; for ὀνομάζειν and compounds, see 180d8, 212c2, 3, 218a4. It is interesting to note that, of the fourteen instances of ὄνομα in the *Symposium*, six occur in Diotima's speech—the highest count; the next highest is Aristophanes, with four; as we have already seen in the *Clouds* (p. 15), Aristophanes seems to have had a professed interest in exploring (the gender of) names.

seal her point about the universality of the desire for *kleos*. "People love getting a name for themselves," she says, "and 'garnering immortal glory for all time'" (208c4–6).[132] This second half of her articulation of what people want is a quote in hexameter verse, that is, a bit of poetry, evoking Homer.[133] But what is interesting about it is that it is not a line we know from anywhere else. And this means that it is quite possible that Diotima is being depicted here as citing, or composing, *her own poetry*.[134]

It seems, then, that the point that Diotima is making is not only in the content of the poetry, but also in the statement of composing poetry itself, and the implications that might have for Diotima's own desire to "get a name." Diotima is, perhaps, also a poet-figure within the dialogue, just like Agathon— who also quotes his own poetry, but who does, by contrast, get the accolade of being called a (male) *poiētēs*, as does Aristophanes. Diotima's argument thus seems to run beneath the surface of her speech, in a subtext to the apparent debate around what people desire, the importance of immortality and "getting a name." She has already shown the importance of understanding the full range of the word *poiētēs*, and the fact that it covers people and practices beyond those it is usually applied to. Now, she subtly critiques Socrates's own act of naming; she argues for the centrality of being given a name with the same terminology she had used for the naming of the *poiētēs*; and, most importantly of all, she demonstrates her own identity as a potential poet with a poetic citation of her own. In other words, she, too, wants to get a name, and she, too, can be a *poiētēs*—it is simply that the word to describe what she is, as a female poet, does not exist within the bounds of current usage. The potential capaciousness of *poiēsis* and *poiētēs* is used, in practice, just like *erōs*, in a narrowed sense—in this case, to delimit her name, her identity, and her gender.

The fact that this is all about gender is underlined by the wider context of Diotima's argument. Immediately following the definitional work on love (and, incidentally, poets) at 205b–c, Diotima asks what the precise mechanism for the pursuit of the true type of love (that is, love of the good) might be (206b).[135] In response, she comes up with one of her most striking (and gender-loaded)

132. ἔρωτι τοῦ ὀνομαστοὶ γενέσθαι καὶ κλέος ἐς τὸν ἀεὶ χρόνον ἀθάνατον καταθέσθαι, *Symp.* 208c4–6.

133. Achilles's κλέος is ἄφθιτον (undying), at *Il.* 9.413; see Nagy 1979: 95.

134. Lamb 1925: 197; Rowe 1998 ad loc. suggests that this may be a poetic composition of Socrates's, rather than Diotima's.

135. See Rowe 1998 ad 206b1–3, contra, e.g., Waterfield 1994: 86.

observations: that love is "giving birth in the beautiful, both in body and soul" (206b7–8).[136] She then goes on to engage in a rich, yet dissonant, metaphor for the productivity of men: pregnancy.[137] "All humans [*anthrōpoi*]," she argues, "are pregnant [*kuousin*] in both body and soul" (206c1–3).[138] This pregnancy, and the desire to procreate, is stimulated by beauty and has the aim of immortality: either in the body by producing children, or in the soul by producing ideas (such as poems and laws).[139] Strikingly, it is men, and not women, who are the focus of this metaphor of pregnancy and birth. "Men who are pregnant in their bodies take up with women," she says, and get children (and thus a kind of immortality) in that way (208e); while "men who are pregnant in their souls are pregnant with and give birth to" abstract virtues, rather than physical children, which ensure their immortality (208e–209a).[140] The emphasis is purely on men as the pregnant actors, as the masculine-gendered definite articles and the necessity of "taking up with women" to actually do the business of giving birth makes clear.[141] The gender paradox is obvious: men cannot be pregnant, and Diotima—the only woman to "speak" in the dialogue—endows them with androgyny to enable them to be pregnant and give birth to both literal and metaphorical children.

This is interesting from a gender perspective in and of itself, in terms of the move made by a woman to endow men with her own uniquely gendered qualities of child-bearing to make her point: both to bring her own gendered

136. ἔστι γὰρ τοῦτο τόκος ἐν καλῷ καὶ κατὰ τὸ σῶμα καὶ κατὰ τὴν ψυχήν, *Symp.* 206b7–8.

137. On the metaphor of pregnancy here, see Plass 1978, Vlastos 1981: 21 n. 59, duBois 1988: 169–83, Pender 1992, Sheffield 2001, Evans 2006: 13–16. Dover 1980 ad 206b1–207a4 notes the innovation of using the verb κυεῖν, elsewhere only reserved for pregnancy in women, to apply to men; though note Aesch. fr. 44 *TrGF*, which shows that in the aorist κυεῖν could be used causally for men (see LSJ s.v., Evans 2006: 25 n. 12). For the idea of thought as conception in Plato, see Edie 1963: 554–56. For the potential incongruity of the birth metaphor in the pederastic context of the symposium, see Plass 1978: 48, though note Halperin 1990: 142–45.

138. κυοῦσιν γάρ, ἔφη, ὦ Σώκρατες, πάντες ἄνθρωποι καὶ κατὰ τὸ σῶμα καὶ κατὰ τὴν ψυχήν, *Symp.* 206c1–3.

139. Dover 1980 ad 208b7–209e4 includes philosophy as the product of creative achievement; see contra Rowe 1998 ad 208c2–209e4.

140. οἱ μὲν οὖν ἐγκύμονες, ἔφη, κατὰ σώματα ὄντες πρὸς τὰς γυναῖκας μᾶλλον τρέπονται, *Symp.* 208e1–3; οἱ δὲ κατὰ τὴν ψυχήν—εἰσὶ γὰρ οὖν, ἔφη, οἳ ἐν ταῖς ψυχαῖς κυοῦσιν ἔτι μᾶλλον ἢ ἐν τοῖς σώμασιν, ἃ ψυχῇ προσήκει καὶ κυῆσαι καὶ τεκεῖν· τί οὖν προσήκει; φρόνησίν τε καὶ τὴν ἄλλην ἀρετήν, *Symp.* 208e5–209a4.

141. As Pender 1992: 76 also notes, cf. Hunter 2004a: 89.

perspective to bear on the philosophical topic at hand, as well as to signal the appropriation of female experiences and bodies by men.[142] (As we will see below, these interpretations of Diotima's gender—both enabling her to push beyond the limits of conventional imagery, and allowing for her colonization and appropriation by men—sit side by side in the *Symposium*.) But it also has important ramifications for her earlier discussion around poetry: because the first example Diotima gives of "men who are pregnant in their souls" is none other than poets themselves. "The begetters [*gennētores*] of these [meta-phorical children]," she says, "are all the poets [*poiētai*], and those craftsmen [*dēmiourgōn*] we call inventors" (209a).[143] She goes on to take the analogy further: the poems of "Homer and Hesiod and all the other good poets" can be seen as their "children" (*ekgona*), and endow them with lasting *kleos* (209d).[144] Interestingly—paying attention to the valency of naming—the poets are called *gennētores*, "begetters," a term which (cognate with *gennan* and *gennēsis*) can be used of both the male "begetters" and the female "bearers" of children.[145] The word therefore gestures to the androgyny which Diotima constructs for these poets, as *both* male begetters and feminine bearers of their "children" poems. (In this sense, Diotima seems to be "looking ahead" to Aristophanes's vision of androgynous bodies in the *Symposium*.)[146] But it also

142. See Halperin 1990: 113–51 on the relevance of Diotima's gender, esp. pp. 142–45 on the male appropriation of the female experience and body; see further duBois 1988: 169–83, and cf. Freeman 1986: 172, W. Brown 1988: 607. At the same time, it is also possible to read the restriction of pregnancy to men as due in part to Plato's endorsement of male homoerotic love as the preferred model for the intellectual love he is trying to describe: see, e.g., Dover 1980: 137, Vlastos 1981: 22–23, Halperin 1990: 113–14, Pender 1992: 79, though note Nye 1990: 142.

143. ὧν δή εἰσι καὶ οἱ ποιηταὶ πάντες γεννήτορες καὶ τῶν δημιουργῶν ὅσοι λέγονται εὑρετικοὶ εἶναι, *Symp.* 209a4–5; see Pender 1992: 77. On the relationship between Diotima's vision of poetic creativity and Plato's other dialogues, see Asmis 1992: 344–47.

144. καὶ εἰς Ὅμηρον ἀποβλέψας καὶ Ἡσίοδον καὶ τοὺς ἄλλους ποιητὰς τοὺς ἀγαθοὺς ζηλῶν, οἷα ἔκγονα ἑαυτῶν καταλείπουσιν, ἃ ἐκείνοις ἀθάνατον κλέος καὶ μνήμην παρέχεται (Just looking at Homer and Hesiod and all the other good poets, and envying the kinds of children they leave behind which give them undying glory and remembrance), *Symp.* 209d1–4.

145. Dover 1980 ad 206b1–207a4, Evans 2006: 14–15; cf. Rowe 1998 ad 209c4–7. Pender 1992: 80 suggests this is an attempt to avoid the awkwardness of the image of a pregnant male poet and connect to the (much more common) metaphor of fatherhood and poetry (on which see chapter 5, n. 154).

146. For Socrates's Diotima making apparently proleptic references to Aristophanes's speech, see Halperin 1990: 147, Rowe 1998 ad 201d1–204c8. For Aristophanes's narrative of original androgyny, see S. Rosen 1999: 120–58, Nussbaum 2001: 171–76, Corbeill 2015: 147.

suggests that the term *poiētēs*, with its connection to *poiēsis* as "creation" explored earlier in the dialogue, is being deliberately linked to the term *gennētōr* to expand its semantic range to that of "begetter" and "creator" in the widest sense of the word, as well as a maker-craftsman. Diotima is pushing the resonance of *poiētēs* to its limits to explore its full creative, gender-crossing capacities—and it is for this reason, perhaps, that the *poiētēs* is the first on her list of paradoxically pregnant men.

The irony, of course, is that women are completely ousted by this move: the poet-*gennētōr* is capable of both begetting and delivering his child-poems, without the need to "take up with a woman," as is the case with physical childbirth.[147] This is mirrored in the vision Diotima puts forth for the homoerotic relationship between the older philosopher and the younger man who allows him to bear and nourish his philosophical children: in this relationship, women are no longer necessary for (metaphorical) child-bearing.[148] Yet there is, potentially, a more positive way of reading Diotima's gendered move for poets here. Just as she argues that the word for *poiētēs* is more expansive than the way in which it is used, we might be able to read the gender-crossing of the male poets into the female sphere of pregnancy and childbirth as a roadmap for ways in which women, too, might cross back over into the male realm of being a *poiētēs*. In essence, as we have seen, this is what the figure of Diotima is *already* doing, by speaking up in a male-dominated dialogue and citing (or even creating) poetry. The gift of androgyny to the male poets is thus, perhaps, not a loss of power for the woman at all, but a clever bargaining chip in which Diotima blurs the boundaries between sex and gender, between male and female, and subtly allows female qualities to imbue the figure of the stereotypical male *poiētēs*. The act of writing women out of the metaphor of the pregnant male poet sits, for the moment, side by side with the challenge to gendered divisions that Diotima and her imagery represents.

The move made here by a woman to use the birth metaphor for male poets is marked in its gender dynamics; but, of course, there is nothing new to the metaphor of birth for poetic creativity. We have seen it already in Aristophanes's *Clouds*, where the poet envisions himself as a *parthenos* who couldn't

147. Note also the way in which Plato skates over the question of the spiritual partners of the poets and attempts to soften the metaphor by presenting the poets as "fathers/begetters": see Pender 1992: 80 with n. 20, Rowe 1998 ad 209c4–7.

148. See Dover 1980 ad 208b7–209e4, and cf. chapter 5, n. 142.

(or shouldn't) give birth, exposing his "child" to be brought up by others.[149] Similarly, Euripides has a male "hymn-maker" (*hymnopoios*) "giving birth to songs and enjoying giving birth" in his *Suppliant Women*, produced in the late 420s BCE (and possibly in 423, the same year as the *Clouds*); while, in the *Frogs*, Aristophanes imagines Aeschylus claiming to "give birth to words."[150] Now, in the *Symposium*, Diotima takes this image and runs with it to explore in full the paradox of a male poet who is pregnant and gives birth. There is an interesting contrast with Plato's use of birth imagery elsewhere in the *Theaetetus*, where Socrates describes himself as a "midwife" delivering the philosophical ideas of other young men whose souls "give birth" (*Tht.* 150b8).[151] In contrast to Diotima's vision of the pregnant older philosopher and the pregnant poet, in the *Theaetetus* Socrates deliberately makes the point that, like a midwife, he himself is "sterile" (*agonos*, *Tht.* 150c4), while it is the ideas themselves which are described as "fertile" (*gonimos*), and notably not the young men from whom he delivers them.[152]

It seems, again, that it is (the construction of) Diotima's marked female gender and her connection to poetry—drawing on the images of poets giving birth in Aristophanes and Euripides—which enable her to take the birth metaphor further than Socrates, or indeed any other figure in the Platonic corpus, to apply it fully and paradoxically to the philosopher, and of course, the poet too.[153] In the voices of Plato's male protagonists elsewhere, it is not birth imagery (*mother* to child) which structures the metaphor of the relationship

149. See pp. 105–8.

150. Eur. *Supp.* 180–81, τόν θ' ὑμνοποιὸν αὐτὸς ἂν τίκτῃ μέλη / χαίροντα τίκτειν; Ar. *Ran.* 1059, τὰ ῥήματα τίκτειν, on which see Wright 2010: 167–68; see also Eur. *Andr.* 476, τεκόντοιν θ' ὕμνον ἐργάταιν δυοῖν ("two craftsmen who have given birth to a song," with Wilamowitz's text), on which see Wright 2010: 174–75, Torrance 2013: 191–206; *HF* 767, ἔτεκον ἀοιδάς (have brought forth songs). For a precedent in the myth of creative "birth" by a male, see Zeus' swallowing of Mētis and birth of Athena, see Detienne and Vernant 1991: 107–30. For more discussion, see pp. 244–47.

151. On this passage, see Edie 1963: 554–55, duBois 1988: 180–81; for a comparison between the images in the *Theaetetus* and *Symposium*, see Burnyeat 1977.

152. On the ideas (not the "young man" [τοῦ νέου, 150c2]) as γόνιμος, see *Tht.* 150c3, 151e6, 157d3 and Dover 1980: 151; on Socrates as sterile, see Edie 1963: 555.

153. Halperin 1990: 117, 137–42. Note that I take this as about the construction of gender "as" feminine: I am not suggesting that there is anything intrinsically feminine to the metaphor of pregnancy, just as there is nothing intrinsically masculine to being a poet; see Halperin 1990: 203 n. 149 by way of comparison.

between poet and poem, but the lineage of *father* to child.[154] One of the guests at the symposium, Phaedrus, has, in fact, been called "the father of the discourse [*logou*]" earlier on in the *Symposium* itself (*Symp.* 177d).[155] The opening of the *Republic* sees Socrates comparing the relationship between poet and poems to that between father and son ("just as poets love their own poems, and fathers their sons," *Rep.* 1.330c), playing on the similar-sounding *poiētai* and *pateres* to generate an image of a male-only lineage of the poet as father to his (male) poem-sons.[156] In the *Phaedrus*, the image of poem as child is fleshed out in an unusual metaphor where the maligned written text is imagined running back to its "father" to defend it (*Phdr.* 275e); while, in the *Theaetetus*, the work of a "father" author who is no longer around to defend his progeny is envisioned as an "orphan" (*Tht.* 164e). Meanwhile, in the *Lysis*, Socrates takes the *poiētai-pateres* connection to its furthest extent, saying that the poets are "like our fathers and guides in wisdom" (*Lysis* 214a).[157] Here the poets are not only fathers to their poems, but to their audience, too, bringing poet and audience together into a male circle where the father-poets hand down wisdom to other men.

Diotima's difference as a woman appears to be what gives her access to a figurative landscape for poetry based on the visceral, physical female experience of pregnancy and birth. At the same time, just as Diotima's gender opens up the image of birth as a striking contribution to the development of the gendering of the *poiētēs*—in a way that pushes past the figure of the hypermale poet-as-father which dominates Plato's other dialogues—her ventriloquization and subordination by the male means that that image is also appropriated and colonized into the experience of men.[158] This is not unique to the metaphor of pregnancy: it is a tactic which, in fact, as we have seen, structures and punctuates Diotima's entire speech, and its relation to the dialogue of men (and poets) that goes on around it. Only men are poets in the *Symposium*: Diotima invents no new term to expand on the capaciousness of *poiēsis* to

154. Pender 1992: 80, Steiner 1994: 112–13, and Ford 2002: 247 n. 38 discuss metaphors of paternity and fertility for poetic authorship; see especially the figuration of Homer as "father" (Hunter 2004b: 235–41), and see further chapter 8, n. 46. For Greek notions of paternity, see Harlow 1998: 156–59.

155. πατὴρ τοῦ λόγου, *Symp.* 177d5; see Pender 1992: 80.

156. ὥσπερ γὰρ οἱ ποιηταὶ τὰ αὑτῶν ποιήματα καὶ οἱ πατέρες τοὺς παῖδας ἀγαπῶσιν, *Rep.* 1.330c3–4. Cf. Arist. *Eth. Nic.* 1120b14, 1168a1, also *Poet.* 1448b20.

157. οὗτοι γὰρ ἡμῖν ὥσπερ πατέρες τῆς σοφίας εἰσὶν καὶ ἡγεμόνες, *Lysis* 214a1–2.

158. Halperin 1990: 143–44, 146.

apply to female poets; she does not even claim her potential poetic composition as her own. Only men are given acknowledgment with terms that describe what they do: Diotima receives no admission of her identity as female prophet, priest, poet, or philosopher, in direct contravention of her invitation to see the *poiētēs* in new semantic and gendered ways, and is described only once in comparison to a group of male sophists to whom Socrates's relationship is complex at best. Only men speak within the text: Diotima's voice, artfully incorporated as it is, is ventriloquized entirely through a man. And only men, not women—as hard as Diotima has to work to stretch the metaphor to transcend biological barriers—are envisioned as being pregnant with poetry.

And yet, even though Diotima is inescapably ventriloquized, ignored in her call for a wider application of poet-terms, and written out of her own metaphor, at the same time, she represents a new impulse: an attempt by a male writer, voicing a female, to work through the poet-terms which had grown up in the battleground of (male) gender. She opens up the conversation in which men learn how to categorize and conceptualize a differently gendered relationship to poetry—and even, perhaps, to begin to conceptualize women *as* poets, for the first time. It is, therefore, fitting that it is Diotima who leads us to the next part of the book: the beginnings of a name, in the words of men, for women poets.

PART III

Wreath

THE FEMALE HOMER: TOWARD A LANGUAGE FOR WOMEN POETS

6

Into the Otherworld

SINGING WOMEN IN EURIPIDES

AROUND 100 BCE, Meleager of Gadara collected a group of epigrams by forty-seven different Greek poets, male and female, which he called his "Garland" or "Wreath" (*Stephanos*).[1] The anthology begins with a long proem (1 G-P = *Anth. Pal.* 4.1), introducing each poet in the metaphorical "wreath of song-makers" (*hymnothetan stephanon*, 4.1.2) by name and comparing them to a different flower. It might seem remarkable that, given the long history of male poets, Meleager chooses to begin his *Garland* with a list of women (4.1.1–6):[2]

> My Muse, to whom do you bring this song with all kinds of fruit—
> or who was the man who crafted this wreath of song-makers
>   [*hymnothetan*]?
> Meleager did it; he produced this gift
> as a keepsake for the famous Diocles.
> He wove in many white lilies of Anyte, and many red
> lilies of Moero, and only a few of Sappho's—but they are roses.

After Anyte (a Hellenistic epigrammatist), Moero (a Hellenistic poet of epigrams, hexameter, and, perhaps, lyric) and, of course, Sappho, Meleager goes

---

1. On Meleager's *Garland*, see Gow and Page 1965: 1:xiv–xxvii, Gutzwiller 1997a, 1998: 276–322.

2. Μοῦσα φίλα, τίνι τάνδε φέρεις πάγκαρπον ἀοιδάν, / ἢ τίς ὁ καὶ τεύξας ὑμνοθετᾶν / στέφανον; / ἄνυσε μὲν Μελέαγρος, ἀριζάλῳ δὲ Διοκλεῖ / μναμόσυνον ταύταν ἐξεπόνησε / χάριν, / πολλὰ μὲν ἐμπλέξας Ἀνύτης κρίνα, πολλὰ δὲ Μοιροῦς / λείρια, καὶ Σαπφοῦς / βαιὰ μέν ἀλλὰ ῥόδα, Meleager 1.1–6 G-P = *Anth. Pal.* 4.1.1–6.

on to list two other women poets before launching into the catalogue of men: the "iris" of Nossis, another Hellenistic epigrammatist (4.1.9–10); and the "virgin-colored saffron" (4.1.12) of Erinna, author of a fragmentary hexameter poem called *The Distaff*.[3]

It is with Meleager's *Garland* that we turn for the first time to observe the systematic attempt by men to come up with a way to talk about women poets. Where, in the previous chapters, we have seen archaic poets wrestling with the male-gendering of the bard, and fifth- and fourth-century Athenians taking an androcentric view of poets as the educators of men in the state, Hellenistic male poets began to innovate by experimenting with adopting female voices, channeling female subjects and "inner" values, and inhabiting female domestic spaces in their poetry.[4] (This has as much to do with gender stereotyping and appropriation of the woman for the male poet's purposes, as we will see, as it does an attempt to investigate or express "authentic" female experience.)[5] At the same time, more women poets (though still not many) began to enter the scene, particularly in the written genre of epigram.[6] Of course, Sappho—the famous exception to the rule and the prototypical female poet—had challenged the norm of the male poet from the beginning, as we will see.[7] But it is in the Hellenistic period that we first find women writers, as a group, being acknowledged by men in their own right: in fact, Meleager's *Garland*, with its list of star women poets, represents one of the first attempts (though, as we will see below, it is not without its problems).[8] In this climate, male writers

3. σὺν δ᾽ ἀναμὶξ πλέξας μυρόπνουν εὐάνθεμον ἶριν / Νοσσίδος, ἧς δέλτοις κηρὸν ἔτηξεν Ἔρως (And he wove in together with them the sweet-perfumed blossoming iris of Nossis: Eros melted the wax for her writing-tablets)", *Anth. Pal.* 4.1.9–10; καὶ γλυκὺν Ἠρίννης παρθενόχρωτα κρόκον (and the sweet virgin-colored saffron of Erinna), 4.1.12. On these women poets see Barnard 1978, Snyder 1989: 64–98; see further chapter 6, n. 6, and pp. 3–4 with introduction, n. 7. On specific women poets, see pp. 235–44 and pp. 261–63 (on Sappho); chapter 7, n. 80 (on Erinna); pp. 281–85 with chapter 9, n. 71 (on Anyte); pp. 271–81 with chapter 9, n. 38 (on Nossis); pp. 267–71 with chapter 9, n. 28 (on Corinna).

4. B. Fowler 1989: 4, Snyder 1989: 65–66, Skinner 2001: 206, 221, Skinner 2005a: 187–88, Murray and Rowland 2007: 212–13, Warwick 2020: 334.

5. Pace Murray and Rowland 2007: 213.

6. Snyder 1989: 66. On women poets and epigram, see Murray and Rowland 2007; cf. Williamson 1995: 16–17, Gutzwiller 1997b: 202–3.

7. See chapters 8 and 9. Note, as another example of an archaic female poet, Megalostrata, mentioned at Alcm. fr. 59b *PMGF*; see Plant 2004: 246, West 2014a: 317.

8. A later example is Antipater of Thessalonica's canon of nine female poets, *Anth. Pal.* 9.26 (on which see chapter 7, n. 85); see Bowman 2004: 7–9 for problematization of this list as evi-

began to explore how to talk about women poets, when there were no words to do so—when the very words for poet, *aoidos* and *poiētēs* chief among them, had been forged in grammar, and ringfenced in practice, as rightfully male. We are able, then, to observe and dissect the different strategies which men used to categorize and name women poets, as they came to terms with, explored, and, in some cases, attempted to control, the collocation between female gender and poetic identity.

This part of the book takes an in-depth look at the various strategies which male writers took to come up with words to describe women poets, in a context where a language for connecting the categories "woman" and "poet" had not yet been invented, and where there was a constant tension between women poets' gender and the history of the masculinization of poetry. Before we begin, however, it must be acknowledged that the most common feature in early discussions of women poets is the absence of poet-terms—and that is when women poets are mentioned at all. Even Sappho, who had the rare privilege of being a woman writer who *was* acknowledged within the canon, is only called a poet twice—as we will see—in five hundred years of extant Greek literature by men.[9] But moving beyond this inescapable fact, when women poets do garner a mention and receive a term labeling them as poets, one approach involves a hybrid form of gendering—where masculine poet-terms (in particular *aoidos*) are applied to women poets, but turned into grammatically feminine forms, demonstrated by agreement with feminine adjectives and participles. We can read this, variously, as an acknowledgment of women's ability to be a poet on an equal level with men by granting them the same poet-vocabulary as male poets; an attempt to shoehorn women into male terms, which carry with them the implicit history of the male-gendering of the poet; or a compromise which highlights women's difference while still suggesting a level of subordination to norms of male poetry. (We will see, during the course of the next two chapters, how each of these plays out in turn in the hands of different male authors.) By contrast, another approach, which gains ground later in the Hellenistic period, is to attribute to women feminized forms of

---

dence of a women's tradition (on which see further pp. 281–85); for the politics of grouping female poets, see de Vos 2014: 428–29. For Sappho's inclusion in the canon of nine (male) lyric poets, see *Anth. Pal.* 9.184, 9.571, and see Barbantani 1993: 28–47 for discussion, also Skinner 1993: 128–29. On the Hellenistic canon of lyric poets generally, see Acosta-Hughes and Barbantani 2007: 429–31.

9. See pp. 216–18.

male terms, like *poiētria*—which might seem either a subordination of the female *poiētria* to the male *poiētēs*, or, perhaps, in some cases, as we will discover, a recognition of women's gender status as poets worthy of being compared to men.

The proem to Meleager's *Garland* provides a useful starting point to observe some of these different approaches to naming and representing women poets, which will be explored in more detail in the chapters that follow. The first and most obvious of Meleager's strategies toward women poets is that of abstraction—here, in the *Garland* proem, through the figuration of their poetry as flowers. (Though it is important to note that this is not exclusive to women: the works of male poets are also figured as flowers, leaves, and plants in the conceit of Meleager's "wreath.") The association between Sappho and roses, in particular (*Anth. Pal.* 4.1.2), is a clear reference to Sappho's "roses of Pieria" (fr. 55.2–3 L-P), a striking image for the poetic gifts of the Muses.[10] But the fact that Meleager opens his catalogue with Sappho, and other women poets, suggests that female authors are being used for a specific associative purpose here, beyond the intertextual link to Sappho's "roses." The ease of their abstraction into flowers through the association between femininity and flowers, as well as the general tendency of abstracting the feminine—from female gods like the Muses to concepts like Chance—enables Meleager to lead into the image of the wreath which structures the proem.[11] Women poets, in other words, are being manipulated to shore up the male poet's metaphor. (We will see other metaphors like this, particularly that of the Muse and the nightingale, cropping up throughout the following chapters.) Another strategy is the application of male-gendered terms to women poets, here with the generalizing masculine plural, "song-makers" (*hymnothetan*, 4.1.2), to describe the poets to be included in Meleager's wreath—eliding the gender of the female poets (who actually, and ironically, are mentioned before any male poets) with a masculine-gendered term, *hymnothetēs*. This elision points to Meleager's final

---

10. οὐ γὰρ πεδέχηις βρόδων / τὼν ἐκ Πιερίας, Sappho fr. 55.2–3 L-P. Stobaeus, our source, says that the lines were addressed "to an uneducated woman" (Stob. 3.4.12); cf. Plut. *Coniug. praec.* 145f–146a, *Quaest. conv.* 646e–f. See Gosetti-Murrayjohn 2006: 21, 22 with n. 4.

11. On the abstraction/personification of the feminine, see chapter 2, n. 31. On the metaphor of plaiting a wreath as feminine-gendered, see Acosta-Hughes 2010: 83 n. 75. Gutzwiller 1998: 79 notes that Nossis is the first directly to associate a poetry collection with flowers (τἄνθεα ποῖα ῥόδα, "what kind of flowers roses are," Nossis 1.4 G-P): Meleager's appropriation of the flowers-as-collection metaphor can thus be read as an appropriation of a female poet's metaphor (Gutzwiller 1998: 87).

strategy: omission. We might laud Meleager for beginning his *Garland* with women poets—but is five women among forty-two men really an impressive number? What about other female epigrammatists (of whose work we now have only fragmentary knowledge), like Eurydice (of whom we will hear more later)? And can we assume that the male term *hymnothetēs* at the proem's start really applies to women poets at all? Sappho's contemporary Alcaeus is associated later in the *Garland* proem with "song-composers" (*hymnopolois*, 4.1.13), suggesting that the "song-makers" (*hymnotheteis*) of the opening might be meant to be connected to male poets like Alcaeus; while none of the female poets are associated with any poet-terms at all.[12] If anything, if we contrast Alcaeus's association with "song-composers" against Erinna's gender-charged "virgin-colored saffron" (4.1.12)—"virgin" (*parthenos*) is used specifically of unmarried girls—we seem to find that, for Meleager, at least, women poets were seen first as women, and then as poets.[13] The clustering of a few female poets at the proem's opening thus seems to serve less as an announcement of women's equal share on the stage as poets and more as a separate categorization of women as apart from men and defined by their gender, to be surrounded by other women and judged alongside them.[14]

But before diving into the rich, imagistic world of Hellenistic epigram, we need to take a few steps back to earlier Greek literature in order to trace the (scant) history of giving female poets poet-terms—and, even before that, in the earliest periods of Greek literature, the few instances where male poet-terms are feminized and applied to nonhuman singing women. For, as we have seen (and will be explored in the following chapter), it is not until Herodotus in the late fifth century BCE that the first term by a male author for a woman poet enters the scene. Before that, we can trace a strange earlier story, where *aoidos*—the term used of Homer, Hesiod, and the tradition of male poets—is used to flesh out and explore, not women poets, but creatures, objects, and ideas that might be associated with feminine creativity and the female voice, from nightingales to Muses, Sphinxes to shuttles. Here, we look not so much at the ways in which

---

12. Ἀλκαίου τε λάληθρον ἐν ὑμνοπόλοις ὑάκινθον (Alcaeus's hyacinth, talkative among the song-composers), *Anth. Pal.* 4.1.13.

13. At the same time, this is a reference to the tradition that Erinna wrote her epic *The Distaff* at the age of nineteen (cf. *Anth. Pal.* 7.11, 9.190) and her early death as a virgin, recorded in the *Suda*.

14. Rosenmeyer 1997: 135, de Vos 2014: 428–29.

women are turned into poets, as the deeper, more associative web of vocabulary between poetics and femininity, where men start to explore the ways in which the language of the poet might be applied to women.

The earliest instances of the feminine *aoidos*, as we have seen, occur in archaic literature in situations of marked gender conflict and poetic resonance. Hesiod's nightingale in the *Works and Days* is called an *aoidos*, complicating the etymological link between the feminine *aēdōn* and the masculine *aoidos* through the clash between the nightingale's gender and her singing ability. Silenced and dominated by the male hawk, the nightingale ends up without a voice and back under male control—yet there is still a latent discomfort in the inevitable parallel between the nightingale *aoidos* and the *aoidos* Hesiod of the *Theogony*. In the *Homeric Hymn to Hermes*, meanwhile, the female tortoise is disemboweled by the male god Hermes, who appropriates and displaces her creative powers as an *aoidos* to make himself the preeminent singer. Both texts, notably, apply *aoidos* in the feminine only to female creatures, perhaps exploring the awareness of the suppleness and creativity of the female voice—as with Helen, the Sirens, and the powerful female lamenters of *Iliad* 24—in the safe space of the animal world. And yet, at the same time, as the silencing of the nightingale and disemboweling of the tortoise show, we cannot afford to miss the distinct and disturbing drive to control and appropriate the female *aoidos* (in both cases, through violence) into the service of the male.

There is one further instance of the feminine *aoidos* in the archaic period. The lyric poet Alcman, of the mid-seventh century BCE (and so a near-contemporary of Sappho), was best known for his *partheneia*, songs composed for a chorus of young unmarried girls.[15] A fragment of his lyric which may come from a *partheneion* (though many are difficult to classify) addresses the Muse: "Come Muse, clear-voiced much-singing Muse, singer [*aoide*] always, begin [*arche*] a new song for the young girls [*parsenois*] to sing" (fr. 14a).[16] Here, in the context of a choral song to be sung by young girls, the poet turns the Muse into an *aoidos*. The "new song" which this Muse inspires thus suggests both the standard invocation to begin the next song in a sequence, and also an

---

15. For Alcman's dates, see Campbell 1967: 192–93; West 1965: 188–94, 1993: xii (followed by Calame 1997: 10) dates instead to the late seventh century BCE, making him a contemporary of Sappho; see also Hutchinson 2001: 71.

16. Μῶσ' ἄγε, Μῶσα λίγηα πολυμμελές / αἰὲν ἀοιδὲ μέλος / νεοχμὸν ἄρχε παρσένοις ἀείδην, Alcm. fr. 14a *PMGF*. On Alcman's *partheneia*, see West 1965, Calame 1997: esp. 2–3, 58–59, 226–27, Hutchinson 2001: 71–112.

acknowledgment of the unusualness of the idea of a song by a female *aoidos*—underlining the novelty of applying *aoidos* to a woman. Yet the verb *archein*, "begin/lead," has a specific meaning in the choral context that indicates a chorus leader signaling the start of the song and dance—so that the term *aoidos* is reduced in scope through the association with *archein* from "composer of songs" to "chorus leader," limiting the Muse's power to inspiration and, perhaps, at most, participation as leader of the chorus.[17] And the poet of the fragment is unequivocally Alcman himself, *not* the Muse. The poem celebrates and performs his (male) poetic composition, even as (or by) invoking the Muse: calling on a male poetic tradition of invocations to the Muses that goes back to Hesiod and Homer, Alcman demonstrates his identity as a poet and flags up the fact that the Muses cannot, in fact, sing among mortals as the male poet does (as we saw in Hesiod). As with Hesiod's nightingale and the *Homeric Hymn*'s tortoise, then, the feminine association with song is explored in the realm of nonthreatening females (here, the female Muses), before, ultimately, being undercut and then appropriated by the male poet.

It is with Euripides, in the late fifth century BCE, that the exploration of the feminine *aoidos* reaches its peak. This was the tragedian who—as we have already seen—was famed for taking the women's point of view, and lampooned for it in Aristophanes. Euripides's identity as a "woman hater" became something of a trope in his reception—and yet, at the same time, it is Euripides, more than any other poet, who represents and explores a wide range of women's experiences. His women are by no means all negatively represented (we might think of his Iphigenia, or Alcestis), while one can argue quite persuasively that even those to whom Aristophanes's women most object, like Medea, are treated in ways that demonstrate an element of compassion rather than judgment.[18] Meanwhile, there are moments, as we will see, where Euripides's women characters step out of the historical context of women's silence and constraint to make impassioned speeches which advocate for the women's point of view. As often, the answer is most likely more complex than a crude

17. On the role of the chorus leader (χορηγός), see Calame 1997: 43–73. For the Muses as χορηγοί, cf. Hes. *Theog.* 7, Pl. *Leg.* 665a3–6; see Calame 1997: 46, 52 (who mentions this fragment). On the verb ἄρχειν/ἐξάρχειν as characteristic of the chorus leader who gives the signal for the beginning of the song/dance, see Calame 1997: 43, 47–48.

18. March 1990; see also Goff 1995, Zeitlin 1996: 364–65, 416, Zelenak 1998: 99–110, McClure 1999a: e.g., 160, 263, Saxonhouse 2005, Lamari 2007, Luschnig 2007, Mossman 2011: 28–48, Chong-Gossard and Ng 2018: 72–73, Sissa 2020, Roisman 2021: 212–13. For a summary of approaches to reading women in Greek drama, see H. Foley 2001: 6–12.

categorization of Euripides as either a misogynist or a feminist before his time: what we see from his poetry, rather, is a multiplicity of explorations of the experiences and voices of women as well as men, in much of their complexity, circumscribed by the historical realities of being a man writing about women, and embedded in the problematic context of the male acknowledgment of female power "in order to control" it.[19] It is not simply, however, I would argue, on the macrolevel of theme or character which Euripides investigates female gender and its relationship to poetry: he does so in pushing the boundaries of the very word for poet itself, and manipulating it into the feminine—more than any other poet had before—to explore the interrelationship between female creativity, speech, and poetic song.[20]

Muses

The term *aoidos* occurs twelve times in Euripides—eight in the masculine, and four in the feminine.[21] These are suitably striking numbers, particularly when compared to the three instances of *aoidos* in the feminine in all previous extant Greek literature—and they demonstrate the extent of Euripides's innovation with feminine *aoidos*.[22] Even the occurrences of *aoidos* in the masculine often imply a preoccupation with feminine gender: in the *Children of Heracles*, for example, the generic masculine plural *aoidoi* seems to include women, while even in the masculine singular, as in the *Alcestis*, *Medea*, or *Heracles*, the term arises in markedly gendered contexts that draw attention to the male-gendering

---

19. Rabinowitz 1993: 26; cf. Mastronarde 2010: 246–47 and Mueller 2017 on the "complexity and diversity" (Mueller 2017: 512) of Euripides's handling of women, also E. Segal 1983 on Euripides as a "poet of paradox."

20. For an excellent study of metapoetry in Euripides, see Torrance 2013; on Euripides and literary criticism, see Wright 2010.

21. ἀοιδός in the feminine: Eur. *Hipp.* 743, *Tro.* 385, *Phoen.* 1507, fr. 528a *TrGF*. In the masculine, but in a gendered context: *Alc.* 454, *Med.* 421, *HF* 678, 692. In the masculine plural: *Heracl.* 403. In the masculine: *HF* 110, 1315, 1346). This count excludes the *Rhesus*, on which see chapter 6, n. 24; cf. also *Hel.* 1109 for ἀοιδός as an adjective, on which see pp. 181–82. Ford 2002: 137 n. 23 gives a count of over thirty instances of ἀοιδός in Euripides, which I am unable to replicate; Collard 1971 notes two more doubtful instances at *Hel.* 358 and fr. 523 *TrGF*. For ποιητής in Euripides (only once), see fr. 663 *TrGF* (quoted at chapter 5, n. 109). Note also the reference to the poet as ἐργάτης at *Andr.* 476: see Wright 2010: 174–75, Torrance 2013: 191–206.

22. Euripides uses ἀοιδός in general more frequently than the other tragedians, though this does not tell us much, given that a greater number of Euripides's plays are extant. The term occurs once in Aeschylus (*Supp.* 695) and three times in Sophocles (fr. 852 *TrGF*, *Trach.* 1000, *OT* 36).

of poetry.[23] We turn first to the most traditional application of feminine *aoidos* in Euripides: its attribution to the Muse, looking back to Alcman's *Mōsa aoidos*.[24] In the *Trojan Women*, Euripides's tragedy of 415 BCE which stages the fate of the women of Troy after the Trojan War, Cassandra—the famous Trojan prophet who was cursed with never being believed—anticipates the impending doom of the Greeks, and describes the losses they have already suffered. She ends her catalogue with a final (and contested) cap: "It is better to keep silent about shameful things: let my Muse [*mousa*] not be a bard [*aoidos*] who sings of evil things" (*Tro.* 384–85).[25] There is significant power in the fact that it is a female character here who calls on the Muse as her personal inspiration—and, specifically, that she reclaims the Muse as a bard, an *aoidos*.[26] Divine inspiration and poetic production, which were forced apart along gendered lines from Hesiod on, merge here, to give the woman the power to be *both* inspirer and poet. This parallels Cassandra's combination of divinely inspired knowledge (she is "possessed by the god," *Tro.* 366) and her performance here within Euripides's play, as she literally speaks in poetry— albeit poetry composed by the poet Euripides, whose presence as the male *aoidos* of the tragedy silently and subtly contrasts with the poet-status of the

---

23. On *Heracl.* 403, see chapter 6, n. 59. *Alc.* 454 is in the context of a choral ode in praise of Alcestis: note that the chorus anticipates Alcestis being hymned by μουσοπόλοι (445), a term which, as we will see, has a gendered history in Sappho at fr. 150 L-P (see chapter 8); see further C. Segal 1993b: 37–50, esp. 46–47. At *HF* 110, 678, and 692 we have the phrase γέρων ἀοιδός (though note the textual uncertainty: Nauck's emendation γέρων for γόων in the MS is accepted by Bond 1981 ad loc. and in Diggle's OCT), while at both 673–86 and 687–95 we have a feminine choral context being evoked (first the Muses, then the Delian women); see Wright 2010: 172–73. For ἀοιδός at *Med.* 421, see pp. 182–89.

24. Note that there is also an occurrence of the Muse as ἀοιδός in the *Rhesus* (ὁ Στρυμόνιος πῶλος ἀοιδοῦ / Μούσης, 386–87), a play whose authenticity and date has long been questioned, and therefore not included here: see Fantuzzi 2021: 16–23 for a comprehensive discussion, also Liapis 2012: lxx and Mattison 2015: 485 n. 1.

25. σιγᾶν ἄμεινον τἀισχρά, μηδὲ μοῦσά μοι / γένοιτ᾽ ἀοιδὸς ἥτις ὑμνήσει κακά, *Tro.* 384–85. Diggle in the OCT (1981) and Kovacs's Loeb edition (1999) both athetize these lines, following Reichenberger. However, Biehl 1989 ad loc. argues persuasively that they fit thematically with the rest of Cassandra's speech; Lee 1976 accepts them without comment. Cf. also C. Segal 1993b: 21–22, Torrance 2013: 242.

26. Cassandra also looks ahead to the choral invocation of the Muse at *Tro.* 512–15; see Loraux 2002: 68–69, Torrance 2013: 163, Fanfani 2018: 244–48. On the Muse in Euripides, see Fantuzzi 2007, Wright 2010: 166 with n. 8, and, on the Muse in the *Trojan Women*, see Fanfani 2018: 245–46.

Muse here.[27] But there is an even deeper gendered game going on here. Cassandra gives the Muse the masculine term *aoidos*, but turns it conspicuously feminine, juxtaposing it with the feminine relative pronoun "who" (*hētis*, 385). The uncomfortable femininity of *aoidos*, in other words, is being deliberately exploited here, with the juxtaposition of the masculine-looking (and historically male-gendered) *aoidos* alongside the feminine pronoun, "she who"—so that the gnomic expression reads in the Greek as a striking oxymoronic gender statement, "may my female Muse not be a male bard, the kind of woman who sings of evil things."

There is a final twist to this apparent rewriting of the gendered history of *aoidos*. Cassandra's statement, as much as it breaks down barriers between Muse and poet, male and female, is expressed, significantly, in the negative—"may my Muse *not* be . . ."—and it is prefaced by a call for silence ("it is better to keep silent [*sigan*] about shameful things," 384). The invocation of the Muse here is thus more of an anti-invocation: the Muse will *not* be summoned, as silence is better than singing about tragedy.[28] Cassandra's apparently radical call for her Muse to be an *aoidos* is turned on its head as nothing less than a female act of self-silencing—the highly gendered stereotype of women as better seen and not heard, which recalls Telemachus's silencing of Penelope in the *Odyssey*, and Ajax's words to Tecmessa in Sophocles's drama *Ajax*: "Silence is a woman's adornment" (Soph. *Aj.* 293). The force of *aoidos* here, then, is more to limit and curtail Cassandra's speech than it is a liberation of the Muse as poet. The paradox of the female Muse being a male bard is, in fact, what brings Cassandra's speech about the doom of the Greeks to a close, and effects her transition into the next section to the praise of Troy (Eur. *Tro.* 386–405). The implication, in the end, seems to be that a Muse cannot be a bard, a woman should not speak as a man does—there are limits to what a woman should, and should not, speak about, and "shameful things" are one of them—and thus Cassandra's assertion that silence is better is both proved, and enforced, by the Muses' anti-invocation. The contrast is particularly strong if we look at the chorus of the old men of Thebes in the *Heracles*, produced a year or so

<hr/>

27. Cassandra is ἔνθεος, *Tro.* 366. Cassandra's comment also, more broadly, slots into the exploration of the relationship between the Muse and lament, both in this tragedy and elsewhere in Euripides's plays: see C. Segal 1993b: 13–34, Loraux 2002: 68–69, Fantuzzi 2007, Fanfani 2018: 243–48.

28. Fanfani 2018: 245 suggests that this is similar to Sappho fr. 150 L-P (on which see pp. 235–44); but, importantly, this is a silencing of the Muse herself, not the μουσοπόλοι of Sappho.

before the *Trojan Women* in around 416 BCE, who term themselves (masculine) *aoidoi* several times—and who do so to sing in a full range of tragic genres, from lament to celebration (inspired by the Muses) to hymns of praise.[29] Cassandra's comment about her Muse not being an *aoidos* suggests, by contrast, that women cannot be *aoidoi* of tragedy in the same way that men can; and the very act of trying to assert the paradox of a Muse who is also a female bard is sufficient to silence Cassandra's attempt to write her own tragedy.

Female Gods

This fantasy of a female god who might, in another world, be an *aoidos*, is picked up elsewhere in Euripides. In the *Hippolytus*, produced in 428 BCE, Phaedra, wife of Theseus and stepmother of Hippolytus—for whom she has conceived an illicit passion—has determined to kill herself as the only way out of the shameful situation. While Phaedra departs into the palace to commit the deed, the chorus of women of Troezen responds with a song known as the "escape ode" (lines 732–75)—a fantastical evocation of their desire to fly to the mythical ends of the earth, to escape the horror of their present.[30] "If only I could reach the apple-planted shore of the Hesperides, the female singers [*tān aoidōn*]," they say (*Hipp.* 742–43), referring to the divine female guardians of Hera's golden apples who were said to dwell at the edge of the earth.[31] The unusualness of the presentation of the Hesperides as singers is underlined by the fact that in several of the manuscripts "singers" (*aoidōn*, usually masculine) is corrupted to the feminine "songs" (*aoidān*), to agree with the feminine definite article—demonstrating the discomfort with the feminization of *aoidos* here and its application to these three female gods.[32] This is not the only time,

---

29. See chapter 6, n. 23.

30. See Barlow 1971: 38–39, Padel 1974, Swift 2009 esp. 369–71; Barrett 1964: 298 calls it "fairyland."

31. Ἑσπερίδων δ᾽ ἐπὶ μηλόσπορον ἀκτὰν / ἀνύσαιμι τᾶν ἀοιδῶν, *Hipp.* 742–43. Note the sexual and feminine erotic connotations of μηλόσπορον: on the erotic undertones of μῆλον, see Winkler 1990: 183, while the -σπορον suffix (from σπείρω, "sow, beget") suggests feminine creative birth. See further Swift 2009: 369–70.

32. See Barrett 1964 ad loc., who notes the same corruption at *Med.* 422; see chapter 6, n. 62. This is particularly interesting as different manuscripts often tend to normalize Doric or other dialects into Attic rather than the other way around (see Probert 2019, who also comments on the modern tendency to see Attic as the "common form" in e.g., LSJ), suggesting a concerted attempt to avoid the (Attic) female ἀοιδῶν in the MS tradition.

however, that Euripides associates the Hesperides with the term *aoidos*: in the *Heracles*, they are called *hymnōidoi* (*HF* 394), "hymn-singing" or "hymn-singers" (depending on whether we take the term adjectivally or substantively), a combination of *hymnos* (hymn) and *aoidos*.[33] Here in the *Hippolytus*, the women of Troezen grant the Hesperides the full (and hallowed) title *aoidos*; but this is a fantasy land, a desired escape to an otherworld articulated in the optative ("if only I could . . .") which does not exist. The reality of the situation, to which the chorus returns in the following two verses, is Phaedra's powerlessness and the inescapable fact of her suicide, as the only way in which she can claim agency in an impossible situation.[34] The ideal of the woman as *aoidos* belongs, in other words, in fairyland—not the real world. Phaedra's reality is a silenced voice; the chorus's wish that a woman might be an *aoidos* remains a starkly defined fantasy. After this ode, Phaedra speaks no more.

Satyrs and Foreigners

Female *aoidoi* at the far ends of the world crop up in another tragedian, a contemporary of Euripides: Ion of Chios, who competed in the major dramatic festivals at Athens from around 450 BCE onward.[35] His *Omphale* (of uncertain date) remains only in fragmentary quotations by later authors, from which we have to piece together what we can about the play.[36] We know that it was a satyr play, and that it told the story of the myth of Hercules's punishment for killing Iphitus, his sentence by the Delphic oracle to be sold as a slave, and his purchase by the Lydian queen Omphale. One fragment has Omphale (most likely) addressing what seems to be the chorus—probably, as Pat Easterling proposes, the satyrs, doubling up as Omphale's female slaves: "Come on, Lydian harp-girls [*psaltriai*], singers [*aoidoi*] of old hymns, adorn [*kosmēsate*] the foreigner!"[37] There is a lot to unpack in these two lines. Firstly, we have a feminine term for the chorus's musicianship, designating them as *psaltriai*,

---

33. ὑμνῳδούς τε κόρας ("hymn-singing girls" or "hymn-singer girls"), *HF* 394; Bond 1981 ad loc. also connects the two passages.

34. On female suicide in tragedy, see Loraux 1987; for the link between female suicide and silence, see Chong-Gossard 2008: 113–54, and on "the escape song as a death wish," see Garrison 1995: 80–101, and pp. 89–93 in particular on the *Hippolytus*.

35. On Ion of Chios see Dover 1986, Jennings and Katsaros 2007, Wright 2016: 29–34.

36. For an overview, see Easterling 2007.

37. <ΟΜΦ.> ἀλλ᾽ εἶα, Λυδαὶ ψάλτριαι, παλαιθέτων / ὕμνων ἀοιδοί, τὸν ξένον κοσμήσατε, Ion of Chios fr. 22 *TrGF* = Ath. 634ef. See Easterling 2007: 288.

"harp-girls"—as well as the feminine *Ludai*, "Lydian." The context is quite clearly defined as a female-gendered one, characterizing Omphale and her court as highly feminine—which matches both the mythology behind Omphale as a sole female ruler (depending on the account, she is either a virgin or a widow), and the common fifth-century stereotype of eastern effeminacy and exotic luxury.[38] This feminine-gendered court of female musicians led by a female ruler is, then, what allows Omphale to call her singers *aoidoi*, appropriating the masculine term into this otherworld where women rule and where *aoidos* can go feminine. But this is not only an emphatically different land with different gender rules, it is also a different time: the female Lydian *aoidoi* are specifically marked as belonging to an older, mythological era by Omphale's designation of their songs as "old." Being out of time and place, then, in a fantasy eastern land of myth where women are on top, enables a boundary-crossing of the masculine *aoidoi* for feminine harp-girls.

The otherness of the situation is underlined by Omphale's labeling Hercules as a "foreigner," a *xenos*. Here, it is Greeks who are foreigners or strangers, not the eastern Lydians whom the Athenian audience of the play would label *xenoi*. Moreover, the girls are told to "adorn" the stranger, with the verb *kosmein*. Easterling glosses this as "celebrate," a valid translation which picks up on the chorus's identification as harp-players and suggests that Omphale is commanding them metaphorically to "adorn" or "embellish" Hercules in song.[39] At the same time, the term can also suggest the adornment or dressing of women (we see it as such, for example, in the dressing of Pandora in Hesiod's *Works and Days*)—and it is hard not to see it as at the very least a double entendre, a veiled reference to the well-known myth of Omphale's cross-dressing of Hercules as a woman.[40] There is no specific evidence for the presence of this aspect of the myth—which became particularly popular into the fourth century and beyond into Roman times—in Ion's version, but we know that it was current at the time, as evidenced by its portrayal on two late fifth-century vases.[41] And other fragments from Ion's play do suggest some kind of "elaborate dressing-up scene," with references to perfume, cosmetics, and

---

38. Easterling 2007: 284, 287.

39. Easterling 2007: 288.

40. ζῶσε δὲ καὶ κόσμησε θεὰ γλαυκῶπις Ἀθήνη, Hes. *Op.* 72. On the myth of Hercules's cross-dressing, see Cyrino 1998: 214–26; see further chapter 4, n. 23.

41. ARV 2 1134.7, London E370, and Staatliche Museen zu Berlin inv. 3414: see Cyrino 1998: 215, Lada-Richards 1999: 18–21, though note Loraux 1990: 35 n. 56 for citations of a later date.

mascara.[42] There is, then, at the very least, some resonance of effeminate dress, if not downright cross-dressing, going on in the command to "adorn the stranger," playing on the pun between the embellishment of a hero's name in song and dressing him up as a woman or effeminate easterner. In this topsy-turvy world of gender-bending, where a woman rules alone, a man dresses like a woman, and a Greek becomes a *xenos*, the application of the usually masculine *aoidos* to the Lydian harp-girls thus seems to fit entirely. Giving the term *aoidos*, normally the preserve of high-flown Greek male poets, to a raucous band of satyrs posing as Lydian harp-girls, acts as a microcosmic reflection of the upside-down nature of this gender-bending otherworld.[43]

Ion's *Omphale* might, then, appear to be the first text in extant Greek literature to apply *aoidos* to human "women." Yet it is important to remember the dramatic context: these are, in fact, if we follow Easterling's conjecture, (men enacting) satyrs posing as non-Greek women. They are thus "other" in three respects (beast vs. man; non-Greek vs. Greek; woman vs. man), set within a context that turns all the norms of the male Greek world upside-down—and, ultimately, not female, in both the context of the fiction (satyrs acting women) and the reality of the drama (male actors acting satyrs acting women).[44] The references to cross-dressing remind us that it is not only potentially Hercules who is engaging in transvestism here, but the chorus too: the male actors and male satyrs are playing an elaborate dress-up game as Lydian women. It therefore seems that it is not only the otherworld of Omphale's court, but the specific gender-bending of the satyrs mimicking women, that is precisely what enables *aoidos* to cross gender and category boundaries here—to be applied, in the end, to *men*, acting satyrs, acting women.

Sphinxes

The final three instances of feminine *aoidos* in Euripides, like the cross-dressing satyrs of *Omphale*, also apply to nonhumans: one a mythical creature, one a bird, and one an inanimate object. We begin with the mythical creature, the Sphinx. In the *Phoenician Women*, probably produced around 410 or 409 BCE, Euripides dramatizes the siege of Thebes and the tragic deaths of Eteocles and

---

42. Easterling 2007: 287, referring to Ion of Chios fr. 24 *TrGF* = Ath. 690b, fr. 25 *TrGF*.

43. On women in Greek theater as "other" to the masculine self, see Zeitlin 1996: 341–74; on the construction of Greeks versus barbarians, see Hall 1989b, Harrison 2002.

44. See chapter 4, n. 39.

Polynices, brothers of Antigone, whom we find near the play's close delivering a lament for her dead brothers and mother. The beginning of the tragedy, she claims, was when Oedipus "solved the intelligible riddle of the unintelligible, savage Sphinx, the singer [*aoidou*], and slayed her body" (Eur. *Phoen.* 1505–7).[45] This was not the first time that the Sphinx—the legendary creature with the head of a woman and body of a lion who guarded the entrance to Thebes and posed a riddle to any traveler who wanted to pass—had been called an *aoidos* in Greek drama.[46] Sophocles calls her a "cruel *aoidos*" in his *Oedipus Tyrannus*, in the voice of the priest (*sklēras aoidou*, Soph. *OT* 36)—but other characters in Sophocles's play have other things to say: she is also a "rhapsode-dog," according to Oedipus (*hē rhapsōidos . . . kuōn*, 391), a "prophecy-singing hooked-clawed virgin," according to the chorus of old Theban men (*tan gampsōnucha parthenon / chrēsmōidon*, 1199–1200), and—the only time she is actually named in the *Oedipus*—"the varied-singing Sphinx," according to Creon (*hē poikilōidos Sphinx*, 130).[47] The terms she receives in Sophocles emphasize, in concert, her monstrosity ("cruel," "hooked-clawed," "dog"); her gender ("virgin," along with the feminine definite articles); and her connection to song (*aoidos*, "rhapsode," "prophecy-singing," "varied-singing"). Both adjectives for song applied to her, *chrēsmōidos* and *poikilōidos*, are cognate with *aoidos*, while both the poet-terms she receives, *aoidos* and *rhapsōidos*, are typically masculine terms. In other words, as a terrible, savage monster who is beyond human, her riddling voice can be connected with the qualities of the *aoidos*, precisely because she is not a normal human woman. Her otherness, her paradoxicality (as Euripides identifies: "the intelligible riddle of the unintelligible Sphinx"), her monstrosity, enable her to cross the bounds of her gender to ally her troublingly powerful voice with that of the male bard.

Yet, at the same time, this is hardly a positive example of an *aoidos*: a monstrous "dog," "cruel," with "hooked claws" (in Sophocles), "savage," and "unintelligible" (in Euripides), who rips into those who fail to solve her riddle. The

45. τᾶς ἀγρίας ὅτε / δυσξυνέτου ξυνετὸν μέλος ἔγνω / Σφιγγὸς ἀοιδοῦ σῶμα φονεύσας, *Phoen.* 1505–7; I follow Mastronarde's text here (1994).

46. On the Sphinx as singer elsewhere in Euripides, see fr. 540a *TrGF*, which includes the fragmentary line [πειπου̃σ' ἐξά[μ]ετ[ρ(α) (speaking hexameters) of the Sphinx (line 6); see Collard, Cropp, and Gibert 2004: 116–17, 126. My thanks to Matthew Wright for pointing this passage out to me.

47. See Finglass 2018 ad 35–39, March 2020 ad 36. On ἀοιδός in Sophocles (only three times), see chapter 6, n. 22. Sophocles's *OT* was likely produced in the 430s BCE (see Finglass 2018: 3); Euripides's use of ἀοιδός in the *Phoenissae* probably looks back to Sophocles's play.

implication in both tragedians is that, if a woman becomes an *aoidos*, this is what she looks like. Moreover, like the Muses and the Hesperides in Euripides, the application of *aoidos* to a mythic creature rather than a human woman goes further, to suggest that a normal woman could not, in any case, become an *aoidos*: *aoidos* in the feminine is the preserve of divine women whose otherness enables them to cross human gender boundaries, or—in Ion's *Omphale*—cross-dressing satyrs who already inhabit an other-realm between man and beast. And finally, Antigone's description of the Sphinx's fate in Euripides's *Phoenician Women* details the troubling end for a woman *aoidos* who oversteps the mark: her song is "solved" or "interpreted" by the man, who thus takes control of her poetry, and in an act of final retribution, her body (*sōma phoneusas*, "slaying her body," Eur. *Phoen.* 1507)—by killing her.[48] Her song interpreted, her body conquered, the man takes control of the woman *aoidos*'s voice and body, and the female *aoidos* is no more.[49]

Shuttles

The next example is neither a monster nor a god—it is not even a creature. It is an inanimate object. It comes from a single line of Euripides, preserved among a jumble of Euripidean lyrics (juxtaposed for humorous effect) in Aristophanes's *Frogs* as Aeschylus mocks his rival poet: "the pursuits of the singer-shuttle [*kerkidos aoidou*]" (Ar. *Ran.* 1316 = Eur. fr. 528a *TrGF*).[50] The idea of turning the shuttle into an *aoidos* most likely stems, as Giovanni Fanfani points

48. Or by inducing her to commit suicide: see March 2020: 8 n. 24, 282.

49. Note that Antigone continues her lament with a cognate of ἀοιδός: at *Phoen.* 1518, she calls on a bird to be συνῳδός (joint-singing) with her. This is clearly a reference to the nightingale, with the corrupt text at 1517–18 containing some allusion to the bird's identity as a "solitary, bereaved mother" (Mastronarde 1994 ad loc.), and thus to the myth of Procne: see Loraux 1998: 63, and see also chapter 2, n. 55. At *Phoen.* 1499 we have two more references to poet-vocabulary: προσῳδόν (following Mastronarde and Diggle's text), also adjectival and also cognate with ἀοιδός, and μουσοπόλον, both used of Antigone's song; Mastronarde 1994 ad loc. suggests that these could also be read as substantives ("accompanist or poet"). Either way, it is suggestive that none of these poet-terms is applied to the human woman Antigone in the same way that the bestial other-woman Sphinx is labeled an ἀοιδός. Note that μουσοπόλον is particularly resonant from a gendered perspective as an echo of Sappho fr. 150 L-P: see pp. 235–44 with chapter 8, n. 21; and cf. the μουσοπόλοι who are anticipated to lament Alcestis at Eur. *Alc.* 445, see chapter 6, n. 23.

50. κερκίδος ἀοιδοῦ μελέτας, Ar. *Ran.* 1316 = fr. 528a *TrGF*. See Fanfani 2017: 429–30; the fragment is ascribed to the *Meleager*, on which see Wright 2018: 187–90.

out, from the noise made by the shuttle as it hits the threads on the loom; two fragments of Sophocles refer to the "voice" or "songs" of the shuttle.[51] Here in Euripides, however, the shuttle is personified as an actual poet, an *aoidos*. There are multiple plays on gender going on here. Firstly, the feminine shuttle (*kerkis*) is allied with a noun, *aoidos*, which is usually masculine.[52] Secondly, as we have seen, the task of weaving in antiquity was indubitably feminine and (in literature) feminine gendered, from Helen's appearance as a weaver in the *Iliad* onward—while the status of poet, *aoidos*, was just as emphatically gendered male. Feminine noun does battle against masculine noun, female sphere of activity against male. On the one hand, we might be reminded of the use of *aoidos* for an inanimate female object in the *Homeric Hymn to Hermes*, and the exploitation of the female association with creativity for male ends. On the other, we can read this as an example of the often-made comparison between weaving and the composition of poetry, which resonates from Helen's meta-poetic weaving of the Trojan War in *Iliad* 3 to the imagery of poet-as-craftsman from Pindar on.[53] In this sense, the female realm is brought into the male, or the male imposed on the female (whichever way we want to read it), assimilating women's work with men's poetic craft. And the fact that women often sang while weaving—as we see Calypso singing at her loom at *Odyssey* 5.61–62 and Circe at *Odyssey* 10.221, for example—reminds us of the hidden female song traditions associated with women's work, crossing the label of canonical male epic poetic composition into the sphere of women's everyday work songs.[54]

Birds

Another instance which resonates with the archaic use of feminine *aoidos* occurs in the *Helen*, Euripides's play of 412 BCE dramatizing the alternative story of Helen of Troy. In the second half of the play, the chorus of Greek slave

51. Stieber 2011: 315–16, Fanfani 2017: 429–30 with n. 50; see Soph. fr. 595 *TrGF* (κερκίδος φωνή) and fr. 890 *TrGF* (κερκίδος ὕμνους).

52. Though it is worth noting that, as in Hes. *Op.* 208, ἀοιδός could be a two-termination adjective: see pp. 57–61 with chapter 2, n. 62; see also chapter 6, n. 56.

53. On female weaving and its connection to singing/poetry in Euripides, see Fletcher 2009, Wright 2010: 171–72 with n. 39, Torrance 2013: 16–18, 26–28, 40–41, 152–57; on craftsmanship metaphors for the poet in Pindar, see Steiner 1986: 41–52, Shapiro 1994: 72–98, C. Segal 1998: 149–54, Ford 2002: 113–30, and in Euripides, see Stieber 2011; see also chapter 3, n. 34 and chapter 6, n. 68.

54. See p. 12 with introduction, n. 45.

women embarks on an ode, calling on the nightingale to help them sing the woes of Helen and the Trojan women: "most songful, melodious bird, nightingale of tears" (*Hel.* 1109–10).[55] Here it is the adjective *aoidos* in the superlative applied to the nightingale, not the noun.[56] As with Hesiod's nightingale, we see a connection being made between the *aoidos* nightingale and the etymology of the word for nightingale, *aēdōn*. Turning *aoidos* into a superlative neatly sidesteps the controversy in Hesiod over whether *aoidos* is a two-termination adjective or a noun—and it also usefully supplies the word with a visibly feminine ending, *aoidotatan*. This is particularly appropriate for the female nightingale, the *aēdōn*, but also for the context, where the female chorus calls on a female bird to sing of women's fate: the invocation to the feminine nightingale as *aoidotata*, "most songful," seems to echo the chorus's own song.[57] Euripides thus seems to manage to turn *aoidos* feminine. But it is at the cost of taking away its status as a noun, as a label for poetic identity. And, once again, the word is applied, not to human women or women singers, but to a bird.[58]

"Singing Back a Song to His-story*": Critiquing the Male Poet*

Euripides's deployment of feminine *aoidos* shows an exploration and problematization of the relationship between women and poetry, and the lack of words to describe them. The application of *aoidos* only to female gods, mythical monsters, birds, and even inanimate objects, demonstrates the tension and discomfort with turning *aoidos* feminine. Nowhere—with the exception, perhaps, of one passage in the *Children of Heracles* where women might lurk hidden behind the generalizing masculine plural for "singers" of oracles (*Heracl.* 403)—does *aoidos* refer to real, living women.[59] But real women do need to be addressed.

---

55. τὰν ἀοιδοτάταν / ὄρνιθα μελῳδὸν ἀηδόνα δακρυόεσσαν, Eur. *Hel.* 1109–10; see Weiss 2018: 158–67. Note the term μελῳδόν at 1109, cognate with ἀοιδός: cf. *IT* 1104 (of the swan), *IA* 1045; cf. also the description of the nightingale as προσῳδός and συνῳδός at *Phoen.* 1499 and 1518, see chapter 6, n. 49.

56. Cf. Theoc. *Id.* 12.7 on the nightingale as συμπάντων λιγύφωνος ἀοιδοτάτη πετεηνῶν (the most songful and clear-voiced of all birds); also Alcm. fr. 1.96–7 *PMGF*: ἁ δὲ τᾶν Σηρην[ί]δων / ἀοιδοτέρα μ[ὲν οὐχί (she is not more songful than the Sirens).

57. Allan 2008 ad 1111–12, Weiss 2018: 145, 160.

58. Cf. *Phoen.* 1499 and 1518: see chapter 6, n. 49.

59. χρησμῶν δ᾽ ἀοιδοὺς πάντας (all the singers of oracles), *Heracl.* 403; on the female oracle at Delphi, see pp. 250–53.

With Euripides's *Medea*, produced in 431 BCE, we arrive at last at one of the most powerful critiques of the tradition and vocabulary of the male *aoidos*. The first choral ode (lines 410–45) sees the chorus of Corinthian women responding to Jason's faithlessness to Medea, asserting that the world has turned upside down.[60] In this new upside-down world, they claim, where rivers flow backward to their sources (line 410), the traditional discourse of misogyny will also be reversed and "the female gender" (*gunaikeiōi genei*, 417–18) will be recognized (415–19).[61] This vision of an otherworld where order is reversed might remind us of the escape to the Hesperides in the *Hippolytus*, or Ion of Chios's court of Lydian satyrs. We might, therefore, be able to anticipate the move that the chorus makes next: the identification of the source of this misogynistic discourse as the long history of male-dominated literature and the tradition of male poets, *aoidoi* (421–30):[62]

> The Muses of the old male poets [*aoidōn*]
> will stop telling tales where *I* was unfaithful.
> Apollo, lord-leader of song, never gave us the chance
> to sing to the lyre:
> if he had, I'd have sung back [*antachēs'*] a song to rival
> *his*-story [lit., "the masculine gender/race," *arsenōn gennai*]. There's a
>   lot of history,
> and lots to say about us—
> as much as the men [*andrōn*].

There is a huge amount to unpack here in this programmatic passage for the male domination of poetry and the recovery of women's voices. The first, and

---

60. For an introduction to this ode see Mastronarde 2002: 239–40, Mossman 2011: 257; see also Barlow 1989: 161–62, McClure 1999b: 388–90, Allan 2002: 57–58, Luschnig 2007: 144–47, Swift 2010: 120–21.

61. τὰν δ᾽ ἐμὰν εὔκλειαν ἔχειν βιοτὰν στρέψουσι φᾶμαι· / ἔρχεται τιμὰ γυναικείωι γένει (What people say will turn my life around to have a good reputation; honor is coming to the female gender/race), *Med.* 415–19. Note the use of γένος, which can mean both "race, class, category" and, more specifically, "gender" (see p. 14); for examples of "the misogynistic tradition in Greek poetry," see Mastronarde 2002 ad 419–20, cf. Knox 1977: 223.

62. μοῦσαι δὲ παλαιγενέων λήξουσ᾽ ἀοιδῶν / τὰν ἐμὰν ὑμνεῦσαι ἀπιστοσύναν. / οὐ γὰρ ἐν ἁμετέραι γνώμαι λύρας / ὤπασε θέσπιν ἀοιδὰν / Φοῖβος ἁγήτωρ μελέων· ἐπεὶ ἀντάχησ᾽ ἂν ὕμνον / ἀρσένων γένναι. μακρὸς δ᾽ αἰὼν ἔχει / πολλὰ μὲν ἁμετέραν ἀνδρῶν τε μοῖραν εἰπεῖν, *Med.* 421–30. Barrett 1964 ad *Hipp.* 743 notes the corruption of ἀοιδῶν to ἀοιδᾶν in the MS tradition in the *Hippolytus* and here at *Med.* 422: see chapter 6, n. 32.

most basic, is that we have a statement being made about the lot of women in the voice of a chorus of (ostensibly) women—in similar fashion to other gendered commentaries in the play, like Medea's famous complaint against women's oppression in marriage and the trauma of childbirth (230–51). Of course, the reality hiding behind the play, as with all dramatic fictions in antiquity, is the voice of a male poet performed by male actors and male chorus. Yet this need not be as limiting as it seems. Laura McClure has shown how we can identify the exploitation of women's gendered discourse in Athenian drama: an interest, if not in the authentic portrayal of "real" women's voices, then at least in exploring and deploying women's speech and speech genres.[63] In this choral ode, the "women" of the play step forward and take their gendered speech to a new level to reflect on the gendering of speech itself, in the presentation of "the female gender" (417–18) and their response to the songs told about "the male gender" (428–29). This radical critique of gendered speech focuses on the male-dominated tradition of poetry. It begins by framing the traditional gender relations of poetry, setting the stage for a gendered reading of poets: the female Muses (*Mousai*) inspire the male bards (*aoidōn*, 421–22). The fact that we are looking back to the beginning of a long-standing male tradition is emphasized, not only by the adjective "old" (*palaigeneōn*, 421–22), but by the reference a few lines below to the chorus's desire to sing a "divine song" (*thespin aoidan*, 425), reminding us of Hesiod's "divine voice" granted to him by the Muses (*audē thespis*, Hes. *Theog.* 31–32).[64] And it also looks back to the Homeric bard, where "divine song" was described as an attribute of both the bards Phemius and Demodocus in the *Odyssey* (Hom. *Od.* 1.328, 8.498); while in Eumaeus's list of craftsmen at *Od.* 17.383–85, the bard is even called a *thespis aoidos*, "divine bard."[65] The description of these old male bards as *aoidoi* is thus perfectly fitting for Hesiod and Homer, the grandfathers of the masculine poetic tradition, who both shaped the gendered relationship between the female Muse and male bard, and fashioned and bounded the term *aoidos* as the preserve of men. (They also, incidentally, initiated the "negative

63. McClure 1999a; cf., on women's voices in tragedy, Williamson 1990 (on Euripides's *Medea*), McClure 1995, Zeitlin 1996: 361–63, McClure 1999b, Mossman 2001, Lardinois and McClure 2001; see also chapter 6, n. 68 for Medea appropriating male-gendered speech, and see further, introduction, n. 63.

64. See p. 49 with chapter 2, n. 15.

65. See Mastronarde 2002 ad 424–25. On Phemius at Hom. *Od.* 1.325–64, see pp. 26–30; on Demodocus in *Odyssey* 8, see pp. 33–35; on *Od.* 17.385, see chapter 1, n. 6.

discourse" which the chorus critiques [*duskelados phama*, 419–20], the misogynistic stereotypes in male poets' depictions of women—most notably Hesiod's Pandora.)[66] This "old" world of gender is evoked by the adjective *palaigenēs*, literally "old-born," with its -*genēs* ending cognate with *genos* ("race," "offspring," but also "gender"—as we are reminded at lines 417–18 and 428–29, where *genos* is used of female and male gender respectively). These poets are not just "old," then, but, the adjective suggests, deeply symbolic of "the old systems of gender" (*palai-genos*).

The chorus is determined to change this traditional gendered poetic world. In their vision, the Muses, they claim, will abandon male poets and stop their negative discourse around women. There are two radical aspects to this projection: the first, the rejection by the Muses of male poets as gatekeepers of poetry, and the transfer of their allegiance from men to women; and secondly, the attribution of the power of song *to the Muses themselves* ("the Muses will stop telling tales," 421–23).[67] As we will recall from the appearance of the Muses elsewhere, particularly in Hesiod's *Theogony*, this is in stark contrast to the usual (male-enforced) passivity of the Muses as inspirers, but not producers, of song. Here, the female chorus envisions them "singing" (423), and—as they do so, as their voices emerge from the silence—recovering the stories of women, rather than the misogynistic stereotypes perpetrated by men. Women will shift, in other words, from the inspirations and personifications of song, the objects of men's imagination and the (much-maligned) subject matter of their poetry, to become their own singers.

But it is not just the Muses who are imagined as becoming singers in this otherworld of reversals. The chorus of (men acting) women are, themselves, singing the ode that imagines women overtaking men as *aoidoi*. This hints at a performance of their own transformation into new feminine *aoidoi*.[68] This feminization of the *aoidos* is hinted at in the chorus's claim that they have been

---

66. Hes. *Theog.* 570–89, *Op.* 60–95; for the likelihood that Hesiod's invective against women is being challenged here, see Luschnig 2007: 146, and see further chapter 6, n. 61.

67. Cf. Mossman 2011 ad 427.

68. Cf. Zeitlin 1996: 348, Luschnig 2007: 145 with n. 57, Mossman 2011 ad 410–45. This is reminiscent of Medea's appropriation of male speech genres throughout the play: see Knox 1977, Williamson 1990, McClure 1995: 54; on gendered speech in tragedy, see chapter 6, n. 63. Note especially Medea's startling use of the feminine τέκτονες a few lines above, at *Med.* 409, and cf. Clytemnestra at Aesch. *Ag.* 1406: see Stieber 2011: 416. The word τέκτων—usually a masculine noun—had a long history of association with the figure of the poet (Svenbro 1984: 156–79; for τέκτων of poets, see Pind. *Pyth.* 3.113, *Nem.* 3.4, Cratinus 70a.2 K-A = Ar. *Eq.* 530).

denied "divine song" (*thespin aoidan*, 425), with the feminine term *aoidan* in the same position at line end as the masculine plural *aoidōn* at 422.[69] The contrast is clear: male singers are out; female song is in. This song which Apollo—the male god—denied them is not, significantly, the song of male bards, however, but "the divine song of the lyre" (*luras*, 424). The feminine lyre is given the agency over song here, not the male poets, in a move that seems to speak back to the disempowered, disemboweled *aoidos* lyre of the *Homeric Hymn to Hermes* (as well as Pindar's lyre in *Pythian* 1) and give her back her voice. The nature of this song, if it had been granted to women by the male god of song, is imagined in the next line: "I would have sung back [*antachēs'*] a song to rival *his*-story" [lit., "the race of men" or "the masculine gender," *arsenōn gennai*, 427–28].[70] The reclamation of the female voice and rebuttal of the male tradition is announced by the programmatic verb *antēcheō*, "to sing back in response" (427). On the surface, this is a triumphant statement of women finally taking part in the conversation and speaking back to men, with the prefix *anti-* (against, in response) underlining the retaliatory nature of women's imagined discourse here. Meanwhile, the use of *genna* (a poetic variant for *genos*), which can mean "race, class" but also "sex" as well as "grammatical gender," suggests that they are not only singing "against" men, but against the masculinization of language, against the male-dominated tradition which produced male terms ("the gender of men") like *aoidos*.[71] This is a targeted attack, not just on a single man (Jason), or even on the whole "class of men," but on the classification systems which bolster men over women in the very language of poetry.[72]

And yet, there is a more sinister undercurrent to the term *antēcheō*, which reveals that the victory may not be as easily taken by the women of the chorus as it seems. The verb *ēcheō* is connected etymologically to both *ēchē*, "cry," and *ēchō*, "echo," and thus, through personification, the female god Echo (*Ēchō*). Medea's cry of pain earlier at her misfortune was described by the chorus as an *ēchē* (149), while elsewhere in Sophocles's *Electra* (a late Sophoclean play and therefore postdating Euripides's *Medea*), we have *ēchō*

69. The polyptoton is noted by Mossman 2011 ad 421–26. On the corruption of ἀοιδῶν to ἀοιδᾶν in the MS tradition, see chapter 6, n. 62.

70. My translation refers to another intervention in female renaming, the feminist revisioning of "history" as "herstory": see Spongberg 2002: 172–88.

71. On γέννα/γένος here, see chapter 6, n. 61.

72. Cf. Williamson 1990: 28–29.

used of the cry of the nightingale's lament, to which Electra compares herself (Soph. *El.* 107–9). When applied to men, on the other hand, *ēchē* describes the manly cries of warriors, the clash of war din, most commonly in the *Iliad* and, later, in Euripides's *Phoenician Women*.[73] There therefore seems to be a gendered aspect to the use of *ēchē/ēchō*, describing the speech genres associated with and typifying each gender: masculine battle cries for men, and feminine lament for women.[74] Perhaps the chorus are trying to appropriate the masculine term into their vocabulary; but the use of a word with such strong gender prescriptions—not to mention one which the chorus had already used to describe Medea's female cry of grief—seems to delimit the women within the gendered confines of the language they speak, even as they try to break free from it.[75] They literally echo their own words from earlier in the play: they are thus caught within their own gendered discourse.

The hidden presence of Echo is the other gendered undertone to the verb. The chorus claim that they will "echo back" a song to men: but, far from turning female speech into a viable opposing discourse to that of men, the example of Echo threatens to turn them into an invisible woman who is doomed forever to repeat men's speech.[76] We know from Euripides's later play, his *Andromeda* (though it was produced much later than the *Medea* in 412 BCE, and preserved only in fragments, including in Aristophanes's parody in the *Women at the Thesmophoria*), that he had an interest in staging the mythical figure of Echo.[77] The play seems to have opened with Andromeda, bound to a rock

73. In Homer of cries of warriors: *Il.* 2.209, 8.159, 12.252, 13.834, 13.837, 15.355, 15.590, *Od.* 3.150; elsewhere of the crashing of trees (*Il.* 16.769), of the sound of the wind (*Il.* 23.213), of the cries of the souls in the Underworld (*Od.* 11.633). At Eur. *Phoen.* 1148 ἠχή is used of the call of Tydeus to rally the Greeks, similar to Homer's usage. See Chantraine s.v.

74. On lament in tragedy, see Holst-Warhaft 1992: 104–37, McClure 1999a: 40–47, Dué 2006: 8–21; see further chapter 1, n. 43.

75. Note that ἠχή also appears in Euripides of instruments (*Phoen.* 1378 of the cry of the σάλπιγξ); we might also be reminded of the "ringing" of the tortoise-lyre in the *Hymn. Hom. Merc.* 53–54. The "echoing" of the chorus of women here thus hints, perhaps, at their transfiguration in male hands into inanimate instruments (like the lyre, Eur. *Med.* 424, λύρας) that ring out on male command.

76. For examples of Echo, see *Hymn. Hom. Pan.* 21, Hes. [*Sc.*] 279, 348, Pind. *Ol.* 14.21 (the first definite instance of personification), Aesch. *Pers.* 391, Eur. *Hec.* 1111, fr. 118 *TrGF*, Ar. *Thesm.* 1056–97; see Germany 2005: 187–88.

77. See Collard, Cropp, and Gibert 2004: 133–68, Wright 2018: 155–56; on Aristophanes's reception of Euripides's Echo, see chapter 4, n. 67.

and powerless, lamenting her fate; her words were repeated back to her by an offstage Echo.[78] Female powerlessness and loss of voice are literally performed in this female back-and-forth between a chained woman and a speech-constrained god, with Echo not even appearing on stage and condemned to repeat others' words. In the *Medea*, then, the chorus tries to claim a new discourse for women and a new agency; but their choice of words seems to doom them to the opposite, a speaking identity where they passively "echo back" what men say. (We could also read these lines, "I would echo back a song to men.") And this kind of "echoing back" is, in fact, precisely what they are doing, as (male) actors performing a script written for them by a male poet. Indeed—if we look back to the start of the verse—the chorus ends up inadvertently underlining their channeling of the masculine discourse precisely in their use of the word *aoidoi*, "male poets," in line 422. By focusing their critique on the "old *male* poets," they foreground and thus implicitly endorse the term which—in the "old poets" before Euripides—had been shored up as masculine, by the ring-fencing of the male identity of the bard and the appropriation and silencing of female voices from Hesiod's captive nightingale to Hermes's eviscerated tortoise.[79]

What started off as a rewriting of the tradition of male poets thus ends up trapping the chorus, through the very language that they use, into stereotypes about male poets and male imaginings of female personifications. The problem is exactly as they identify it: there is no song, there are no words, to tell their story. They end up imprisoned in the very language which they are trying to reinvent.[80] And this predicts the failure of their new vision, and the irony in their affirmation of a novel world order: as Donald Mastronarde puts it, "They proclaim the arrival of a new discourse about women and men, while with its wider perspective the audience understands that this anticipation of

---

78. Eur. *Andromeda* frr. 114–18 *TrGF*. For the evidence that Echo was offstage, see Bubel 1991: 8–23; cf. Collard, Cropp, and Gibert 2004: 134–35.

79. Mastronarde 2002 ad 424 on ignoring female poets (cf. Allan 2002: 57); Mossman 2011 ad 423–27 sidesteps the issue by suggesting that the (mythical) dramatic date of the play predates these archaic and classical female poets.

80. We might compare Soph. *El.* 983, where Electra anticipates her own fame because of her ἀνδρεία ("courage," but also "manliness"), demonstrating her entrapment within the vocabulary of male κλέος: see Bassi 2003: 40–42. Note Barlow 1989: 164, 169 on Medea as trapped within feminine stereotypes (see esp. p. 169, "Medea's very ἀνδρεία helps to create her tragic situation").

female fame is doomed to frustration."[81] We know the reputation which Medea will end up with from Euripides's play, as a monstrous child killer (no matter what Euripides may or may not have intended); we see precisely these kinds of criticisms being leveled in Aristophanes's *Women at the Thesmophoria*. The *Medea* becomes, in other words, exactly that kind of "negative discourse" (*duskelados phama*, *Med.* 419–20) which the chorus critiques as the misogynistic stereotypes of old poetry.[82] In the end, the world order of gendered poetry is not turned upside down as the chorus envisages: instead, the ultimate irony is that, as products of the male poet themselves and accessories of the play in which Medea was to become vilified as the murderer of her own children, the chorus becomes complicit in the very act of negative gender stereotyping which they claim they want to stop.[83] The echo chamber of gendered language means that they cannot do anything else.

We can read the treatment of *aoidos* in Euripides in different ways: for instance, we might be tempted to see the placement of feminine *aoidoi* in the otherworld, and the *Medea* chorus's failure to break free of the cycle of gendered language, as a deliberate limitation by Euripides of what women can or should do. But we can also see it—along with the chorus of the *Medea*—as a confrontation of the boundaries imposed upon women's voices within a context where the vocabulary for women poets, the recovery of women's stories, and the normalization of women writers on an equal footing to men simply did not exist. The feminization of *aoidos* in Euripides, and its situation in the otherworlds at the ends of the earth, may, then, be nothing less than an insistent exploration of precisely what it means to be "other" as a woman: either (depending on how we read it) a lesson in othering women, even as they appear to be incorporated into male-gendered vocabulary; or an exposition of the gendered systems of thought and language through which women have been, and continue to be, othered.

81. Mastronarde 2002: 239; cf. Williamson 1990: 29, McClure 1999b: 390, Luschnig 2007: 147 with n. 63, and contrast Knox 1977: 224.

82. Mossman 2011 ad 410–45 makes a similar point.

83. The most notable example of the vilification of Medea in reception is Seneca's *Medea*, which became influential particularly in the Renaissance: see Lauriola 2015: 385–88. For the reception of Euripides's *Medea*, see Clauss and Johnston 1997, Mastronarde 2002: 64–70, Bartel and Simon 2010 (esp. pp. 1–2 on the seminal place of Euripides's *Medea* in creating the trajectory of different Medeas), Mossman 2011: 53–58, Lauriola 2015.

Euripides's *Medea* was produced in 431 BCE. In the early to mid-420s BCE, another writer took to the challenge of naming women poets (or rather, one specific woman poet): Herodotus, whose *Histories* were published around 425 BCE. It is with Herodotus that we turn from the feminization of *aoidos*, and the problems and challenges that brings, to the first time a woman poet—Sappho—ever receives a poet-term from a man.

7

A Woman, or a Poet?

WORDS FOR WOMEN POETS,
FROM HERODOTUS TO ANTIPATER

AROUND THE SAME time as Euripides was problematizing and exploring *aoidos* in the feminine, we find the first occurrence of a term for a woman poet by a man in extant Greek literature, in Herodotus's *Histories* (published around the mid-420s BCE).[1] At this point, as we begin to look at poet-terminology being applied (by men) to women for the first time, we need to look back to the different possible approaches, addressed in the introduction, to naming women poets in a gendered language—particularly against a background where poetry was typically male. Would the application of a male-gendered term like *aoidos* to a woman be a way of leveling the playing field of gender (as with the use of "poet" in contemporary English usage)? Or does the fact that ancient Greek was structured around grammatical gender—in contrast to modern English—mean that we should anticipate female-equivalent terms for women ("poetess"), as in contemporary French?[2] Or should we expect the exploration or invention of entirely new terms, to avoid the history of male-gendering inherent in poet-terminology after centuries of building up an association between masculinity and being a poet, in order to meet women on their own terms?

1. See Hornblower 2006: 307 for a publication date around 425 BCE (following, e.g., Rau 1967: 40, Dover 1972: 87, Cobet 1977); Fornara 1971 argues for a later date, around 414 BCE; see, however, contra Cobet 1977, and note Sansone 1985, who argues for a progressive publication of the *Histories*, beginning in the mid-420s BCE.

2. See pp. 4–8 for discussion.

To this end, there is an important question which we need to address in understanding how their male contemporaries thought (and wrote) about women poets. Patricia Rosenmeyer puts it particularly well. (She is writing about Sappho, but it applies equally to other female poets—particularly with the tendency of male writers, as we will see, to pigeonhole female poets with Sappho and assume that all women poets were, in some sense, Sapphos.)[3] "Is Sappho's identity as a woman more important to her or her contemporaries than her identity as a poet?" Rosenmeyer asks. "Do we read her as a woman writing poetry or as a poet who happens to be female?"[4] This question is particularly salient to the application of poetic terms to women, where gender was encoded both in the grammar of the term, and in the deeply embedded associations of male gender with poet-terms like *aoidos* and *poiētēs*. If Sappho's identity as a woman was more important to her male peers than her identity as a poet, we must ask, could she ever be called a male-gendered, semantically male *aoidos*? If her identity as a poet was more significant, could the male-gendering of *aoidos* be ignored sufficiently to apply to her as a poet, irrespective of her gender? Could the categories of "woman" and "poet" ever intersect in language, even if they came to do so in practice, given the long history of the male-gendering of the poet? Would these categories compete with each other, complement each other, or change one another—and how could they be described in a language that, up till now, had no words to describe a female poet?

Herodotus's Sappho: The Beginning (and End) of a Terminology for Women Poets

To answer these questions, we need to turn to the first time in extant Greek literature that a woman poet receives a poet-term, to understand how the language around women poets begins. In book 2 of his *Histories*, Herodotus has been laying out an ethnography of Egypt, discussing its topography, geography, religious customs, history, and social organization.[5] Toward the end of

---

3. See Gutzwiller 1998: 54 n. 23, who observes the tendency to call all female poets μελοποιοί (lyric poets) through association with Sappho; cf. Gow and Page 1965: 2:89, also de Vos 2014: 411, 422, Lardinois 2021a.

4. Rosenmeyer 1997: 133. Cf. Snyder 1989: 8, also Yatromanolakis 2007: 167.

5. For a comprehensive commentary on book 2, see Lloyd 1975–1988; see further Redfield 1985: 103–10, Harrison 2003, Moyer 2011: 42–83, Coulon, Giovanelli-Jouanna, and Kimmel-Clauzet 2013, E. Bowie 2018.

the book, during a discussion of the history of Egypt, he moves to dispel a connection between Rhodopis, a famous courtesan of Naucratis in Egypt, and the building of the third pyramid at Giza (Hdt. 2.134).[6] A brief biography of Rhodopis is given by way of evidence (2.135): she came to Egypt as a slave, Herodotus says, and was subsequently freed by Charaxus, "the brother of Sappho, the poet [*tēs mousopoiou*]" (2.135.1), for which "Sappho heaped abuse on him [*katekertomēse*] in a song" (2.135.6).[7] As Joel Lidov has shown—in contrast to the biographical tendency in both ancient and modern commentators, who have tended to try to square Herodotus's story with Sappho's own poetry to read back a biographical element into the Sapphic fragments—this tells us far more about Herodotus's own goals and literary interests than it does about Sappho's biography, or even her poetry.[8] My interpretation will take much the same approach, reading this not as a biographical note on Sappho or an explication of Sappho's poetry, but rather as evidence of Herodotus's use of the figure of the female poet for his own literary ends, and the development by a male writer of a gender-differentiated vocabulary for women poets.

In order to understand the precise force of the term Herodotus uses to call Sappho a "poet"—*mousopoios*—there is a fair amount of context that needs to be filled in. We need to appreciate where Herodotus stands within the tradition of Greek poet-terminology. We need to understand the other poet-terms given to male poets in the *Histories*, as well as the attitudes expressed toward them. We need to address Sappho's own use of poet-terms and Herodotus's relationship to her choice of words for herself (does he listen to Sappho, ignore her, or write against her?); and we need to understand the history of the term *mousopoios* itself. It is only then that we can, finally, look at the word in Herodotus itself and what it says about his treatment of Sappho—and how the murky beginnings of a vocabulary for women poets establish the ground rules for how to talk about women and poetry.

---

6. See Lloyd 1988: 84–85, Lidov 2002: 206–15, Konstantakos 2018, and esp. Nagy 2018 on Rhodopis's building of the third pyramid.

7. ἀδελφεοῦ δὲ Σαπφοῦς τῆς μουσοποιοῦ, 2.135.1; ἐν μέλεϊ Σαπφὼ πολλὰ κατεκερτόμησέ μιν, 2.135.6. For Sappho's brother and Rhodopis (equated with Sappho's Doricha in the later tradition), see Sappho frr. 5, 15 L-P.

8. Lidov 2002: 214 with n. 24, and cf. Coo 2021: 263–66. Contrast Yatromanolakis 2007: 328–37, who (following Page 1955: 49–51) argues that ἐν μέλεϊ at Hdt. 2.135.6 should be taken as a citation of his source as a Sapphic poem; cf. Lloyd 1988: 86. See further, for arguments for a lost group of Sapphic blame poems, chapter 7, n. 34, and on Sappho as an iambist, Rosenmeyer 2006, Martin 2016, Steiner 2021: 78–83.

As we have already seen, Herodotus was one of the first writers to demonstrate the range and ubiquity of the new terminology for male poets in the late fifth century, from *poiein* (to compose poetry) to *poiētēs* (maker, poet).⁹ As John Marincola points out, with the advent of the (relatively) new medium of prose, Herodotus seems to have been particularly aware of the need to differentiate prose from poetry—and, at the same time, particularly cognizant of the kinds of vocabulary that surrounded poetic versus prose composition.¹⁰ He uses *poiētēs* six times in the *Histories*, of Homer, Alcaeus, Aeschylus, and poets in general.¹¹ Compounds made up of the *-poios* suffix also occur, setting up generic divides between poets and prose-writers: we have *epopoios*, "epic poet" (of Homer and epic poets in general); *logopoios*, "prose-writer" (literally "word-maker," of the historian Hecataeus and the fabulist Aesop); and *mousopoios*, "poet" (literally "music-maker," only of Sappho).¹² The question of genre differentiation, between poets on the one hand and prose-writers on the other, leaps out from Herodotus's terminological division between *poiētai/epopoioi/mousopoioi*, on the one hand, and *logopoioi*, on the other.¹³ And yet

9. For ποιεῖν as composing poetry: Hdt. 2.116.2 (of Homer), 3.38.4 (of Pindar), 4.13.1 (of Aristaeus), 5.95.2 (of Alcaeus). For ποίησις as poetry: 2.23.1, 2.82.1. See Ford 2002: 133–34 with 134 n. 6, Yatromanolakis 2007: 318–20, esp. 318 n. 150 and 319 n. 151. See further pp. 83–86.

10. Marincola 2006: 13, cf. Goldhill 2002, Ford 2002: 133. Note that Goldhill 2002: 10 points out that Herodotus was preceded by at least a generation of prose-writers (see also R. L. Fowler 2006); the *Histories* are, however, our earliest extant extended example of Greek prose. See further chapter 7, n. 13.

11. ποιητής in Herodotus: Hdt. 2.23.1, 2.53.3, 2.156.6, 3.115.2, 5.95.1, 6.52.1. See Lateiner 1989: 106–7 for a list of passages citing epic and other poets. For Herodotus's attitude toward the poets (particularly in the critique of the Helen *logos* at 2.112–20), see Verdin 1977, Lateiner 1989: 99–100, 106, Ford 2002: 146–52, Marincola 2006, Ford 2007, Grintser 2018; on Herodotus and Homer, see Pelling 2006, Marincola 2007 (on the *Odyssey* in particular); on Herodotus and Pindar, see Nagy 1990a: 314–38, Kingsley 2018. On Herodotus as himself employing poetic techniques, see Herington 1991, Calame 1995: 90–91; for Herodotus's similarity to Homer, particularly in his presentation of battle narratives, see Marincola 2018; and for a comparison between the discursive aims of Herodotus and Pindar as controllers of the authority of speech and κλέος, see Nagy 1990a: 215–49, 314–38. For examples of the rejection of poets as historical sources in Herodotus, see Lateiner 1989: 99, 106 (cf. Ford 2002: 146–47), and for the potential negative connotations of ποιεῖν and -ποιός in Herodotus, see Hartog 1988: 296–97, Lidov 2002: 212 n. 18, Kurke 2011: 376–82 (on λογοποιός specifically).

12. ἐποποιός: 2.120.3, 7.161.3; cf. the noun ἐποποιίη at 2.116. λογοποιός: 2.134.3, 2.143.1, 5.36.2, 5.125.1. μουσοποιός: 2.135.1.

13. This is in contrast, as we have seen, to Plato's use of the term: see pp. 137–38 with chapter 5, n. 67. For discussion of the term λογοποιός in Herodotus, see R. L. Fowler 2006: 37. On

genre is not the only fault line in terms of literary-critical vocabulary which Herodotus crosses. From a gender perspective, it is impossible to miss the fact that Sappho is the only female poet mentioned in Herodotus; that she is not called a *poiētēs*; and that, conversely, she is the only one to receive the term *mousopoios*. The avoidance of the term *poiētēs* for Sappho accords with the gender-marking of *poiētēs* as emphatically masculine which we see in the contemporary plays of Aristophanes: we might compare the first-person *anēr poiētēs* of the *Clouds* parabasis, or the ideal "man-poet" of the *Frogs*.[14] The historic association forged between masculinity and the poet, begun with *aoidos* and picked up in the shift to *poiētēs*, seems to hold true here. Instead of calling Sappho a *poiētēs*, which Herodotus marked earlier in the same book of the *Histories* as the preserve of male poets like Homer, he applies a differentiated term for her—one which is marked out as gendered, as the only occurrence of the word in the *Histories*, conjoined to the only female poet: "perhaps," as Dimitrios Yatromanolakis argues, "the earliest case in our written sources of a subtle differentiation between male poets and Sappho."[15] And yet is not enough to point out the difference. The real question is what the precise force of that differentiation is, what gender dynamics are at play; for Herodotus, staking out the terms of poetry, had a choice to make as to what term he used for the only female poet in the *Histories*—a female poet who had never, in extant literature, received a poet-term from her male peers. The stakes, for the historian who was leading the way in systematizing and exploring *poiein* vocabulary for poets (the "father of philology," as Andrew Ford calls him), were high.[16]

There are several different possible approaches to reading the gender politics in Herodotus's use of *mousopoios* here. Does Herodotus's act of differentiation work to recognize Sappho on her own terms? Does it, perhaps, engage with some kind of preexisting language around *mousopoios* and women? Or does it

---

Herodotus's view of ποίησις as specifically qualified by making metrical verse, and the contrast between poetic verse-making and λογοποιός as "prose-writer," see Ford 2002: 135. Note that Nagy 1990a: 221–22 argues that λόγιοι at Hdt. 1.1.1 should be seen as an implicit reference to Herodotus himself. On Aesop as λογοποιός in Herodotus, see Kurke 2011: 370–82, and see further chapter 7, n. 22. On Hecataeus as λογοποιός, see Hartog 1988: 296, Nagy 1990a: 325, 225, Yatromanolakis 2007: 318 n. 149, and, for an argument that the term has pejorative connotations in Herodotus, see Kurke 2011: 376–82; for Herodotus on Hecataeus in general, see Dillery 2018.

14. See pp. 103–8, 114–21.

15. Yatromanolakis 2007: 319.

16. Ford 2002: 148, referring to Diels 1910: 25; see chapter 7, n. 21.

generate a new vocabulary (whether positive or negative) that articulates the relationship between women and poetry? Does it serve, ultimately, to celebrate the female poet, or to contrast and segregate her?

Let's start with the first hypothesis—that Herodotus is meeting Sappho on her own terms. Yatromanolakis notices (and it is hard to miss) that Herodotus's *mousopoios* is reminiscent of a term which Sappho uses in her own poetry, and (as we will see) to describe her own gender identity as a poet: *mousopolos*, or "one who serves the Muses" (fr. 150 L-P).[17] The precise power of this term will be analyzed at length when we come to look at Sappho's fragments in the next chapter; for now, it is simply worth noting the similarities and differences between Sappho's language and that of Herodotus. At first, Herodotus's *mousopoios* might appear to be a twin for Sappho's *mousopolos*: both begin with the *mouso-* prefix, both have a suffix that begins in *po-*, and both are two-termination forms ending in *-os*. But there are some crucial differences between the two. The suffix *-poios* in Herodotus's noun, "maker" (from *poiein*)—a typical example of the classical *-poios*-suffixes in action—has a significant impact on the translation of the prefix *mous-* here in Herodotus: it forces *mousa* to mean "music" or "song," in the abstract sense which the noun *Mousa* can also denote. The alternative meaning of *Mousa* as "Muse," as personified gods, cannot be retained while at the same time making sense of the suffix *-poios*: to put it crudely, one can make music, but not Muses. The noun thus translates more or less straightforwardly as "music-maker" or (in Gregory Nagy's translation) "artisan of song," taken by most translators of Herodotus to mean "poet" or, more specifically, "lyric poet."[18] Translations of *mousopolos* in Sappho, on the other hand, range from Diane Rayor's "those who serve the Muses" to Jim Powell's "the Muses' servants" to Alex Hardie's "those who busy themselves with the Muses," which, as we will see, seems to capture the sense of the *-polos* suffix most closely.[19] Despite their differences in attempting to render *-polos* into English, it is clear from all these translations that Sappho's *mousopolos* entertains—indeed, encourages—the interpretative possibility of reading the

17. ἐν μοισοπόλων <δόμωι>, fr. 150.1 L-P. See pp. 235–44; on the text, see chapter 8, n. 18.

18. Nagy 1990a: 325 (though note a slightly different translation, "maker of songs," at Nagy 2018: 118, which emphasizes the -ποιός suffix). Macaulay 1890 has "lyric poet"; Godley 1920 gives "poetess"; Waterfield 1998 has "poet"; Purvis (in Strassler and Purvis 2007) gives "lyric songstress."

19. Rayor 2014: 81 (and cf. Snyder 1997: 118); J. Powell 2019: 39; Hardie 2005: 14. Contrast Carson 2002: 303, who translates as simply "in a house of the Muses." See further p. 237, and for critical interpretations of the term, see chapter 8, n. 23.

mous- prefix as referring to the Muses, as well as the abstract "music": the combination of physical proximity and active engagement suggested by *-polos* retains the sense both of service to a real deity and of occupation with the craft of music. What the comparison makes clear, then, is the interpretative richness of Sappho's epithet, which Herodotus loses (or dismantles) by switching the suffix. *Mousopolos* subtly retains the ambiguity of the noun *Mousa* and suggests a more intimate connection between female poet and god than Herodotus's more prosaic noun allows. *Mousopoios*, on the other hand, takes away the woman poet's intimate feminine access to the Muses and turns her into a "music-maker." This move is a concerted act of poetic gendering. It both labels the female poet *as* feminine, through the gendered association in the prefix with the female Muses, and yet at the same time denies her access to the Muses through the restrictive force of the suffix—for access to and appropriation of the Muses, as we have seen, had already been claimed by the male *aoidoi* as their special privilege.[20] *Mousopoios* thus serves both to segregate the female poet through her gender, and to delimit her capacities, by virtue of her gender as a nonmale poet. She is not an *epopoios* with access to the Muses: she is a *mousopoios*, a woman, like a Muse, but disconnected from the Muses.

Herodotus was, of course, writing after Sappho, and so would likely have been aware of Sappho's use of *mousopolos*: the similarity between the two terms and the specificity of the application of *mousopoios* to Sappho suggests that he was.[21] Jesper Svenbro has suggested that Herodotus may have originally intended *mousopolos*, and that the term could have been edited to *mousopoios* through a scribal error, in analogy to *logopoios* for Aesop at 2.134.3.[22] But with no evidence for such a change, and an analogy for other nouns ending in *-poios* elsewhere in Herodotus (e.g., *epopoios*) and the increasing commonness of *poiein* cognates, the argument for *mousopoios* seems to stand.[23]

20. See pp. 46–56.

21. Herodotus was clearly a close reader of poetry: see Ford 2002: 146–52, Marincola 2006: 13, Grintser 2018, and see Diels 1910: 25 on Herodotus as the father of the philological method; see further chapter 7, n. 11. Yatromanolakis 2007: 319 comments on the similarity between the two terms.

22. Svenbro 1984: 171. The analogy between Aesop as λογοποιός and Sappho as μουσοποιός is, however, interesting in its own right: as a gender differentiation (see above, Yatromanolakis 2007: 319; cf. Lidov 2002: 212 n. 18, "Aesop is not Sappho"), but also as a marker of genre differentiation; see Kurke 2011: 371 with n. 40. Nagy 1990a: 325 notes the similarity between the λογοποιός/μουσοποιός juxtaposition in Herodotus and λόγιος/ἀοιδός in Pind. *Pyth.* 1.

23. Ford 2002: 134 n. 6, Yatromanolakis 2007: 319 with n. 154.

Moreover, the term *mousopoios* has its own gendered history, contemporary with Herodotus's usage. This suggests another potential reading for Herodotus's use of *mousopoios* here—the second of the possible approaches to understanding *mousopoios* listed above: a potential engagement with a preexisting language connecting *mousopoios* and women. The term first appears in Euripides, once in *Hippolytus* (428 BCE) and again in the *Trojan Women* (415 BCE).[24] Both times, it refers to future memorialization—but, more significantly from a gendered perspective, the term is spoken in both instances in women's voices (Artemis in *Hippolytus*, Hecuba in *Trojan Women*).[25] In the *Hippolytus* it actually refers to women's song: "the music-making pursuit of virgin girls" (Eur. *Hipp.* 1428–29).[26] Meanwhile, in the *Trojan Women*, we find *mousopoios* appearing as a noun, as Hecuba laments the death of Astyanax: "What could a poet [*mousopoios*] write on your tomb?" (*Tro.* 1188–89).[27] The use of the two-termination *mousopoios*, which looks the same in the masculine and feminine, suggests the possibility that, in this play of women where Muses can become *aoidoi*, Hecuba might be calling on a *female* poet to write the epitaph—perhaps, even, if Herodotus's *Histories* was published by this point, Sappho herself, referring directly to Herodotus's use of *mousopoios*.[28] At the same time, we are also aware that Hecuba herself is performing the lament for Astyanax here, suggesting that she, too, is a type of *mousopoios* (just like her claim to be a potential *aoidos* in *Iliad* 24): in some sense, the answer to her question, "what could a *mousopoios* write on your tomb?" is answered by her own (female) lament for Astyanax (captured in a male poet's text, enacted by

---

24. Eur. *Hipp.* 1428, *Tro.* 1188–89; other instances at Hdt. 2.135.1, Theoc. *Epigr.* 19.1, 22.3, Dio Chrys. *Or.* 2.33, Ael. *NA* 7.35; cf. chapter 4, n. 9. Note also μουσοποιεῖν at Soph. fr. 245 *TrGF* of Thamyris/Thamyras (known for his contest with the Muses), which suggests a play on the μουσ- stem.

25. Yatromanolakis 2007: 320.

26. ἀεὶ δὲ μουσοποιὸς ἐς σὲ παρθένων / ἔσται μέριμνα (The music-making pursuit of virgin girls will always make you its theme), *Hipp.* 1428–29. Note, interestingly, that it is a man (Hippolytus) who will be the subject matter of song; on this passage, see further Wright 2010: 169–70.

27. τί καί ποτε / γράψειεν ἄν σε μουσοποιὸς ἐν τάφῳ, *Tro.* 1188–89. See Ford 2002: 138.

28. On the Muse as ἀοιδός, see pp. 172–75. For Herodotus's date in relation to Euripides, see chapter 7, n. 1. The suggestion that Euripides's Hecuba may be (anachronistically) thinking of Sappho as a writer of Astyanax's epitaph is strengthened by the fact that Sappho commemorates the wedding of Hector and Andromache in fr. 44 L-P; perhaps Hecuba is thus thinking of Sappho as a particularly appropriate song-maker for Andromache's son's epitaph. Compare the μουσοπόλοι at Eur. *Alc.* 445, who can be read as potential female poets: see chapter 6, n. 23.

a male actor pretending to be a woman), and she becomes the *mousopoios* upon whom she calls. The link to the gendered use of *mousopoios* in Euripides suggests that Herodotus's labeling of Sappho is not, then, simply a connection to the theme of memorialization in the neighboring chapters of the *Histories* (though this is certainly one strand), but a tightly controlled delineation of women's song as connected to the label *mousopoios*. This connection is both intertextual (with Euripides), semantic (through the latent connection between the term's prefix *mous-*, the Muses, and femininity), and defined by its gender politics (the act of delimitation the word represents as a male rebranding of a Sapphic-sounding term, similar to Sappho's *mousopolos*). By all these readings, *mousopoios* here becomes a type of gender-segregated term connected to women's song that both identifies the woman by her gender and delimits her access to the Muses.

So much for the first two potential approaches to *mousopoios* in Herodotus, then—Herodotus's relationship to Sappho's terminology, and his intertextuality with the use of *mousopoios* in other poets. What about the third approach— the suggestion that Herodotus may be generating a new vocabulary, within the *Histories*, that attempts to define the relationship between women and poetry? For this, we need to look more closely at the context of the term within the *Histories*, and examine the kinds of gendered linguistic strategies it represents for Herodotus. Firstly and most fundamentally, it must be pointed out that Herodotus endows Sappho with a poet-term—and he is the first to do so in all extant Greek literature.[29] As we have already seen, the term *mousopoios* is a two-termination adjective used as a substantive, which means that the ending looks grammatically masculine, but is used with a feminine definite article to mark it as grammatically feminine (*tēs mousopoiou*, Hdt. 2.135.1). This might appear to strike a good balance—between the feminine connotations of the term, linked to the Muses through the *mous-* prefix, and its masculine-looking ending, with a term that could apply both to men and to women, and with a word that fits women into the typically masculine vocabulary of *-poios* and yet differentiates them at the same time.[30] We might even perhaps argue that Herodotus is attempting, by using a two-termination substantive adjective for

29. She is also identified by her proper name: see S. Larson 2006 on the suppression of the names of the wives of Candaules and Gyges (as well as other women's names, see pp. 229–34).

30. As noted above, however, there are only three instances of the term in the classical period, two in Euripides and one in Herodotus—and of those, two (Eur. *Hipp.* 1428 and Hdt.

Sappho rather than a deeply embedded masculine noun like *poiētēs*, to encourage a new kind of vocabulary—one that does not impinge on male identity, but which takes off from it and sets up a new world for women poets.

This is one possible close-up view of *mousopoios*. But it leaves out the strategy of silencing Sappho's own vocabulary for herself, which hides behind the word choice here; it forgets the power of the -*poios* suffix to limit Sappho's relationship to the Muses; and it also omits to situate the word in its context in the *Histories*. And this leads us into different way of reading. There are troubling signs, even in the surrounding passage. Sappho is introduced, not by virtue of her poetry, but because of her brother, Charaxus (Rhodopis, Herodotus tells us, was freed by Charaxus, "brother of Sappho the music-maker," 2.135.1). Later in the chapter, Herodotus claims that she "violently attacked" (*katekertomēse*, 2.135.6) Charaxus "in a song."[31] Most critics have focused on whether this provides evidence for a lost Sapphic poem (or indeed, an interpretation of the fragments we do have).[32] Few have read it as evidence for Herodotus's shaping of Sappho, even though some have noticed the intratextual resonance of the verb *katakertomeō* here, which is used elsewhere in Herodotus only of the vengeful Harpagus's taunting of Astyages after forcing him to eat his own son.[33] This verb, with the prefix *kata-*, is quite different from the light mockery suggested by *kertomeō*, which is often adduced here by way of comparison—either to suggest a lost group of blame poems by Sappho, a risqué Sapphic poem which teases her brother in ironic fashion, or the reperformance of Sappho in the context of men's festivities.[34] But the presence of the prefix *kata-* makes this a much more emotive version of *kertomeō*.[35] Far from evoking light-hearted

---

2.135.1) certainly refer to women. It is not until Theoc. *Epigr.* 19.1 that we have μουσοποιός referring definitively to a male poet (Hipponax).

31. ἐν μέλεϊ Σαπφὼ πολλὰ κατεκερτόμησέ μιν, Hdt. 2.135.6.

32. See chapter 7, nn. 8 and 34.

33. Hdt. 1.129.1; see Kurke 1999: 225–62, Lidov 2002: 231. Lidov notes (231 n. 67) that the verb is not used again until the late Hellenistic period.

34. Aloni 1997: lxvi–lxxv argues that this refers to a group of lost blame poems by Sappho (cf. Yatromanolakis 2007: 334; see further Rosenmeyer 2006, Martin 2016 on Sappho as engaging in the tradition of *iambos*, and see Donelli 2021: 19–22, who connects to Sappho fr. 55 L-P). Lidov 2002: 232 n. 70 argues that the evidence for such poems is quite thin, and suggests rather (pp. 231–32) that it implies a risqué teasing of her brother by Sappho, by analogy to *Hymn. Hom. Merc.* 4.54–56; Yatromanolakis 2007: 325 n. 178, 343 n. 256 also connects κερτομέω to the *Homeric Hymn to Hermes* and the context of festivities of men.

35. As Lidov in fact notes (2002: 231). See LSJ s.v., with the translation "rail violently."

ribaldry, its intratextual associations connect Sappho with a vengeful foreigner belittling his enemy for a monstrous act of cannibalism. It suggests, through its verbal resonances with Harpagus, an othering of Sappho's discourse, a transferal from Greek song into the realm of Persian, "other," stereotyped negative speech.[36] In other words, if it is used to mark Harpagus's other-speech as a foreigner who engaged in cannibalism, it seems to mark Sappho as a gendered stereotype. And, in this context, it anticipates the ranting baker-women of Aristophanes's *Frogs*, "railing at each other" (*loidoresthai*, Ar. *Ran.* 857) in a way that should not be imitated by "men-poets."[37] Sappho seems to be associated with an othered discourse that belongs both to ranting, vengeful foreigners and to low-bred, abusive women.

The gender-stereotyped undertones of *katakertomēse* at 2.135.6 to describe Sappho's discourse connects to another aspect of her characterization: her alignment with negative, highly sexualized female stereotypes in the surrounding chapters.[38] A specific critique of Homer's version of Helen's story at 2.112–20 introduces the figure of Helen, the ultimate sexualized female prize; at 2.121 we have the Egyptian pharaoh Rhampsinitus's daughter, who was commanded by her father to pretend to be a prostitute in order to catch a thief; and at 2.126 we have Rhampsinitus's successor, Kheops, putting his daughter in a brothel to pay for his pyramid. This forms the transition to the tale of Rhodopis, the famous courtesan of Naucratis, who was freed by Sappho's brother Charaxus. These sexualized women are connected by their desire (unusual for a woman) to leave behind a memorial of themselves: Kheops's daughter, Herodotus reports, asked for a block of stone from each man she slept with so she could build a small pyramid of her own "to leave behind a memorial [*mnēmēion*] of her own" (2.126.1); the story of Rhodopis is also about her desire "to leave behind a memorial [*mnēmēion*] of herself" in Delphi (2.135.3).[39] But Rhodopis's memorial is not just called a *mnēmēion*—Herodotus goes on

---

36. Kurke 1999: 226 argues, suggestively, for a fracture of genre rather than gender here (cf. Gilhuly 2018: 102). On the "other" in Herodotus, see Redfield 1985, Hartog 1988: 212–59, Gray 1995, Bichler 2000, Goldhill 2002: 16–20. See further chapter 6, n. 43.

37. See pp. 114–16; Kurke 1999: 226 with n. 11 also makes the connection to the proverbial abusive tone of Greek breadwomen.

38. Lidov 2002: 228–29, Yatromanolakis 2007: 315–16; cf. Gilhuly 2018: 101–3.

39. ἰδίῃ δὲ καὶ αὐτὴν διανοηθῆναι μνημήιον καταλιπέσθαι, Hdt. 2.126.1; ἐπεθύμησε γὰρ Ῥοδῶπις μνημήιον ἑωυτῆς ἐν τῇ Ἑλλάδι καταλιπέσθαι, ποίημα ποιησαμένη, 2.135.3. On Rhodopis, Sappho, and memorialization, see Yatromanolakis 2007: 320; for bibliography on Rhodopis's dedication, see Yatromanolakis 2007: 320 n. 157.

to define it: *poiēma poiēsamenē*, "she had a work made" (2.135.3). Yatromanolakis notes the double sense of *poiēma* here, as "a word denoting both a 'made thing' and a 'poem' that eventually connects Rhodopis' and Sappho's *poiêmata*."[40] But there is another etymological and verbal link—between Rhodopis as a "maker" of a monument (*poiēsamenē*, with a feminine participle, 2.135.3) and Sappho as a "maker" of music, with the *-poios* suffix (*mousopoiou*, 2.135.1).

This connection between Rhodopis "making a *poiēma*" and Sappho as *mousopoios* is particularly important, as it sheds new light on Sappho's characterization as *mousopoios*, gendering the term in the context of notorious, sexualized women who step beyond the bounds of normal social convention to become "makers" of their own fame. The explicit connection between fame in a monument and fame in song is explored toward the end of the chapter, where Herodotus discusses the famous "name" (*ounoma*, 2.135.5) of Rhodopis, and claims that she was "celebrated" (*kleinē*, 2.135.5) alongside another prostitute, Archidice, who was "sung of" in Greece (*aoidimos*, 2.135.5). Both are words associated with epic—*kleinē* is cognate with *kleos*, while *aoidimos* inevitably reminds us of Helen's self-description as the subject matter of poetry in *Iliad* book 6 (the first time a word related to poet-vocabulary is given in a woman's voice in Greek poetry).[41] With the connection to Helen's description of her self-memorialization in the *Iliad*, an intricate thematic interweaving is achieved between the sexualized women of the surrounding chapters of the *Histories* (Helen, Rhampsinitus's and Kheops's daughters, Rhodopis, and Archidice), poet-vocabulary, poetic creation, memorialization, and notoriety in song. And this is capped by the paradigmatic example of Sappho. As a poet-figure and representative of women's self-memorialization in song, she is the obvious example. We also know that her sexuality was central to her later reception, particularly in comedy, while there is enough of an indication that Sappho is being sexualized here simply through the thematic connection to the other female figures surrounding her, as well as the fact that Rhodopis and Archidice are called *hetairai* (2.135.5), the term which Sappho used of her female companions but which came to mean "courtesans," and which probably in turn

---

40. Yatromanolakis 2007: 320, who notes that ποίημα in the sense of "poem" already occurs at Cratinus fr. 198.5 K-A.

41. See Steiner 1994: 139, Lidov 2002: 211, Yatromanolakis 2007: 323. Kurke 1999: 224 argues that these terms are deliberately "tongue-in-cheek" parodies of the ἑταῖραι (and at p. 225 makes the connection to Helen, "in some sense the prototype of every courtesan"). Donelli 2021: 23–27 suggests that the evocation of Helen is intended to recall Sappho fr. 16 L-P.

fueled Sappho's sexualized reception.[42] In this context, *mousopoios*, "music-maker," might be reminiscent of the *hetairai* and flute-girls who often accompanied men at symposia, at which Herodotus seems to suggest the prostitutes Archidice and Rhodopis were fantasized about by men.[43] The whole of chapter 135 thus acts as a ring composition that circles around Sappho and generates a very specific context for the sexualized, gendered interpretation of *mousopoios*: introduced in the opening section (2.135.1), Sappho is drawn into the parallel example of Rhodopis as *poiēsamenē* (2.135.3) and prostitutes who are *aoidimos* (2.135.5), connecting her back to Helen and other *hetairai* who have tried to memorialize themselves, before the final gendered stereotyping of her discourse and her song (*katekertomēse*, 2.135.6) at the chapter's end. This suggests a further interpretation for the verb *katekertomēse*: women's place, Herodotus seems to suggest, with the description of Rhodopis as *kleinē* and Archidice as *aoidimos*, is to be "told of in song" (*aoidimos*), and not to do the singing. (This is, in fact, how the *Histories* itself starts, turning women into the subject matter of Herodotus's inquiry, with the discussion of female rapes from Helen on.)[44] With Sappho, however, the gender roles are uncomfortably reversed: the woman becomes the singer, and the male (her brother) becomes the subject of song.

This, then, seems to point to the fourth approach to interpreting Sappho as *mousopoios* advanced above—that, rather than celebrating Sappho's poetic identity, *mousopoios*, with all its resonances and subtexts, sets up a marked contrast between Sappho and male poets, turning her into a gender-stereotyped, sexualized, nonmale poet. In sum, the balance sheet for Herodotus's attribution

---

42. On comic representations of Sappho, see Robinson 1924: 122, Williamson 1995: 15–16, Most 1995: 17, Yatromanolakis 2007: 295–312, Kivilo 2010: 189–90, Dover 2016: 174, Coo 2021: 269–75; cf. Yatromanolakis 2007: 248–51 on the recontextualization of Sappho's use of ἑταίρα in the context of the symposium, also Schlesier 2013, Gilhuly 2018: 101–16. On the term ἑταίρα here and its potential connection to Sappho, see Lidov 2002: 228–30; on Rhodopis's characterization as ἑταίρα, see Kurke 1999: 220–27, and on ἑταῖραι in general, see chapter 3, n. 23.

43. Yatromanolakis 2007: 322–26 suggests that περιλεσχήνευτος at 2.135.5 indicates men's sympotic talk; see also Nagy 2018: 119 on the λέσχη as a "men's club," and cf. Kurke 1999: 225. On the masculinity of the symposium, see chapter 3, n. 24.

44. See, e.g., Larson 2006: 229, cf. Walcot 1978: 139. For the argument that narratives around women structure the *Histories*, see Wolff 1964, Larson 2006, and on Helen in Herodotus, see Blondell 2013: 142–63. For Herodotus's treatment of other women in the *Histories*, see Dewald 1986, Blok 2002.

of *mousopoios* to Sappho is a decided negative.[45] Although he grants her a poet-term, that term works to set her apart from the male *poiētai* and *epopoioi* who appear elsewhere in the *Histories*. She is given a different word from all the other male poets in the *Histories*: she is not a *poiētēs*, with its associations between masculinity and man-making. She is denied her own vocabulary of *mousopolos*; and, although she is labeled with a *-poios* term in its place, its conjunction with *mous-* diminishes the power of the prefix and dismantles the term which Sappho had used of herself, undercutting its interpretative power. Finally, Herodotus connects her identity as a *mousopoios* to the sexualized, negatively gender-stereotyped women of the surrounding chapters who have broken through the bounds of convention to attempt to ensure their own self-memorialization in poetry, to turn her brand of "making" into a grab for attention by eroticized women whose job it is to be told of in men's talk—not to do the singing themselves.

Bridging the Gap: Prawns and Parades

It would be another three centuries before a woman poet (again, Sappho) received a poet-term in literature by men. The experiment with *mousopoios* in the *Histories* definitively puts an end to the vocabulary of female poets as *mousopoioi*: feminine *mousopoios* does not occur again in extant Greek literature.[46] (Other examples, like *melopoios*, "song-maker," which tie women poets to Sappho as predominantly lyric poets, do not become common until much later.)[47]

In the meantime, there are two other instances of the exploration of feminizing poet-vocabulary that bridge the Hellenistic period. Both follow Euripides (and the archaic tradition before him) in choosing to feminize *aoidos*, rather than attempting to broach the all-masculine *poiētēs* and *-poios* vocabulary. The first is a Hellenistic mock epic by Matro called *The Attic Dinner*, quoted at length by Athenaeus, which catalogs the food served at a ban-

---

45. Pace Coo 2021: 266.

46. See chapter 7, n. 24.

47. E.g., Dion. Hal. *Comp.* 23.51–52, Lucian *Imagines* 18.2. On the term μελοποιός, see chapter 4, n. 42. For the tendency to call all women poets lyricists, see Gutzwiller 1998: 54 n. 23; for examples, see μελοποιός applied to female poets in the *Anth. Pal.* MSS titles, e.g., Anyte at 4, 5, 7, 8, 12, 16 G-P (cf. Ἀνύτης λυρικῆς at 9 G-P); Nossis at 10 G-P. Note also [Eur.] *Rhes.* 550 where the adjectival form is applied to the song of the feminine nightingale (ὑμνεῖ . . . / μελοποιὸν ἀηδονὶς μέριμναν, 548–50).

quet for a group of late fourth-century BCE Athenian politicians.[48] Describing the prawns (*karides*, a feminine noun in Greek), Matro dubs them "the singers [*hai ... aoidoi*] of Olympian Zeus" (fr. 1.63 Olson-Sens); elsewhere, he uses the same phrase of *bolbinai*, an obscure kind of (grammatically feminine) flower.[49] Clearly, Matro is picking up on the feminization of *aoidos*—probably in Euripides—and parodying it by applying it to feminine nouns to which it palpably does not apply, extending ad absurdum Euripides's attribution of *aoidos* to the inanimate shuttle.[50] Meanwhile, the appellation "of Olympian Zeus" reminds us of the "kings and singers" passage in Hesiod's *Theogony*, where *aoidoi* are said to be from the Muses and kings are "from Zeus" (Hes. *Theog.* 94–96).[51] Here in Matro, the bards come from Zeus, and it is feminine prawns, not sacralized male poets, who are doing the singing. For Matro, clearly, the idea of a female *aoidos* is quite as funny as the thought that a prawn might sing.[52]

The second example comes from a rather better-known Hellenistic poet, Theocritus, who was active in Alexandria in the early third century BCE. *Idyll* 15 describes two women, Praxinoa and Gorgo, who attend the festival of Adonis, where they hear a woman reciting the Adonis song.[53] The female singer is unnamed, but is called a *poluidris aoidos*, "a very knowledgeable female bard" (Theoc. *Id.* 15.97).[54] She is given multiple female determiners: a

48. For an introduction and commentary, see Olson and Sens 1999; see also Degani 1995, McClure 2003: 34.

49. καρῖδές θ᾽, αἳ Ζηνὸς Ὀλυμπίου εἰσὶν ἀοιδοί (and prawns, which are the singers of Olympian Zeus), Matro fr. 1.63 Olson-Sens = Ath. 4.136a; βολβῖνας θ᾽, αἳ Ζηνὸς Ὀλυμπίου εἰσὶν ἀοιδοί (and bolbinai, which are the singers of Olympian Zeus), fr. 3.3 Olson-Sens = Ath. 2.64c. For other suggestions as to why the prawns are called ἀοιδοί, see Olson and Sens 1999 ad loc.

50. See pp. 180–81.

51. See pp. 49–50 with chapter 2, n. 19.

52. It is worth noting that ἀοιδός retains its prestige in the masculine: it is never used in the masculine of objects or foodstuffs.

53. On *Idyll* 15, see Gow 1952: 2:262–304, Griffiths 1979: 82–85, Dover 1985: 197–215, Goldhill 1994b: 216–23, Burton 1995 esp. 93–122, Davies 1995, Whitehorne 1995, Hunter 1996: 110–38, Skinner 2001, Lambert 2001, Foster 2006, Hunter 2008. On the Adonis song, see Gow 1952 ad 15.96; see further chapter 7, n. 56.

54. ἁ τᾶς Ἀργείας θυγάτηρ, πολύιδρις ἀοιδός, Theoc. *Id.* 15.97; the text is cited from Gow 1952. It is worth noting that ποιητής becomes less common in the Hellenistic period in comparison to ἀοιδός: ἀοιδός appears twenty times in Theocritus, versus ποιητής only once (*Epigr.* 21.1, see chapter 9, n. 21); we have ἀοιδός thirteen times in Callimachus, and again, only one

feminine definite article; the term "daughter" (*thugatēr*: she is identified as "the daughter of Argeia / an Argive woman"); and a feminine adjective, *poluidris*. All these female markers tell us that *aoidos*, in this context, is meant to be taken as emphatically feminine.[55] At the same time, the context is also demonstrably "feminine"-gendered: the festival of Adonis was a women's festival, and this one is no exception (it has been convened by Ptolemy's queen, Arsinoe, and attended by women including Praxinoa and Gorgo).[56] In this sense, it seems that the overt gendering of the context is sufficient to pull *aoidos* over into the female sphere, and to endow this woman with the time-honored vocabulary of male authorship.[57] And there is another feature which might enable *aoidos* to become feminine here. Gorgo goes on to give more details about the female *aoidos*: she "did best in the lament last year," Gorgo says (97–98).[58] This "lament" is, in fact, the next (and last) day of the festival, which the female singer anticipates toward the end of her song: "tomorrow morning all we women [*athroai*] . . . will untie our hair, let our robes fall to our ankles to show our breasts, and begin our keening songs [*aoidas*]" (132–35).[59] The female *aoidos* calls the lament an *aoidē*, a song—by etymological association, thus also connecting her own title of "singer"/*aoidos* to the act of lament, which was—as we have seen, and as the festival of Adonis shows—one of the few public

---

instance of ποιητής (*Epigr.* 10.1). Note esp. Theoc. *Id.* 16.73 and Callim. *Aet.* 1.23, where ἀοιδός is used as a self-reference by the poet. For another female musician in Theocritus, see Theoc. *Id.* 4.30–31, where Corydon boasts that he is a "musician" (μελικτάς, 30) and "able to strike up Glauce's tunes" (κεῦ μὲν τὰ Γλαύκας ἀγκρούομαι, 31). Glauce was a well-known female musician contemporary to Theocritus (see Bulloch 1989: 32).

55. Gorgo underlines this at the end of the song: τὸ χρῆμα σοφώτατον ἀ θήλεια (The woman's a wonder!), *Id.* 15.145; note the substantive ἀ θήλεια. Skinner 2001: 216 makes the interesting suggestion that the use of the matronymic may be a reference to Nossis's self-identification through her double matronymic as the daughter of "Theophilis daughter of Cleocha" (Θευφιλὶς ἀ Κλεόχας) at 3.3–4 G-P; see further pp. 248–49 with chapter 8, n. 54.

56. On women at the Adonia, see J. Larson 2007: 124, Neils 2008: 245–46; on the festival of Adonis in Athens (with discussion of Theoc. *Id.* 15 at pp. 3–6, 53–56, 121), see Reitzammer 2016. Gow 1952 ad 15.143 notes the feminine participles/adjectives in the song of the female ἀοιδός (ἀθρόαι, 132; εὐθυμεύσαις, 143), referring to the women attending the festival (though some men appear to have got through, as evidenced by Praxinoa's interlocutors at 71, 74, 87–88: see Skinner 2001: 212–13).

57. Dover's (1985 ad *Id.* 15.97) hesitation in response to the scholiast's suggestion that ἀοιδός here could signify that this female singer was also a poet, composer of her own songs, speaks as much of his own assumptions as those made by Theocritus.

58. πολύϊδρις ἀοιδός, / ἅτις καὶ πέρυσιν τὸν ἰάλεμον ἀρίστευσε, *Id.* 15.97–98.

59. ἀῶθεν δ' ἄμμες . . . ἀθρόαι . . . / λύσασαι δὲ κόμαν καὶ ἐπὶ σφυρὰ κόλπον ἀνεῖσαι / στήθεσι φαινομένοις λιγυρᾶς ἀρξεύμεθ' ἀοιδᾶς, *Id.* 15.132–35.

speech genres to which women could lay claim.[60] This identification between a skillful female *aoidos* and her powerful lament recalls the three potential female *aoidoi* of *Iliad* 24, where the term *aoidos* was subliminally used to explore the richness and reach of the women's voices in lament. Here in Theocritus, then, where women perform to women in a feminine-gendered context and female-gendered genre, *aoidos* in the feminine seems to provide a Homerically endorsed avenue for men to explore ways in which women singers, and the power of women's voices, might be recognized.[61]

Antipater's Sappho: Not as Good as Homer

This feminization of *aoidos* is picked up again toward the end of the Hellenistic period, with the second application of a poet-term to a real, named female poet—and once again, it is Sappho, as in Herodotus, who is the recipient. It is worth reiterating that Sappho's primacy among women poets (both as the earliest and the best-known female poet), and her extraordinary position as a woman in the mostly male canon of Greek literature, means that the majority of times a woman poet is mentioned in ancient texts, it is Sappho. It is thus, perhaps, unsurprising that when Antipater of Sidon, an epigrammatist of the latter half of the second century BCE, chooses to use *aoidos* for a named female poet for the first time in the history of Greek literature, it comes in an epitaph for Sappho (*Anth. Pal.* 7.14 = 11 G-P):[62]

> Aeolian land, you cover Sappho, who is sung of [*aeidomenan*]
> as a mortal Muse among the immortal Muses:
> Aphrodite and Eros reared her together, and with her Persuasion

---

60. Hunter 2008: 244, following Cairns 1992: 14, notes that the foreshadowing of the lament here in effect transfers the properties of the upcoming choral lament back onto the (monodic) Adonis song that follows. On lament as a women's genre, see chapter 1, n. 43.

61. Although the hymn of the female singer has received criticism from its (male) critics, based on the extraordinary claim that Theocritus may "have written it not by his standards, but by hers" (Gow 1938: 202, cf. Gow 1952 ad 15.97); see Hunter 1996: 123–24 for a summary of critical positions to the Adonis hymn and responses.

62. Σαπφώ τοι κεύθεις, χθὼν Αἰολί, τὰν μετὰ Μούσαις / ἀθανάταις θνατὰν Μοῦσαν ἀειδομέναν, / ἂν Κύπρις καὶ Ἔρως συνάμ᾽ ἔτραφον, ἇς μέτα Πειθὼ / ἔπλεκ᾽ ἀείζωον Πιερίδων στέφανον, / Ἑλλάδι μὲν τέρψιν, σοὶ δὲ κλέος. ὦ τριέλικτον / Μοῖραι δινεῦσαι νῆμα κατ᾽ ἠλακάτας, / πῶς οὐκ ἐκλώσασθε πανάφθιτον ἦμαρ ἀοιδῷ / ἄφθιτα μησαμένᾳ δῶρ᾽ Ἑλικωνιάδων; *Anth. Pal.* 7.14 = Antip. Sid. G-P 11. The text is cited from Gow and Page 1965. For Antipater's date, see Gutzwiller 1998: 236 n. 20, and see in general Gutzwiller 1998: 236–76.

wove the ever-living garland of the Pierides,
a source of joy to Greece, and fame [*kleos*] to you. You Fates,   5
spinning your three threads on your distaffs,
how did you not spin an all-undying [*panaphthiton*] day for the singer
   [*aoidōi*]
who made the undying [*aphthita*] gifts of the daughters of Helicon

This epigram represents perhaps the earliest instance of a sustained attempt, by a male author, to come up with a language to identify a woman poet—and, as such, it is full of elements to unpack. The most obvious motif running through the poem is the comparison of Sappho to the Muses: she is "a mortal Muse among the immortal Muses" (lines 1–2), who wove "the ever-living garland of the Pierides" (a patronymic or locational term for the Muses, 4), and "made the undying gifts of the daughters of Helicon" (another locale of the Muses, 8).[63] The analogy between Sappho and the Muses was, by Antipater's time, a well-known trope in Hellenistic epigram.[64] Perhaps the most famous example is an epigram ascribed to Plato, but most likely written around 250 BCE: "Some say there are nine Muses; how careless! See—Sappho of Lesbos is the tenth" (*Anth. Pal.* 9.506).[65] The comparison draws on the representation of the female Muses as inspirers of song to articulate the nexus of gender and poetics represented by a woman poet. At the same time, it also enables male authors to tie into a long and distinguished pedigree, stretching back to Homer's invocation of the Muses and Hesiod's self-identification as a *Mousaōn therapōn*.

On the face of it, calling a woman poet a Muse might seem a compliment, elevating her above male poets' subordination to the Muses (like Hesiod's *Mousaōn therapōn*) by associating her with the female divinities of song and the hallowed tradition of poetic invocations to the Muse.[66] And yet, as Alison

63. Note the alternative myth of the Pierides as the nine daughters of Pierus who challenged the Muses to a song contest (Ov. *Met.* 5.294–678); Πιερίδες, however, is also an appellation for the Muses; see Smith 1886: 307.

64. *Anth. Pal.* 9.506, 7.407, 7.14, 9.66, 9.571, 9.189. On Sappho as Muse in Hellenistic epigram, see Gosetti-Murrayjohn 2006; see also Hallett 1979: 447 with n. 1, Williamson 1995: 14–18, Rosenmeyer 1997: 133–34, Acosta-Hughes 2010: 86–87 with 86 n. 89. Cf. Catull. 35.16 *Sapphica...Musa*, Plut. *Amat.* 762f. For a comparison between Erinna and the Muses, see *Anth. Pal.* 7.12.5–6.

65. For the date, see Ludwig 1963, Page 1981: 126, which Gosetti-Murrayjohn 2006: 32 n. 29 notes would make it the first extant example of the Sappho as tenth Muse trope.

66. Snyder 1989: 155, Barbantani 1993: 34, Gosetti-Murrayjohn 2006: 31; cf. de Vos 2014: 415–16, esp. 416 n. 22.

Sharrock points out, "the ancient and modern practice of calling Sappho 'the tenth Muse' should be deeply troubling . . . because it has the effect, albeit subliminal, of crossing out or undermining the active creative function of woman poets. It is only a small step from calling a woman poet 'a Muse' to constructing her as 'poetry' rather than 'poet', as the page who 'is a poem rather than being someone who writes a poem.'"[67] For another thing, it is the very "obviousness" of calling Sappho a Muse which we need to call into question.[68] The figuration of Sappho as a Muse is inherently gendered from the beginning: what connects the two is their gender, rather than, in the first instance, their relationship with poetry.[69] We can see this most clearly through the fact that, by contrast, male poets are never compared to Muses— demonstrating that it is gender, more than poetry, which relates Sappho and the Muse in male authors' imaginations.[70] Alcaeus of Messene (not the archaic poet of Lesbos of the same name) writes an epigram on Homer, calling him "the star of the Muses and Graces" (as well as, it is worth noting, an *aoidos*; 11.8 G-P = *Anth. Pal.* 7.1.8). Homer is not a Muse; he is an *aoidos*, and the Muses' "star." Elsewhere in Hellenistic epigram, Homer sings "equal to the Muses" (*Anth Pal.* 7.2.1); he is a *poiētēs* who is "honored by the Muses" (*Anth. Pal.* 7.2B.3–4); and a "herald" and *prophētēs* who is the "light of the Muses" (*Anth. Pal.* 7.6.3). Pindar is "the sacred mouth of the Muses" (*Anth. Pal.* 9.184) and the "servant of the sweet-voiced Muses" (*Anth. Pal.* 7.35.2), while Anacreon is "most delightful to the Muses" (*Anth. Pal.* 7.31.3). For men, in other words, the gendered relationship set up from Homer and Hesiod on, between female Muse and male poet, still holds. A man could never be a Muse.

Here, too, in Antipater's epigram, there are signs that the comparison is not altogether in Sappho's favor. A consistent theme threading through the poem is the contrast between Sappho's mortality, on the one hand, and the immortality of both the Muses ("the immortal Muses," 1–2) and her poetry ("the ever-living garland," 4; "the undying gifts," 8) on the other. Sappho does not, ultimately, achieve the status of Muse, precisely by virtue of her death which the epitaph commemorates. The poem lamenting Sappho's death thus serves,

67. Sharrock 2002: 208.

68. Hallett 1979: 447, Williamson 1995: 15, Rosenmeyer 1997: 134. See p. 51 with chapter 2, n. 25 for further discussion of the problematization of the Muses.

69. The same point is made by Williamson 1995: 15, Rosenmeyer 1997: 134 n. 40, Gosetti-Murrayjohn 2006: 40.

70. Gosetti-Murrayjohn 2006: 36 n. 37, 40.

paradoxically, as a way of staging Sappho's inability to become a Muse, even as the male poet affects to compare her to them. The paradox of the second line, with the juxtaposition of "immortal" and "mortal" (*athanatais thnatan*, 2), demonstrates the extent to which Sappho is *not* a Muse; and the final couplet, with the contrast between the "all-undying [*panaphthiton*] day" which Sappho failed to achieve (7) and the "undying [*aphthita*] gifts" of the Muses (8), hammers it home. Immortality is extracted from the female poet and given to her poetry, which in turn is dislodged from the woman poet and attributed instead to the Muses: "the undying gifts of the daughters of Helicon" (8).[71]

This disenfranchisement of the female poet goes beyond the comparison to a Muse: it is signaled throughout the epigram as Antipater makes a series of literary-allusive moves that put Sappho into the background, using her instead as a vehicle for the male poet's own poetry and poetic fame, by generating a lineage that stretches back from himself to the archaic male poets. The most compelling example of this is the contrast between the term given to Sappho in line 7—*aoidōi*, "singer"—and the passive participle in line 2, "sung of" (*aeidomenan*). On the one hand, the labeling of Sappho as an *aoidos* in the final couplet of the poem is the first time that either of the two major poet-terms, *aoidos* and *poiētēs*, is applied to a woman by a man—the first application, in other words, of male poet-vocabulary to a real female poet in Greek literature. And yet the use of *aeidomenan* at the poem's opening acts as a guide as to how Sappho's designation as an *aoidos* should, in fact, be read. The participle *aeidomenan*, "sung of," from *aeidein*, comes from the same root as *aoidos*, linking the two and creating a ring composition around the poem. (Both words stand at line end in the second and penultimate lines.) But, crucially, *aeidomenan* is a passive form: "sung of," not "singing," turning Sappho into the subject matter of song rather than the singer. This is, in fact, quite conspicuously the case: Sappho is the genuine object of Antipater's song, with her name opening the epigram in the accusative (*Sapphō*, 1). At the same time, *aeidomenan*, as a participle, can be declined as a first-declension feminine form in a way that the noun *aoidos* cannot. It thus generates, at the epigram's opening, a gendered vocabulary around the female poet's connection to poetry that specifically transforms her into the subject matter of song. It serves both to signal Anti-

71. This echoes an epigram by Dioscorides, where Sappho's songs are called her "immortal daughters" (ἀθανάτας . . . θυγατέρας), *Anth. Pal.* 7.407.10 = 18.10 G-P; cf. *Anth. Pal.* 7.16 for a later (probably first-century CE) example. On this trope in Hellenistic receptions of Sappho, see Hunter 2021: 278–79.

pater's appropriation of Sappho as subject, and to reference the male epigrammatic tradition of writing about Sappho to which the "Sappho-as-Muse" trope gestures. We are not discussing Sappho's poetry here, in other words, but Sappho *as* (male) poetry—in the same way as her personification as a Muse serves to diminish her identity as a poet and turn her into an abstraction of the male imagination.[72] (We might compare an anonymous epigram of uncertain date, in which Sappho is listed alongside eight of the canonical male lyric poets— "Sappho was not the ninth among men [*andrōn*], but is written up [*katagraphetai*] as the tenth Muse among the lovely Muses" [*Anth. Pal.* 9.571.7–8]"—where Sappho is set in contrast with male poets and "written up" [*katagraphetai*] into the male voice to bolster and reference the male tradition of representing Sappho as the tenth Muse.)[73] Moreover, there is a gendered literary lineage to *aeidomenan* here in Antipater's epigram, with a clear resonance (both etymological and semantic) between Antipater's *aeidomenan* and the *aoidimos* (subject of song) Helen in *Iliad* book 6, who refers to her future memorialization by male poets—including the *aoidos* Homer. Rather than being celebrated as an *aoidos*, Sappho is, just like Helen—just like the Muses, in fact—being appropriated into the male poet's poem as the subject of his song, guarantor of his status as the *aoidos* who turns women into his subject matter.

The connection to Homer's Helen is not an accidental one. The appropriation of Sappho as a subject of song is a critical vehicle for the demonstration of Antipater's own literary skill, and a way of forging a connection to other male *aoidoi* like Homer and Hesiod.[74] Intertextual resonances abound throughout the epigram, with typical Hellenistic allusivity.[75] The description of the Muses as *Pierides* in line 4 looks back to the first line of Hesiod's *Works and Days*, where the Muses are said to come "from Pieria," as well as a possible

72. It is worth noting that all personifications except Ἔρως (the Muses, Aphrodite, Persuasion, and the Fates) are feminine in Greek.

73. ἀνδρῶν δ᾽ οὐκ ἐνάτη Σαπφὼ πέλεν, ἀλλ᾽ ἐρατειναῖς / ἐν Μούσαις δεκάτη Μοῦσα καταγράφεται, adesp. *Anth. Pal.* 9.571.7–8. See Page 1981: 340–43, Barbantani 1993: 8–10, Gosetti-Murrayjohn 2006: 42, Acosta-Hughes 2010: 85, de Vos 2014: 416–17. On the Alexandrian canon of lyric poets, see chapter 6, n. 8.

74. On the production of epigrams (and fictional epitaphs) on famous poets, as a means to construct the poet's place in the literary tradition, see Bing 1988, Gutzwiller 1998: 259–65, Sens 2007: 375, and cf. chapter 7, n. 82.

75. On allusion and intertextuality as a key feature of Hellenistic poetry, see Bing 1988, Hopkinson 2020: 7–9, and in Hellenistic epigram in particular, see Sens 2007, Klooster 2011: 15–42.

reference to the "roses of Pieria" of Sappho fr. 55.2–3 L-P; while the Muses' depiction in line 8 as coming "from Helicon" references the first line of Hesiod's *Theogony*.[76] At the same time, the *terpsis* (joy) in Antipater's description of Sappho's song in line 5 recalls the "joy in song" (*terpsis aoidēs*) of the Muses toward the end of the *Theogony*, forging another link between Sappho and her personification as a (less-than) Muse.[77] Moving to Homer, the *kleos* which Sappho's song is said to bring (line 5) draws on the Homeric conception of *kleos* as the proper subject of poetry (Achilles's *klea andrōn* at *Iliad* 9.189, for example)—particularly when conjoined with the adjective *aphthita* a few lines below (line 8), which inevitably recalls Achilles's prediction of his *kleos aphthiton*, his "undying glory" (Hom. *Il.* 9.413). We might argue that *kleos aphthiton* is a phrase that is also used by Sappho in the context of the wedding of Hector and Andromache (Sappho fr. 44.4 L-P), and that this could therefore be seen as a nod to Sappho's poetics: but there is a crucial difference.[78] In both Homer and Sappho, the phrase is used to endow the characters depicted in their poetry with glory (*kleos*), that then reflects on, and is substantiated in, the poetry which tells that glory—so that the poetry itself becomes a form of *kleos* (from *kluein*, "that which is heard").[79]

Here in Antipater's epigram, however, the accusative *kleos* can be read in multiple ways. It can stand in apposition either to the "garland" woven by Persuasion (an image for Sappho's poetry), or, importantly, to Sappho herself, who opens the entire poem in the accusative. In this second sense, it is *Sappho herself*, and not her poetry, who is the source of *kleos*. This might seem to be a compliment to Sappho—until, that is, we remember that it is Achilles (in Homer) and Hector and Andromache (in Sappho) who are the recipients of *kleos* in the words of the poet; critically, it is the poet who bestows *kleos*. Sappho has thus been turned into a character of Antipater's poem here, twisted from the author of *kleos* in her own poetry to a recipient of *kleos* in the male poet's poem—and thus the *kleos* becomes her attribute and his poetry, just as

76. Hes. *Op.* 1: Μοῦσαι Πιερίηθεν ἀοιδῇσι κλείουσαι (Muses of Pieria who give glory in song); Gosetti-Murrayjohn 2006: 35 also notes Hes. [*Sc.*] 206, Μοῦσαι Πιερίδες. For Sappho's "roses of Pieria," see p. 168 with chapter 6, n. 10. Hes. *Theog.* 1: Μουσάων Ἑλικωνιάδων ἀρχώμεθ᾽ ἀείδειν (let me start to sing from the Muses of Helicon), see pp. 48–49; cf. Hes. *Op.* 658, Pind. *Isthm.* 2.34, *Pae.* 7b.19.

77. Μοῦσαι ... / ἐννέα, τῇσιν ἄδον θαλίαι καὶ τέρψις ἀοιδῆς (the nine Muses, who love feasts and the joy of song), Hes. *Theog.* 916–17.

78. Gosetti-Murrayjohn 2006: 36 n. 36 notes the Sapphic allusion.

79. See pp. 27–28 with chapter 1, n. 9.

Achilles's *kleos* is sung of in Homer's epic, or Hector and Andromache's fame is depicted in Sappho's poems. In other words, by virtue of turning Sappho into the subject matter of poetry, Antipater has wrenched the *kleos*-endowing power of poetry away from her, using Sappho as a tool to demonstrate his own skill in literary allusivity, at the same time as she generates the *kleos* of his own poem. It is a telling role reversal: on the surface, the male poet seems to gesture to Sappho's fame and her ability to tell of *kleos* in her poetry; but by turning her into an object, a feature of his poem, it is, in fact, his *own* poetry-as-*kleos* which is bolstered here.

We might argue back, against this rather bleak picture of Sappho's appropriation by the male poet, that there are positive images for women's poetic composition in the epigram: the consistent imagery of weaving, for example, which structures the poem, from Persuasion who "wove the ever-living garland of the Pierides" with Sappho (line 4), to the weaving of the Fates in lines 5–7. This recalls Helen's association with weaving in the *Iliad* and the alignment of Helen's web with the subject matter of Homer's epic; while the mention of the Fates' distaff might recall the Hellenistic poet Erinna, who composed a hexameter epic titled *The Distaff* which celebrates women's weaving, and for whom Antipater himself wrote an epigram (*Anth. Pal.* 7.713).[80] Yet the poem ends with the ultimate failure of women's weaving—the lament that the Fates were unable to spin an immortal life "for the *aoidos*" Sappho in lines 5–8. It seems that, if we are to take the metaphor of weaving as a symbol for women's poetry seriously, the Fates' failure to turn Sappho into an immortal like the Muses appears to indicate the ultimate inadequacy of women's poetry—and thus, also, their ambition to "spin" Sappho into an *aoidos* in her own right.

The lament for the failed weaving of the Fates at the poem's close is, then, ultimately, an exposition of the appropriation of the female poet's claim to become an *aoidos*: it is the male poet's poetry which guarantees the female poet immortality, through the epitaph which celebrates her as the object of his poetry. The irony is that Antipater's prediction is entirely true: the vast majority

80. On Erinna, see West 1977 (who argues against Erinna's authorship of *The Distaff* as well as the epigrams attributed to her); see contra, Pomeroy 1978, and see further, chapter 8, n. 57. See also Cameron and Cameron 1969, Barnard 1978: 204–8, Arthur 1980, Skinner 1982, Snyder 1989: 86–97, Gutzwiller 1997b, Stehle 2001, Neri 2003, Rayor 2005, Manwell 2005, Murray and Rowland 2007: 213–26, Levaniouk 2008, Gutzwiller 2017a. On women's weaving, see chapter 1, n. 58, and, for Helen's weaving in the *Iliad*, see p. 41 with chapter 1, n. 59; on the common trope of weaving as a metaphor for poetry, see chapter 1, n. 60. For the comparison of Sappho and Erinna, see *Anth. Pal.* 9.190.7–8: see chapter 7, n. 86.

of Sappho's poetry, her "undying gifts," survives in quotations in texts by men, from scholiasts to grammarians to historians.[81] In a sense, then, endowing her with the word *aoidos* becomes a conclusive statement of the precise extent of the male poet's power. He is the one who preserves her memory—both of the female poet and her poetry.[82] The way the female poet can become an *aoidos* is through him. And this means that she is set in counterpoint and contrast to men—as the use of the term *aoidos*, with its masculine grammatical form, its literary heritage stretching back to Homer and Hesiod, and the literary allusions to the (male) archaic poets which pepper the epigram, demonstrate only too well. There is an inherent comparison and contrast to male poets baked into the term; and calling Sappho an *aoidos* only serves to set her contrast and difference to men into relief.

And this is made clear in a second epigram by Antipater, which gets straight to the point of the difference between Sappho and Homer as *aoidoi*. The epigram, a brief two-liner, runs thus: "My name is Sappho. I surpassed women [*thēleian*] in song [*aoidōn*] as much as Homer surpassed men [*andrōn*]" (*Anth. Pal.* 7.15).[83] Here, neatly summed up, is the inherent gender contrast between Sappho and Homer that underlies Antipater's designation of Sappho as *aoidos* in the previous epigram.[84] We might compare the later description of "the female Homer" in Antipater of Thessalonica's canon of nine female poets, or Galen's famous opposition of Homer and Sappho:

81. Note de Vos 2014: 422–23, 430–31 on the "selective transmission of the works of women poets" by men; see further pp. 281–85. See also Most 1995: 33 for a different angle.

82. Cf. Gutzwiller 1998: 240 on Antipater's collection of epigrams as a "projection of the author as an interpreter of earlier Greek texts and culture"; for a similar point (though with reference to Antipater's epitaph for Anacreon, *Anth. Pal.* 7.30 = 17 G-P), see Gutzwiller 1998: 265.

83. οὔνομά μευ Σαπφώ, τόσσον δ᾽ ὑπερέσχον ἀοιδῶν / θηλειᾶν ἀνδρῶν ὅσσον ὁ Μαιονίδας, *Anth. Pal.* 7.15 = Antip. [Thess.] 73 G-P. The text follows Gow and Page 1968; Setti 1890: 72 gives ἀοιδάν, as does Dübner; see Gow and Page 1968: 2:77 in defense of ἀοιδῶν. For the attribution to Antipater of Sidon (as opposed to Antipater of Thessalonica), see Setti 1890: 73, Argentieri 2003: 103–4, Acosta-Hughes and Barbantani 2007: 440–41, and note Setti 1890, Gutzwiller 1998: 236–37 with 237 n. 21, Argentieri 2003 on the problem of the ascription of epigrams assigned to "Antipater" without an ethnic determiner.

84. Rosenmeyer 1997: 134–35, cf. Gosetti-Murrayjohn 2006: 37. Rosenmeyer (1997: 135) makes the excellent point that the contrast could have been presented as one of genre, as in the opposition between Erinna (epic) and Sappho (lyric) at *Anth. Pal.* 9.190 (see chapter 7, n. 86), but it is not: when Sappho is set against Homer, it is her gender, not her identity as a lyric poet, that comes to the fore.

"When people say 'the poet said this, the poetess said that'—we all hear 'Homer' in the word 'poet,' and 'Sappho' in 'poetess.'"[85] Sappho is limited by her gender in Antipater's epigram to the category of women (*thēleian*, line 2) and is therefore inherently different from Homer—as the correlative pronouns contrasting the two (*tosson . . . hosson*, lines 1–2) and the juxtaposition between "women" and "men" (*thēleian andrōn*, line 2) indicate.[86] At the same time, the use of *thēleia* for "woman" in line 2—an adjective (we might remember it from Protagoras's division of the grammatical genders in the introduction) being used as a substantive—creates an ambiguity. If we take it as a substantive, the epigram translates as above, "surpassed women in song." But if we read it adjectivally, then we could translate the opening as "excelled in women's song."[87] In this sense, we have a deeper segregation: not only is Sappho contrasted with Homer, dividing women poets from men, but poetry about and for women is seen as entirely separate from men's poetry. Not only Sappho's gender as a poet, but the gendering of her poetry, is at stake—and it is this, her inherent "femaleness," which disqualifies her from competing with an *aoidos* like Homer.

It is not only the male poet who pronounces Sappho's contrast and difference as a woman, however. Antipater goes further, creating a fictional voice for Sappho that forces her, in the first person, to acknowledge her own gendered inferiority ("my name is Sappho . . .").[88] Not content simply to relegate her to second place to Homer, he appropriates her female voice and asks her to ventriloquize his own statement about her inferiority as a woman poet. This appropriation of Sappho's voice is signaled by Antipater's reinterpretation of a Sapphic fragment for his own purposes. In fr. 106 L-P, Sappho comments on the "superiority" of "the Lesbian *aoidos*"—a statement which, as we will see in chapter 9, can be read as a veiled commentary on her own identity as an *aoidos*

85. *Anth. Pal.* 9.26.3: θῆλυν Ὅμηρον. (There is debate over the reference, see Werner 1994; Rosenmeyer 1997: 134 n. 41 takes it with Anyte, Gosetti-Murrayjohn 2006: 38–39 with Sappho.) Gal. *Quod animi mores* 4.771: ὅταν εἴπωσιν ὑπὸ μὲν τοῦ ποιητοῦ λελέχθαι τόδε τὸ ἔπος, ὑπὸ δὲ τῆς ποιητρίας τόδε· πάντες γὰρ ἀκούομεν Ὅμηρον <μὲν> λέγεσθαι ποιητήν, Σαπφὼ δὲ ποιήτριαν.

86. For a comparison with similar language, see *Anth. Pal.* 9.190.7–8: Σαπφὼ δ᾽ Ἠρίννης ὅσσον μελέεσσιν ἀμείνων, / Ἤριννα Σαπφοῦς τόσσον ἐν ἑξαμέτροις (Sappho surpasses Erinna as much in lyrics, as Erinna does Sappho in hexameters). See West 1977: 95 n. 1, Murray and Rowland 2007: 215–16, Klooster 2011: 68–69, Cairns 2016: 154–55.

87. As Gosetti-Murrayjohn 2006: 37 notes.

88. Cf. Rosenmeyer 1997: 135.

of Lesbos.[89] Where Sappho hides her identity beneath the male "*aoidos* of Lesbos," and subtly suggests that she, too, might be considered an *aoidos* to rival men, Antipater does the opposite: he takes her statement of "superiority" or "surpassing" in fr. 106 L-P and makes her qualify the statement in the fiction of her first-person voice, to put herself in her gendered place—she surpasses others, yes, but only women. This Sappho, in other words, admits that she is *not* quite as good as Homer; this Lesbian poet does not surpass others. And this is exactly why, in this epigram, she does not qualify for the term *aoidos*: in contrast to Sappho's fr. 106 L-P, or even Antipater's own epitaph for Sappho (*Anth. Pal.* 7.14), she is not given a poet-term here at *Anth. Pal.* 7.15—in spite of the opening statement of her "name," *ounoma*, which signals a specific interest in naming and terminology. Instead, the poet says that she "surpassed women in song" (*aoidōn*, 1), using the feminine noun *aoidē* (cognate with *aoidos*). The feminine *aoidē* explicitly denies Sappho the vocabulary of *aoidos*: she cannot be like Homer, and cannot be an *aoidos*, because she is a woman; the closest she can get is feminine "song." And if Sappho, the paradigmatic example of a woman poet and "women's song" (as both this epigram and the reception of Sappho's poetry argue), cannot achieve equality with male poets, then, the epigram implies, no other woman can. In a single word, Antipater sums up the history of the gender segregation of poetry—and demonstrates why a woman cannot be an *aoidos*.

Names Not Given: The Case of Sappho

It is worth pausing at this point to reflect that, with Antipater of Sidon, we reach the last time that Sappho is called a "poet" by men, in all extant male-authored literature to the end of the Hellenistic period.[90] The problem with looking at descriptions of women poets by men is that, more often than not, it is a case of the terms that *are not* used, rather than those that are. The cultural conditions which made women's writing much less common in the first

---

89. πέρροχος, ὡς ὅτ' ἄοιδος ὁ Λέσβιος ἀλλοδάποισιν, Sappho fr. 106 L-P; see pp. 261–63.

90. For Sappho's ancient reception, see Williamson 1995: 5–33, Most 1995: 15–20, Yatromanolakis 2007, Kivilo 2010: 183–84, Gilhuly 2018: 101–7, Kivilo 2021, Finglass and Kelly 2021: 263–319; on Sappho's reception in Hellenistic epigram, see Barbantani 1993: 28–47, Gosetti-Murrayjohn 2006, Acosta-Hughes and Barbantani 2007: 438–42, Acosta-Hughes 2010: 82–92, de Vos 2014. On Sappho as ποιήτρια in the imperial period, see chapter 7, n. 107; as μελοποιός, see chapter 7, n. 47.

place, and set it up as second-class to men's, did not just mean that women poets were less likely to be mentioned, or that, in the beginning, a language to describe women poets did not exist—or that, when a language was invented, it was still inherently set in opposition to that of men (though all of these are true). It also meant that male authors were much more reluctant to give women poet-terms at all. One of the most predominant figurations of Sappho—and by far more common than her acknowledgment as a poet—is as a Muse, as we saw in Antipater's depiction of Sappho as "a mortal Muse" (*Anth. Pal.* 7.14.2) and the anonymous epigram where Sappho is "written up as the tenth Muse" (*Anth. Pal.* 9.571.8). Elsewhere, we have seen her called "beautiful" (in Plato's *Phaedrus*), while her poems are "roses" in the proem to Meleager's *Garland*.[91] And in the chapters to come, we will come across Sappho as "a theme of song" (*Anth. Pal.* 9.521.5), a "nightingale" (Hermesianax fr. 7 Powell), and even singled out for praise "in spite of being a woman" (Arist. *Rh.* 1398b).[92]

These strategies of abstraction as a Muse, sexualization, objectification as a "theme of song" to bolster male poets' own literary claims, and limitation as a "woman" serve to absent and silence Sappho as a poet. In many places, as we will see in the next chapter in Hermesianax's catalogue of poets, the process of this denial of poet-terms to Sappho is explicitly spelled out. Only twice—in Herodotus's *mousopoios*, and Antipater's *aoidos*—is Sappho called a poet by men. Even here, the context makes clear that the terms are being used either to gender segregate Sappho from her male peers and deny her her own vocabulary (as in Herodotus), or to set her up in contrast with the male poets whom she can never equal, and identify her as a tool in the male poet's own self-canonization (as Antipater does). These two instances stand alone among thirty-three independent references to Sappho in the extant corpus of Greek literature until the end of the Hellenistic period (thirty-eight if we include anonymous, undated epigrams).[93] Two poet-terms in thirty-eight mentions is a troubling figure for the most famous female poet of the ancient world: not simply in terms of the infrequency with which Sappho is mentioned in general, but the fact that she is rarely acknowledged with any term that even

91. Pl. *Phdr.* 235c3–4: see pp. 133–35 with chapter 5, n. 51. On Meleager's *Garland*, see pp. 165–69.

92. On *Anth. Pal.* 9.521, see p. 220 with chapter 7, n. 101; see p. 277 with chapter 9, n. 62 on Hermesianax; pp. 268–69 with chapter 9, n. 29 on Aristotle.

93. This does not include play titles with Sappho's name or visual representations, on which see Yatromanolakis 2001, Yatromanolakis 2007: 51–164, also Kivilo 2010: 172–73.

attempts to articulate her poetic identity. By contrast, Homer—who, if we read Antipater of Sidon at face value in *Anth. Pal.* 7.15, should be Sappho's closest male equivalent—is mentioned by name forty-four times in Plato's *Republic* alone, exceeding *all* of Sappho's mentions over six centuries in a single text; while Homer is explicitly called a *poiētēs* seven times in the *Republic*, more than tripling the count of all Sappho's poet-terms with one term in one text by one author.[94] Sappho, on the other hand, as we have seen, is mentioned once in the entire Platonic corpus, and is characterized, typically, not by her identity as a poet, but by her physical (sexualized) appearance, and her gender as a woman. Not only are men spoken about more often, then—but, when they are, they are far more likely to be identified as a poet. In this sense, Antipater's description of Homer outstripping Sappho becomes predictive of Homer's far greater reach and acknowledgment as a poet than his female counterpart. Sappho's silencing by men—both by the denial of poet-terms, and the strategies of sexualization, objectification, contrast, abstraction, and appropriation—seems to be absolute.

Beyond the Bard: New Words for Women Poets

Yet this is not where the story ends. As the feminized vocabulary of *aoidos* seems to run itself into the ground, with male poets undermining the feminine *aoidos* and reclaiming the title of *aoidos* for their own, we see different words for female poets begin to spring up, as male writers start to explore different avenues for a vocabulary for women's writing. At first, these new words for women poets remain close to the terminology of *aoidos*—as the first example, an epigram for Erinna, shows. It is attributed either to Leonidas of Tarentum (an epigrammatist of the early third century BCE) or Meleager of Gadara (epigrammatist and compiler of the *Garland*, from the early first century BCE) (*Anth. Pal.* 7.13 = Leonidas 98 G-P):[95]

94. ποιητής of Homer: *Rep.* 3.392e3, 3.393a6, 3.393c10, 3.394b5, 4.424c1, 10.606e3, 10.606e4–5 (note that this is the final occurrence of ποιητής in the *Republic*). For a wider count, including the phrase Ὅμηρος καὶ οἱ ἄλλοι ποιηταί: *Rep.* 2.377d3–4, 2.379c9–d1, 3.387b1–2, 3.388a5, 3.393c7–8, 10.599b9–c1.

95. Παρθενικὴν νεάοιδον ἐν ὑμνοπόλοισι μέλισσαν / Ἤρινναν Μουσέων ἄνθεα δρεπτομένην / Ἅδας εἰς ὑμέναιον ἀνάρπασεν· ἦ ῥα τόδ᾽ ἔμφρων / εἶπ᾽ ἐτύμως ἁ παῖς, ʻΒάσκανος ἔσσ᾽, Ἀΐδα,ʼ *Anth. Pal.* 7.13 = Leonidas 98 G-P. Gutzwiller 1998: 77, Cairns 2016: 154 and Sens 2018: 105 n. 11 take the epigram as Leonidean, as do Gow and Page 1965; see further Neri 1996: 213–16, 2003: 192.

As the virgin [*parthenikēn*] honeybee, the new-singer [*neaoidon*]
   among the song-composers [*hymnopoloisi*],
Erinna, was gathering the flowers of the Muses,
Hades snatched her off for marriage. When she was alive,
   the girl said rightly: "You are envious, Hades."

The imagery of Erinna as a honeybee among the flowers of the Muses demon-
strates the strategy of abstracting female poets into (literally) flowery imagery,
as we saw with the proem to Meleager's *Garland*. The bee is also a particularly
common metaphor for the poet, and occurs in several other epigrams on
Erinna.[96] In terms of poet-words, however, what is particularly interesting is
the other term applied to Erinna in the first line: *neaoidos* (new-singer). Camillo
Neri has observed that this neologism—the first time the word occurs in ex-
tant Greek literature—can be read multiple ways: both as a reference to the
novelty of Erinna's poetry, and to her youth (the adjective *neos* means both
"new" and "young").[97] Alexander Sens suggests further that there is an em-
phasis on the quality of Erinna's work here in the neologism, with novelty
identified as a key "desideratum" of poetry, and that the epigram thus functions
as a whole as "an endorsement of her poetic voice."[98] What seems particularly
interesting about the term *neaoidos*, from a gender perspective, however, is the
way in which the author of the epigram is attempting to find a new vocabulary
for women poets—and literally signposts it by appending the adjective *neos*,
"new," to the old word *aoidos*. This is even more slippery than simply adding
"new" to an old word: like Hesiod's *aoidos* for the nightingale, at the very be-
ginning of the feminization of *aoidos*, this could be read as either a two-
termination adjective, or a feminine noun standing in its own right in apposition
to Erinna's name.[99] In other words, this is a new coinage for a new idea—a new
type of poet-term, in the feminine, that reframes the old masculine associa-
tions with *aoidos*. The gendered aspect of this "new term" is signposted by the
adjective appended to it, *parthenikēn*, "virgin-girl," which—like Meleager's
designation of Erinna's "virgin-colored saffron" in the proem to the *Garland*

96. See *Anth. Pal.* 2.110, 7.12.1, 7.13.1–2, 9.190.1–2; see Gutzwiller 1997b: 214, Gutzwiller 1998:
77, Nünlist 1998: 60–63.

97. Neri 2003 ad loc.; on the text and accentation, see Neri 1996: 215–16.

98. Sens 2018: 107.

99. Note that Erinna is described with another common noun, παῖς, at the end of the epi-
gram (line 4, gendered feminine with the definite article), thus creating a ring composition with
νεάοιδον and underlining the flexibility of gendered vocabulary.

(*Anth. Pal.* 4.1.12)—specifically genders Erinna as a female poet, both semantically and grammatically, and demonstrates that *neaoidos* is to be read here as unmistakably feminine.[100] Moreover, as in the *Garland* proem where Alcaeus is envisioned singing "among song-composers" (*en hymnopolois*, 4.1.13), the female-gendered term that emphasizes Erinna's identity as a young girl is set in opposition to the masculine plural *hymnopoloi* that gestures to the community of male poets: this "new-female-poet" sings "among [male] song-composers" (*en hymnopoloisi, Anth. Pal.* 7.13.1). Finally, the entire epigram is set within the highly gendered context of a literary rape scene—Hades's rape of Persephone, looking back to the *Homeric Hymn to Demeter* and reminiscent, too, of Hermes's evisceration of the tortoise in the *Homeric Hymn to Hermes*. The context and contrast are clear: one female, many males; a new term for a woman poet, a familiar term for male poets, set within the context of the gendered history of Greek literature—both in terms of the subject matter and the singers and mechanisms of poetry. There are clear signals that a new kind of vocabulary for women poets is being played with here.

Another cousin to *aoidos* which is briefly explored in application to women poets is *aoidimos*, "sung of," the term which Helen had used of herself in book 6 of the *Iliad*. For Helen, it signaled her status as the object of male song, at the same time as it also gestured to the male bard's complex dependence on her as his subject matter. An anonymous epigram of uncertain date has Sappho being addressed by the Muses: "You will be sung of as a theme of song [*aoidimos*] among all mortals" (*Anth. Pal.* 9.521.5).[101] Antipater of Sidon apostrophizes Sappho as *aeidomenan* (sung of) in *Anth. Pal.* 7.14.2, turning her into the passive object of men's poetry; here, the passive force of *aoidimos* is driven home with the passive verb *melpsei* ("you will be sung of," *Anth. Pal.* 9.521.5).[102] Meanwhile, Sappho is deprived of any poet-term; like Helen in the *Iliad*, *aoidimos* is as close as she gets. So far, *aoidimos* seems to be restricted to the

---

100. See pp. 165–69 with chapter 6, n. 13.

101. μέλψῃ δ᾽ ἐν πάντεσσιν ἀοίδιμος ἀμερίοισιν, *Anth. Pal.* 9.521.5. The epigram is not included in Gow and Page 1965 or 1968; Stadtmüller 1906: 519 suggests either Alcaeus of Messene or Dioscorides as potential authors. Cf. Barbantani 1993: 37, who compares the language to *Anth. Pal.* 7.14 = Antip. Sid. 11 G-P. Note that the epigram is addressed to Sappho from the Muses: for the trope of Sappho as Muse, see pp. 208–12 with chapter 7, n. 64.

102. Cf. the passive here with ἀειδομέναν at *Anth. Pal.* 7.14.2 = Antip. Sid. 11.2 G-P, and καταγράφεται at *Anth. Pal.* 9.571.8 (see p. 211).

objectification of women by male poets, shoring up the male writers who depict them as the only ones who qualify to be *aoidoi*.

Yet an inscription dated (tentatively) to the third or second centuries BCE provides a suggestively different future for *aoidimos* and women poets. It is an epigram honoring a poet named Delphis, from a statue base on the island of Cos. Although the text is hard to reconstruct, lines 3–4 appear to read (according to Paton and Hicks's reconstruction): "The poet [*aoidimos*] grew up [sc. here in Cos], Delphis, since s/he engaged with the Olympian Muses."[103] The definition of Delphis's "engagement with the Olympian Muses" seems to clinch the unusual translation of *aoidimos* as "poet" here. So who was Delphis? Paton and Hicks, who reproduce the text of the epigram in their *Inscriptions of Cos*, assume that Delphis must have been a male poet.[104] Yet there is plenty of evidence for Delphis as a female name, and Kerstin Höghammar has argued persuasively that Delphis should be taken as female here.[105] From the standpoint of the evidence of the inscription itself, the history of the connection between *aoidimos* and the female voice—from Helen to Sappho—suggests that a reading of *aoidimos* as "female poet" is not only valid, but warranted. And the public context of the statue's dedication might argue for *aoidimos* as the ideal term to encapsulate the female Delphis's engagement with song, alongside her reputation and memorialization in public (male) circles—just like Homer's Helen in the *Iliad*.

This is the only example, however, in which the resonant *aoidimos* is used of a woman poet.[106] By the end of the Hellenistic period, the experiment with

103. ἀ]οίδιμος ἅδε ἀνέτειλε, / Δελφίς, ἐπεὶ Μου[σ]ᾶν [ἄψ]α[τ]ο Ὀλυμπιάδων, *IG* XII,4 2:845.3–4 = *SEG* 54.783.3–4 = Paton-Hicks 137.3–4; see Höghammar 1993: 60, 170. Cf. a later (first-century CE) inscription for an unknown female poet of Old Comedy from Alexandria and Cos, who is called a ποιήτριαν κω[μῳδίας] / ἀρχαίας, *IG* XII,4 2:845.3–4 = *SEG* 54.787.3–4; Bosnakis 2004: 105 suggests that the mention of a Δελφίς at lines 9–10 may be a reference back to the earlier female poet of *IG* XII,4 2:845 = *SEG* 54.783.

104. Paton and Hicks 1891: 156.

105. Höghammar 1997: 129–31, who notes that the name Δελφίς is attested in Cos for another woman; she also identifies Delphis the (female) poet with the Delphis of Paton-Hicks 10. The *Lexicon of Greek Personal Names* gives fourteen occurrences of the name Δελφίς, five male and nine female (two from Cos); the poet Delphis is included as a female example.

106. A later example of ἀοιδός-vocabulary for a female poet occurs at *Anth. Pal.* 7.17 = Laurea 1 G-P in Tullius Laureas's fictive epitaph for Sappho, where she is termed ἀοιδοπόλος (line 2): see Rosenmeyer 1997: 131, Nisbet 2019: 266–67. For an intriguing example of ἀοίδιμος in female speech applied to a male poet (Archilochus, P-W 231 = *SEG* 15.517), see pp. 263–64 with chapter 9,

the feminization of *aoidos* seems to have run its course. Looking for another way to talk about women poets, and a new family of vocabulary through which to conceptualize women's relationship to poetry, it is natural, perhaps, that male authors turn to the other most common term for poet—*poiētēs*. Rather than trying to adopt the masculine term into the female realm, as with *aoidos*, however, a new feminine form of the masculine appears instead for the first time: *poiētria* (female poet).[107] This feminine form is, on one level, a step forward in the journey of naming women poets, and—as we will see—represents a different approach to gendering that makes space for some women poets to be honored in their own right. Perhaps, in some cases, the generation of a feminine equivalent was a way in which the uniqueness of women's roles and gender could be recognized. At the same time, *poiētria* also represents the strategy of contrast which we saw in Antipater: Galen's later division of Homer as the quintessential *poiētēs* versus Sappho as the *poiētria* is perhaps the clearest articulation of the contrastive nature of the word.[108] This gendered differentiation continues in its usage: as we will see in the next part of the book, the term *poiētria* is never used by women poets to describe themselves. This seems to be suggestive evidence that the word did not speak to women, or, at least in their eyes, represent their gendered identity and relationship to poetry; it might even imply (if we want to take it further) that the term could have been perceived as a negative one, pigeonholing women by virtue of their gender at the same time as it attempted to shoehorn them into the mold of male poet-terminology. Conversely, there are no occurrences of a woman being called a *poiētēs* in the singular by a man: while women are included in generic masculine plurals as *poiētai*, no woman is

---

n. 15. For examples of women using ἀοιδός (adjectivally) and ἀοίδιμος, including for a male poet, see chapter 9, n. 27.

107. According to the TLG, ποιήτρια occurs ninety-six times in the Greek corpus (ninety removing repetitions), and thirty times before 230 CE, with the first instance in Alexis in the mid-fourth century BCE. See, e.g., Strabo 17.1.33 (of Sappho); Plut. *De mul. vir.* 245c (of Telesilla); Plut. *Quaest. Graec.* 300f (of Myrtis); Dio Chrys. *Or.* 33.45 (in a discussion of feminized professions); Paus. 8.18.5 (of Sappho); Gal. *Quod animi mores* 4.771 (of Sappho, see chapter 7, n. 85); Clem. Al. *Strom.* 4.19.120.3 (of Telesilla); Clem. Al. *Strom.* 4.19.122.4 (of Corinna, Telesilla, Myia, Sappho); P. Oxy. 2438 col. ii (of Corinna); Ael. *VH* 12.19 (of Sappho); Ath. 10.450e, 13.596e, 15.687a (of Sappho, though only three times in thirty-one mentions of the female poet, vs. four times where she is called ἡ καλή, as in Plato's *Phaedrus*; see Schlesier 2019).

108. See chapter 7, n. 5.

ever a *poiētēs*.[109] *Poiētēs* and *poiētria* seem, then, to retain, at least in some sense, the contrastive gendered models of poetic authorship set up by grammar and enforced in practice.

The first extant occurrence of the term *poiētria* is a single-word title of a play by the poet Alexis, a playwright who was active probably from the 350s BCE on.[110] It is difficult to speculate about a play of which we only know the title, *Poiētria*, and a fragment of one line: and yet there are still interesting things to be said. The first is that we know that Alexis also wrote another play (or plays) called *Poiētai* and/or *Poiētēs*.[111] The occurrence of (at least) one play titled in the masculine, *Poiētēs/Poiētai*, and another with the feminine of *poiētēs*, *Poiētria*, suggests a contrast between the masculine and feminine versions of the term, and implies that, already at this early period, *poiētēs* and *poiētria* were envisioned as exclusive enough of each other to warrant a separate term. Moreover, if we focus on the plural *Poiētai* (one version of the male-poet play's title given in Athenaeus), the contrast between the masculine plural and the feminine singular *Poiētria* underlines the way in which female poets were always gender-marked, versus the masculine plural which acted as a generalizing term for "poets," and could subsume the female. Finally, the derivation of the term *poiētria* (like *poiētēs*) from the verb *poiein* is explicitly signaled in the only surviving line of the play: "I do [*poiō*] this for the most part" (fr. 189 K-A).[112] We do not know whether the speaker was male or female; either way, the use of *poiein* clearly underlines the etymology of the play's title. But the emphasis on "doing" also throws a spanner in the works for the interpretation of *Poiētria*: do we translate the title as "female poet" (the common later meaning of *poiētria*), or do we see it rather as pointing to a "female contriver" (such as a "scheming female slave," with a feminized version of *poiētēs* along the lines of, for example, the historian Xenophon's "contriver [*poiētēs*] of stratagems against the enemy")?[113] Even the very beginnings of the use of *poiētria* shroud it in ambiguity.

109. Examples of masculine plurals of ποιητής in which women poets (in all cases, Sappho) are explicitly included: Dion. Hal. *Comp.* 23, *Dem.* 40, Gal. *De simpl. med.* 11.586.

110. On Alexis, see Arnott 1996: 3–33. On ποιήτρια as a later Hellenistic coinage, see Chantraine s.v. ποιέω, Yatromanolakis 2007: 319 n. 152.

111. See Arnott 1996: 551, who notes that these could either be references to two different plays, or to the same with the ending corrupted in one of the references in Athenaeus.

112. Ὡς ἐπὶ τὰ πολλὰ τοῦτο ποιῶ, Alexis fr. 189 K-A.

113. Xen. *Cyr.* 1.6.38, ποιητὴν ... τῶν πρὸς τοὺς πολεμίους μηχανημάτων. Arnott 1996: 555 gives the later example of Heliodorus 2.8.2 for ποιήτρια in the sense of "female contriver,"

The next instance of *poiētria*, meanwhile, occurs nested in a double quotation. Stobaeus, a late antique anthologist of around the fifth century CE, collected an anthology of excerpts from prose and poetry, including the only known testimony of the "lectures" of the Cynic philosopher Teles (fl. c. 235 BCE).[114] One of these has Teles citing another, earlier philosopher, Bion of Borysthenes (of the late fourth/early third centuries BCE).[115] The passage begins with what seems to be Teles's own maxim: "The good man [*andra*]—just like a good actor, who has to do the best he can in the dramatic contests with whatever character the poet [*poiētēs*] gives him—has, similarly, to perform whatever role Chance gives him. For she, Bion says, like a poetess [*poiētria*], sometimes gives the role of protagonist, and other times a secondary character; sometimes a king, and sometimes a beggar. Don't, then, long for the role of protagonist when you're a secondary character; otherwise, you won't act [*poiēseis*] according to the part."[116] Here, then, we have Stobaeus, citing Teles, citing Bion—who uses the term *poiētria*. Bion's image of Chance—a feminine noun and common personification in Greek (*Tuchē*)—as a *poiētria* is picked up by Teles and illustrated with an example that makes the simile easier to understand: think, he says, of the male *poiētēs* in the dramatic contests, who hands out parts to his male actors (*hupokritēs*). The situation of the male actors, Teles argues, is similar to that of "the good man [*andra*]." It is interesting that Teles seems to feel the need to explain Bion's metaphor of Chance as a female poet by replacing her, in his own analogy and own words, with a male poet (*poiētēs*)—while simultaneously underlining the masculinity of both the male actors of the analogy and his real target audience, as "good men." Where Bion's quotation picks up on

---

and points out that this should be "a warning against the automatic assumption that Alexis' title figure was a poetess rather than e.g. a scheming female slave like Habrotonon in Men. *Epitr.*"

114. On Teles, see Fuentes González 1998a, and for text and commentary, see Fuentes González 1998b.

115. On Bion, see Kindstrand 1976.

116. Δεῖ ὥσπερ τὸν ἀγαθὸν ὑποκριτὴν ὅ τι ἂν ὁ ποιητὴς περιθῇ πρόσωπον τοῦτο ἀγωνίζεσθαι καλῶς, οὕτω καὶ τὸν ἀγαθὸν ἄνδρα ὅ τι ἂν περιθῇ ἡ τύχη. καὶ γὰρ αὕτη, φησὶν ὁ Βίων, ὥσπερ ποιήτρια, ὀτὲ μὲν πρωτολόγου, ὀτὲ δὲ ὑστερολόγου περιτίθησι πρόσωπον, καὶ ὀτὲ μὲν βασιλέως, ὀτὲ δὲ ἀλήτου. μὴ οὖν βούλου δευτερολόγος ὢν τὸ πρωτολόγου πρόσωπον· εἰ δὲ μή, ἀνάρμοστόν τι ποιήσεις, Teles fr. 2.5–6 Hense; the text is cited from Fuentes González 1998b. Fuentes Gonzalez 1998a: 8 (following Hoogvliet 1821: 20) argues convincingly that the quotation from Bion is limited to the sentence καὶ γὰρ αὕτη ... ὀτὲ δὲ ἀλήτου.

Chance's femininity and assigns her a feminine noun, and even the agency to hand out parts and roles to men, Teles undercuts the simile by replacing it with his own, all-male lived reality of a male poet and male actor. At the same time, the chain of literary transmission here—Bion to Teles, Teles to Stobaeus—is male, underlining the masculinity of authorship, even as reference is made to *Tuchē* as a female poet, and emphasizing the embeddedness and reliance of the language of women poets as *poiētriai* on male discourses. Teles seals this with his parting words: you need to "act" (*poiēseis*), he says, according to your part. The second-person singular conjures the explicit audience, the "good man" whom Teles is trying to shape.[117] In other words, the vocabulary of *poieō*—which briefly entered the territory of the female in Bion's analogy—is brought firmly back into the masculine realm, in the real world of male philosophers making good men.

The title of Alexis's lost play and Teles's citation (and reappropriation) of Bion's *poiētria* are the only two occurrences of the term in extant Hellenistic literature. This suggests that the search for a vocabulary of women poets was not yet at an end, and that *poiētria* had yet to take root as a mainstream term. But we see it being picked up somewhere else, and in a rather different way—not as an appropriation of the abstract feminine into the realm of the male, as in Teles, but as a way of honoring and foregrounding a real, celebrated female poet. It hints at a new direction for the vocabulary of *poiētria*, as an honorific recognition of an outstanding woman's professional success—and demonstrates, perhaps, how *poiētria* came to gain in popularity, after the Hellenistic period, as a means to talk about women poets beyond the literary mechanisms of appropriation, contrast, and canonicity which we have seen dominating the works of male writers thus far.

To find these instances, we have to turn to the inscriptional evidence: a pair of decrees honoring a female poet by the name of Aristodama, who is given the title "female poet [*poiētria*] of epic" in both inscriptions.[118] The first (*IG* IX 2:62 = *SIG* 532) is from 218/17 BCE, passed by the city of Lamia to proclaim a series of honors for "Aristodama of Smyrna, the *poiētria* of epic,"

---

117. On the second-person singular, see Fuentes González 1998a: 8.

118. On Aristodama, see Rutherford 2009, also Stephanis 1988: 75, Snyder 1989: 97, Ferrandini Troisi 1998 (see esp. pp. 211–13 on the title ποιήτρια ἐπέωμ and links to Ionian epic), Skinner 2005c: 111 n. 48, Yatromanolakis 2007: 319 n. 152; see Rutherford 2009: 237 n. 2 for further bibliography.

who performed poems celebrating the Aetolians.[119] The second (*SEG* 2.263), also of the late third century BCE but this time from the west Locrian city of Chaleion, similarly hails Aristodama as a "*poiētria* of epic" and gives her another set of honors (including a garland and a slice of meat).[120] Both are fascinating examples of the term *poiētria* being applied to a named female poet, for the very first time in extant Greek. The honorific context and inscriptional evidence make this one of the earliest instances we can identify of the term being used to label a woman poet's métier, in a context that goes beyond the literary works of male poets with their vested interest in the vocabulary of the *poiētēs/poiētria*. The Lamia inscription seems to show an overt interest in the etymology—and, perhaps, the novelty (in the feminine form)—of the term *poiētria*, parsing its relationship to the verb *poieō*: "Aristodama of Smyrna in Ionia, daughter of Amyntas, the female poet [*poiētria*] of epic, visited our city and made [*epoiēsato*] many performances of her own poems [*poiēmatōn*]" (lines 3–5).[121] The emphasis that these were Aristodama's "own" poems also serves to underline the fact that *poiētria* is being used here to emphasize Aristodama's identity as an agentic, creative composer of poetry, rather than a singer or reciter of the poems of men, endowing her with an agency and authorship which is rarely seen in earlier poet-terminology for women. *Poiētria* is thus both a professional title, describing what Aristodama does, and an honorific, praising her creativity and identity as a woman poet and acknowledging her role, justifying the gift of honors to her.

This justification is particularly important in the Lamia inscription—because one of the honors granted to Aristodama is an unusual one: the gift of citizenship.[122] Ian Rutherford suggests that "granting citizenship to a woman is conceptually highly awkward in a society which does not, generally

---

119. ἐπειδὴ Ἀριστο[δ]άμα Ἀμύντα Ζμυρναία ἀπ' Ἰω[νίας] ποιήτρια ἐπ[έ]ω[μ] πα[ρα]γ[ε]νομ[έ]να ἐν τὰμ πόλιν πλείονας ἐ[πιδείξεις] ἐποιήσατο τῶν ἰδίωμ ποιημάτων (since Aristodama of Smyrna in Ionia, daughter of Amyntas, the female poet of epic, visited our city and made many performances of her own poems), *IG* IX 2:62.3–5 = *SIG* 532.3–5.

120. ἐπειδὴ [Ἀριστοδ]άμ[α Ἀμ]ύντα Ζμυρναί[α] ἀπ' Ἰωνίας [ἐπέωμ] ποιήτρι[α] παρα[γε]γομ[έ]να (since Aristodama of Smyrna in Ionia, daughter of Amyntas, the female poet of epic, visited [our city]), *SEG* 2.263.2–4. Note that this is a Delphic copy of a Chaleian decree: see Rutherford 2009: 238.

121. Yatromanolakis 2007: 319 n. 152 notes that the Lamia inscription "(as it is restored) refers to the mode of her performances."

122. δεδόσθαι δ' αὐτᾶ[ι κ]αὶ πολιτείαν (and that citizenship should be granted to her), *IG* IX 2:62.8 = *SIG* 532.8.

speaking, allow that women can be citizens at all. . . . Thus, the possibility arises that in virtue of her profession she might have come to enjoy in the broader Greek world a political status denied to her in her own community."[123] Yet, as Josine Blok has reminded us, women could be and were citizens of ancient Greek city-states; what they lacked was the narrower, political definition of citizenship, that is, the ability to participate in politics and hold office in the state.[124] The attribution of *politeia*, "citizenship," to Aristodama here refers, probably, to membership of the "city," the *polis*, not necessarily (in fact, likely not) political engagement.[125] What *is* unusual is the gift of citizenship to a female poet at all: this is the only recorded instance of citizenship being granted to a woman poet before the Roman period.[126] By contrast, we have multiple examples of male poets being awarded citizenship as an honor.[127] In a sense, then, it is, perhaps, the uniqueness of being a woman and a poet—a *poiētria*—which pinpoints, in a single term, the way in which Aristodama steps outside the conventions of her gender to receive an honor that was usually granted to male poets. At the same time, the generic context of the honorific inscription elides the identity of the inscription's "author"—in counterpoint to the literary texts that have dominated this book, which work to write their authors into the tradition of Greek literature—and uplifts its honorand. Aristodama's example shows, for the first time, the power of the term *poiētria*—in contrast to previous attempts to name women poets, from Herodotus's *mousopoios* to Antipater's *aoidos*—to encapsulate the unusualness of a woman's gender as a poet, her relation to and yet unique difference from male *poiētai*, and the connection between her agency (as a performer of her own poetry and awardee of honorary citizenship in her own right) and authorship. With this new term—which occurs (tentatively) only once more (again of a women

123. Rutherford 2009: 238.

124. Blok 2017: 4, 30–31, 47–99: see further, chapter 4, n. 136.

125. For the difference between broad and narrow definitions of πολιτεία, see Blok 2017: 152, 155.

126. The three other examples of women poets being granted citizenship come from the Roman period, and in only one of these is the (unknown) female poet called a ποιήτρια (*IG* XII,4 2:845 = *SEG* 54.787): see Rutherford 2009: 244. Note that Aristodama is not granted citizenship in the Chaleion inscription.

127. Though, of course, this is also due to the far greater number of male poets than female: in both cases, it demonstrates how unusual Aristodama was. For examples of male poets being granted citizenship, see, e.g., *IG* IX 2:63, *SEG* 33.106, *SEG* 33.195; see further Hardie 1983: 26, Petrovic 2009: 215–16.

poet, Alcinoe, named on an inscription) before the imperial period—we seem
to see a different context and reach for the *poiētria*: one where she can, per-
haps, be honored as an equal, not in contrast, to men.[128]

This is where the story of men giving poet-terms to women in Greek ends—
for the moment at least, before the shift into the imperial period, and a change
in the practices of female poetic naming that sees the rise of *poiētria* and the
final death of female *aoidos*.[129] It has been a long and winding road from He-
siod's strung-up and silenced *aoidos* nightingale, to Euripides's female *aoidoi*
of the otherworld; from Herodotus's *mousopoios* Sappho set against her male
peers, to Antipater of Sidon's second-class Sappho *aoidos*; through the explora-
tions of different variations on *aoidos* in epigram and inscription; and finally,
to the invention of the new vocabulary of the feminized *poiētria*. The thread
running through all these strategies, and uniting them, is that it is women's
gender relationship to poetry, and the opposition between masculine- and
feminine-gendered models for the poet, which men alternately wrestle with,
subvert, or emphasize. To the male authors of Greek literature, Sappho, and
women poets like her—like Aristodama—are first and foremost women: gen-
der is always in the front line.

And yet, it is important to remember that this only tells one side of the
story. At the same time as men were searching for new ways to talk about
women poets, those female poets were, themselves, engaging in the same
quest for a name—often in counterpoint to their male peers. In the final part
of the book, then, we turn at last to the voices of the women poets. We hear
for the first time how, in a world of male poets and female silencing where
women writers were rarely acknowledged, women poets came up with a new
kind of vocabulary to talk about themselves—in their own words.

128. *IG* XII,5 812.4: the text is largely reconstructed, and H. Bouvier 1980 argues that the
restorations are uncertain and should not lead to the conclusion that a female poet is being
honored, but see contra Jeanne and Louis Robert in the *Bulletin épigraphique* 1981 no. 362, where
Alcinoe is called "une poétesse." See also Skinner 2005c: 111 n. 48, Rutherford 2009: 241. Cf. the
later (first-century CE) inscription for an unknown female poet of Old Comedy (ποιήτριαν
κω[μῳδίας] ἀρχαίας), *IG* XII,4 2:845.3–4 = *SEG* 54.787.3–4: see further chapter 7, n. 103.

129. See chapter 7, n. 107; ἀοιδός does not occur in the feminine again after Antipater of
Sidon (*Anth. Pal.* 7.14 = 11 G-P).

PART IV

Bird

A NEW KIND OF LANGUAGE:
WOMEN POETS IN THEIR
OWN WORDS

8

Mother Sappho

CREATING WOMEN POETS

IF WE were able, at least in part, to trace the presence of poet-terms for women in men's writing, then women's writing is all about absence.[1] The fragmentary condition of Sappho's poetry is, perhaps, the best-known example of the "gaps" in our knowledge of female literary production; other female poets' works are reduced to a few scattered lines, at best, and sometimes all we know is their names.[2] At the same time, the number of attested women poets is vanishingly small compared to the count of male poets—a testimony to the normative culture against women's education and access to poetry, and the silencing of women's voices.[3] But this is not the only aspect to the topic of female authorship in the ancient world that makes it a challenging site of exploration. If the first difficulty is the scarcity of the source material, the second leads directly from it: the tension between gender and self-expression that arises when women speak, perform, and/or write—challenging cultural expectations about women's silence in public—inevitably, as we saw in the introduction, becomes an integral feature of the few surviving female-authored texts that cannot be ignored.[4] And then there is the issue of the ways in which these texts are handed down to us: the layered, fragmentary, mediated

---

1. The chapters in this part of the book are revised and expanded versions of an article that originally appeared in *Ramus* in 2016 (Hauser 2016a) and are gratefully reprinted with permission; for a companion study of women writers in Rome, see Hauser 2016b.

2. See Gubar 1984: 46–47.

3. See pp. 3–4.

4. See Skinner 1993, Stehle 1997 (on gender and performance) and Lardinois and McClure 2001.

tradition in which we receive female-authored texts—for the most part, not recorded at all, and if they are, only partially quoted in male-authored texts and unreliably transmitted by male scribes—requires that we problematize the extent to which we can, or should, attempt to recover an "authentic" female voice in the works of ancient Greek women poets.[5] Finally, there is the inevitable problem with which this book has wrestled from the beginning—the fact that women had no words to talk about themselves, that they were, by the very vocabulary of poetic authorship, denied access to the canon of male literature. In a sense, absence was what defined a woman writer: if she wanted to talk about herself, she either had to come up with a new vocabulary, or learn to speak subliminally, coding her gendered identity beneath the surface of the text. All this makes poet-terms for women incredibly hard to find. Absence of women writers in the first place, absence of women in the transmission process, and the absence of a language to describe what it meant to be a woman and a poet, conspire to portray the picture that women could not be poets in the same way as men could. In response, much of the (important) work that has been done on women writers has had to piece together fragmentary glimpses of women's "voice," or "style," or "views," focusing on the language or the metaphors or the myths of the various fragments that remain to us, to try to access an idea of the woman-as-poet.[6]

But there is, I think, the possibility of a different way of reading: one that is suggested by the rich history of poet-terms and their interaction with gender which has been traced in this book. The long association of the forging of poetic identity at the site of gender allows us to take a specific look at the words that women poets use to describe themselves and their poetic identity, and provides a new way in to reading these fragmentary, often-forgotten women writers— because the fact that the word for a woman poet did not exist did not, in fact, hinder them; quite the opposite. As we will see in the chapters that follow, the circumscription of gender that surrounded male poet-terms like *aoidos* and *poiētēs* actually stimulated the development of a whole new range of fertile and supple words by and for women poets—often richer in their interpretative possibilities than those of their male counterparts. I am not arguing for some

5. The question of the "femaleness" of the voice in ancient women poets has centered mostly around Sappho: see Winkler 1990: 165, Skinner 1993, Greene 1994, Lardinois 2001, Greene 2008, and cf. Skinner 2005b on Nossis; see further pp. 281–85.

6. E.g., Snyder 1989: 152–56; W. Henderson 1995: 36 on Corinna's "views on poetry"; Skinner 2005b: 112 on "the peculiarly female timbre of Nossis' poetic voice."

kind of gender-circumscribed "female style" here (along the lines of Cixous's *écriture féminine*), but rather a conscious, performative, and agentic discourse around women poets' identity, developed in direct response to the history of the masculinization of the poet that stretched back to Homer.[7] To be a woman poet in antiquity brought with it an inevitable awareness of the normative male-gendering of poetry—not just in the cultural constructs surrounding literary production, not just in the fact that the canon of Greek literature was over-whelmingly populated by men writing about men, but in the very words that labeled "the poet." We can read women poets in ancient Greece, then, as experiencing what Sandra Gilbert and Susan Gubar have termed "anxiety of authorship."[8] In contrast to men, "the 'anxiety of influence' that a male poet experiences [in his relationship to his male precursors] is felt by a female poet as an even more primary 'anxiety of authorship'—a radical fear that she cannot create, that because she can never become a 'precursor' the act of writing will isolate or destroy her."[9] Gilbert and Gubar point out, quite rightly, women's exclusion from the gendered mechanisms of the male relationship with the Muse—a woman "cannot 'beget' art upon the (female) body of the muse."[10] Yet, in ancient Greek, "anxiety of authorship" was about more than the exclusion of women from the canon, patriarchal definitions of "literary authority," and a relationship with artistic inspiration through the Muses—it was also defined by women's exclusion from the very word for "poet" itself. Seen in this light, we can, then, watch women as they work to come up with new ways of naming themselves that respond to, challenge, avoid, allude to, or undermine the old masculine systems of poetic naming, while generating a new identity for themselves—as women who wrote.

In the chapters that follow, I look at the interrelationship between gender and authorship in the works of different women poets, from Sappho to anonymous oracles giving prophecies in verse to little-known epigrammatists, through the terminology they use to describe their own gendered identity as women poets. The focus here is on the subtle and suggestive use of language by women in a culture where poetic identity had been marked and dominated by men. Seeing women's manipulation of language as a performative process,

7. See introduction, n. 65; on gendered speech, see introduction, n. 63; chapter 4, n. 34; chapter 6, n. 63.

8. Pace Snyder 1989: 154–55.

9. Gilbert and Gubar 1979: 48–49; cf. Gubar 1984: 45, Downes 2010: 23.

10. Gilbert and Gubar 1979: 49; see p. 51 for further discussion.

I uncover a "subversive mask" of language used by female poets to create a double layering that talks about their own gendered poetic authorship. I also show how female poets reformulate the gendered relationship between male poet and female Muse to suggest a subversive connection of motherhood, Muses, and memory. Male authors, as we saw in chapter 2, had already delimited a very specific gendered relationship between female Muse and male poet, while at the same time marking out the image of female poets-as-Muses as one of passive abstraction and appropriation. In the following chapters, however, I suggest that women poets generate a new type of connection to the Muses by simultaneously claiming a close association with the Muses through their gender, but also layering it with notions of maternity, community, and authorial identity—thereby circumventing the sexualized, agentic male / passive female, bard/Muse opposition which we saw from Hesiod on, as well as the abstraction of female poets as Muses.[11]

In this chapter, I focus on words around motherhood in female-authored poetic texts as a claim for women's creativity, a metaphor for poetic production, and a figuration of a female poetic community.[12] I move from a discussion of Sappho's *mousopolos* in fr. 150 L-P to a Delphic oracle on Homer's mother, to an epigram which subverts expectations of motherhood to lay claim to female creativity through words. Moving beyond the generalized instances of symbolic motherhood or birthing imagery which have been the focus of previous work on women poets' metaphors of motherhood, I hone in on those specific moments where female poets claim the word "mother" itself as a poetic term—and assess the power of that move, in the delineation both of women's poetic identity, and in the creation of a lineage of women poets in engagement with, and to rival, that of men. Chapter 9 then circles back to the book's beginnings with the term *aoidos*—showing how women, from Sappho to Nossis, responded to the long history of the male-gendering of poetic authorship to come up with a vocabulary for women poets that commented on and subverted masculine terms, laying claim to a new gendered dynamic between women and song. In both chapters, the refiguration of the relationship with the Muses through gender is key, as is the knowing, intertextual exchange with the masculine language of authorship. Given the paucity

11. On Sappho as Muse, see pp. 208–12 with chapter 7, n. 64.

12. For an introduction to modern theorizations of motherhood and recent research on mothers in the ancient world, see Keith, McAuley, and Sharrock 2020; see further chapter 8, n. 80.

of surviving female-authored texts from antiquity, it would be difficult—perhaps impossible—to create any kind of exhaustive survey of women's poetic self-representation, and all we are ever likely to get are glimpses of moments where women's self-identification filters through the gaps, tracing occasional recurrences of themes or linguistic echoes where they arise, but most often catching only a brief word here or there. Instead, then, I suggest that each reading allows us to see these female poets seeking an authentic lexicon and definition for their role within a male-dominated realm—a performative, processual enacting of the self, as women and as authors, through the layering of language and the assumption of a subversive mask which enacts and creates multiple meanings.

Sappho: Rewriting the Muse into the Mother

Sappho's "I"—the construction of Sappho's authorial persona, the "Sappho" we came across in the introduction in fr. 160 L-P who claims to "sing these songs beautifully to delight my female companions"—has occasioned much controversy.[13] Is this "Sappho" a remnant of the poems' original performance context (the well-worn *Sapphofrage*)?[14] A generic style marker of lyric, signposting a more "personal" style than that of epic? An indication that we can read first-person statements as instances of Sappho's own autobiography? Or a deliberate narratological position, as Alex Purves has argued?[15] Here—as throughout this book—we are not in search of the "real" Sappho, but Sappho as she is presented, depicted, curated through words in her poetry: the mask

13. See p. 9.

14. Lardinois 1996 gives a concise and thoughtful analysis of the debate; he suggests that Sappho's poetry was performed mostly in public, either by a singing and dancing χορός or by a soloist in concert with a choral performance; see F. Ferrari 2021 for a similar conclusion and overview of the evidence. On the performance context of choral lyric, see Davies 1988, C. Segal 1989, Calame 1997, Stehle 1997, Carey 2009, Athanassaki and Bowie 2011. On the performance context of Sappho, see, inter alia, Gentili 1988: esp. 216–22, Snyder 1991, Calame 1996, Lardinois 1996, Stehle 1997: 262–318, Kurke 2000, Nagy 2007, Yatromanolakis 2009, E. Bowie 2016, D'Alessio 2018. On the much-studied use of the first person in choral lyric (particularly Alcman and Pindar), see Davies 1988a: esp. 54–55, Danielewicz 1990, D'Alessio 1994, Klinck 2001, Hauser 2022. For the suggestion that at least some of Sappho's poetry was created as text, see Stehle 1997: 294, 297, 301, and 310–11.

15. Purves 2014. For the argument for personal statements as engaging with the performance context, see Lardinois 1996, Lardinois 2021b; for the autobiographical reading, see Bowra 1961: 176–240.

and persona of the gendered poet. There is a complex staging of gender and poetics in Sappho's poetry, at once masking her gender and, at the same time, exploring oppositions between male and female spheres, both in their social roles and spaces, and in the space of poetic intertext.[16] Indeed, it is particularly in Sappho's engagement with male poets' gendered poetics that critics have seen Sappho's gendered authorial construction coming to the fore. John Winkler demonstrates a gendered modality between different spheres of "public" and "private" in Sappho's poetry which shows an ability to engage with both male and female gendered social consciousness (what Winkler calls "Sappho's double consciousness"). And he identifies this particularly in Sappho's poetic intertextuality with male bards, in particular Homer—"a kind of test case for the issue of women's consciousness of themselves as participants without a poetic voice of their own at the public recitations of traditional Greek heroism."[17]

We have already seen this kind of divisionality between male and female poets and poetic discourse happening in reverse: Antipater sets up Sappho against Homer, while Herodotus's *mousopoios* constructs Sappho's gendered difference in comparison to the other male poets who make an appearance in the *Histories*. And this provides us with the clue as to where to start: fr. 150 L-P, and Sappho's *mousopolos*, which—in Herodotus's subtly altered version— already seems to have been read in antiquity as a gender-marked poet-term. Fragment 150 is, at first glance, a cryptic example of Sapphic lyric with a troubled textual transmission:[18]

> for it is not right in the house of those who serve the Muses [*moisopolōn*] that there should be lamentation. . . . That would not be fitting for us.

16. Sappho's gendered persona is notoriously difficult to pin down: see DeJean 1989: 21, Most 1995: 32 with n. 88, Stehle 1997: 317.

17. Winkler 1990: 169; for other discussions of Sappho's intertext with Homer, see Rissman 1983, Schrenk 1994, Rosenmeyer 1997, duBois 1997: 98–126, Snyder 1997: 63–77, Blondell 2010b, Purves 2014, Spelman 2017, Kelly 2021; and note Mueller (forthcoming) for a reparative reading.

18. οὐ γὰρ θέμις ἐν μοισοπόλων <δόμωι> / θρῆνον ἔμμεν' <. . . . . . .> οὔ κ' ἄμμι πρέποι τάδε, Sappho fr. 150 L-P. I prefer Campbell's text here (1982) over Lobel and Page, who print †οἰκίαι instead of δόμωι; see Voigt 1971: 140, Lardinois 1996: 155 and Calame 1997: 210 n. 12, who accept the replacement δόμωι. Whatever the solution to the line end, the phrase ἐν μοισοπόλων (as Lardinois 1996: 155 n. 25 points out) "means by itself 'in the abode of the servants of the Muses.'". On this fragment, see Hardie 2005: 14–17 and 20–22, also Page 1955: 133, Lanata 1996: 14, Snyder 1997: 118, Ford 2002: 13–14, F. Ferrari 2010: 143–47.

According to Maximus of Tyre, who preserved the fragment for us, Sappho is addressing her daughter, leading most scholars to the conclusion that the "house" spoken of here is Sappho's own.[19] It is the noun that precedes it, however, *moisopolōn*—*mousopolōn* in the Attic dialect, "those who serve the Muses"—that is of interest here.[20] We have already seen how later male authors label Sappho with a whole range of terms, from *mousopoios* to *aoidos* to "Muse"; but not once in any author's description of Sappho's status as poet do we get the fertile combination of the prefix *mous-* and the suffix *-polos*; indeed, this is the first time that the word occurs in the entire corpus of Greek literature, which makes it possible that Sappho may have coined the term herself.[21] Moreover, if we take the "house" here to be her own, and Sappho as the speaker (as Maximus of Tyre tells us), then Sappho is using *mousopolos* here to refer to herself (or rather, her persona as poet). So why does Sappho choose to use this specific noun here—one of the few clear instances in the surviving fragments where she refers to her poetic persona and her poetry in connection to the Muses, and the earliest instance of any reference by a female poet to her own poetic identity?[22]

Various interpretations have been put forward as to what *mousopolos* might refer to, from a "professional musician" (Alex Hardie) to a "cultic association" (Giuliana Lanata) to "a place of education" (Anne Burnett).[23] A brief exploration of the etymology of the word, however, and its literary resonances,

19. Wilamowitz-Moellendorff 1913: 73, Kranz 1939: 88, Burnett 1983: 211.

20. I use the Attic spelling of *mousopolos* (Aeolic *moisopolos*) in the main text to avoid confusion.

21. Note the occurrence of μουσοπόλος in a second-century BCE inscription referring to a theatrical group (ἐσθλὴ τεχνιτῶν μουσοπόλων σύνοδος), *IG* VII 2484.5–6; see Le Guen 2001: 84–86, Hardie 2005: 15, Aneziri 2020. For other instances of μουσοπόλος, see Eur. *Alc.* 445 (see chapter 6, n. 23), *Phoen.* 1499 (see chapter 6, n. 49), both in the context of lament; also Telestes fr. 805b.2 *PMG*, Castorion fr. 310.5, Hermesianax fr. 7.27 Powell (see p. 277), *Anth. Pal.* 9.248. Degani and Burzacchini 1977: 185 argue that μουσοπόλος becomes "[un] semplice equivalente di ποιητής, solo meno prosastico"; see also Svenbro 1984: 208 n. 93, Calame 1997: 210, Ford 2002: 134 n. 6.

22. For another example, see the βρόδων / τὼν ἐκ Πιερίας at fr. 55.2–3 L-P (see chapter 6, n. 10); on Sappho's allusions to her poetics, see Peponi 1997.

23. Hardie 2005: 15, Lanata 1996: 14, Burnett 1983: 211. Other scholars who favor the cultic reading of μουσοπόλοι include Wilamowitz-Moellendorff 1913: 73, 78, Degani and Burzacchini 1977: 185, Gentili 1988: 84; see contra Page 1955: 139–40, Hardie 2005: 15–17, F. Ferrari 2010: 147. Calame 1997: 210–14 reads the term as evidence for Sappho's "circle" (see contra Stehle 1997: 273).

serves to show that the clues to its interpretation may rest within the noun itself. If we look at the usage of *-polos* ("one who busies themselves about something," from the verb *pelomai*) in extant ancient Greek literature, it becomes clear that the suffix seems to suggest a sense of physical proximity, an actual rather than a metaphorical (i.e., status-based) attendance (for example, *aipolos* [goatherd], *boupolos* [cowherd], *epipolos* [companion], *mētropolos* [mother-helper], or *naopolos* [temple overseer]).[24] The *-polos* suffix thus seems to suggest an active element of "being nearby" and "overseeing," an engagement with the prefix of the noun that specifically constructs the person named as a participant in the province of their attendance. The precise power of the suffix becomes clear, as we have seen, when we set it against Herodotus's reception of Sappho's term—*mousopoios*, rather than *mousopolos*.[25] Herodotus's replacement of a single letter in the suffix, *-poios* instead of *-polos*, changes the entire semantic range of the prefix. As a *mousopolos*, Sappho in her poetry could be an overseer, an attendant of the Muses as embodied gods. As a *mousopoios*, the "maker" suffix forces the *mous-* prefix to mean "music" alone (in the sense that *mousa* could mean by metonymy). The Muses are completely erased from Sappho's term, along with the network of proximity, expertise, care, and attendance suggested by her choice of word, and Herodotus's Sappho becomes a prosaic "music-maker."

We have already seen the strategic gender policing that this represents in Herodotus's reception of Sappho. For Sappho's part, what the comparison with Herodotus does is to make clear, by contrast, the rich interpretative power of the term she chooses to represent herself—a word that may have been her own invention. Sappho's *mousopolos* implies both a physical proximity to and active engagement with the female gods of song, at the same time as she also articulates a metaphorical occupation with and expertise in the poetic craft they represent. The flexibility of the term allows *mous-* to refer to

---

24. I am grateful to Egbert Bakker for pointing out that the πολ- formations derive from the IE root *kʷel(H)-, which originally had the meaning "move, twist, turn" (see further Fortson 2010: 130). This became weakened in ancient Greek πέλω/πέλομαι (be/be constituted), but was retained with derived words in the agricultural or ritual sphere (αἰπόλος, βούκολος, θειοπόλος, ἱεραπόλος, μελισσοπόλος, μουσοπόλος, οἰοπόλος, and so on). For ἀοιδοπόλος (busied with song, poet), see chapter 7, n. 106; for ὑμνοπόλος (composing songs of praise; poet), see Meleager 1.13 G-P = *Anth. Pal.* 4.1.13, with discussion at p. 169; see also Leonidas 98.1 G-P = *Anth. Pal.* 7.13.1, at pp. 218–20 with chapter 7, n. 95, and cf. *Anth. Pal.* 7.18.6.

25. See pp. 192–204.

both personified gods and their attribute, song, while at the same time gesturing toward an intimate connection between female poet and god.[26]

The intimacy of this relationship is set in contrast to another poet who also claimed to "serve" the Muses—and this link shows Sappho interacting directly with her (male) poetic forebears, and gives the term a distinctly literary flavor. The poet, of course, is Hesiod, and his chosen term *Mousaōn therapōn*— "servant of the Muses," as we saw in chapter 2.[27] In the *Theogony*, the male poet lays claim to the inspiration by the Muses, and specifically defines the *aoidos* as a "servant of the Muses" (*Mousaōn therapōn*, 99–100).[28] This term, as we have seen, suggests a combination of privileged access and inferior status, an element of differential status and distance between the god and the mortal servant. At first glance, this may not look too different to Sappho's *mousopolos*, which is often translated as "one who serves the Muses." But a passage from a later author, the imperial orator and philosopher Dio Chrysostom, can help to clarify the exact meaning of Hesiod's *Mousaōn therapōn*, and allow us to start to pin down its exact semantic relationship to *mousopolos* (Dio Chrys. *Or.* 36.33):[29]

> We can think of [poets] as simply like servants at the rites, who stand outside the doors, decorating the doorways and altars which are in full view and making other similar preparations, but never going inside. Indeed, that is why they call [*onomazousin*] themselves "servants of the Muses" [*therapontas Mousōn*], not initiates or any other sacred name [*onoma*].

Dio Chrysostom's first-century CE explanation of a common poetic name (*onoma*) serves to expound on the meaning of *Mousaōn therapōn* in Hesiod. Dio emphasizes that poets call themselves *therapontes*, "servants," because "they most likely haven't been properly initiated . . . we can think of them as

---

26. On Sappho and the Muses, Campbell 1983: 261, Snyder 1997: 118, Hardie 2005: 14 n. 10. Cf. Sappho frr. 32, 55.3 L-P.

27. For another example of intertextuality with Hesiod in Sappho, see Clay 1980 (on fr. 104a L-P); see also De Martino 1987, West 2002: 215. on the connection between Sappho's μουσοπόλος and Hesiod's Μουσάων θεράπων, see Aloni 1997: 248, F. Ferrari 2010: 147.

28. See pp. 50–56 with chapter 2, n. 21.

29. ἀτεχνῶς δὲ ἔοικεν ὅμοιον εἶναι τοῖς ἔξω περὶ θύρας ὑπηρέταις τῶν τελετῶν, πρόθυρα κοσμοῦσι καὶ βωμοὺς τοὺς ἐν τῷ φανερῷ καὶ τὰ ἄλλα τὰ τοιαῦτα παρασκευάζουσιν, οὐδέ ποτ᾽ ἔνδον παριοῦσιν. ὅθεν δὴ καὶ θεράποντας Μουσῶν αὑτοὺς ὀνομάζουσιν, οὐ μύστας οὐδὲ ἄλλο σεμνὸν ὄνομα, Dio Chrys. *Or.* 36.33.

simply like servants at the rites, who stand outside the doors."[30] The vivid image confirms the sense of physical distance between god and *therapōn* which we see borne out in Hesiod's description of the Muses' distance, both physically on Mount Olympus and figuratively in the gap between the Muses' immortal powers and knowledge and the lowly mortal shepherd. And yet, at the same time, as we saw, the gender clash between male servant and female god, and the emphasis on the fact that only men can be singers in the *Theogony*, demonstrates—in contrast to comparable passages in the *Iliad* where warriors act as *therapontes* to each other or to the war-god—that there is an ironic or posturing element to Hesiod's use of the term. Although he poses as a distanced servant, he uses the juxtaposition between *aoidos* and *Mousaōn therapōn* to point out the fact that the power is, in fact, in his hands—that, as a man and an *aoidos*, he is, in fact, the only one who can engage in song.

Seen in this light, we can read Sappho's *mousopolos* as a considered response to Hesiod's *Mousaōn therapōn* and the gender polemics it represents. Sappho takes Hesiod's *therapōn*—with its implications of formal inferiority and physical distance from the Muses, as well as its provocative intimation that it is, in fact, the male *aoidos* who holds all the power—and turns the term on its head. Sappho's formulation, *mousopolos*, with its -*polos* suffix, creates a new relationship of proximity and engaged activity, and a dynamic of care and guardianship toward the Muses.[31] In fact, the word demonstrates and performs the interconnectedness between poet and Muse, fusing the two into a single term, in stark contrast to Hesiod's oppositional binary of female *Mousa* and male *therapōn*. Moreover, in contrast to Hesiod, who underlines the distanced "Olympian homes" of the Muses (*Theog.* 75, 101), Sappho enacts and performs her understanding of this relationship with the Muses within the stage of the feminine space of the "house." As a woman, the house is her assigned province—indeed, it is the province of all the women of her family, as the fragment, addressed to herself and her daughter, shows.[32]

And this leads to another innovation represented by Sappho's *mousopolos*: in contrast to Hesiod's figure of the lone chosen male poet, Sappho's term is in the plural, "in the house of those who serve the Muses" (*moisopolōn*,

30. Tim Whitmarsh suggests to me that Dio might be introducing a wordplay between θεράπων and θύρα, which I think is likely.

31. Compare Page duBois's analysis of Sappho's intimacy with Aphrodite at duBois 1995: 24, 80, cf. Skinner 1991.

32. See, in particular, Stehle 1981 and Winkler 1981; see also Snyder 1997: 58. On the symbolic, gendered space of house and temple in ancient Greece, see Pomeroy 1975: 79–83, Cole 2004.

fr. 150.1 L-P). If we accept Maximus of Tyre's context for the fragment, then *mousopoloi* here refers to Sappho and her daughter: two women, connected by both their female gender and their mother-daughter bond, set within the context of the female sphere of the home and linked in proximate, engaged service to the female Muses. There are several layers to this that need to be teased out. The first is that the plural, encompassing Sappho and her daughter, works to create a demonstrably female-gendered context for Sappho's new poet-term for herself. This, in turn, connects the femininity of the Muses to the female poet in new ways that rewrite the gendered polemics of Hesiod's phrase. The group of two women enshrined in the plural become fused with the female Muses that are encapsulated in the very word *mousopolos*. The contrast with Hesiod's term could not be more pronounced: single male poet versus community of women; female Muse set apart from and in contrast to the male poet's gender, versus feminine Muse enclosed within and integral to the term that declares the female poet(s). This emphasis on community and collectivity is seen throughout Sappho's lyrics, and is encapsulated in the plural *mousopoloi* here.[33] We might compare fr. 147 L-P, "I say that someone will remember [*mnasesthai*] us."[34] The interaction between Sappho's singular "I say" and the plural, "us" not only hints at her poetic community and a collective of women, but also, at a metapoetic level, looks to the tradition of women's self-awareness of their representation in poetry—echoing Helen's prediction that she will be *aoidimos* in *Iliad* 6. Meanwhile, the use of the verb *mnasesthai*—cognate with Mnemosyne, Memory, mother of the Muses—suggests another link between Sappho's poetic identity, motherhood, and the Muses. This interconnected depiction of Sappho's poetic community and her relationship to the Muses hints at a "community of practice" (to borrow Penelope Eckert and Sally McConnell-Ginet's term)—"an aggregate of people who come together around mutual engagement in an endeavor."[35] This is, in fact, a much more accurate description of the construction of poetic authorship in the context of archaic Greek literary culture than Hesiod's lone poetic genius: the poet's identity was constructed within social and communal frameworks—the feast,

---

33. See Stehle 1997: 262–318 (Stehle calls this "the women's circle," p. 262); see also Hallett 1979, L. Wilson 1996. See further, on Sappho's circle, chapter 8, n. 23; on the performance of Sappho's poems, see chapter 8, n. 14.

34. μνάσεσθαί τινά φαιμι †καὶ ἕτερον† ἀμμέων, Sappho fr. 147 L-P.

35. Eckert and McConnell-Ginet 1992a: 464; see also Eckert and McConnell-Ginet 1992b, Holmes and Meyerhoff 1999, Meyerhoff 2001, McElhinny 2003: 29–30, McConnell-Ginet 2003: 71.

the symposium, the festival.[36] Authorship in antiquity was a "community of practice": a shared practice of literary endeavor, where language was used to create and shape identities toward, around, in engagement with, and against other members of that community. Sappho's plural *mousopoloi* thus generates a female community that rewrites the relationship to the Muse and looks back to a tradition of women's poetic engagement. It argues against Hesiod's statement that only men can be poets (the *andres aoidoi* of *Theog.* 94) to show that communal poetry can belong to women.

A second layer to the term, in its reference to Sappho and her daughter, sets up the mother-daughter relationship as a metaphor for the poet. The creativity and generativity of the mother, in giving birth to her daughter, echoes the female poet's creativity. This radically rewrites the relationship between the male poet and female Muse, who, as we saw in both Hesiod and Aristophanes, is commonly sexualized by male poets, turning the male poet–female Muse interaction into an erotically charged assault whereby the male poet "begets" his song on the female Muse. Here, rather than birthing song on the Muse, Sappho's relationship with her daughter acts as a metaphor for her own poetic creativity. We see this connection between her relationship with her daughter and poetic metaphor elsewhere in Sappho's poetry: fr. 98b L-P, for example, has Sappho wishing for a "many-colored headband" for her daughter Kleis, which in fr. 98a L-P we hear was recommended by Sappho's own mother.[37] The image of the woven *poikilos* headband, linking weaving and poetic creation, and the signal of *poikilia* as a quality of Sappho's own poetry (the famous depiction of Aphrodite as *poikilothronos*, "rainbow-throned," in the opening line of Sappho fr. 1 L-P can be seen as programmatic for Sappho's poems), makes the resonant image of the women down the generations of Sappho's family, grandmother to mother to daughter, a clear metaphor for poetic creativity.[38] At the same time, her daughter's name—Kleis—has its root in *kleos*, the glory that is celebrated in poetry and, also, the poetry itself—suggesting

36. Ford emphasizes literary criticism as a "social activity" (2002: x), and introduces the helpful term "literary culture" (2002: 4); cf. Nagy 1989: 1 on "the social function of early Greek poetry." See further, introduction, n. 26.

37. ποικίλαν / ... μιτράν<αν>, Sappho fr. 98b.1–3; μ]ιτράναν ... / ποικίλαν, fr. 98a.10–11.

38. See Snyder 1997: 80, 91–95, who argues for ποικιλία as a specifically Sapphic aesthetic, cf. Acosta-Hughes 2010: 13. On these fragments, see F. Ferrari 2010: 3–6, and for the connection between weaving, metapoetics, and the mother-daughter relationship, see further pp. 247–49. For Kleis elsewhere in Sappho, see fr. 132 L-P; for another suggestive connection linking Kleis

that Kleis's involvement in Sappho's poetic metaphors is more than incidental, and connecting her directly as a figure for Sappho's poetry.[39] Here in fr. 150 L-P, meanwhile, the generative position of mother enables Sappho to align with the Muse as an active female author, rather than (like a male poet) making use of the Muse as a passive instrument to generate song. The relationship of poet and Muse is no longer an antagonistic assault of male poet begetting his poetry on the female Muse, but a collaborative community of women who share the creative capacity of birth.

The final aspect to the mother-daughter relationship here is the missing piece to the puzzle of the context: Why is Sappho telling her daughter not to mourn? Maximus of Tyre tells us that it was because Sappho was dying, and Sappho was instructing her daughter not to grieve for her. Eva Stehle observes that "if that was the projected situation in the poem, the most likely subject was Sappho's belief in her poetic immortality. The term 'servants of the Muses' then constitutes the reason not to mourn, namely that Sappho will live on through her poetry."[40] But there is more to it than this: because the plurality of *mousopoloi* means that it is not simply that Sappho lives on through her poetry, but that she also lives on through her *daughter*, who is included in the term that summons up this female community. The immortal continuity of Sappho is guaranteed as much by the female generativity of birth, which will allow her to live through her daughter, as by the survival of her poems. She lives on, in other words, both as a mother and as a poet. The contrast with male formulations of Sappho as a Muse in Hellenistic epigram, where we have seen Sappho's poems granted immortality as in Antipater's poem—and even called "her daughters" in an epigram by Dioscorides (*Anth. Pal.* 7.407)—while Sappho herself is relegated to the mortal sphere, is turned on its head here.[41] It is not the poems which are her daughters; rather, it is her daughter who is both a fellow poet in the community of *mousopoloi* and akin to her poems, a feminine ("Kleis") part of Sappho's *kleos*, through the female poet's generativity and creativity through birth. Here Sappho is able to live on precisely because she is a woman and a mother: it is her birth-giving ability, in the presence of her daughter, that allows her to make a community together with her daughter

---

with her grandmother, see P. Oxy. 1800 fr.1 col. i.15–16 = Sappho T 252 V (text in Grenfell and Hunt 1922: 138), where Kleis is said to have the same name as Sappho's mother.

39. Svenbro 1993: 153.

40. Stehle 1997: 273.

41. See chapter 7, n. 71.

in service of the Muses, and which—through her daughter, and through her poems—will continue her legacy as a woman poet after her death.

While the *Mousaōn therapōn* in Hesiod is distanced from the Muses and places himself apart from them as a single, chosen male, articulating both his inferior status in the presence of a higher power and arguing for his unique power as a male *aoidos*, then, Sappho transfers her understanding of the interrelationship between her gender and her authorship to the feminine, enclosed stage of the house, in the communal context of her relationship with her daughter. She translates the singular *Mousaōn therapōn* into a community of female *mousopoloi*, connected by the mother-daughter bond, who, together, take part in the intimate project of caring for and engaging with the Muses. There are many gendered innovations to the term Sappho chooses to describe herself. She emphasizes her proximity to and active engagement with the Muses, in contrast to Hesiod's distance. She transforms the house into the sacred space, metaphorical or not, in which women can perform their identity by singing their own poetry in their own voices, vouchsafed by their privileged relationship with the Muses. She rewrites Hesiod's gendered polemics to bring Muse and female poet closer together, underlining their proximity through their shared gender in a female community, turning the male poet's erotic assault on the Muses to beget his poetry into a collaborative circle of women who share the creative ability to give birth. She transforms the mother-daughter bond into a metaphor for poetic creation, aligning the identity of mother and poet in the legacy she leaves behind. Through all this construction of a new relationship to the Muses and establishment of a new kind of female community for poetry, meanwhile, Sappho engages head-on with the tradition of male poetry, setting herself against male systems of gendered naming and arguing against the male-gendering of the poet. Creating her own vocabulary and poetic terminology, she invents a language for female poetic authorship that both plays upon male tropes and embellishes them with uniquely female spaces and relationships, to construct a self-definition that is uniquely and incontrovertibly her own.

Men on Mothers

Sappho's figuration of the mother-daughter bond within a community of poets does not go unnoticed—nor does the fertile metaphor of birth for poetry. We have already seen how Aristophanes figured himself in the *Clouds* as a *parthenos* who could not (or should not) give birth, who has to expose his "child" to be brought up by others (530–32).[42] Meanwhile, Euripides has a poet "giving birth to songs" (*Supp.* 180) and "craftsmen who have given birth to a song" (*Andr.* 476); and Aristophanes figures Aeschylus's mind "giving birth to words" (*Ran.* 1059).[43] This appropriation of the female body and the metaphor of birth as a means to beget the poem refigures the sexualized relationship between poet and Muse—and, as we saw, was turned by Diotima, in Plato's *Symposium*, into the extraordinary image of pregnant male poets.[44] Yet, as we discussed in chapter 5, the father-child metaphor became the governing image (particularly in Plato) for male poets' relationship to their poetry.[45] Homer becomes the "father" of poets and poetry, indeed of all subsequent literature; and the conception of author as "father" becomes so prevalent that later authors can programmatically refer to themselves as the "father" of their books.[46]

If male poets visualized themselves as fathers of their poetry, they did occasionally formulate women poets—in particular, Sappho—as connected to birth, perhaps drawing on the mother-daughter relationship in Sappho's *mousopolos* and her depiction of her gendered poetic identity as a mother and a poet. The comic poet Antiphanes, who began writing in the early 380s BCE, has a fragment from his lost comedy *Sappho* where "Sappho" is presented as posing a riddle (fr. 194 K-A = Ath. 10.450e–f):[47]

> There is a female [*thēleia*] being that hides her newborns inside
> her, and though they have no voice they make their cries sound loud
> across the swell of the sea and over the whole earth
> to whomever they want, and people who aren't there can
> hear them—even those who are deaf.

42. See pp. 103–8.

43. See p. 159 with chapter 5, n. 150.

44. See pp. 156–61.

45. See p. 160 with chapter 5, n. 154.

46. On Homer as "father," see Philostr. *VS* 620.9, Nonnus *Dion.* 25.265; see further Hunter 2004b: 235–41, and cf. Aristid. *Or.* 2.47. For authors as the "father" of their books, see Ath. 1.1a; for poets as "sons," see Lucian *Imagines* 9, and cf. Maximus *Diss.* 33.8b, Clem. Al. *Protr.* 2.25.4, Ael. *NA* 14.16.

47. ἔστι φύσις θήλεια βρέφη σῴζουσ᾽ ὑπὸ κόλποις / αὑτῆς, ὄντα δ᾽ ἄφωνα βοὴν ἵστησι γεγωνὸν / καὶ διὰ πόντιον οἶδμα καὶ ἠπείρου διὰ πάσης / οἷς ἐθέλει θνητῶν, τοῖς δ᾽ οὐδὲ παροῦσιν ἀκούειν / ἔξεστιν· κωφὴν δ᾽ ἀκοῆς αἴσθησιν ἔχουσιν, Antiphanes fr. 194.1–5 K-A = Ath. 10.450e–f. On this fragment, see Svenbro 1993: 158–59, Steiner 1994: 113–14, Prins 1996: 46–48, Yatromanolakis 2007: 300–305, Ceccarelli 2013: 244–57, Coo 2021: 270–75.

This is the riddle—what, then, is the solution? The answer, Antiphanes's Sappho goes on to say, is a written letter:[48]

> The female being is a letter [*epistolē*]:
> the newborns she carries around inside her are the letters of the alphabet,
> and although they have no voice they speak to people far away,
> whoever they want; and if another person happens to be standing nearby
> someone reading, they won't hear them.

As Yopie Prins points out, "The riddle revolves around *epistolē* as a feminine noun: the female creature is an epistle, containing inside of itself letters of the alphabet that will speak to the reader who voices them. These letters are figured as infants born into speech, and the letter bearing them (in all senses of the word) as a female body about to give birth."[49] Here, we see Antiphanes playing on the feminine grammar of the "written letter" (*epistolē*), to turn it from a feminine noun (*thēleia*)—the same word that, as we saw in the introduction, Protagoras had used to classify his three grammatical genders—into a "female being" that can give birth. There is more to this than the simple joke around the transformation from grammatically feminine object to animate female being. In the voice of the female poet, the riddle takes on a deeper meaning. It connects Sappho's gender as a woman and her creativity as a poet with her ability to give birth, and suggests that the riddle's "answer" of the "female being" that "carries around inside her the letters of the alphabet" might just as well apply to Sappho and her written poems. Meanwhile, the mid-third-century BCE poet Herodas, composer of mimiambs, gives a parodic reference in one of his mimes to a "Nossis, daughter of Erinna" who owns an illicit leather dildo (6.20).[50] This is, as has often been pointed out, a clear reference to women's poetry, reimagining the Hellenistic poet Nossis's poetic debt and relationship to Erinna as a mother-daughter relationship. At the same time, the introduction of the dildo suggests (as Celsiana Warwick has argued) both an accusation against female poetry as a theft of the masculine poetic tradition, and a contrast between male productivity in poetry and unproductive female

---

48. θήλεια μὲν νῦν ἐστι φύσις ἐπιστολή, / βρέφη δ᾽ ἐν αὐτῇ περιφέρει τὰ γράμματα· / ἄφωνα δ᾽ ὄντα <ταῦτα> τοῖς πόρρω λαλεῖ / οἷς βούλεθ᾽· ἕτερος δ᾽ ἂν τύχῃ τις πλησίον / ἑστὼς ἀναγιγνώσκοντος οὐκ ἀκούσεται, Antiphanes fr. 194.17–21 K-A = Ath. 10.451a–b. See Coo 2021: 271, cf. Yatromanolakis 2007: 304.

49. Prins 1996: 47; cf. Svenbro 1993: 159.

50. Νοσσὶς . . . ἠρίννης, Herod. 6.20.

masturbation, in which women require the male phallus (that is, the male poetic tradition) in order to be generative.[51]

Mothers and Daughters: Creating Women Poets

We can draw on Antiphanes's and Herodas's parodic figurations of female poets to identify two aspects to the depiction of women poets as mothers, which we find reimagined and explored in female poets' own discourse. One is the metaphor for the construction of a lineage of female-authored poetry (as we see in Herodas); the other is the connection of female generativity with women's gendered poetic identity (as we find in Antiphanes). Marilyn Skinner, arguing for a separate women's oral tradition, sees the figuration of the mother-daughter relationship in female-authored poetry as a literal mechanism for the dissemination of women's poetry.[52] Yet this literal reading of the mother-daughter link as a functional process fundamentally misses the way in which the role of mother is connected to the role of poet, as a form of self-labeling, claiming authority, intricate allusion to male metaphors of poetic production, and gendered identity formation—as we have seen in Sappho's *mousopolos*.[53] This is much more than a strategy of dissemination: it is a construction of equivalent authoritative identities that inform and play into each other, bringing together women's gender and creativity as both birth-givers and producers of poems, and in direct response to male models of fatherhood (and, occasionally, birth) as a metaphor for poetic production.

We have already observed the mother-daughter relationship figuring in Sappho's collective address to herself and her daughter Kleis as *mousopoloi* in fr. 150 L-P, and the way in which the mother-daughter bond becomes a foundational aspect of Sappho's gendered poetic persona, merging the identities of mother and poet in her and her daughter's joint legacy as cocreators in a community of those who serve the Muses. Other instances of mother-daughter imagery in female poets are more symbolic. In Nossis's third epigram, she uses "the fine linen cloak, which Theophilis, daughter of Cleocha, wove together

---

51. Warwick 2020; see also Skinner 1987: 40–41, 2001: 216–17, 2005b: 127–28.

52. Skinner 1993: 135, and cf. Skinner 1987: 42; for her arguments for a female-only audience for this kind of women's poetry, see Skinner 1983: 13, 1987: 41–42, 1993, 2005b: 122, 129–30. Bowman (2004: 4) calls this "the segregated tradition." For further discussion, see pp. 281–85.

53. For a modern parallel, see Wodak 1995, Kendall 2003: 603 for sociological studies on women using the language of motherhood in the workplace.

with Nossis, her noble daughter" to gesture to a female community of creators from grandmother to mother to daughter, tying in the imagery of weaving-as-poetry and its feminine associations to become a symbol for her own poetic creation (3.3–4 G-P = *Anth. Pal.* 6.265.3–4).[54] This looks back both to Erinna's *Distaff* (with a similar "constellation of elements—a bride, her mother, the rite marking a transition from childhood to adulthood, and weaving as a reflexive emblem of the written text"), as well as to Sappho frr. 98a–b L-P, where Kleis's *poikilos* headband figures for Sappho's poetry, and the tradition from grandmother to mother to daughter symbolizes a lineage of creative women.[55] Intertextuality between women writers—Sappho to Erinna to Nossis—is thus literally figured in the image of weaving passed down from mother to daughter, inscribing the intertextual connection between female authors onto the mother-daughter relationship. This mother-daughter relationship is referenced several times in Nossis's epigrams: not only in 3 G-P with the woven cloak, but also in 8 G-P (= *Anth. Pal.* 6.353) where an image of a woman named Melinna inspires the author to comment that "the daughter truly resembles her mother [*materi*] in every respect; what a good thing it is when children are like their parents!" (lines 3–4).[56] The point of the epigram is not simply to say that Melinna looks like her biological mother, but that the painted Melinna (the "daughter") looks like the real Melinna (the "mother"). An analogy is thus drawn between the reality described by an artwork and the created object, and the mother-daughter relationship—suggesting, similarly, that Nossis's poem, which also "depicts" or "creates" (*tetuktai*, 1) Melinna through ekphrasis and her memorialization in song, should be read as Nossis's poetic

54. βύσσινον εἷμα τό τοι μετὰ παιδὸς ἀγαυᾶς / Νοσσίδος ὕφανεν Θευφιλὶς ἁ Κλεόχας, Nossis 3.3–4 G-P = *Anth. Pal.* 6.265.3–4. On the gendered metapoetics in these lines, see Skinner 1987: 40–41, 1989: 5–6, 2005b: 114–16, Coughlan 2020: 615–19. On weaving as a symbol for women's poetic creativity, see Skinner 2001: 214–16; for the connection between weaving and poetry in general, see chapter 1, n. 60.

55. For the similarity to Erinna's *Distaff*, see Skinner 2001: 215; for Sappho frr. 98a–b L-P, see pp. 242–43. The connection between weaving, motherhood, and a community of women is also seen in Sappho fr. 102 L-P, where the speaker complains: "My dear mother, I cannot weave my web, broken as I am by my desire for a boy because of slender Aphrodite" (γλύκηα μᾶτερ, οὔτοι δύναμαι κρέκην τὸν ἴστον / πόθῳ δάμεισα παῖδος βραδίναν δι' Ἀφροδίταν).

56. ὡς ἐτύμως θυγάτηρ τᾷ ματέρι πάντα ποτῴκει· / ἦ καλὸν ὄκκα πέλῃ τέκνα γονεῦσιν ἴσα, Nossis 8.3–4 G-P = *Anth. Pal.* 6.353.3–4. On the gendered perspective of women's viewing in female-authored ekphrastic epigrams, see Skinner 2001: 206–11; for a survey of the theme of resemblance across Nossis's epigrams, see Tueller 2008: 166–77.

"daughter." At the same time, the idea of an epigram admiring a woman's portrait derives from an epigram by Erinna, celebrating the artistic realism of a portrait of a young girl, Agatharchis (3 G-P = *Anth. Pal.* 6.352).[57] Nossis's identification of a painting "looking like its mother" thus, again, creates a commentary on her own intertextual relationship with Erinna, and the similarity between her epigram, the "daughter," and Erinna's "mother" poem. An equivalent web of association between motherhood and intertext with her female poetic forebears structures Nossis's relationship with Sappho: Nossis's self-introduction in 11 G-P (= *Anth. Pal.* 7.718) via the stranger who visits Sappho's Mytilene presents her as "a woman dear to the Muses" to whom "a Locrian woman gave birth" (lines 3–4), similarly connecting the relationship between mother and daughter with Nossis's reception of Sappho and turning Sappho into Nossis's poetic "mother."[58]

Mother and child feature again in an epigram by Nossis's contemporary Moero, where a vine is pictured as a "mother" who "gives birth" to its leaves and grapes (1 G-P = *Anth. Pal.* 6.119).[59] And in a fragment of Corinna (fr. 674 *PMG*), the town of Thespia in Boeotia is called "fair-birthing" (*kalligenethle*) and "loved by the Muses" (*mōsophileite*).[60] Both words appear here for the first time in Greek literature, suggesting that—like Sappho's *mousopolos*—they may be Corinna's own inventions.[61] As well as referencing the town's origins, the complex and original adjectives also serve to connect childbirth and creativity, birth-giving and the Muses—and they link into Corinna's own identity

57. On the relationship between Nossis 8 G-P and Erinna 3 G-P, see Gutzwiller 1997b: 214, Gutzwiller 1998: 77 78 with 77 n. 81, Skinner 2001: 207–9; on Erinna 3 G-P, see Rayor 2005: 69, Murray and Rowland 2007: 223–25, Gutzwiller 2017a: 280–81. West 1977: 114–15 argues against Erinna's authorship of this epigram (as well as the *Distaff*); for a convincing defense of Erinna's authorship, see Pomeroy 1978, also Gutzwiller 1998: 77 n. 81, and cf. Rayor 2005: 70 n. 5. For Nossis's intertextual relationship with Erinna (as well as Sappho), see Gutzwiller 1997b and 1998: 77–78.

58. See pp. 279–80 with chapter 9, n. 69. For Sappho as Nossis's "mother poet" here, see Gutzwiller 1998: 86, Bowman 1998: 41, Coughlan 2020: 615. See further chapter 9, n. 70.

59. οὐδ' ἔτι τοι μάτηρ ἐρατὸν περὶ κλῆμα βαλοῦσα / φύσει ὑπὲρ κρατὸς νεκτάρεον πέταλον (your mother will no longer cast her lovely branch around you or give birth to sweet leaves over your head), Moero 1.3–4 G-P = *Anth. Pal.* 6.119.3–4. Skinner 2005c: 101 argues that the epigram should be seen as a tragic parody; see also Snyder 1989: 85, Gutzwiller 2017b: 409–11.

60. Θέσπια καλλιγένεθλε φιλόξενε μωσοφίλειτε, Corinna fr. 674 *PMG*.

61. W. Henderson 1995: 30, 37 n. 9; West 1990: 557 suggests that καλλιγένεθλε should be seen as a learned allusion to Thespia's origins.

as also Boeotian, also feminine, also generative, and also linked to poetic production.[62]

Homer's Mother

All these examples are important evidence of the centrality of the mother-daughter metaphor for figuring women's poetic creation, as well as intertextual relationships between women poets (as with Nossis, Erinna, and Sappho). Yet Sappho's *mousopolos*—which works to link her identity as poet directly to her identity as mother in the joint address to herself and her daughter—demonstrates that the figuration of poet-as-mother is, at the same time, more than just a metaphor: it is about connecting the very language of the "poet" to that of the "mother."

There are other moments in extant women's poetry where the terminology for the woman as poet, and her self-labeling as a mother, fuse to become one—so that the word for "mother" can become the word for "poet." The first instance harks back to Antiphanes's Sappho, in that it also concerns a woman's riddle.[63] It comes from the Delphic oracles—collections of sometimes historical, sometimes legendary, and sometimes entirely fictional oracles delivered by the female oracle at Delphi.[64] The long-time orthodoxy that the Pythia's incoherent speech was translated into verse by male "interpreters" has been dismantled, and replaced with a vision of the female oracle that sees her speaking clearly and coherently, and in verse, delivering her oracles directly to her inquirers.[65] Some, like Michael Flower, believe that

---

62. On Corinna and the Muses, see also fr. 676a *PMG*, ἐς Μωσάων; fr. 654a ii.13–14 *PMG* with Page's reconstruction, Μω[σάων . . .] / δῶ[ρ-, potentially referring to Corinna's own gift of poetry and relation to the Muses; fr. 655.1 *PMG*, where Terpsichore appears to summon Corinna; fr. 692 fr. 36 *PMG*, μωσα (though note W. Henderson 1995: 36 n. 5, "too uncertain to be useful"). See further W. Henderson 1995: 29–32.

63. Note the association elsewhere between women's speech and riddling: a woman named Cleobulina was renowned in the ancient world as a creator of hexameter riddles (Plant 2004: 29–32, Coo 2021: 272), while ἑταῖραι may have posed riddles to men in the context of the symposium (McClure 2003: 81, Schlesier 2019: 353, Coo 2021: 272). Cf. the riddle of the Sphinx: see pp. 178–80.

64. The oracles are collected in Parke and Wormell (P-W) 1956, and in translation in Fontenrose (F) 1978.

65. For a summary of the debate, see Flower 2007: 215–17; see also Fontenrose 1978: 212–24, Price 1985, Nagy 1989: 26, Maurizio 1995.

they can see distinct "styles" in the different Pythias, as their oracles are reported to us (in Herodotus); others, like Lisa Maurizio, caution that the Delphic oracles participate in an oral medium and transmission, and identify "ambiguity" as their defining trait.[66] As examples of women's poetic speech, however, they provide an interesting different angle to the question of women's poetic naming—because several oracles make mention of male poets.[67] One such example is a verse reply said to have been given to Homer by the Delphic oracle, which Pausanias—the second-century CE traveler and chronicler—records was positioned under Homer's statue in the temple of Apollo at Delphi (P-W 317–19). This oracle—in marked contrast, as we will see, to male oracles on Homer—makes no mention of Homer's poetic identity, and gives him no poet-term.[68] Instead, the female oracle focuses on structuring her response through the relationship between mother and child (P-W 317):[69]

> You seek your fatherland [*patrida*]? You have a motherland [*mētris*],
>   not a fatherland [*patris*].
> The island of Ios is your mother's [*mētros*] fatherland [*patris*], which
>   will receive you
> when you die. But beware the riddle [*ainigma*] of the young children
>   [*paidōn*].

The female oracle, proclaiming verse in hexameter just like the *aoidos*, denies the male poet Homer a poet-term: his identity as a poet—his most famous identifying feature—is entirely and conspicuously omitted. Instead, the oracle's hexameter verses, set beneath the statue of a male hexameter poet, stand

---

66. Flower 2007: 211–39; Maurizio 2001. See further Hafner 2022.

67. See pp. 263–67 with chapter 9, n. 13.

68. See pp. 265–67 with chapter 9, n. 24.

69. πατρίδα δίζηαι; μητρὶς δέ τοι, οὐ πατρίς ἐστιν. / ἔστιν Ἴος νῆσος μητρὸς πατρίς, ἥ σε θανόντα / δέξεται. ἀλλὰ νέων παίδων αἴνιγμα φύλαξαι, P-W 317 = F L80 = Arist. fr. 76.16–17 Rose = [Plut.] *Vit. Hom.* 4 = Paus. 10.24.2. See Parke and Wormell 1956: 127, and, for other versions of the oracle, see P-W 318–19. Both Fontenrose and Parke and Wormell classify the oracle as legendary/fictitious; Parke and Wormell date it to the Sixth Period, up to 300 BCE. There are, however, issues with the methods used to determine "real" and "fictitious" oracles in both volumes; see Maurizio 2001: 39 n. 4. For the purposes of this book, I analyze all oracles (attributed to the Pythia, rather than paraphrases) as evidence of the oracle's female speech. See further, Fontenrose 1978: 83 n. 49, Graziosi 2002: 130 n. 15, 154–55 n. 85, Arafat 2016: 212; we will come across this oracle again at §12.3.3.

as a tribute to the female oracle's ability to compose poetry just like a man. But the Delphic oracle does not simply demonstrate her comparable ability to that of Homer: defying the (reasonable) expectation that the statue of Homer should be captioned by his own verses, she in fact manages to oust him entirely from the poetic contest, and publicly puts her own hexameter poetry on display instead. Meanwhile, by refusing Homer a poet-term in the verses that describe him, she replicates male strategies of denying women access to a poetic identity in their poetry.

The gendered polemic of the oracle is explicitly brought out by the birth imagery which pervades the verses.[70] The first two lines revolve around the opposition between "motherland" and "fatherland," and the ironic juxtaposition of "mother's fatherland" in line 2, which highlights the gender politics inherent in terms like "fatherland." Yet the joke on gender here is not purely semantic—it is grammatical too: *patris* (or *patrida* in the accusative, which is the first word of the oracle) is a grammatically feminine noun which describes a semantically masculine concept (the labeling of a country as a place where one's "fathers" have lived). The oracle brings grammar and semantics into line by taking away the *patris* from Homer and replacing it with a much less common term, a *mētris*, a "motherland."[71] At the same time, she demonstrates the persistence of patriarchal terms like *patris*. In line 2, on the other hand, having introduced the term *mētris*, she ironically goes on to call Ios Homer's "mother's fatherland" (*mētros patris*)—both performing the difficulty of getting rid of gender stereotypes represented in words like *patris*, and showing how such words deny recognition to "mothers." (The similarity between *mētros*, "of your mother," and *mētris*, "motherland," makes this much clear.)

But there is more to the oracle's replacement of "fatherland" with "motherland" than abstract gender politics. The fact that it is Homer's "father/motherland" at stake, and the female oracle's competing verse poetry, also suggests a poetic dimension to the gendering going on here. We have already remarked that the oracle omits any male poet-term like *aoidos* to describe Homer; now she deprives the poet of the masculine terminology that connects him to patriarchal structures, like the *patris*. At the same time, she interjects female terms, like *mētris*, and places a central importance on Homer's mother, to

70. See Maurizio 2001: 49 on birthing imagery in the oracles.
71. Cf. Pl. *Rep.* 9.575d5–6 for the Cretans calling their πατρίς a μητρίς.

generate a connection between being a poet and being a mother. Of course, Homer, as a male poet, can never become a mother: but the Delphic oracle is a woman—and, in this sense, her foregrounding of the role of mother underlines the female-gendered and agonistic aspect of her poem.

This, in turn, is what allows us to read the "riddle [*ainigma*] of the young children" in line 3 as more than a prophetic reference to Homer's death.[72] It is, at the same time—in the kind of subliminal reading which we will come to see is a feature of women's discourse about their own poetic identity—a reference to the Pythia's *own* riddling speech. The word *ainigma*, "riddle," was often used of oracular speech, which was well known for its ambiguity.[73] It was also commonly used of another female's speech—the Sphinx, whom we saw both problematized and bestialized as an *aoidos* in Sophocles and Euripides.[74] And of course, we observed the connection being drawn between riddles, female speech, and birth imagery through Antiphanes's Sappho, where the letters of the alphabet were visualized in riddle form as the "newborn children" of a "female being." Here, the Delphic oracle girds her poem with birth imagery—from motherland in line 1, to mother in line 2, to children in line 3—and suggests that the male poet's inability to understand, not only the words of the children, but also *her own* riddling speech, will be his downfall. Connecting the riddling ambiguity of her prophetic words to that of the children who will overcome Homer, she thus demonstrates the fact that this is a poetic contest in which her verses themselves, as a surrogate for the riddling children, will defeat her poetic rival. Motherhood and riddling female speech come together in the final line, at the same time as the oracle predicts the male poet's downfall through his inability to understand the complex, enigmatic speech of her "children"—her words. The oracle thus becomes both a mother and a female poet, capable of producing and understanding riddles, generating hexameter verse which defeats that of the canonical male poet, and—through her female gender and her connection to riddling speech—besting him in the poetic contest.

72. According to the biographical tradition, this was a riddle posed to Homer by two young fishing boys, which Homer was unable to solve: see Levine 2002, Graziosi 2002: 162–63.

73. For αἴνιγμα of oracular speech, see Parke and Wormell 1956: 2:xxviii; Maurizio 2001 comments on ambiguity as the defining feature of the Pythia, and cf. Levine 2002: 143.

74. See pp. 178–80; for αἴνιγμα of the Sphinx, see Eur. *Phoen.* 1731, 1759, Plut. fr. 136.29, Dio Chrys. *Or.* 10.31.1–2.

Mother of Words

Our final example comes from a little-known woman poet: Eurydice of Macedon. Eurydice's reputation as a poet is, as often, in proportion to the number of fragments that survive. We have only one extant poem belonging to her, quoted in Plutarch's *Moralia*:[75]

> Eurydice of Hierapolis dedicated this
> to the Muses when she fulfilled the longing for knowledge in her soul.
> For she, delighted mother [*mētēr*] of healthy [*hēbōntōn*] sons, worked
>   hard
> to learn letters, the record [*mnēmeia*] of speech [*logōn*].

Eurydice I of Macedon was born around 410 BCE. She was the granddaughter of a king of Lyncestae in northern Greece, wife of the king of Macedon, Amyntas III, and (as we see in the epigram above) mother of three sons, each of whom became the king of Macedon. Indeed, one of them was Philip II, father of Alexander the Great, thus making Eurydice Alexander's grandmother.[76] But it is not her impressive pedigree that earns her a place here; it is her writing, which, as she tells us, she "worked hard to learn" (4).

On the surface, the dedicatory inscription falls into the category of a standard votive offering: the incorporation of the name of the dedicator and the gods to whom it is given are both standard votive fare.[77] There are some other pieces of information given, in addition to Eurydice's name. The first is Eurydice's motherhood, and the description of her "healthy sons" (4); the second, the fact that she learned to read and write, "work[ing] hard to learn letters, the record of speech."[78] Plutarch records the epigram as an example of Eurydice's model status as a mother, educating herself in order to pass it on to her sons.[79] And indeed, there are many ways in which the epigram presents Eurydice in the light of model womanhood. Her status as a mother—consistently emphasized

---

75. Εὐρυδίκη Ἱεραπολιῆτις τόνδ᾽ ἀνέθηκε / Μούσαις εὔιστον ψυχῇ ἑλοῦσα πόθον. / γράμματα γὰρ μνημεῖα λόγων μήτηρ γεγαυῖα / παίδων ἡβώντων ἐξεπόνησε μαθεῖν, Plut. *De lib. ed.* 14b–c. The text quoted here is that given at Wilamowitz-Moellendorff 1919: 71; for discussion, see Wilamowitz-Moellendorff 1919: 71–72, Plant 2004: 44.

76. On Eurydice's background, see Carney 2000: 38–50.

77. Mikalson 2005: 14–15.

78. On the evidence for female literacy in the Hellenistic world, see Pomeroy 1977 and 1984, Cole 1981; see further, introduction, n. 11.

79. Plut. *De lib. ed.* 14b9–10; cf. Quintilian's similar recommendation (Quint. *Inst.* 1.1.6).

as the ideal role for a woman in the ancient world—is foregrounded, and her willing compliance with her task emphasized with the participle "delighted" (3).[80] Her fertility and ability to produce many male children are suggested in the plural "sons," while the fact that they have all reached adulthood—another hallmark of the ideal mother—is explicitly pointed out with the word "healthy" (*hēbōntōn*, 4), which literally translates as "having achieved adulthood" or "being in the prime of life."[81]

And yet there is quite a different way of reading the epigram—for, as Ian Plant notes, in spite of Plutarch's citation of Eurydice's educating herself to support her sons, Eurydice "speaks only of the benefits of the learning for herself."[82] Plant's observation suggests that there is more going on. The two aspects of her personality—her womanhood, and her writing—are in fact deeply implicated in the structure of the poem, with the subclause "delighted mother of healthy sons" (3–4) embedded across a line break within the main clause, "for she . . . worked hard to learn letters, the record of speech" (3–4). The effect is as if the two are so deeply implicated in one another that they cannot be separated. The juxtaposition of the two clauses creates a particularly interesting collocation at its heart which serves to define Eurydice's attitude toward her poetry, and which allows us to begin to comprehend her understanding of her relationship to writing. At the very center of the clause, framed by a rhyming noun and perfect participle, we have the collocation "mother of words" (*logōn mētēr*, 3). The line break between "mother" and "healthy sons" makes this juxtaposition particularly hard to miss, and it would be an easy mistake to make, upon first reading the epigram, to assume that the two—the noun *mētēr* and the genitive plural *logōn* placed beside it—belong together. Indeed, this reading only continues with the genitive *paidōn*, which can be read in apposition to *logōn*: "the mother of words, her healthy children." In this sense, Eurydice's *logoi* are, in fact, the sons in question—an identification reinforced by the grammatical masculinity of *logoi* aligning with the maleness of Eurydice's "sons."

So why does this matter? I want to suggest that Eurydice is performing a version of literary gender here that implicates her female authorship with her

80. On motherhood as the ideal woman's role in antiquity, see Pomeroy 1975: 84–86, Vivante 1999: 239, Keith, McAuley, and Sharrock 2020: 27. For examples, see Lys. 1.6, Xen. *Oec.* 7.10–11, and see chapter 8, n. 12.

81. See Chantraine s.v. ἥβη.

82. Plant 2004: 44.

motherhood. As we have already seen, the association between motherhood and female authorship is by no means a modern one: the riddle posed by Antiphanes's Sappho demonstrates that much—and Antiphanes was, in fact, a close contemporary of Eurydice's. In addition to demonstrating a contemporary connection between motherhood and "letters," however, there are also several striking similarities between Eurydice's epigram and Antiphanes's Sappho's answer to the riddle, which create a suggestive literary parallel between the two texts. The second line of Antiphanes's Sappho's response, in particular— "the newborns she carries around inside her are the letters of the alphabet" (*brephē d'en hautēi peripherei ta grammata*, fr. 194.2 K-A)—shares similarities with the third and fourth lines of Eurydice's epigram: the mirroring of "new-borns" (*brephē*) and "letters" (*grammata*) at line start and end in Antiphanes is echoed in the pairing between Eurydice's "letters" (*grammata*) at the start of the third line (note the same word) and "sons" (*paidōn*) at the start of the fourth. Children, motherhood, "letters," and women's poetic identity seem to be linked together in a web of associations that relates being a mother to being a female poet.

Within this framework, then, we can begin to read Eurydice's epigram as playing into a contemporary associative imagery connecting motherhood, women poets, and writing. Rather than positing her learning and writing as a constraint of her position as a woman, valid only inasmuch as it is passed onto her children, the collocation *logōn mētēr*, "mother of words," at the heart of the inscription subtly hints at the fact that it is precisely Eurydice's femininity and motherhood that qualify her for a deep and enduring (note "in her soul," 2) connection to literature. This is only reinforced by the fact that her dedication is to the Muses, female gods who, as we have seen through the example of Sappho's *mousopolos*, were presented as intimately connected to the female literary project.[83] This is underlined by the juxtaposition of the plural noun "record" (*mnēmeia*, 3) next to the collocation *logōn mētēr*, which—in close proximity to the mention of the Muses—implicitly recalls the mother of the Muses themselves, Mnemosyne (cognate with *mnēmeia*).[84] Just as Mnemo-syne mothered the Muses, gods of literature and poetry, so Eurydice, too, is a mother of poetry, a *logōn mētēr*. The words of the poem itself literally inscribe

83. The Muses are directly connected to Eurydice by the pairing of the two nouns at the beginning of the lines of the first distich (Εὐρυδίκη ... Μούσαις, 1–2).

84. For the birth of the Muses by Mnemosyne, see Hes. *Theog.* 53–62; on Mnemosyne, see Notopoulos 1938, and see also p. 241.

the dedication into a genealogy of memory and motherhood that goes back to the Muses and Mnemosyne, as well as Sappho *mousopolos* and her daughter, through the connection of motherhood and poetic authorship—the bearing of children, and the production of words.

Eurydice's epigram, short as it is, thus serves to define female authorship in a subtle, multilayered text that allows for multiple meanings. On the surface of the poem, Eurydice denotes herself as a good mother who has learned letters to educate her sons, articulating the values and desires expected of a woman. In another layer, her poem opens up a discourse on femininity, motherhood, creativity and its relationship to literature and authorship. And at the deepest layer, reading the *mnēmeia*-function of Eurydice's "letters" as a connection to Mnemosyne, the mother of the Muses, the dedicatory inscription itself becomes a claim to a connection with the Muses that is deeply implicated in motherhood, language, and memory. As Susan Sniader Lanser puts it in reference to the coded speech of the female voice, "the 'feminine style' of the surface text, that 'powerless,' non-authoritative term called 'women's language,' here becomes a powerfully subversive mask for telling secrets to a woman under the watchful eyes of a man . . . it deliberately adopts a 'feminine' position that is exaggerated into subversion by exposing the mechanisms of its own abjection."[85] Eurydice's poem, in other words, conforms on one level to the expected literary ambitions of a woman, and, on another level, contains within itself an entirely different meaning and voice that can only be read by the knowing reader who is able to read between the lines to the subversive connection of motherhood, Muses, and memory—and the trajectory that that draws back to other female poets, like Sappho, who have made the same associations between motherhood and Muses, as well as male writers, who manipulated the metaphor of birth and paternity to refer to their poetic production. Motherhood thus becomes an identity that allows a woman to encode her creativity behind a "subversive mask" that appears to conform to gendered norms—while at the same time linking the female poet to her poetic forebears, and identifying a woman poet's generativity through birth with her creativity in poetry. Being a mother genders a woman's poetic creativity female—and demonstrates that a woman poet is, through the connection between her gender, her generativity, and her literary creativity, the only one qualified to be a "mother of words."

85. Lanser 1992: 11; see also Irigaray 1985: 76–78. For a similar reading of the "hidden transcripts" behind "powerless" voices, see Scott 1990.

9

Bards and Birds

OLD TERMS ON HER TERMS,
FROM SAPPHO TO NOSSIS

THE LAST CHAPTER began with the effect of Sappho's word choice in calling herself a *mousopolos*, and the ramifications that has for our understanding of Sappho's gendered relationship with the Muses and the construction of the poetics of motherhood. Yet it is also worth noting the terms that Sappho rejects—for this is just as powerful a statement of gendered poetics. As we have already seen, the supple, interpretatively rich *mousopolos* is, in fact, just as important in its representation of the refusal to accept male terms: while we might translate both Hesiod's *Mousaōn therapōn* and Sappho's *mousopolos* into English as "servant of the Muses," we cannot afford to miss the fact that, with *mousopolos*, Sappho dismisses Hesiod's vocabulary and comes up with an entirely new term for herself. While, on the surface, the semantics might seem the same, then, the choice of words is, in fact, crucially different, and (as we have seen) each brings with them different resonances, effects, and gender politics.

This rewriting of Hesiod's term as a new word was, importantly, a lexical choice. It is not the case that Sappho could not have used Hesiod's term, *therapōn*, because of her gender: the masculine *therapōn* could have been feminized to *therapaina* (female servant)—the word we came across in chapter 3 to describe the Delian women in the *Homeric Hymn to Apollo*.[1] That this female equivalent to Hesiod's *therapōn* was available to Sappho is demonstrated by the fact that we find it in a fragment ascribed to Sappho, describing the "gold-shining servant [*therapaina*] of Aphrodite" (Sappho/Alcaeus

---

1. See p. 63.

fr. 23 L-P).² (By way of comparison, in another fragment, we find Sappho mock-
ing a "country girl" [*agroiōtis*, fr. 57 L-P], using—for the first time in extant
Greek literature—the feminized form of the masculine *agroiōtēs*, which we
find in Homer.)³ With both *therapaina* and *agroiōtis*, we see Sappho using
feminized versions of male terms—in both cases, the earliest instances of the
feminine term in extant Greek. In other words, if Sappho wanted to create
female-gendered versions of male nouns, she not only had a framework for
doing so: she demonstrates, elsewhere, her ability to mold the Greek language
to incorporate feminine versions of male terms, terms which had been used
and canonized in the masculine by the male poets Hesiod and Homer.⁴

Yet Sappho does not take the route of feminizing male terms when it comes
to describing her gendered identity as a poet. (It is interesting that later au-
thors, who frequently call Sappho a *poiētria*, thus contravene Sappho's own
performed practice of self-naming.) Instead, she articulates her opposition to
Hesiod's gendered poetic identity by generating a new term for herself which
develops a different relationship to the Muses, and articulates her layered
poetic identity as a woman. Meanwhile, from a grammatical perspective,
mousopolos is an interesting choice as a two-termination adjectival substantive
(gendered feminine, in this case, but with a masculine-looking ending).
Rather than tying down her identity as a woman poet to grammatical gender
(by using a word with an overtly grammatically feminine ending, or by femi-
nizing a masculine poet-term), then, Sappho allows the semantics and social
context of the word to speak for itself.

And this leads us to what might seem one of the most obvious candidates in
the history of gendered poet-terms for women's self-naming: *aoidos*. This was
a word which, as we have seen, was forged in the crucible of gender in the epics
of Homer and had already been tried out for size in the feminine, from Hom-
er's lamenting women to Hesiod's nightingale to the tortoise of the *Homeric
Hymn to Hermes*. Following the foray into the invention of a new vocabulary

---

2. χρυσοφάην θερ[άπαιν]αν Ἀφροδίτ[ας, Sappho vel Alcaeus fr. 23 L-P. Campbell 1982:
451 n. 1, following Bergk and Gomperz, notes that the ascription to Sappho is usually accepted.
Note that this is the earliest instance of θεράπαινα in extant Greek (though cf. θεράπνη at
Hymn. Hom. Ap. 157): for later examples, see Pherec. DK 7 B 2.6–7, Hdt. 3.134.5, Xen. *Cyr.* 6.4.11.

3. τίς δ᾽ ἀγροῖωτις θέλγει νόον . . . / ἀγροῖωτιν ἐπεμμένα στόλαν . . . (what country girl
enchants your mind . . . wearing country dress), Sappho fr. 57.1–2 L-P. For ἀγροιώτης in Homer,
see *Il.* 11.549, 11.676, 15.272, *Od.* 11.293, 21.85; also Hes. [*Sc.*] 39, Hes. fr. 66.7 M-W, fr. 195.39 M-W;
cf. Alcm. fr. 16.1 *PMGF*, Alc. fr. 130.17 L-P.

4. Cf. Corinna fr. 664b *PMG*: see p. 270.

by female poets around the poetics of motherhood in the previous chapter, then, this chapter turns to look at women poets' response to a very old term indeed. It examines the gendering of the *aoidos* in female poets' discourse, and the ways in which women poets either adopted, adapted, or discarded the word as a way to articulate their gendered poetic identity. In so doing, it explores the different ways in which women poets might have responded to the discourse surrounding the male-gendering of authorship in words like *aoidos*. Did they use such terms to describe male authors, for instance? Did they feel that *aoidos* was an old term they could use for themselves, on their terms? Or did the history of the male-gendering of the *aoidos*, combined with the disturbing appropriation of those females who tried to be *aoidoi* like Hesiod's nightingale and Hermes's tortoise, lead women poets to conclude that the existing lexicon of poetic authorship was not open to them, or one they wanted to adopt? And, if that was the case, did they reject the old term entirely—or did they work around it to come up with new, resonant words that were able to hint at the tradition of the *aoidos*, but also stake out a new place for women poets in the tradition of gendered poetry?

The performativity of gender has, in many ways, influenced much of the reading of the gender strategies throughout this book. At the heart of this chapter, in particular, as we return to where the book began on the battleground of the *aoidos*, lies the concept of the performance of gender and poetic authorship, as a way of articulating both women's approaches to the male-gendering of authorship and their staging of their own gendered authorship. As Judith Butler (whose theorization of the performativity of gender continues to be both controversial and influential) explains, "a performative is that discursive practice that enacts or produces that which it names."[5] The concept of performativity thus has an important part to play in our understanding of the construction of gender in relationship to authorship, as an identity rather than as a purely grammatical entity. Butler's understanding of gender as a continuous series of "constituting acts" maps neatly onto the performativity of authorship and gender in ancient Greek poetry, and in women poets in particular: each "performance" of her poetic identity by a woman poet constitutes both a statement and a development of her gender identity, and vice versa.[6] Meanwhile, "performing" takes on another meaning when we look at the ways in

5. Butler 1993: 13. On speech act theory, see Austin 1962, further developed in Searle 1969 and 1979.
6. See pp. 12–13 with introduction, n. 49.

which women poets responded to the persona of the poet—the persona of the *aoidos*—which had been constructed by male authors as male, in a word that was gendered masculine. In some cases, we will see women donning the mask of male-gendered authorship in order to deconstruct the terms that forced female poets to impersonate masculine gender. In others, we will see women both appearing to perform their socialized gendered role, while at the same time subversively breaking the mold.

On His Terms: Bards

We begin, again, with Sappho. While no external evidence survives as to what Sappho's male contemporaries might have called her (perhaps, as we have seen in chapter 7, due to the fact that in many cases they chose not to give her a poet-term at all), fr. 106 L-P provides a useful way to show that Sappho was aware of the issues at stake in deploying traditional authorship terminology, and the fact that it was—most often—applied to (and by) men. In this fragment, she speaks of an *aoidos* from Lesbos—using the term which had become the standard formulation for "(male) poet" in the archaic period:[7]

> superior, as the poet [*aoidos*] from Lesbos [*ho Lesbios*] is to those of
> other lands

Given the fragmentary condition of much of Sapphic transmission, we are not told to whom Sappho is referring here, or, indeed, if she is referring to anyone in particular. The author who preserved this fragment for us tells us that Sappho is talking about "an outstanding man [*andros*]"—thus making the implicit grammatical gender of Sappho's *aoidos* explicit.[8] Most later (male) commentators have taken it for granted that Sappho is speaking of a particular male poet here, and have suggested as candidates either Alcaeus or Terpander, both archaic poets of Lesbos with towering reputations.[9]

Yet surely the critical jump from *aoidos* to male poet, in the work of one of the most influential female poets of antiquity, is one which we should regard with suspicion. Why does Sappho have to be talking about a man here

---

7. πέρροχος, ὡς ὅτ᾽ ἄοιδος ὁ Λέσβιος ἀλλοδάποισιν, Sappho fr. 106 L-P.

8. Demetr. *Eloc.* 146: see Innes 1995: 310–19.

9. Bowra 1961: 132 suggests Alcaeus (as well as Sappho); Treu 1963: 223 suggests Terpander; cf. Power 2010: 335 with n. 41. The phrase μετὰ Λέσβιον ᾠδόν later became proverbial: see Boterf 2017: 91 with n. 45.

at all—or at least, why *only* a man? Is it not questionable that male scholars have read this as a woman poet acknowledging the "superiority" of a male poet—transforming this fragment into not simply a commendation of Lesbian poets, but an admission of the superiority of male *aoidos* over female? By contrast, it is quite possible that Sappho is using the grammatical masculine here, not in the referential sense (referring to a specific man), but as a generic masculine—reinforced by her usage of the generalizing "as when"—to refer, less to a particular male poet of Lesbos and more to "der alten, ruhmreichen Sangestradition auf Lesbos," of which she, naturally, is a part.[10] (A better translation of the fragment might then read, "superior, as poets from Lesbos are to those of other lands.") Of course, Sappho herself, being both from Lesbos and a poet, would fit both the qualifications necessary to come under the generalizing umbrella of "the poet from Lesbos"—and it would only be her sex as a woman that would be hidden within the generic masculine due to the lexical "invisibility of feminine/female expressions."[11]

This reading suggests a couple of interesting aspects to women poets' approach to the male-gendered terms, like *aoidos*, that had been used by men. For one thing, it demonstrates Sappho's awareness of poet-vocabulary, and her engagement with the conversation around gendered poetic identities that stretches back to Homer. We see Sappho bringing the term into her own voice, refusing to allow it to be a possession of male poets alone. At the same time, the polyvalency of its interpretation—oscillating between what might appear to be a deferential acknowledgment of the superiority of her male poetic colleagues, and, on the other hand, a subtle intimation that she should be included *among* the group of superior Lesbian *aoidoi*—suggests that Sappho is donning a performative mask here that allows us to read the fragment, and its statement of poetic identity, in multiple ways.[12] Shifting between masculine and feminine referents, situating herself within the predominantly masculine sphere of poets (*aoidoi*), and playing with linguistic gender, we seem to see an

10. Treu 1963: 223; cf. Klinck 2008: 146, Lardinois 2014: 129. Maslov 2009: 14, asserting that "in the surviving texts neither lyric nor elegiac poets speak of themselves—or are spoken of—as ἀοιδοί," seems to skate over this instance; at p. 9 he suggests that Sappho fr. 106 L-P "most likely refers to professional performers, rather than to poet-composers (but possibly to both)," but note p. 10 "the term is never applied to the poets themselves." Maslov also elides the gender component: the only reference to a potential gendering in the history of ἀοιδός is at Maslov 2009: 22 n. 47, where ἀοιδός can have "common animate gender," but only as an adjective.

11. Hellinger and Bußmann 2001: 10; see chapter 1, n. 52.

12. This is similar to Winkler's "double consciousness" (1990: 162–87); cf. Skinner 1993.

intertextual performativity of the gendered self here that both acknowledges the history of the masculinization of the *aoidos* and enacts Sappho's demand for admission into the realm of *aoidoi*, through—and in the medium of—her poetry. Whether the *aoidos* from Lesbos is a specific personality or a representative of the masculine-gendered tradition to which Sappho herself belongs, then, what is certain is that Sappho clearly does not lack a vocabulary for authorship—nor is she blind to it. It is simply gendered male.

On His Terms: Oracles

An interesting comparison to Sappho's engagement with the tradition of male poetic naming is provided by the Delphic oracle, whom we came across in the last chapter. These oracles pronouncing on male poets like Homer, Hesiod, and Archilochus constitute some of the only instances, aside from Sappho's *aoidos* in fr. 106 L-P, that we find women talking in verse about male poets—which makes them a rich testimony and source for women's responses to traditions of male poetic naming.[13]

A third-century BCE inscription from a shrine dedicated to Archilochus on the island of Paros gives details of an oracle which the shrine's dedicator, Mnesiepes, seems to have obtained from Delphi. The oracle apparently ordered Mnesiepes, according to one line of the inscription, "to honor Archilochus the poet [*tom poiētan*]" (F H74).[14] Although this seems to be a paraphrase of the oracle's words, and so only indirect evidence for the oracle's speech, it is a tantalizing example of the use of a poet-term for a specific male poet by a woman. Archilochus in fact receives two other poet-terms from the Delphic oracle within our period. The first is an oracle in verse, recorded on the same inscription on Paros: in it, Telesicles, Archilochus's father, is told by the oracle that his son will be "immortal and sung-of [*aoidimos*]" (P-W 231).[15] The word

13. Two further examples of references to male poets/craftsmen are P-W 279 = F H25, and P-W 349 = F H52. See also F H32 (P-W p.116 *ad* 284).

14. Μνησιέπει ὁ θεός ἔχρησε λῶιον καὶ ἄμεινον εἶμεν / [τι]μῶντι Ἀρχίλοχον τὸμ ποιητάν, καθ᾽ ἃ ἐπινοεῖ (the god gave an oracle to Mnesiepes that it is better to honour Archilochus the poet, as he intends), *SEG* 15.517 A, i.14–15 = F H74. The text is cited from Rivoli 2020; see also Nagy 1979: 303–8, Swift 2019: 58–63.

15. ἀθάνατός σοι παῖς καὶ ἀοίδιμος, ὦ Τελεσίκλεις, P-W 231.1 = F Q56 = *SEG* 15.517 A, ii.50. Parke and Wormell, who see the oracle as fictitious, place it in the Fifth Period, i.e., pre–373 BCE; Fontenrose also identifies as mythical/quasi-historical and gives a date in brackets [c. 680 BCE].

blurs between active "singer"—on the analogy of *aoidos*—and passive "sung-of," fusing Archilochus's status and reputation as a poet with his poetic identity. Interestingly, the oracle's use of the word *aoidimos* connects her verse with a tradition of female speech going back to Helen's use of *aoidimos* in *Iliad* book 6, as well as the inscription of the female poet Delphis from the island of Cos, dated to roughly the same time, where the word *aoidimos* identifies her as a "poet."[16] The female oracle thus draws on a gendered tradition of the use of *aoidimos*, signaling the gender differential between her poetic verse and the male poet, Archilochus. But she also hints at a female tradition of self-labeling as *aoidimos*, and women's awareness of their subordination to male poets (like Helen's acknowledgment of her creation in song); as well as their attempts—like Delphis—to rename themselves.

The third oracle on Archilochus gives him yet another poet-term, and a very familiar one at that: *Mousaōn therapōn*. The story goes that Archilochus was killed in battle by a man known as Corax, who tried to enter the temple at Delphi and was told by the Pythia: "You killed the servant of the Muses [*Mousaōn theraponta*]; leave the temple" (P-W 4).[17] The fact that this was supposed to be a spontaneous address by the Pythia, rather than the delivery of a formal oracle from Apollo, makes this a fascinating instance of unfettered female speech.[18] And it shows the Pythia demonstrating some deft literary intertextuality. The phrase *Mousaōn therapōn* recalls, not only Hesiod, but also Archilochus himself, who had used a close paraphrase of the term to describe his poetic persona in the first fragment of his poetry: "I am the servant [*therapōn*] of the lord of war, and skilled in the lovely gift of the Muses [*Mouseōn*]" (fr. 1 *IEG*).[19] Instead of

16. See pp. 43–44, p. 221; see also see chapter 9, n. 27.

17. Μουσάων θεράποντα κατέκτανες· ἔξιθι νηοῦ, P-W 4 = F Q58. Parke and Wormell accept this oracle as historical; Fontenrose classifies as quasi-historical. See further Nagy 1979: 301–8, Swift 2019: 5–7. For Archilochus's life and biographical tradition, see Burnett 1983: 15–32, Swift 2019: 3–8; for testimonia on Archilochus's death, see Gerber 1999b: 38–45 (Loeb T12–18).

18. For the Pythia as author of this phrase, see Heraclid. Lemb. π. πολιτείων (p. 22 Dilts), Plut. *De sera* 17.560e, Ael. fr. 80 = *Suda* s.v. Ἀρχίλοχος, Oenomaus ap. Euseb. *Praep. evang.* 5.33.8–9; note, however, that Dio Chrys. *Or.* 33.11–12, Aristid. *Or.* 46 (ii. 380 Dindorf), Gal. *Protr.* 9.22, Origen *C. Cels.* 3.25 have Apollo as the speaker, rather than the Pythia. For the text of individual passages, see Parke and Wormell 1956: 3–4.

19. εἰμὶ δ᾽ ἐγὼ θεράπων μὲν Ἐνυαλίοιο ἄνακτος / καὶ Μουσέων ἐρατὸν δῶρον ἐπιστάμενος, Archilochus fr. 1 *IEG*. See Nagy 1979: 304–5, Burnett 1983: 33–34, Marmodoro and Hill 2013: v, Swift 2019: 205–6.

simply adopting Hesiod's term, however, Archilochus makes himself into a *therapōn* of Ares—recalling, instead, the common Homeric formulation—and places the genitive plural, *Mouseōn*, on the following line, dependent on "gift" ("gift of the Muses") rather than "servant" ("servant of the Muses").[20] Hesiod's relationship of gendered opposition with the Muses is replaced, by Archilochus, with an all-male, Iliadic model of male poets, male warriors, and male gods, with the Muses relegated to their own line as givers of the "gift" of poetic inspiration. The Delphic oracle, on the other hand, moves over Archilochus's self-designation to highlight his poetic influence, Hesiod, labeling him not with his chosen term, but with Hesiod's.[21] She thus demonstrates her literary expertise and—by skillfully manipulating the term herself, in her own poetry—both differentiates her voice, reinstates the importance of the (female) Muses, and places herself, and her oracle, in a (male) literary lineage that goes back through Archilochus to Hesiod.[22]

Just as interesting, however, are the instances where the Pythia chooses *not* to give poetic vocabulary—as well as the gendered divisions between different oracles. We have another spontaneous address by the Pythia, this time apparently to a poet himself: Hesiod. Here, Hesiod is addressed by the oracle in terms that describe his poetry and poetic associations: he is "honored by the immortal Muses" (P-W 206.2), will have *kleos* (3), and is a "fortunate man [*anēr*]" (1), underlining the masculinity that the Pythia associates with his poetry.[23] Yet he receives no actual poet-term—no *aoidos*, no *Mousaōn therapōn* as Hesiod gave himself (and as the Pythia granted Archilochus). This absence of poet-terms becomes more pronounced in the oracle delivered to Hesiod's rival, Homer, which we have already come across in the last chapter—the reply given to Homer by the oracle at Delphi, which was placed under his statue in the temple of Apollo. In this oracle, as we have seen, Homer not only receives no poet-term from the Pythia, but his identity as a poet, and his fame

---

20. See pp. 50–56 with chapter 2, n. 42.

21. Contrast Theoc. *Epigr.* 21.1 for Archilochus as ποιητής.

22. Μοῦσα appears in the extant oracles elsewhere only at P-W 206.2 (of Hesiod) and P-W 473.4, 8, 50 (of Apollo singing with the Muses).

23. ὄλβιος οὗτος ἀνὴρ, ὃς ἐμὸν δόμον ἀμφιπολεύει, / Ἡσίοδος Μούσῃσι τετιμένος ἀθανάτῃσιν· / τοῦ δ᾽ ἤ τοι κλέος ἔσται ὅσην τ᾽ ἐπικίδναται ἠώς (this man is blessed, who visits my house, Hesiod, honored by the immortal Muses; his glory will reach as far as the dawn spreads), P-W 206.1–3 = F L41. The *Certamen* (13) presents this as a spontaneous address by the Pythia; both Fontenrose and Parke and Wormell classify as a legendary oracle.

for his poetry, are not even mentioned.[24] But Pausanias (who records the verses for us) documents another oracle on Homer, immediately after his record of the Delphic pronouncement: and this is an oracle delivered by a male seer, by the name of Euclus (Paus. 10.24.3).[25] In contrast to the Pythia's scant attribution of poetic credentials to Homer, Euclus's oracle opens by naming Homer as an *aoidos* in the very first line; he goes on to praise his fame (*polukleiton*, "very famous," line 3), his song (*aeisas*, "singing," line 5), and his immortality (line 6). The male oracle, then, does not hesitate to endow Homer with the masculine vocabulary of *aoidos*; the female oracle, by contrast, does not mention the poetic connections of the most famous male poet of antiquity. It is hard not to see this—particularly given the oracles' juxtaposition in Pausanias—as a competing public discourse in poetry, a statement of the two oracles' different gendered identities through the ways in which they relate to another poet. The male oracle, a man producing his own hexameter poetry, assimilates himself easily into the tradition of the *aoidos*. The female oracle, by contrast, differentiates her verses by silencing Homer (in a neat reverse move that replicates the silencing of women's voices)—thus sidestepping traditional male norms of epic authorship.

So if this is what the oracle calls (or does not call) male poets, does she give herself any terms to describe her own gendered engagement in poetic verse? The short answer is—at least in the extant oracles—no.[26] Yet, as with Lisa Maurizio's argument for the oracles' defining ambiguity, we can see this lack of terminology as a stylistic choice—a part of the riddle of the Delphic oracle.

24. See pp. 250–53. By contrast, some later oracles elsewhere do label Homer an ἀοιδός: *Or. Sib.* 11.163, Lucian *Alex.* 33.6. Cf. another example of a Delphic oracle on Homer from the Hadrianic period, where Homer is called a Σειρήν: P-W 465.2 = F H 65; for other examples of male poets as Sirens, see Paus. 1.21.1, *Anth. Pal.* 9.184.1.

25. καὶ τότ᾽ ἐν εἰναλίῃ Κύπρῳ μέγας ἔσσετ᾽ ἀοιδός, / ὅν τε Θεμιστὼ τέξει ἐπ᾽ ἀγροῦ / δῖα γυναικῶν / νόσφι πολυκτεάνοιο πολύκλειτον Σαλαμῖνος. / Κύπρον δὲ προλιπὼν διερός θ᾽ ὑπὸ κύμασιν ἀρθείς, / Ἑλλάδος εὐρυχόροιο μοῦνος κακὰ πρῶτος ἀείσας / ἔσσεται ἀθάνατος καὶ ἀγήραος ἤματα πάντα (And then, in sea-girt Cyprus, there will be a great bard, far-famed, to whom Themisto, noblest of women, will give birth in a field far from wealthy Salamis. Leaving Cyprus, wet and tossed by the waves, the first and only to sing of the troubles of Greece with its wide plains, he will be immortal and ageless for all time), Paus. 10.24.3. Pausanias comments that Euclus was one of the few male oracles (10.12.11), and places him before the birth of Homer; on male seers, see Flower 2007 esp. 29–30.

26. Although not a poet-term, note P-W 473.1 = Porph. *Plot.* 22.13 (ἄμβροτα φορμίζειν ἀναβάλλομαι ὕμνον ἀοιδῆς, "I begin to strike up on the lyre an immortal hymn of song"); the voice of the first person is, however, subsequently identified as Apollo's (P-W 473.10).

Rather than making a clear statement about their gendered relationship to poetry—which, in any case is a highly complex one, inspired by the male Apollo, performed by the female oracle, broadcast by the male *prophētai*—the oracle performs her gendered poetry and, through the poetic names she gives (or chooses not to give) to men, obliquely challenges the norms of male poetry. The tradition of male poets' self-naming is indirectly problematized through the denial of terms to the most canonical of poets—in contrast to the male oracle's strategy—while, when the female oracle does hand out male poet-terms, her choice of words both displays and performs her poetic mastery, and inserts *her* poetry into the canon.

Not on His Terms

All this goes to show—from the limited evidence we have—that women poets were very much aware of the words which male authors used to refer to themselves, and the discourse of masculinity that went with them. But this raises as many questions as it answers: because no woman poet (or at least, no extant woman poet) ever seems to use *aoidos, Mousōn therapōn, poiētēs,* or any of the other terms favored by men (and used by women to describe men), *for herself.*[27] Sappho, as we have seen, rejects Hesiod's *Mousaōn therapōn* and rewrites it with a word that may have been her own invention, *mousopolos.* Meanwhile, she uses *aoidos* in the masculine to gesture to the overbearing masculinization of the poetic tradition, as well as—by the very performance of her poetry—to subtly interject herself into that tradition, thereby commenting on and showing up the exclusionary nature of the term. The Delphic oracles take a similar approach, challenging the male-gendering of poets, denying them terms in the same way that women are denied poet-vocabulary, and deploying words for authorship in strategic ways that insert female verse into the male canon.

Following in Sappho's footsteps, women poets across Greek literature reject male poet-terms. No woman poet ever calls herself an *aoidos.* No woman poet writes of herself as a *poiētēs,* or a *poiētria.* No woman poet ever calls herself a *Mousōn therapōn,* or any of the other words we have seen male poets using to

27. For some later imperial examples of women using ἀοιδός (adjectivally) or ἀοίδιμος, see *IK* 89.31–6 = *Anth. Pal.* 15.8, also *SEG* 47.1509; for a fascinating example of the use of ἀοίδιμος as "poet" by a woman for a man, in contrast to φιλόμουσος for herself, see *IGR* 3:958 with Fraser 1984: 279, Hussein and Raffa 2016.

mark out their poetic identity. Nor does she ever use any of the terms which men employ to label women poets, like *mousopoios*. Why?

One of the main reasons, I think, is precisely the success of the strategies of male-gendering traced throughout this book. From the very beginnings of Greek literature, male poets had worked hard to bound and define poetic terms as male, and had left little space within the semantic range of the words, forged and hammered in the discourse of masculinity, to include women. The connection between masculinity, man-making, and male agency which came to be enshrined in the term *poiētēs*, in particular, meant that women could never lay claim to be a *poiētēs*—not simply because it was male-gendered by virtue of its grammar, but also (as Diotima points out in the *Symposium*) because it was tied up in a male discourse of poetic and political agency.

At the same time, just like Diotima, women poets seem to have been very much aware of the fact that their gendered poetic identity was always placed in contrast to that of men (as we saw with the formulation of Sappho as a kind of inferior "female Homer" in chapter 7). Direct evidence of this comes from a fragment of Corinna, the third-century BCE lyric poet from Boeotia, which shows the female poet bluntly commenting on women's relegation to second place after men: "I blame [*memphomē*] clear-sounding [*ligouran*] Myrtis, because—as a woman [*bana*]—she went into competition [*erin*] with Pindar" (fr. 664a *PMG*).[28] In these lines, Corinna poses as a critic of her fellow female poet, Myrtis—a fifth-century BCE lyric poet, also from Boeotia—and suggests that, as a woman (*bana* is the Boeotian for Attic *gunē*), she should not have gone up against the (male) Pindar. Here the noun "woman" becomes not only the sole definer of the woman poet, but her downfall, her one shortcoming. (We might compare Aristotle's quotation of the fourth-century BCE rhetorician and sophist Alcidamas, rival of Isocrates—"the Mytileneans honored Sappho even though she was a woman [*gunaika*]" [Arist. *Rh.* 1398b]—where Sappho is singled out as succeeding in spite of the hindrance of "being

---

28. μέμφομη δὲ κὴ λιγουρὰν / Μουρτίδ᾽ ἰώνγ᾽ ὅτι βανὰ φοῦ- / σ᾽ ἔβα Πινδάροι πὸτ ἔριν, fr. 664a *PMG*. On this fragment see Snyder 1989: 52–53, Clayman 1993, Rayor 1993: 228–29, W. Henderson 1995: 32, Bowman 2004: 20, Collins 2006: 20–21, West 2014a: 333. For a mid-fifth-century BCE date for Corinna, see Bowra 1931, Latte 1956, Davies 1988b, Snyder 1989: 44, Collins 2006: 19–20; for the later date, see Lobel 1930, Page 1953: 65–84, West 1970, West 1990, Clayman 1993, C. Segal 1998: 315–23, Plant 2004: 92; and for further bibliography, see Snyder 1989: 165 n. 14, Henderson 1995 36 n. 4, McPhee 2018: 198 n. 1. On Corinna and her poetry, see Skinner 1983, Snyder 1989: 41–54, Rayor 1993, W. Henderson 1995, Larmour 2005, Collins 2006, Klinck 2008: 152–64, Berman 2010, J. Heath 2013 and 2017, McPhee 2018.

a woman.")[29] This is not, then, necessarily an evocation of a real "contest" between the two poets, or a metaphorical evocation of legendary poetic contests like those between Apollo and Marsyas, or Homer and Hesiod, or even the contest of Helicon and Cithaeron related in Corinna fr. 654a.i *PMG*.[30] Nor should we make the mistake of taking Corinna's critique of Myrtis at face value.[31] Rather, we can read it—given Corinna's pointedly, almost acerbically, gendered description of Myrtis "as a woman"—as a criticism of the gendered status quo, in which women poets are constantly placed in counterpoint, and second place, to men.[32] (There is therefore a certain irony to the fact that a later—male-authored—tradition imagined Corinna defeating Pindar in competition.)[33] By this reading, Corinna is not criticizing or "blaming" (*memphomē*) her fellow female poet. She is, rather, critiquing the system through which women are continually compared to men: by ventriloquizing the male criticism of women poets, she is able to find fault with the kind of negative criticism, focused on their gender, to which women poets are subjected. In this sense, the *eris* between Myrtis and Pindar is not an actual competition, nor is it between those two poets alone: it is the poetic battle of the sexes, where women—including Corinna—are judged, not on their own terms, but in comparison and contrast to men. Interestingly, however, there is a subtle subversion of the implied outcome of Myrtis's battle against Pindar— not only because she is being memorialized in the poetry of another woman poet, but also because it is Myrtis, and not Pindar, who receives an acknowledgment of the quality of her speech (*ligouran*, "clear-sounding").[34] In a

29. Μυτιληναῖοι Σαπφὼ καίπερ γυναῖκα οὖσαν, Arist. *Rh.* 1398b13–14; see Yatromanolakis 2007: 166–67.

30. Snyder 1989: 52–53 notes that ἔρις can mean "strife/quarrel" as well as the specialized sense of "musical contest" (see contra W. Henderson 1995: 32). For further discussion, see Guillon 1958: 53 n. 4, Clayman 1993: 639, Rayor 1993: 229, Collins 2006: 21. The contest of Helicon and Cithaeron at Corinna fr. 654a.i *PMG* has been interpreted as a refraction of Corinna's relationship to Pindar: see Clayman 1993, Larmour 2005.

31. W. Henderson 1995: 32; compare Skinner 1983: 15, Snyder 1989: 53, and see contra Klinck 2008: 152.

32. Clayman 1993: 641, Rayor 1993: 226, Larmour 2005: 40–53; pace Latte 1956: 66–67.

33. Plut. *De glor. Ath.* 4.347f–348a, Paus. 9.22.3, Ael. *VH* 13.25; see Clayman 1993.

34. A "Hellenistic . . . keyword indicating the 'slight' or 'plain' style," as Clayman 1993: 640 notes: see Callim. *Aet.* 1.29, and cf. Corinna's self-description of her λιγουροκωτίλυς (clear-coaxing) voice at fr. 655.5 *PMG* (on which see West 1970: 285, W. Henderson 1995: 31, C. Segal 1998: 317). For an interesting comparison for the use of λιγυρός elsewhere of the female voice, see Hom. *Od.* 12.44, 183 of the Sirens.

sense, then, it is the female poet, and not the male, who ends up winning in Corinna's gendered staging of the battle of the sexes.

A second fragment of Corinna's makes clear the precise connection between the rejection of the male-female contrast, and the shunning of masculine poet-vocabulary in women's choice for the terms of their own self-naming. Tellingly, it is quoted in the same source alongside fr. 664a: "I [tell of] the excellences of heroes [*heirōōn*] and heroines [*cheirōadōn*]" (fr. 664b *PMG*).[35] Corinna describes her subject matter as a poet by setting up a polarity between masculine hero (*hērōs*) and feminine heroine (*hērōis*), using the gendered versions of each of the pair. We might be reminded of Sappho's demonstration of her ability to use feminized versions of masculine nouns with the *therapaina* of Sappho/Alcaeus fr. 23 L-P and the *agroiōtis* of fr. 57 L-P.[36] Both female poets show that they know of, and can use, feminine equivalents of masculine nouns; Corinna even does so in describing her poetic subject matter. And yet they choose not to use feminine equivalents of male terms (*aoidos* in the feminine, *poiētria*, *therapaina*) in naming themselves as poets. Corinna's fr. 664a seems to explain why: women poets don't want to be set against male poets and labeled "as a woman" (*bana phous'*, fr. 664a.2–3 *PMG*).[37] They don't want to be the female-gendered and second-class version of the male equivalent.

So if terms like *aoidos* and *poiētēs* had a problematic history of male-gendering that excluded women, and women poets chose not to use feminized versions of the terms in order to sidestep the inevitable contrast with their male counterparts, what could a woman call herself? What do women poets replace the discourse of the male *aoidos* and the male *poiētēs* with, if not the same words or their feminine equivalents? We have already seen one answer, in Sappho's riposte to Hesiod with her *mousopolos* of fr. 150 L-P. But Sappho's move, to deploy an entirely new word that rewrites the gendered mechanisms of Hesiod's term *Mousaōn therapōn*, is not the only way which women poets choose to describe their own poetic identity. And for that, we need to turn away from the *Mousaōn therapōn*, and back to the *aoidos*—to watch as women

35. ἰώνει δ᾽ εἰρώων ἀρετὰς / χείρωάδων, fr. 664b *PMG*. See Snyder 1984, also Rayor 1993: 222–23, who interprets the use of the first person as evidence of a "woman-identified" approach.

36. See pp. 258–59.

37. See Collins 2006: 20 n. 16 on the translation of φοῦσα.

poets rewrite the gendering of the *aoidos* by using a subtly similar word with an old literary pedigree, that encapsulates both their gender, and their relationship to song, in a new way.

On Her Terms: Birds

The word of choice is the nightingale, *aēdōn*. This is, perhaps, surprising, given how the nightingale fares in Hesiod's *Works and Days* and its tragic fate as an *aoidos*. In the hands of the third-century BCE Hellenistic epigrammatist, Nossis, however, the nightingale is both deftly problematized and reclaimed into female poetics, in a way that shows Nossis—like Sappho—engaging with male poet-terms and replacing them with her own.

Nossis was an important Hellenistic female poet, and, like Sappho, was included in both Meleager's *Garland* and Antipater of Thessalonica's canon of nine female poets.[38] Despite the fact that only twelve of her epigrams survive, they are enough to give us an idea of Nossis's "woman-centered, erotically charged world" and Sapphic poetics.[39] Nossis's third epigram, as we saw in the previous chapter, pays tribute to her mother and grandmother's influence in her literary upbringing and education (reminding us of Sappho's relationship with her daughter), hinting strongly at "an alternative cultural environment set apart, to some degree, from the male-dominated public order."[40] Her poems are, then, a promising site for looking for a statement of female poetic authorship.

---

38. For Meleager's *Garland*, see pp. 165–69; for Antipater of Thessalonica's canon of women poets, see chapter 7, n. 85. The majority of the bibliography on Nossis either focuses on her relationship to Sappho or her "feminine" voice and context: for the former, see Maas 1936, Gow and Page 1965: 2:442, Barnard 1978: 210, Skinner 1989, Skinner 1991, Williamson 1995: 18–20, Bowman 1998, Skinner 2005b: 124–30, Acosta-Hughes 2010: 85–86, de Vos 2014: 412–14, Coughlan 2020: 608–19 (and see further chapter 9, nn. 69 and 70); on the latter, see Skinner 1987, Gutzwiller 1998: 74–88, Snyder 1989: 77–84, Furiani 1991, Skinner 2005b, Cappelletti 2018. On Nossis's Hellenistic context, see Gigante 1974, and on her relation to the epigrammatic genre, Gutzwiller 1997b: 211–22 and 1998: 74–88, Murray and Rowland 2007: 226–29. There is some contention around Nossis's date, see Carugno 1957 for discussion: for the generally accepted Hellenistic date, with a floruit of around 300 BCE, see Maas 1936, Gow and Page 1965: 2:434.

39. Skinner 2005b: 128.

40. Skinner 2005b: 115; on Nossis 3 G-P = *Anth. Pal.* 6.265, see pp. 247–48 with chapter 8, n. 54.

It is in the tenth epigram that we come across the nightingale (10 G-P = *Anth. Pal.* 7.414):[41]

> As you pass by, laugh out loud and say a friendly
> word to me. I am Rhinthon of Syracuse,
> the tiny nightingale-ess [*aēdonis*] of the Muses [*Mousaōn*]—but from
>   our tragic burlesques we plucked our own ivy.

The epigram is spoken in the voice of Rhinthon of Syracuse, a male Hellenistic dramatist who composed "tragic burlesques," imitating an epitaph for the poet where the passerby is addressed and asked to stop beside the tomb.[42] On one level, of course, this can be read as a conventional epitaphic epigram, a tribute (as Oliver Taplin sees it) from Nossis to her fellow poet Rhinthon.[43] The statement "I am Rhinthon" thus acts as the stock epitaphic assertion of identity, where the epitaph appears to speak to the reader in the first person, bringing its subject back to life.[44] If this is the case, we would have to explore why Nossis chooses Rhinthon for this act of homage—rather than one of the better-known, or more canonical, male poets (as with Sappho's interaction with Hesiod). Marilyn Skinner suggests that Nossis sees herself as identifying with Rhinthon, a poet who engaged with a so-called "inferior" form who nevertheless won fame and approval for his work (in the form of the Dionysiac garlands referred to with the "ivy" in lines 3–4). Their shared Hellenistic aesthetic of smallness and purity (hinted at in the adjective "tiny" in line 3), as Skinner points out, is represented in the form of the small, female nightingale: "Nossis 10 is therefore a literary manifesto in which the figure of Rhinthon, the hyperfeminine *aêdonis*, fronts for the author, who tacitly professes her own allegiance to that emerging principle of Hellenistic taste that renounces magnitude and high seriousness in

41. καὶ καπυρὸν γελάσας παραμείβεο, καὶ φίλον εἰπὼν / ῥῆμ᾽ ἐπ᾽ ἐμοί. Ῥίνθων εἴμ᾽ ὁ Συρακόσιος, / Μουσάων ὀλίγη τις ἀηδονίς, ἀλλὰ φλυάκων / ἐκ τραγικῶν ἴδιον κισσὸν ἐδρεψάμεθα, Nossis 10 G-P = *Anth. Pal.* 7.414. On this epigram, see Snyder 1989: 82–83, Gutzwiller 1998: 84–85, Skinner 2005b: 123–24, Tueller 2008: 63–68.

42. On Rhinthon of Syracuse, see Gow and Page 1965: 2:441–42. As Bowman 1998: 40 points out, the conventions of the epigrammatic epitaph were well established by the time of Nossis. See further Lattimore 1962: 230–37, Meyer 2007: 191, Tueller 2008: 65–94, and esp. 63–68 on Nossis, for the motif of epitaphs appealing to passersby.

43. Taplin 1993: 49–50.

44. See Burzachechi 1962, Svenbro 2004: 79–80, Tueller 2008: 16–27.

favor of a deft and playful textual finesse."[45] In a subtle turn, the description of the ivy as "our *own* ivy" (line 4, my emphasis), and the switch from first-person singular to plural ("I am Rhinthon" in line 2 to "we plucked" in line 4) thus serves to bind the two poets together. On the surface, "Rhinthon" appears to claim in the epigram that he achieved recognition from his tragic burlesques; simultaneously, Nossis, by identifying herself with him and by writing an epigram that binds them together, gains her own "garland" from the implication of her work with his.

And yet it is the term *aēdonis*, "nightingale," which suggests that Nossis is doing more than simply paying tribute to Rhinthon by identifying with her fellow poet. Skinner has suggested that, by adding the feminine -*is* suffix to the already grammatically feminine noun *aēdōn* (nightingale) in apposition to Rhinthon's name, Nossis hyperfeminizes an attribute which is allegedly supposed to belong to the male poet Rhinthon. By doing so, Nossis therefore creates a double grammatical female-ness to the noun that "call[s] attention to the female poetic presence behind the male mask."[46] The fact that Nossis is enacting Rhinthon, and that she is hiding/revealing her identity through the performance of her own gender/identity, is further suggested both by her frequent self-naming elsewhere in the surviving corpus of her work (three times within the twelve remaining epigrams), and in her pervasive use of a distinctly "personalized authorial voice"—implying that the reader is meant to be well aware that it is Nossis speaking behind the fictive Rhinthon. As Kathryn Gutzwiller argues, "The voice heard in the epigrams once they have been gathered into a poetry book, far from being the anonymous voice of traditional dedicatory style, now seems to emanate from a single personality."[47] Taking Gutzwiller's argument a step further, Jackie Murray and Jonathan Rowland suggest that the pervasive presence of many masculine-voice epigrams within Nossis's surviving works suggests that this interplay and deconstruction of masculine and feminine voices was a conscious theme in Nossis's work. Describing Nossis's voice as "simultaneously masculine and feminine," they suggest that her "transgendering" of her vocality serves to problematize divisions between masculine/feminine gender and authorship.[48] Nossis is thus not only identifying with Rhinthon in this epigram—she is also *performing* him, in a process

---

45. Skinner 2005b: 124.

46. Skinner 2005b: 124.

47. Gutzwiller 1997b: 219, cf. Snyder 1989: 77.

48. Murray and Rowland 2007: 213.

which thereby calls attention to the performativity of the self, of the gendered voice, and of poetic authorship itself.

And this performance of gendered poetic authorship focuses on the term *aēdonis*, "nightingale," which Nossis—through Rhinthon—uses in the first-person singular: "I am a tiny nightingale-ess of the Muses" (3). We have already seen how, in Hesiod, the nightingale (*aēdōn*) is associated with the figure of the *aoidos* through a connection between the etymologies of the two words and the nightingale's association with song. The figure of the nightingale recurs as a trope for song and poetry in Greek literature—for male poets, as well as female. We see male poets calling themselves students of the nightingale, or even dubbing themselves actual nightingales: the fifth-century BCE epinician poet Bacchylides, contemporary of Pindar, for example, calls himself "the honey-voiced nightingale of Keos" (*Kēias aēdonos*, 3.97–98), while Euripides is labeled "the honey-voiced nightingale" in an epigram ascribed to Ion of Chios (*Anth. Pal.* 7.44.3).[49] Meanwhile, the fifth-century BCE philosopher Democritus saw the nightingale as the inventor of song, and human poets as merely the nightingale's "students."[50] And the word "nightingales" becomes a synonym for "poems" in both a Callimachean epitaph for a fellow poet ("your nightingales live on," Callim. *Epigr.* 2.6), and in an anonymous canon of the nine lyric poets, where Alcman's poetry is called the "female-singing nightingales of Alcman" (*Anth. Pal.* 9.184.9).[51]

And yet it is not enough to see the "nightingale-as-poet" trope as a metaphor for song, plain and simple—for this is to miss the gendered move going on here. The use of *aēdōn* as a synonym for "poet" by some male poets is yet another sign and symptom of the male appropriation of female speech—not only because *aēdōn* is a feminine noun, but also because the nightingale is specifically associated with female speech and song throughout Greek literature.[52] We see this already in Hesiod, with the female nightingale given the

49. Bacchyl. 3.97–98 S-M, *Anth. Pal.* 7.44.3 (the only classical instance of ἀηδών in the masculine); cf. Thgn. 939. On the nightingale as a figure for the (male) poet, see Nagy 1996 esp. 59–60 with 60 n. 2, Hünemörder 2006: 750, Nelson 2019. On the connection between nightingales and poetry, see pp. 58–59 with chapter 2, n. 55.

50. Democritus DK 68 B 154; cf. Alcm. fr. 39 *PMGF* = Ath. 9.930a on poets' imitation of partridges; Chamaeleon fr. 24 Wehrli = Ath. 9.390a.

51. Cf. *Anth. Pal.* 10.92.2–3, and compare Erinna's "my Sirens" at *Anth. Pal.* 7.710.1 = Erinna 1.1 G-P.

52. Another bird associated with female song is the Siren: see Hom. *Od.* 12.184–91 (see chapter 1, n. 56), Alcm. fr. 1.96–97 *PMGF* (see chapter 6, n. 56), Alcm. fr. 30 *PMGF*, Pind. fr. 94b.13 S-M

term *aoidos* and set against the male hawk. In Homer, too, the nightingale is directly connected to female speech. In book 19 of the *Odyssey*, Penelope compares her weeping to the mourning of the nightingale (*aēdōn*, Hom. *Od.* 19.518).[53] In this earliest occurrence of the nightingale in Greek literature, we see the bird being described in a female character's discourse, and used as a metaphor for women's lament. This recurrent association with female song, and specifically, female lament, stems chiefly from the depiction of the nightingale in the myth of Procne.[54] The myth (at least in the Greek version) relates that Procne was turned into a nightingale after her sister, Philomela, was assaulted and mutilated by her husband, Tereus. Though Tereus cut out Philomela's tongue so that she could not tell of the crime he had committed, Philomela relayed the story to her sister by weaving the tale into a tapestry. The two women then killed Itys, Procne's son by Tereus, and were transformed into birds—Procne into a nightingale, and Philomela into a swallow. Procne's tale figured as a trope throughout ancient Greek literature (and beyond), from Homer's *Odyssey* to Aeschylus's *Agamemnon* to Sophocles's lost *Tereus*, as an example of female lament, with the nightingale's song thought to figure as Procne's constant lament for Itys—and of course, as we have seen throughout this book, lament was deeply connected to the female voice as "an art of women."[55] Nicole Loraux traces the trope of the nightingale's connection to female lament through Penelope in the *Odyssey* to the Danaids in Aeschylus's *Suppliant Women*, to Electra, Antigone, and Cassandra, suggesting that the extraordinary generativity of the symbol of the nightingale for women suggests that it is "as if all feminine roles, with the exception of that of a mother, can be explained by referring to the figure of the nightingale."[56]

(on which see Stehle 1997: 96–97), Eur. *Hel.* 169 (on which see Swift 2010: 224–25, Weiss 2018: 145–56), and Erinna 1.1 G-P (on which see chapter 9, n. 51). See also Alcm. fr. 1.87 *PMGF* where the voice of the girls in the *partheneion* compares itself to that of an owl; see Klinck 2001: 276. For comparisons of male poets to Sirens, see chapter 9, n. 24.

    53. See chapter 2, n. 56.

    54. See Loraux 1998: 57–65.

    55. Holst-Warhaft 1992: 1; see further chapter 1, n. 43. For individual passages, see Hom. *Od.* 19.518–23, Aesch. *Ag.* 1142–48, and see P. Oxy. 3013.31–32 for a fragmentary hypothesis of Soph. *Tereus*; cf. also Aesch. *Supp.* 58–71, Soph. *Aj.* 622–34, Ar. *Av.* 737, Eur. *Hel.* 1109–10 (see pp. 181–82), Eur. *Phoen.* 1518 (see chapter 6, n. 49). On the nightingale and lament, see Nelson 2019, Loraux 1998: 57–65; on the nightingale in tragedy, see Weiss 2017: 253–63, and in Euripides in particular, Weiss 2018: 158–67.

    56. Loraux 1998: 60.

And one of those roles is the role of poet. The connection between female nightingale and female poet, between *aēdōn* and *aoidos* in the feminine, is already one that is made by male authors. Hesiod's *aēdōn* becomes a feminine *aoidos* through the interlinked etymology between the two words at *Works and Days* 208.[57] Unsurprisingly, Euripides—who we saw in chapter 6 exploring the feminization of *aoidos*—picks up on this to make a similar move in his *Helen*, where the (female) chorus calls on the "most-singing nightingale" (*aoidotatan... aēdona*) to help them sing the woes of Helen and the Trojan women (Eur. *Hel.* 1109–10).[58] In the *Helen*, in the voice of women (as with Penelope in the *Odyssey*), the nightingale is called on to aid the female lament—and, through the adjective *aoidotatē*, the bird is connected directly to the bard, linking *aēdōn* and *aoidos* once again. By turning *aoidos* explicitly into an adjective, and placing it in the superlative, Euripides enables the two-termination adjective to gain a feminine ending, thus generating an interesting feminine equivalent for *aoidos* that draws out the femininity of the nightingale, the female chorus, and the female subjects of their song. Similarly, Theocritus, following Euripides, calls the nightingale "most-singing" (*aoidotatē*, Theoc. *Id.* 12.7), again associating *aēdōn* with *aoidos*.[59] This association between the nightingale and women's speech extends even to male poets—so that we see Alcman's poems, in the epigram from *Anth. Pal.* 9.184, described as his "female-singing nightingales" (*thēlumeleis... aēdones*, line 9). Alcman's subject matter as a writer of *partheneia* means that his poetry, by association, is turned into explicitly female-gendered, "female-singing" nightingales.[60] Indeed, this emphasis on the femininity of the nightingale and its association with female lament means that, in spite of the proliferation of the nightingale as a poetic image for lament and its connection with poetry (as in Democritus), it is only used twice for a male poet (Bacchylides and Euripides, as we saw above)—and, for Euripides at least, given his fame as a dramatist of women, there may well have been a female-gendered component to the term.

57. See pp. 57–61.

58. See pp. 181–82.

59. ὅσσον ἀηδών / συμπάντων λιγύφωνος ἀοιδοτάτη πετεηνῶν (as the nightingale is the most songful and clear-voiced of all birds), Theoc. *Id.* 12.6–7.

60. And note the avian references to the female performers of the *partheneion* as Sirens and owls in Alcm. fr. 1.87 and 1.96 *PMGF*, esp. with the adjective ἀοιδοτέρα at 1.97: see chapter 9, n. 52.

The conclusion drawn by male poets, however, is not the one we might anticipate—that is, an association between female nightingale and female poets. The connections between the nightingale and female song are most often indirect, related to the feminine speech genre of lament, rather than women's poetry. In fact, a woman poet is only ever once called an *aēdōn* by a man, in the early third-century BCE poet Hermesianax's description of Sappho—and there it is in pointed contrast to the application of *aoidos* to a male poet, Alcaeus.[61] The passage in question comes from a fragment of an elegiac poem in which poets' love interests are being catalogued: "The bard [*aoidos*] loved the nightingale [*aēdonos*], and caused / the man [*andra*] of Teos pain by the eloquence of his songs" (Hermesianax fr. 7.49–50 Powell).[62] Following a tradition of linking Sappho erotically to male poets—and thereby "heteroeroticizing" her—Sappho is imagined in a love triangle with Alcaeus (the "bard," 49) and Anacreon (the "man of Teos," 50).[63] While Alcaeus is called an *aoidos*, Sappho, however, is described as an *aēdōn*, a nightingale (49). The two words are juxtaposed in Greek (*aoidos aēdonos*, 49), bringing out the phonetic and etymological similarities between them—as well as their differences. Alcaeus receives a poet-term with a long pedigree; Sappho, meanwhile, is hidden behind the metaphor of the nightingale (with the feminine noun, and the nightingale's association with song, acting as a proxy for the idea of a "singing woman"), so that Hermesianax can allude to Sappho's association with song without actually attributing her a poet-identity. Moreover, the juxtaposition of *aoidos aēdonos* cannot fail to evoke the description of the nightingale as *aoidos* in Hesiod's *Works and Days*, and the failed outcome of the nightingale's attempt to challenge the male hawk. Paralleling the two words thus demonstrates how Hermesianax both denies Sappho the term *aoidos*, and turns her into a nightingale destined to be silenced by the male voice like Hesiod's singer-bird.

It is up to women poets to take the indirect association between the nightingale and female speech and male poets' appropriation of the nightingale

---

61. For a second-century CE epigraphic example of a woman as a "nightingale of the Muses," see conclusion, n. 2. For Erinna as a swan, see *Anth. Pal.* 7.713 = Antipater of Sidon 58 G-P.

62. ὁ δ' ἀοιδὸς ἀηδόνος ἠράσαθ', ὕμνων / Τήϊον ἀλγύνων ἄνδρα πολυφραδίῃ, Hermesianax fr. 7.49–50 Powell = Ath. 13.597b–599b. On the textual difficulties, see J. U. Powell 1925: 102, Yatromanolakis 2007: 348 n. 277. The quotation comes from the third book of Hermesianax's *Leontion*: see Caspers 2006, Yatromanolakis 2007: 348–51, Boyd 2017: 183–86.

63. Cf. Diphilus fr. 71 K-A; see Kivilo 2010: 190, also Gilhuly 2018: 103–5 on the "metaliterary heteroerotics" of this fragment.

trope, and to redirect it, reclaim it, as a word that could signify a "female poet" in a new sense of the word. And this is precisely what Nossis does in her tenth epigram. Nossis is not only calling on a motif that is associated with poetry and song; she is utilizing one that is specifically connected to women's song and women's roles in the articulation and delineation of her authorship— while simultaneously reclaiming it from male authors who tried to appropriate the term, and turning it into "her own" (*idion*, Nossis 10.4 G-P) positive image of female authorship. The etymology of *aēdōn* and its connection to *aoidos*— made explicit from Hesiod to Euripides to Theocritus to Hermesianax— means that Nossis is laying claim to a different, yet highly charged, word for poetic authorship with a strong literary pedigree, that nevertheless has associations with female song. Just like Sappho, Nossis responds to and exploits the gendered poet-vocabulary of male poets to generate a new vocabulary for female poets. And, like Sappho, Hesiod is a big player here, both with the connection between *aēdon-aoidos* in *Works and Days*, and with Nossis's identification of the nightingale as "of the Muses" (*Mousaōn*, 3), which recalls Hesiod's *Mousaōn therapōn* from the *Theogony*. Nossis's new poet-term thus fuses Hesiod's two major gendered terms for the male poet—*Mousaōn therapōn* and *aoidos*—and creates a new poet-term for women poets by playing off Hesiod's only female poet, the silenced nightingale. She thereby generates a double chain of reception—not only placing herself as Hesiod's successor and replacing his poet-terms with her own, but also copying the strategies of Sappho to demonstrate a lineage of women's receptions and recreations of male poet-terms to create a space for female voices, and the tactics of rewriting the masculinized past which that involves.[64]

Yet there is even more to unpack here—because Nossis does not simply use the word *aēdōn*: she adds a feminine suffix, -*is*, to the already feminine word, to make the hyperfeminine *aēdonis*, "nightingale-ess" (3).[65] The etymology of *aēdōn*, from *aeidō*, and its history of associations with *aoidos*, means that it can already be translated as "female singer."[66] By a similar logic, the hyperfeminized noun *aēdonis* might be seen as equivalent here to something

64. For Nossis's "substitution of Sappho for Hesiod as her primary archaic model," see Gutzwiller 1997b: 213, 1998: 76.

65. Cf. [Eur.] *Rhes.* 548–50, ὑμνεῖ . . . / μελοποιὸν ἀηδονὶς μέριμναν (the female nightingale sings her song-making lament).

66. LSJ s.v. give the gendered "songstress."

like "female poetess." The line in the epigram of Nossis thus might be better translated as: "I am Rhinthon of Syracuse, a female poetess of the Muses." This is not only an additional drawing out of the paradox enshrined in the contrast between the hyperfemininity of the suffix of *aēdonis* and Rhinthon's masculinity, ventriloquized by Nossis. It also, at another level, draws attention to Nossis's poetic mask, emphasizing the femininity of the female poet behind the "male" statement. Simultaneously, the tragic resonances of the nightingale suggest that Nossis here, in her performance of Rhinthon, is engaging in her own tragic farce (as we saw above in her appropriation of the "own ivy"), appropriating Rhinthon's area of expertise as a writer of tragic farces—in the same way that male poets across Greek literature had appropriated women for their own ends.[67] Nossis thus both invokes "traditional" male assumptions about female song as expressed in lament through the figure of the nightingale, performing them beneath the mask of the male voice, while simultaneously replacing it with her own hyperfeminized vision of female gender and its relationship, both to the Muses, and to authorship as a whole. Even more importantly, she hints at a potential lexicon for female authorship that is both cognate with the masculine *aoidos* and which comments on the deep association between nightingale imagery and female speech.

The new gendered poetics represented by Nossis's hyperfeminine nightingale is heightened by its explicit connection to the Muses as a "nightingale of the Muses" (*Mousaōn . . . aēdonis*, 3).[68] The addition of *Mousaōn* as a qualifier for the nightingale not only resonates with Hesiod's *Mousaōn therapōn*—it also links in to Sappho's recreation of the relationship between female poet and female Muse in her new term for her poetic authorship, *mousopolos*. This connection between Nossis's poet-term and that of Sappho, through the Muses, is made explicit in Nossis's epigram 11, where the poet explicitly instructs a stranger visiting Sappho's Mytilene to introduce Nossis as a woman who is

---

67. There is even further significance in the fact that Nossis has chosen to write in elegiac couplets, which are never used in tragedy, suggesting the appropriation of Rhinthon into her own voice; while the nightingale is programmatically associated with elegy (see Monella 2005, Nelson 2019). The nightingale thus also becomes a sign of Nossis's own generic/gender-transformative power. See Murray and Rowland 2007: 226–29 for Nossis's "transgendered poetics."

68. The phrase appears in only one other instance in Greek literature, in a fragment of Euripides's *Palamedes* quoted at Diog. Laert. 2.44.5 = Eur. fr. 588 *TrGF* (see Wright 2018: 194), though note the second-century CE inscription at *IGUR* III.1342.1–2: see conclusion, n. 2.

"dear to the Muses" (*Mousaisi philan*, 11.3 G-P = *Anth. Pal.* 7.718).[69] Here—in an epigram that is notable as both the earliest surviving epigrammatic treatment of Sappho, and also the only instance in extant literature up to the end of the Hellenistic period that Sappho is mentioned by a woman—Nossis identifies herself to Sappho through the Muses, using the female gods of poetry as her ticket of introduction to her fellow female poet, and demonstrating explicitly that she sees their relationship to the Muses as a common denominator between the two women poets.[70] This, then, seals the link between Nossis's *Mousaōn aēdonis* and Sappho's *mousopolos*: both rewriting male canonical poet-terms, both reframing the relationship between women poets and the Muses, in very different ways. In so doing, Nossis forges a lineage of women poets who use the Muses to self-define their gendered identity as poets.

Nossis's *aēdonis*, with its overt female gendering, its referentiality to male figurations of female speech genres, its lineage to Sappho through the strategies of rewriting male terms and reconnecting to the Muses, and its linguistic and literary connection to *aoidos*, thus has the potential for interpretation as "female poet" in a sense equivalent to the terms used for male poetic authorship. In Nossis's epigram, however, the term is wrapped in layers of irony in a "now you see it, now you don't" play of metaphor, image, and performed identity in which female authorship is both hinted at and hidden under the rich interpretative mask of the nightingale. We see Nossis, on the one hand, playing up the hyperfeminized nightingale while, at the same time, subtly and at a deeper level laying claim to a connection between song, the Muses, and poetic authorship that rivals even that of the male poets. Thus Nossis beats Rhinthon at his own game, turning an epitaph for the male poet into an enunciation of her own poetic ability and aims. The "tiny nightingale-ess of the Muses" becomes a

---

69. ὦ ξεῖν᾽, εἰ τύ γε πλεῖς ποτὶ καλλίχορον Μυτιλάναν / τὰν Σαπφοῦς χαρίτων ἄνθος ἐναυσόμενος / εἰπεῖν ὡς Μούσαισι φίλαν τήνᾳ τε Λόκρισσα / τίκτεν· ἴσαις δ᾽ ὅτι μοι τοὔνομα Νοσσίς, ἴθι (If you, stranger, are sailing to Mitylene where dances are lovely in order to borrow the flower of Sappho's graces, announce that a Locrian woman bore one dear to the Muses and to her. You should know that my name is Nossis. Now go. [tr. Gutzwiller]), Nossis 11 G-P = *Anth. Pal.* 7.718. The text of lines 3–4 follows Gallavotti 1971: 243, 245–46; see Gutzwiller 1998: 85 n. 96, Acosta-Hughes 2010: 85 n. 82, both of whom follow Gallavotti. For discussion of this epigram, see Cazzaniga 1970, Gallavotti 1971, Barbantani 1993: 30–31, Bowman 1998, Gutzwiller 1998: 85–86, Skinner 2005b: 126–27, Acosta-Hughes 2010: 85–86, de Vos 2014: 413–14, Licciardello 2016, Coughlan 2020: 612–16.

70. See Gutzwiller 1998: 86, Bowman 1998: 40–42. On Nossis's reception of Sappho, see chapter 9, n. 38; on Sappho as Nossis's poetic "mother," see chapter 8, n. 58.

symbol for Nossis herself: slighted as small by male poets but easily capable of singing her own tune; silenced by the male voice, but capable of transformation through performance into female-gendered speech; connected through her gender to other female poets, all struggling to define their identity in words; and just as good as the male dramatists at making a tragic pun or two.

Coda: A Line of Birds?

Nossis's nightingale is not, however, alone. We find the nightingale again in an epigram by another female poet, Anyte, a contemporary of Nossis.[71] The context is suggestively metapoetic: Anyte describes a girl, named Myro, lamenting the death of her pets—a grasshopper, which is called "the nightingale [*aēdoni*] of the fields" (line 1), and a cicada (Anyte 20 G-P = *Anth. Pal.* 7.190).[72] Marilyn Skinner reads the depiction of Myro, a girl with singing pets, as a masked allusion to Anyte's fellow female poet, Moero (whose name was given as both Moero and Myro in antiquity).[73] The metapoetic undertones are, indeed, hard to miss: the association of both animals with song (and thus, poetry); the grasshopper's identification as a "nightingale" (with all the history of its association with poets which that evokes); the literary allusions of the reference to the cicada as "oak-dwelling," which recalls both Homer and Hesiod's evocations of cicadas "sitting in trees"; the echo of Erinna's reproach to Hades ("you are envious, Hades," Erinna 2.3 G-P = *Anth. Pal.* 7.712.3) in the closing line of the epigram, where Hades is called "hard to persuade."[74] Although "Myro" is not identified as a singer or nightingale, her association with songster-pets and

71. For Anyte's date, see Gow and Page 1965: 2:89–90, Page 1975: x, Gutzwiller 1998: 54 n. 22. On Anyte, see Geoghegan 1979, Barnard 1991, Gutzwiller 1993, Gutzwiller 1998: 54–74, Greene 2000, Skinner 2001: 209–10, Murray and Rowland 2007: 229–32.

72. ἀκρίδι τᾷ κατ᾽ ἄρουραν ἀηδόνι, καὶ δρυοκοίτᾳ / τέττιγι ξυνὸν τύμβον ἔτευξε Μυρώ / παρθένιον στάξασα κόρα δάκρυ, δισσὰ γὰρ αὐτᾶς / παίγνι᾽ ὁ δυσπειθὴς ᾤχετ᾽ ἔχων Ἀίδας (The girl Myro made a joint tomb for her grasshopper, the nightingale of the fields, and her oak-dwelling cicada, shedding a little-girl tear; for Hades, hard to persuade, took away her two pets), Anyte 20 G-P = *Anth. Pal.* 7.190. The epigram is ascribed to both Anyte and Leonidas of Tarentum in the *Anthology*, but is usually attributed to Anyte, see Gow and Page 1965: 2:101.

73. Skinner 2005c: 104–5, following Baale 1903: 35–39. For the different spellings of Moero's name, see Gow and Page 1965: 2:413–14, Plant 2004: 61, Gutzwiller 2017b: 405.

74. On the song of the grasshopper and cicada, see Gutzwiller 1998: 66 n. 55, Skinner 2005c: 105. For the allusions to Homer and Hesiod, see Hom. *Il.* 3.152, Hes. *Op.* 583. Gutzwiller 1998: 66 with n. 53 suggests that the entire epigram may have been based on a lost poem by Erinna.

the multiple literary allusions to both male and female poetic traditions suggest, as Skinner points out, a literary undertone to the epigram, and invite a reading of "Myro" as a (masked) depiction of the female poet Moero here. At the same time, I would add that the addition of the image of the nightingale, *aēdōn*, and its association with women's voices, lament, and poetry, builds further on the metapoetic vocabulary to hint at a connection between "Myro"/ Moero and her identity as a feminine *aēdōn/aoidos*. There seems to be an implicit awareness of the female-gendering of the term *aēdōn* here: it is associated with the grammatically feminine of the two pets, the *akris*, rather than the masculine *tettix* which—given its literary pedigree in Homer and Hesiod—we might expect to be associated instead with the poetically resonant *aēdōn*. We might even see an echo of Nossis's use of *aēdonis*—a similar kind of masking and unmasking of the female poet in the resonant use of *aēdōn* to hint at her relationship to song, figurations of the female voice, and the discourse around the *aoidos*.

Yet this invites an important question, which forms something of a coda to this part of the book's broad survey of women's poetic identity, taking in, as it has, different women poets and different literary contexts from Sappho to Nossis, from archaic performance contexts to Hellenistic literary epigram. The question is this: Are we to read these female poets responding to each other in their use of poet-related vocabulary—and, if so, to what extent are we to understand this as a "women's tradition" of poetry? Early feminist readings of women poets took a literal, and exclusionary, view toward a female tradition of poetry in the ancient world. As we saw in the last chapter, Marilyn Skinner goes perhaps the furthest to posit a segregated oral tradition of women's songs, performed by and among women, which occasionally manifests itself in intertextual citations between female poets in the surviving textual tradition, but which existed largely on the margins.[75] This conceptualization of a "women's tradition" became a part of the critical mainstream, and led to a frequent—but unexamined, in terms of the models of transmission, the self-positioning and performance of the gendered voice, or the types of gendered engagement with male poets—labeling of the "women's tradition" of poetry.[76] Recent work has cautioned against the pitfalls of this kind of generalization of women's poetry, in favor of acknowledging women poets'

75. See p. 147 with chapter 8, n. 52.

76. Such that Snyder 1989: 152–56 identifies a separation of women poets in terms of their genres, themes, and style; cf. Barnard 1978: 204, Hallett 1979: 460, Skinner 1983: 13 (on Sappho),

text-based engagement with the male literary tradition, exploring the adoption of transgendered voices and "masculine"-gendered stances by female poets, and emphasizing the importance of acknowledging the hands of men in the construction of the "female" tradition.[77] Like these recent critics, I think it is not only incorrect to suggest that the concept of a "women's tradition" should be seen in the exclusive sense of being defined (or limited) by female gender to "write like a woman," or to posit, on the basis of the surviving evidence, a segregated community of women performing what are seen as "feminine" themes, subjects, and styles—it also misrepresents the gendered dynamics in the surviving text-based tradition.

The examination of poet-terms in the preceding chapters instead gives us a new way into this question. As always, it is a case of the extant evidence, and Mieke de Vos is right to remind us that the texts we have were likely curated by men in order to privilege (male-perceived) "feminine" modes of expression—while Laurel Bowman cautions that "the likely existence of an internal tradition of song in the women's subculture . . . does not mean that the surviving female-authored poems are examples of such a tradition."[78] Given the evidence available, however, and acknowledging that what we are dealing with is a troubled, text-based, transmitted tradition, it is at the very least suggestive that in the instances in which we do find poet-terms among female poets, we do not find them simply attempting to imitate men—calling themselves *aoidos* or *poiētēs*—but coming up with a new vocabulary that is, nevertheless, deeply embedded in male histories of talking about poets and poetry, like the nightingale. In engagement with her fellow female poet Moero, Anyte brings in the image of the nightingale, not only potentially conversing with Nossis's own figuration of the female nightingale as a mask for her identity as a poet, but also responding to centuries of male-generated images of gendered song from Homer to Hesiod to the tragedians.[79] In other words, in calling on the nightingale, she is crossing between gendered figures of speech, and gendered mechanisms of literary allusion. Nossis's figuration of the nightingale as "of the Muses," meanwhile, as we have seen,

---

Skinner 1989: 11 n. 15, Rayor 1993 (on Corinna), Gutzwiller 1997b: 203 (citing Skinner 1993) and 220, Gutzwiller 1998: 86 (on Nossis as part of a female tradition).

77. Bowman 2004, Murray and Rowland 2007, de Vos 2014.

78. Bowman 2004: 3.

79. Similarly, Greene 2000 argues for a balance between "masculine" and "feminine" influences and concerns in Anyte's epigrams, in opposition to the standard reading of her poetry as traditionally "masculine" (e.g., Wilamowitz-Moellendorf 1924: 1:136).

responds to both Hesiod's *Mousaōn therapōn* and Sappho's feminine-encoded *mousopolos*; and Sappho's *mousopolos* is, in turn a rejoinder to Hesiod's *Mousaōn therapōn*. Women poets, then, both look to each other—as we find Corinna looking back to Myrtis, Anyte to Moero, Nossis to Erinna, or Nossis to Sappho—and write against men (as Sappho and Nossis write against Hesiod; Corinna sets Myrtis against Pindar; Nossis performs against Rhinthon) in their generation of and commentary upon poet-terms. And the words they come up with to define themselves have a deeply rooted history in male-gendered poet-terminology—*mousopolos* and *Mousaōn therapōn*; *aēdonis* and *aoidos*—at the same time as they rewrite the story of gendered poetry to allow for the inclusion of women poets.

The subtle, coded ways in which women poets engage with poet-terms, then, gives us a new approach to the question of whether we can read a "female tradition" of poetry, and pinpoints the issue with reading a "feminine-only" poetics. The problem with the phrase "female tradition" is that it suggests something apart, different, segregated. What we find, in fact, when we look at women's manipulation of poet-terms on the ground, is a conscious, complex, and informed engagement with the tradition of male-authored poetry and poet-terms like *aoidos* and *Mousaōn therapōn*, alongside the generation of images and words which attempt to encapsulate what it means to be a woman poet. Women poets are deeply embedded in—not apart from—the poetic tradition in which they participate.[80] It is precisely a feature, then, of the "anxiety of authorship" experienced by women writers—the lack of poet-terms for women, the lack of space for women within the male-authored canon—that women poets undergo a double-coded approach to generating their gendered poetic identity in order to make space for themselves within the tradition: both engaging with male terms, and then subverting and rewriting them to perform and birth their own identity as gendered poets.[81] When we think of women poets as a "line of birds"—one nightingale, like Anyte's, responding to another, like Nossis's—we inevitably hear "bards," too. And we are meant to: it is part of these women poet's bid for inclusion and engagement with the male tradition that they demonstrate their ability to rewrite male terms, at the same time as they perform their own gendered identity. Where male poets set

80. Cf. Bowman 2004: 23.
81. See Winkler 1990: 162–87 on Sappho's "double consciousness." On the "anxiety of authorship" experienced by women writers, see p. 233 with chapter 8, n. 9, and cf. Gutzwiller 1997b: 220 who identifies "anxiety of authorship" in Nossis's relationship to men's depictions of Erinna.

women in contrast to men, then, women poets deliberately engage with the preexisting gendered canon, and gendered norms of "being a (male) poet"—to create their own tradition and lineage that could hold up to (and counteract) male norms of poetic identity.

In the absence of norms of female authorship and words to describe the woman poet, then, we begin to see what really matters for female poets as they struggle to come up with a language that defines their literary projects and gendered identities. We see them utilizing language as a subversive mask for female self-definition, performing the role of the male poet or the dutiful mother while simultaneously outlining and defining their poetic projects. We see them weaving subtle connections between the figures of the Muses, motherhood, and creativity, emphasizing proximity to the Muses as the special province of the female *mousopoloi*, associating motherhood with Memory, and connecting female poetry through the nightingale's lament to the female gods of song. We gain a privileged insight into their response to the male-centric authorial models established by Homer and Hesiod; we see how they juggle the expectations of a society that saw motherhood as a woman's sole purpose with their desire to produce literature; and we watch as they adopt the mask of a male poet to explore the connection between gender, authorship, and voice. More than anything, it is through relationship—to each other and their poetic communities, their families, their roles in society, and their male counterparts—and in the performative, processual enacting of the self, as women and as poets, that these female poets define and construct their understanding of their poetic authorship, not simply through the descriptive force of what they do. It is a language of intertext that they create, in which the words used to define the "poet" become a battleground in which to challenge assumptions about gender and its relationship to poetry. Being a female poet thus becomes a shared experience—a process of engagement, self-construction, and continuous interrelationship and change, where the terms for women poets are as varied, and as distinctive, as the women who created them.

CONCLUSION

Beyond Words

THIS BOOK began with a simple question: What did Sappho call herself? In a world where the poet was gendered male through the shaping of language, society, and culture, in a language where the very word for poet was embedded in masculinity, and no terms existed to identify a woman who was also a poet—what language did Sappho use to describe herself, to understand her gendered identity, and to articulate what she did? Given the inescapable reality that women were far less likely than men to achieve the status of "poet," the words available for the description of literary identity unavoidably came to reflect the cultural status quo, and shifted to emphasize and construct male authoriality. And yet, this book has argued, it is precisely this linguistic-cultural atmosphere which makes the study of what women and men poets in the ancient world called themselves such a fertile site of recovery. It is what allows us, in other words, to trace the story of the invention of the gendered poet. In the absence of a predefined vocabulary for female authorship, we are able to watch the process by which female poets envisioned their engagement with notions of literary production and gender, and their construction of a vocabulary for and between themselves. In the face of a lack of words to describe their female counterparts, we can observe male poets wrestling with ways to talk about, neutralize, and come to terms with women's identity as poets. And on the gendered battleground of literary production, where women's mimetic creativity and powerful voices acted in counterpoint to male poets, we can watch as men constructed an artifice of the inevitability of the masculinity of poetry from the very beginning.

This is an artifice that has been only too successful. It has led to the masculinity of poetic authorship, and the story around the gendering of Greek literature, going unchallenged—as if the word "poet" (*aoidos, poiētēs*) did not always carry with it a rich and complex tale of gender circumscription, navigation,

286

creation. As a direct result of these strategies of male-gendering, the masculine gender of the poet has become so (dangerously) normal as to be invisible. And yet, as this book has demonstrated, there is a long history to the masculiniza-tion of the poet, a concerted effort to make the poet male that has made the equation of "man" and "poet" look effortless. It is a history that we cannot af-ford to ignore, since these gendered strategies, as this book has attempted to show, underpin the story of Greek literature. At the same time, in direct con-nection to these strategies of male-gendering, we have seen women respond-ing by rewriting their position in the gendered poetic tradition, engaging with the language of men and creating their own supple, fertile terms through the generative fields of new kinds of metaphors and relationships, new connec-tions to the Muse, knowing intertexts with their male counterparts, and ambi-tious, subversive female song.

What emerges, then, is a new literary history that takes gender as its starting point, and rewrites the traditional story of the poet as a concerted strategy of masculinization, a silencing and appropriation of the female, and women's verbal challenges in response. Throughout, I have attempted to argue that we cannot afford to ignore the gendering of Greek poetry. Words do not just come into being. We cannot afford to look at words like "poet"—both then and now—and be blind to the history of the gender contest that they represent. The works of literature that have been handed down to us are the product of a conscious system of gender construction and enforcement, and a resistance to those systems of gender, which were key to the development of Greek lit-erature. And understanding that gives us the key to reading old texts in pro-vocative new ways. As Adrienne Rich's epigraph to this book argues, this kind of work is an essential springboard, not just for our understanding of ancient literature, but for our deeper appreciation of how language conditions—and can set free—the ways in which we see and talk about ourselves. "A radical critique of literature, feminist in its impulse, would take the work first of all as a clue to how we live, how we have been living, how we have been led to imag-ine ourselves, how our language has trapped as well as liberated us, how the very act of naming has been till now a male prerogative, and how we can begin to see and name—and therefore live—afresh."[1]

This acknowledgment has a profound effect on our understanding of the ancient canon of male authors, the precedent it set for later times, and our relationship to it. It did not have to be that way. Men consciously chose to

1. Rich [1971] 1979: 35.

frame a relationship between their gender identity and their identity as poets, and the words they chose to do so set up a boundary which excluded anyone "other" from the circle—not just on the grounds of gender, which has been the focus of this book, but also race, ethnicity, and enslavement. (There would be scope for many more books on these topics.) The strategies of masculinization that have been identified in each chapter, structure—and were intended to structure—the ways in which we read Greek literature: from the exploration of the masculinity of the bard against the challenge of women's voices in Homer, to the abstraction of the Muses into personifications in Hesiod, to the appropriation of the female voice and body in the *Homeric Hymns*, the embodiment of the ideal man-poet in Aristophanes, and the censorship of women's voices in Plato to ensure the correct kind of male poet in the city-state. Similar gendered strategies were deployed in the search for words for women poets—from Euripides's exploration of the othering of female attempts to become singers like men, to the built-in contrast between male and female poets relegating women to second place. At the same time, women poets engaged in their own strategies of gendered naming, rewriting the canon of male literature by refiguring the terms and relationships of male poetry, performing a male-gendered voice as a way to demonstrate the subversive mask of their feminine poetics, and birthing a new tradition of women's poetry through the interconnection of women's gender, generativity, and poetic identity in motherhood.

But the story does not end here. The gendering of poet-terms goes on into the imperial period and beyond; it continues to be an area of both contention and of rich engagement and generation of new vocabularies. It can be traced in Latin literature as well as Greek—and even, in some cases, in the intersection between the two.[2] And it continues to be an issue today. I have chosen throughout the book to call women "poets"—not "poetesses"—as a conscious approach, in my own particular linguistic and cultural context, toward gender neutrality in my own words, to acknowledge the equal claim of men and women to be poets and writers, irrespective of their gender. In choosing to do

---

2. For a suggestive example, see the bilingual funerary inscription from the second century CE commemorating Aucta, which labels her, in Greek (but not Latin), as τὴν Μουσέων χαρίεσσαν ἀηδόνα, τὴν μελίγηρυν / Αὔκταν (honey-voiced Aucta, the graceful nightingale of the Muses), *IGUR* III.1342.1–2; there may also be a hint of a bilingual pun on Aucta's name, with Latin *auctor*. On this inscription, see Hutchinson 2013: 320. On the phrase "nightingale of the Muses," cf. Nossis 10.3 G-P and see pp. 271–81 with chapter 9, n. 68.

so, this book has been actively participating in the debate around gender and naming that has its roots in the epics of Homer and the lyrics of Sappho, that is performed in the dramas of Aristophanes and discussed in the philosophy of Plato. This is not, then, just a case of reading ancient texts in a kind of philological vacuum, separate from modern practices: the modern practice informs the reading of the ancient texts, and the ancient texts make us ask questions about how we practice gendered naming today. It is, I hope, just the start of the conversation about the importance of the words we use for ourselves, and for each other—to interrogate our past, and rewrite our future.

REFERENCES

Académie française. 2019. "La féminisation des noms de métiers et de fonctions." March 1, 2019. https://www.academie-francaise.fr/actualites/la-feminisation-des-noms-de-metiers-et-de-fonctions.

Acosta-Hughes, Benjamin. 2010. *Arion's Lyre: Archaic Lyric into Hellenistic Poetry*. Princeton NJ: Princeton University Press.

Acosta-Hughes, Benjamin, and Silvia Barbantani. 2007. "Inscribing Lyric." In *Brill's Companion to Hellenistic Epigram*, ed. P. Bing and J. S. Bruss, pp. 429–57. Leiden: Brill.

Ademollo, Francesco. 2011. *The Cratylus of Plato: A Commentary*. Cambridge: Cambridge University Press.

Alexiou, Margaret. 2002. *The Ritual Lament in Greek Tradition*. 2nd ed. Oxford: Rowman and Littlefield.

Alford, Richard D. 1987. *Naming and Identity: A Cross-Cultural Study of Personal Naming Practices*. New Haven CT: Yale University Press.

Allan, William. 2002. *Euripides: Medea*. London: Duckworth.

———, ed. 2008. *Euripides: Helen*. Cambridge: Cambridge University Press.

Allen, Christine Garside. 1975. "Plato on Women." *Feminist Studies* 2 (2/3): 131–38.

Aloni, Antonio. 1989. *L'aedo e i tiranni: Ricerche sull'inno Omerico a Apollo*. Rome: Ateneo.

———, ed. 1997. *Saffo: Frammenti*. Florence: Giunti.

Anderson, John M. 2007. *The Grammar of Names*. Oxford: Oxford University Press.

Aneziri, Sophia. 2020. "Artists of Dionysus: The First Professional Associations in the Ancient Greek World." In *Skilled Labour and Professionalism in Ancient Greece and Rome*, ed. E. Stewart, E. Harris and D. Lewis, pp. 293–312. Cambridge: Cambridge University Press.

Annas, Julia. 1976. "Plato's *Republic* and Feminism." *Philosophy* 51: 307–21.

Arafat, Karim. 2016. "Pausanias and Homer." In *Homeric Receptions across Generic and Cultural Contexts*, ed. A. Efstathiou and I. Karamanou, pp. 205–14. Berlin: de Gruyter.

Argentieri, Lorenzo. 2003. *Gli epigrammi degli Antipatri*. Bari: Levante.

Arnold, John H., and Sean Brady, eds. 2011. *What Is Masculinity? Historical Dynamics from Antiquity to the Contemporary World*. Basingstoke: Palgrave Macmillan.

Arnott, William G., ed. 1996. *Alexis: The Fragments*. Cambridge: Cambridge University Press.

———. 2007. *Birds in the Ancient World from A to Z*. London, New York: Routledge.

Arthur, Marilyn B. 1980. "The Tortoise and the Mirror: Erinna PSI 1090." *The Classical World* 74 (2): 53–65.

———. 1981. "The Divided World of *Iliad* VI." *Women's Studies* 8 (1/2): 21–46.

Arthur, Marilyn B. 1983. "The Dream of a World without Women: Poetics and the Circles of Order in the *Theogony* Prooemium." *Arethusa* 16 (1/2): 97–116.

Asmis, Elizabeth. 1992. "Plato on Poetic Creativity." In *The Cambridge Companion to Plato*, ed. R. Kraut, pp. 338–64. Cambridge: Cambridge University Press.

Assaël, Jacqueline. 1985. "Misogynie et féminisme chez Aristophane et chez Euripide." *Pallas* 32: 91–103.

Athanassaki, Lucia. 2009. "Narratology, Deixis, and the Performance of Choral Lyric: On Pindar's *First Pythian Ode*." In *Narratology and Interpretation: The Content of Narrative Form in Ancient Literature*, ed. J. Grethlein and A. Rengakos, pp. 241–74. Berlin: de Gruyter.

Athanassaki, Lucia, and Ewen Bowie, eds. 2011. *Archaic and Classical Choral Song: Performance, Politics and Dissemination*. Berlin: de Gruyter.

Austin, Colin. 1990. "Observations critiques sur les *Thesmophories* d'Aristophane." *Dodone* 19 (2): 9–29.

Austin, Colin, and S. Douglas Olson, eds. 2004. *Aristophanes: Thesmophoriazusae*. Oxford: Oxford University Press.

Austin, John L. 1962. *How to Do Things with Words*. Oxford: Clarendon.

Baale, Maria J. 1903. *Studia in Anytes poetriae vitam et carminum reliquias*. Haarlem: Kleynenberg.

Bagnall, Roger S., and Raffaella Cribiore. 2006. *Women's Letters from Ancient Egypt, 300 BC–AD 800*. Ann Arbor: University of Michigan Press.

Baker, Paul. 2008. *Sexed Texts: Language, Gender and Sexuality*. London: Equinox.

Bakker, Egbert J. 2009. "Homer, Odysseus, and the Narratology of Performance." In *Narratology and Interpretation: The Content of Narrative Form in Ancient Literature*, ed. J. Grethlein and A. Rengakos, pp. 117–36. Berlin: de Gruyter.

———, ed. 2017. *Authorship and Greek Song: Authority, Authenticity, and Performance*. Leiden, Boston: Brill.

Bakola, Emmanuela. 2008. "The Drunk, the Reformer and the Teacher: Agonistic Poetics and the Construction of Persona in the Comic Poets of the Fifth Century." *Cambridge Classical Journal* 54: 1–29.

———. 2010. *Cratinus and the Art of Comedy*. Oxford: Clarendon.

Bakola, Emmanuela, Lucia Prauscello, and Mario Telò, eds. 2013. *Greek Comedy and the Discourse of Genres*. Cambridge: Cambridge University Press.

Barbantani, Silvia. 1993. "I poeti lirici del canone alessandrino nell' epigrammistica." *Aevum Antiquum* 6: 5–97.

Barber, Elizabeth Wayland. 1994. *Women's Work: The First 20,000 Years*. New York: W. W. Norton.

Barlow, Shirley A. 1971. *The Imagery of Euripides: A Study in the Dramatic Use of Pictorial Language*. London: Methuen.

———. 1989. "Stereotype and Reversal in Euripides' *Medea*." *Greece and Rome* 36 (2): 158–71.

Barnard, Sylvia. 1978. "Hellenistic Women Poets." *Classical Journal* 73 (3): 204–13.

———. 1991. "Anyte: Poet of Children and Animals." In *Rose di Pieria*, ed. F. De Martino, pp. 165–76. Bari: Levante.

Barrett, W. S., ed. 1964. *Euripides: Hippolytus*. Oxford: Clarendon.

Bartel, Heike, and Anne Simon, eds. 2010. *Unbinding Medea: Interdisciplinary Approaches to a Classical Myth from Antiquity to the 21st Century*. London: Legenda.

Barthes, Roland. 1968. "La mort de l'auteur." *Manteia* 5: 12–17.

Bas-Wohlert, Camille. 2012. "Gender-Neutral Pronoun Debate Rocks Sweden." *The Local Se*, October 8, 2012. https://www.thelocal.se/20121008/43676/.

Bassi, Karen. 1998. *Acting like Men: Gender, Drama, and Nostalgia in Ancient Greece*. Ann Arbor: University of Michigan Press.

———. 2003. "The Semantics of Manliness in Ancient Greece." In *Andreia: Studies in Manliness and Courage in Classical Antiquity*, ed. R. Rosen and I. Sluiter, pp. 25–58. Leiden: Brill.

Baumgarten, Nicole, Inke Du Bois, and Juliane House, eds. 2012. *Subjectivity in Language and Discourse*. Leiden: Brill.

Beard, Mary. 2017. *Women and Power: A Manifesto*. London: Profile Books and London Review of Books.

Beck, Deborah. 2005. "Odysseus: Narrator, Storyteller, Poet?" *Classical Philology* 100 (3): 213–27.

Beck, Frederick A. G. 1964. *Greek Education, 450–350 BC*. London: Methuen.

Beecroft, Alexander. 2010. *Authorship and Cultural Identity in Early Greece and China*. Cambridge: Cambridge University Press.

Behme, Timothy Donald. 2007. "Norms of Authorship in Ancient Greece: Case Studies of Herodotus, Isocrates, and Plato." PhD diss., University of Minnesota.

Belfiore, Elizabeth. 1982. "Plato's Greatest Accusation against Poetry." *Canadian Journal of Philosophy* 13 (sup. 1): 39–62.

———. 2011. "Poets at the Symposium." In *Plato and the Poets*, ed. P. Destrée and F.-G. Herrmann, pp. 155–74. Leiden, Boston: Brill.

Benson, Hugh H. 2013. "The Priority of Definition." In *The Bloomsbury Companion to Socrates*, ed. J. Bussanich and N. D. Smith, pp. 136–55. London, New York: Bloomsbury.

Benveniste, Émile. 1971. *Problems in General Linguistics*. Translated by M. E. Meek. Miami FL: University of Miami Press.

Bergren, Ann. 1979. "Helen's Web: Time and Tableau in the *Iliad*." *Helios* 7: 19–34.

———. 1982. "Sacred Apostrophe: Re-presentation and Imitation in the Homeric Hymns." *Arethusa* 15 (1/2): 83–108.

———. 1983. "Language and the Female in Early Greek Thought." *Arethusa* 16: 69–95.

Berman, Daniel W. 2010. "The Landscape and Language of Korinna." *Greek, Roman and Byzantine Studies* 50: 41–62.

Bichler, Reinhold. 2000. *Herodots Welt: Der Aufbau der Historie am Bild der fremden Länder und Völker, ihrer Zivilisation und ihrer Geschichte*. Berlin: Akademie Verlag.

Biehl, Werner, ed. 1989. *Euripides: Troades*. Heidelberg: Carl Winter.

Biles, Zachary P. 2011. *Aristophanes and the Poetics of Competition*. Cambridge: Cambridge University Press.

Biles, Zachary P., and S. Douglas Olson, eds. 2015. *Aristophanes: Wasps*. Oxford: Oxford University Press.

Bing, Peter. 1988. *The Well-Read Muse: Present and Past in Callimachus and the Hellenistic Poets*. Göttingen: Vandenhoeck und Ruprecht.

Bing, Peter. 1993. "Impersonation of Voice in Callimachus' Hymn to Apollo." *Transactions of the American Philological Association* 123: 181–98.

Black, Sandra E., and Chinhui Juhn. 2000. "The Rise of Female Professionals: Are Women Responding to Skill Demand?" *The American Economic Review* 90 (2): 450–55.

Blank, David. 2000. "The Organization of Grammar in Ancient Greece." In *History of the Language Sciences*, vol. 1, ed. S. Auroux, E. F. K. Koerner, H.-J. Niederehe, and K. Versteegh, pp. 400–417. Berlin: de Gruyter.

Blankenship, J. David. 1996. "Education and the Arts in Plato's *Republic*." *The Journal of Education* 178 (3): 67–98.

Blok, Josine. 2002. "Women in Herodotus' *Histories*." In *Brill's Companion to Herodotus*, ed. E. J. Bakker, I. J. F. de Jong, and H. van Wees, pp. 225–42. Leiden: Brill.

———. 2017. *Citizenship in Classical Athens*. Cambridge: Cambridge University Press.

Blondell, Ruby. 2002. *The Play of Character in Plato's Dialogues*. Cambridge: Cambridge University Press.

———. 2010a. "'Bitch That I Am': Self-Blame and Self-Assertion in the *Iliad*." *Transactions of the American Philological Association* 140 (1): 1–32.

———. 2010b. "Refractions of Homer's Helen in Archaic Lyric." *American Journal of Philology* 131: 349–91.

———. 2013. *Helen of Troy: Beauty, Myth, Devastation*. Oxford, New York: Oxford University Press.

———. 2018. "Helen and the Divine Defense: Homer, Gorgias, Euripides." *Classical Philology* 113: 113–33.

Bloom, Allan, ed. 1991. *The Republic of Plato*. 2nd ed. New York: Basic Books.

Bobrick, Elizabeth. 1997. "The Tyranny of Roles: Playacting and Privilege in Aristophanes' *Thesmophoriazusae*." In *The City as Comedy: Society and Representation in Athenian Drama*, ed. G. Dobrov, pp. 177–97. Chapel Hill: University of North Carolina Press.

Bond, Godfrey W., ed. 1981. *Euripides: Heracles*. Oxford: Clarendon.

Bosnakis, Dimitris. 2004. "Zwei Dichterinnen aus Kos: Ein neues inschriftliches Zeugnis über das öffentliche Auftreten von Frauen." In *The Hellenistic "Polis" of Kos: State, Economy and Culture*, ed. K. Höghammar, pp. 99–108. Uppsala: Acta Universitatis Upsaliensis.

Boterf, Nicholas. 2017. "Placing the Poet: The Topography of Authorship." In *Authorship and Greek Song: Authority, Authenticity, and Performance*, ed. E. Bakker, pp. 80–98. Leiden, Boston: Brill.

Bouvier, David. 2003. "Quand le poète était encore un charpentier . . . : Aux origines du concept de 'poésie.'" *Études de lettres* 3: 85–105.

———. 2004. "'Rendre l'homme meilleur!' ou quand la comédie interroge la tragédie sur sa finalité: À propos des *Grenouilles* d'Aristophane." In *Poétique d'Aristophane et langue d'Euripide en dialogue*, ed. C. Calame, pp. 9–26. Lausanne: Études de Lettres.

Bouvier, H. 1980. "Une intruse dans la littérature grecque." *Zeitschrift für Papyrologie und Epigraphik* 40: 36–38.

Bowie, A. M. 1982. "The Parabasis in Aristophanes: Prolegomena, *Acharnians*." *Classical Quarterly* 32 (1): 27–40.

Bowie, Ewen L. 2011. "Alcman's First *Partheneion* and the Song the Sirens Sang." In *Archaic and Classical Choral Song: Performance, Politics and Dissemination*, ed. L. Athanassaki and E. Bowie, pp. 33–66. Berlin: de Gruyter.

———. 2016. "How Did Sappho's Songs Get into the Male Sympotic Repertoire?" In *The Newest Sappho: P. Sapph. Obbink and P. GC inv. 105, frs. 1–4*, ed. A. Bierl and A. Lardinois, pp. 148–64. Leiden, Boston: Brill.

———. 2018. "The Lesson of Book 2." In *Interpreting Herodotus*, ed. T. Harrison and E. Irwin, pp. 53–74. Oxford: Oxford University Press.

Bowman, Laurel. 1998. "Nossis, Sappho and Hellenistic Poetry." *Ramus* 27: 39–59.

———. 2004. "The 'Women's Tradition' in Greek Poetry." *Phoenix* 58 (1/2): 1–27.

Bowra, C. M. 1931. "The Date of Corinna." *Classical Review* 45: 4–5.

———. 1961. *Greek Lyric Poetry: From Alcman to Simonides*. 2nd ed. Oxford: Oxford University Press.

Boyancé, Pierre. 1937. *Le culte des Muses chez les philosophes grecs: Études d'histoire et de psychologie religieuse*. Paris: E. de Boccard.

Boyd, Barbara Weiden. 2017. *Ovid's Homer: Authority, Repetition, and Reception*. Oxford, New York: Oxford University Press.

Bragg, Melvyn. 2015. "Sappho." *In Our Time*, BBC Radio 4, April 9, 2015. Audio, 46:02. http://www.bbc.co.uk/programmes/b05pqsk4.

Braun, Alfonsina. 1938. "I verbi del fare nel greco." *Studi italiani di filología classica* 15: 242–96.

Bremmer, Jan N. 1996. "The Status and Symbolic Capital of the Seer." In *The Role of Religion in the Early Greek Polis*, ed. R. Hägg, pp. 97–109. Jonsered: Åströms Förlag.

Brillante, Carlo. 1999. "L'invenzione della lira nell'inno omerico a Hermes." *Studi classici e orientali* 47 (1): 95–128.

Brisson, Luc. 1998. *Plato the Myth Maker*. Chicago: University of Chicago Press.

———. 2002. *Sexual Ambivalence: Androgyny and Hermaphroditism in Graeco-Roman Antiquity*. Berkeley: University of California Press.

———. 2012. "Women in Plato's *Republic*." *Études Platoniciennes* 9: 129–36.

Broadie, Sarah. 2003. "The Sophists and Socrates." In *The Cambridge Companion to Greek and Roman Philosophy*, ed. D. Sedley, pp. 73–97. Cambridge: Cambridge University Press.

Brown, Norman O. 1947. *Hermes the Thief*. Madison: University of Wisconsin Press.

Brown, Wendy. 1988. "'Supposing Truth Were a Woman . . .': Plato's Subversion of Masculine Discourse." *Political Theory* 16 (4): 594–616.

Brunschwig, Jacques. 1984. "Remarques sur la théorie stoïcienne du nom propre." *Histoire épistémologie langage* 6 (1): 3–19.

Bubel, Frank, ed. 1991. *Euripides: Andromeda*. Stuttgart: Steiner.

Buchan, Morag. 1999. *Women in Plato's Political Theory*. London, New York: Routledge.

Bucholtz, Mary, and Kira Hall. 2005. "Identity and Interaction: A Sociocultural and Linguistic Approach." *Discourse Studies* 7 (4–5): 585–614.

Bulloch, A. W. 1989. "Hellenistic Poetry." In *The Cambridge History of Classical Literature*, Vol. 1, Part 4, *The Hellenistic Period and the Empire*, ed. P. E. Easterling and B. M. W. Knox, pp. 1–81. Cambridge: Cambridge University Press.

Bundrick, Sheramy D. 2005. *Music and Image in Classical Athens*. Cambridge: Cambridge University Press.

Burke, Seán. 1992. *The Death and Return of the Author: Criticism and Subjectivity in Barthes, Foucault and Derrida*. Edinburgh: Edinburgh University Press.

Burkert, Walter. 1987. "The Making of Homer in the Sixth Century BC: Rhapsodes versus Stesichorus." In *Papers on the Amasis Painter and His World*, ed. J. Walsh, pp. 43–62. Malibu: Getty Publications.

Burnett, Anne Pippin. 1983. *Three Archaic Poets: Archilochus, Alcaeus, Sappho*. London: Duckworth.

Burnyeat, Myles F. 1977. "Socratic Midwifery, Platonic Inspiration." *Bulletin of the Institute of Classical Studies* 24: 7–16.

Burr, Elisabeth. 2003. "Gender and Language Politics in France." In *Gender across Languages: The Linguistic Representation of Women and Men*, ed. M. Hellinger and H. Bußmann, vol. 3, pp. 119–39. Amsterdam: John Benjamins.

Burton, Joan B. 1995. *Theocritus's Urban Mimes: Mobility, Gender, and Patronage*. Berkeley: University of California Press.

Burzachechi, Mario. 1962. "Oggetti parlanti nelle epigrafi greche." *Epigraphica* 24: 3–54.

Butler, Judith. 1988. "Performative Acts and Gender Constitution: An Essay in Phenomenology and Feminist Theory." *Theatre Journal* 40: 519–31.

———. 1990. *Gender Trouble: Feminism and the Subversion of Identity*. London, New York: Routledge.

———. 1993. *Bodies That Matter: On the Discursive Limits of "Sex."* London, New York: Routledge.

Buxton, Richard. 1994. *Imaginary Greece: The Contexts of Mythology*. Cambridge: Cambridge University Press.

———, ed. 2001. *From Myth to Reason? Studies in the Development of Greek Thought*. Oxford: Oxford University Press.

Bynum, David E. 1976. "The Generic Nature of Oral Epic Poetry." In *Folklore Genres*, ed. D. Ben-Amos, pp. 35–58. Austin: University of Texas Press.

Cairns, Francis. 1992. "Theocritus, *Idyll* 26." *Proceedings of the Cambridge Philological Society* 38: 1–38.

———. 2016. *Hellenistic Epigram: Contexts of Exploration*. Cambridge: Cambridge University Press.

Calame, Claude. 1982. "Énonciation, véracité ou convention littéraire? L'inspiration des Muses dans la Théogonie." *Actes sémiotiques* 34: 5–24.

———. 1995. *The Craft of Poetic Speech in Ancient Greece*. Translated by Janice Orion. Ithaca NY: Cornell University Press.

———. 1996. "Sappho's Group: An Initiation into Womanhood." In *Reading Sappho: Contemporary Approaches*, ed. E. Greene, pp. 113–24. Berkeley: University of California Press.

———. 1997. *Choruses of Young Women in Ancient Greece: Their Morphology, Religious Role, and Social Function*. Translated by Derek Collins and Janice Orion. Lanham, Boulder: Rowman and Littlefield.

———. 2001. "The Rhetoric of *Muthos* and *Logos*: Forms of Figurative Discourse." In *From Myth to Reason? Studies in the Development of Greek Thought*, ed. R. Buxton, pp. 119–44. Oxford: Oxford University Press.

———. 2004a. "Identités d'auteur à l'exemple de la Grèce classique: Signatures, énonciations, citations." In *Identités d'auteur dans l'antiquité et la tradition européenne*, ed. C. Calame and R. Chartier, pp. 11–40. Grenoble: Millon.

———, ed. 2004b. *Poétique d'Aristophane et langue d'Euripide en dialogue*. Lausanne: Études de Lettres.

Calame, Claude, and Roger Chartier, eds. 2004. *Identités d'auteur dans l'antiquité et la tradition européenne*. Grenoble: Millon.

Calhoun, G. M. 1938. "The Poet and the Muses in Homer." *Classical Philology* 33: 157–66.

Calvert, Brian. 1975. "Plato and the Equality of Women." *Phoenix* 29: 231–43.

Camerer, Colin F. 2003. *Behavioral Game Theory: Experiments in Strategic Interaction*. Princeton NJ: Princeton University Press.

Cameron, Averil, and Alan Cameron. 1969. "Erinna's Distaff." *Classical Quarterly* 19 (2): 285–88.

Campanile, Domitilla, Filippo Carlà-Uhink, and Margherita Facella, eds. 2017. *TransAntiquity: Cross-Dressing and Transgender Dynamics in the Ancient World*. Abingdon, New York: Routledge.

Campbell, David A., ed. 1967. *Greek Lyric Poetry: A Selection*. London: Macmillan.

———, ed. 1982. *Greek Lyric I: Sappho, Alcaeus*. Cambridge MA: Harvard University Press.

———. 1983. *The Golden Lyre: The Themes of the Greek Lyric Poets*. London: Duckworth.

Canto, Monique. 1985. "The Politics of Women's Bodies: Reflections on Plato." In *The Female Body in Western Culture: Contemporary Perspectives*, ed. S. R. Suleiman, pp. 339–53. Translated by Arthur Goldhammer. Cambridge MA: Harvard University Press.

Cappelletti, Loredana. 2018. "Esclusive notizie locresi in Nosside (*Anth. Pal.* 6, 132 e 265)." *Athenaeum* 106 (2): 474–90.

Carey, Chris. 1993. "The Purpose of Aristophanes' *Acharnians*." *Rheinisches Museum* 136: 245–63.

———. 2009. "Genre, Occasion and Performance." In *The Cambridge Companion to Greek Lyric*, ed. F. Budelmann, pp. 21–38. Cambridge: Cambridge University Press.

———. 2019. "Drama and Democracy." In *Poet and Orator: A Symbiotic Relationship in Democratic Athens*, ed. A. Markantonatos and E. Volonaki, pp. 233–48. Berlin: de Gruyter.

Carney, Elizabeth Donnelly. 2000. *Women and Monarchy in Macedonia*. Norman: University of Oklahoma Press.

Caroll, John B., Stephen C. Levinson, and Penny Lee, eds. 2012. *Language, Thought, and Reality: Selected Writings of Benjamin Lee Whorf*. 2nd ed. Cambridge MA: MIT Press.

Carson, Anne, transl. 2002. *If Not, Winter: Fragments of Sappho*. New York: Knopf.

Carter, Duncan M., ed. 2011. *Why Athens? A Reappraisal of Tragic Politics*. Oxford: Oxford University Press.

Cartledge, Paul. 2000. "Greek Political Thought: The Historical Context." In *The Cambridge History of Greek and Roman Political Thought*, ed. C. Rowe and M. Schofield, pp. 11–22, Cambridge: Cambridge University Press.

Carugno, Guido. 1957. "Nosside." *Giornale Italiano de filologia* 10: 324–35.

Case, Sue-Ellen. 1990. *Performing Feminisms: Feminist Critical Theory and Theatre*. Baltimore: Johns Hopkins University Press.

Caspers, Christiaan L. 2006. "The Loves of the Poets: Allusions in Hermesianax fr. 7 Powell." In *Beyond the Canon*, ed. M. A. Harder, R. F. Regtuit, and G. C. Wakker, pp. 21–42. Leuven, Dudley MA: Peeters.

Cavarero, Adriana. 2002. "The Envied Muse: Plato versus Homer." In *Cultivating the Muse: Struggles for Power and Inspiration in Classical Literature*, ed. E. Spentzou and D. Fowler, pp. 47–68. Oxford: Oxford University Press.

Cavarero, Adriana. 2005. *For More than One Voice: Toward a Philosophy of Vocal Expression.* Stanford CA: Stanford University Press.

Cazzaniga, Ignazio. 1970. "Critica testuale ed esegesi a Nosside A.P. VII 718." *La parola del passato* 25: 431–45.

Ceccarelli, Paola. 2013. *Ancient Greek Letter Writing: A Cultural History (600 BC–150 BC).* Oxford: Oxford University Press.

Chandler, Albert R. 1934. "The Nightingale in Greek and Latin Poetry." *Classical Journal* 30 (2): 78–84.

Chappell, Mike 2011. "The *Homeric Hymn to Apollo*: The Question of Unity." In *The Homeric Hymns: Interpretative Essays*, ed. A. Faulkner, pp. 59–81. Oxford: Oxford University Press.

Cheshire, Jenny. 1985. "A Question of Masculine Bias." *English Today* 1 (1): 22–26.

———. 2008. "Still a Gender-Biased Language?" *English Today* 24 (1): 7–10.

Chong-Gossard, J. H. Kim On. 2008. *Gender and Communication in Euripides' Plays: Between Song and Silence.* Leiden, Boston: Brill.

Cingano, Ettore. 2017. "Interpreting Epic and Lyric Fragments: Stesichorus, Simonides, Corinna, the Theban Epics, the Hesiodic Corpus and Other Epic Fragments." *Lexis* 35: 28–57.

Cixous, Hélène. 1976. "The Laugh of the Medusa." *Signs* 1 (4): 875–93.

Clackson, James. 2015. *Language and Society in the Greek and Roman Worlds.* Cambridge: Cambridge University Press.

Clader, Linda L. 1976. *Helen: The Evolution from Divine to Heroic in Greek Epic Tradition.* Leiden: Brill.

Clauss, James J., and Sarah Iles Johnston, eds. 1997. *Medea: Essays on Medea in Myth, Literature, Philosophy, and Art.* Princeton NJ: Princeton University Press.

Clay, Jenny Strauss. 1980. "Sappho's Hesperus and Hesiod's Dawn." *Philologus* 124: 302–5.

———. 1988. "What the Muses Sang: *Theogony* 1–115." *Greek, Roman and Byzantine Studies* 29: 323–33.

———. 1989. *The Politics of Olympus: Form and Meaning in the Major Homeric Hymns.* Princeton NJ: Princeton University Press.

———. 2003. *Hesiod's Cosmos.* Cambridge: Cambridge University Press.

Clayman, Dee L. 1993. "Corinna and Pindar." In *Nomodeiktes: Greek Studies in Honor of Martin Ostwald*, ed. R. M. Rosen and J. Farrell, pp. 633–42. Ann Arbor: University of Michigan Press.

Clements, Ashley. 2014. *Aristophanes' Thesmophoriazusae: Philosophizing Theatre and the Politics of Perception in Late Fifth-Century Athens.* Cambridge: Cambridge University Press.

Cobet, Justus. 1977. "Wann wurde Herodots Darstellung der Perserkriege publiziert?" *Hermes* 105: 2–27.

Cohen, Beth, ed. 1995. *The Distaff Side: Representing the Female in Homer's Odyssey.* Oxford: Oxford University Press.

Cohen, Edward E. 2006. "Free and Unfree Sexual Work: An Economic Analysis of Athenian Prostitution." In *Prostitutes and Courtesans in the Ancient World*, ed. C. A. Faraone and L. McClure, pp. 95–124. Madison: University of Wisconsin Press.

Cole, Susan G. 1981. "Could Greek Women Read and Write?" In *Reflections of Women in Antiquity*, ed. H. Foley, pp. 219–46. New York: Gordon and Breach.

————. 2004. *Landscapes, Gender, and Ritual Space: The Ancient Greek Experience.* Berkeley: University of California Press.

Colesanti, Giulio. 2014. "Two Cases of Submerged Monodic Lyric: Sympotic Poetry and Lullabies." In *Submerged Literature in Ancient Greek Culture: An Introduction,* ed. G. Colesanti and M. Giordano, pp. 90–106. Berlin: de Gruyter.

Collard, Christopher. 1971. *Supplement to the Allen and Italie Concordance to Euripides.* Groningen: Hakkert.

Collard, Christopher, Martin J. Cropp, and John Gibert, eds. 2004. *Euripides: Selected Fragmentary Plays.* Vol. 2. Oxford: Aris and Phillips.

Collins, Derek. 1999. "Hesiod and the Divine Voice of the Muses." *Arethusa* 32 (3): 241–62.

————. 2006. "Corinna and Mythological Innovation." *Classical Quarterly* 56 (1): 19–32.

Collobert, Catherine, Pierre Destrée, and Francisco J. Gonzales, eds. 2012. *Plato and Myth: Studies on the Use and Status of Platonic Myths.* Leiden, Boston: Brill.

Coo, Lyndsay. 2021. "Sappho in Fifth- and Fourth-Century Greek Literature." In *The Cambridge Companion to Sappho,* ed. P. J. Finglass and A. Kelly, pp. 263–76. Cambridge: Cambridge University Press.

Corbeill, Anthony. 2015. *Sexing the World: Grammatical Gender and Biological Sex in Ancient Rome.* Princeton NJ: Princeton University Press.

Corbett, Greville G. 1991. *Gender.* Cambridge: Cambridge University Press.

Coughlan, Taylor S. 2020. "The Poetics of Dialect in the Self-Epitaphs of Nossis and Leonidas of Tarentum." *Classical Philology* 115 (4): 607–29.

Coulon, Laurent, Pascale Giovanelli-Jouanna, and Flore Kimmel-Clauzet, eds. 2013. *Hérodote et l'Égypte: Regards croisés sur livre II de l'enquête d'Hérodote.* Lyon: Maison de l'Orient et de la Méditerranée.

Crane, Gregory. 1988. *Calypso: Backgrounds and Conventions of the Odyssey.* Frankfurt: Athenaeum.

Cyrino, Monica Silveira. 1998. "Heroes in D(u)ress: Transvestism and Power in the Myths of Herakles and Achilles." *Arethusa* 31(2): 207–41.

D'Alessio, Giambattista B. 1994. "First-Person Problems in Pindar." *Bulletin of the Institute of Classical Studies* 41: 117–39.

————. 2018. "Fiction and Pragmatics in Ancient Greek Lyric: The Case of Sappho." In *Textual Events: Performance and the Lyric in Early Greece,* ed. F. Budelmann and T. Phillips, pp. 31–62. Oxford: Oxford University Press.

Dancy, R. M. 2004. *Plato's Introduction of Forms.* Cambridge: Cambridge University Press.

D'Angour, Armand. 2019. *Socrates in Love: The Making of a Philosopher.* London, New York: Bloomsbury.

Danielewicz, Jerzy. 1990. "Deixis in Greek Choral Lyric." *Quaderni urbinati di cultura classica* 34: 7–17.

Davidson, James. 2007. *The Greeks and Greek Love: A Radical Reappraisal of Homosexuality in Ancient Greece.* London: Phoenix.

Davies, Malcolm. 1988a. "Monody, Choral Lyric, and the Tyranny of the Hand-Book." *Classical Quarterly* 38: 52–64.

————. 1988b. "Corinna's Date Revisited." *Studi Italiani di filologia classica* 6: 186–94.

————. 1995. "Theocritus' *Adoniazusae.*" *Greece and Rome* 42 (2): 152–58.

de Beauvoir, Simone. [1949] 2011. *The Second Sex*. Translated by Constance Borde and Sheila Malovany-Chevallier. 2nd ed. London: Vintage.

de Jong, Irene J. F. 2001. *A Narratological Commentary on the Odyssey*. Cambridge: Cambridge University Press.

De Martino, Francesco. 1987. "Saffo ed Esiodo (Fr. 1,21–24 Voigt)." *Giornale filologico Ferrarese* 10: 51–55.

———, ed. 1991. *Rose di Pieria*. Bari: Levante.

De Simone, Mariella. 2008. "The 'Lesbian' Muse in Tragedy: Euripides μελοποιός in Aristoph. *Ra.* 1301–28." *Classical Quarterly* 58 (2): 479–90.

de Vos, Mieke. 2014. "From Lesbos She Took Her Honeycomb: Sappho and the 'Female Tradition' in Hellenistic Poetry." In *Valuing the Past in the Greco-Roman World*, ed. C. Pieper and J. Ker, pp. 410–34. Leiden: Brill.

Degani, Enzo. 1995. "Problems in Greek Gastronomic Poetry: On Matro's *Attikon Deipnon*." In *Food in Antiquity*, ed. J. Wilkins, D. Harvey, M. Dobson and A. Davidson, pp. 413–28. Exeter: University of Exeter Press.

Degani, Enzo, and Gabriele Burzacchini, eds. 1977. *Lirici greci: Antologia*. Florence: La Nuova Italia.

DeJean, Joan. 1989. *Fictions of Sappho, 1546–1937*. Chicago: University of Chicago Press.

Demand, Nancy. 1975. "The Nomothetes of the *Cratylus*." *Phronesis* 20 (2): 106–9.

Denniston, J. D. 1927. "Technical Terms in Aristophanes." *Classical Quarterly* 21 (3/4): 113–21.

Denyer, Nicholas. 1991. *Language, Thought and Falsehood in Ancient Greek Philosophy*. London: Routledge.

Destrée, Pierre, and Fritz-Gregor Herrmann, eds. 2011. *Plato and the Poets*. Leiden: Brill.

Detienne, Marcel, and Jean-Pierre Vernant. 1991. *Cunning Intelligence in Greek Culture and Society*. Translated by Janet Lloyd. Chicago: University of Chicago Press.

Dewald, Carolyn. 1986. "Women and Culture in Herodotus' *Histories*." In *Reflections of Women in Antiquity*, ed. H. P. Foley, pp. 91–125. New York: Gordon and Breach.

Diehl, E. 1940. "Fuerunt Ante Homerum Poetae." *Rheinisches Museum für Philologie*, 89 (2): 81–114.

Diels, Herman. 1910. "Die Anfänge der Philologie bei den Griechen." *Neue Jahrbücher für das klassische Altertum* 13: 1–25.

Dihle, Albrecht. 1994. *A History of Greek Literature: From Homer to the Hellenistic Period*. Translated by Clare Krojzl. London, New York: Routledge.

Dillery, John. 2018. "Making *Logoi*: Herodotus' Book 2 and Hecataeus of Miletus." In *Interpreting Herodotus*, ed. T. Harrison and E. Irwin, pp. 17–52. Oxford: Oxford University Press.

Dillon, Matthew. 2014. "Engendering the Scroll: Girls' and Women's Literacy in Classical Greece." In *The Oxford Handbook of Childhood and Education in the Classical World*, ed. J. Evans Grubb and T. Parkin, pp. 396–417. Oxford: Oxford University Press.

Dion, Kenneth L. 1983. "Names, Identity, and Self." *Names* 31 (4): 245–57.

Doherty, Lillian E. 1991. "The Internal and Implied Audiences of *Odyssey* 11." *Arethusa* 24 (2): 145–76.

———. 1992. "Gender and Internal Audiences in the *Odyssey*." *The American Journal of Philology* 113 (2): 161–77.

———. 1995a. "Sirens, Muses and Female Narrators in the *Odyssey*." In *The Distaff Side: Representing the Female in Homer's Odyssey*, ed. B. Cohen, pp. 81–92. Oxford: Oxford University Press.

———. 1995b. *Siren Songs: Gender, Audiences, and Narrators in the Odyssey*. Ann Arbor: University of Michigan Press.

Donelli, Giulia. 2021. "Herodotus, the Old Sappho and the Newest Sappho." *Lexis* 39 (1): 13–34.

Dornseiff, Franz. 1933. *Die archaische Mythenerzählung: Folgerungen aus dem homerischen Apollonhymnos*. Berlin: de Gruyter.

Dover, Kenneth J., ed. 1968. *Aristophanes: Clouds*. Oxford: Oxford University Press.

———. 1972. *Aristophanic Comedy*. Berkeley: University of California Press.

———. 1974. *Greek Popular Morality in the Time of Plato and Aristotle*. Oxford: Blackwell.

———, ed. 1980. *Plato: Symposium*. Cambridge: Cambridge University Press.

———, ed. 1985. *Theocritus: Select Poems*. Bristol: Bristol Classical Press.

———. 1986. "Ion of Chios: His Place in the History of Greek Literature." In *Chios: A Conference at the Homereion in Chios 1984*, ed. J. Boardman and C. E. Vaphopoulou-Richardson, pp. 27–37. Oxford: Clarendon.

———, ed. 1993. *Aristophanes: Frogs*. Oxford: Oxford University Press.

———. 2016. *Greek Homosexuality*. 3rd ed. London, New York: Bloomsbury.

Downes, Jeremy M. 2010. *The Female Homer: An Exploration of Women's Epic Poetry*. Newark: University of Delaware Press.

Duban, Jeffrey M. 1980. "Poets and Kings in the *Theogony* Invocation." *Quaderni urbinati di cultura classica* 4: 7–21.

duBois, Page. 1988. *Sowing the Body: Psychoanalysis and Ancient Representations of Women*. Chicago: University of Chicago Press.

———. 1995. *Sappho Is Burning*. Chicago: University of Chicago Press.

Dué, Casey. 2006. *The Captive Woman's Lament in Greek Tragedy*. Austin: University of Texas Press.

Duncan, Anne. 2006 *Performance and Identity in the Classical World*. Cambridge: Cambridge University Press.

Durante, Marcello. 1976. *Sulla preistoria della tradizione poetica greca. Parte seconda: Risultanze della comparazione indoeuropea*. Rome: Ateneo.

During, Simon. 1992. *Foucault and Literature: Towards a Genealogy of Writing*. London, New York: Routledge.

Easterling, Patricia E. 1991. "Men's κλέος and Women's γόος: Female Voices in the *Iliad*." *Journal of Modern Greek Studies* 9: 145–51.

———. 2007. "Looking for Omphale." In *The World of Ion of Chios*, ed. V. Jennings and A. Katsaros, pp. 282–94. Leiden, Boston: Brill.

Eckert, Penelope, and Sally McConnell-Ginet. 1992a. "Think Practically and Look Locally: Language and Gender as Community-Based Practice." *Annual Review of Anthropology* 21: 461–90.

———. 1992b. "Communities of Practice: Where Language, Gender and Power All Live." In *Locating Power: Proceedings of the Second Berkeley Women and Language Conference*, ed. K. Hall, M. Bucholtz, and B. Moonwomon, pp. 89–99. Berkeley: University of California Press.

Eckert, Penelope, and Sally McConnell-Ginet. 2013. *Language and Gender*. Cambridge: Cambridge University Press.

Edie, James M. 1963. "Expression and Metaphor." *Philosophy and Phenomenological Research* 23 (4): 538–61.

Edmunds, Lowell. 1980. "Aristophanes' *Acharnians*." *Yale Classical Studies* 26: 1–41.

Edmunds, Lowell, and Robert W. Wallace, eds. 1997. *Poet, Public, and Performance in Ancient Greece*. Baltimore: John Hopkins University Press.

Edwards, Mark W., ed. 1991. *The Iliad: A Commentary*. Vol. 5, *Books 17–20*. Cambridge: Cambridge University Press.

Ehrlich, Susan, Miriam Meyerhoff, and Janet Holmes, eds. 2017. *The Handbook of Language, Gender and Sexuality*. 2nd ed. Oxford: Wiley-Blackwell.

Elias, Julius A. 1984. *Plato's Defence of Poetry*. Albany: State University of New York Press.

Elmer, David. 2005. "Helen *Epigrammatopoios*." *Classical Antiquity* 24 (1): 1–39.

Emlyn-Jones, Chris, and William Preddy, eds. 2013. *Plato: Republic, Books 1–5*. Cambridge MA: Harvard University Press.

Ercoles, Marco. 2014. "Metrics (*métron*), Ancient Theories of." In *Encyclopedia of Ancient Greek Language and Linguistics*. Vol. 2, ed. G. Giannakis, pp. 431–36. Brill: Leiden.

European Parliament. 2018. "Gender-Neutral Language in the European Parliament." July 2018. https://www.europarl.europa.eu/cmsdata/151780/GNL_Guidelines_EN.pdf.

Evans, Nancy. 2006. "Diotima and Demeter as Mystagogues in Plato's *Symposium*." *Hypatia* 21 (2): 1–27.

Fanfani, Giovanni. 2017. "Weaving a Song: Convergences in Greek Poetic Imagery between Textile and Musical Terminology. An Overview on Archaic and Classical Literature." In *Textile Terminologies from the Orient to the Mediterranean and Europe, 1000 BC to 1000 AD*, ed. S. Gaspa, C. Michel, and M.-L. Nosch, pp. 421–36. Lincoln NE: Zea Books.

———. 2018. "What Melos for Troy? Blending of Lyric Genres in the First *Stasimon* of Euripides' *Trojan Women*." In *Paths of Song: The Lyric Dimension of Greek Tragedy*, ed. R. Andújar, T. R. P. Coward and T. A. Hadjimichael, pp. 239–64. Berlin: de Gruyter.

Fantham, Elaine, Helene Foley, Natalie Kampen, Sarah Pomeroy, and Alan H. Shapiro. 1994. *Women in the Classical World: Image and Text*. Oxford and New York: Oxford University Press.

Fantuzzi, Marco. 2007. "La *mousa* del lamento in Euripide, e il lamento della Musa nel *Reso* ascritto a Euripide." *Eikasmos* 18: 173–99.

———, ed. 2021. *The Rhesus attributed to Euripides*. Cambridge: Cambridge University Press.

Faraone, Christopher A. 2006. "Priestess and Courtesan: The Ambivalence of Female Leadership in Aristophanes' *Lysistrata*." In *Prostitutes and Courtesans in the Ancient World*, ed. C. A. Faraone and L. McClure, pp. 207–23. Madison: University of Wisconsin Press.

Farmer, Matthew C. 2017. *Tragedy on the Comic Stage*. Oxford: Oxford University Press.

Farrell, Joseph. 2002. "Greek Lives and Roman Careers in the Classical *Vita* Tradition." In *European Literary Careers*, ed. P. Cheney and F. A. de Armas, pp. 24–46. Toronto: University of Toronto Press.

Fearn, David. 2017. *Pindar's Eyes: Visual and Material Culture in Epinician Poetry*. Oxford: Oxford University Press.

Fehr, B. 1990. "Entertainers at the *Symposion*." In *Sympotica: A Symposium on the Symposion*, ed. O. Murray, pp. 185–95. Oxford: Oxford University Press.

Felson, Nancy. 1994. *Regarding Penelope: From Character to Poetics.* Norman: University of Oklahoma Press.

Felson, Nancy, and Laura Slatkin. 2005. "Gender and Homeric Epic." In *The Cambridge Companion to Homer*, ed. R. Fowler, pp. 91–114. Cambridge: Cambridge University Press.

Ferrandini Troisi, F. 1998. "Aristodama, una poetessa ionica." *Annali della facoltà di lettere e filosofia, Università degli Studi di Bari* 41: 207–13.

Ferrari, Franco. 2010. *Sappho's Gift: The Poet and Her Community.* Translated by Benjamin Acosta-Hughes and Lucia Prauscello. Ann Arbor: Michigan Classical Press.

———. 2021. "Performing Sappho." In *The Cambridge Companion to Sappho*, ed. P. J. Finglass and A. Kelly, pp. 107–20. Cambridge: Cambridge University Press.

Ferrari, Giovanni R. F. 1988. "Hesiod's Mimetic Muses and the Strategies of Deconstruction." In *Post-Structuralist Classics*, ed. A. E. Benjamin, pp. 45–78. Abingdon: Routledge.

———. 1989. "Plato on Poetry." In *The Cambridge History of Literary Criticism*. Vol. 1, *Classical Criticism*, ed. G. A. Kennedy, pp. 92–148. Cambridge: Cambridge University Press.

———. 1992. "Platonic Love." In *The Cambridge Companion to Plato*, ed. R. Kraut, pp. 248–76. Cambridge: Cambridge University Press.

Ferrari, Gloria. 2003. "What Kind of Rite of Passage Was the Ancient Greek Wedding?" In *Initiation in Ancient Greek Rituals and Narratives*, ed. D. Dodd and C. A. Faraone, pp. 27–42. London, New York: Routledge.

Finglass, Patrick J., ed. 2018. *Sophocles: Oedipus the King.* Cambridge: Cambridge University Press.

Finglass, Patrick J., and Adrian Kelly, eds. 2021. *The Cambridge Companion to Sappho.* Cambridge: Cambridge University Press.

Finkelberg, Margalit. 1990. "A Creative Oral Poet and the Muse." *The American Journal of Philology* 111 (3): 293–303.

———. 1998. *The Birth of Literary Fiction in Ancient Greece.* Oxford: Clarendon.

Fisher, N. R. E. 1993. "Multiple Personalities and Dionysia Festivals: Dicaeopolis in Aristophanes' *Acharnians*." *Greece and Rome* 40: 31–47.

Fletcher, Judith. 2008. "A Trickster's Oaths in the *Homeric Hymn to Hermes*." *American Journal of Philology* 129: 19–46.

———. 2009. "Weaving Women's Tales in Euripides' *Ion*." In *The Play of Texts and Fragments: Essays in Honour of Martin Cropp*, ed. J. Cousland and J. Hume, pp. 127–39. Leiden, Boston: Brill.

Fletcher, Richard, and Johanna Hanink, eds. 2016. *Creative Lives in Classical Antiquity.* Cambridge: Cambridge University Press.

Flower, Michael. 2007. *The Seer in Ancient Greece.* Berkeley: University of California Press.

Fögen, Thorsten. 2004. "Gender-Specific Communication in Graeco-Roman Antiquity: With a Research Bibliography." *Historiographia Linguistica* 31 (2–3): 199–276.

Foley, Helene P. 1978. "Reverse Similes and Sex Roles in the *Odyssey*." *Arethusa* 11 (1/2): 7–26.

———. 2001. *Female Acts in Greek Tragedy.* Princeton NJ: Princeton University Press.

Foley, John Miles. 1990. *Traditional Oral Epic: The Odyssey, Beowulf, and the Serbo-Croation Return Song.* Berkeley: University of California Press.

Foley, Richard. 2010. "The Order Question: Climbing the Ladder of Love in Plato's *Symposium*." *Ancient Philosophy* 30 (1): 57–72.

Fontenrose, Joseph. 1978. *The Delphic Oracle: Its Responses and Operations with a Catalogue of Responses*. Berkeley: University of California Press.

Ford, Andrew. 1981. "A Study of Early Greek Terms for Poetry: *Aoidē, Epos* and *Poiēsis*." PhD diss., Yale University.

———. 1985. "The Seal of Theognis: The Politics of Authorship in Archaic Greece." In *Theognis of Megara: Poetry and the Polis*, ed. T. J. Figueira and G. Nagy, pp. 82–95. Baltimore: Johns Hopkins University Press.

———. 1992. *Homer: The Poetry of the Past*. Ithaca NY: Cornell University Press.

———. 2002. *The Origins of Criticism: Literary Culture and Poetic Theory in Classical Greece*. Princeton NJ: Princeton University Press.

———. 2007. "Herodotus and the Poets." In *The Landmark Herodotus: The Histories*, ed. R. Strassler, pp. 816–18. New York: Anchor Books.

Fornara, Charles W. 1971. "Evidence for the Date of Herodotus' Publication." *Journal of Hellenic Studies* 91: 25–34.

Fortson, Benjamin W. 2010. *Indo-European Language and Culture: An Introduction*. Oxford, Malden MA: Wiley-Blackwell.

Foster, J. Andrew. 2006. "Arsinoe II as Epic Queen: Encomiastic Allusion in Theocritus, *Idyll* 15." *Transactions and Proceedings of the American Philological Association* 136 (1): 133–48.

Foucault, Michel. 1977. "What Is an Author?" In *Language, Counter-Memory, Practice*, ed. D. F. Bouchard, pp. 113–38. Translated by D. F. Bouchard and S. Simon. Oxford: Blackwell.

Fowler, Barbara Hughes. 1989. *The Hellenistic Aesthetic*. Madison: The University of Wisconsin Press.

Fowler, Robert L. 1987. *The Nature of Early Greek Lyric*. Toronto: University of Toronto Press.

———. 2005. "The Homeric Question." In *The Cambridge Companion to Homer*, ed. R. Fowler, pp. 220–32. Cambridge: Cambridge University Press.

———. 2006. "Herodotus and His Prose Predecessors." In *The Cambridge Companion to Herodotus*, ed. C. Dewald and J. Marincola, pp. 29–45. Cambridge: Cambridge University Press.

———. 2011. "*Mythos* and *Logos*." *Journal of Hellenic Studies* 131: 45–66.

Fowler, Rowena. 1983. "'On Not Knowing Greek': The Classics and the Woman of Letters." *Classical Journal* 78 (4): 337–49.

Fox, Matthew. 1998. "The Constrained Man." In *Thinking Men: Masculinity and Its Self-Representation in the Classical Tradition*, eds. L. Foxhall and J. Salmon, pp. 6–22. London, New York: Routledge.

Foxhall, Lin, and John Salmon, eds. 1998a. *Thinking Men: Masculinity and Its Self-Representation in the Classical Tradition*. London, New York: Routledge.

———. 1998b. *When Men Were Men: Masculinity, Power and Identity in Classical Antiquity*. London, New York: Routledge.

Fränkel, Hermann. 1951. *Dichtung und Philosophie des frühen Griechentums: Eine Geschichte der griechischen Epik, Lyrik und Prosa bis zur Mitte des fünften Jahrhunderts*. New York: American Philological Association.

Fraser, Peter Marshall. 1984. "A Dedication to L. Septimius Nestor at Old Paphos." In *Report of the Department of Antiquities of Cyprus*, pp. 279–80.

Freeman, Barbara. 1986. "Irigaray at *The Symposium*: Speaking Otherwise." *Oxford Literary Review* 8 (1/2): 170–7.

Friedländer, Paul. 1914. "Das Proömium von Hesiods Theogonie." *Hermes* 49: 1–16.

Frutiger, Perceval. 1930. *Les mythes de Platon: Étude philosophique et littéraire.* Paris: Alcan.

Fuentes González, Pedro P. 1998a. "Teles Reconsidered." *Mnemosyne* 51 (1): 1–19.

———, ed. 1998b. *Les diatribes de Télès: Introduction, texte revu, traduction et commentaire des fragments.* Paris: Vrin.

Fuhrer, Therese, and Lisa Cordes, eds. 2022. *The Gender Parameter in the Shaping of First-Person Discourse in Classical Literature: Shaping a (Gendered) 'I' Persona.* Berlin: de Gruyter.

Furiani, Patrizia L. 1991. "Intimità e socialità in Nosside di Locri." In *Rose di Pieria*, ed. F. De Martino, pp. 179–95. Bari: Levante.

Furley, William D. 2011. "Homeric and Un-Homeric Hexameter Hymns: A Question of Type." In *The Homeric Hymns: Interpretative Essays*, ed. A. Faulkner, pp. 206–31. Oxford: Oxford University Press.

Gallavotti, Carlo. 1971. "L'epigramma biografico di Nosside come esempio di critica testuale." In *Studi filologici e storici in onore di V. de Falco*, pp. 239–50. Naples: Libreria Scientifica Editrice.

Gamel, Mary Kay, ed. 2002. *Performing/Transforming Aristophanes' Thesmophoriazusae. American Journal of Philology* Special Issue 123 (3).

Gantz, Timothy Nolan. 1974. "Pindar's First Pythian: The Fire Within." *Ramus* 3 (2): 143–51.

Garrison, Elise P. 1995. *Groaning Tears: Ethical and Dramatic Aspects of Suicide in Greek Tragedy.* Leiden: Brill.

Gentili, Bruno. 1988. *Poetry and Its Public in Ancient Greece.* Translated by A. T. Cole. Baltimore: Johns Hopkins University Press.

———. 1990. "L' 'io' nella poesia lirica greca." *A.I.O.N. Sez. Filologico-Letteraria* 12: 20–22.

Gentner, Dedre, and Susan Goldin-Meadow, eds. 2003. *Language in Mind: Advances in the Study of Language and Thought.* Cambridge MA: MIT Press.

Geoghegan, D., ed. 1979. *Anyte: The Epigrams.* Roma: Edizioni dell'Ateneo e Bizzarri.

Gerber, Douglas E., ed. 1997. *A Companion to the Greek Lyric Poets.* Leiden: Brill.

———, ed. 1999a. *Greek Elegiac Poetry.* Cambridge MA: Harvard University Press.

———, ed. 1999b. *Greek Iambic Poetry.* Cambridge MA: Harvard University Press.

Germany, Robert. 2005. "The Figure of Echo in the *Homeric Hymn to Pan.*" *American Journal of Philology* 126 (2): 187–208.

Ghert-Zand, Renee. 2018. "In an Increasingly Nonbinary World, Is Gendered Hebrew Willing to Adapt?" *The Times of Israel*, December 9, 2018. https://www.timesofisrael.com/in-an-increasingly-nonbinary-world-is-gendered-hebrew-willing-to-adapt/.

Gigante, Marcello. 1974. "Nosside." *La parola del passato* 29: 22–39.

Gilbert, Sandra, and Susan Gubar. 1979. *The Madwoman in the Attic: The Woman Writer and the Nineteenth-Century Literary Imagination.* New Haven CT: Yale University Press.

Gilhuly, Kate. 2018. *Erotic Geographies in Ancient Greek Literature and Culture.* London, New York: Routledge.

Gill, Christopher. 1990. "Platonic Love and Individuality." In *Polis and Politics: Essays in Greek Moral and Political Philosophy*, ed. A. Loizou and H. Lesser, pp. 69–88. Aldershot VT: Avebury.

———. 2016. "Are the 'Higher Mysteries' of Platonic Love Reserved for Ethical-Educational Pederasty?" In *Plato in Symposium*, ed. M. Tulli and M. Erler, pp. 371–79. Sankt Augustin: Academia.

Gill, Christopher, and Timothy P. Wiseman, eds. 1993. *Lies and Fiction in the Ancient World.* Exeter: University of Exeter Press.

Gilleland, Michael E. 1980. "Female Speech in Greek and Latin." *American Journal of Philology* 101: 180–83.

Gilula, Dwora. 1990. "P.Oxy. 2737 and Aristophanes' Early Career." *Zeitschrift für Papyrologie und Epigraphik* 81: 101–2.

———. 1996. "A Singularly Gifted Actor (Ar. *Th.* 1056–1096)." *Quaderni di storia* 22: 159–64.

———. 1997. "The Poet Faces His Audience." *Quaderni di storia* 23: 131–43.

Given, John. 2007. "The Agathon Scene in Aristophanes' *Thesmophoriazusae.*" *Symbolae Osloenses* 82 (1): 35–51.

Glazebrook, Allison. 2005. "Reading Women: Book Rolls on Attic Vases." *Mouseion* 5:1–46.

Godley, A. D., ed. 1920. *Herodotus, The Persian Wars.* Vol. 1, *Books 1–2.* Cambridge MA: Harvard University Press.

Goff, Barbara. 1995. "Aithra at Eleusis." *Helios* 22 (1): 65–78.

Goldhill, Simon. 1990. "The Great Dionysia and Civic Ideology." In *Nothing to Do with Dionysos? Athenian Drama in Its Social Context,* ed. J. J. Winkler and F. I. Zeitlin, pp. 97–129. Princeton NJ: Princeton University Press.

———. 1991. *The Poet's Voice: Essays on Poetics and Greek Literature.* Cambridge: Cambridge University Press.

———. 1994a. "Representing Democracy: Women at the Great Dionysia." In *Ritual, Finance, Politics: Athenian Democratic Accounts Presented to David Lewis,* ed. R. Osborne and S. Hornblower, pp. 347–69. Oxford: Oxford University Press.

———. 1994b. "The Naive and Knowing Eye: Ekphrasis and the Culture of Viewing in the Hellenistic World." In *Art and Text in Ancient Greek Culture,* ed. S. Goldhill and R. Osborne, pp. 197–223. Cambridge: Cambridge University Press.

———. 2002. *The Invention of Prose. Greece and Rome.* New Surveys in the Classics 32. Oxford: Oxford University Press.

Gosetti-Murrayjohn, Angela. 2006. "Sappho as the Tenth Muse in Hellenistic Epigram." *Arethusa* 39 (1): 21–45.

Gould, Carol S. 1987. "Socratic Intellectualism and the Problem of Courage: An Interpretation of Plato's *Laches.*" *History of Philosophy Quarterly* 4: 265–79.

Gould, John. 1980. "Law, Custom and Myth: Aspects of the Social Position of Women in Classical Athens." *The Journal of Hellenic Studies* 100: 38–59.

Gould, Thomas. 1990. *The Ancient Quarrel between Poetry and Philosophy.* Princeton NJ: Princeton University Press.

Gow, A. S. F. 1938. "The *Adoniazusae* of Theocritus." *Journal of Hellenic Studies* 58 (2): 180–204.

———, ed. 1952. *Theocritus.* 2 vols. Cambridge: Cambridge University Press.

Gow, A. S. F., and D. L. Page, eds. 1965. *The Greek Anthology: Hellenistic Epigrams.* 2 vols. Cambridge: Cambridge University Press.

———, eds. 1968. *The Greek Anthology: The Garland of Philip and Some Contemporary Epigrams.* 2 vols. Cambridge: Cambridge University Press.

Graver, Margaret. 1995. "Dog-Helen and Homeric Insult." *Classical Antiquity* 14 (1): 41–61.

Gray, Vivienne. 1995. "Herodotus and the Rhetoric of Otherness." *American Journal of Philology* 116: 185–211.

Graziosi, Barbara. 2002. *Inventing Homer: The Early Reception of Epic.* Cambridge: Cambridge University Press.

Graziosi, Barbara, and Johannes Haubold. 2003. "Homeric Masculinity: HNOPEH and ΑΓΗΝΟΡΙΗ." *The Journal of Hellenic Studies* 123: 60–76.

Greene, Ellen. 1994. "Apostrophe and Women's Erotics in the Poetry of Sappho." *Transactions and Proceedings of the American Philological Association* 124: 41–56.

———. 2000. "Playing with Tradition: Gender and Innovation in the Epigrams of Anyte." *Helios* 27: 15–32.

———, ed. 2005. *Women Poets in Ancient Greece and Rome.* Norman: University of Oklahoma Press.

———. 2008. "Masculine and Feminine, Public and Private, in the Poetry of Sappho." In *Dialogism and Lyric Self-Fashioning: Bakhtin and the Voices of a Genre*, ed. J. Blevins, pp. 23–45. Selinsgrove PA: Susquehanna University Press.

Grenfell, Bernard P., and Arthur S. Hunt, eds. 1922. *The Oxyrhynchus Papyri: Part XV.* Oxford: Oxford University Press.

Griffin, Jasper. 1998. "The Social Function of Attic Tragedy." *Classical Quarterly* 48 (1): 39–61.

Griffith, Mark. 1983. "Personality in Hesiod." *Classical Antiquity* 2 (1): 37–65.

———. 2001. "Antigone and Her Sister(s): Embodying Women in Greek Tragedy." In *Making Silence Speak: Women's Voices in Greek Literature and Society*, ed. A. Lardinois and L. McClure, pp. 117–37. Princeton NJ: Princeton University Press.

———. 2009. "Apollo, Teiresias, and the Politics of Tragic Prophecy." In *Apolline Politics and Poetics*, ed. L. Athanassaki, R. Martin and J. Miller, pp. 473–500. Athens: Hellenic Ministry of Culture.

———. 2015. "The Earliest Greek Systems of Education." In *A Companion to Ancient Education*, ed. W. M. Bloomer, pp. 26–60. Oxford: Wiley-Blackwell.

Griffiths, Frederick T. 1979. *Theocritus at Court.* Leiden: Brill.

Grintser, Nikolay P. 2018. "Herodotus as a Literary Critic." In *Herodotus: Narrator, Scientist, Historian*, ed. E. Bowie, pp. 157–74. Berlin: de Gruyter.

Griswold, Charles L. 1981. "The Ideas and the Criticism of Poetry in Plato's *Republic*, Book 10." *Journal of the History of Philosophy* 19 (2): 135–50.

———. 2003. "Plato on Rhetoric and Poetry." In *The Stanford Encyclopedia of Philosophy*, ed. E. N. Zalta. https://plato.stanford.edu/archives/spr2020/entries/plato-rhetoric/.

Gubar, Susan. 1981. "'The Blank Page' and the Issues of Female Creativity." *Critical Inquiry* 8 (2): 243–63.

———. 1984. "Sapphistries." *Signs* 10 (1): 43–62.

Guillon, P. 1958. "Corinne et les oracles béotiens: La consultation d'Asôpos." *Bulletin de correspondance hellénique* 82: 47–60.

Gutzwiller, Kathryn J. 1993. "Anyte's Epigram Book." *Syllecta Classica* 4: 71–89.

———. 1997a. "The Poetics of Editing in Meleager's *Garland*." *Transactions and Proceedings of the American Philological Association* 127: 169–200.

Gutzwiller, Kathryn J. 1997b. "Genre Development and Gendered Voices in Nossis and Erinna." In *Dwelling in Possibility: Women Poets and Critics on Poetry*, ed. Y. Prins and M. Shreiber, pp. 202–22. Ithaca NY: Cornell University Press.

———. 1998. *Poetic Garlands: Hellenistic Epigrams in Context*. Berkeley: University of California Press.

———. 2017a. "Erinna." In *Hellenistic Poetry: A Selection*, ed. D. Sider, pp. 277–87. Ann Arbor: University of Michigan Press.

———. 2017b. "Moero." In *Hellenistic Poetry: A Selection*, ed. D. Sider, pp. 405–12. Ann Arbor: University of Michigan Press.

Hafner, Markus. 2022. "Pythia Poetrix? Zur Polyphonie des orakularen 'Ichs.'" In *The Gender Parameter in the Shaping of First-Person Discourse in Classical Literature: Shaping a (Gendered) 'I' Persona*, ed. T. Fuhrer and L. Cordes. Berlin: de Gruyter.

———. Forthcoming. "Funktion, Stimme, Fiktion: Studien zu Konzeptionen kooperativer Autorschaft in frühgriechischer und klassischer Literatur." Habilitation, University of Graz.

Hahm, David E. 1969. "Plato's 'Noble Lie' and Political Brotherhood." *Classica et Mediaevalia* 30: 211–27.

Hall, Edith. 1989a. "The Archer Scene in Aristophanes' *Thesmophoriazusae*." *Philologus* 133: 38–54.

———. 1989b. *Inventing the Barbarian: Greek Self-Definition through Tragedy*. Oxford: Clarendon.

———. 2000. "Female Figures and Metapoetry in Old Comedy." In *The Rivals of Aristophanes: Studies in Athenian Old Comedy*, ed. D. Harvey and J. Wilkins, pp. 407–18. London: Duckworth.

Hall, Joan Kelly. 2012. "Language and Identity." In *Teaching and Researching: Language and Culture*, pp. 30–46. 2nd ed. London: Routledge.

Hallett, Judith P. 1979. "Sappho and Her Social Context: Sense and Sensuality." *Signs* 4 (3): 447–64.

Halliwell, Stephen. 1980. "Aristophanes' Apprenticeship." *Classical Quarterly* 30: 33–45.

———, ed. 1988. *Plato: Republic 10*. Warminster: Aris and Phillips.

———, ed. 1993. *Plato: Republic 5*. Warminster: Aris and Phillips.

———. 2000. "The Subjection of *Muthos* to *Logos*: Plato's Citations of the Poets." *Classical Quarterly* 50: 94–112.

———. 2002. *The Aesthetics of Mimesis: Ancient Texts and Modern Problems*. Princeton NJ: Princeton University Press.

———. 2011. "Antidotes and Incantations: Is There a Cure for Poetry in Plato's *Republic*?" In *Plato and the Poets*, ed. P. Destrée and F.-G. Herrmann, pp. 241–66. Leiden: Brill.

Halperin, David. 1990. *One Hundred Years of Homosexuality, and Other Essays on Greek Love*. London, New York: Routledge.

Hamilton, John T. 2015. "Torture as an Instrument of Music." In *Thresholds of Listening: Sound, Technics, Space*, ed. S. van Maas, pp. 143–52. New York: Fordham University Press.

Hansen, Hardy. 1976. "Aristophanes' *Thesmophoriazusae*: Theme, Structure, and Production." *Philologus* 120: 165–85.

Hardie, Alex. 1983. *Statius and the Silvae: Poets, Patrons, and Epideixis in the Graeco-Roman World*. Liverpool: Cairns.

———. 2005. "Sappho, the Muses, and Life after Death." *Zeitschrift für Papyrologie und Epigraphik* 154: 13–32.

Harlow, Mary. 1998. "In the Name of the Father: Procreation, Paternity and Patriarchy." In *Thinking Men: Masculinity and Its Self-Representation in the Classical Tradition*, ed. L. Foxhall and J. Salmon, pp. 155–69. London and New York: Routledge.

Harrell, Sarah E. 2003. "Marvelous *Andreia*: Politics, Geography, and Ethnicity in Herodotus' *Histories*." In *Andreia: Studies in Manliness and Courage in Classical Antiquity*, ed. R. Rosen and I. Sluiter, pp. 77–94. Leiden: Brill.

Harrison, Thomas, ed. 2002. *Greeks and Barbarians*. Edinburgh: Edinburgh University Press.

———. 2003. "Upside Down and Back to Front: Herodotus and the Greek Encounter with Egypt." In *Ancient Perspectives on Egypt*, ed. R. Matthews and C. Römer, pp. 145–55. London, New York: Routledge.

Hartog, François. 1988. *The Mirror of Herodotus: An Essay on the Interpretation of the Other*. Translated by Janet Lloyd. Berkeley: University of California Press.

Harvey, David. 2000. "Phrynichos and His Muses." In *The Rivals of Aristophanes: Studies in Athenian Old Comedy*, ed. D. Harvey and J. Wilkins, pp. 91–134. London: Duckworth.

Harvey, David, and John Wilkins, eds. 2000. *The Rivals of Aristophanes: Studies in Athenian Old Comedy*. London: Duckworth.

Hauser, Emily. 2016a. "In Her Own Words: The Semantics of Female Authorship in Ancient Greece, from Sappho to Nossis." *Ramus* 45 (2): 133–64.

———. 2016b. "*Optima tu proprii nominis auctor*: The Semantics of Female Authorship in Ancient Rome, from Sulpicia to Proba." *Eugesta* 6: 151–86.

———. 2020. "Putting an End to Song: Penelope, Odysseus, and the Teleologies of the *Odyssey*." *Helios* 47 (1): 39–69.

———. 2022. "Making Men: Gender and the Poet in Pindar." In *The Gender Parameter in the Shaping of First-Person Discourse in Classical Literature: Shaping a (Gendered) 'I' Persona*, ed. T. Fuhrer and L. Cordes, pp. 129–49. Berlin: de Gruyter.

———. Forthcoming. "Women in Homer (and Beyond)." In *The Cambridge Companion to Ancient Greek Epic*, ed. E. Greensmith. Cambridge: Cambridge University Press.

Heath, John. 2013. "Why Corinna?" *Hermes* 141 (2): 155–170.

———. 2017. "Corinna's 'Old Wives' Tales.'" *Harvard Studies in Classical Philology* 109: 83–130.

Heath, Malcolm. 1987. *Political Comedy in Aristophanes*. Göttingen: Vandenhoeck and Ruprecht.

———. 2013. "Aristotle *On Poets*: A Critical Evaluation of Richard Janko's Edition of the Fragments." *Studia Humaniora Tartuensia* 14 (1): 1–27.

Heiden, Bruce. 1991. "Tragedy and Comedy in the *Frogs* of Aristophanes." *Ramus* 20 (1): 95–111.

———. 2007. "The Muses' Uncanny Lies: Hesiod, *Theogony* 27 and Its Translators." *American Journal of Philology* 128 (2): 153–75.

———. 2008a. "Two Notes on the Invocation of the Muses at *Iliad* 2.484–93." *Scripta Classica Israelica* 27: 1–7.

———. 2008b. *Homer's Cosmic Fabrication: Choice and Design in the Iliad*. Oxford: Oxford University Press.

Hellinger, Marlis, and Hadumod Bußmann, eds. 2001–2003. *Gender across Languages: The Linguistic Representation of Women and Men*. 3 vols. Amsterdam: John Benjamins.

Henderson, Jeffrey. 1987a. "Older Women in Attic Old Comedy." *Transactions and Proceedings of the American Philological Association* 117: 105–29.

———, ed. 1987b. *Aristophanes: Lysistrata*. Oxford: Oxford University Press.

———. 1990. "The *Dēmos* and the Comic Competition." In *Nothing to Do with Dionysos? Athenian Drama in its Social Context*, ed. J. J. Winkler and F. I. Zeitlin, pp. 271–313. Princeton NJ: Princeton University Press.

———. 1991. "Women and the Athenian Dramatic Festivals." *Transactions and Proceedings of the American Philological Association* 121: 133–47.

Henderson, William John. 1995. "Corinna of Tanagra on Poetry." *Acta Classica* 38: 29–41.

Herington, John. 1991. "The Poem of Herodotus." *Arion* 1 (3): 5–16.

Heubeck, Alfred, Stephanie West, and J. B. Hainsworth, eds. 1988. *A Commentary on Homer's Odyssey*. Vol. 1, *Introduction and Books I–VIII*. Oxford: Clarendon.

Hobbs, Angela. 2000. *Plato and the Hero: Courage, Manliness and the Impersonal Good*. Cambridge: Cambridge University Press.

Höghammar, Kerstin. 1993. *Sculpture and Society: A Study of the Connection between the Free-Standing Sculpture and Society on Kos in the Hellenistic and Augustan Periods*. Uppsala: Acta Universitatis Upsaliensis.

———. 1997. "Women in Public Space: Cos c. 200 BC to c. AD 15/20." In *Sculptors and Sculpture of Caria and the Dodecanese*, ed. I. Jenkins, Ian, G. B. Waywell, M. Gisler-Hüwiler and P. Higgs, pp. 127–33. London: British Museum Press.

Holmberg, Ingrid Elisabeth. 1997. "The Sign of ΜΗΤΙΣ." *Arethusa* 30 (1): 1–33.

Holmes, Janet, and Miriam Meyerhoff. 1999. "The Community of Practice: Theories and Methodologies in Language and Gender Research." *Language in Society* 28 (2): 173–83.

Holmes, Janet, and Nick Wilson. 2017. *An Introduction to Sociolinguistics*. 5th ed. London, New York: Routledge.

Holmes, Brooke. 2012. *Gender: Antiquity and Its Legacy*. Oxford: Oxford University Press.

Holst-Warhaft, Gail. 1992. *Dangerous Voices: Women's Laments and Greek Literature*. London, New York: Routledge.

Homeyer, Helene. 1977. *Die Spartanische Helene und der Trojanische Krieg*. Wiesbaden: Steiner.

Honko, L. 1998. *Textualizing the Siri Epic*. Helsinki: Academia Scientarum Fennica.

Hoogvliet, J. M. 1821. *Specimen philosopho-criticum, continens Diatriben de Bione Borysthenita*. Leiden: M. Cyfveer.

Hooker, James T. 1977. "ΣΥΝΔΙΚΟΣ in Pindar." *Philologus* 121: 300.

Hopkinson, Neil, ed. 2015. *Theocritus, Moschus, Bion*. Cambridge MA: Harvard University Press.

Hornblower, Simon. 2006. "Herodotus' Influence in Antiquity." In *The Cambridge Companion to Herodotus*, ed. C. Dewald and J. Marincola, pp. 306–18. Cambridge: Cambridge University Press.

Householder, Fred W. 1995a. "Plato and His Predecessors." In *Concise History of the Language Sciences: From the Sumerians to the Cognitivists*, ed. E. F. K. Koerner and R. E. Asher, pp. 90–93. Oxford, New York: Elsevier.

————. 1995b. "Aristotle and the Stoics on Language." In *Concise History of the Language Sciences: From the Sumerians to the Cognitivists*, ed. E. F. K. Koerner and R. E. Asher, pp. 93–99. Oxford, New York: Elsevier.

Hubbard, Thomas K. 1986. "Parabatic Self-Criticism and the Two Versions of Aristophanes' *Clouds*." *Classical Antiquity* 5: 182–97.

————. 1991. *The Mask of Comedy: Aristophanes and the Intertextual Parabasis*. Ithaca NY: Cornell University Press.

————. 1995. "Hesiod's Fable of the Hawk and the Nightingale Reconsidered." *Greek, Roman and Byzantine Studies* 36 (2): 161–71.

Hünemörder, Christian. 2006. "Nightingale." In *Brill's New Pauly*. Vol. 9, ed. H. Cancik and H. Schneider, pp. 749–51. Leiden: Brill.

Hunter, Richard. 1996. *Theocritus and the Archaeology of Greek Poetry*. Cambridge: Cambridge University Press.

————. 2004a. *Plato's Symposium*. Oxford: Oxford University Press.

————. 2004b. "Homer and Greek Literature." In *The Cambridge Companion to Homer*, ed. R. Fowler, pp. 235–53. Cambridge: Cambridge University Press.

————. 2008. "Mime and Mimesis: Theocritus, *Idyll* 15." In *On Coming After: Studies in Post-Classical Greek Literature and Its Reception*, pp. 233–56. Berlin: de Gruyter.

————. 2009. *Critical Moments in Classical Literature: Studies in the Ancient View of Literature and Its Uses*. Cambridge: Cambridge University Press.

————. 2021. "Sappho and Hellenistic Poetry." In *The Cambridge Companion to Sappho*, ed. P. J. Finglass and A. Kelly, pp. 277–89. Cambridge: Cambridge University Press.

Hussein, Ersin, and Massimo Raffa. 2016. "A Musical Note from Roman Cyprus." *Trends in Classics* 8 (1): 124–38.

Hutchinson, Gregory O. 2001. *Greek Lyric Poetry: A Commentary on Selected Larger Pieces*. Oxford: Oxford University Press.

————. 2013. *Greek to Latin: Frameworks and Contexts for Intertextuality*. Oxford: Oxford University Press.

Ibrahim, Muhammad Hasan. 1973. *Grammatical Gender: Its Origin and Development*. The Hague, Paris: Mouton.

Innes, Doreen C. 1995. Introduction to *Aristotle: Poetics, Longinus: On the Sublime, Demetrius: On Style*, ed. S. Halliwell, W. H. Fyfe and D. C. Innes, pp. 309–40. Cambridge MA: Harvard University Press.

Irigaray, Luce. 1985. *This Sex Which Is Not One*. Translated by Catherine Porter with Carolyn Burke. Ithaca NY: Cornell University Press.

————. 1989. "Sorcerer Love: A Reading of Plato's *Symposium*, Diotima's Speech." Translated by Eleanor H. Kuykendall. *Hypatia* 3 (3): 32–44.

Jaillard, Dominique. 2007. *Configurations d'Hermès: Une "théogonie hermaïque."* Kernos Supplément 17. Liège: Kernos.

Janaway, Christopher. 1995. *Images of Excellence: Plato's Critique of the Arts*. Oxford: Oxford University Press.

————. 2006. "Plato and the Arts." In *A Companion to Plato*, ed. H. Benson, pp. 388–400. Oxford and Malden MA: Blackwell.

Janko, Richard. 1982. *Homer, Hesiod, and the Hymns: Diachronic Development in Epic Diction.* Cambridge: Cambridge University Press.

———. 1998. "The Homeric Poems as Oral Dictated Texts." *The Classical Quarterly* 48 (1): 1–13.

———, ed. 2000. *Philodemus: On Poems, Book 1.* Oxford: Oxford University Press.

———, ed. 2011. *Philodemus: On Poems, Books 3–4, with the Fragments of Aristotle: On Poets.* Oxford: Oxford University Press.

Janse, Mark. 2020. "Sex and Agreement: (Mis)matching Natural and Grammatical Gender in Greek." *Keria* 22 (2): 25–55.

Jennings, Victoria, and Andrea Katsaros, eds. 2007. *The World of Ion of Chios.* Leiden, Boston: Brill.

Jensen, Minna Skafte. 2011. *Writing Homer: A Study Based on Results from Modern Fieldwork.* Copenhagen: The Royal Danish Academy of Sciences and Letters.

Johnson, Ian P. 2019. "Gender Neutral Wording Is Making German Ridiculous, Asserts Association." *Die Welle*, March 7, 2019. https://www.dw.com/en/gender-neutral-wording-is-making-german-ridiculous-asserts-association/a-47801450.

Jong, Erica. 1980. "The Artist as Housewife." In *In Her Own Image: Women Working in the Arts,* ed. E. Hedges and I. Wendt, pp. 115–20. New York: Feminist Press.

Kampen, Natalie Boymel. 1998. Preface to *Thinking Men: Masculinity and Its Self-Representation in the Classical Tradition*, ed. L. Foxhall and J. Salmon, pp. x–xi. London and New York: Routledge.

Kaplan, Justin, and Anne Bernays. 1999. *The Language of Names: What We Call Ourselves and Why It Matters.* New York: Touchstone.

Karanika, Andromache. 2014. *Voices at Work: Women, Performance, and Labor in Ancient Greece.* Baltimore: John Hopkins University Press.

Katz, Joshua T., and Katharina Volk. 2000. "'Mere Bellies'? A New Look at *Theogony* 26–8." *The Journal of Hellenic Studies* 120: 122–31.

Katz, Marilyn. 1991. *Penelope's Renown: Meaning and Indeterminacy in the Odyssey.* Princeton NJ: Princeton University Press.

Kelly, Adrian. 2021. "Sappho and Epic." In *The Cambridge Companion to Sappho*, ed. P. J. Finglass and A. Kelly, pp. 53–64. Cambridge: Cambridge University Press.

Kendall, Shari. 2003. "Creating Gendered Demeanors of Authority at Work and at Home." In *The Handbook of Language and Gender*, ed. J. Holmes and M. Meyerhoff, pp. 600–623. Oxford: Blackwell.

Kennedy, George A. 1986. "Helen's Web Unraveled." *Arethusa* 19: 5–14.

Kern, Edith. 1961. "Author or Authoress?" *Yale French Studies* 27: 3–11.

Kindstrand, Jan F., ed. 1976. *Bion of Borysthenes.* Uppsala: Acta Universitatis Upsaliensis.

Kingsley, K. Scarlett. 2018. "Justifying Violence in Herodotus' *Histories* 3.38: *Nomos*, King of All, and Pindaric Poetics." In *Herodotus: Narrator, Scientist, Historian*, ed. E. Bowie, pp. 37–58. Berlin: de Gruyter.

Kirby, John T. 1991. "Mimesis and Diegesis: Foundations of Aesthetic Theory in Plato and Aristotle." *Helios* 18 (2): 113–28.

Kivilo, Maarit. 2010. *Early Greek Poets' Lives: The Shaping of the Tradition.* Leiden: Brill.

———. 2021. "Sappho's Lives." In *The Cambridge Companion to Sappho*, ed. P. J. Finglass and A. Kelly, pp. 11–21. Cambridge: Cambridge University Press.

Klinck, Anne L. 2001. "Male Poets and Maiden Voices: Gender and Genre in Pindar and Alcman." *Hermes* 129 (2): 276–9.

———. 2008. *Woman's Songs in Ancient Greece*. Montreal: McGill-Queen's University Press.

Klooster, Jacqueline. 2011. *Poetry as Window and Mirror: Positioning the Poet in Hellenistic Poetry*. Leiden: Brill.

Knox, Bernard. 1952. "The *Hippolytus* of Euripides." *Yale Classical Studies* 13: 1–31.

———. 1977. "The *Medea* of Euripides." *Yale Classical Studies* 25: 193–225.

Koller, Hermann. 1972. "Epos." *Glotta* 50: 16–24.

Konstantakos, Ioannis M. 2018. "Time, Thy Pyramids: The 'Novella' of Mycerinus (Herodotus 2.129–134)." In *Herodotus: Narrator, Scientist, Historian*, ed. E. Bowie, pp. 77–107. Berlin: de Gruyter.

Kovacs, David, ed. 1999. *Euripides: Trojan Women, Iphigenia among the Taurians, Ion*. Cambridge MA: Harvard University Press.

Kranz, Walter. 1939. *Geschichte der griechischen Literatur*. Leipzig: Dieterich.

Kruschwitz, Peter. 2012. "Language, Sex, and (Lack of) Power: Reassessing the Linguistic Discourse about Female Speech in Latin Sources." *Athenaeum* 100: 197–229.

Kurke, Leslie. 1999. *Coins, Bodies, Games, and Gold: The Politics of Meaning in Archaic Greece*. Princeton NJ: Princeton University Press,

———. 2000. "The Strangeness of 'Song Culture': Archaic Greek Poetry." In *Literature in the Greek and Roman Worlds: A New Perspective*, ed. O. Taplin, pp. 58–87. Oxford: Oxford University Press.

———. 2007. "Archaic Greek Poetry." In *The Cambridge Companion to Archaic Greece*, ed. H. A. Shapiro, pp. 141–68. Cambridge: Cambridge University Press.

———. 2011. *Aesopic Conversations: Popular Tradition, Cultural Dialogue, and the Invention of Greek Prose*. Princeton NJ: Princeton University Press.

Lada-Richards, Ismene. 1999. *Initiating Dionysus: Ritual and Theatre in Aristophanes' Frogs*. Oxford: Oxford University Press.

———. 2002. "Reinscribing the Muse: Greek Drama and the Discourse of Inspired Creativity." In *Cultivating the Muse: Struggles for Power and Inspiration in Classical Literature*, ed. E. Spentzou and D. Fowler, pp. 69–92. Oxford: Oxford University Press.

Lamari, Anna A. 2007. "Aeschylus' *Seven against Thebes* vs. Euripides' *Phoenissae*: Male vs. Female Power." *Wiener Studien* 120: 5–24.

Lamb, W. R. M., ed. 1925. *Plato: Lysis, Symposium, Gorgias*. Cambridge MA: Harvard University Press.

Lambert, Michael. 2001. "Gender and Religion in Theocritus, *Idyll* 15: Prattling Tourists at the *Adonia*." *Acta Classica* 44: 87–103.

Lanata, Giuliana. 1996. "Sappho's Amatory Language." In *Reading Sappho: Contemporary Approaches*, ed. E. Greene, pp. 11–25. Berkeley: University of California Press.

Lanser, Susan Sniader. 1992. *Fictions of Authority: Women Writers and Narrative Voice*. Ithaca NY: Cornell University Press.

Lardinois, André. 1994. "Subject and Circumstance in Sappho's Poetry." *Transactions and Proceedings of the American Philological Association* 124: 57–84.

———. 1996. "Who Sang Sappho's Songs?" In *Reading Sappho: Contemporary Approaches*, ed. E. Greene, pp. 150–72. Berkeley: University of California Press.

Lardinois, André. 2001. "Keening Sappho: Female Speech Genres in Sappho's Poetry." in *Making Silence Speak: Women's Voices in Greek Literature and Society*, ed. A. Lardinois and L. McClure, pp. 75–92. Princeton NJ: Princeton University Press.

———. 2014. "Notes." In *Sappho: A New Translation of the Complete Works*, trans. D. Rayor, pp. 97–154. Cambridge: Cambridge University Press.

———. 2021a. "Sappho as Anchor for Male and Female Greek Poets in the Hellenistic Period." In *Women and Power in Hellenistic Poetry*, ed. M. A. Harder, J. J. H. Klooster, R. F. Regtuit, and G. C. Wakker, pp. 161–92. Leuven: Peeters.

———. 2021b. "Sappho's Personal Poetry." In *The Cambridge Companion to Sappho*, ed. P. J. Finglass and A. Kelly, pp. 163–74. Cambridge: Cambridge University Press.

Lardinois, André, and Laura K. McClure, eds. 2001. *Making Silence Speak: Women's Voices in Greek Literature and Society*. Princeton NJ: Princeton University Press.

Larmour, David H. J. 2005. "Corinna's Poetic *Metis* and the Epinikian Tradition." In *Women Poets in Ancient Greece and Rome*, ed. E. Greene, pp. 25–58. Norman: University of Oklahoma Press.

Larson, Jennifer. 2007. *Ancient Greek Cults: A Guide*. London, New York: Routledge.

Larson, Stephanie. 2006. "Kandaules' Wife, Masistes' Wife: Herodotus' Narrative Strategy in Suppressing Names of Women (Hdt. 1.8–12 and 9.108–13)." *Classical Journal* 101 (3): 225–44.

Lateiner, Donald. 1989. *The Historical Method of Herodotus*. Toronto: University of Toronto Press.

Latte, Kurt. 1956. "Die Lebenszeit der Korinna." *Eranos* 54: 57–67.

Lattimore, Richmond. 1962. *Themes in Greek and Latin Epitaphs*. Urbana: Illinois University Press.

Lauriola, Rosanna. 2015. "Medea." In *Brill's Companion to the Reception of Euripides*, ed. R. Lauriola and K. N. Demetriou, pp. 377–442. Leiden: Brill.

Le Guen, Brigitte. 2001. *Les associations de technites dionysiaques à l'époque hellénistique. I: Corpus documentaire*. Nancy: Association pour la Diffusion de la Recherche sur l'Antiquité.

Lech, Marcel Lysgaard. 2012. "Eupolis and the λῆρος of the Poets: A Note on Eupolis 205 K-A." *The Classical Journal* 107 (3): 283–89.

Lee, Kevin H., ed. 1976. *Euripides: Troades*. Basingstoke: Macmillan.

Lefkowitz, Jeremy B. 2014. "Aesop and Animal Fable." In *The Oxford Handbook of Animals in Classical Thought and Life*, ed. G. Campbell, pp. 1–23. Oxford: Oxford University Press.

Lefkowitz, Mary. 1981a. *Heroines and Hysterics*. London: Duckworth.

———. 1981b. *The Lives of the Greek Poets*. London: Duckworth.

Lefkowitz, Mary, and Maureen B. Fant, eds. 2005. *Women's Life in Greece and Rome: A Source Book in Translation*. 3rd ed. Baltimore: Johns Hopkins University Press.

Levaniouk, Olga. 2008. "Lament and Hymenaios in Erinna's *Distaff*." In *Lament: Studies in the Ancient Mediterranean and Beyond*, ed. A. Suter, pp. 200–232. Oxford: Oxford University Press.

Levine, Daniel B. 2002. "Poetic Justice: Homer's Death in the Ancient Biographical Tradition." *Classical Journal* 98 (2): 141–60.

Liapis, Vayos, ed. 2012. *A Commentary on the Rhesus attributed to Euripides*. Oxford: Oxford University Press.

Licciardello, Flavia. 2016. "Nossis' Auto-Epitaph: Analysing a Controversial Epigram." *Acta Antiqua Academiae Scientiarum Hungaricae* 56 (4): 435–48.

Lidov, Joel. 2002. "Sappho, Herodotus, and the *Hetaira*." *Classical Philology* 97 (3): 203–37.

Lincoln, Bruce. 1997. "Competing Discourses: Rethinking the Prehistory of *Mythos* and *Logos*." *Arethusa* 30 (3): 341–68.

Livia, Anna. 2003. "'One Man in Two is a Woman': Linguistic Approaches to Gender in Literary Texts." In *The Handbook of Language and Gender*, ed. J. Holmes and M. Meyerhoff, pp. 142–58. Oxford: Blackwell.

Llewellyn-Jones, Lloyd. 2003. *Aphrodite's Tortoise: The Veiled Woman of Ancient Greece*. Swansea: Classical Press of Wales.

Lloyd, Alan B. 1975. *Herodotus Book II*. Vol. 1, *Introduction*. Leiden: Brill.

———. 1988. *Herodotus Book II*. Vol. 3, *Commentary 99–182*. Leiden: Brill.

Lobel, Edgar. 1930. "Corinna." *Hermes* 65: 356–65.

Lobel, Edgar, and Denys L. Page, eds. 1963. *Poetarum Lesbiorum fragmenta*. Oxford: Clarendon.

Loraux, Nicole. 1987. *Tragic Ways of Killing a Woman*. Translated by Anthony Forster. Cambridge MA: Harvard University Press.

———. 1990. "Herakles: The Super-Male and the Feminine." In *Before Sexuality: The Construction of Erotic Experience in the Ancient Greek World*, ed. D. M. Halperin, J. J. Winkler, and F. I. Zeitlin, pp. 21–52. Princeton NJ: Princeton University Press.

———. 1993. *The Children of Athena: Athenian Ideas about Citizenship and the Division between the Sexes*. Translated by Caroline Levine. Princeton NJ: Princeton University Press.

———. 1998. *Mothers in Mourning, with the Essay "Of Amnesty and Its Opposite."* Translated by Corinne Pache. Ithaca NY, London: Cornell University Press.

———. 2002. *The Mourning Voice: An Essay on Greek Tragedy*. Translated by Elizabeth Rawlings. Ithaca NY: Cornell University Press.

Loxton, Rachel. 2019. "From Fräulein to the Gender Star: Germany's Language Revolution." *The Local De*, November 1, 2019. https://www.thelocal.de/20190212/from-frulein-to-the-gender-star-germanys-language-revolution/.

Ludwig, Walther. 1963. "Plato's Love Epigrams." *Greek, Roman and Byzantine Studies* 4: 59–82.

Luschnig, Cecelia A. E. 2007. *Granddaughter of the Sun: A Study of Euripides' Medea*. Leiden: Brill.

Lutwack, Leonard. 1994. *Birds in Literature*. Gainesville: University Press of Florida.

Maas, Martha, and Jane McIntosh Snyder. 1989. *Stringed Instruments of Ancient Greece*. New Haven CT: Yale University Press.

Maas, Paul. 1936. "Nossis." *Paulys Realencyclopädie der classischen Altertumswissenschaft* 17.1: 1053–4.

Macaulay, George C., transl. 1890. *The History of Herodotus*. 2 vols. London: Macmillan.

MacDowell, Douglas M., ed. 1971. *Aristophanes: Wasps*. Oxford: Oxford University Press.

———. 1982. "Aristophanes and Kallistratos." *Classical Quarterly* 32: 21–6.

———. 1995. *Aristophanes and Athens: An Introduction to the Plays*. Oxford, New York: Oxford University Press.

Macleod, Colin, ed. 1982. *Homer Iliad Book XXIV*. Cambridge: Cambridge University Press.

Major, Wilfred E. 2013. *The Court of Comedy: Aristophanes, Rhetoric, and Democracy in Fifth-Century Athens*. Columbus: Ohio State University Press.

Manville, Philip B. 1990. *The Origins of Citizenship in Ancient Athens*. Princeton NJ: Princeton University Press.

Manwell, Elizabeth. 2005. "*Dico ergo sum*: Erinna's Voice and Poetic Reality." In *Women Poets in Ancient Greece and Rome*, ed. E. Greene, pp. 72–90. Norman: University of Oklahoma Press.

March, Jennifer R. 1990. "Euripides the Misogynist?" In *Euripides, Women and Sexuality*, ed. A. Powell, pp. 32–75. London, New York: Routledge.

———, ed. 2020. *Sophocles: Oedipus Tyrannus*. Liverpool: Liverpool University Press.

Marelli, Cesare. 2006. "L'autore come personaggio: l'Euripide di Aristofane." In *L'autore e l'opera: Attribuzioni, appropriazioni, apocrifi nella Grecia antica*, ed. F. Roscalla, pp. 133–53. Pisa: ETS.

Marincola, John. 2006. "Herodotus and the Poetry of the Past." In *The Cambridge Companion to Herodotus*, ed. C. Dewald and J. Marincola, pp. 13–28. Cambridge: Cambridge University Press.

———. 2007. "Odysseus and the Historians." *Syllecta Classica* 18: 1–79.

———. 2018. "Ὁμηρικώτατος? Battle Narratives in Herodotus." In *Herodotus: Narrator, Scientist, Historian*, ed. E. Bowie, pp. 3–24. Berlin: de Gruyter.

Marmodoro, Anna, and Jonathan Hill, eds. 2013. *The Author's Voice in Classical and Late Antiquity*. Oxford: Oxford University Press.

Marquardt, Patricia. 1982. "The Two Faces of Hesiod's Muse." *Illinois Classical Studies* 7 (1): 1–12.

Marrou, Henri Irénée. 1975. *Histoire de l'éducation dans l'antiquité*. 7th ed. Paris: Editions de Seuil.

Marshall, Hallie R. 2012. "Clouds, Eupolis and Reperformance." In *No Laughing Matter: Studies in Athenian Comedy*, ed. C. W. Marshall and G. Kovacs, pp. 55–68. London: Bristol Classical Press.

Martin, Richard P. 1989. *The Language of Heroes: Speech and Performance in the Iliad*. Ithaca NY: Cornell University Press.

———. 2001. "Just Like a Woman: Enigmas of the Lyric Voice." In *Making Silence Speak: Women's Voices in Greek Literature and Society*, ed. A. Lardinois and L. McClure, pp. 55–74. Princeton NJ: Princeton University Press.

———. 2016. "Sappho, Iambist: Abusing the Brother." In *The Newest Sappho: P. Sapph. Obbink and P. GC inv. 105, frs. 1–4*, ed. A. Bierl and A. Lardinois, pp. 110–26. Leiden, Boston: Brill.

Marušič, Jera. 2011. "Poets and Mimesis in the *Republic*." In *Plato and the Poets*, ed. P. Destrée and F.-G. Herrmann, pp. 217–40. Leiden, Boston: Brill.

Maslov, Boris. 2009. "The Semantics of Ἀοιδός and Related Compounds: Towards a Historical Poetics of Solo Performance in Archaic Greece." *Classical Antiquity* 28 (1): 1–38.

———. 2015. *Pindar and the Emergence of Literature*. Cambridge: Cambridge University Press.

———. 2016. "The Genealogy of the Muses: An Internal Reconstruction of Archaic Greek Metapoetics." *American Journal of Philology* 137 (3): 411–46.

Masterson, Mark. 2013. "Studies of Ancient Masculinity." In *A Companion to Greek and Roman Sexualities*, ed. T. K. Hubbard, pp. 17–30. Malden MA, Oxford: Wiley-Blackwell.

Mastronarde, Donald, ed. 1994. *Euripides: Phoenissae*. Cambridge: Cambridge University Press.

———, ed. 2002. *Euripides: Medea*. Cambridge: Cambridge University Press.

Mattison, Kathryn. 2015. "*Rhesus* and the Evolution of Tragedy." *Classical World* 108 (4): 485–97.

Maurizio, Lisa. 1995. "Anthropology and Spirit Possession: A Reconsideration of the Pythia's Role at Delphi." *Journal for Hellenic Studies* 115: 69–86.

———. 2001. "The Voice at the Center of the World: The Pythias' Ambiguity and Authority." In *Making Silence Speak: Women's Voices in Greek Literature and Society*, ed. A. Lardinois and L. McClure, pp. 38–54. Princeton NJ: Princeton University Press.

Mayer, Roland G. 2003. "Persona<l> Problems: The Literary Persona in Antiquity Revisited." *Materiali e discussioni per l'analisi dei testi classici* 50: 55–80.

McClure, Laura K. 1995. "Female Speech and Characterization in Euripides." In *Lo spettacolo delle voci*, vol. 2, ed. F. de Martino and A. H. Sommerstein, pp. 35–60. Bari: Levante.

———. 1999a. *Spoken like a Woman: Speech and Gender in Athenian Drama*. Princeton NJ: Princeton University Press.

———. 1999b. "'The Worst Husband': Discourses of Praise and Blame in Euripides' *Medea*." *Classical Philology* 94 (4): 373–94.

———. 2001. Introduction to *Making Silence Speak: Women's Voices in Greek Literature and Society*, ed. A. Lardinois and L. McClure, pp. 3–16. Princeton NJ: Princeton University Press.

———, ed. 2002. *Sexuality and Gender in the Classical World: Readings and Sources*. Oxford, Malden MA: Blackwell.

———. 2003. *Courtesans at Table: Gender and Greek Literary Culture in Athenaeus*. London, New York: Routledge.

McConnell-Ginet, Sally. 2003. "'What's in a Name?' Social Labeling and Gender Practices." In *The Handbook of Language and Gender*, ed. J. Holmes and M. Meyerhoff, pp. 69–97. Oxford: Blackwell.

———. 2014. "Gender and Its Relation to Sex: The Myth of 'Natural' Gender." In *The Expression of Gender*, ed. G. G. Corbett, pp. 3–38. Berlin: de Gruyter.

McDonald, Katherine. 2016. "The Sociolinguistics of Gender, Social Status and Masculinity in Aristophanes." *Journal of Historical Sociolinguistics* 2 (2): 155–88.

McElhinny, Bonnie. 2003. "Theorizing Gender in Sociolinguistics and Linguistic Anthropology." In *The Handbook of Language and Gender*, ed. J. Holmes and M. Meyerhoff, pp. 21–42. Oxford: Blackwell.

McGlew, James F. 2002. *Citizens on Stage: Comedy and Political Culture in the Athenian Democracy*. Ann Arbor: University of Michigan Press.

McManus, Barbara F. 1997. *Classics and Feminism: Gendering the Classics*. New York: Twayne.

McPhee, Brian D. 2018. "Mythological Innovations in Corinna's Asopides poem (fr. 654.ii–iv PMG)." *Greek, Roman and Byzantine Studies* 58 (2): 198–222.

Melberg, Arne. 1995. *Theories of Mimesis*. Cambridge: Cambridge University Press.

Meulder, Marcel. 1992. "L'invocation aux Muses et leur réponse: Platon, *Rép.* VIII, 545d–547c." *Revue de philosophie ancienne* 10: 139–77.

Meyer, Doris. 2007. "The Act of Reading and the Act of Writing in the Hellenistic Epigram." In *Brill's Companion to Hellenistic Epigram*, ed. P. Bing and J. S. Bruss, pp. 185–210. Brill: Leiden.

Meyerhoff, Miriam. 2001. "Communities of Practice." In *Handbook of Language Variation and Change*, ed. J. K. Chambers, P. Trudgill, and N. Schilling-Estes, pp. 526–48. Oxford: Wiley.

Mikalson, Jon D. 2005. *Ancient Greek Religion*. Oxford, Malden MA: Wiley-Blackwell.

Miller, Andrew M. 1979. "The Address to the Delian Maidens in the *Homeric Hymn to Apollo*: Epilogue or Transition?" *Transactions and Proceedings of the American Philological Society* 109: 173–86.

———. 1986. *From Delos to Delphi: A Literary Study of the Homeric Hymn to Apollo*. Leiden: Brill.

Miller, Mitchell H. 1999. "Platonic Mimesis." In *Contextualizing Classics: Ideology, Performance, Dialogue*, ed. T. M. Falkner, N. Felson, and D. Konstan, pp. 253–66. Lanham MD: Rowman and Littlefield.

Millett, Paul. 1984. "Hesiod and His World." *Proceedings of the Cambridge Philological Society* 30: 84–115.

Minchin, Elizabeth. 1995. "The Poet Appeals to His Muse: Homeric Invocations in the Context of Epic Performance." *The Classical Journal* 91 (1): 25–33.

———, ed. 2011. *Orality, Literacy and Performance in the Ancient World*. Leiden: Brill.

Minton, William W. 1960. "Homer's Invocations of the Muses: Traditional Patterns." *Transactions and Proceedings of the American Philological Association* 91: 292–309.

———. 1970. "The Proem-Hymn of Hesiod's *Theogony*." *Transactions and Proceedings of the American Philological Association* 101: 357–77.

Moi, Toril. 1985. *Sexual/Textual Politics*. London: Methuen.

Monella, Paolo. 2005. *Procne e Filomela: Dal mito al simbolo letterario*. Bologna: Patròn Editore.

Morales, Helen. 2020. *Antigone Rising: The Subversive Power of Ancient Myths*. London: Wildfire.

Moravcsik, Julius. 1986. "On Correcting the Poets." *Oxford Studies in Ancient Philosophy* 4: 35–47.

Moravcsik, Julius, and Philip Temko, eds. 1982. *Plato on Beauty, Wisdom, and the Arts*. Totowa NJ: Rowman and Littlefield.

Mordine, Michael. 2006. "Speaking to Kings: Hesiod's *ainos* and the Rhetoric of Allusion in the *Works and Days*." *Classical Quarterly* 56: 363–73.

Morgan, Kathryn A. 1993. "Pindar the Professional and the Rhetoric of the ΚΩΜΟΣ." *Classical Philology* 88 (1): 1–15.

———. 2000. *Myth and Philosophy from the Presocratics to Plato*. Cambridge: Cambridge University Press.

———. 2015. *Pindar and the Construction of the Syracusan Monarchy in the Fifth Century B.C.* Oxford: Oxford University Press.

Moss, Jessica. 2007. "What Is Imitative Poetry and Why Is It Bad?" In *The Cambridge Companion to Plato's Republic*, ed. G. R. F. Ferrari, pp. 415–44. Cambridge: Cambridge University Press.

Mossman, Judith M. 2001. "Women's Speech in Greek Tragedy: The Case of Electra and Clytemnestra in Euripides' *Electra*." *Classical Quarterly* 51 (2): 374–84.

———, ed. 2011. *Euripides: Medea*. Oxford: Aris and Phillips.

Most, Glenn W. 1995. "Reflecting Sappho." *Bulletin of the Institute of Classical Studies* 40: 15–38.

———. 2001. "From *Logos* to *Mythos*." In *From Myth to Reason? Studies in the Development of Greek Thought*, ed. R. Buxton, pp. 25–50. Oxford: Oxford University Press.

———. 2011. "What Ancient Quarrel between Philosophy and Poetry?" In *Plato and the Poets*, ed. P. Destrée and F.-G. Herrmann, pp. 1–20. Leiden: Brill.

Moulton, Carroll. 1981. *Aristophanic Poetry*. Göttingen: Vandenhoeck and Ruprecht.

Moyer, Ian S. 2011. *Egypt and the Limits of Hellenism*. Cambridge: Cambridge University Press.

Muecke, Frances. 1982. "A Portrait of the Artist as a Young Woman." *The Classical Quarterly* 32 (1): 41–55.

Mueller, Melissa. 2007. "Penelope and the Poetics of Remembering." *Arethusa* 40 (3): 337–62.

———. 2010. "Helen's Hands: Weaving for *Kleos* in the *Odyssey*." *Helios* 37 (1): 1–21.

———. 2017. "Gender." In *A Companion to Euripides*, ed. L. McClure, pp. 500–514. Oxford: Wiley-Blackwell.

———. Forthcoming. *Sappho and Homer: A Reparative Reading*. Cambridge: Cambridge University Press.

Munson, Rosaria Vignolo. 1988. "Artemisia in Herodotus." *Classical Antiquity* 7 (1): 91–106.

Murdoch, Iris. 1977. *The Fire and the Sun: Why Plato Banished the Artists*. Oxford: Clarendon.

Murnaghan, Sheila. 1999. "The Poetics of Loss in Greek Epic." In *Epic Traditions in the Contemporary World: The Poetics of Community*, ed. M. Beissinger, J. Tylus, and S. Wofford, pp. 203–20. Berkeley: University of California Press.

———. 2009. "Penelope's *Agnoia*: Knowledge, Power, and Gender in the *Odyssey*." In *Homer's Odyssey*, ed. L. Doherty, pp. 231–46. Oxford: Oxford University Press.

Murray, Jackie, and Jonathan M. Rowland. 2007. "Gendered Voices in Hellenistic Epigram." In *Brill's Companion to Hellenistic Epigram*, ed. P. Bing and J. S. Bruss, pp. 211–32. Brill: Leiden.

Murray, Penelope. 1981. "Poetic Inspiration in Early Greece." *The Journal of Hellenic Studies* 101: 87–100.

———, ed. 1996. *Plato on Poetry*. Cambridge: Cambridge University Press.

———. 1999. "What Is a *Muthos* for Plato?" In *From Myth to Reason? Studies in the Development of Greek Thought*, ed. R. Buxton, pp. 251–62. Oxford: Oxford University Press.

———. 2002. "Plato's Muses: The Goddesses That Endure." In *Cultivating the Muse: Struggles for Power and Inspiration in Classical Literature*, ed. E. Spentzou and D. Fowler, pp. 29–46. Oxford: Oxford University Press.

———. 2004. "The Muses and Their Arts." In *Music and the Muses: The Culture of Mousikē in the Classical Athenian City*, ed. P. Murray and P. Wilson, pp. 365–89. Oxford: Oxford University Press.

———. 2005. "The Muses: Creativity Personified?" In *Personification in the Greek World: From Antiquity to Byzantium*, ed. E. Stafford and J. Herrin, pp. 147–59. Aldershot, Burlington VT: Ashgate.

———. 2006. "Reclaiming the Muse." In *Laughing with Medusa: Classical Myth and Feminist Thought*, ed. V. Zajko and M. Leonard, pp. 327–54. Oxford: Oxford University Press.

———. 2011. "Tragedy, Women and the Family in Plato's *Republic*." In *Plato and the Poets*, ed. P. Destrée and F.-G. Herrmann, pp. 175–93. Leiden, Boston: Brill.

Naddaf, Gerard. 1998. "Translator's Introduction." In *Plato the Myth Maker*, by L. Brisson, pp. vii–liii. Chicago: University of Chicago Press.

Naddaff, Ramona A. 2003. *Exiling the Poets: The Production of Censorship in Plato's Republic*. Chicago: University of Chicago Press.

Nagy, Gregory. 1974. *Comparative Studies in Greek and Indic Meter*. Cambridge MA: Harvard University Press.

Nagy, Gregory. 1979. *The Best of the Achaeans: Concepts of the Hero in Archaic Greek Poetry.* Baltimore: Johns Hopkins University Press.

———. 1989. "Early Greek Views of Poets and Poetry." In *The Cambridge History of Literary Criticism.* Vol. 1, *Classical Criticism*, ed. G. A. Kennedy, pp. 1–77. Cambridge: Cambridge University Press.

———. 1990a. *Pindar's Homer: The Lyric Possession of an Epic Past.* Baltimore: Johns Hopkins University Press.

———. 1990b. *Greek Mythology and Poetics.* Ithaca NY: Cornell University Press.

———. 1992. "Authorisation and Authorship in the Hesiodic Theogony." *Ramus* 21: 119–30.

———. 1996. *Poetry as Performance: Homer and Beyond.* Cambridge: Cambridge University Press.

———. 2001. "Orality and Literacy." In *Encyclopedia of Rhetoric*, ed. T. O. Sloane, pp. 532–38. Oxford: Oxford University Press.

———. 2004a. "L'aède épique en auteur: La tradition des *Vies d'Homère.*" In *Identités d'auteur dans l'antiquité et la tradition européenne*, ed. C. Calame and R. Chartier, pp. 41–68. Grenoble: Millon.

———. 2004b. *Homer's Text and Language.* Urbana, Chicago: University of Illinois Press.

———. 2007. "Did Sappho and Alcaeus Ever Meet? Symmetries of Myth and Ritual in Performing the Songs of Ancient Lesbos." In *Literatur und Religion I: Wege zu einer mythisch–rituellen Poetik bei den Griechen*, ed. A. Bierl, R. Lämmle, and K. Wesselmann, pp. 211–69. Berlin: de Gruyter.

———. 2009a. *Homer the Classic.* Washington, Cambridge MA: Center for Hellenic Studies.

———. 2009b. "Hesiod and the Ancient Biographical Traditions." In *The Brill Companion to Hesiod*, ed. F. Montanari, A. Rengakos, and C. Tsagalis, pp. 271–311. Brill: Leiden.

———. 2010. "Ancient Greek Elegy." In *The Oxford Handbook of the Elegy*, ed. K. Weisman, pp. 13–45. Oxford: Oxford University Press.

———. 2013. "The Delian Maidens and Their Relevance to Choral Mimesis in Classical Drama." In *Choral Mediations in Greek Tragedy*, ed. R. Gagné and M. G. Hopman, pp. 227–56. Cambridge: Cambridge University Press.

———. 2018. "Herodotus on Queens and Courtesans of Egypt." In *Herodotus: Narrator, Scientist, Historian*, ed. E. Bowie, pp. 109–22. Berlin: de Gruyter.

Nehamas, Alexander. 1982. "Plato on Imitation and Poetry in *Republic* 10." In *Plato on Beauty, Wisdom, and the Arts*, ed. J. Moravscik and P. Temko, pp. 47–78. Totowa NJ: Rowman and Littlefield.

Neil, Robert A., ed. 1901. *The Knights of Aristophanes.* Cambridge: Cambridge University Press.

Neils, Jenifer. 2008. "Adonia to Thesmophoria: Women and Athenian Festivals." In *Worshiping Women: Ritual and Reality in Classical Athens*, ed. N. Kaltsas and H. A. Shapiro, pp. 242–65. Athens: National Archaeological Museum.

Nelson, Stephanie. 2016. *Aristophanes and his Tragic Muse: Comedy, Tragedy and the Polis in 5th Century Athens.* Leiden, Boston: Brill.

Nelson, Thomas J. 2019. "'Most Musical, Most Melancholy': Avian Aesthetics of Lament in Greek and Roman Elegy." *Dictynna* 16: http://journals.openedition.org/dictynna/1914.

Neri, Camillo, ed. 1996. *Studi sulle testimonianze di Erinna.* Bologna: Pàtron.

———, ed. 2003. *Erinna: Testimonianze e frammenti*. Bologna: Pàtron.

Nestle, Wilhelm. 1940. *Vom Mythos zu Logos: Die Selbstentfaltung des griechischen Denkens von Homer bis auf die Sophistik und Sokrates*. Stuttgart: Alfred Kröner Verlag.

Nisbet, Gideon. 2019. "Sappho in Roman Epigram." In *Roman Receptions of Sappho*, ed. T. S. Thorsen and S. Harrison, pp. 265–87. Oxford: Oxford University Press.

North, Helen. 1966. *Sophrosyne: Self-Knowledge and Self-Restraint in Greek Literature*. Ithaca NY: Cornell University Press.

Notopoulos, James A. 1938. "Mnemosyne in Oral Literature." *Transactions and Proceedings of the American Philological Association* 69: 465–93.

Noussia-Fantuzzi, Maria. 2010. *Solon the Athenian, the Poetic Fragments*. Leiden: Brill.

Nünlist, René. 1998. *Poetologische Bildersprache in der frühgriechischen Dichtung*. Stuttgart: Teubner.

Nussbaum, Martha C. 2001. *The Fragility of Goodness: Luck and Ethics in Greek Tragedy and Philosophy*. 2nd ed. Cambridge: Cambridge University Press.

Nye, Andrea. 1989. "The Hidden Host: Irigaray and Diotima at Plato's Symposium." *Hypatia* 3 (3): 45–61.

———. 1990. "The Subject of Love: Diotima and Her Critics." *Journal of Value Inquiry* 24: 135–53.

Olson, S. Douglas. 1989. "The Stories of Helen and Menelaus (*Odyssey* 4.240–89) and the Return of Odysseus." *The American Journal of Philology* 110 (3): 387–94.

———. 1995. *Blood and Iron: Stories and Storytelling in Homer's Odyssey*. Leiden: Brill.

———, ed. 2002. *Aristophanes: Acharnians*. Oxford: Oxford University Press.

Olson, S. Douglas, and Alexander Sens, eds. 1999. *Matro of Pitane and the Tradition of Epic Parody in the Fourth Century BCE: Text, Translation, and Commentary*. Oxford: Oxford University Press.

O'Regan, Daphne E. 1992. *Rhetoric, Comedy, and the Violence of Language in Aristophanes' Clouds*. Oxford, New York: Oxford University Press.

Osborne, Catherine. 1994. *Eros Unveiled: Plato and the God of Love*. Oxford: Clarendon.

O'Sullivan, Neil. 1992. *Alcidamas, Aristophanes and the Beginnings of Greek Stylistic Theory*. Stuttgart: Franz Steiner Verlag.

Otto, Walter Friedrich. 1954. *Die Musen und der göttliche Ursprung des Singens und Sagens*. Darmstadt: Wissenschaftliche Buchgemeinschaft.

Padel, Ruth. 1974. "'Imagery of the Elsewhere': Two Choral Odes of Euripides." *Classical Quarterly* 24 (2): 227–41.

Page, Denys L. 1938. *Euripides' Medea*. Oxford: Oxford University Press.

———, ed. 1953. *Corinna*. London: Society for the Promotion of Hellenic Studies.

———. 1955. *Sappho and Alcaeus: An Introduction to the Study of Ancient Lesbian Poetry*. Oxford: Clarendon.

———, ed. 1962. *Poetae melici graeci*. Oxford: Clarendon.

———, ed. 1975. *Epigrammata graeca*. Oxford: Clarendon.

———, ed. 1981. *Further Greek Epigrams: Epigrams before A.D. 50 from the Greek Anthology and Other Sources*. Cambridge: Cambridge University Press.

Pantelia, Maria C. 1993. "Spinning and Weaving: Ideas of Domestic Order in Homer." *The American Journal of Philology* 114 (4): 493–501.

Pantelia, Maria C. 2002. "Helen and the Last Song for Hector." *Transactions of the American Philological Association* 132 (1): 21–27.

Parke, H. W. and D. E. W. Wormell, eds. 1956. *The Delphic Oracle: The History; The Oracular Responses*. 2 vols. Oxford: Blackwell.

Parker, Andrew, and Eve Kosofsky Sedgwick, eds. 1995. *Performativity and Performance*. New York, London: Routledge.

Partee, Morriss Henry. 1970. "Plato's Banishment of Poetry." *Journal of Aesthetics and Art Criticism* 29 (2): 209–22.

———. 1971. "Inspiration in the Aesthetics of Plato." *The Journal of Aesthetics and Art Criticism* 30 (1): 87–95.

———. 1972. "Plato's Theory of Language." *Foundations of Language* 8 (1): 113–32.

Partenie, Catalin, ed. 2009. *Plato's Myths*. Cambridge: Cambridge University Press.

Passmore, Oliver. 2018. "Present, Future and Past in the *Homeric Hymn to Apollo*." *Ramus* 47 (2): 123–51.

Paton, William R., and Edward L. Hicks, eds. 1891. *The Inscriptions of Cos*. Oxford: Clarendon.

Paxson, James J. 1998. "Personification's Gender." *Rhetorica* 16 (2): 149–79.

Pearson, Roger. 2016. *Unacknowledged Legislators: The Poet as Lawgiver in Post-Revolutionary France*. Oxford: Oxford University Press.

Peirano, Irene. 2014. "'Sealing' the Book: Sphragis as Paratext." In *The Roman Paratext*, ed. L. Jansen, pp. 224–42. Cambridge: Cambridge University Press.

Pelling, Christopher. 2006. "Homer and Herodotus." In *Epic Interactions: Perspectives on Homer, Virgil and the Epic Tradition*, ed. M. J. Clarke, B. G. F. Currie, and R. O. A. M. Lyne, pp. 75–104. Oxford: Oxford. University Press.

Pender, Elizabeth E. 1992. "Spiritual Pregnancy in Plato's *Symposium*." *Classical Quarterly* 42 (1): 72–86.

———. 2007. "Sappho and Anacreon in Plato's *Phaedrus*." *Leeds International Classical Studies* 6 (4): 1–57.

Peponi, Anastasia-Erasmia. 1997. "*Mythoplokos Eros*: Sappho's Allusion to Her Poetics." In *Acta: First Panhellenic and International Conference on Ancient Greek Literature*, ed. J.-T. Papademetriou, pp. 139–65. Athens: Hellenic Society for Humanistic Studies.

———. 2009. "*Choreia* and Aesthetics in the *Homeric Hymn to Apollo*: The Performance of the Delian Maidens (Lines 156–64)." *Classical Antiquity* 28 (1): 39–70.

———. 2012. *Frontiers of Pleasure: Models of Aesthetic Response in Archaic and Classical Greek Thought*. Oxford: Oxford University Press.

Perkell, Christine. 2008. "Reading the Laments of *Iliad* 24." In *Lament: Studies in the Ancient Mediterranean and Beyond*, ed. A. Suter, pp. 93–117. Oxford: Oxford University Press.

Perry, B. E. 1962. "Demetrius of Phalerum and the Aesopic Fables." *Transactions and Proceedings of the American Philological Association* 93: 287–346.

Pertusi, Agostino, ed. 1955. *Scholia vetera in Hesiodi Opera et Dies*. Milan: Vita e Pensiero.

Perusino, Franca. 1986. *Dalla commedia antica alla commedia di mezzo: Tre studi su Aristofane*. Urbino: Università degli studi di Urbino.

Petrovic, Andrej. 2009. "Epigrammatic Contests, *Poeti Vaganti* and Local History." In *Wandering Poets in Ancient Greek Culture: Travel, Locality and Pan-Hellenism*, ed. R. Hunter and I. Rutherford, pp. 195–216. Cambridge: Cambridge University Press.

Pfeijffer, Ilja Leonard. 1999. *Three Aeginetan Odes of Pindar: A Commentary on Nemean V, Nemean III, and Pythian VIII*. Leiden: Brill.

Plant, Ian M., ed. 2004. *Women Writers of Ancient Greece and Rome: An Anthology*. Norman: University of Oklahoma Press.

Plass, Paul C. 1978. "Plato's 'Pregnant' Lover." *Symbolae Osloenses* 53: 47–55.

Pomeroy, Sarah B. 1975. *Goddesses, Whores, Wives and Slaves: Women in Classical Antiquity*. New York: Schocken.

———. 1977. "*Technikai kai mousikai*: The Education of Women in the Fourth Century and in the Hellenistic Period." *American Journal of Ancient History* 2: 51–68.

———. 1978. "Supplementary Notes on Erinna." *Zeitschrift für Papyrologie und Epigraphik* 32 (1978): 17–22.

Powell, Jim, transl. 2019. *The Poetry of Sappho: An Expanded Edition, Featuring Newly Discovered Poems*. 2nd ed. Oxford: Oxford University Press.

Powell, John U., ed. 1925. *Collectanea Alexandrina*. Oxford: Clarendon.

Power, Timothy. 2010. *The Culture of Kitharôidia*. Cambridge MA: Harvard University Press.

Pratt, Louise. 1995. "The Seal of Theognis, Writing, and Oral Poetry." *The American Journal of Philology* 116 (2): 171–84.

Price, Simon. 1985. "Delphi and Divination." In *Greek Religion and Society*, ed. P. Easterling and J. V. Muir, pp. 128–54. Cambridge: Cambridge University Press.

Prins, Yopie. 1996. "Sappho's Afterlife in Translation." In *Re-Reading Sappho: Reception and Transmission*, ed. E. Greene, pp. 36–67. Berkeley: University of California Press.

———. 1999. *Victorian Sappho*. Princeton NJ: Princeton University Press.

Probert, Philomen. 2019. "Greek Dialects in the Lexicon." In *Liddell and Scott: The History, Methodology, and Languages of the World's Leading Lexicon of Ancient Greek*, ed. C. Stray, M. Clarke, and J. T. Katz, pp. 200–25. Oxford: Oxford University Press.

Pucci, Pietro. 1977. *Hesiod and the Language of Poetry*. Baltimore: Johns Hopkins University Press.

———. 1987. *Odysseus Polutropos: Intertextual Readings in the Odyssey and the Iliad*. Ithaca NY: Cornell University Press.

———. 1998. *The Song of the Sirens: Essays on Homer*. Lanham: Rowman and Littlefield.

Puelma, Mario. 1972. "Sänger und König zum Verständnis von Hesiods Tierfabel." *Museum Helveticum* 29: 86–109.

Purves, Alex. 2014. "Who, Sappho?" In *Defining Greek Narrative*, ed. D. Cairns and R. Scodel, pp. 175–96. Edinburgh: Edinburgh University Press.

Rabinowitz, Nancy Sorkin. 1993. *Anxiety Veiled: Euripides and the Traffic in Women*. Ithaca NY: Cornell University Press.

Rabinowitz, Nancy Sorkin, and Amy Richlin, eds. 1993. *Feminist Theory and the Classics*. London, New York: Routledge.

Race, William H., ed. 1997. *Pindar: Nemean Odes, Isthmian Odes, Fragments*. Cambridge MA: Harvard University Press.

Rademaker, Adriaan. 2003. "'Most Citizens Are *euruprôktoi* Now': (Un)manliness in Aristophanes." In *Andreia: Studies in Manliness and Courage in Classical Antiquity*, ed. R. Rosen and I. Sluiter, pp. 115–25. Leiden: Brill.

Rademaker, Adriaan. 2013. "The Most Correct Account: Protagoras on Language." In *Protagoras of Abdera: The Man, His Measure*, ed. J. M. van Ophuijsen, M. van Raalte, and P. Stork, pp. 87–111. Leiden: Brill.

Railton, Stephen. 1991. *Authorship and Audience: Literary Performance in the American Renaissance*. Princeton NJ: Princeton University Press.

Rankine, Patrice. 2011. "Odysseus as Slave: The Ritual of Domination and Social Death in Homeric Society." In *Reading Ancient Slavery*, ed. R. Alston, E. Hall and L. Proffitt, pp. 34–50. London: Bristol Classical Press.

Rau, Peter. 1967. *Paratragodia: Untersuchung einer komischen Form des Aristophanes*. Munich: Beck.

Rayor, Diane J. 1993. "Korinna: Gender and the Narrative Tradition." *Arethusa* 26: 219–31.

———. 2005. "The Power of Memory in Erinna and Sappho." In *Women Poets in Ancient Greece and Rome*, ed. E. Greene, pp. 59–71. Norman: University of Oklahoma Press.

———, transl. 2014. *Sappho: A New Translation of the Complete Works*. With introduction and notes by André Lardinois. Cambridge: Cambridge University Press.

Redfield, James. 1982. "Notes on the Greek Wedding." *Arethusa* 15 (1/2): 181–201.

———. 1985. "Herodotus the Tourist." *Classical Philology* 80 (2): 97–118.

Reed, T. James. 2020. *Genesis: The Making of Literary Works from Homer to Christa Wolf*. Woodbridge: Boydell and Brewer.

Reitzammer, Laurialan. 2016. *The Athenian Adonia in Context: The Adonis Festival as Cultural Practice*. Madison: University of Wisconsin Press.

Revermann, Martin. 2006. *Comic Business: Theatricality, Dramatic Technique, and Performance Contexts of Aristophanic Comedy*. Oxford: Oxford University Press.

———. 2010. "On Misunderstanding the *Lysistrata*, Productively." In *Looking at Lysistrata: Eight Essays and a New Version of Aristophanes' Provocative Comedy*, ed. D. Stuttard, pp. 70–79. London: Bristol Classical Press.

Rhodes, P. J. 2003. "Nothing to Do with Democracy: Athenian Drama and the Polis." *Journal of Hellenic Studies* 123: 104–19.

Riad, Tomas. 2014. "Metron." In *Encyclopedia of Ancient Greek Language and Linguistics*. Vol. 3, ed. G. Giannakis, pp. 436–40. Brill: Leiden.

Rich, Adrienne. [1971] 1979. "When We Dead Awaken: Writing as Re-Vision." In *On Lies, Secrets, and Silence: Selected Prose*, pp. 33–50. New York, London: W. W. Norton.

Richardson, Nicholas, ed. 1993. *The Iliad: A Commentary*. Vol. 4, *Books 21–24*. Cambridge: Cambridge University Press.

———, ed. 2010. *Three Homeric Hymns: To Apollo, Hermes, and Aphrodite*. Cambridge: Cambridge University Press.

Rissman, Leah. 1983. *Love as War: Homeric Allusion in the Poetry of Sappho*. Königstein: Hain.

Rivoli, Matteo. 2020. "L'iscrizione di Mnesiepes dall'*Archilocheion* di Paro." *Axon* 4 (1): 141–64.

Roberts, W. Rhys. 1900. "Aristophanes and Agathon." *Journal of Hellenic Studies* 20: 44–56.

Robinson, David M. 1924. *Sappho and Her Influence*. Norwood MA: Plimpton Press.

Rogers, Brett M. 2014. "Why Didaskalia?: The Language of Production in (and Its Many Meanings for) Greek Drama." Didaskalia *10.12*. https://www.didaskalia.net/issues/10/12/.

Roisman, Hanna. 2006. "Helen in the *Iliad*: *Causa Belli* and Victim of War: From Silent Weaver to Public Speaker." *American Journal of Philology* 127 (1): 1–36.

———. 2021. *Tragic Heroines in Ancient Greek Drama*. London, New York: Bloomsbury.

Romaine, Suzanne. 2001. "A Corpus-Based View of Gender in British and American English." In *Gender across Languages: The Linguistic Representation of Women and Men*, ed. M. Hellinger and H. Bußmann, vol. 1, pp. 153–76. Amsterdam: John Benjamins.

Romani Mistretta, Marco. 2017. "Hermes the Craftsman: The Invention of the Lyre." *Gaia* 20: 5–22.

Rosen, Ralph M. 2004. "Aristophanes' *Frogs* and the *Contest of Homer and Hesiod*." *Transactions of the American Philological Association* 134: 295–322.

Rosen, Ralph M. and Ineke Sluiter, eds. 2003. *Andreia: Studies in Manliness and Courage in Classical Antiquity*. Leiden: Brill.

Rosen, Stanley. 1999. *Plato's Symposium*. 2nd ed. South Bend IN: St. Augustine's Press.

Rosenmeyer, Patricia A. 1997. "Her Master's Voice: Sappho's Dialogue with Homer." *Materiali e discussioni per l'analisi dei testi classici* 39: 123–49.

———. 2006. "Sappho's Iambics." *Letras clássicas* 10: 11–36.

Roth, Catharine P. 1976. "Kings and Muses in Hesiod's *Theogony*." *Transactions and Proceedings of the American Philological Association* 106: 331–38.

Rowe, Christopher J., ed. 1986. *Plato: Phaedrus*. Warminster: Aris and Phillips.

———, ed. 1998. *Plato: Symposium*. Warminster: Aris and Phillips.

Rubarth, Scott. 2014. "Competing Constructions of Masculinity in Ancient Greece." *Athens Journal of Humanities and Arts* 1 (1): 21–32.

Russell, Anna. 2019. *So Here I Am: Speeches by Great Women to Empower and Inspire*. London: White Lion.

———. 2020. *Parole aux femmes! Discours inspirants pour éveiller les consciences*. Translated by Laurence Taillebois. Quebec: Hurtubise.

Russo, Carlo Ferdinando. 1962. *Aristofane, autore di teatro*. Florence: Sansoni.

Russo, Joseph, Manuel Fernandez-Galiano and Alfred Heubeck, eds. 1993. *A Commentary on Homer's Odyssey*. Vol. 3, *Books XVII–XXIV*. Oxford: Clarendon.

Rüter, Klaus. 1969. *Odysseeinterpretationen: Untersuchungen zum ersten Buch und zur Phaiakis*. Göttingen: Vandenhoeck and Ruprecht.

Rutherford, Ian. 2009. "Aristodama and the Aetolians: An Itinerant Poetess and Her Agenda." In *Wandering Poets in Ancient Greek Culture: Travel, Locality and Pan-Hellenism*, ed. R. Hunter and I. Rutherford, pp. 237–48. Cambridge: Cambridge University Press.

Saetta Cottone, Rossella. 2003. "Agathon, Euripide et le thème de la μίμησις dramatique dans les Thesmophories d'Aristophane." *Revue des études grecques* 116: 445–69.

Sansone, David. 1985. "The Date of Herodotus' Publication." *Illinois Classical Studies* 10 (1): 1–9.

Saxonhouse, Arlene W. 1994. "The Philosopher and the Female in the Political Thought of Plato." In *Feminist Interpretations of Plato*, ed. N. Tuana, pp. 67–86. University Park: The Pennsylvania State University Press.

———. 2005. "Another Antigone: The Emergence of the Female Political Actor in Euripides' *Phoenician Women*." *Political Theory* 33 (4): 472–94.

Schein, Seth. 1984. *The Mortal Hero: An Introduction to Homer's Iliad*. Berkeley: University of California Press.

Schein, Seth. 1995. "Female Representations and Interpreting the *Odyssey*." In *The Distaff Side: Representing the Female in Homer's Odyssey*, ed. B. Cohen, pp. 17–27. Oxford: Oxford University Press.

Schironi, Francesca. 2018. *The Best of the Grammarians: Aristarchus of Samothrace on the Iliad*. Ann Arbor: University of Michigan Press.

Schlesier, Renate. 2013. "Atthis, Gyrinno, and Other *Hetairai*: Female Personal Names in Sappho's Poetry." *Philologus* 157 (2): 199–222.

———. 2019. "A Sophisticated *hetaira* at Table: Athenaeus' Sappho." In *The Reception of Greek Lyric Poetry in the Ancient World: Transmission, Canonization and Paratext*, ed. B. Currie and I. Rutherford, pp. 342–72. Leiden: Brill.

Schmid, Walter T. 1992. *On Manly Courage: A Study of Plato's Laches*. Carbondale, Edwardsville: Southern Illinois University Press.

Schmitzer, Ulrich. 2007. "Authors." In *Brill's New Pauly*, ed. H. Cancik and H. Schneider, pp. 399–403. Leiden: Brill.

Schofield, Malcolm. 2007. "The Noble Lie." In *The Cambridge Companion to Plato's Republic*, ed. G. R. F. Ferrari, pp. 138–64. Cambridge: Cambridge University Press.

Schrenk, Lawrence P. 1994. "Sappho Frag. 44 and the *Iliad*." *Hermes* 122: 144–50.

Scodel, Ruth. 2001. "Poetic Authority and Oral Tradition in Hesiod and Pindar." In *Speaking Volumes: Orality and Literacy in the Greek and Roman World*, ed. J. Watson, pp. 109–37. Leiden: Brill.

Scott, James C. 1990. *Domination and the Arts of Resistance: Hidden Transcripts*. New Haven CT: Yale University Press.

Scully, Stephen P. 1981. "The Bard as the Custodian of Homeric Society: *Odyssey* 3.263–272." *Quaderni urbinati di cultura classica* 8: 67–83.

Searle, John. 1969. *Speech Acts: An Essay in the Philosophy of Language*. Cambridge: Cambridge University Press.

Sedley, David. 2003. *Plato's Cratylus*. Cambridge Studies in the Dialogues of Plato. Cambridge: Cambridge University Press.

Segal, Charles P. 1969. "Aristophanes' Cloud-Chorus." *Arethusa* 2 (2): 143–61.

———. 1989. "Archaic Choral Lyric." In *The Cambridge History of Classical Literature*. Vol. 1, *Greek Literature*, ed. P. Easterling and B. Knox, pp. 165–201. Cambridge: Cambridge University Press.

———. 1993a. "The Female Voice and Its Ambiguities: From Homer to Tragedy." In *Religio Graeco-Romana: Festschrift für Walter Pötscher*, ed. J. Dalfen, G. Petersmann, and F. F. Schwarz, pp. 57–75. Horn: F. Berger und Söhne.

———. 1993b. *Euripides and the Poetics of Sorrow: Art, Gender, and Commemoration in Alcestis, Hippolytus, and Hecuba*. Durham NC: Duke University Press.

———. 1994a. *Singers, Heroes, and Gods in the Odyssey*. Ithaca NY: Cornell University Press.

———. 1994b. "Classical Criticism and the Canon, or, Why Read the Ancient Critics?" In *Reading World Literature: Theory, History, Practice*, ed. S. Lawall, pp. 87–112. Austin: University of Texas Press.

———. 1996. "Euripides' *Medea*: Vengeance, Reversal and Closure." *Pallas* 45: 15–44.

———. 1998. *Aglaia: The Poetry of Alcman, Sappho, Pindar, Bacchylides, and Corinna*. Lanham MD: Rowman and Littlefield.

Segal, Erich. 1983. "Euripides: Poet of Paradox." In *Oxford Readings in Greek Tragedy*, ed. E. Segal, pp. 244–54. Oxford: Oxford University Press.

Sens, Alexander. 2007. "One Things [sic] Leads (Back) to Another: Allusion and the Invention of Tradition in Hellenistic Epigrams." In *Brill's Companion to Hellenistic Epigram*, ed. P. Bing and J. S. Bruss, pp. 371–90. Leiden: Brill.

———. 2018. "Envy and Closure in the Greek Anthology." In *They Keep It All Hid: Augustan Poetry, Its Antecedents and Reception*, ed. P. E. Knox, H. Pelliccia and A. Sens, pp. 101–15. Berlin: de Gruyter.

Setti, Giovanni. 1890. *Studi sulla Antologia Greca: Gli epigrammi degli Antipatri*. Turin: Loescher.

Shapiro, H. Alan. 1994. *Myth into Art: Poet and Painter in Classical Greece*. London, New York: Routledge.

Sharrock, Alison R. 1997. "Re(ge)ndering Gender(ed) Studies." *Gender and History* 9: 603–14.

———. 2002. "An A-musing Tale: Gender, Genre, and Ovid." In *Cultivating the Muse: Struggles for Power and Inspiration in Classical Literature*, ed. E. Spentzou and D. Fowler, pp. 207–28. Oxford: Oxford University Press.

Sheffield, Frisbee C. C. 2001. "Psychic Pregnancy and Platonic Epistemology." *Oxford Studies in Ancient Philosophy* 20: 1–33.

———. 2006. *Plato's Symposium: The Ethics of Desire*. Oxford: Oxford University Press.

Shelmerdine, Susan C. 1984. "Hermes and the Tortoise: A Prelude to the Cult." *Greek, Roman and Byzantine Studies* 25: 201–8.

Shelton, John. 2019. "City of Hanover Overhauls Gender Language Usage in Official Texts." *Die Welle*, January 22, 2019. https://www.dw.com/en/city-of-hanover-overhauls-gender-language-usage-in-official-texts/a-47188002.

Shorey, Paul, ed. 1930. *The Republic, I: Books I–V*. Cambridge MA: Harvard University Press.

Sidwell, Keith. 2009. *Aristophanes the Democrat: The Politics of Satirical Comedy during the Peloponnesian War*. Cambridge: Cambridge University Press.

Silk, Michael S. 2000. "Aristophanes versus the Rest: Comic Poetry in Old Comedy." In *The Rivals of Aristophanes: Studies in Athenian Old Comedy*, ed. D. Harvey and J. Wilkins, pp. 299–316. London: Duckworth.

———. 2002. *Aristophanes and the Definition of Comedy*. Oxford: Oxford University Press.

Sissa, Giulia. 1990. *Greek Virginity*. Translated by A. Goldhammer. Cambridge MA: Harvard University Press.

———. 2020. "Mighty Mothers: Female Political Theorists in Euripides' *Suppliant Women* and *Phoenician Women*." In *Maternal Conceptions in Classical Literature and Philosophy*, ed. A. Sharrock and A. Keith, pp. 193–223. Toronto: University of Toronto Press.

Skempis, Marios, and Ioannis Ziogas. 2009. "Arete's Words: Etymology, *Ehoie*-Poetry and Gendered Narrative in the *Odyssey*." In *Narratology and Interpretation: The Content of Narrative Form in Ancient Literature*, ed. J. Grethlein and A. Rengakos, pp. 213–240. Berlin: de Gruyter.

Skinner, Marilyn B. 1982. "Briseis, the Trojan Women, and Erinna." *Classical World* 75: 265–69.

———. 1983. "Corinna of Tanagra and Her Audience." *Tulsa Studies in Women's Literature* 2: 9–20.

———. 1987. "Greek Women and the Metronymic: A Note on an Epigram by Nossis." *Ancient History Bulletin* 19: 39–42.

Skinner, Marilyn B. 1989. "Sapphic Nossis." *Arethusa* 22: 5–18.

———. 1991. "Aphrodite Garlanded: Eros and Poetic Creativity in Sappho and Nossis." In *Rose di Pieria*, ed. F. De Martino, pp. 79–96. Bari: Levante.

———. 1993. "Women and Language in Archaic Greece, or, Why Is Sappho a Woman?" In *Feminist Theory and the Classics*, ed. N. S. Rabinowitz and A. Richlin, pp. 125–44. London, New York: Routledge.

———. 2001. "Ladies' Day at the Art Institute: Theocritus, Herodas, and the Gendered Gaze." In *Making Silence Speak: Women's Voices in Greek Literature and Society*, ed. A. Lardinois and L. McClure, pp. 201–22. Princeton NJ: Princeton University Press.

———. 2005a. *Sexuality in Greek and Roman Culture*. Oxford: Blackwell.

———. 2005b. "Nossis *Thêlyglôssos*: The Private Text and the Public Book." In *Women Poets in Ancient Greece and Rome*, ed. E. Greene, pp. 112–38. Norman: University of Oklahoma Press.

———. 2005c. "Homer's Mother." In *Women Poets in Ancient Greece and Rome*, ed. E. Greene, pp. 91–111. Norman: University of Oklahoma Press.

Skulsky, S. D. 1975. "Πολλῶν Πείρατα Συντανύσαις: Language and Meaning in *Pythian* 1." *Classical Philology* 70: 8–31.

Slatkin, L. 2011. "Composition by Theme and the *Metis* of the *Odyssey*." In *The Power of Thetis and Selected Essays*, pp. 139–56. Washington, DC: Center for Hellenic Studies.

Sluiter, Ineke. 1990. *Ancient Grammar in Context: Contributions to the Study of Ancient Linguistic Thought*. Amsterdam: VU University Press.

Sluiter, Ineke, and Ralph M. Rosen. 2003. "General Introduction." In *Andreia: Studies in Manliness and Courage in Classical Antiquity*, ed. R. Rosen and I. Sluiter, pp. 1–24. Leiden: Brill.

Smith, William. 1886. *A Smaller Classical Dictionary of Biography, Mythology, and Geography*. New York: Harper and Brothers.

Smoes, Etienne. 1995. *Le courage chez les Grecs, d'Homère à Aristote*. Brussels: Ousia.

Snell, Bruno. 1982. *The Discovery of the Mind in Greek Philosophy and Literature*. 2nd ed. New York: Dover.

Snyder, Jane McIntosh. 1974. "Aristophanes' Agathon as Anacreon." *Hermes* 102 (2): 244–46.

———. 1981. "The Web of Song: Weaving Imagery in Homer and the Lyric Poets." *The Classical Journal* 76 (3): 193–96.

———. 1984. "Korinna's 'Glorious Songs of Heroes.'" *Eranos* 82: 1–10.

———. 1989. *The Woman and the Lyre: Women Writers in Classical Greece and Rome*. Bristol: Bristol Classical Press.

———. 1991. "Public Occasion and Private Passion in the Lyrics of Sappho of Lesbos." In *Women's History and Ancient History*, ed. S. B. Pomeroy, pp. 1–19. Chapel Hill: University of North Carolina Press.

———. 1997. *Lesbian Desire in the Lyrics of Sappho*. New York: Columbia University Press.

Sommerstein, Alan H. 1977. "Aristophanes and the Events of 411." *Journal of Hellenic Studies* 97: 112–26.

———, ed. 1981. *Aristophanes: Knights*. Warminster: Aris and Phillips.

———, ed. 1982. *Aristophanes: Clouds*. Warminster: Aris and Phillips.

———, ed. 1990. *Aristophanes: Lysistrata*. Warminster: Aris and Phillips.

———, ed. 1994. *Aristophanes: Thesmophoriazusae*. Warminster: Aris and Phillips.

———. 1995. "The Language of Athenian Women." In *Lo spettacolo delle voci*, ed. F. de Martino and A. H. Sommerstein, pp. 61–85. Bari: Levante.

Spelman, Henry. 2017. "Sappho 44: Trojan Myth and Literary History." *Mnemosyne* 70: 740–57.

Spentzou, Efrossini, and Don Fowler, eds. 2002. *Cultivating the Muse: Struggles for Power and Inspiration in Classical Literature*. Oxford: Oxford University Press.

Spongberg, Mary. 2002. *Writing Women's History since the Renaissance*. Basingstoke: Palgrave Macmillan.

Stadtmüller, Hugo, ed. 1906. *Anthologia Graeca epigrammatum Palatina cum Planudea*. Vol. 3. Leipzig: Teubner.

Stafford, Emma. 1998. "Masculine Values, Feminine Forms: On the Gender of Personified Abstractions." In *Thinking Men: Masculinity and Its Self-Representation in the Classical Tradition*, ed. L. Foxhall and J. Salmon, pp. 43–56. London, New York: Routledge.

Stafford, Emma, and Judith Herrin, eds. 2005. *Personification in the Greek World: From Antiquity to Byzantium*. Aldershot, Burlington VT: Ashgate.

Starkie, William J. M., ed. 1897. *The Wasps of Aristophanes: With Introduction, Metrical Analysis, Critical Notes, and Commentary*. London: Macmillan.

Stehle, Eva. 1981. "Sappho's Private World." *Women's Studies* 8: 47–63.

———. 1997. *Performance and Gender in Ancient Greece: Nondramatic Poetry in Its Setting*. Princeton NJ: Princeton University Press.

———. 2001. "The Good Daughter: Mothers' Tutelage in Erinna's *Distaff* and Fourth-Century Epitaphs." In *Making Silence Speak: Women's Voices in Greek Literature and Society*, ed. A. Lardinois and L. McClure, pp. 179–200. Princeton NJ: Princeton University Press.

———. 2002. "The Body and Its Representation in Aristophanes' *Thesmophoriazousai*: Where Does the Costume End?" *American Journal of Philology* 123: 369–406.

Steiner, Deborah. 1986. *The Crown of Song: Metaphor in Pindar*. Oxford: Oxford University Press.

———. 1994. *The Tyrant's Writ: Myths and Images of Writing in Ancient Greece*. Princeton NJ: Princeton University Press.

———. 2015. "Figures of the Poet in Greek Epic and Lyric." In *A Companion to Ancient Aesthetics*, ed. P. Destrée and P. Murray, pp. 31–46. Oxford, Malden MA: Wiley-Blackwell.

———. 2021. "Sappho and Archaic Greek Song Culture." In *The Cambridge Companion to Sappho*, ed. P. J. Finglass and A. Kelly, pp. 77–90. Cambridge: Cambridge University Press.

Stephanis, Ioannis E. 1988. Διονυσιακοὶ Τεχνῖται. Συμβολὲς στὴν προσωπογραφία τοῦ θεάτρου καὶ τῆς μουσικῆς τῶν ἀρχαίων Ἑλλήνων. Heraklion: Crete University Press.

Stern-Gillet, Suzanne. 2004. "On (Mis)Interpreting Plato's *Ion*." *Phronesis* 49 (2): 169–201.

Stewart, Edmund, Edward Harris, and David Lewis, eds. 2020. *Skilled Labour and Professionalism in Ancient Greece and Rome*. Cambridge: Cambridge University Press.

Stieber, Mary C. 2011. *Euripides and the Language of Craft*. Leiden: Brill.

Stoddard, Kathryn B. 2003. "The Programmatic Message of the 'Kings and Singers' Passage: Hesiod, *Theogony* 80–103." *Transactions of the American Philological Association* 133 (1): 1–16.

Strassler, Robert B., ed., and Andrea L. Purvis, transl. *The Landmark Herodotus: The Histories*. New York: Anchor Books.

Stroup, Sarah Culpepper. 2004. "Designing Women: Aristophanes' *Lysistrata* and the 'Hetairiza-tion' of the Greek Wife." *Arethusa* 37: 37–73.

Suter, Ann, ed. 2008. *Lament: Studies in the Ancient Mediterranean and Beyond*. Oxford: Oxford University Press.

Suzuki, Mihoko. 1989. *Metamorphoses of Helen: Authority, Difference, and the Epic*. Ithaca NY: Cornell University Press.

Svenbro, Jesper. 1984. *La parola e il marmo: Alle origini della poetica greca*. Torino: Boringhieri.

———. 1993. *Phrasikleia: An Anthropology of Reading in Ancient Greece*. Translated by Janet Lloyd. Ithaca NY: Cornell University Press.

———. 2004. "La naissance de l'auteur dans une inscription grecque (*Anthologie palatine* 6, 197)." In *Identités d'auteur dans l'antiquité et la tradition européenne*, ed. C. Calame and R. Chartier, pp. 77–88. Grenoble: Millon.

Swift, Laura A. 2009. "The Symbolism of Space in Euripidean Choral Fantasy (*Hipp.* 732–75, *Med.* 824–65, *Bacch.* 370–433)." *Classical Quarterly* 59 (2): 364–82.

———. 2010. *The Hidden Chorus: Echoes of Genre in Tragic Lyric*. Oxford: Oxford University Press.

———, ed. 2019. *Archilochus: The Poems*. Oxford: Oxford University Press.

Swiggers, Pierre, and Alfons Wouters. 2002. "Grammatical Theory and Philosophy of Language in Antiquity: Introduction." In *Grammatical Theory and Philosophy of Language in Antiquity*, pp. 9–20. Leuven, Paris, Sterling VA: Peeters.

Taaffe, Lauren K. 1993. *Aristophanes and Women*. Oxford, New York: Routledge.

Tammaro, Vinicio. 2006. "Poeti tragici come personaggi comici in Aristofane." In *Κωμωιδοτραγωιδία: Intersezioni del tragico e del comico nel teatro del V secolo a.C.*, ed. E. Medda, M. S. Mirto, and M. P. Pattoni, pp. 249–62. Pisa: Edizioni della Normale.

Taplin, Oliver. 1983. "Tragedy and Trugedy." *Classical Quarterly* 33: 331–33.

———. 1986. "Fifth-Century Tragedy and Comedy: A Synkrisis." *Journal of Hellenic Studies* 106: 163–74.

———. 1993. *Comic Angels and Other Approaches to Greek Drama through Vase Paintings*. Oxford: Oxford University Press.

Tarrant, Harold. 1991. "*Clouds* I: Steps towards Reconstruction." *Arctos: Acta Philologica Fennica* 25: 157–81.

Tate, J. 1928. "'Imitation' in Plato's *Republic*." *Classical Quarterly* 22 (1): 16–23.

———. 1932. "Plato and 'Imitation.'" *Classical Quarterly* 26 (3–4): 161–69.

Taylor, Daniel. 1995. "Classical Linguistics: An Overview." In *Concise History of the Language Sciences: From the Sumerians to the Cognitivists*, ed. E. F. K. Koerner and R. E. Asher, pp. 83–90. Oxford, New York: Elsevier.

Tessitore, Aristide. 1994. "Courage and Comedy in Plato's *Laches*." *The Journal of Politics* 56: 115–33.

Thalmann, William. 1984. *Conventions of Form and Thought in Early Greek Epic Poetry*. Baltimore: Johns Hopkins University Press.

Tobin, Yishai. 2001. "Gender Switch in Modern Hebrew." In *Gender across Languages: The Linguistic Representation of Women and Men*, ed. M. Hellinger and H. Bußmann, vol. 1, pp. 177–98. Amsterdam: John Benjamins.

Torrance, Isabelle. 2013. *Metapoetry in Euripides*. Oxford: Oxford University Press.

Treu, Max, ed. 1963. *Sappho*. Munich: Heimeran.

Tsagalis, Christos. 2004. *Epic Grief: Personal Laments in Homer's Iliad*. Berlin: de Gruyter.

———. 2009. "Poetry and Poetics in the Hesiodic Corpus." In *Brill's Companion to Hesiod*, ed. F. Montanari, A. Rengakos, and C. Tsagalis, pp. 131–77. Leiden: Brill.

Tsitsibakou-Vasalos, Evanthia. 2009. "Chance or Design? Language and Plot Management in the *Odyssey*: Klytaimnestra ἄλοχος μνηστὴ ἐμήσατο." In *Narratology and Interpretation: The Content of Narrative Form in Ancient Literature*, ed. J. Grethlein and A. Rengakos, pp. 177–212. Berlin: de Gruyter.

Tuana, Nancy, ed. 1994. *Feminist Interpretations of Plato*. University Park: The Pennsylvania State University Press.

Tueller, Michael A. 2008. *Look Who's Talking: Innovations in Voice and Identity in Hellenistic Epigram*. Leuven: Peeters.

Uchida, Tsugunobu. 1992. "Aristophanes als Freund der Muse: Zur Parabase des *Friedens*." *Rheinisches Museum für Philologie* 135 (3/4): 225–34.

Ugolini, Giuseppe. 1923. "L'evoluzione della critica letteraria d'Aristofane." *Studi Italiani di filologia classica* 3: 215–46.

Vaahtera, Jaana. 2008. "On Grammatical Gender in Ancient Linguistics: The Order of Genders." *Arctos* 42: 247–66.

Van Brock, Nadia. 1959. "Subsitution rituelle." *Revue hittite et asianique* 65: 117–46.

van Groningen, Bernhard Abraham. 1966, ed. *Théognis. Le premier livre, édité avec un commentaire*. Amsterdam: N.V. Noord-Hollandsche.

Verdin, Herman. 1977. "Les remarques critiques d'Hérodote et de Thucydide sur la poésie en tant que source historique." In *Historiographia Antiqua: Commentationes Lovanienses in honorem W. Peremans septuagenarii editae*, ed. T. Reekmans, E. Van't Dack, and H. Verdin, pp. 53–76. Leuven: University Press.

Vergados, Athanassios. 2007. "The *Homeric Hymn to Hermes* 51 and Antigonus of Carystus." *Classical Quarterly* 57: 737–42.

———. 2011a. "The *Homeric Hymn to Hermes*: Humour and Epiphany." In *The Homeric Hymns: Interpretative Essays*, ed. A. Faulkner, pp. 82–104. Oxford: Oxford University Press.

———. 2011b. "Shifting Focalization in the *Homeric Hymn to Hermes*: The Case of Hermes' Cave." *Greek, Roman and Byzantine Studies* 51 (1): 1–25.

———, ed. 2013. *The Homeric Hymn to Hermes: Introduction, Text and Commentary*. Berlin: de Gruyter.

Vicaire, Paul. 1964. *Recherches sur les mots désignant la poésie et le poète dans l'oeuvre de Platon*. Paris: Presses Universitaires de France.

Vivante, Bella, ed. 1999. *Women's Roles in Ancient Civilizations: A Reference Guide*. Westport CT: Greenwood Press.

Vlastos, Gregory. 1981. "The Individual as an Object of Love in Plato." In *Platonic Studies*, pp. 3–42. 2nd ed. Princeton NJ: Princeton University Press.

———. 1989. "Was Plato a Feminist?" *Times Literary Supplement* 276: 288–89.

Voigt, Eva-Maria, ed. 1971. *Sappho et Alcaeus, Fragmenta*. Amsterdam: Polak and van Gennep.

Wackernagel, Jacob. 1926–1928. *Vorlesungen über Syntax*. 2 vols. 2nd ed. Basel: Birkhäuser.

Walcot, Peter. 1978. "Herodotus on Rape." *Arethusa* 11 (1/2): 137–47.

Warner, Marina. 1985. *Monuments and Maidens: The Allegory of the Female Form*. New York: Atheneum.

Warwick, Celsiana. 2020. "Nossis' Dildo: A Metapoetic Attack on Female Poetry in Herodas's Sixth *Mime*." *Transactions and Proceedings of the American Philological Association* 150 (2): 333–56.

Waterfield, Robin, transl. 1994. *Plato: Symposium*. Oxford: Oxford University Press.

———, transl. 1998. *Herodotus: The Histories*. Oxford: Oxford University Press.

Weil, Henri. 1884. "De l'origine du mot 'poète.'" *Annuaire de l'association pour l'encouragement des études grecques en france* 18: 1–7.

Weiss, Naomi A. 2017. "Noise, Music, Speech: The Representation of Lament in Greek Tragedy." *American Journal of Philology* 138: 243–66.

———. 2018. *The Music of Tragedy: Performance and Imagination in Euripidean Theater*. Berkeley: University of California Press.

Werner, Jürgen. 1994. "Der weibliche Homer: Sappho oder Anyte?" *Philologus* 138: 252–59.

West, Candace, and Don H. Zimmerman. 1987. "Doing Gender." *Gender and Society* 1: 125–51.

West, Martin L. 1965. "Alcmanica." *Classical Quarterly* 15 (2): 188–202.

———. 1966. *Theogony*. Oxford: Clarendon.

———. 1970. "Corinna." *Classical Quarterly* 20: 277–87.

———. 1974. *Studies in Greek Elegy and Iambus*. Berlin: de Gruyter.

———. 1975. "Cynaethus' Hymn to Apollo." *Classical Quarterly* 25: 161–70.

———. 1977. "Erinna." *Zeitschrift für Papyrologie und Epigraphik* 25: 95–119.

———. 1990. "Dating Corinna." *Classical Quarterly* 40: 553–57.

———. 1992. *Ancient Greek Music*. Oxford: Oxford University Press.

———. 2002. "The View from Lesbos." In *Epea pteroenta: Beiträge zur Homerforschung*, ed. M. Reichel and A. Rengakos, pp. 207–19. Stuttgart: Steiner.

———, ed. 2003. *Homeric Hymns, Homeric Apocrypha, Lives of Homer*. Cambridge MA: Harvard University Press.

———. 2011. *The Making of the Iliad*. Oxford: Oxford University Press.

———. 2014a. "The Greek Poetess: Her Role and Image." In *Hellenica*, Vol. 3, *Philosophy, Music and Metre, Literary Byways, Varia*, pp. 315–40. Oxford: Oxford University Press.

———. 2014b. *The Making of the Odyssey*. Oxford: Oxford University Press.

Whitaker, C. W. A. 2002. *Aristotle's De Interpretatione: Contradiction and Dialectic*. Oxford: Oxford University Press.

Whitehead, Alfred N. 1978. *Process and Reality: An Essay in Cosmology*. Corrected ed. New York: The Free Press.

Whitehorne, John E. G. 1995. "Women's Work in Theocritus, *Idyll* 15." *Hermes* 123 (1): 63–75.

Whitmarsh, Tim. 2004. *Ancient Greek Literature*. Cambridge, Malden MA: Polity.

Wider, Kathleen. 1986. "Women Philosophers in the Ancient Greek World: Donning the Mantle." *Hypatia* 1 (1): 21–62.

Wilamowitz-Moellendorff, Ulrich von. 1913. *Sappho und Simonides: Untersuchungen über griechische Lyriker*. Berlin: Weidmann.

———. 1919. "Lesefrüchte." *Hermes* 54: 46–74.

Wilberding, James. 2012. "Curbing One's Appetites in Plato's *Republic*." In *Plato and the Divided Self*, ed. R. Barney, T. Brennan, and C. Brittain, pp. 128–49. Cambridge: Cambridge University Press.

Willi, Andreas. 2003. *The Languages of Aristophanes: Aspects of Linguistic Variation in Classical Attic Greek*. Oxford: Oxford University Press.

Williamson, Margaret. 1990. "A Woman's Place in Euripides' *Medea*." In *Euripides, Women and Sexuality*, ed. A. Powell, pp. 16–31. London, New York: Routledge.

———. 1995. *Sappho's Immortal Daughters*. Cambridge MA: Harvard University Press.

Wilson, Adrian. 2004. "Foucault on the 'Question of the Author': A Critical Exegesis." *The Modern Language Review* 99 (2): 339–63.

Wilson, Emily, transl. 2018. *Homer: The Odyssey*. New York: W. W. Norton.

Wilson, Lyn H. 1996. *Sappho's Sweetbitter Songs: Configurations of Female and Male in Ancient Greek Lyric*. London, New York: Routledge.

Wilson, N. G., ed. 2007. *Aristophanis fabulae, Vols. I–II*. Oxford: Oxford University Press.

Winkler, John J. 1981. "Gardens of Nymphs: Public and Private in Sappho's Lyrics." In *Reflections of Women in Antiquity*, ed. H. P. Foley, pp. 63–89. New York: Gordon and Breach.

———. 1990. *The Constraints of Desire: The Anthropology of Sex and Gender in Ancient Greece*. New York, London: Routledge.

Winkler, John J., and Froma I. Zeitlin, eds. 1990. *Nothing to Do with Dionysos? Athenian Drama in Its Social Context*. Princeton NJ: Princeton University Press.

Wittig, Monique. 1985. "The Mark of Gender." *Feminist Issues* 5 (2): 3–12.

Wodak, Ruth. 1995. "Power, Discourse, and Styles of Female Leadership in School Committee Meetings." In *Discourse and Power in Educational Organizations*, ed. D. Corson, pp. 31–54. Cresskill NJ: Hampton.

Wohl, Victoria. 1993. "Standing by the *Stathmos*: The Creation of Sexual Ideology in the *Odyssey*." *Arethusa* 26: 19–50.

Wolff, Erwin. 1964. "Das Weib des Masistes." *Hermes* 92 (1): 51–58.

Wolfsdorf, David. 2003. "Socrates' Pursuit of Definitions." *Phronesis* 48 (4): 271–312.

Wolicki, Aleksander. 2015. "The Education of Women in Ancient Greece." In *A Companion to Ancient Education*, ed. W. M. Bloomer, pp. 305–20. Oxford: Wiley-Blackwell.

Woodbury, Leonard. 1952. "The Seal of Theognis." In *Studies in Honour of Gilbert Norwood*, ed. M. E. White, pp. 20–41. Toronto: University of Toronto Press.

Woolf, Virginia. [1929] 1989. *A Room of One's Own*. 2nd ed. San Diego, New York, London: Harcourt.

Worman, Nancy. 2001. "This Voice Which Is Not One: Helen's Verbal Guises in Homeric Epic." In *Making Silence Speak: Women's Voices in Greek Literature and Society*, ed. A. Lardinois and L. McClure, pp. 19–37. Princeton NJ: Princeton University Press.

———. 2002. *The Cast of Character: Style in Greek Literature*. Austin: University of Texas Press.

Wright, Matthew. 2010. "The Tragedian as Critic: Euripides and Early Greek Poetics." *Journal of Hellenic Studies* 130: 165–84.

———. 2012. *The Comedian as Critic: Greek Old Comedy and Poetics*. London: Bristol Classical Press.

———, ed. 2016. *The Lost Plays of Greek Tragedy*. Vol. 1, *Neglected Authors*. London, New York: Bloomsbury.

———, ed. 2018. *The Lost Plays of Greek Tragedy*. Vol. 2, *Aeschylus, Sophocles and Euripides*. London, New York: Bloomsbury.

Wyke, Maria, ed. 1998. *Gender and the Body in the Ancient Mediterranean*. Oxford: Blackwell.

Yarrow, Simon. 2011. "Masculinity as a World Historical Category of Analysis." In *What Is Masculinity? Historical Dynamics from Antiquity to the Contemporary World*, ed. J. H. Arnold and S. Brady, pp. 114–38. Basingstoke: Palgrave Macmillan.

Yatromanolakis, Dimitrios. 2001. "Visualizing Poetry: An Early Representation of Sappho." *Classical Philology* 96 (2): 159–68.

———. 2007. *Sappho in the Making: The Early Reception*. Cambridge MA, Washington DC: Center for Hellenic Studies.

———. 2009. "Alcaeus and Sappho." In *The Cambridge Companion to Greek Lyric*, ed. F. Budelmann, pp. 204–26. Cambridge: Cambridge University Press.

Yunis, Harvey, ed. 2011. *Plato: Phaedrus*. Cambridge: Cambridge University Press.

Zajko, Vanda. 2008. "'What Difference Was Made?': Feminist Models of Reception." In *A Companion to Classical Receptions*, ed. L. Hardwick and C. Stray, pp. 195–206. Oxford, Malden MA: Blackwell.

Zajko, Vanda, and Miriam Leonard, eds. 2006. *Laughing with Medusa: Classical Myth and Feminist Thought*. Oxford: Oxford University Press.

Zanetto, Giuseppe. 2006. "*Tragōdia* versus *trugodia*: la rivalità letteraria nella commedia attica." In *Κωμωιδοτραγωιδία: Intersezioni del tragico e del comico nel teatro del V secolo a.C.*, ed. E. Medda, M. S. Mirto, and M. P. Pattoni, pp. 307–25. Pisa: Edizioni della Normale.

Zeitlin, Froma I. 1996. *Playing the Other: Gender and Society in Classical Greek Literature*. Chicago: University of Chicago Press.

Zelenak, Michael X. 1998. *Gender and Politics in Greek Tragedy*. New York: Peter Lang.

Zimman, Lal. 2017. "Transgender Language Reform: Some Challenges and Strategies for Promoting Trans-Affirming, Gender-Inclusive Language." *Journal of Language and Discrimination* 1 (1): 83–104.

Zoller, Coleen P. 2021. "Plato and Equality for Women across Social Class." *Journal of Ancient Philosophy* 15 (1): 35–62.

INDEX OF PASSAGES

GENERAL INDEX

Meleager of Gadara, 165–66, 168–69, 218–19, 271

melopoios, 87, 92–95, 93n42, 204

Meno, 134

meter, 72, 141. *See also metrios*

metrios, 141. *See also* meter

mimēsis, 42, 127, 127n24. *See also* imitation

Mimnermus, 83

misogyny, 88–89, 97, 99, 103, 183, 185

Mnemosyne, 241, 256

Mnesiepes, 263

Moero, 165, 249, 281–82

morals, 31, 141. *See also* virtue

mortality, 210, 243. *See also* immortality

mother-daughter relationship, 19, 242–50

motherhood, 19–21, 68, 105–7, 137, 156, 233–34, 234n12, 241–43, 246, 247n43, 250, 252–56, 285. *See also* authorship

Mousaōn therapōn, 54–56, 83–84, 208, 239–40, 244, 258, 264, 270, 278–79. *See also* Muses

mousopoios, 195–200, 202–4, 228, 236, 238. See also *mousopolos*

mousopolos, 18–19, 195–97, 234, 236–37, 237n21, 238, 240–41, 245, 247, 250, 256–58, 270, 279–80. See also *mousopoios*

Murray, Jackie, 273

Murray, Penelope, 50–51, 132, 148

Musaeus, 119

Muses: and Apollo, 52n35; collaborative relationship with, 242–44, 247, 279; femininity of, 55, 147, 197, 241; gender of, 92–94, 173–74; in Hesiod, 18, 49–50, 52–54, 62–63, 171, 184, 205, 209, 211–12, 239–40, 244, 258; in Homer, 47–50, 47n8, 52–53, 171, 184, 208–9; inspirational power of, 33–34, 46–47, 57, 170–73, 184–85, 233; limited power of, 52–53, 55–56; and mortality, 47–48, 208; and motherhood, 233–34; and the nightingale, 283; objectification of, 51, 56, 61; personification of, 113n114, 288; proximity to, 197, 244, 256; relationship to the poet, 18, 20–21, 48–50, 66; in Sappho, 248–49, 280–81, 285; servants to, 196–97, 236–40, 258, 264–65;

sexuality of, 51–52, 112–14. See also *Mousaōn therapōn*

Myrtis, 269

mythologos, 129, 129n34, 144–45

mythopoios, 124, 136, 138

mythos, 29–30, 67, 72, 75, 129, 136, 143; *versus logos,* 143n84

Nagy, Gregory, 54–55, 60

names: ambiguity of, 10; and gender, 91, 99, 101–3; and identity, 6n21; makers of, 125; and the self, 6–7. *See also* professional terms; proper names

Naucratis, 193, 201

Nausicaa, 34

Neri, Camillo, 219

nightingale: as *aoidos,* 182, 219, 228, 259–60, 274–75; fables of, 57–58; as female, 58–59, 64–65, 274–76; and lament, 180n49, 275–76, 275n55; as male poet, 274, 274n49; silencing of, 61, 170; women reclaiming, 271–74, 283; and women's voices, 18, 20, 59, 59n56, 277–78. See also *aēdōn; aēdonis;* hawks

Nossis, 1–2, 166, 246, 248–49, 271–73, 278–84

Noussia-Fantuzzi, Maria, 83n1

Odysseus, 28, 31–32, 34–36, 41–42, 129

Oedipus, 179

Olson, S. Douglas, 93

oracles, 250–52, 263–65. *See also* Delphic oracles

Origins of Criticism, The (Ford), 2–3

Orpheus, 119

othering, 178, 178n43, 201, 288. *See also* foreigners

Patroclus, 54–55, 119

Pausanias, 104n79, 251, 266

Pender, Elizabeth, 134

Penelope, 28–32, 32n25, 36, 44, 59, 61, 98, 174, 275–76

Theognis, 56, 83–84
Theophilis, 247–48
Theseus, 175
Thucydides, 62n3, 84–85, 138
tortoise, 63–70, 72, 73n40, 170, 259–60.
    See also lyre
tragedy, 8, 87, 89n27, 279n67
translation, 34n29, 62n3, 65n12, 69n27,
    77n54, 106n89, 142n79, 196, 250
transvestism, 87–92, 88n23, 97, 99, 151n119
trauma, 35
Tsagalis, Christos, 39

Van Brock, Nadia, 54
Vicaire, Paul, 130
virtue, 31, 128, 141–42, 145. *See also* morals
voice. *See* women's voices

Warwick, Celsiana, 246–47
weaving, 29, 41, 41n58–41n59, 181, 212, 242,
    242n38, 248, 275; as poetry, 41n60, 181n53,
    242, 248n54. *See also* shuttles
Whitmarsh, Tim, 240n30
Winkler, John, 236, 262n12, 284n81
women: and citizenship, 226–27; depictions
    of, 42, 88–89, 281–82; and female-marked
    spaces, 28; and fidelity, 31–32; imitation
    of, 88, 91–92, 96–97, 99, 102–4, 106, 108,
    121, 130–31, 133, 139, 171; and literacy, 4,

4n11; and masculinity, 6, 16; and mother-
hood, 105–6, 254–55, 285; objectification
of, 51, 56, 64, 68–74, 76, 111, 209, 211; over-
powering of creativity, 68–69; perceived
threat of, 33, 61, 185, 252–53, 286; as poets,
3–4, 3n7, 19, 44, 134, 140, 155, 167, 169–71,
173–80, 189, 195, 204, 206–7, 210, 214, 216,
218, 222–24, 228, 262–63, 267–68, 270–71;
professional roles of, 115n125; self-naming
of, 270; and sexuality, 68, 202–3, 217;
silencing of, 3–4, 4n10, 18, 29–30, 41, 51–52,
61, 67n18, 69, 131–32, 136, 147, 170, 174, 188,
228, 278, 280–81; and song, 25–26; stereo-
types of, 109, 201; subordination of, 18–19,
50–51, 61, 137–38, 157, 189; vocabulary for,
231–32, 235, 279. *See also* femininity
women's tradition, 3n4, 247, 282–84
women's voices, 17–18, 30, 33, 37n43, 40–42,
    44–45, 57, 62–63, 77, 250n63. *See also*
    lament; speech, gendered
Woolf, Virginia, 1
Works and Days, 61, 170, 177, 278

Xenophon, 223–24

Yatromanolakis, Dimitrios, 195–96,
    202

Zeus, 49–50, 55, 75, 77

A NOTE ON THE TYPE

This book has been composed in Arno, an Old-style serif typeface in the
classic Venetian tradition, designed by Robert Slimbach at Adobe.